ECONOMICS AND OTHER BRANCHES – IN THE SHADE OF THE OAK TREE: ESSAYS IN HONOUR OF PASCAL BRIDEL

ECONOMICS AND OTHER BRANCHES – IN THE SHADE OF THE OAK TREE: ESSAYS IN HONOUR OF PASCAL BRIDEL

Edited by

Roberto Baranzini and François Allisson

Routledge
Taylor & Francis Group

LONDON AND NEW YORK

First published 2014 by Pickering & Chatto (Publishers) Limited

2 Park Square, Milton Park, Abingdon, Oxfordshire OX14 4RN
52 Vanderbilt Avenue, New York, NY 10017

Routledge is an imprint of the Taylor & Francis Group, an informa business

First issued in paperback 2020

BRITISH LIBRARY CATALOGUING IN PUBLICATION DATA

Economics and other branches – in the shade of the oak tree: essays in honour
of Pascal Bridel.
1. Economics.
I. Allisson, Francois, editor. II. Baranzini, Roberto editor. III. Bridel, Pascal,
1948 – honouree.
330-dc23

ISBN-13: 978-1-84893-533-4 (hbk)
ISBN-13: 978-0-367-66939-3 (pbk)

Typeset by Pickering & Chatto (Publishers) Limited

CONTENTS

LIST OF CONTRIBUTORS

Amanar Akhabbar is Professor of Economics at ESSCA School of Management and Lecturer at the *Collège des humanités*, Swiss Federal Institute of Technology, Lausanne.

François Allisson is Lecturer at the *Centre Walras-Pareto d'études interdisciplinaires de la pensée économique et politique*, University of Lausanne.

Richard Arena is Professor of Economics at *Institut d'économie et de management*, University of Nice Sophia Antipolis.

Roger E. Backhouse is Professor of the History and Philosophy of Economics at the University of Birmingham (UK) and Erasmus University Rotterdam.

Roberto Baranzini is Professor of Economics and History of Economic Thought at the University of Lausanne, and Director of the *Centre Walras-Pareto d'études interdisciplinaires de la pensée économique et politique*.

Sandrine Baume is Professor of Political Science at the *Centre de droit public*, University of Lausanne.

Daniele Besomi is Senior Research Fellow at the *Centre Walras-Pareto d'études interdisciplinaires de la pensée économique et politique*, University of Lausanne.

Giovanni Busino is Professor Emeritus of Sociology at the University of Lausanne.

Jean Cartelier is Professor Emeritus of Economics at the Université Paris-Ouest La Défense.

Jacques Coenen-Huther is retired Lecturer in Sociology at the University of Geneva.

Francesca Dal Degan is Senior Researcher at the *Centre Walras-Pareto d'études interdisciplinaires de la pensée économique et politique* and teacher of History of Economic Thought at the Sophia University Institute.

Jean-Pierre Danthine is Vice-Chairman of the Governing Board, Swiss National Bank and Head of Department II (Financial Stability, Cash, Finance and Risk).

Michel De Vroey is Professor Emeritus at the Université catholique de Louvain and Visiting Professor at the Université Saint-Louis.

Pierre Dockès is Professor Emeritus at the Université Lumière-Lyon 2.

Nathalie Dongois is Senior Lecturer at the *Institut de criminologie et de droit pénal*, University of Lausanne.

Rodolphe Dos Santos Ferreira is Professor Emeritus at the University of Strasbourg and member of the *Bureau d'Economie Théorique et Appliquée*.

Biancamaria Fontana is Professor of History of political thought and Political philosophy at the *Institut d'études politiques et internationales*, University of Lausanne.

Jean Pierre Gaudin is Professor Emeritus of Political Science at Sciences-Po Aix.

Bruna Ingrao is Professor of History of Economic Thought at the *Dipartimento di scienze sociali e economiche*, University of Rome 'La Sapienza'.

David Laidler is Professor Emeritus of Economics at the University of Western Ontario, London, Canada.

Jérôme Lallement is Professor of Economics at the University Paris Descartes, and Fellow at the *Centre d'économie de la Sorbonne (CNRS-Université Paris1)*.

Pierre Livet is Emeritus Professor of Philosophy and Epistemology at the University of Aix-Marseille.

Maria Cristina Marcuzzo is Professor of Economics at the *Dipartimento di scienze statistiche*, University of Rome 'La Sapienza'.

Steven G. Medema is University Distinguished Professor of Economics at the Department of Economics, University of Colorado Denver.

Pierre Moor is Professor Emeritus of Administrative Law at the University of Lausanne.

Fiorenzo Mornati is Professor of Economics at the *Dipartimento di economia e statistica 'Cognetti de Martiis'*, University of Torino.

Solène Morvant-Roux is Assistant Professor at the *Département d'économie politique*, University of Fribourg.

Emmanuel Picavet is Professor of Applied Ethics at the University of Paris 1 Panthéon-Sorbonne and a Member of the Sorbonne Centre for Contemporary Philosophy.

Pier Luigi Porta is Professor of Economics at the University of Milano-Bicocca, a Member of Christ's College and Visiting Fellow of Wolfson College at Cambridge University.

Jean-Pierre Potier is Professor of Economics at the University Lumière-Lyon 2, and Member of the CNRS research team *Triangle. Action, discours et pensée politique et économique.*

Jean-Michel Servet is Professor of Development Studies at the Graduate Institute of Geneva.

Francesca Sofia is Professor of History of Political Institutions at the *Dipartimento di storia, culture, civiltà*, University of Bologna.

Philippe Steiner is Professor of Sociology at the University of Paris-Sorbonne and Senior member of the *Institut universitaire de France.*

Sophie Swaton is Lecturer at the *Centre Walras-Pareto d'études interdisciplinaires de la pensée économique et politique*, University of Lausanne.

Maria Tortajada is Professor of History and Aesthetics of Film at the *Section d'histoire et esthétique du cinema*, University of Lausanne.

Jan van Daal is Professor Emeritus and Member of the CNRS research team *Triangle. Action, discours et pensée politique et économique*, University Lumière-Lyon 2.

Donald Walker is Professor Emeritus of Economics at the Indiana University of Pennsylvania.

Amos Witztum is Professor of Economics and Research Associate at the Centre for Philosophy of Social and Natural Sciences, London School of Economics.

LIST OF FIGURES AND TABLES

INTRODUCTION: ECONOMICS AND OTHER BRANCHES – IN THE SHADE OF THE OAK TREE: ESSAYS IN HONOUR OF PASCAL BRIDEL

Roberto Baranzini and François Allisson

Introduction

In one of his *notes d'humeur* – casual annotations scribbled on a piece of paper – Léon Walras once wrote:

> One must know what one is doing. If one wants to harvest promptly, one should plant carrots and salads; if one has the ambition to plant oak trees, one must be wise enough to say: [posterity] will owe me this shade.[1]

This formula is famous among Walrasian scholars: 'carrots' and 'salads' are good only for those working under the limiting framework of partial analysis; while those working, like Walras, on general equilibrium stay wisely 'in the shade of the oak tree'.

This volume celebrates Pascal Bridel's academic career on the occasion of his retirement. It collects thirty-two essays written by his colleagues and friends and illustrates the wide range of his academic interests. It offers at the same time a comprehensive survey of recent research in his areas of expertise: history of economic thought, economic theory (especially monetary theory), and the relations between economics and its neighbouring disciplines. Given Bridel's original and stimulating academic personality, he would be disappointed if this was not the case.

Pascal Bridel was born on 11 July 1948 in Lausanne, Switzerland. He was educated in Lausanne, and graduated from University of Lausanne in Political Science (1971) and in Economics (1972). He obtained his first PhD in economics from Lausanne University in 1976 with a dissertation entitled 'Loi des débouchés et principe de la demande effective. Essai de contribution à l'histoire de l'analyse économique', showing from the start an interest in the history of economic thought.

This first doctoral work was followed by a decisive period in his formation: from 1976 to 1981 he carried out his research at Trinity College, Cambridge. Cambridge in the 1970s was unique in the way economic theory and history of economic thought interrelated: this could not leave Bridel indifferent, and indeed it gave shape to the main themes of his academic career. At the time Cambridge was still a Keynesian world: Donald Moggridge was completing the *Collected Writings of John Maynard Keynes*; Bridel himself collaborated with John Eatwell, Murray Milgate and Peter Newman to the edition of *The New Palgrave: A Dictionary of Economics* (1987). But the more lasting analytic influence came from one of his teachers at Cambridge, Frank Horace Hahn, who, together with Don Patinkin, introduced him to an issue that was to stay with him for the rest of his career: the impossible integration of money into general equilibrium. Cambridge was also the place where Bridel met several scholars with whom he would maintain life-long academic and personal contacts; some of these old Cambridge friends contribute to this volume. Two essays in particular are dedicated to classical Cambridge themes: Maria Cristina Marcuzzo illustrates the fate of the Keynesian multiplier, while Pier Luigi Porta recalls the Italian tradition within Cambridge economics.

At the end of this period Bridel completed his Cambridge PhD, 'Some Aspects of the Saving-Investment Technique of Analysis' (published in 1987 by Macmillan with the title *Cambridge Monetary Thought: Development of Saving-Investment Analysis from Marshall to Keynes*). He then pursued his interest in monetary theory with an experience in central banking. From 1981 to 1986 he was first researcher, and then economic advisor and head of the department for international monetary relations, at the Swiss National Bank in Zurich. There he took part in meetings with the OECD, the Bank for International Settlement and the IMF. Since then, he has always kept up-to-date with monetary theory and policy. Four essays in this volume recall this phase in his career. Jean-Pierre Danthine, former colleague at the University of Lausanne and presently Vice-Chairman of the Governing Board of the Swiss National Bank, sets forth the case for a macro-prudential approach to financial stability. David Laidler revisits two important events in economic history through Irving Fisher's well-known equation. Jean Cartelier, echoing a neo-Mengerian theme widely developed by Bridel in his lectures, explores the possible endogenous nature of money in search models. Finally, Solène Morvant-Roux and Jean-Michel Servet outline an alternative paradigm for money, in which economics interacts with anthropology.

In 1986 Bridel was appointed Full Professor of Economics at the Law Faculty of Lausanne University, thus becoming the fifth holder of this Chair after Walras, and the fourth after Pareto. In 1990, he created the *Centre d'études interdisciplinaires Walras-Pareto*, that he directed from 1990 to 2012. The *Centre Walras-Pareto* was initially created to rescue the archives and highlight the value of the personal libraries of Walras and Pareto. An important product of this bibliographical and archival material was the publication, in 1996, of *Le Chêne et l'architecte*, an annotated collection of a century of reviews of Walras's *Elements of Pure Economics*. In 1997 Bridel published the remarkable *Money and General Equilibrium Theory. From Walras to Pareto (1870–1923)*, a work centred on the Lausanne School, and more specifically on Léon Walras's economic thought, with a distinctive emphasis on the integration of money into general equilibrium. Several essays in this volume reflect this line of research. The section entitled Léon Walras's Economic Thought shows how Bridel's research on Walras in the 1990s was carried out in parallel with the publication by a team of scholars at Lyon, of Auguste and Léon Walras's *Œuvres économiques complètes* (to which he contributed) and in the context of a renewal of the historiography on Walras and general equilibrium. This collective effort has been realized by *Association Internationale Walras* (that Bridel chaired with Jean-Pierre Potier in 2010–12), and in the framework of the research project (CRNS-FNS) on *L'équilibre général comme savoir*, jointly developed by the GRESE (Paris 1 Panthéon-Sorbonne) and the *Centre Walras-Pareto*.

In this volume, Jérôme Lallement unravels Walras's position on the dichotomy between individualism and holism. Rodolphe Dos Santos Ferreira reassesses Bertrand's critique of Walras. Pierre Dockès compares the philosophy of history of Walras and Marx. Richard Arena discusses to what degree Sraffa's theory is not Walrasian. Two other sections approach Walras from the angle of the history of economic thought. Roger Backhouse and Steven Medema present the reception of Walras in the Anglo-Saxon – Marshallian – world. Jan van Daal and Donald Walker revisit their translation of Walras's *Studies in Social Economy* of 2010 that contributed to this reception. On the Lausanne School, Fiorenzo Mornati explores the question of social complexity, by introducing the reader to Pareto's second approximation. François Allisson provides for the first time a study of the work of Basile Samsonoff, a forgotten PhD student of Pareto.

At the University of Lausanne Bridel was in charge of the teaching of history of economic thought, monetary theory and policy, and political economy for lawyers. He was also visiting professor at the universities of Paris 1-Panthéon-Sorbonne, Lyon 2 and Paul-Cézanne Aix III. For several years (between 1985–8 and 1991–2) he gave advanced lectures on monetary theory on behalf of the Ministry of Finance and the People's Bank of China. Between 2000 and 2014, he taught history of economic thought at the University of Geneva. Under his auspices, the *Centre Walras-Pareto* organized several conferences, notably on the edition of economists (1991), on the socialist calculation debate (1992), on general equilibrium (1998), on Don Patinkin (2001) and on Léon Walras (2006). In 2014 the *Centre Walras-Pareto* continues this tradition by hosting the annual conference of the European Society for the History of Economic Thought, which brings together about two hundred and fifty historians of economic thought.

Besides pursuing his own research, Bridel contributed to a series of collective projects. He sat on various editorial boards: *The European Journal of the History of Economic Thought*, *Économie et société (série PE)*, *Revue européenne des sciences sociales*, *Œconomia*; he was member of the advisory board of the second edition of *The New Palgrave Dictionary of Economics*, and member of the executive committee and treasurer of the European Society for the History of Economic Thought. He also served as Vice-Dean of the Faculty of Law, and as Vice-Rector of the University of Lausanne. Since its foundation the size of *Centre Walras-Pareto* has grown, from including just Pascal Bridel and one assistant, to a team of sixteen scholars in 2014, engaged in research and teaching activities in the history of economic thought, economic philosophy and the history of political thought.

This development reflects the diversification of Bridel's interests, and his engagement first with methodology, then with interdisciplinary studies. Several contributions in this volume illustrate this preoccupation with economic methodology. Amos Witztum looks into the relations between economics and ethics in Adam Smith's work. Pierre Livet explores the role of history within philosophy and economics. Emmanuel Picavet revisits economic themes using a Hobbesian methodology. Daniele Besomi describes the use of meteorological metaphors in the theories of economic crises. Amanar Akhabbar stresses the striking methodological similarities between two of Samuelson's theorems.

Bridel's engagement with interdisciplinary studies resulted in his long involvement in the research group *Raison et Rationalité* (several members of which contribute to this volume), and in his active participation to Giovanni Busino's *Revue européenne des sciences sociales (Cahiers Vilfredo Pareto)*, of which he edited several special issues. Bridel has always been very interested in the problem of the coordination of human actions, a question to which economics can provide only a partial frame of understanding. This led him to compare how various disciplines – sociology, law, political sciences, but also fine arts – addressed these theoretical problems. In this volume, Jacques Coenen-Huther discusses the relation between economics and sociology by illustrating the distinction between two ideal-types – the *homo œconomicus* and the *homo sociologicus*. Jean-Pierre Gaudin analyses how interdisciplinary and trans-disciplinary approaches can handle complex social issues in today's academic context. Giovanni Busino provides a dismal account of the current state of sociology. From the perspective of the history of political thought, Biancamaria Fontana presents a sceptical approach to the issue of accountability and Sandrine Baume revisits the concept of transparency in political thought. From the law perspective, Pierre Moor reveals the normative power of law as a system and Nathalie Dongois and Sophie Swaton show how criminal law could handle the social responsibility of firms in front of the environmental challenge. In the domain of visual arts, Bruna Ingrao makes a distinction between cognition in the visual arts, and rationality in economics. Maria Tortajada transposes the dichotomy, well known to economists, between realism and reality, to film history and aesthetics. Finally, Michel De Vroey raises the difficult question of what civil society can expect from macroeconomic theory. These interdisciplinary studies reflect Bridel's search for intellectually stimulating topics, to enrich his own contributions as a historian of economic thought.

One of most recent volumes edited by Bridel, *General Equilibrium Analysis: A Century after Walras* (2011), published on the centenary of the death of Léon Walras, attests that Bridel's main area of expertise remains general equilibrium analysis, and that, in this domain, he is close to a group of distinguished economists: Arrow, Baumol, Kirman, Guesnerie, Posner, Solow – all contributors to the volume, and all, like him, firmly 'in the shade of the oak tree'.

More recently, Bridel has been engaged with Francesca Dal Degan and Nicolas Eyguesier in the publication of Simonde de Sismondi's *Œuvres économiques complètes*, the first two volumes of which feature in the partial bibliography (until 2013) given at the end of this introduction. Three contributions reflect this editorial project: Philippe Steiner looks at the political aspects of Quesnay's political economy, Francesca Dal Degan and Francesca Sofia present Benjamin Constant as reader of Sismondi, and Jean-Pierre Potier examines how French liberal economists thought about the 'social question' during the 1848 Revolution.

The book is organized in six parts – Léon Walras's Economic Thought, The Spreading of Thought, Monetary Theory, Methodology, Economics and Humanities, Economics and Civil Society. All the essays have been specifically composed in honour of Pascal Bridel.

We are very grateful to the *Faculté de Droit, des sciences criminelles et d'administration publique* of the University of Lausanne for having initiated this project, which would have been impossible without its support. We would also like to thank all the contributors, as well as all the members of the *Centre Walras-Pareto* for their help in the preparation of this volume.

Roberto Baranzini and François Allisson
*Centre Walras-Pareto d'études interdisciplinaires
de la pensée économique et politique*
University of Lausanne

PASCAL BRIDEL'S BIBLIOGRAPHY (UP TO 2013)

Bridel, P., 'Book Review: Une entreprise horlogère du Val-de-Travers. Fleurier Watch Co. SA, by François Jequier', *Revue économique et sociale*, 31 (1973), pp. 215–16.

—, 'Loi des débouchés et principe de la demande effective. Essai de contribution à l'histoire de l'analyse économique' (PhD dissertation, University of Lausanne, Lausanne: Tex, 1977).

—, 'Temps et science économique', *Skepsis*, 1 (1977), pp. 12–18.

—, 'On Keynes's Quotations from Mill: A Note', *Economic Journal*, 89:355 (1979), pp. 660–2.

—, 'Some Notes on Marshall's Theory of Interest', *Studi Economici*, 18 (1982), pp. 91–113.

—, 'Essai d'estimation de la part suisse à l'activité financière internationale', *Monnaie et Conjoncture*, 2 (1984), pp. 61–71.

Bridel, P. and F. Leutwiler, 'Toward a Solution of the International Debt Problem: A Pragmatic Appoach', *Monnaie et Conjoncture*, 2 (1984), pp. 51–8.

Bridel, P., 'Book Review: The Economics of Supply and Demand, by L. R. Klein', *Contributions to Political Economy*, 4 (1985), pp. 101–4.

—, *Cambridge Monetary Thought: The Development of Saving-Investment Analysis from Marshall to Keynes* (London: Macmillan, 1987).

—, 'Chevalier, Michel', in J. Eatwell, M. Milgate and P. Newman (eds), *The New Palgrave Dictionary of Economics* (London: Macmillan, 1987), p. 412.

—, 'Credit Cycle', in Eatwell, Milgate and Newman (eds), *The New Palgrave Dictionary of Economics*, pp. 717–19.

—, 'Currency und Bankingtheorie', in E. Albisetti et al. (eds), *Handbuch des Geld-Bank und Börsenwesens der Schweiz* (Thoune: Ott Verlag, 1987).

—, 'Ganilh, Charles', in Eatwell, Milgate and Newman (eds), *The New Palgrave Dictionary of Economics*, p. 483.

—, 'Goschen, George', in Eatwell, Milgate and Newman (eds), *The New Palgrave Dictionary of Economics*, p. 550.

—, 'Lavington, Frederick', in Eatwell, Milgate and Newman (eds), *The New Palgrave Dictionary of Economics*, pp. 142–3.

—, 'Lender-of-Last-Resort', in E. Albisetti et al. (eds), *Handbuch des Geld-Bank und Börsenwesens der Schweiz* (Thoune: Ott Verlag, 1987).

—, 'Léon Walras: Théorie et politique économiques', in G. Busino and P. Bridel (eds), *L'école de Lausanne de Léon Walras à Pasquale Boninsegni* (Lausanne: Université de Lausanne, 1987), pp. 13–28.

—, 'Montchrétien, Antoyne', in Eatwell, Milgate and Newman (eds), *The New Palgrave Dictionary of Economics*, pp. 546–7.

—, 'Price Level', in Eatwell, Milgate and Newman (eds), *The New Palgrave Dictionary of Economics*, pp. 955–7.

—, 'Public Works', in Eatwell, Milgate and Newman (eds), *The New Palgrave Dictionary of Economics*, pp. 1072–3.

—, 'Saving Equals Investment', in Eatwell, Milgate and Newman (eds), *The New Palgrave Dictionary of Economics*, pp. 246–8.

—, 'Widow's Cruse', in Eatwell, Milgate and Newman (eds), *The New Palgrave Dictionary of Economics*, pp. 919–20.

Busino, G. and P. Bridel, *L'école de Lausanne de Léon Walras à Pasquale Boninsegni* (Lausanne: Université de Lausanne, 1987).

Bridel, P., 'Banque centrale, système de taux de change et relations économiques extérieures: quelques réflexions sur le cas de la Banque nationale suisse depuis la seconde guerre mondiale', *Relations Internationales*, 56 (1988), pp. 487–511.

Bridel, P. and R. Cippà, 'Alcune riflessioni sulla crisi dell'indebitamento internazionale', in M. Baranzini and A. Cencini (eds), *Contributi di analisi economica* (Bellinzona: Edizioni Casagrande, 1987), pp. 265–88.

Bridel, P., 'Book Review: Structures of Inquiry and Economic Theory, by M. Baranzini and R. Scazzieri (eds), Oxford, 1986', *Revue suisse d'économie politique et de statistique*, 124 (1988), pp. 79–81.

—, 'Quelques réflexions sur l'idée de "main invisible"', *Revue européenne des sciences sociales*, 26:82 (1988), pp. 79–98.

—, *Cambridge Monetary Thought: The Development of Saving-Investment Analysis from Marshall to Keynes* (London: Macmillan, 1989).

—, 'Price Level', in J. Eatwell, M. Milgate and P. Newman (eds), *Money* (London: Macmillan, 1989), pp. 298–302.

—, 'Équilibre, statique et analyse dynamique chez Vilfredo Pareto. Remarques sur la contribution de Siro Lombardini', *Revue européenne des sciences sociales*, 28:88 (1990), pp. 183–91.

—, 'Equilibrio, statica comparata e analisi dinamica in Pareto', in G. Busino (ed.), *Pareto Oggi* (Bologna: Il Mulino, 1991), pp. 43–52.

—, 'La contribution de Walras à la théorie du monopole de l'émission de monnaie', in *Hommage à un européen offert à Henri Rieben à l'occasion de son 70ème anniversaire* (Lausanne: Ecole des HEC/Centre de recherches européennes, 1991), pp. 303–15.

—, 'L'épargne des ménages dans le système de prévoyance d'une société vieillissante. Note de synthèse', in O. Blanc and P. Gilliand (eds), *Suisse 2000. Enjeux démographiques* (Lausanne: Réalités sociales, 1991), pp. 23–34.

—, 'Credit Cycle', in J. Eatwell, M. Milgate and P. Newman (eds), *The New Palgrave Dictionary of Money and Finance* (London: Macmillan, 1992), pp. 527–9.

— (ed.), 'Editing Economists and Economists as Editors', *Revue européenne des sciences sociales*, special issue, 30:92 (Geneva and Paris: Droz, 1992).

—, 'Gibson Paradox', in Eatwell, Milgate and Newman (eds), *The New Palgrave Dictionary of Money and Finance*, pp. 239–40.

—, 'Introduction', *Revue européenne des sciences sociales*, 30:92 (1992), pp. 5–7.

—, 'La politica monetaria svizzera nella prospettiva dell'unione monetaria europea', in R. Chopard (ed.), *Europa '93! E la piazza finanziaria svizzera?* (Lugano: Meta Edizioni, 1992).

—, 'The Lausanne Lectures in Pure Economics: From Walras to Pareto (How and What to Publish, if Anything at all!)', *Revue européenne des sciences sociales*, 30:92 (1992), pp. 145–69.

—, 'Transmission Mechanism and the Price Level', in Eatwell, Milgate and Newman (eds), *The New Palgrave Dictionary of Money and Finance*, pp. 693–6.

—, 'Widow's Cruse', in Eatwell, Milgate and Newman (eds), *The New Palgrave Dictionary of Money and Finance*, pp. 800–1.

—, 'Book Review: The Golden Age of the Quantity Theory, by Laidler, D.', *European Journal of the History of Economic Thought*, 1:1 (1993), pp. 186–9.

—, 'Comment on Ulrich Camen: "The Swiss Share in International Markets for Bank Deposits and Bonds"', in N. Blattner, H. Genberg and A. Swoboda (eds), *Banking in Switzerland* (Heidelberg and New York: Physica Verlag, 1993), pp. 297–301.

—, 'Introduction', *Revue européenne des sciences sociales*, 31:86 (1993), pp. 5–12.

— (ed.), *The Socialist Calculation Debate after the Upheavals in Eastern Europe. Papers Given at a Conference Held at the Centre d'Etudes Interdisciplinaires Walras-Pareto, nces sociales*, special issue, 31:96 (1993).

—, 'Dépréciation de la monnaie et épargne forcée. Une contribution négligée de Walras à la théorie monétaire des cycles', *Economies et Sociétés*, 28:10–11 (1994), pp. 89–114.

—, 'Book Review: Vilfredo Pareto: Neoclassical Synthesis of Economics and Sociology, by A. de Pietri-Tonelli and G. Bousquet', *Economic Journal*, 105:430 (1995), p. 798.

—, 'Book Review: Non-Natural Sciences: Reflecting on the Entreprise of More Heat than Light, edited by N. De Marchi', *Economic Journal*, 106:436 (1996), pp. 737–39.

Bridel, P., P. Dockès and J.-P. Potier (eds), 'Cours d'économie sociale. Cours d'économie politique appliquée. Matériaux du cours d'économie politique pure', vol. 12 of *Auguste et Léon Walras, Œuvres économiques complètes* (Paris: Economica, 1996).

Bridel, P., 'Book Review: The Notion of Equilibrium in the Keynesian Theory, edited by M. Sebastiani', *Economic Journal*, 107:440 (1996), p. 262.

—, 'L'économie normative épinglée', *Revue européenne des sciences sociales*, 34:104 (1996), pp. 229–32.

Bridel, P. and R. Baranzini, *Le Chêne et l'architecte: un siècle de comptes rendus bibliographiques des 'Eléments d'économie politique pure' de Léon Walras* (Geneva: Droz, 1996).

—, 'On Pareto's First Lectures on Pure Economics at Lausanne', *History of Economic Ideas*, 5:3 (1997), pp. 65–87.

Bridel, P., 'Book Review: The Economics of Joan Robinson, edited by Marcuzzo, C., Pasinetti, L. and Roncaglia, A.', *Economic Journal*, 107:445 (1997), pp. 1923–4.

—, 'Book Review: The Evolutionist Economics of Léon Walras, by Albert Jolink', *European Journal of the History of Economic Thought*, 4:3 (1997), pp. 530–3.

—, *Money and General Equilibrium Theory: From Walras to Pareto (1870–1923)* (Cheltenham: Edward Elgar, 1997).

Bridel, P. and J. Presley, 'John Maynard Keynes and the French Connection', *Manchester School of Economic and Social Studies*, 65:4 (1997), pp. 452–65.

Bridel, P., 'Book Review: Les Revues économiques en France. Genèse et actualité (1751–1994), by Marco, L.', *European Journal of the History of Economic Thought*, 5:3 (1998), pp. 554–70.

—, 'Book Review: Walras's Market Models, by Donald A. Walker', *Journal of Economic Literature*, 36:1 (1998), pp. 231–3.

—, 'Homo Œconomicus: Rerum cognoscere causas? ou du principe de rationalité comme instrument de connaissance en théorie économique', *Revue européenne des sciences sociales*, 37:113 (1999), pp. 149–67.

—, 'Une note d'humeur de Léon Walras. Commentaire', *Economies et Societes*, 28 (1999), pp. 161–4.

Bridel, P. and E. Tatti, 'Introduction', *Revue européenne des sciences sociales*, 37:116 (1999), pp. 5–9.

— (eds), 'L'équilibre général entre économie et sociologie', *Revue européenne des sciences sociales*, special issue, 37:116 (1999).

Bridel, P., 'From Walras's to Pareto's Teaching: the case of Monetary Theory', in C. Malandrino and R. Marchionatti (eds), *Economia, sociologia e politica nell'opera de Vilfredo Pareto* (Florence: L. S. Olschki, 2000), pp. 123–39.

— (ed.), 'La peur de l'impensable dans les sciences sociales, VIè séminaire interdisciplinaire du Groupe d'Etudes "Raison et Rationalités"', *Revue européenne des sciences sociales*, special issue, 38:119 (2000), 157 p.

—, 'L'Homo Œconomicus aurait-il peur de l'homo sapiens? Ou la peur de l'irrationnel peut-elle amener à l'obscurantisme?', *Revue européenne des sciences sociales*, 38:119 (2000), pp. 45–64.

—, 'Book Review: Les traditions économiques françaises (1848–1939), P. Dockès et al. (eds)', *History of Political Economy*, 33:3 (2001), pp. 664–7.

— (ed.), *The Foundations of Price Theory*, 6 vols (London: Pickering & Chatto, 2001), xviii + 403, xiv + 365, 359, 340, xxvi + 369, 280 p.

— (ed.), 'L'acteur. Un concept sur la scène des sciences sociales, VIIè séminaire interdisciplinaire du Groupe d'Etudes 'Raison et Rationalités'', *Revue européenne des sciences sociales*, special issue, 39:121 (2001), 139 p.

—, 'Introduction', in *Revue européenne des sciences sociales*, special issue, 39:121 (2001), pp. 5–6.

—, 'The Endogeneity of Money: Walras and the "Moderns"', in B. Schefold (ed.), *Exogeneity and Endogeneity: The Quantity Theory of Money in the History of Economic Thought and in Modern Policy* (Marburg: Metropolis, 2002), pp. 227–47.

Bridel, P. and M. De Vroey (eds), 'Patinkin and the Development of Modern Economic Theory', *European Journal of the History of Economic Thought*, special issue, 9:2 (2002), pp. 155–326.

—, 'Introduction', in 'Patinkin and the Development of Modern Economic Theory', *European Journal of the History of Economic Thought*, special issue, 9:2 (2002), pp. 155–60.

Bridel, P., 'Patinkin, Walras and the "Money-in-the-Utility-Function" Tradition', in 'Patinkin and the Development of Modern Economic Theory', *European Journal of the History of Economic Thought*, special issue, 9:2 (2002), pp. 268–92.

—, 'Wicksell and the Gibson Paradox', in P. L. Porta and G. Vaggi (eds), *Employment, Technology and Institutions in the Process of Structural Change*, Working Paper 51 (Milan: Università degli Studi di Milano-Bicocca, July 2002), pp. 99–103.

—, 'Book Review: Studies in the History of French Political Economy: From Bodin to Walras, edited by Gilbert Facarello', *Economic Journal*, 112:483 (2002), pp. 578–81.

Bridel, P. and E. Huck, 'Yet another Look at Léon Walras's Theory of Tâtonnement', *European Journal of the History of Economic Thought*, 9:4 (2002), pp. 513–40.

—, 'Walras's Tâtonnement: A Reply to Rebeyrol and Costa', *European Journal of the History of Economic Thought*, 9:4 (2002), pp. 559–67.

Bridel, P., 'Say et le débat sur l'épargne forcée: une note', in J.-P. Potier and A. Tiran (eds), *Jean-Baptiste Say, Nouveaux regards sur son œuvre* (Paris: Economica, 2003), pp. 471–93.

—, 'Book Review: Competition, edited by Jack High', *Journal of the History of Economic Thought*, 25:3 (2003), pp. 367–9.

— (ed.), 'La preuve en sciences sociales, IXè séminaire interdisciplinaire du Groupe d'Etudes 'Raison et Rationalités'', *Revue européenne des sciences sociales*, special issue, 41:128 (2003), 171 p.

Bridel, P. and C. Salvat, 'Reason and Sentiments: Review of Emma Rothschild's Economic Sentiments: Adam Smith, Condorcet and the Enlightenment', *European Journal of the History of Economic Thought*, 11:1 (2004), pp. 131–45.

Bridel, P. (ed.), *L'invention dans les sciences humaines. Hommage à Giovanni Busino* (Geneva: Labor et Fides, 2004), 216 p.

—, 'L'invention en théorie économique: stabilité, instabilité et transfert', in P. Bridel (ed.), *L'invention dans les sciences humaines. Hommage à Giovanni Busino* (Geneva: Labor et Fides, 2004), pp. 126–41.

—, 'Book Review: Vilfredo Pareto and the Birth of Modern Microeconomics by Luigino Bruni', *History of Political Economy*, 36:4 (2004), pp. 763–5.

—, 'Cherbuliez, Antoine-Elisée', in *Dictionnaire historique de la Suisse, Vol. 3* (Hauterive: Gilles Attinger, 2004).

—, 'Lavington, Frederick', in *Oxford Dictionary of National Biography, Vol. 10* (Oxford: Oxford University Press, 2004).

— (ed.), 'La cumulativité des savoirs en sciences sociales, Xè colloque interdisciplinaire du Groupe d'Etudes "Raison et Rationalités"', *Revue européenne des sciences sociales*, special issue, 43:131 (2005), 145 p.

—, 'Cumulativité des connaissances et science économique: Que cherche-t-on exactement à cumuler?', *Revue européenne des sciences sociales*, special issue, 43:131 (2005), pp. 63–79.

—, 'Pourquoi la monnaie a-t-elle une valeur positive?', in B. Bovary and M. S. Nguyen (eds), *Mélanges Pierre Moor* (Berne: Staempfli, 2005), pp. 21–9.

Bridel, P. and R. Baranzini, 'L'Ecole de Lausanne, l'utilité marginale moyenne et l'idée de marché', in G. Bensimon (ed.), *Histoire des représentations du marché* (Paris: Houdiard, 2005), pp. 347–65.

Bridel, P., 'Lausanne (École de)', in M. Borlandi, R. Boudon, R. Cherkaoui and B. Valade (eds), *Dictionnaire de la pensée sociologique* (Paris: PUF, 2005), pp. 387–9.

Bridel, P. and B. Ingrao, 'Managing Cambridge Economics: The Correspondence between Keynes and Pigou', in M. C. Marcuzzo and A. Rosselli (eds), *Economists in Cambridge: A Study through their Correspondence. 1907–1946* (London: Routledge, 2005), pp. 149–73.

Bridel, P., 'Review of Fabio Petri, General Equilibrium, Capital and Macroeconomics: A Key to Recent Controversies in Equilibrium Theory', *History of Economic Ideas*, 13 (2006), pp. 151–6.

— (ed.), 'Devant la loi, XIè colloque interdisciplinaire du Groupe d'Etudes "Raison et Rationalités"', *Revue européenne des sciences sociales*, special issue, 44:133 (2006), 162 p.

—, 'Avant-propos', *Revue européenne des sciences sociales*, special issue, 44:133 (2006), p. 5.

—, 'Review of Thomas J. Sargent and François R. Velde, The Big Problem of Small Change', *Economica*, 73 (2006), pp. 547–8.

—, 'Credit Cycles and the Rate of Interest', in T. Rafaelli, G. Becattini and M. Dardi (eds), *The Elgar Companion to Alfred Marshall* (Cheltenham: Elgar, 2006), pp. 445–52.

—, 'La théorie monétaire après Walras: une logique.... Walrassienne', *Economies et Sociétés*, 38 (2006), pp. 1693–704.

— (ed.), 'Evaluation en sciences sociales: concepts, mesures et comparaisons, XIIè colloque interdisciplinaire du Groupe d'Etudes "Raison et Rationalités"', *Revue européenne des sciences sociales*, special issue, 45:138 (2007), 152 p.

—, 'Avant-Propos', *Revue européenne des sciences sociales*, special issue, 45:138 (2007), p. 5.

—, 'Le rôle de la mesure dans la construction de l'objet théorique et comment l'objet théorique devient ... mesure', *Revue européenne des sciences sociales*, special issue, 45:138 (2007), pp. 143–52.

— (ed.), 'Processus d'évaluation des sciences sociales: acteurs et valeurs, XIIIè colloque interdisciplinaire du Groupe d'Etudes 'Raison et Rationalités', *Revue européenne des sciences sociales*, special issue, 46:141 (2008), 111 p.

—, 'Avant-Propos', *Revue européenne des sciences sociales*, special issue, 46:141 (2008), p. 5.

—, 'Bortkiewicz et Walras. Notes sur une collaboration intellectuelle avortée', *Revue d'économie politique*, 118 (2008), pp. 711–42.

—, 'Lausanne, école de', in *Dictionnaire historique de la Suisse, Vol. 7* (Hauterive: Gilles Attinger, 2008).

—, 'Review of James Macdonald, A Free Nation Deep in Debt. The Financial Roots of Democracy', *Economica*, 76 (2009), pp. 402–3.

— (ed.), 'Rationalités et émotions: un examen critique, XIVè colloque interdisciplinaire du Groupe d'Etudes "Raison et Rationalités"', *Revue européenne des sciences sociales*, special issue, 47:144 (2009), 162 p.

—, 'Avant Propos', *Revue européenne des sciences sociales*, special issue, 47:144 (2009), p. 5.

—, '"Passions et intérêts" revisités: la suppression des" sentiments" est-elle à l'origine de l'économie politique', *Revue européenne des sciences sociales*, special issue, 47:144 (2009), pp. 135–50.

Bridel, P. and F. Mornati, 'De l'équilibre général comme "branche de la métaphysique"; ou de l'opinion de Pareto sur le projet walrasien', *Revue économique*, 60 (2009), pp. 869–90.

Bridel, P., 'Théorie économique et philosophie politique: quelques réflexions préliminaires sur la réédition de l'oeuvre scientifique de Sismondi', *Cahiers d'économie politique*, 57 (2009), pp. 127–46.

Bridel, P., and M. Dal-Pont Legrand (eds), 'Clément Juglar (1819–1905). Les origines de la théorie des cycles', *Revue européenne des sciences sociales*, special issue, 47:143 (2009), 124 p.

Bridel, P., F. Allisson and L. Breban, 'Bibliographie de Clément Juglar', *Revue européenne des sciences sociales*, special issue, 47:143 (2009), pp. 107–24.

Bridel, P., and M. Dal-Pont Legrand, 'Introduction', *Revue européenne des sciences sociales*, special issue, 47:143 (2009), pp. 7–11.

Bridel, P., 'Juglar, Walras et Pareto: Measurement without Theory vs Theory without Measurement', *Revue européenne des sciences sociales*, special issue, 47:143 (2009), pp. 87–94.

—, 'Barbeyrac, ou le droit (naturel) saisi par le jeu (économique?): une note', in D. Tappy, B. Kahil-Wolff and L. Bruchez (eds), *300 ans d'enseignement du droit à Lausanne* (Geneva: Schulthess, 2010), pp. 81–9.

—, 'A propos de l'idée d'"École de Lausanne"', *Revue européenne des sciences sociales*, 48:146 (2010), pp. 89–92.

— (ed.), *General Equilibrium Analysis: A Century after Walras* (London: Routledge, 2011), xix + 148 p.

—, 'Introduction', in Bridel (ed.), *General Equilibrium Analysis: A Century after Walras*, pp. xv–xix.

—, 'The Normative Origins of General Equilibrium Theory; or, Walras's Attempts at Reconciling Economic Efficiency with Social Justice', in Bridel (ed.), *General Equilibrium Analysis: A Century after Walras*, pp. 15–23.

—, 'Of the "Old" Palgrave Entries on Crises', in D. Besomi (ed.), *Crises and Cycles in Economic Dictionaries and Encyclopaedias* (London: Routledge, 2011), pp. 332–42.

—, 'Origines et détermination du "prix de chaque chose": la Richesse commerciale entre le coût de production de Smith et la "catallactique" de l'offre et de la demande de Canard', *Il pensiero economico italiano*, 19 (2011), pp. 85–92.

Bridel, P. and N. Dongois, 'Transmission du VIH et traitement de l'information: une tentative d'analyse économique de l'art. 231 CP', in M. A. Niggli and M. Jendly (eds), *Système pénal et discours publics: entre justice câline et justice répressive* (Berne: Editions Stämpfli, 2012), pp. 39–62.

Bridel, P., 'Walras and Pareto on the Connection between the Trade Cycle and General Equilibrium Theory', in H. M. Krämer, H. D. Kurz and H. M. Trautwein (eds), *Festschrift in honour of Harald Hagemann: Macroeconomics and the History of Thought* (London: Routledge, 2012), pp. 78–95.

Bridel, P. and B. Kapossy (eds), 'Sismondi: Républicanisme moderne et libéralisme critique-Modern Republicanism and Critical Liberalism', *Travaux et recherches de l'Institut Benjamin Constant*, 14 (Geneva: Slatkine, 2013), 244 p.

Bridel, P., 'Sismondi on Paper Money and Public Debt (1810): Or, a Missed (?) Opportunity to Join the Bullionist Controversy', in 'Sismondi: Républicanisme moderne et libéralisme critique-Modern Republicanism and Critical Liberalism', *Travaux et recherches de l'Institut Benjamin Constant*, 14 (Geneva: Slatkine, 2013), pp. 165–77.

Sismondi, J. C. L., *J.C.L. Sismondi, Œuvres economiques completes*, Vol. 2, *De la richesse commerciale*, ed. P. Bridel, F. Dal Degan and N. Eyguesier (Paris: Economica, 2012).

—, *J.C.L. Sismondi, Œuvres economiques completes*, Vol. 3, *Ecrits d'economie politique 1799–1815*, ed. P. Bridel, F. Dal Degan and N. Eyguesier (Paris: Economica, 2012).

1 WALRAS BETWEEN HOLISM AND INDIVIDUALISM

Jérôme Lallement

When an example is to be found of the way methodological individualism is used in economics, mention is made of the theory of general equilibrium as the canonical example of an individualistic approach to economic phenomena.[1]

The overall equilibrium is based on a representation of society. Society is composed of free and equal individuals. Though equal in rights, these individuals may differ from each other only because they do not have the same tastes or resources. These individuals are supposed to be rational, free and independent of each other (isolated). Socializing these isolated individuals can be done through markets. Exchanges on markets allow individuals to maximize their satisfaction or profit. If there is such a thing as the general equilibrium, it is a situation in which, after trading, each agent obtains the highest satisfaction possible, in light of his or her initial resources. This equilibrium is deemed good for society insofar as it is an optimum. Thus presented, the overall equilibrium is fully compliant with methodological individualism standards: a collective phenomenon, the system of price equilibrium, can be completely accounted for by individuals' behaviours. As noted by Kenneth J. Arrow, economists today have overwhelmingly rallied to methodological individualism:[2] 'It is a touchstone of accepted economics that all explanations must run in terms of the actions and reactions of individuals.'[3]

Because he is the inventor of general equilibrium, Walras is credited with the methodological individualism that is at work in today's microeconomics. Yet Walras is quite explicit in his rejection of methodological individualism in favour of a synthetic position between individualism and holism.[4] Portraying Walras as an advocate of methodological individualism results from hasty and abusive assimilation between the theory of general equilibrium, as outlined in the *Elements of Pure Economics* (1874–7), and the classic representation of a market as the place where isolated individuals can socialize. In a market, individuals meet; they are isolated and independent of each other, and confront their individual choices. Some supply, others demand, and the market is precisely the means by which supply and demand balance each other. At equilibrium price, all buyers willing to pay that price will find sellers willing to sell them as much as they wish to buy and, symmetrically, all sellers will find buyers willing to buy them all they are willing to sell at that price. Since Smith, the virtues of the market have often been highlighted. Here is a process that takes as explanatory data the agents' actions and that, from these strictly individual data can explain a collective phenomenon, the market clearing price. Sometimes, this market equilibrium is assimilated to the expression of a law, the law of supply and demand. In case of insufficient supply, prices rise and demand falls because buyers reduce their personal demand; and supply increases because higher prices encourage producers to increase their production. Individual behaviours contribute to restoring balance. The market is therefore a perfect example of the implementation of methodological individualism: a social phenomenon (the market clearing price) is fully explained by individual behaviours. In this line of interpretation, the overall balance is the extension of the analysis of a single market to an economy composed of a multitude of interrelated markets. And methodological individualism is again carefully implemented.

The objective here is to show that Walras was radically hostile to individualism in all its forms (ontological as well as methodological). Most often implicitly, all modern formulations of general equilibrium consider methodological individualism as a methodological principle accepted without discussion. Walras's position deserves special treatment to the extent that it adopts a very explicit social philosophy incompatible with methodological individualism. Some of Walras's paradoxical theses, such as his refusal of consent to taxation or advocating a flat tax, the same for all, can be explained by his ontological and methodological positions. First, Walras's world view should be clarified, since he bases his methodological choices on a realistic ontology (see Walras's World Vision, pp. 16–19). Walras developed a theory of the just society that is also a true theory of society (see The True Theory of a Just Society, pp. 20–3). The specificity of Walras's position is that it is neither individualistic nor holistic (see Considerations of Walras's Holism and Individualism, pp. 23–6). Hence there is a very special view of the role of the state, in complete contradiction with methodological individualism (see The Role of the State according to Walras, pp. 27–30).

Walras's World Vision

Walras first develops a theory of the individual and society and of their relationships. Then, on the basis of this theory, he constructs methodological principles consistent with this ontology, but very different from methodological individualism.

Ontology

Walras's world view is based on an opposition between two radically different entities: man and nature. It is necessary to contrast two types of events: natural facts and human facts. The first are the result of nature's blind and fatal forces, while the second are the product of human beings' free and conscious activity. This dichotomy is based on an, essential, ontological distinction between men and things; it implies an epistemological difference between the methods needed to address the facts of nature and those suitable for the study of human facts.

The distinction between man and nature is so important to Walras that he presents it at the very beginning of *Elements of Pure Political Economy*, in order to give a definition of political economy. This distinction was already made as early on as the *General Theory of Society* (1867–8) and will never be later denied by Walras.[5] The fundamental difference between man and nature introduces a dual characterization of man. Man is part of nature and is subject to the laws of nature as an animal, that is to say as a thing; but he also exists as a moral being since he is as man proper, that is to say a moral person. According to Walras, this dual characterization of man, as an animal but especially a moral person, implies a specificity that is irreducible to all knowledge on human beings.

Walras meant to build up the social science that was still lacking in the nineteenth century,[6] and, to this end, he first set out the methodological rules needed to address humanitarian facts – rules that must obviously be consistent with his ontology.[7] As opposed to natural facts, which are the result of blind and fatal forces, humanitarian facts are, by definition, the product of human action. These humanitarian facts have two specific human traits: first, man's ability for division of labour and, second, his moral personality.[8]

Man's aptitude for a division of labour pertains to physiology insofar as it is rooted in the peculiarities of the human anatomy.[9] Man's moral personality is expressed through his sensitivity, intelligence and will.[10] But it is especially the third feature of the human personality, his will, which interests the science of society. As an animal, man feels and knows that he is, feels and has knowledge; but man can boast something that no animal has:

> He has a purpose he strives to achieve, but he does so knowing he has a purpose and that it is up to him to pursue it; that is why we say that man accomplishes a free destiny and is fully aware he does, and that he is not a thing but a person.[11]

Finally, man himself is characterized by four features: his ability to division of labour, his sensitivity, his intelligence and his will. Walras then defines man as 'a moral person'[12] as opposed to animals (which are things). These four traits result in four types of humanitarian facts: Art (which includes the sum of friendly and aesthetic emotions, or all connections of human sensitivity with people or things), Science (or all the connections of human intelligence with nature), Labour (or Industry, i.e. all the social relations men have to satisfy their needs) and Mores (all the relations that men have with each other as moral persons to pursue their ends and fulfill their destinies). Each of these categories of facts is regulated by specific principles which are, respectively, the Beautiful for Art, the True for Science, the Useful for Industry and the Good (or Right) for Mores.

This is an initial classification of humanitarian facts, their specificities and regulatory principles. Thereafter, this categorization is somewhat simplified in the *Elements of Pure Political Economy* (1874–7) to result in the famous trilogy: 'art, science and morals', which is sufficient for political economy to cover all aspects of social wealth[13] and specify what are applied economics, pure economics and social economics. When he speaks of political economics, Walras slightly modifies his terminology: the word 'art' replaces 'industry' (with the same regulative principle, the useful) and mores become morals;[14] as human emotions and feelings are not immediately relevant in the field of political economics, the aesthetic dimension is ignored by Walras in the *Elements of Pure Political Economics.*[15]

Individual and Society

Once this view of human facts has been presented,[16] Walras discusses the matter of the individual and society. 'In the same way as stars or celestial bodies are engaged with each other in action and reaction or gravitation, men or personal or moral beings are attached to each other by relations of right and duty or society'.[17] Just as there is a science – astronomy – to account for gravity, 'there can and should be a science to define, classify and determine social relations: that science is social science'.[18] But this social science, which does not yet exist and that Walras's mission is to build up, will be different from natural science. Natural science determines 'objective and real laws' while social science determines subjective and ideal laws;[19]

> suffice it to say, in the first case, what is; and in the second case must be said what should be. This difference is the one between moral truth and physical truth; but we believe that, be it physical or moral, truth must still be in the nature of science.[20]

Every science must first rely on demonstrations to establish truths; after which these truths become universally necessary, by force of reason. For social science, the challenge is that nobody has yet established universal truths, and knowledge in political economics, as in all social sciences, is not established with certainty.[21] In economics, there is not yet a sufficient body of accepted knowledge that can be considered as definitive truths; there is

> only a literature and economic and social opinions. It must be different from now on; but for evil to be opposed to good, and good to evil, in moral science – as the false

is opposed to the true, and true to false, in mathematics or physical sciences – good needs be distinguished from evil in morals, in the same way the true can be discerned from the false in mathematics and physics.[22]

It is in terms of social truth that Walras's position is imparted all its specificity: Walras is convinced that there are social truths that can be demonstrated rationally or experimentally, such as physical or mathematical truths. These truths are the 'work of collective reason and not individual feeling'[23] and they gradually emerge from past human experience. Walras adds that he joins his efforts 'to those among contemporary authors who claim they are the founders of social science'.[24] Afterwards, to prove movement by trying to walk, he gives his version of truth about society.

According to Walras, the starting point for the analysis of society is the issue of the origins of society. Walras considered three possibilities: that origin can be either divine or human or natural. He rejects the first option in the name of the separation of morals and theodicy.[25] The second solution (the human origin of society) is based on social contract theories that consider society to be a conventional or free fact, not a natural or necessary one. Walras discards this position he calls exclusive empiricism and absolute individualism, because this means assuming that man could be a moral person outside society.

> Remove all moral people from society and it is bound to disappear; but, if you remove society, there are no more moral people: though each person is an essential element of society, society is an essential element of any moral person. We are therefore in the social state in the same way as St. Paul says that we are in God: – In eo vivimus, and movemur sumus; we live, act and exist in him only.[26]

Walras does not wonder about the origin of man, and his reflection starts from an observation: there are men, and there is a society. These are two irrefutable facts that need only be observed; they are two inseparable facts: moral persons presuppose society, but society presupposes there are moral people. Walras draws the conclusion that society has a natural origin. To imagine a society without individuals does not make sense, just as it would not make sense to imagine individuals without society (the fiction of the state of nature advocated by social contract theories), because these individuals could never be moral persons.[27] Each moral person is part of a long history, necessarily a collective one; they enjoy at birth all that previous generations have achieved and, when they die, they bequeath to mankind the fruit of their labours. How might moral persons exist 'otherwise than within morals and thanks to morals', that is to say in society and thanks to society? People and society are two distinct facts, and they are inseparable.

The True Theory of a Just Society

The first requirement for the construction of a theory of society is the formulation of a criterion of truth that is the yardstick by which can be assessed whether a society is more or less a just one. In other words, we must find the standards of a truth of justice that allow to develop, on the basis of truths demonstrated 'by rational or experimental proof',[28] a true theory of the just society.

The solution to this issue was provided by the French Revolution, in two words that sum up both all the ideas that inspired the Declaration of Rights and all the principles upon which the 1791 Constitution rests, namely: Liberty, Equality'.[29] These two ideals are the two defining criteria of a just society. Society may be said to be just if it meets these two requirements, freedom and equality. Two remarks on these ideals:

(1) Freedom and equality are universal truths that have gradually emerged in the history of mankind. Proof of their truth comes from mankind's cumulative experience. Their effective implementation will give rise to a just society. Such unwavering faith in progress as expressed by Walras about property and government applies to all social phenomena: 'humanity has always patiently marched from the initial disorder of facts to the final order of principles'.[30] Walras asserts that history gives us an experimental proof of the definition of justice. Freedom and equality, which characterize justice, are products of history. They emerge gradually from the initial confusion of facts and become increasingly true over time, although their emergence is long and difficult.[31]

(2) Truth is still evolving, and these two ideals warrant social science is true. The truth of the two foundations of justice turns social theory into a theory that can claim it is the truth because it is built on the basis of accurate premises from which a demonstration, as a rigorous one as a geometry demonstration, permits to develop true conclusions.[32]

Walras still needs to define four concepts to establish the theory of society. The *individual* is a legal person 'performing his or her destiny independently of all other (people)'. *General social conditions* are 'the social environment of individual activity. The State is 'the set of all moral people considered as achieving their own destiny in solidarity with each other'.[33] Finally, *particular personal positions* designate the individual situations that moral persons achieve thanks to their activities in given social conditions.

To reconcile equality and freedom, society must solve two problems: determine the respective roles of the State and of the individual. The first problem is a matter of order, specifying which areas are within individual initiative and what areas require State intervention. The second issue is one of justice, of determining when individuals should individually benefit from their own efforts to fulfill their destinies; and when to collectively benefit from these efforts. Walras's solution of these problems is to combine the four concepts he has just set, so as to comply with both revolutionary ideals: freedom and equality. The formulation of a comprehensive solution to these two problems allows Walras to specify very precisely what a just society is.

The Problem of Order

Disorder settles in society when individuals undertake activities pertaining to the State or, symmetrically, when the State takes on initiatives that are individuals' responsibilities. The issue of order is to assign the individual and the State separate fields of initiative, and the question is obviously where to draw the line between the two. Walras solves this problem by first resorting to the principle of freedom. Individuals must be free to do and undertake all that has to do with striving for, obtaining and maintaining their personal positions, as this is each individual's moral personality. Such freedom to act (which is nothing other than free enterprise) is fundamental in order to comply with the first 1789 principle. Yet, symmetrically, it is appropriate that the State should enjoy the necessary authority to establish, maintain and improve general social conditions identical for all, i.e. the institutional framework for individual operations. This means, in modern terms, that the State takes on the production of public goods and the definition of the legal framework of economic activity, while individuals are free to undertake whatever private activities they deem profitable.

In accordance with the definitions Walras has provided above, the individual and the State are both natural and necessary facts. It follows that these are two equal and symmetrical social types, 'and that, in all social classes, the State's natural law is the individual's natural right'.[34] However, these observations should be completed as they articulate only one side of the individual's natural rights and the natural right of the State. Freedom, Walras says, cannot exist without its opposite, authority. Similarly, equality also implies inequality. While freedom is an unquestionable natural right of the individual, authority is no less an undeniable natural right of the State. If equality is an undeniable right of the state, inequality is no less an indisputable right of the individual.[35]

> I bow to the sacred name of liberty, and I declare that it is supremely contrary to order that the State should breach my individual responsibilities, and meddle to weigh, measure and choose my food, my clothes, my home, monitor and control my tastes, my thoughts, and it is most ridiculous when it forces me to smoke its tobacco and cigars, while it is abhorrent when it tries to dictate my religion and beliefs.[36]

This would spell despotism. However, it would be as bad if people declared war or peace instead of the State; would administer justice or take from Peter to pay Paul. That would mean anarchy. Despotism and anarchy are both as bad, because they ignore the distinction between individual initiative and state initiative. We must therefore recognize the State has a scope that is specific, in the same way as we acknowledge the individual enjoys a sphere of free activities.

Authority and freedom easily combine once the respective jurisdictions of the State and individuals are clearly defined by the distinction between general social conditions – which pertain to the State – and individual positions, which fall under each one of us. While individual initiative is to be defended in the name of freedom, State initiative is based on the authority it should have to undertake all that is within its jurisdiction, namely to create equal general terms and conditions for all.[37]

We see here that Walras's position combines the fundamental principle of liberalism (freedom of enterprise and trade), with a necessary space allocated to the State to organize the conditions of individual operations. Here we find Walras's great idea, which illustrates his 'method for conciliation or synthesis': the individual and the State are complementary.

The Problem of Justice

The second 1789 principle, equality, solves the second problem of society, the matter of justice. While equality is synonymous with social justice, Walras also justifies a number of inequalities as necessary for justice. To that end, he uses the Aristotelian distinction between distributive justice and commutative justice. Commutative justice presides over trade and provides that what is given should be equivalent (in the proper sense, namely equal in value) to what is received. It is a characteristic feature of prices as determined by the overall balance that this commutative justice should be complied with.[38] Distributive justice concerns the distribution of wealth and we know that Walras deemed as in conformity to natural law that people be owners of their work capabilities (hence, of the price of their work) as well as of all property they can acquire on a market. Land, however, in the name equality for all, must be owned by the State. Indeed, land is in limited supply and, to protect equality among individuals, it must belong to all mankind – past, present and future. As owner of the land, the State earns the annuities relating to its rental and thereby gets the resources to fulfill its mission, while individuals take full advantage of the fruits of their own efforts, since all taxes have been scrapped.

Freedom to act in an institutional framework identical for all may lead some to be more industrious, thriftier; others to work less and spend their income without trying to accumulate a fortune. This will result in inequality among individual positions (a differentiation of personal situations) perfectly consistent with justice.

> To sum up, the individual's role is to voluntarily fulfill their destinies, feel, think, act and work, either alone or in association with others, to be a farmer, industrialist, businessman, scientist, artist or public servant, and to do so in a position related to his

efforts and his merit. The role of the state is to shape the environment wherein to fulfill personal destinies, ensure external and internal security, to make, execute and enforce laws, to open channels of communication, to promote the progress of science and arts, and to organize the conditions of existence of society. Individuals' rights consist to be able to act freely and obtain unequal positions. The right of the State is to exert its authority and establish equal conditions for all. *Freedom of the individual; state authority; equal conditions; unequal positions.* This is therefore ultimately the higher law of society's organization on the basis of order and justice.[39]

Again, complementarity of state and individuals is the key.

Considerations of Walras's Holism and Individualism

Once the theory of the just society has been constructed, it is possible to assess the distance between the individualism credited to Walras by assimilation with current standard microeconomics and the standpoints he explicitly supports. All the arguments put forward by Walras show, first, that he rejects methodological individualism, but on the other hand, in a way, he also discards holism (what he calls collectivism or communism).

Ontologically, Walras considers that society and the individual have always already been there. Society is not a creation by individuals, contrary to what is asserted by social contract theories, whose extreme individualism Walras rejects. As archetypes of methodological individualism, social contract theories posit that individuals came first and society second; that society cannot be imagined outside individuals and that it is nothing else but the sum of the individuals who compose it. Walras systematically embraces the opposite stance to these positions by postulating that individuals and society are two factual givens, denying the pre-existence of one of these givens in relation to the other, while asserting that the individual and society are coextensive: one cannot exist without the other; there is no society without individuals, but even more so, there are no people without society either. This position departs from extreme holism, which sees individuals as entirely determined by society, but also radically differs from methodological individualism, which posits the primacy of the individual over society. Pierre Dockès speaks of 'synthetic holism' to characterize Walras's position.[40] The formulation refers to what Walras himself called the 'Method of conciliation or of synthesis'.[41] However, Dockès's formulation does not seem to correctly characterize Walras's position, as he also rejects individualism as explicitly as communism. Unlike holism, Walras does not relegate the individual to the background and, contrary to individualism, he does not relegate the State to the background either; therefore, it seems we should rather say Walras is neither holistic nor individualistic, or that he is both at once, since he places the individual and the State on the same ontological footing. Nevertheless, in the eyes of methodological individualism as well as methodological holism, it is a contradiction in terms to argue that one is simultaneously both. Hence, Walras should rather be considered as neither holistic nor individualistic. This leads Walras to adopt singular stands on the State, the individual, property and taxation.

It should first be stressed that Walras does not always seem to clearly distinguish the State from society and he often equates the two concepts by providing them with identical characteristics. Such assimilation is evident in the *General Theory of Society*. In the sixth lesson of the *General Theory*, Walras defines the State as 'the natural and necessary agent for the institution of general social conditions'.[42]

In this sixth lesson, Walras compares society to an army, in order to emphasize that society, like the army, is much more than the sum of the individuals who compose it. 'Let me remind you first that the individual in society, like a soldier in the army, is nothing by himself, and that he owes half his value to the society he is only an element of'. Walras continues his comparison:

> A society could not exist without individuals, no more than an army without soldiers ... but it is also true that individuals, even industrious, intelligent and wise ones, would be as helpless without a satisfactory social organization, like soldiers – however brave and strong – without a good military organization, without a determined and implemented plan, without superior tactics.[43]

At this juncture in his argument, though he has hitherto never introduced the State in his analyses, Walras, without any justification, moves on from society to the State. Indeed, in the sentence immediately following the above quotation, Walras writes:

> I carry this comparison further and add now that, therefore, the State is not a mere collection of individuals, just as the army is not the mere collection of its soldiers, and that the State's interests and rights are not merely all individuals' interest and rights as opposed to each person's interest and right, no more than the army's interest is merely the interests of all soldiers as opposed to each soldier's interests.

Walras's rhetoric is very subtle because the evocation of an organization, a plan, a tactic for soldiers suggests, rather than an army, what is usually called 'a Military Staff'. The transition from the Staff, who heads the army, to the State, which governs society, seems so obvious to Walras that he does not feel he needs to add more details. However, a sign that all is not perfectly clear (is it society or the state?) is that Walras, when discussing the State, then uses exactly the same words as about society: 'the State has a life of its own and even exceeds the sum of the lives of all the individuals who belong to it'.[44] The State, just like society, is a factual given about whose origin nothing needs be said. Society is a natural fact and Walras extends this characterization to the State.

The distinction between society and the State comes a little later in Walras's writings, when he introduces a new relationship: no longer between the individual and the State, modeled on the relationship between the individual and society, but a relationship between all three terms – society, the individual and the State:

> Since society is a natural and necessary fact, not a conventional and free one, the individual and the State are two equivalent social types, and, in all social classes, the natural right of the State is worth the same as the individual's natural right.[45]

This new articulation this time no longer opposes the individual and society (both natural and inseparable given facts), but the State and the individual, as they are both natural and inseparable givens as well. Suddenly, the whole society becomes a somewhat ghostly and distant whole, which looks like the meeting point between the individual and the State. In his 'Method of Conciliation or Synthesis', Walras maintains the ambiguity by defining the State as 'the organ of society that is separate from each of the men who compose it'.[46]

This rather wobbly construction that assigns very similar characteristics to society and the State led Walras to assign the State as the holder of the public interest (is it society's interest?).

> I hold, for my part, that when the State makes laws and applies them, when it pierces roads and digs canals, when it opens libraries and museums, it is in the interest of all members of a society where some are living, but a far larger number of others like them are not yet of this world, and, consequently, not pursuant to a law that the State holds not from all the individuals it is composed of but by its very nature.[47]

Here one might recall Walras's words, already mentioned above: 'the State is not the mere collection of individuals and ... the interest and right of the State are not simply the interests and rights of all individuals as opposed to the interest and right of each individual'. The State and individuals are on the same ontological footing, and one cannot be reduced to the other.

Walras underlines his views are as radically opposed to individualism as to communism (holism). He explicitly criticizes the extreme positions that claim to arbitrate between freedom and equality.

> One particularly believes in liberty; and as freedom causes inequality, he relinquishes both equality and authority. He annihilates the State in the individual's presence; for him, society is merely an association that everyone joins to make the most of it, or simply as an insurance that protects against all risks. This is absolute individualism (of the Mr. Emile de Girardin type). The other mainly strives at equality, and since equality results from authority, he gives up both liberty and inequality. He absorbs the individual into the State; and society as a whole is for him a community where everyone depends on everyone and where no one belongs to oneself any longer. This is absolute communism (of the Mr. Louis Blanc type).[48]

Comparing Walras's positions with Hayek's or Popper's individualistic theories speaks volumes: they are opposed in all possible ways. Popper refers to the debate about universals to defend opposite views to Walras's.[49] Collective entities do not exist: 'Even 'war' or 'the army' are abstract concepts, strange as it may seem. What is concrete is all those who get killed, or people in uniforms, etc'.[50] Popper calls realism (Plato's, hence Walras's) essentialism. Such essentialism attributes to universals as real an existence as that of real objects, and seeks to eliminate the accidental features of phenomena to penetrate the essence of things in order to explain them away. Against essentialism, Popper argues that society, like all universals, has no independent existence and is only a theoretical model that we mistake for reality. The program of methodological individualism is precisely 'to construct and carefully analyse our sociological models [e.g. the army or society, JL] in descriptive or nominalist terms, i.e. in terms of individuals, their attitudes, expectations, relationships, etc'.[51]

On this point, Hayek's position is identical to Popper's. He refuses

> the notions that the popular mind has devised on aggregates such as 'society' or 'the economy', 'capitalism' or 'imperialism', or such other collective entities that the researcher must, in social sciences, consider as mere provisional theories, popular abstractions, which he should not erroneously mistake for facts.[52]

From this ontological position, Hayek draws a method – methodological individualism:

> Let [the social scientist, JL] refrain logically from addressing these pseudo-entities as facts, and let him systematically start from concepts that guide individuals in their actions and not from the results of their theoretical reflection on their actions – that is the characteristic feature of this methodological individualism, closely related as it is to the subjectivism of social sciences.[53]

This statement of methodological individualism is accompanied by criticism of methodological totalism (holism):

> the error in the totalist vision is to misunderstand as facts what is nothing but tentative theories, models constructed by mere common sense to explain the links between a number of individual phenomena under our scrutiny.[54]

Walras refuses nominalism and develops a kind of essentialism that is the antithesis of the nominalism claimed by Popper and Hayek. To empiricists who argue that 'man varies ... from country to country, from century to century, [that] there are no men ... there are only the French, the Germans, etc.', Walras replies that 'underlying the differences in places and times, essential unity exists and that, if it were true that there were no men, but only French and German people, then it would be true that there are no such things as French or German people, but only individuals called Peter, Paul, Wilhelm, Friedrich, etc.'.[55] While Walras supports the reality of the existence of such collectives as society or the State as well as individuals, Popper asserts diametrically opposed positions: universals do not exist, and therefore society does not either.[56]

The Role of the State According to Walras

Social contract theories assume, and so does holism, that there is a contradiction between the individual and society. Methodological individualism postulates that society has been invented by individuals, who are first. Holism is attributed the inverse symmetrical position: society is first and society dictates individuals' behaviours.[57] Walras refuses this dilemma and goes beyond the opposition between the individual and society by denying the primacy of one over the other, and assuming the necessary and simultaneous existence of both,[58] which does not preclude a tension between the respective weights of individuals and society. But, most importantly, this tension is displaced once a third term is taken into account: the State. It has already been pointed out (see above, pp. 24ff.) that, as Walras puts it, society is often equated with the State. What is important is the tension between the State and the individual. Walras dismisses both the exclusive zealots of the State and the devotees of the individual, because of the aberrations inherent to their initial assumptions; he then suggests the only possible solution he can support: a synthesis of the two.

> One thing has not been tried yet: the agreement of freedom and authority in order; the agreement of equality and inequality in justice; the separation and reconciliation of the individual and the State by the separation and reconciliation of individualism and communism.[59]

This is an original synthesis because, in the same way as when regarding the individual and society, Walras precludes any primacy of the individual or of the State: both are coextensive. The holistic (communist) ideal of ancient republics used to sacrifice the individual to the State, and freedom to authority.

> In Athens, Sparta or Rome, the word 'city', 'republic' or 'res publica' (public thing), used to have a meaning and scope such as they will never have for us: it expressed precisely that absorption of man in the citizen; of the individual in the State. Instead, our common sense today claims the individual is everything, and that the State, a mere collection of individuals, is nothing.

Yet, Walras observes, 'achieving absolute individualism is as impossible as reaching absolute communism'.[60] The truth is the necessary coexistence of the individual and the State, the only question being how to find the right balance between the State's rights and duties and the individual's rights and duties.

This view of the state led Walras to hold sometimes surprising positions. The State is not the emanation of individuals' wills, contrary to what is postulated by social contract theories. The state is 'natural and necessary'.[61] The State is a fact, as much so as society or individuals are natural and necessary givens. Walras draws radical logical conclusions. The State has rights to hold social wealth to ensure its existence, just as individuals have rights to social wealth to ensure their existence. The individual's and the State's natural characters imply that the distribution of social wealth leads Walras to evoke individuals' natural rights to own their personal capabilities, their work, and the price of their work, just as it is in accordance with natural law, i.e. the nature of things, that the state should own all the land on behalf of all mankind, the present but also the past and future ones.

Hence some statements by Walras, which seem to contradict his exaltation of 'the tradition of the Revolution [of] the ideal of democracy'.[62] Between the individual and the state, which stand at either ends of the spectrum, there is the family and the government, whose theory is yet to be developed. About the family, Walras acknowledges that there is still no satisfactory theory, but he mentions 'the Belgian school's fine work on national representation', which provides an organic representation of all different producers' interests, 'which would rid us of our deplorable current universal suffrage; it would then suffice to find an organization of legislative and executive powers that might also rid us of our no less deplorable parliamentary system'.[63]

If these political issues concerning the form of the State or how governments should be chosen (only very briefly mentioned by Walras), two economic problems are yet to be solved: first, what role should the State play in a market economy and, second, what income can the State claim to perform its functions.

The Role of the State in the Working of a Market Economy

We know that it is up to the State to use its authority to enforce people's equal conditions. These powers of the State are, Walras believes, the logical and necessary consequence of the definition of a just society as described above. But Walras goes much further by conferring to the state a fundamental role in a sphere of activity in which individual initiative is the rule, in the name of individuals' freedom to take any action regarding their personal positions. The State must play a key role in an area where, *a priori*, individuals' freedom should be complete and the state should not intervene.

Walras demonstrates that there is a general equilibrium corresponding to maximum satisfaction assuming there is 'hypothetically absolute free competition'.[64] However, such a competitive situation is not a spontaneous state of the economy. Free competition does not at all mean there should be no government intervention. First of all, this intervention is necessary to establish and maintain free competition wherever possible.[65] Entrepreneurs' natural tendency is to establish monopolies to ensure windfall profits at the expense of consumers and at no benefit to society. Under these conditions, the introduction of competition is an essential function of the State, acting now as the guarantor of the general interest. 'Again, let us insist that instituting and maintaining free economic competition in a society is to be achieved through legislation – and very complicated legislation as well – and it is therefore up to the State to do it'.[66] The prime role of the State with respect to the organization of the market competition is not very clear in Walras, but one can simply refer to the current intervention by the State in favour of competition to realize the magnitude of the task.

Moreover, Walras lists many other situations where government intervention is needed to get effectively operating markets: the currency, natural monopolies, situations where appreciating usefulness is impossible for the individual (public utilities) and where quality assessments are impossible for the individual (some private services).[67] This is the subject of applied economics.

Nothing more is needed to show that the applied theory of industry is far from being summarized in just these few words: *Laisser faire*, just let it be and let go; and that, on the contrary, it boasts a long series of studies on sharing responsibilities between the State and the individual in the production of wealth.[68] A fundamental asymmetry can be noticed here: markets should not intervene in the sphere where State authority is necessary to create equal conditions, whereas the state must intervene to organize the production of some goods or services normally left to markets and private initiative. This leads Walras to say: 'Collectivism is half the truth in applied economics, like communism in social economics'. It means that if, indeed, entrepreneurial freedom is a natural human right that must be respected for private activities, it is also true that the intervention of the State, grounded on its authority, is indispensable to the proper functioning of markets, which cannot do without it.[69] At the end of the day, this reinforces the image of a less liberal Walras than suggested by the current image put across by the simplistic theory of general equilibrium.

The State Revenue

The first consequences of the claim that society is as natural as the individual have to do with taxation. Walras wonders what the fairest taxation method might be. Common answers are based on an initial assumption under which all social wealth (land, personal capabilities, fixed assets, …) are appropriated by individuals; and this initial assumption itself is the result of an individualistic position where individuals are first. According to social contract theories, which advocate such positions, State resources can only be drawn from a levy on income (or capital) that is all in the individuals' hands. It is then necessary to obtain people's voluntary consent. Then the question arises whether to resort to a poll tax, a proportional tax or a progressive tax.

> If the State is a mere collection of moral persons, all unequal [as individualists postulate, JL], I admit it should be equated to a company of shareholders, all holders of a greater or lesser number of shares, and we should aim at distributing both the benefits and burdens of State services in proportion to specific personal situations, just like the dividends or losses of any trade or business – *pro rata* to share capital.[70]

Walras takes Adolphe Thiers as the representative of this position, and the social-ist proposals for a progressive tax subsequently went far beyond that.[71] Walras rejects both possibilities and argues in favour of the 'principle (of an) equal and compulsory contribution'.[72] Through a strictly equal-for-all tax, he does not advocate a form of capitation; he merely accepts the logical consequences of his initial choice, especially his ontology of the individual and society. Against indi-vidualism, Walras constantly defends the same position, saying:

> If, on the contrary, the State is a community of legal persons, all considered equal, I ask that it be rather compared to a community of members with all the same rights and the same duties ... I say, let there be no rich or poor in the State, but citizens with the same rights and duties with respect to the general social conditions.[73]

This ideal vision assigns individuals ownership of their personal capabilities and the State ownership of the land. Therefore, the State, through its income from the land, will have the resources needed to fulfill its functions (security, organ-izing competition and producing utilities).[74] This is the way Walras understands 'the principle of equal and compulsory contribution': as all citizens are all col-lectively (through the State) joint owners of the land, and as the State, like every owner of a capital, can enjoy the revenue of its capitals, i.e. property rents, it is therefore clear that 'men in society necessarily contribute an equal share to the burdens of State services, just as they necessarily share equally in the benefits of these services provided by the State'.[75]

Conclusion

Walras relies on a realistic ontology that puts man and society, the individual and the state, at the same level. Assuming that both entities are as real as the other, and inseparable, he rejects individualism and communism (holism) all at once. He disqualifies individualism and methodological holism, since it accepts explanations made in individual terms as well as those involving collective enti-ties such as society, the family and the State. However, by giving the State and the individual the same reality, he shakes the very foundations of economic theory. On one hand, he gives the state a central role in the functioning of markets, as it organizes competition and overcomes market failures (public goods, natural monopolies, ...). On the other hand, he recasts taxation, abandoning both the principle of consent to taxation and the issue of proportionality or progressive taxation. The natural existence of the State implies that it, like the individual, has natural rights to own resources to provide for itself. Land ownership by the State solves the problem of State resources and *a priori* gives it the means to achieve its natural missions. These positions frontally contradict methodological indi-vidualism, on grounds that, beyond the method, implement an ontology that, though Walras made it explicit, was rarely discussed by economists.

2 THE CASE AGAINST MARKET PERFECTION: THE TWO BERTRANDS' OBJECTIONS ARE ONE

Rodolphe Dos Santos Ferreira

Introduction

The path is strange that led Bertrand to the economists' Hall of Fame. As a mathematician, he made a single well-known incursion in our discipline, which was presumably designed as an attack against the use of mathematics in economics. This attack was accomplished in 1883 in a ten-page article of the *Journal des Savants* reviewing Walras's *Mathematical Theory of Social Wealth*, published in the same year, together with Cournot's *Researches into the Mathematical Principles of the Theory of Wealth* (1838), viewed as the main source of Walras's work.[1] Each one of these two reviews contains one main *objection*, the first to Cournot's concept of duopolistic equilibrium, the second to Walras's analysis of the adjustment to equilibrium. These two objections became two independent sources of an astoundingly strong recognition (if we take into account the brevity of Bertrand's statements) by two communities working in two distinct fields that may be traced back to Cournot and Walras: industrial organization and general equilibrium theory, respectively.

As concerns industrial organization, with twenty lines criticizing three pages of one of the most important books in the history of economics, Bertrand attained with respect to the author of the *Researches* an almost symmetric position, assigned by supposedly opposite choices as regards the two main strategy variables that may be adopted by the competitors, namely prices and quantities. Yet Bertrand himself attributed to Cournot the approach to competition with which his name has since been associated, and objected to it, arguing that what we now call 'Bertrand equilibrium' does not exist. Moreover, having also lent his name to the paradox that two competitors (one of which might even be a potential entrant) are enough to implement the perfectly competitive outcome, provided they compete in prices, he appears in some sense as the champion of neoclassical orthodoxy under the assaults of oligopolistic competition. This, in spite of presenting the collusive solution as more reasonable than a price war triggered by competition, and in spite of building his critique on the rejection of one of the main ingredients of the neoclassical paradigm, namely market perfection, entailing permanent fulfilment of the law of one price.

As to general equilibrium theory, the impact of Bertrand's objection was immediate since it touched Walras himself, forcing him to make explicit the nature of the adjustment to equilibrium he had in mind.[2] Bertrand's objection concerned the distributional effects of disequilibrium transactions, resulting in hysteresis and ultimately in equilibrium indeterminacy. Walras's reaction consisted in explicitly excluding trade out of equilibrium from the second edition (1889) of the *Éléments* onwards: '*Theoretically*, the exchange should be suspended' until the equilibrium price is established, as he writes when analysing the exchange of two commodities one for each other.[3] The sense of Bertrand's objection is precisely that in *real, imperfect*, markets, transactions do take place at prices differing from *the* market balancing price, an observation which also happens to be the basis of his objection to Cournot.

Thus, although formulated in two contexts that were going to fall apart as two separate fields, both Bertrand's objections stem from the same observation and share the same distaste for the assumption of market perfection. In the following, I shall successively examine the objection to Cournot and the objection to Walras, and then conclude in favour of the fundamental unity of the two.

The Objection to Cournot

The objection formulated by Bertrand (1883) to Chapter 7 of the *Researches into the Mathematical Principles of the Theory of Wealth*[4] is frequently thought to concern the choice of producers' strategy variables: Bertrand would supposedly advocate prices instead of quantities, favoured by Cournot.[5] This idea is a myth[6] that does not resist the reading, however cursory, of Bertrand,[7] and that has been demolished by Magnan de Bornier.[8] In spite of this welcome clarification, the nature of Bertrand's objection remains confused in the minds of most economists.

Cournot's Competition of Producers in a Perfect Market

The analysis of producers' competition in Chapter 7 of the *Researches*[9] concerns a market supplied by the proprietors of two (more generally n) springs of identical quality.

> By *market* the economists mean, not a certain place where purchases and sales are carried on, but the entire territory of which the parts are so united by the relations of [free trade] that prices there take the same level throughout, with ease and rapidity.[10]

As an approximation, the market we consider can accordingly be viewed as *perfect*, its working continuously verifying the *law of one price*. Hence, 'the price is necessarily the same for each proprietor',[11] a condition which is implicitly supposed to be satisfied in and *out of* equilibrium. Indeed, taking into account the sales target D_2 determined by proprietor (2), on which he 'can have no direct influence', proprietor (1) chooses 'for D_1 the value which is best for him, [a value that] he will be able to accomplish *by properly adjusting [the] price*'.[12] Of course, proprietor (2), 'seeing himself *forced to accept this price* and this value of D_1, may adopt a new value for D_2, more favourable to his interests than the preceding one'.[13] So, each producer i chooses the profit-maximizing value of his own sales target D_i, given his competitor's sales target D_j and conjecturing, under the law of one price and the law of demand F, the corresponding *market clearing* price p, such that $D_i + D_j = F(p)$.

Under these conditions, 'it will be convenient to adopt the inverse notation',[14] and suppose that producer i chooses D_i so as to maximize (at zero cost) D_i $F^{-1}(D_i + D_j)$, given D_j. Cournot remains however silent about the way the law of one price is actually enforced and, more precisely, about the way the market clearing price arises. It has become usual to refer in this context to an auctioneer, or else to a two-stage game with producers setting quantities at the first stage, and competing in prices at the second.[15] The inverse demand function F^{-1} then describes the auctioneer's price setting conduct in the former case, the expected second stage (conditional) equilibrium in the latter. Equivalently, one can also discard the 'convenient' reference to the inverse demand, and suppose that each producer i computes the price which maximizes the value of his residual demand $(F(p) - D_j)\,p$, given his competitor's sales target D_j, and again under the law of one price and the law of demand.[16] Of course, simply computing the optimal price is not enough for producer i, who must have access to some way of implementing it.[17] I shall not elaborate on this point and just record Cournot's silence, but I shall add to the two fundamental features of Cournot competition, namely the fact that each proprietor 'can have no direct influence' on his competitor's sales target and the fact that 'the price is necessarily the same for each proprietor', as a third fundamental feature, the free and complete individual price manipulability, under the law of demand.

Bertrand's Competition of Producers in an Imperfect Market

In his critique of Cournot, Bertrand recalls the collusive solution, discarded as unsustainable by Cournot, and then wrongly attributes to him price undercutting strategies supposedly pursued by the competitors: 'Cournot conjectures that one of the competitors will lower *his* price to attract buyers, and that the other, in order to bring them back, will lower *his* more. They will continue until each of them will no longer gain anything more by lowering *his* price'.[18] Clearly, for Bertrand, the law of one price does not apply. As a consequence, the undercutting competitor is assumed to be able, in spite of product homogeneity, to keep a lower price for his output long enough to increase sales by diverting customers' demand to his advantage. This market imperfection destroys the sustainability of any situation with a common positive price. Indeed,

> a peremptory objection arises: With this hypothesis a solution is impossible; the price reduction would have no limit. In fact, whatever jointly determined price were adopted, if only one of the competitors lowers his, he gains, disregarding all unimportant exceptions, all the sales, and he will double his returns if his competitor allows him to do so.[19]

Bertrand describes a limitless price war, ignoring that it would naturally converge to what is now paradoxically called 'Bertrand equilibrium', with competitors setting a zero price. Also, in spite of the reservation 'if his competitor allows him to do so', Bertrand neglects the possibility of automatic price matching strategies (for instance, through a best price guarantee), restoring the law of one price and making price undercutting unprofitable.

Thus, Bertrand's 'peremptory objection' to Cournot does not address the latter's choice of quantities as strategy variables, on which the competitors 'can have no direct influence'. It is true that he points to 'a peculiar oversight' in Cournot's approach, through which the latter

> introduces under the names D and D' [*sic*] the quantities sold by the two competitors, and treating them as independent variables, he assumes that the one quantity happening to change through the will of one owner, the other would remain constant. The contrary is obviously true'.[20]

As a matter of fact, Cournot's strategy variables D_1 and D_2 are not *sold quantities* but *sales targets* that are made compatible by an appropriate adjustment of the market price, which Bertrand ignores. The point I want to stress is, however, that Bertrand's objection addresses the inexistence of an equilibrium: 'a solution is impossible; the price reduction would have no limit'. And such inexistence, or rather the unsustainability of Cournot's solution, results from the price undercutting strategies that are only possible in an imperfect market, where the law of one price does not apply, so that purchases and sales can be carried on even when prices diverge and the market is not cleared.

The Objection to Walras

The *Mathematical Theory of Social Wealth* covers the theories of exchange, of production and of capitalization and credit, each one being the object of a different memoir, among the first four that compose the book. Bertrand's objection, although virtually applying to the whole of Walrasian theory, is, however, directed to the simplest expression of the theory of exchange, the exchange between two commodities discussed in the very first memoir. I shall accordingly stick to this simple expression, and shall not consider the extension of the objection to a more general setting.[21]

Walras's Tâtonnement: Price Adjustment with Suspended Exchange in Perfect Markets

Walras's mathematical theory of exchange, as exposed in the first memoir[22] of Walras (1883), is structured in a manner that is in some sense reminiscent of Cournot (1838), mentioned in section 1 as an important methodological source. Walras distinguishes two problems, namely:

1. *'Given two commodities (A) and (B), and the demand curves of these two commodities for one in terms of the other, to determine the respective equilibrium prices'.*[23]

2. *'Given two commodities (A) and (B), and the utility for each trader of each one of these commodities, as well as the quantity of each one of them possessed by each holder, to determine the demand curves'.*[24]

The second problem is not addressed in the *Researches*, where the law of demand is taken as a datum, but it transposes producers' profit-maximizing decisions studied by Cournot into commodity holders' utility maximizing decisions: 'the demand curves result mathematically from the utility curves and from the [possessed commodity] quantities since each holder aims to obtain the maximum satisfaction of his needs'.[25] Aggregation of the individual demand curves then results in total (net) demand curves defined by the equations $D_a = F_a (p_a)$ and $D_b = F_b (p_b)$, where p_a is the price of commodity (A) in terms of commodity (B), so that $p_b = 1/p_a$. Considering the exchange from the point of view of commodity (A), the demand curve D_a may be confronted to the offer curve $O_a = F_b (p_b) p_b = F_b (1/p_a) (1/p_a)$. The first problem is then to determine the solution to the market clearing equation $F_a (p_a) = F_b (1/p_a) (1/p_a)$: 'the prices result mathematically from the demand curves since *one should not have in the market more than one price*, that for which *total effective demand is equal to total effective supply*'.[26] Thus, the first problem exactly coincides with Cournot's problem of determining, under the law of one price and the law of demand, the market clearing price, the problem that is implicit in the convenient adoption of the inverse notation.

Now, in order to justify the assumed market perfection, Cournot referred to *free trade*, which ensures that prices adjust in practice 'with ease and rapidity'. Similarly, Walras refers to *free competition*, working in rigorous conditions, that allow 'to make abstraction of small disruptive circumstances'.[27] Free competition ensures that the problem consisting in determining, given the demand curves, the equilibrium prices, a problem which is 'evidently solvable, at least in principle, by the mathematical procedure', is also 'actually solvable, in the market, by the empirical procedure of over- and underbidding', 'a way to solve by groping (*tâtonnement*) the system of exchange equations'.[28]

Bids are made either by the buyers and sellers themselves or by 'agents such as stockbrokers, commercial brokers' who 'are the simple executors of orders inscribed in order books' and represented by the demand curves.[29] Because of the assumed market perfection, Cournot was able to suppose that his producers, when considering all the potential values of their sales targets, were always referring to the corresponding market clearing price. In a similar way, Walras is able to suppose that his commodity holders, when considering all the potential prices at which to give their corresponding market orders, can treat these prices as if they were market clearing prices, excluding any quantity rationing. This is of course only possible if prices are instantaneously adjusted to their market clearing values, before any exchange actually takes place. As noted by Walras himself, a calculator would be able to determine mathematically the equilibrium prices from the order books, given 'all the necessary time'.[30] But how to contract 'all the necessary time' for the completion of 'the empirical procedure of over- and underbidding' into the instantaneity of the adjustment supposed to be performed in perfect markets? Walras's tentative answer to this question, which is his response to Bertrand's objection, is given in a footnote of his article on Gossen:

> *in the theoretical market*, in case of an excess of demand over supply or of supply over demand, no order is met, the exchange staying *suspended* until the over- and underbidding have brought supply and demand to equality; after that, every order is met.[31]

But what about the *real* market?

Bertrand's Price Adjustment with Ongoing Exchange in Imperfect Markets

Bertrand's objection involves again market imperfection. What are the consequences of ongoing exchanges at non-clearing prices during the process of price adjustment? The first consequence pointed out by Bertrand is the illegitimacy of aggregation: 'It is not permissible to replace all the buyers by a single one'.[32] To prove this statement, Bertrand considers the example of two buyers willing to purchase the same quantity q at the same price p, but with different demand curves, say $q = f_1(p) = f_2(p)$, but with $f_1 \neq f_2$. If quantity q is sold at price p as a result of a first transaction, so that one of the two buyers can withdraw from the market, it is clearly not indifferent for the final outcome which of the two buyers 1 or 2 has been satisfied, since we are then left with demand f_2 or f_1, respectively. This is, however, immaterial if p is precisely the market clearing price, that is, if the supply at p when the market opens is $2q$, so that no price adjustment has to take place.

In this example, it is not so much aggregation that is at stake, but much more the path followed by out-of-equilibrium transactions. Indeed, as Bertrand writes,

> it must be noted that the curves representing the buyers' orders at various prices must necessarily vary for each one of them during the duration of the market without their intentions having changed. The resultant curves whose intersection solves the problem constantly change shape and one can easily demonstrate the necessary variation of the abscissa of the point where they intersect.[33]

Because of the income effects associated with transactions at non-clearing prices, 'the curve that represents the orders must be calculated and remade after each transaction'. Then, 'Mr. Walras's theorem loses its geometric character, the final result depending on the haphazard circumstances that one had claimed to have eliminated'.[34] In other words, as soon as exchange is not suspended until the market clearing price is found and can be applied, as soon as purchases and sales can be carried on before the market clears, *path dependency* generally occurs. Bertrand's objection to Cournot focused on equilibrium inexistence. His objection to Walras ends up in the demonstration of equilibrium *indeterminacy*.

Conclusion

In spite of a prominent and seemingly undeserved success obtained by criticizing Cournot, Bertrand is still largely unrecognized for what he really did. Even if his reading of Cournot was defective and his critique certainly less than fair, his objection touched a sensitive issue. Cournot's analysis of producers' competition very much depends on their supposed capacity to conjecture and implement the market clearing price corresponding to each possible configuration of sales targets, yet it remains silent about the way prices are actually set. This silence is masked by the convenient adoption of the inverse demand function, letting the job be done by the impersonal forces of the market. If on the contrary prices are personally posted by the competitors, the question of the way by which the law of one price is enforced and price undercutting prohibited can no more be ignored. In the case of price-setting competitors and if the market is less than perfect, that is, if transactions can take place at non-clearing prices, an undercutting competitor is *a priori* able to increase sales by stealing customers from his rival(s). Cournot equilibrium is then unsustainable, and the way is open for an endless price war.

Bertrand's objection to Walras also addresses the way prices are set, supposedly fast enough for transactions to remain suspended during the process of price adjustment. If that is not the case, if transactions do take place during that process, before *tâtonnement* succeeds, income is redistributed among transactors, thus introducing path dependency and eventually equilibrium indeterminacy. Again, the possibility for the competitors to perform disequilibrium transactions, in the course of the adjustment process, destroys fulfilment, if not existence, of Walras equilibrium as determined *ex ante* by the *mathematical procedure*. The objection to Walras has precisely the same foundation as the objection to Cournot, namely that real markets are imperfect and accommodate transactions at non-clearing prices.

3 WALRAS, MARX AND THE PHILOSOPHY OF HISTORY

Pierre Dockès

If a comparison between Marx and Walras may bring to light certain proximities or oppositions, it is clear that the communism of the first bore an importance unlike the liberal socialism of the other and that, *in this field of history*, they don't belong to the same category. With his academic philosophical culture, a knowledge of history limited to a few great works of vulgarized histories, Walras did not fight on equal terms with Marx. Moreover, while history was central to the first, the essential was evidently elsewhere to the other. However, the pregnancy of the *Zeitgeist* on these two intellectual heirs of the Enlightenment and Revolution is considerable and makes connections possible.

History is at the centre of the Marxian system. Socialism is made scientific by the laws of history: the historic evolution that results from forces that are developed within all modes of production undergoes a general law, the only universal law. It conveys a univocal succession of modes of production within which categories and theories are put into perspective. Communism is the final stage.

The status of Walrasian history is more difficult to grasp. It is not, to say the least, an important field of study and Walras remains, in his domain, an enlightened amateur. But his role in the Walrasian system is crucial, for his pure political and social economy, this ideal in the matter of interest and justice (an abstraction drawn from reality that is already always there as an *Idea*), will necessarily become reality. There is a Walrasian philosophy of history, a pure historic science that is *a priori* in essence, but history is also an empirical science, if not the concrete science *par excellence*. In the end, as knowledge of our relative and imperfect world, it dominates practice[1] thereby withdrawing from the field of science.

We witness here the sketch of a general construction that flows from Walras's conception of science. *A priori* history gives him the *achievement* process of the Social Ideal; concrete history provides him with real types (the inductive moment) from which he can abstract ideal types, the base to the construction of his theories on economy and ideal or rational society. Finally, practical history confers upon him the world of imperfection and provides him with the bases to his liberalism.

This chapter will not examine their vision of real history, of 'reasoned history', but will focus on their philosophy of history instead. *In a first part, the goal of the journey* will be clarified: end of history or ultimate rational society. *In a second part, the forces that thrust the ship* will be defined. The paradox is that he (Marx) who provides the forces at play in history – its laws – refuses to boil 'the [Comtist?] cauldrons of the future'[2] in order to give us the characteristics of a communist society, and he (Walras) who does not really seek to determine those laws gives us the characteristics of the ideal City of the future that he thinks he can draw from the knowledge of human nature 'on the good old terrain of natural law'.[3]

The Goal of the Journey: End of History versus Ultimate Rational Society

On the Ground of Method, Léon Walras is Essentially Idealist[4] and Karl Marx Fundamentally Materialist

However, they both see themselves as partisans of synthesis: Walrasian synthesis is fundamentally eclectic ('synthetic socialism, or synthesism'[5]), in contrast with Marx's dialectic method. Marx's materialism forbids him to try to define an ideal society that conforms to an absolute justice, to equity. There are as many concepts of equity as there are modes of production. Marx refuses to accept utopia. He does not want to provide the characteristics of an ideal society. It's only a question of explaining which mode of production history will achieve necessarily, and to activate it.

Walras,[6] on the other hand, extracts this Idea – the ideal city – from the nature of men. He draws real types from the concrete real, from which he further abstracts ideal types. Then, reasoning *a priori* about them, he defines absolute justice and absolute interest, thus enabling him to provide the characteristics of an ideal society. Socialism, to him, is the belief in a moral science capable of defining the social Ideal. He maintains having demonstrated that 'the best according to justice' and 'the best according to interest' are necessarily compatible in absolute. That is how he deduces his general social formula: 'liberty of the individual, authority of the State, equality of conditions, inequality of positions'. He argues that he is able to define the characteristics of the ideal city from this basis. Although history is to achieve it, he does not explain the modalities of this history's development.

Walras claims to be representative of scientific socialism[7]; Marx appears to have been reticent to use the expression borrowed from Proudhon, even if he retains the idea (Engels will not hesitate to use it himself). For the idealist Walras, the social Ideal must be determined in accordance with human nature, based on natural law. To Marxists, the laws of history must be revealed, explained and this new science – which Marx considers as related to Darwinian evolutionism (evolutionism also influenced Walras) – elaborated.

What are the Main Characteristics of the Ideal Society of Walras?

In his early *Seeking the Social Ideal* (*Recherche de l'Idéal social*, 1863), in the late 'Theory of Property' ('Théorie de la Propriété', 1896), and in several other texts that constitute *Studies in Social Economics* (*Études d'économie sociale*), Walras explains what the right method is and which conclusions may be obtained by it.[8]

Rational society is essentially – but only – founded on an economy of small merchant production. A society in which, first and foremost, land and natural riches are collective, which corresponds to 'a first social reform' (he proposes a plan for the purchase of land by the State); a society in which artificial monopolies will have been eliminated thanks to the State and natural monopolies nationalized or duly controlled by the State (a 'second social reform'). The only – temporary – private monopolies remaining would be linked to invention. Taxes would be abolished and the State would live off its own revenues (tenant farmings and capital interests[9] from its savings). A great number of cooperatives and insurances would associate with producers who wished to do so.

Moreover, free competition would be made general for all markets when it can be *indefinite* – including the labour market – whilst subsisting natural monopolies would be State managed at unique prices resulting from outbidding ('à l'enchère') or underbidding ('au rabais').[10]

Entrepreneur's benefits would be almost inexistent (except for inventors). If inequalities between men were to subsist according to merit (work, qualification, savings), they would be moderate since equality of conditions would be respected (collectivization of natural riches): if men would be free to improve their conditions, the State would authoritatively guarantee equality of conditions. There would be no more great fortunes, and if inheritance was maintained by Walras (oddly a natural right because man is free to dispose of his own goods), it would necessarily be moderate.

Is it possible to go further? Léon Walras admits in his mature years[11] the possibility of a generalized collectivism if the market economy is respected: all collective firms would be managed by upwards and downwards (on the markets of productive services and of product markets). He goes as far as believing that the future could well lead to a situation in which the field of collective production would be much wider and he even proposes a vast experiment[12] to discover which system would be best in terms of interest. He personally believes that society wishes to favour dynamism – the place of ownership must be important – and if it wishes for more tradition and respect, the collective field must be more significant.

This rational society which the scholar is able to reveal would be achieved by reforms that science is able to define. The State would not have to introduce them authoritatively, but wait until public opinion was ready and enlightened. If it appears to be impossible, the risk of a tragic revolution would increase. So, Walras's socialism is a 'liberal socialism'.

However, Marx's Texts on Socialist ('Communist Society in its Lower Phase') or Communist Societies ('Upper-Stage Communism') are Rare, Vague, at Times Ambiguous, often Written to Answer a Political Issue.

These are mainly a sketch in the *Manifesto of the Communist Party* of 1848, a few lines in *Capital* (1867), and brief developments in *Critique of the Gotha Programme* (1875).

There are also a few words in *The Civil War in France* (1871), written after the Paris Commune, a moment when Marx, undoubtedly driven by the movement, was more libertarian than ever. The communal Constitution is thus considered as exemplary: decentralized, in the end federative according to Proudhon's model (even though of course not admittedly so), constructed on the basis of local communities managing their problems and sending their representatives (who can be revoked at any moment and are bound to an imperative mandate) up to the departmental level, and then to the central government level, it constitutes the 'political form finally found to allow the achievement of the economic emancipation of work'.[13]

We learn in the *Manifesto*[14] that they will be the first ten post-revolutionary measures. It is interesting to note that if some of them could have been appreciated by Walras (and the following measure foremost: the expropriation of land ownership[15] and the allocation of rent to the State's expenditure, free public education), others would be radically rejected by the Master of Lausanne (progressive income tax, 'equal liability of all to work', the recourse to industrial armies, nationalization of credit and its centralization in a State monopoly), or rejected moderately (abolition of inheritance), others are questionable (State monopolization of the means of transport, 'extension of factories and instruments of production owned by the State').

On the political terrain 'the proletariat must first of all seize political power, must rise as a national class, must constitute itself as a nation'.

What follows these emergency measures remains a bit vague.

How would communist appropriation (collectivism in terms of repartition according to Walras) and communist production (collectivism in terms of production according to Walras) be achieved?

As for the first point, we know that it is fundamentally a matter of abolition of 'bourgeois property', of transforming capital in a collective ownership.[16] How? 'The proletariat will use its political supremacy to wrest, by degree, all capital from the bourgeoisie'

Once this communist appropriation is achieved, what will be the forms of communist production? It is necessary to 'centralise all the means of production in the hands of the State – proletariat organised as the dominant class' in order to 'increase the mass of productive forces as rapidly as possible'.[17] Marx adds that 'all production will be concentrated in the hands of associated individuals',[18] which is purposefully ambiguous: what would be the role of these associations?

Finally, Marx and Engels accept the ultimate disappearance (an extinction) of the State on the political level ('political government of men'), and the latter would only subsist on an economic level ('the administration of things and direction of productive operations'[19]). Marx had already explained in *The Poverty of Philosophy* that the State as political power has to disappear with the disappearance of the antagonism between social classes.[20] In the *Manifesto*, he writes: 'in the course of development, class distinctions have disappeared, and all production has been concentrated in the hands of a vast association of the whole nation, the public power will lose its political character'.

In Volume 1 of *Capital*[21] – written in 1867 – Marx is more specific, not in order to describe communist society but to unveil the secret of the 'the *fetishism* of commodities'.[22] In a communist society with common means of production, individual labour forces would be spent – according to a concerted plan – as only one force of social labour (producers' associations seem forgotten). It will be distributed between the different kinds of works in proportion of the various *social* wants (as Robinson distributing his time between different works in proportion of various *individual* wants).

Part of social production would be allocated to reproduction, the rest being distributed for individual consumption according to a variable distribution key, dependant on the producing organism of society and on the degree of development achieved. This could be, *for example* (merely for the sake of a parallel with the bourgeois production of commodities), 'to each according to his labour' (implicitly, the idea that another distribution key will become possible when the development of productive forces will be sufficient thus appears).

Labour time would thus play a dual role: in production, as the key to distribution of social labour according to the various social needs, and in distribution, as the key to distribution of each individual's share of common labour.

It is worth noting that in 1872, as he participated in the debate over the issue of land nationalization,[23] Marx specifies that 'there will no longer be a government, or State power, distinct from society itself' (which remains ambiguous). And especially that '*the national centralization of the means of production* will serve as the national basis of a society formed by free and equal producers' associations which will advance social affairs according to a common and rational plan'.[24] We thereby find the nationalized means of production, producer associations (cooperatives?) and a plan to coordinate the whole system.

In *Critique of the Gotha Programme*, written in 1875,[25] Marx is compelled to clarify his viewpoint further by criticizing the Lassalian position and particularly the use of – unscientific – 'soft expressions', expressing 'socialist kind feelings' such as: workers are entitled to *equitable distribution*, the equal rights of all members of society to the *complete fruits of their labour*.

On 'equitable distribution' first. Don't members of the bourgeoisie believe that current distribution is equitable? Isn't equitability based on current modes of production? There are as many conceptions of equity as there are modes of production. Besides, there are several with 'sectarian socialists'. Marx is not an idealist – there is no absolute Justice that can be determined scientifically – contrary to Walras's beliefs.

As for *the complete fruits of their labour*, shouldn't the elements necessary to an expanded reproduction as well as reserve funds and insurance be subtracted from production? It has nothing to do with equity but is an economic problem (Walras would call it a question of social interest). As for what remains for consumption before it is distributed between individuals, apart from general expenses unlinked to production, shouldn't the goods consumed as a community and necessary to those who cannot work (public assistance) be subtracted also?

The most interesting is the way that the consumable part (a surplus, a 'partial product' and not integral) will be distributed. *In a communist society in its first phase*, the stigmata of the former order cannot but remain present. Not only will the 'dictatorship of the proletariat' impose itself on the political level, but the law of value will also apply to the economic level: the individual producer will receive only what he gave, that is the amount of labour achieved. The bourgeois principle remains in force: 'an amount of labour in one form is exchanged against a similar amount of labour in another form'.[26] How? Society – practically the State – gives each individual a bond certifying the amount of labour achieved (after deduction of the amount of labour achieved towards collective funds) and he uses this bond to draw a certain amount of diverse products (according to their labour value) in the social reserves[27] (there is no longer subject 'free and equal producers' associations'). What has changed in comparison with capitalism? Individuals can deliver labour only and can only deliver labour (no bonds, except for public assistance, to non-workers) and no one can become owner except for ownership of the means of consumption. Thus there is an obvious inequality, a repercussion of the bourgeois economic order that shouldn't be measured in terms of equity but rather material necessity or existing mode of production.

A radical difference with Walras is that savings for capital accumulation are no longer individual but socially decided above the distribution to individuals. Individual savings cannot be accumulated, only saved – hoarded – for later consumption: inequality is only a question of quantity or quality of labour and not an effort of abstinence (one knows how ironic Marx is about this abstinence).

It is only in a superior phase of communist society, when 'the sources of cooperative wealth will flow in abundance'[28] and that man will be truly free, prosperous, liberated from the constraints of the division of labour, that he will work only because work will be 'the first need of life' and that we will move from the concept of 'each according to his capacities' to that of 'each according to his needs'. An ultimate Marxian concession to the old utopia? Undoubtedly, but also the progressive confidence in the explosion of the productive power of the liberated man, the belief in the disappearance of the work sentence, with only creative labour remaining.

Walras was Very Critical of Marxian Collectivism

Walras was very critical of Marxian collectivism in his *Theory of Property* of 1896: that of Marx[29] himself concerning the first communist phase (even though he did not have access to *Critique of the Gotha Programme*), and that of Marxists (who got access to this *Critique* in its 1891 publication or via Wilhelm Bracke to whom Marx sent the *Critique* many years before it was published).

Walras wrote: 'I declare collectivism possible under certain conditions only, I contest its equity and usefulness'.[30] However, Marxian collectivism could only work efficiently, even by the use of its consubstantial constraint, because its base – a theory of value founded on labour and not on 'scarcity' – is erroneous.

The Marxian theory of labour value leads to consider tenant farming and interests as 'exactions of the capitalist-entrepreneur' in detriment to the 'worker-consumer'. Marxian collectivism will impose commodities prices that only retain the sole value of labour to eradicate these exactions.[31] He points out that in a Marxist system the entrepreneurial State buys a time length and distributes numeral work bonds guaranteeing products containing an equal length of labour. The prices of products only retain the wages paid. They are fixed and do not vary with supply and demand.

He notes *first* that for commodities to be sold at costs reflecting wages only, the State must necessarily be the sole owner of capital and land, the only entrepreneur: Marxian distribution thus imposes a collectivist organization of production.

Then, Walras – who completely rejects the idea of coordination via a 'concerted plan'[32] – will reason through this hypothesis to show which kind of economy it leads to.

He admits that since the total amount of wages paid will be equal to the total amount of revenues distributed, global supply will equal global demand. But this needs not be true of particular supplies and demands of commodities. How will the State reach the equilibrium if the prices only contain wages and are fixed?

He also accepts a State that could know the production levels of various products and stocks as well as the evolution of their demand, even that the State could partially move certain producer services from one branch to the next: if it cannot transform already made tools and already trained men, it can play on new capital and the training of men. In spite of this the Marxian 'concerted plan' cannot succeed.

As the State cannot move lands to the Bordeaux region, the absolutely limited amount of 'rent' of these lands can only conflict with the great use of their produce (Château-Lafite): Bordeaux region vineyards can only produce 20,000 bottles, the price of each bottle is constant (it equals the value of labour) and the demand will be of one million bottles! Nobody will drink it since a Marxist State cannot resort to arbitrary rationing (for friends) or luck (lotteries) and it will no longer be produced (as apple trees or hops will be planted instead!)[33] If, more generally, the 'rare' service of rent is made free, its demand will inevitably be superior to offer and there will be no criteria to distribute this service amongst the different products.

Walras adds that an identical problem exists for 'artificial capital goods' that could not be distributed if their price were to be null.[34] In fact, the problem is not exactly the same because, contrary to land, capital goods can only be partially transferred (thanks to 'new capital goods') from sectors for which net demand is negative to sectors for which net demand is positive. However, Walras considers that the State lacks a distribution criterion for lack of competition.

In the end, Walras is a *'semi-collectivist'* (only natural riches). And if full collectivism is possible, it's only with free competition markets *or* at least functioning *'as if'*. Marxist collectivists still remain to be convinced of their mistake, a task that is not impossible since they already accept individual ownership of personal skills.

Will they understand:

that it is preferable to let the prices of goods and services be set freely on free trade markets? According to Walras, collectivism in terms of production – even in the absolute form of a State having become the sole entrepreneur – does not mean the end of a wage system defined as 'lump sum sale of labour on the service market' (*'vente au forfait du travail sur le marché des services'*). It is still possible, fair and useful to determine prices according to bidding up (*'à l'enchère'*) or underbidding (*'au rabais'*) mechanisms;[35]

that if there is an agreement to collectivize land, capital goods must be collective or individual whether they are produced by the State's savings (on tenant farming for the most part) or individuals?

And if Marxists' wish to give the State ownership of all capital goods stems from the fear of witnessing a renaissance 'of an oppressive financial feudalism in new society', they may rest assured! The wealth of billionaires only comes from the appropriation of private lands, rent raises in progressive societies, speculation on real estates and natural or artificial monopolies. Rational society, according to Walras, will forbid these misplaced and in fact artificial demonstrations of inequality.

The Laws of History

It is widely acknowledged that Marx's philosophy of history owes much to Hegel's. It is less known that Walras's – fundamentally idealistic – conception of history sees itself as close to the great philosopher's. He would thus be the source of both philosophies of history even if Marx himself considers having re-established it on its feet. Indeed, the influence of the German philosopher's idealism was exerted on Walras via Etienne Vacherot,[36] although Walras considered that he had moved beyond Vacherot's system and that the necessary achievement of a social Ideal through history was one of his major contributions beyond the latter's doctrine.[37]

The Marxian presentation of mode of production will serve as a starting point before it is set in relation to the Walrasian conception of social relationships. The general law of historic evolution given by Marx will then be evoked. Finally, Walras's philosophy of history will be clarified.

Marx and the Mode of Production, Walras and Social Relationships

Marx distinguishes between the relations of man to nature and those between men themselves. The first are mediatized by labour, hence labour division and cooperation and hence the use of modes of production. But men only produce the material means of their existence – a question of productive power – in relation to the modalities of production's social organization, the 'social relations of production'. Modes of production are therefore defined by the coherence of a development stage of productive forces and by a kind of production relations. Ownership and political relationships first, then ideas, representations, conscience facts, form a superstructure that only reflects this mode of production.

Let's compare this conception to Léon Walras's. The latter also distinguishes between the relations of men to things and those between men themselves, facts of industry and of morals. The first are relations of subordination of things to men, and labour is also the means of man's power over nature. When trying to define the nature of man, as he distinguishes between its two aspects, Walras notes that according to the first, man is an animal that divides labour to produce its own means of existence. *The criterion here is interest.* As for the relations between men themselves, they mainly stem from the second aspect of the nature of man: man is a moral person (a rational being endowed with sensibility and free will). Ownership relations – human institutions that preside over the distribution – emerge from this second aspect. *The criterion here is justice.* Contrary to Marx, social relations are not determined within the sphere of production, ownership rules being in the sphere of justice, not interest. In a nutshell, as opposed to the Marxian pyramid based on mode of production, a Walrasian construction stands on a double base: (1) division of labour and production, (2) moral person and ownership relations, and therefore distribution of social wealth.

In fact, the Walrasian construction is more complex because division of labour implies social relations that thereby emerge from the criterion of interest. And the main problem is that these social relations, which could be qualified as relations of production, could stand in contradiction with social relations stemming from the moral persona of man. Although with Marx, social and ownership relations only respond to determination – that is, productive forces – with Walras there is a potential tension between two types of determination of social relations – that is between interest and justice. But if, at what Walras considers to be the practical level – that is factual history – this tension is expressed effectively, it disappears at the ideal or absolute level. There cannot be any contradiction between interest and justice at this level.

Besides, there is no strict symmetry between the two Walrasian aspects. In his youth especially, the materialistic, economic, even biological, dimension of division of labour prevailed; it appeared to impose itself over the moral dimension, involve it. 'The fact of division of labour' thus takes on such an importance in early writings that it appears to determine all of man in society.[38] But then (as early as 1863 in *Recherche de l'idéal social*), a certain balance is found. One must not conclude from this that concerning the voluntarist action of men, interest should prevail over justice. On the contrary – if there were to be a contradiction – Walras considers that justice should be favoured.

Marxian Philosophy of History

Marxian writings are numerous. The *Manuscripts* of 1844 especially should be mentioned, as well as the *Theses on Feuerbach* of 1845, *The German Ideology* of 1845–6, *Poverty of Philosophy* of 1847, the *Manifesto of the Communist Party* of 1848 and finally the foreword to *Critique of Political Economy* of 1859.[39] At this point, the essential doctrine was forged.

In Marx, to the *double correspondence* between productive forces and social relations that define the mode of production (or infrastructure) on the one hand, and between mode of production and a whole superstructure on the other hand, is added a double determination from which these dynamics – history – stem:

production relations between men are determined by the social production of their existence, the degree of development of productive forces,

on this basis is built the entire judicial and political structure as well as the determined forces of social conscience, thus consecrating the *domination* of production of material life. Not that, as with Feuerbach, men are the fruits of circumstances and material background only, but 'it is precisely men who transform circumstances,'[40] that is, who develop productive forces and lead class struggles, hence evolution.

Society evolves towards a determined end, but in an uneven way. The development of productive power is vitalized by social relations when they correspond.

This particular development can only produce a contradiction between the two constituent parts of the mode of production; social relations, then, become hindrances to the development of productive forces, hence increasing tensions and, finally, social revolution and the fall of the superstructure, the formation of new production relations – and therefore new judicial and political relations – and new forms of social conscience in correspondence with the superior degree attained by productive power. In the end, we face a conception of the movement of history in which the 'internal contradictions' of all modes of production spur historical development, even the success of a mode of production producing these contradictions, and thus its disintegration, to give birth to a new mode of production. A necessary, fatal, movement which has an *end*: the disappearance of class antagonism with the end of the bourgeois mode of production and the transformation of the proletariat as a universal class: the end of prehistory and birth of a reconciled era.

The fatality of the course of history questions the role of men themselves in this evolution, a question parallel to that of the role of free will in the necessary development of history in Walras. First, they develop productive forces but have no other alternative: a first necessity. Then they lead class struggles. From the Marxist point of view, there is neither interest nor collective will of the whole of men in a given society (at least before the final stage), antagonism is at the heart of social issues. To state that men make their own history[41] comes down to maintaining that they act by class struggles.

Is there a contradiction between history predetermined – even as a last resort Engels would say – by economic conditions[42] and the statement according to which 'the history of any society until today is the history of class struggles'?[43] Indeed, whatever the details added later by Marx and Engels, class struggles only appear to hold a limited position (in this general theory at least): it shouldn't succeed in making the ancient mode of production disappear as long as its capacity to develop productive power has not disappeared (which was, of course, a problem to revolutionaries before and after 1917), it can only play the role of midwife of a new society, and perhaps advance the time of delivery or be used as forceps!

Moreover, class struggles are not the expression of an active liberty of man, of his 'free will',[44] because they are themselves determined, part of the whole mechanics. As soon as humanity gets out of primitive communism – under the pressure of the development of productive forces – classes form (already in embryo in the primitive mode), antagonistic social relations of production. The necessity of classes and therefore of their antagonism (until the final stage) is not inferior to that of the development of productive forces. Men can only develop social struggles. They do it according to their class interests and thereby make history without knowing what kind of history they are making because historical reason – even materialistic reason – contrives to reach the ultimate destination beyond the horizon of real men. The 'free will' of men is only asserted at the end of the path, where the 'reign of necessity' ends. Indeed, the path can differ according to 'historic circumstances', but the general direction, the progressive process and the communist ends are necessary: 'capitalist production generates its own negation with the fatality that presides over the metamorphoses of nature'.[45]

Walras's Philosophy of History

The fatality that presides over the metamorphoses of nature. It sends us back to Léon Walras, who wrote in *L'économie politique et la justice*: 'historical facts are achieved within humanity, just as natural facts are achieved within nature, and are tinged, similarly to natural facts, of a fatalistic or even providential character'.[46]

Walras explains in the same early writings that there exist moral facts between 'natural facts' and 'historical facts'. Contrary to the latter two, they do not have a fatalistic character as they are founded on the free will of man. The problem, therefore, is: *how can moral facts founded on free will lead to a necessary historic destiny of man*?

Because history is defined by Walras as 'pure moral science', he is compelled to resolve this contradiction. He writes 'The effects of human will serve as the object of ... a study which shall be entitled pure moral science or history' and these effects are the necessary achievement of the Idea, the social Ideal that Reason could define.[47]

The economic and social Ideal that the scholar can apprehend on the basis of his knowledge of the nature of man in society will necessarily be achieved through the effort of human will. As in Quesnay – who he and his father consider to be a precursor – 'the natural and essential order' of societies exists ontologically. This order is Ideal in both senses of the term: ideal in the sense that it is a Platonician idea and ideal in the sense of perfection. It becomes knowledge for the philosopher or scholar that 'unveils' it little by little thanks to the 'efforts' of reason. If it is to lead the voluntary actions of men, the future will necessarily achieve it. The philosophy of history of Walras, pure moral science,[48] will be in charge of theorizing this process.

How can it resolve the free will/necessity aporia? In other words, if the destiny of man, conforming to his nature, pre-exists as an Idea, if it is knowable (thanks to the scholar) and necessarily achieved, how will this necessity be realized – voluntarily and freely – by free will?[49]

First, according to Walras, free will is not as free as it believes it is, *it is largely illusory*.[50] If its existence needs be temporarily acknowledged because it is a 'fact of experience', it remains a social science that is ('at least in part') 'mechanics of moral forces, that is an abstract and deductive science as much as – if not more than – mechanics of physical forces'.[51] Freedom is transformed in necessity!

This transformation admittedly rests on the banal distinction between individual and collective: freedom of the individual which can drive the latter to stray away from his trajectory and determination of humanity that comes down to an implicit determinism by the 'law of large numbers'. Humanity will inevitably attain its ideal:

> it is what we would do, possibly in spite of ourselves; for if, individually, man is free to desert the accomplishment of his destiny, humanity as a whole is not free to act against interest and justice, that is against its own nature.[52]

The end of this quote shows that there exists more than determinism by the 'law of large numbers': if the moral persona of man is endowed with reason and free will, if the social Ideal of absolute interest and justice is the rational expression of this human nature, how could free will refuse what conforms to human nature, to seek the achievement of its essence? Therefore, if the North wind will be able to freeze some of humanity's hopes for a certain length of time, 'the impossible would be for scientific and liberal socialism not to harvest'.[53] Although he does not claim to provide the rules of this theology, they exist and can only achieve the Ideal. Walras – being Hegelian in this respect – considers history as the achievement of the Idea that the scholar can have access to because it is rational.

Then, and in spite of its inherent contradictions, free will is not only illusory, it is even indispensable for history to advance. Mechanicism is not only nuanced, but, moreover, it cannot be reduced to spontaneism, *on the contrary*. If he considers that humanity comes gradually closer to the social ideal, history is not only an unconscious process. To Walras, history does not only proceed from 'trial and error' or by 'tâtonnement', it is also voluntarist (of a collective will) and in part rational.[54]

He is very 'French' in this respect, in the line of Jean-Jacques Rousseau. But if 'men make their own history', history remains determined. Free will enlightened by reason *acts* human history, history could not be made without it, but it is not free to move in any direction or to achieve any kind of utopia: only 'good' reforms can succeed permanently, those that go in the direction of history, and free will is only free to advance history towards the rational city.

In the end, Walrasian free will plays the role of Marxist class struggles or, to put it differently, class struggle is the form that 'free will' takes on with Marx. History would not be made without one or the other because history does not correspond to spontaneous mechanics of trial and error but is voluntarist, even though, to Walras as to Marx, they are largely determined; in the end they are only free to go in the right direction.

Walras did not provide – or imagine being able to provide – contrary to Marx, the laws of history. Although Walras sometimes considered *selection* as the great engine of history, this is rather nuanced. He writes:

The power of selection is indisputably one of the greatest facts – if it manages to evolve from the state of hypothesis to that of demonstrated truth – that physiology will have brought to light this century and thanks to which humanity tends to move closer to its current ideal and maybe to conceive another ulterior ideal.[55]

It is also important to note the importance given by Léon Walras to the development of productive forces in the course of humanity and specifically in the progressive transformation of social relations, which reinforces a certain proximity with Marx.

Slavery, serfdom, appear to him as imposed by the economic necessity of their time and the 'Industrial Revolution'; 'steam and machines' or 'modern industry' have led to the disappearance of slavery and serfdom, after having made them useless or even detrimental, much more efficiently than philosophers' or moralists' attacks would have done.[56]

The issue of the wage system is raised today in a similar fashion with the pursuit of machine development. However, these are not materialistic mechanics. Social progress starts with ideas, which requires the development of social sciences first. When commenting on the possibility of suppressing the proletariat thanks to millions of mechanical slaves, he adds: 'would a complete ideal thus be achieved? No, but it would be perceived by science as it is able to seize the absolute.'[57] Machines change the relative interest but the absolute interest – necessarily conform to absolute justice – imposes the final stop to proletariat: ideas are realized whilst the dynamics of productive forces only serve as support.

4 SRAFFA WITHOUT WALRAS

Richard Arena

This contribution is an attempt to evaluate the impact of the works of Léon Walras on the development of the economic theory of Italian author Piero Sraffa, and in particular on his book *Production of Commodities by Means of Commodities (PCC)*.[1] It could not have been written fifteen years earlier. As a matter of fact, Sraffa's publications and, in particular *PCC*, do not contain any direct or explicit reference to the work of Léon Walras. However, after Trinity College has opened the Sraffa Archives (SA), the Wren Library of Cambridge University made it possible for researchers to also access Sraffa's manuscripts and private library. These archives are extraordinarily rich and reveal much about Sraffa's life and work. Given this, it seemed interesting – for the occasion of this book dedicated to Pascal Bridel – to search the SA and Sraffa's private library for traces of any influence that Léon Walras might have had on his economic work and how he interpreted Walras's work.

Before presenting the results of our research, it is necessary to elaborate, in a first section, on its purpose: why was there reason to believe that Léon Walras could have influenced Sraffa's critique of marginalist economic theory as well as the elaboration of *PCC*? To answer this question, we have to go back in time, to the period 1960 to 1980 during which the first reactions to Sraffa's *Prelude to a Critique of Economic Theory* emerged. The second part of this text then gives an overview of what the SA and Sraffa's private library reveal about Sraffa's perspective on the work of Léon Walras – aiming to be as exhaustive as possible without drawing any undue inferences. Indeed, we confined ourselves to present with the most possible accuracy what is said in our sources to allow the reader to form his own opinion. It is only in the conclusion that we propose our own interpretation of the available materials and in this vein attempt to provide an answer to the question how the work of Léon Walras could have influenced Piero Sraffa.

Why Do We Suspect that the Work of Léon Walras Might Have had an Influence on Piero Sraffa's 'Critique of Economic Theory' and the Elaboration of *PCC*?

As we alluded to in the introduction, to answer this question, we have to go back in time, more precisely to the period between 1960 and 1980, during which both *PCC* as well as the Cambridge Capital Controversies are debated.[2] During this period, numerous economists made a link between the theoretical approaches of Walras and Sraffa, even though – as we highlighted already – there is no direct reference to Walras in the publications of Sraffa. This is for two reasons which the following sections will briefly recall.

PCC – Another Theory of General Equilibrium?

PCC provoked numerous comments as well as literature reviews and, in a first instance, caused perplexity among its readers. Reactions varied and focused on different aspects. Some economists who are favourable to Sraffa's theses have interpreted *PCC* as the basis for a theory of general equilibrium to rival those which were constructed by Walras and Pareto and strengthened, in the modern period, by Debreu.

A first such interpretation can be found in Claudio Napoleoni's 1965 publication *L'Equilibrio Economico Generale*,[3] which draws on a course in mathematical economics that the author gave at the University of Ancona. Lecture notes were quickly transformed into a textbook widely used by students and lecturers, especially in Italy. The book starts with a number of didactic chapters laying out Walras's theory of general equilibrium. The first chapter, entitled 'The General Formulation of Walras's Theory of Production and Exchange' and the fifth chapter, entitled 'The Equilibrium System with Constant Technical Coefficients' are brief, yet very close representations of Walras's *Elements of Pure Economics*. They are followed by an examination of Leontief's and von Neumann's multi-sector models. The book concludes with an analysis of the system of determination of relative prices and of Sraffa's distribution variables. It gives the impression that modern theory of prices underwent a progressive yet natural evolution from Walras to Sraffa, of which multi-sector models would only be first stages. According to this narrative, the trajectory began with Walras's model of production and exchange with fixed coefficients of production. The need for simplification and the rejection of utility value theory led to the price theory in Leontief's closed model, which is then followed by Leontief's dynamic model accounting for fixed capital, and finally by von Neumann's model which accounts for the joint choice of technology and production. Sraffa's system of prices and distribution is the final point in this sequence of progressive transformation of models of price determination as it achieves a more objective and accurate analysis of 'real' capitalist economies. Napoleoni's interpretation of this trajectory is organized around one constant: the attempt to account for the general interdependence of prices by means of 'algebraic systems of linear equations'.[4] In that sense, Sraffa's system offers the basis for a new theory of general equilibrium that replaces the notion of scarcity by the notion of reproduction.

Our second example dates from 1980, more precisely a publication by Vivian Walsh and Harvey Gram called *Classical and Neo-Classical Theories of General Equilibrium*.[5] It is interesting to note that this book was published fifteen years after Napoleoni's textbook, i.e. at a moment in time when most economists were not yet aware of the decline of neo-Walrasian theory of general equilibrium, even though the theory had been challenged in the mid-1960s by insolvable problems of stability and in the mid-1970s by the devastating consequences of the Debreu–Sonnenschein–Mantel theorem (DSM). Put differently, the book was published at a time when most economists still believed in a possible evolution of the so-called neo-Ricardian research programme and when, for most theorists, general equilibrium theory still constituted the unavoidable horizon and analytical framework that structured economic analysis. In the introduction to the book the authors indicate for that matter, that 'The chosen topics ... cover the main span of basic economic theory as it exists to-day'.[6]

The idea is simple: contrary to the generally held opinion, there existed *two* and not *one* theories of general equilibrium – one of 'classical' the other of 'neo-classical' inspiration:

> A sharp distinction can be drawn in the theory of general equilibrium between the classical theme of the accumulation and allocation of surplus output, and the neo-classical theme of the allocation of given resources among alternative uses. Without this distinction neither the history of economic analysis nor the structure of modern mathematical models of general equilibrium can be clearly understood.[7]

The authors analyse the historical roots of the two theoretical traditions and then present two distinct canonical models. This allows them to single out what, according to them, are the fundamental differences between the two models. To facilitate comparison, the 'neo-classical model' is presented in a simplified way as a linear two-sector model with fixed production coefficients, constant returns to scale and two factors of production (capital and labour).[8] This is contrasted to the 'classical model' which has the same properties, but does not distinguish primary factors of production (a separate chapter analyses the distribution between profits and wages[9]). None of the two models, therefore, is strictly speaking 'Walrasian' or 'Sraffian'. Léon Walras's actual theory is introduced in a preliminary chapter in which the authors review the *Elements* with undeniable meticulousness. The formalization they propose in the later chapter is, however, more audacious insofar as it rests on a dual price-quantity model in order to prepare for what is to follow. Piero Sraffa is less adequately presented than Léon Walras. The conventional but dismal Leontief–Sraffa model is sufficient to present equations for price and quantity and, once more, the key to the proposed solutions lies in the properties of duality. For our subject, in any case, the conclusion is simple: Léon Walras and Piero Sraffa are presented like two essential authors, who – both in their own way – made contributions to two competing theories of general equilibrium.

The publications of Napoleoni and of Walsh and Gram therefore constitute significant examples of the tendency prevalent in the 1960s and 1970s to make of Piero Sraffa the architect of a dissident theory of general equilibrium.

This thesis met certain sympathies among the so-called neo-Ricardians although it never became predominant among them. Paradoxically, unexpected support came from the opposite camp, in the figure of Frank Hahn: 'I assert the following: there is not a single formal proposition in Sraffa's book which is not also true in a General Equilibrium model constructed on his assumptions'.[10]

Hahn's thesis, which he put forward in his 1982 article treating those he considers 'neo-Ricardians', is well known.[11] According to him, Sraffa's general system of production prices can be assimilated to an inter-temporal general equilibrium model in which the rate of profit becomes an interest rate. This is, however, a strange scenario given that in general – as we know – inter-temporal equilibria allow for a multitude of interest rates. The only possible interpretation of such an inter-temporal model *à la* Sraffa is thus that the quantities in Sraffa's system are not random and cannot be chosen in an arbitrary way; they are not independent variables, but reflect an extremely specific configuration of initial endowments and of the technology that is available to economic agents. Hence, Sraffa's price system is 'one very specific case of the economy'[12] and 'the neoclassical economist who is always happy to consider interesting special cases sets to work to find a proper equilibrium for Mr Sraffa'.[13]

In that sense, Sraffa's system of production prices would be a *curiosum* of inter-temporal general equilibrium theory.

It goes without saying that the interpretations of *PCC* by Napoleoni as well as Walsh and Gram on the one hand and that of Hahn on the other hand are perfectly contradictory. As we have already pointed out, the former make of Sraffa a dissident theorist of general equilibrium whose theory cannot be associated solely to neo-classical tradition. For Hahn, on the other hand, Sraffa's system of prices is a minor contribution to general equilibrium theory and is entirely neo-classical in the sense that he gives to this term.[14] This, however, is not the problem. Our aim is not to discuss here the correctness and respective merits of these different publications, but to highlight that despite their fundamental differences, these publications have contributed to establish the idea that Sraffa's system of production prices has a 'family resemblance' to general equilibrium theory as constructed by Walras. Many economists concluded from this – without evident proof – that Sraffa could not have ignored Walras's work when constructing his own theory and that Walras's system of general equilibrium played a role in the formulation of Sraffa's theory of production prices.

Sraffa and the Critique of General Equilibrium

We obviously know about the destructive impact of Sraffa's critique of Marshallian theory of competition and prices in the context of partial equilibrium. We also know that – as expressed in his 1926 article – Sraffa briefly considered using general equilibrium theory in order to get out of the resulting dead end before he renounced it because it is 'well-known conception, whose complexity, however, prevents it from bearing fruit, at least in the present state of our knowledge, which does not permit of even much simpler schemata being applied to the study of real conditions'.[15]

However, some economists favourable to Sraffa's theoretical approach always maintained that Walrasian general equilibrium theory was never exempt of the criticisms that could be constructed based on the notion of capital developed in *PCC*, or from the critique that Sraffa had addressed to Marshall's theory.

Among the former figures was undoubtedly Pierangelo Garegnani, who towards the end of the 1950s and – it should be noted – independently of *PCC* had developed an original critique of Walrasian capitalization theory which was, in its concept, close to the Cambridge critique of aggregated neo-classical capital theory[16] and gave rise to numerous debates.[17]

Among the latter one could mention Bertram Schefold, who argued that the modern versions of general equilibrium theory are not exempt of Sraffa's critiques. He offered several lines of reasoning in support of his argument. The first one is rooted in the absence of a genuine theory of the firm in Gérard Debreu's *Theory of Value*:

> According to Debreu, the prices emerging from the equilibrium are only signals that indicate for a whole branch of industry the production quantity corresponding to the profit maximum. The prices give no clue as to how the quantity produced by the industry along with the factor distribution to the individual firms, should be determined. An infinite number of divisions of the total turnover of the branch to the individual firms is in general mathematically compatible with equilibrium. So Sraffa's problem is not solved even in the framework of the modern theory of general economic equilibrium of the short period in perfect competition.[18]

The second line of argument put forward by Schefold concerns the difficulty of general equilibrium theory to account for increasing returns to scale – which are nonetheless widespread, in particular among innovating firms.[19] This criticism is part of a wider, more general criticism concerning the degree of abstraction of

Walrasian equilibrium theory: 'Walras proceeds in a formal and deductive way within a narrow horizon, so that a *logical* critique cannot show how many *real* phenomena remain poorly understood in his work'.[20]

Finally, Schefold raises the problem of the role of capital goods and the necessity to reproduce them within the system of initial factor endowments of the individual agent.

> The essential difficulties with Walrasian models (including Debreu) originate ... from the following assumption: they all take the quantities of the various capital goods is given from the beginning ... Because capital goods depreciate they have to be reproduced. Their prices of production have to contain interest according to a uniform rate of the money capital advanced for production. Since the supply prices for existing capital goods, which depend on the conditions of scarcity and the potential uses of capital goods in production, do not stand in a genuine relation to prices of production of reproduced capital goods in the model, an ambiguous double price determination occurs.[21]

We will not evaluate the reach of the critiques of Walrasian and neo-Walrasian constructions formulated by Garegnani and Schefold nor the debates they initiated within contemporary economic analysis. We merely state that economists associated very closely with Piero Sraffa when he was alive, were convinced that Sraffa's *Prelude to a Critique of Economic Theory* could be used to understand the limitations faced by general equilibrium theory. Although, to our knowledge, neither Garegnani nor Schefold wrote this explicitly, this belief can lead one to think – correctly or not – that the study of Léon Walras's work has left its marks on the economic thinking of Piero Sraffa.

Which Traces of Walras's Influence on the Author of PCC can be Found in the SA as well as in Sraffa's Private Library and What is Sraffa's Own Perspectives on the Work of Léon Walras?

The research we have undertaken in the Wren Library has been as exhaustive as possible, but we can obviously not exclude the possibility that one or two documents may have escaped our attention. However, as reiterated in the third part of this contribution, we do not believe that an unattended discovery could turn our conclusions upside down and all the evidence at hand points towards one interpretation only. In the meantime, in the following section, we will not immediately interpret our findings, but rather content ourselves with indicating their intrinsic value. Three different types of traces of Walrasian influence on Sraffa will be distinguished in what is to follow.

Sraffa's Own Knowledge of Léon Walras's Work

We refer here to the books and articles of Léon Walras, which have been available to Sraffa in his own personal library in Cambridge.

This library contains six volumes by Léon Walras. First of all, Sraffa owned *Elements of Pure Economics* (1900, in French, published by Pichon, Paris and Rouge, Lausanne).[22] On the cover of the book, Sraffa noted with pencil '4th edition' above the year 1900 and attached his bookplate. Inside the book, there are, however, no signs of annotations by Sraffa. Sraffa's library also comprises *Summary of the Elements of Pure Economics* (in French with commentary and revisions by G. Leduc) published in Pichon et Durand-Auzias, Paris et Rouge et Cie, Lausanne in 1938.[23] Once again, Sraffa has attached his bookplate, but other than this there are no signs of annotations from Sraffa inside Walras's *Summary of the Elements of Pure Economics*. In the same library, we can also find an English copy of *Elements of Pure Economics* published by George Allen and Unwin in 1954.[24] Once again, other than his bookplate, there are no visible comments by Sraffa inside the book. There are also French copies of *Studies in Social Economics* published by Pichon, Paris et Rouge, Lausanne in 1896[25] and *Studies in Applied Economics* published by Pichon, Paris et Rouge, Lausanne in 1898.[26] On the former, Sraffa underlined the words 'Economics', 'social', 'Walras's and '1896' with a pencil. Once again he attached his bookplate. Other than that, he has again refrained from any handwritten comments. Finally, the library also comprises the English version of *Correspondences of Léon Walras and Related Papers*, prepared by William Jaffé in three volumes, published by North Holland in Amsterdam in 1965.[27] Here as well, we cannot find any handwritten annotation other than the usual bookplate. We know, however, that on page 529 of Volume 1, W. Jaffé wrote the following in the second note concerning a letter of Charles Letort to Léon Walras dated 17 February 1877: 'Mr. Piero Sraffa of Cambridge very kindly communicated to me a photocopy of this letter the autograph of which is in his possession'.[28]

Sraffa, even though he was usually very attentive to the references other scholars made to himself in their publications and articles, has not made any particular handwritten annotation to Jaffé's note no. 2.

It should be noted that the exchange between Jaffé and Sraffa with regards to Walras did not end there. Indeed, the SA reveal that on 20 September 1956, William Jaffé sent a letter to Sraffa in which he writes the following:

> At the moment I am in Italy living on a Fulbright Lecturing award, but I am principally concerned with gathering materials on Léon Walras's relations with Italian economists of his time. This, I believe, should make an interesting chapter in a book I am preparing on the Life and works of Léon Walras. I already have photocopies of the Walras Correspondence which I found at Lausanne and Lyons, but this has only

served to whet my appetite for more documentation which should be existent in Italy. I imagine the papers and letters of Pantaleoni, Pareto and Barone must be held somewhere. It would interest me particularly to find the manuscript of Barone's Note on Wicksteed which was written at Edgeworth's request in 1895 and then turned down when submitted for publication in the Economic Journal. Could you possibly tell me who in Italy might be of help in this search?[29]

Sraffa's answer to Jaffé dates from 1 October, and comprises essentially the following:

Trinity College, Cambridge, 1st October 1956,

Dear Mr. Jaffé,

Thank you for your letter. I too had seen with pleasure that we were being noticed together as fellow-editors of old economists, and of course I shall be glad to help you if I can.

I feel that, being in Italy, you are really much better placed than I am, to find out about the papers of the Italian economists. However, here are some scraps of information – although much of it is from memory and may well, after so many years, be inaccurate.

The first thing is the correspondence of Pareto with Walras, the originals of which I believe were deposited before the war with the 'Département cantonal de l'instruction publique' at Lausanne.

In Italy Pareto did not have many friends. You may however be able to contact one of these (if he is still living) Professor Sensini of Pisa University. He printed several years ago (with some omissions) the letters he had received from Pareto, including two bitter ones referring to Walras' enmity towards Pareto himself. These you must certainly get hold of.

Beyond this I can only suggest that you try to get in touch with Pareto's second wife, Mme Regis, who was a Frenchwoman, or her family. Professor G. H. Bousquet would be the person more likely to be able to help you in this. (I have the impression that he was at the University of Algiers, but was compelled to leave the place during the present troubles).

As to Pantaleoni, his colleagues at the University of Rome can no doubt help you to find his family. A son (Demetrio I believe) went to live in the U.S.A. just before the war – I think he was in the shipping business.

If my memory is not at fault (after more than 30 years) Pantaleoni's library at his death went to the Italian Ministry of Finance. The Librarian of the Ministry at the time was Prof. Gangemi, now of the Faculty of Economics at Naples University. He may be able to help.

For Barone's papers you should get in touch with Dr Francesco Spinedi, who was his assistant, and who edited his works in 1936. His address is (or was in 1948) Corso Vittorio Emanuele 142, Roma.[30]

Jaffé concludes this exchange with a letter dated 9 November, summarized in the following paragraphs:

I am still groping in Italy. As for the Walras–Pareto correspondance [*sic*], I made photocopies of the complete exchange of letters some time ago in Lausanne, and I have nearly finished deciphering Walras's dreadful rough drafts of the letters he sent. I propose before long to annotate and publish not only this correspondance [*sic*], but the Walras–Barone and the Walras–Pantaleoni letters as well. It is for the sake of the annotations that I am looking for further manuscript material in England and Italy.

I already have Sensini's Corrispondenza di Vilfredo Pareto. Sensini, I am told, is still living, but he is said to be difficult to approach. I shall, nevertheless, try.

I know Professor Bousquet quite well. In fact I accepted an invitation to teach at the University of Algiers last Spring mainly because I hoped that in the course of my personal contacts with him, he would shed some light on the problems I am working on. Unfortunately, he turned out to be so much absorbed in political activity and in purely sociological questions that he proved of little help. I was in Algiers at the time of his expulsion from Algeria, and since then he seems to be lost from sight.

I am now in correspondance [*sic*] with Dr. Spinedi, but apparently he has little to offer.

As you see, it is not only the competitive market which operates by 'tâtonnements'. Following your suggestions, I am writing to Madame Régis and to Professor Gangemi; I am also writing to Professor Einaudi. I have learned at least to groan in Italian: 'Pazienza !'[31]

These first indications based on the examination of Sraffa's personal library and the exchange of letters with Jaffé show that Sraffa was certainly an economist with a greater than average knowledge of Léon Walras's work, especially when compared to UK universities and Cambridge in particular. He was fluent in French and was in possession of both the English and French version of *Elements of Pure Economics*, as well as the *Summary*. He also had direct access to the *Studies in Applied Economics* as well as *Social Economics* and he is clearly familiar with Walras's correspondences. His answers to Jaffé's questions show again that he is not ignorant about Walras's social and intellectual environment. Besides, his reputation as connoisseur of Walras is also attested to in a remark from Joan Robinson to Bertram Schefold regarding the Sraffa's only reference to general equilibrium theory in his 1926 article[32]

> The allusion to the theory of Walras and Pareto occurs without mentioning their names. [Sraffa] had, however, worked on both and was, according to an oral report by Joan Robinson, *the first* to lecture on them in Cambridge towards the end of the 1920s.[33]

However, we should be careful about not pushing the hypothesis of Sraffa as well-informed expert of Walras too far. On the one hand, we cannot find any handwritten annotation or even underlined words or text passages in any of the books authored by Walras that were in Sraffa's possession. This is not necessarily conclusive evidence, but it should be pointed out that such annotations and profound comments exist in books by other authors (Alfred Marshall, for instance). In other words, Sraffa's library could just indicate that he was, quite simply, a bibliophile.

In the same way, the exchange of letters between Jaffé and Sraffa does not necessarily indicate that Sraffa had a profound knowledge of Walras's work and scientific environment. Jaffé seems to be aware of this and the tone of his response resembles that of someone whose expectations have been disappointed ('Pazienzia!').

To summarize, no matter whether we lean towards the hypothesis of Sraffa as assiduous student of the works of Walras or rather of Sraffa as bibliophile scholar, these first indications are worth noting but do not reveal anything certain about the influence Léon Walras's work may have had on Sraffa's projects.

The Role of the Theory of General Equilibrium in the 'Lectures on the Advanced Theory of Value'

Piero Sraffa began to teach his 'Lectures on the Advanced Theory of Value' in 1928. He structured them as a veritable history of value theory from François Quesnay and William Petty to the marginalist theories of utility which he associates mainly with the names of Jevons, Menger and Walras. In the lectures, a rather modest role is given to general equilibrium theory. The theory is confined to the end of the course and, repeatedly, it becomes clear that Sraffa lacks the time to outline for his students what he would have preferred to teach them.[34] The beginning of his lecture notes on general equilibrium theory sets the tone:

> I shall now say something about the theory of general equilibrium of all commodities at the same time. Of course I shall not expound it in detail, but just say as much as it is necessary to show its general method of approach, and the sort of technique it uses.[35]

Sraffa's teaching has two characteristic traits. On the one hand, he is basing his notes almost exclusively on Pareto's *Manual of Political Economy*. The *Elements* are only formally cited as a possibility for enhanced reading and Sraffa actually commits an error in his list of enhanced reading: 'Those who want to follow it up, may read Pareto's Manuel d'E.P. (text non math., app. mat.) or Walras, **Princ. D'E.P. Pure** [*sic*] – Cassel, Th. of S.E.'.[36]

The *Elements* have thus become *Principles*! ... and the study of the problems of general equilibrium theory is based on Pareto's text without ever going back to the points made in the work of Walras.

On the other hand, it is interesting to note that Sraffa highlights questions of a rather general nature in his lectures, such as the question of how utility can be measured or the coherence conditions which are required to hold in an approach which favours interdependence between agents and goods. He is thus not so much interested in the logic and content of general equilibrium theory, rather in questions affecting directly the development of a positive theory in which he was engaged at the end of the 1920s.

For instance, indifference curves are one of the two main tools Sraffa highlights in his text. Having explained how to interpret these types of curves and how they differ from traditional utility functions and demand curves, Sraffa highlights in particular the passage from cardinal to ordinal utility theory:

> In this way, which is sufficient for many problems, we do not make any assumptions as to utility being or being not a measurable quantity. We proceed as when we are arranging in order of intelligence a number of men, or in order of beauty a number of pictures – without implying that intelligence and beauty are measurable quantities and that we can say that a man is twice as intelligent as another or a picture seven times as beautiful.[37]

While this question is not unimportant in the context of general equilibrium theory, it is not a central question. The fact that Sraffa chooses to highlight this nevertheless is a reflection of his objections to the notion of measurable utility, as shown by the following extract from the Archives:

> The quantities involved in econ. theory may be classed in 3 groups:
>
> 1. Those which cannot possibly be measured because they are more defined in terms of the method of measuring them, e.g. marg. utility and sacrifice. (No definition at all is given for measuring them in the case of several individuals: in the case of one individual, they are defined as being proportional to certain quantities, i.e. prices, but this is, as Cairnes says 'merely giving a name to the unknown causes of price'). Such quantities must be excluded altogether: at the worst, they may be used as a fictitious device for solving problems, but must not appear either in the premises, nor in the conclusions.[38]

Sraffa's preoccupation with the legitimacy of the concept of indifference curves is thus closely tied in with his own vision of the world, but it is not a question to which general equilibrium theory necessarily has to have an answer. That Sraffa brings it up is rather a result of his own reflections, at the time, on how to (re) construct an objectivist tradition in political economy.

At the same time, Sraffa tries to establish and satisfy the conditions for the existence of a determined solution of prices and quantities, i.e. what he calls the problem of 'equilibrium equations in exchange'.[39] The idea behind this is simple: why would, in any given economy, the number of goods and the number of agents be such that the system of equations of prices and quantities can be fully determined? Won't the general equilibrium approach lead into a 'vicious circle' if we try to determine the totality of prices and quantities in an economy?[40] This is the old problem that has been considered by Marshall and Walras, in their different manners, and that has been taken up again by Edgeworth in a more specific context. Sraffa's lectures confirm, however, that Sraffa's starting point in this question is not Walras, but Pareto: 'The point Pareto is trying to prove is that the number of conditions given is equal to the number of unknowns.'[41]

Therefore, it is not surprising to find a reference to Pareto's doubts regarding the chances of resolving a Walras-style equation system with the number of variables and independent relationships being, somehow, estimated quantitatively:

> The disadvantage, as compared with the simpler scheme [that of partial equilibrium] is however very great; it is much more removed from any possible practical application. Even if all the knowledge of circumstances which it assumes will be obtained, the system of equations would be so intricate that, as Pareto says, the resources of algebra would not be equal to the task of solving them.[42]

Sraffa quotes, in this context, Pareto's authentic and famous line that 'The solution of a system of 70699 equations would be beyond the resources of algebra'.[43] From these difficulties, he draws a much more negative conclusion than Pareto:

> NB. It must be clear that there is no question in all this of objective indeterminateness, i.e., one doesn't mean that in the actual market the price will be indeterminate, whatever that may mean. It simply means that the economists have gone too far in making their abstractions, they have simplified too much: in trying to make it simple, they have gone so far as to ignore some condition which is essential to the determination of the problem. Therefore the proof of indeterminateness only can prove the inadequacy of the assumptions made.[44]

This reflects a methodological stance which was already apparent in the structure of Sraffa's articles from 1925 and 1926. As he did for Marshallian-inspired price theory in those articles, Sraffa now criticizes the theory of general equilibrium and its capacity to explain observable phenomena in real capitalist market economies.

As for price theory before, Sraffa raises the excess of abstraction and the lack of practical applicability of general equilibrium theory. This comment confirms our initial interpretation. Sraffa does not search to enter into the details of the internal logic of general equilibrium theory, but looks for components that could be useful to the construction of his own theory. This is also confirmed by Sraffa's research and work in preparation of the 1926 paper. We know that, effectively, in 1926, when faced with the limitations of Marshallian price theory, Sraffa looked to abandon partial equilibrium analysis in favour of general equilibrium. Sraffa found the Marshallian model with its diminishing marginal returns to be incompatible with the notion of *ceteris paribus*, because one cannot reasonably assume that small variations in the production of one single good cannot affect factor utilization across the whole economy. General equilibrium seemed promising, but Sraffa rejected it for the reasons discussed above. Another example for the excessive abstraction of general equilibrium theory was, according to Sraffa, the notion of marginal utilities. For him, it was not reasonable that the marginal utility of one good should depend on the quantity of other goods one consumes. What is more, building on his research on the interaction between the individual and the group, he notes:

> It should here be added that it is not sufficient to make utility of one commodity function of quantity of all others consumed by individual but also by community! It

would be as if in astronomy we said the movement of each star depends upon all others, but we have not the faintest idea of the shape of the functions![45]

From this examination of Sraffa's published and non-published writings at the end of the 1920s, we have to draw the conclusion that he was, among the economists of the time and in his academic environment, one of the best informed as regards general equilibrium theory. However, this knowledge was based on the works of Pareto, not Walras, and was mainly instrumental, that is to say, directly related to Sraffa's own endeavours in the 1920s. As Sraffa was critical of general equilibrium theory, one would be allowed to think that he did not further deepen his understanding of this theory, because he never though it to be convincing in the first place.

The Role of General Equilibrium Theory in the Remainder of the Sraffa Archives

General equilibrium theory in general, and Léon Walras in particular, do not appear much in the Archives and where they do, it is mainly for pedagogical reasons. For instance, and most likely due to direct influence from Léon Walras himself, Sraffa often refers to Walras together with Menger and Jevons, when talking about the marginalist revolution. As an example, consider these short remarks:

> Immediate (?) simultaneous success of utility with Jevons, Menger, Walras. It always happens with discoveries: and, as always, it is later found that unsuccessful predecessors had already discovered the whole thing.[46]

Or:

> As to Marx, the fact that the utility theory of value had been found several times before (by Dupuit, Gossen) and had fallen flat while, when it was again almost simultaneously published by Jevons, Menger and Walras in the years immediately following the publication of Vol. 1 of Capital, it suddenly found a large body of opinion prepared to accept it and support it, is significant enough (Ashley, Present Pos. of P.E., Ec. J. 1910 ?).[47]

Similarly, if more surprisingly, Sraffa links the marginalist revolution to some contemporary historical events:

> 1870
> Comune di Parigi
> Internazionale
> Caduta 2° Impero
> Fondaz. Imp. Germ.
> Fine potere temp. Papi
> Regno d'Italia

Jevons-Menger-Walras
Abandono arg. Metallo
e inizio caduta prezzi
(dura 20 anni, poi per 20 anni cadonno)
Alison[48]

Walras also appears in a small number of short reading notes, for example on the correspondence between Poincaré and Walras[49] or the debate between Bertrand and Walras.

Finally, one could suggest that the question of Walras's capitalization theory could have incited some reflection, especially given that Pierangelo Garegnani wrote part of a much-debated book[50] on this topic. However, it is interesting to note that no hint on any such reflection could be found in the archives despite the presence of the two first editions of Garegnani's book (with no annotations by Sraffa) in Sraffa's personal library as well as the existence of letters between Sraffa and Garegnani which also do not mention the book, except to discuss the possibility of it being published in English. One can also note that Sraffa sent some texts on capitalization (which are also in the library and also do not have any annotations) to Boffito, another participant in the discussion about capitalization theory.

The scarcity of references to Walras in the remainder of the Archives seems to confirm the very limited role of Léon Walras in the scientific life of Piero Sraffa. What remains to be done, is to draw some more general conclusions from this.

Concluding Remarks

All the different indications which we have assembled seem to point to the same conclusion. Contrary to what one could have thought before the Sraffa Archives were opened, the works of Léon Walras do not seem to have played a major role in the development of the work of Piero Sraffa, not even as object of a critique. On the one hand, some of the topics of Walras's work are totally absent from Sraffa's writings. While Sraffa owned a copy of Walras's *Etudes*, he never referred to it in his own writings, be it positively or negatively. Similarly, the question of stability of different Walrasian equilibria was of no interest to Sraffa. On the other hand, Sraffa sees the rare topics that he and Walras have in common through a Pareto filter and appropriates them, as we have seen, in a critical way and only as minor contributions to his own intellectual edifice.

A posteriori, these results are hardly surprising. Sraffa was first a Marshallian because he was Italian and from Turin and then lived and worked in Cambridge. His only contact with Walras could be through the Italian marginalists, which is why Pantaleoni and Pareto have a much bigger place than Walras in Sraffa's published or unpublished writings.

It should also be noted that Sraffa was not a mathematician-economist as we understand today. His relationship with the mathematicians of Cambridge was marked by a complicated and slow dialogue during which Sraffa had bespoke tools created for him, which he then adjusted to his needs. Sraffa never just took a ready-made system of equations from elsewhere and imported it into his work. Finally, he has a very specific way of constructing his equations. He never used multi-sector models used by mathematician-economists such as Walras, Pareto, Cassel, Dmitrieff, Bortkiewicz, von Neumann, Wald or Leontief. Recent work by authors such as Kurz, Salvadori, Gilibert or De Vivo who work on the Sraffa Archives may have diverging views on some points, but on this they agree. Therefore, from now on, we may have to get used to letting Sraffa be Sraffa without Walras.

5 WALRAS IN THE AGE OF MARSHALL: AN ANALYSIS OF ENGLISH-LANGUAGE JOURNALS, 1890–1939

Roger E. Backhouse and Steven G. Medema

Introduction

It is generally accepted that Léon Walras's greatest influence on American and British economics began only in the 1930s. While there is a significant element of truth to this, it begs the question of the degree to which Walras's work was known in the English-speaking world prior to the 1930s. Economists sometimes write as if there was a rediscovery of Walras in the 1930s, which raises the question of what American economists already knew about his work and how they had responded to it. Pascal Bridel has tackled this problem through analysing the reviews of Walras's books, and Walker has provided both a brief overview of these connections and a selection of the more recent literature illustrating Walras's influence.[1] This essay extends this work through a systematic analysis of how his ideas were received in the main English-language journals.

The period chosen is 1890 to 1939, which coincides with what might be described, somewhat loosely, as the 'Age of Marshall' in English-speaking economics. This epoch began with the publication of his *Principles of Economics* (1890), the influence of which on British and American economics was unparalleled for more than two decades. By the 1930s, however, Marshall's work was being widely challenged and some looked to Walras in developing an alternative way forward. Our starting point is also dictated by the timeframe within which specialist academic journals began to appear: the *Publications of the American Economic Association*, predecessor of the *American Economic Review* (1886), the *Quarterly Journal of Economics* (1887), the *Economic Journal* (1890), and the *Journal of Political Economy* (1893). The end point is the date of John Hicks's *Value and Capital* (1939) as, by this time, interest in Walrasian general equilibrium theory was becoming well established.

Walras was *always* a familiar name to readers of English-language journals. He was, from the beginning, a well-known figure in British and American economics, who carried on an extensive correspondence with British and American economists,[2] whose work was reviewed, who was made an honorary member of the American Economic Association,[3] whose retirement from the Chair at Lausanne was noted, and who was the subject of substantial obituaries in English-language journals.[4] His first publication in English, translated by Irving Fisher, appeared in the *Annals of the Academy of Political and Social Science* in 1892. Walras and his successor at Lausanne, Pareto, were contributors to English-language journals, and books published in the major languages of continental Europe were routinely reviewed in these journals. In short, from the 1890s onwards, Walras was never an obscure economist in the English-speaking world. His name may have appeared in the journals much less frequently than Marshall or Keynes, but it was far from unknown, as Table 5.1 makes clear.

Table 5.1: Occurrences of prominent names in JSTOR, 1890–1944.

Name	JSTOR hits
Marshall	2,164
Keynes	1,431
Jevons	986
Pigou	855
Cassel	623
Knight	609
Pareto	406
Hayek	362
Walras	361
Wicksell	317
Schumpeter	284
Menger	252

Source: dfr.jstor.org, subject 'economics' [accessed 21 March 2013]. Note that initials are not given as some names will catch a number of economists (e.g. Neville and Maynard Keynes; Auguste and Léon Walras). Though we believe that the numbers are not seriously misleading, they should be treated as rough approximations.

Our sample consists of the articles identified in the journals archived in JSTOR that discuss Walras. It was obtained by searching for all articles in which the words 'Walras' or 'Walrasian' appeared and then reading them to determine whether there was a discussion of the work of Léon Walras, and if so what was said about it. The size of the database is shown in Table 5.2 and Figures 5.1 to 5.3, below. Table 5.2 gives the number of articles in each English-language journal by half-decade.[5] Figure 5.1 plots the data for the leading American journals; Figure 5.2 aggregates North American and British journals; and Figure 5.3 places English-language journals in the context of equivalent figures for German/Scandinavian and Italian journals. The general pattern, *in all languages*, is of a gradual decline after the 1890s – after Walras had completed his main work – and of a sharp revival of interest in the late 1920s. The dramatic rise in discussions of Walras is focused, as one might expect, on newly established journals, in particular, *Economica* and *Econometrica*, which had cited his work extensively since they were first established.

The sample of journals and articles has limitations, which is why our results need to be considered alongside other types of evidence, such as Bridel.[6] Most significantly, there are no French journals included. There are further factors, such as the effects of war. Even where publication continued during wartime, the urgency to discuss wartime problems will have affected the material under discussion, and hence the authors likely to be cited. There were also important changes in the types of article published, in that there was an increasing tendency to discuss economic theory as something separate from application – in short, to argue in terms of what we now call 'models'.[7] However, this is not something that can be separated from increased interest in Walras; indeed, they are closely tied.

Table 5.2: Articles discussing Walras in English-language journals, 1890–1939.

	AEA/AER	JPE	QJE	Ann	Ecta	JFE	SEJ	Can	RESt	USA	Eca	EJ	RES	UK	Total
1890–4	4	1	1	7	–				–	13	–	8	–	8	21
1895–9	2	3	2	4	–				–	11	–	17	–	17	28
1900–4	3	2	5	1	–				–	11	–	6	–	6	17
1905–9	1	1	4	0	–				–	6	–	2	–	2	8
1910–14	7	0	0	0	–				–	7	–	7	–	7	14
1915–19	2	0	1	0	–				–	3	–	3	–	3	6
1920–4	2	2	1	0	–				–	5		9	–	9	14
1925–9	5	8	8	1	–				–	22	1	6	–	7	29
1930–4	9	17	5	0	19				0	50	15	12	4	31	81
1935–9	11	16	4	3	23	4	3	6	5	75	22	13	4	39	119

Source: These are articles and reviews in JSTOR that we have identified as discussing Léon Walras. AEA/AER = journals published by the American Economic Association; JPE = *Journal of Political Economy*; QJE = *Quarterly Journal of Economics*; Ann = *Annals of the American Association of American Academy of Political and Social Science*; Ecta = *Econometrica*; SEJ = *Southern Economic Journal*; Can = *Canadian Journal of Economics*; RESt = *Review of Economics and Statistics*; Eca = *Economica*; EJ = *Economic Journal*; RES = *Review of Economic Studies*. The presence of a '–' means' the journal did not exist in the relevant period. Note that *Econometrica* is counted as 'English-language' even though it carried some articles in French.

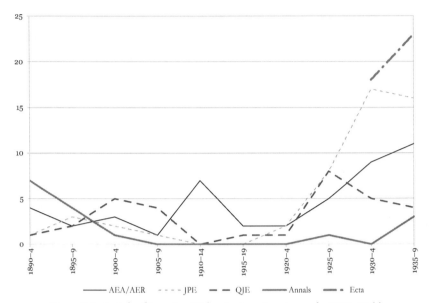

**Figure 5.1: Articles discussing Walras in American journals, 1890–1944.
Source as in Table 5.2.**

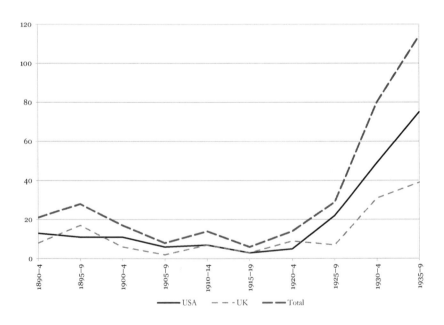

**Figure 5.2: Articles mentioning Walras in the USA and UK, 1890–1944. Source as in
Table 5.2. Note that the count for 'USA' includes a very small number of citations of the
Canadian Journal.**

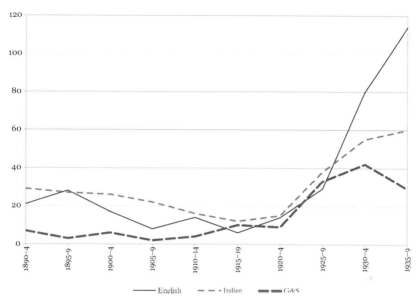

Figure 5.3: Articles mentioning Walras in English-language, German/Scandinavian and Italian journals, 1890–1944. Source as in Table 5.2.

Discussion of Walras in his Lifetime

There were over sixty references to Walras in the English-language journal literature in the last two decades of his life, including a translation by Irving Fisher of his 'Geometrical Theory of the Determination of Prices' in the *Annals of the American Academy of Political and Social Science* (hereinafter, *Annals*). Of these, roughly forty appeared in 1890–9 and only twenty over the period 1900–9. The vast majority of these early references involved no more than a passing mention, such as saying that a work had been influenced by Walras.[8] Discussions rarely went beyond a paragraph and some were simply notes regarding recent publications by Walras.[9] Many references linked him to fellow marginalists, Jevons, Menger and sometimes Marshall. His work was clearly linked to mathematical economics, which was beginning to gain currency in this period. However, his name was linked with many other topics and, in complete contrast with the 1930s, it is notable how few references were made to general equilibrium.

When Walras's retirement (for health reasons) from his chair at Lausanne was noted in the *Annals*, reference was made to his contribution to developing a 'pure economics ... created in mathematical forms'[10] and to the 'cordial acknowledgment' of his work in Italy, Belgium, Holland, Russia, Austria and America – as against its very minimal influence in his homeland, France.[11] Shortly afterwards, Oncken's 'Letter from Switzerland' in the *Economic Journal* noted that the second edition of Walras's *Elements* illustrated 'the diffusion of the taste for the mathematical treatment of economic problem'.[12] Of course, the number of scholars and students equipped to profit from Walras's analysis was not large, which led Edgeworth to welcome Irving Fisher's *Brief Introduction to Infinitesimal Calculus*, noting its utility in enabling 'a person without special mathematical training or aptitude to understand the works of Jevons, Walras, Marshall, or Pareto, or the mathematical articles constantly appearing in leading journals'.[13]

Walras's proper place in the development of the mathematical approach was much discussed. Two of the main American supporters of Walras, Fisher and Moore, emphasized that it was Cournot, not Walras, who deserved credit as the 'principal founder' of the 'mathematical school'.[14] Indeed, Moore noted that Walras had reproached his French countrymen for ignoring Cournot's fundamentally important contributions.[15] Seligman[16] pointed to the early origins of the theory of marginal utility in Lloyd, Dupuit and Gossen, and that this notion was only rediscovered by Jevons, Menger and Walras. However, far from minimizing Walras's originality, Moore pointed out that Boccardo, Jevons and Walras 'independently began the elaboration of the mathematical method',[17] and Fisher noted that Cournot's work 'differs materially from the modern mathematical economists' such as Jevons and Walras.[18] Similarly, Schumpeter described Walras, along with Jevons, as among the 'founders of what is usually called the "modern" system of theory'.[19]

When it came to matters of technical detail and of application of the mathematical approach, Walras was seen by some as providing a more refined explication of certain fundamental concepts, in relation to both pioneers such as Cournot and his contemporaries. Fisher noted that Walras and his followers went 'deeper into the analysis' of demand than had Cournot or more recent figures such as Jevons, building up from utility and quantities to individual demands and from individual demands to the 'general demand curve used by Cournot'.[20] Moore, reviewing Pareto's *Cours* in the *Annals*, objected to Pareto's 'frequently unnecessary and confusing use of mathematics', noting that if one was not familiar with a work such as Walras's *Elements*, Pareto's analysis would be 'absolutely unintelligible'.[21] Fiamingo, in the *JPE*, echoed this sentiment, pointing to Walras's 'splendid demonstration and elucidation' of the equation of exchange, in contrast to the spare analytics of Gossen and Jevons.[22]

Others were less charitable. Flux, for example, praised Wicksell's simplicity and clarity as against 'the bewildering complexity of Walras' work'.[23] Flux held the same view of Walras as against Pareto,[24] though he also noted in a review of the *Cours* that the former had 'rendered illustrious' the chair now held by the latter. Merritt, also reviewing the *Cours*, considered Pareto and Walras to be similar in subject matter and approach, but said that Pareto 'omitted much of [Walras's] unnecessary detail', pointing out that, like Marshall, Pareto was content to throw mathematical details into footnotes.[25]

Attention was also paid to the specifics of Walras's analysis. Edgeworth was foremost in drawing upon Walras in his work. He noted the relevance of the work of Walras and Pareto on domestic trade for the analysis of trade between nations – as well as his own disagreement with aspects of Walras's analysis of the exchange process.[26] Edgeworth also drew on Walras in analysing distribution, utilizing his concepts of a numéraire[27] and a zero-profit equilibrium (where 'the entrepreneur makes neither gain nor loss') – the latter idea having been the source of a good deal of confusion in the literature, which mystified Edgeworth).[28] And where Edgeworth found Walras's analysis of tax incidence useful for his own work, Seligman thought it 'too simple'[29] and lamented the mathematical school's failure to develop a fully worked-out theory.

English-speaking economists also noted Walras's work on monopoly. Pigou pointed to his demonstration of the possibility of sellers practicing price discrimination.[30] Johnson lauded the contributions of Walras, along with Marshall, Ely and Hobson to 'the formulation of the law of monopoly price'[31] and noted that the advance of this work on the classical view leaves one 'forced to admit that substantial progress can be made even by the methods of "pure theory"'.[32]

Walras's monetary analysis also received no small amount of attention during this period, with six allusions to his work on money and, in particular, bimetallism, all in the *QJE* and *EJ*, between 1893 and 1904. Walras's 'The Theory of Money' and his opinions on Indian currency had been presented to the British Association for the Advancement of Science in 1887, and it was noted six years later in both the *Annals* and the *EJ* that his proposal seems to have been adopted, at least in part, by the British government.[33] Walras's advocacy of a bimetallic system, which would combine a gold standard with 'a token coinage of silver' adjusted as necessary to maintain stable prices, was lauded in the *Annals* as being 'derived from the principles of pure political economy' and as such served 'as a striking proof of the importance of a method which he has given so much of his life to elaborate'. Sanger, a student of Marshall's, noted his pleasure in finding that Wicksell had discussed Walras's proposal along with bimetallism,[34] and he praised Walras's scheme for its potential feasibility and benefits while chiding another writer for failing to take Walras's ideas into account.[35] In the United States, Commons mentioned a proposal for a bimetallic, elastic currency system proposed by a 'distinguished Swiss professor of political economy'[36] and pointed out that Benjamin Andrews, the president of Brown University and an American delegate to the Brussels Conference, was proposing a monetary system that was substantially the same.[37]

Walras's analysis of capital was also referenced on multiple occasions during this period, most often by Irving Fisher, who, in citing Walras among many others in a long list of definitions of capital by leading scholars going back to Turgot, placed him in the Smithian tradition of defining capital as 'that portion of stock not devoted to immediate consumption'.[38] He pointed favourably to Walras's classification of all wealth into capital and income, where the latter is consumed by a single use while the former serves more than one use[39] – an aspect of Walras's theory also noted approvingly by Fetter[40] – and that Pareto's conception of capital followed closely that put forward by Walras.[41] Fisher said that Walras came 'very close to' getting at the distinction between stocks and flows, the former being the things and the latter being the services generated by those things (which include capital),[42] though he also suggested that Walras misunderstood the important role of the time element here. Fisher also found Walras's discussion of the relationship between income (from wealth), or services, and wealth itself – a relationship Fisher called 'correlative and inseparable'[43] – an important contribution to the theory of distribution,[44] noting that his own theory of income laid out in this 1897 article 'was suggested by the pregnant remarks of Walras and particularly of Cannan'.[45]

A final interesting group of references to Walras – evident in the literature only during this early period – related to his links with the cooperative movement in France and his interest in elements of socialism. This aspect of Walras's life and work was remarked upon a half-dozen times between 1890 and 1904, with five of those references coming from European scholars who were publishing works in US/UK journals. The one American to comment on this work, Harvard's Edward Cummings on cooperative production movements in France and England, noted that the success of the cooperative bank[46] *Caisse d'escompte des associations populaires*, founded by Leon Say and Walras at Lyon, was at the head of a second wave of French interest in cooperatives. While the press considered this movement 'the surest and most generous remedy for the errors and perils of socialism',[47] Walras himself, as Oncken noted,[48] was motivated by a desire to synthesize socialism and liberalism and to avoid the extremes evidenced by the 'fanatics' of both.

As Gide was later to note, Walras's affirmative discussion of these cooperative ventures contrasted sharply with other opinions evidenced in the French journals of the period.[49] But Gide also saw an important link between Walras's cooperative ventures and his theory of general competitive equilibrium, arguing that the latter lent indirect support to the cooperative movement. This movement abolishes profit and 'ideal system of free competition' essentially does the same, as Walras and others had shown, and does so 'automatically, without needing the constraining force of competition'.[50]

As in the previous period, there was also no settled view of Walras's place in the spectrum of economic analysis, though he was still generally linked to marginalism, and seen as proposing theories similar to Marshall's. The sense of a Lausanne School was also emerging during this period and is reflected in moves to link – sometimes by way of contrast – Walras and Pareto. One of the most lengthy early discussions of Walras in the English-language literature was by Pareto himself. The 'discovery of a general system of equations to express the economic equilibrium' was his 'great contribution', though Pareto parted company with Walras on the utility of deriving 'economic deductions from metaphysical principles of jurisprudence', as in the *Etudes d'economie sociale*.[51] Oncken, too, noted both the agreement between Walras and Pareto on the 'economico-mathematical method' and 'pure political economy' as well as Pareto's rejection 'as absurd and unscientific every teleological method of observation, everything utopian or idealistic in the sense of Plato's Republic'.[52] Several people related Pantaleoni to Walras and Lausanne,[53] against Pantaleoni's claims that he did not adhere to any particular school of thought.

It was also not uncommon to see Walras connected with the Austrian approach. Weiser, for example, in laying out the essentials of the Austrian school, wrote of the commonalities between Walras and the Austrian tradition: both simplified reality, as the geographer does with a map.[54] Böhm-Bawerk[55] and Henrietta Leonard considered separating Walras from the Austrians, though admitting that they reached similar conclusions. Not surprisingly, they noted that the approach of Jevons and Walras 'has considerable deficiencies' in relation to Austrian analysis. Edgeworth, on the other hand, found Weiser's framework less effective than the mathematical ones employed by Marshall and Walras[56] and Fisher, in a similar vein, noted that the value theory of Davenport, a supporter of the Austrians, was previously derived by 'mathematical economists' including Walras, and he criticizes him for not having drawn more heavily on their work.[57]

The Two Decades after Walras's Death

As Figure 5.2 shows, English-language mentions of Walras reached a low point in the decade and a half after his death. The figures would be even lower were it not for a significant number of obituaries and memorial articles. The death of Walras in January 1910 was noted in the AEA's *Economic Bulletin* that March, and a full-scale obituary by Irving Fisher followed in June, hailing him, along with Jevons, as 'founding modern mathematical economics'.[58] Fisher argued that 'Walras surpassed Jevons in neatness and brevity of expression, and succeeded far more than Jevons in constructing a complete and coherent system': he merited 'an exalted place in the history of economic thought and one which is likely to grow more rather than less conspicuous with time'.[59] Pareto paid tribute to a wider range of contributions, but also emphasized his contributions to a mathematical science of economics, suggesting that 'Walras did for political economy that which Lagrange effected for rational mechanics'[60] – a sentiment echoed by Laughlin.[61] Both Fisher and Pareto emphasized that Walras's mathematical approach highlighted the interdependencies among the variables in the system and was more useful in that regard than as a method for solving concrete problems – a discussion noted approvingly by Edgeworth.[62]

Young, reviewing the revised edition of Jevons's *Theory of Political Economy*, focused on the connections between Walras and Jevons, and sometimes with Menger, as marginalists,[63] but there were writers who sought to distinguish Walras's work from theirs. Pareto criticized those who would lump all mathematical economists together and for not understanding the 'substantial differences' between Marshall, Edgeworth, Walras and Pareto.[64] Similarly, Mitchell contrasted the hedonism of Jevons and his followers with the more general approach of Walras, who, like Menger and Clark, avoided what he considered an improper foundation for economic analysis.[65]

In the early 1920s, a significant proportion of mentions of Walras were still in obituaries, this time of Carl Menger, Pareto and Marshall. Others were overwhelmingly in book reviews, the books reviewed including histories of economic thought and textbooks on elementary economics. References to Walras were in almost all cases incidental, not reflecting serious engagement with his ideas. Of the references to his ideas, one, referred to his attempt, along with Pareto, to define 'the general conditions of economic equilibrium by sets of simultaneous equations'[66] in the course of discussing the mathematical appendix to Marshall's *Principles*. Edgeworth also cited his mathematical analysis of markets in the context of reviewing Gustav Cassel's simplification of the Walrasian equations.[67] Another attributed to him the idea of constant production coefficients, ascribing to Pareto the idea that they might be variable (something with which Walras clearly agreed).[68] Fisher, a supporter of Walras in general, cited him critically, for an absurd definition of capital, and Fetter criticized Wesley Mitchell for not departing far enough from the pure the pure theory of Walras and Pareto, and failing to explore what lay behind peoples' choices.[69] Marjorie Tappan also cited Walras as someone who wanted to abandon psychological explanations of behaviour in terms of confining attention to supply and demand schedules.[70]

This pattern, in which most references to Walras were incidental, citing a historical figure or using his name to locate a particular approach, usually with his theory of markets in mind, though occasionally his quantity theory, began to be challenged in the second half of the 1920s. E. B. Wilson was clearly implying that economists ought to pay more attention to Walras when he wrote,

> Collegiate texts on economics do not flock to follow Walras and Pareto. With the large numbers of youth, euphemistically termed students, who crowd into the general collegiate courses, all but the few most resolutely cruel teachers will give up the fight for high intellectual standards.[71]

Similarly, Schumpeter took Walras seriously when he spent time arguing that the approaches of the 'schools' of Marshall and Walras were fundamentally the same.[72] However, it was Moore, who had supported Walras so enthusiastically in his last years, Charles Roos, and Henry Schultz who engaged with Walras's ideas more seriously than American economists had done for some years.

In the first of three articles published in the *Quarterly Journal of Economics* in 1926, Moore simply cited Walras, along with Pareto, as the investigating simultaneous equilibrium in markets for all commodities.[73] In the second, he cited Pantaleoni's inspiration in inducing Pareto to investigate 'what lay buried in the complex researches of Léon Walras'.[74] In describing Pantaleoni as prescient in seeing where economics was going, Moore indicated that he believed the future of economics lay with the Walrasian approach. However, in the third article he presented a theory of 'economic oscillations' that rested explicitly on Walras's theory.

> In the ensuing pages I shall carry the statical theory of general equilibrium elaborated by Walras and Pareto to the stage of a synthetic, realistic view of a moving general equilibrium; methods for determining numerically the necessary constants in the equations will be presented; and the conclusion will be reached that economic oscillations, other than periodic, are simply the results of perturbations in a system striving, under the influence of statical forces, toward a moving general economic equilibrium.[75]

Walras was, for Moore, the starting point for a new form of realistic, quantitative economics. In presenting the 'Walrasian equations', he stated that Walras's claim to 'scientific immortality' did not lie in his being a co-discoverer of marginal utility, but 'in his having established for the first time the conditions of a general economic equilibrium'.[76] He outlined the equations of Walras's system before going on to show how this system could be transformed, by assuming that demand and production functions had specific functional forms, into a system the parameters of which could be estimated from price and quantity data and used to analyse oscillations in the system. Moore himself could not achieve this in his article, but he sketched out a clear programme, attributing a crucial and important stage in that programme to Walras.

Roos, a mathematician at Chicago who had discussed his work with Schultz, and who cited Moore's pioneering work on the use of correlation analysis, also had the goal of constructing a dynamic theory, seeing Walras as having discussed the static theory that had to precede it.[77] Furthermore, like Moore, he made extensive use of Walrasian equations in his attempt to construct a dynamic theory. Though he was clearly trying to go beyond either of them, in places he implied that Walras's formulations of the theory of economic equilibrium were more useful than Pareto's.

Schultz, whose goal was to estimate demands statistically, heaped praise on Walras as having

> succeeded both in completely surveying the interrelated factors in exchange, production, and distribution in such a way as to give a truer insight into the complexity of our economic system, and in paving the way for subsequent applications of the quantitative method to the problem of measuring the relative strength of the different economic forces.[78]

His discoveries, said Schultz, were 'epoch-making'. Citing both Moore and Roos, he discussed ways of constructing a dynamic system, clearly endorsing their view that Walras's equations formed the starting point. The following year, in a book review, he reiterated his view that the work of Walras was epoch-making, and that it was being 'unified, amended, completed and surpassed'.[79] A year after that, his article on marginal productivity theory presented a long (45-page), detailed mathematical analysis of Walras's theory of distribution, deriving technical coefficients from various production functions, including the Cobb–Douglas function.[80]

By the end of the 1920s, Moore, Schultz and Roos had made a very strong case that the Walrasian system of general equilibrium was the foundation on which a new mathematical and quantitative economics should be built, in two of the leading American journals – Roos and Moore in the *Quarterly Journal of Economics* and Schultz in the *Journal of Political Economy*. Readers would not have found the same mathematical arguments in the pages of the *American Economic Review* but, if they read carefully, they would have encountered the same sentiments, expressed more allusively, by Schultz and Wilson.

1930 to the Centenary of Walras's Birth

When we look to the citation data from the 1930s, as found in Table 5.2, two journals stand out: *Economica* and *Econometrica*. Prior to the 1930s, Walras had been mentioned only once in *Economica* (established at the London School of Economics in 1921), in a book review that, tangentially, cited Walras, along with Fisher and Schumpeter, as having abandoned the attempt to provide a psychological explanation of supply and demand schedules.[81] However, after the arrival of Lionel Robbins and Friedrich Hayek, both of whom were critics of the insularity of the Cambridge school, Walras's name began to appear frequently in its pages. Initially, Walras was treated along with his contemporaries, in the manner found in earlier work. For example, Hayek echoed Wicksell's view that 'Walras's unfortunately difficult work' had been as influential as that of the subject of his article, Carl Menger.[82] Amongst the younger, more mathematically inclined generation, Roy Allen referred mostly to Pareto and Fisher when he formulated a 'mathematical theory of exchange',[83] and even Jevons was more extensively discussed than Walras, who was mentioned merely in a footnote.

It was an article by Hicks that elevated Walras and the Lausanne School above their contemporaries.[84] Whilst Walras's was one among many theories of income distribution, along with those of Clark, Marshall, Wicksteed, Wicksell, Barone and Pareto, Hicks picked out the 'Lausanne school method' as being particularly important:

> It is one of the great advantages of the Lausanne analysis, that in it the 'individualistic' method, which has been described by Dr. Hayek as one of the greatest assets of neo-classical economics, is carried to its most complete fulfilment.[85]

The Walras–Pareto system determined an equilibrium system of prices in which no individual had any incentive to anything different from what he had done in the past. Attention was drawn to Hicks's discussion of Walras by Schultz,[86] whose work Hicks had bracketed with Pareto's as unsatisfactory. Schultz sought to challenge Hicks's talk of the 'Walras–Cassel' system, arguing that there were important differences between the two. In particular, Walras, unlike Cassel, did not take supplies of factors as given. This gave Hicks the opportunity to reiterate his admiration for the Lausanne School – 'there are few economists whom I admire more than I do the masters of Lausanne'[87] – and to imply that his talk of a Walras–Cassel system was to emphasize Walras's role. Hicks was offering an argument about how an economy would respond to changes in wages that was often attributed to Cassel even though the core of the argument was in Walras and, he said, 'I dislike Cassel getting the credit for it'.[88]

Walras was praised even more strongly in the first issue of *Econometrica*. In the lead article, Schumpeter, who was now in the United States, at Harvard, in an apologia for econometrics (then understood to encompass mathematical economics) wrote,

> I for one shall always look up to Léon Walras as the greatest of all economists. In his theory of equilibrium he gave a powerful basis to all our work. It is true that while he made the decisive step in the *quantitative*, he failed to move in the *numerical* line, the *junction* of which two is characteristic of econometrics. But we have been taught of late to look more hopefully even on the 'numerical' possibilities of that most general and most abstract part of our science which is equilibrium theory in Walras's sense.[89]

Recent work, including pioneering work by Fisher and Moore, had taken the system much further, to the extent that 'when we now look at the Walrasian system, [we feel] very much as we feel when beholding the model of a motor car constructed forty years ago'.[90] Though René Roy,[91] in the next article, sought to praise Cournot, part of the reason why Roy considered him so important was his influence on Walras.

Other writers in *Econometrica* linked Walras to econometrics and the attempt to implement the theory empirically. Ezekiel referred to 'the general theories of Pareto, Walras and Moore' in which demands are a function of the prices of all products, placing it together with 'the neoclassical theory' of Marshall in which the price of one commodity depends on the supply of all commodities.[92] Bousquet referenced to the 'immortal studies' of Walras and Pareto in a paper arguing for more dynamic conceptions of equilibrium.[93] Thus by the mid-1930s, general equilibrium, formulated mathematically, was considered the appropriate starting point by many writers in *Econometrica*. For example, Tinbergen wrote that 'the Walrasian theory of market price' could be taken as 'the starting point' for static theories.[94] The journal was committed to the use of mathematical methods, and Walras's analysis provided a theory that could be and was used.

To find explicit hostility to Walras (as opposed to silence) we have to turn to the longer-established journals. Paul Homan's remark in the *American Economic Review* that it was 'sheer folly' to think that economic phenomena could be explained by the methods of Cournot and Walras came in a defense of institutionalism.[95] However, the *AER* also contained a statement of the case for mathematical economics, which endorsed these methods.[96] Other discussions of Walras used his work as a starting point without making any issue out of the fact. Thus William Jaffe grounded discussion of imperfect competition and oligopoly in Walras, seeing his equations as representing pure, frictionless competition.[97] Paul Ellsworth,[98] meanwhile, drew attention to Ohlin's[99] having started from the 'Walras–Pareto–Cassel mutual interdependence theory of pricing' and having extended it to incorporate the notion of space.

Amongst the long established journals, much attention was paid to Walras in the *JPE*, where his work was clearly seen as important. Wright provided a very substantial appraisal of Moore's *Synthetic Economics* (1929), in which Moore's work was presented as building on the starting point provided by Walras and Pareto.[100] Roos echoed Moore's position when he simply referred to Walras, *en passant*, as having offered no more than a static theory, but his mathematical analysis implied clear endorsement of Walrasian methods.[101] Similarly, Whitman's 1934 article on statistical demand techniques implied support despite containing no more than an incidental mention of Walras. Schultz's (1931) survey of the 'Italian school of mathematical economics' also provided a clear endorsement as did Umberto Ricci's (1932) analysis of the law of demand. Walras's theory was, Schultz argued, a theory that needed to be much better understood,[102] and he criticized Ragnar Frisch for not citing Walras when discussing the measurement of utility.[103] In a similar vein, Schumpeter noted that Joan Robinson was resolutely Marshallian, not so much as noting Walras's existence.[104] Though he said that he did not mean to imply adverse criticism – he admired Marshall too much for that – he implied that Walrasian methods might overcome some of the imperfections implicit in Robinson's methods. Arthur Marget considered Walras's monetary theory to merit detailed analysis and along with Whitney, credited Walras with anticipating Keynes's equation of exchange by some four decades.[105] There was but one critical article on Walras, again by someone with institutionalist leanings, Leo Rogin.[106] His claim was that the Lausanne School had brought an atomistic approach into economic theory, and that the resemblance with physics brought about by the use of mathematics gave a sense of assurance that was unwarranted. References to Walras in the *QJE* were far fewer than in the *JPE* but the pattern was the same.[107]

The year 1934 marked the centenary of Walras's birth, which further stimulated interest in his work.[108] The centenary was celebrated in Lausanne, the Econometric Society sending a fulsome tribute signed by 317 of its members. This recognized the service the University of Lausanne had rendered to science by funding a chair devoted to the theory of economic equilibrium.[109] *Econometrica* carried a facsimile of the tribute, even though it had already published the text. It had also carried a specimen of Walras's correspondence and handwriting and published Walras's correspondence with Cournot and Jevons.[110] In September there was a meeting of the Econometric Society in Lausanne, at which papers on macro dynamics by Frisch and on particular and general equilibria by Lange made use of Walras's work. In December, there was a session on Walras at the joint meeting of the Econometric Society and the American Statistical Association, chaired by Schumpeter and with papers by Jaffe, Marget, Oskar Lange and Fisher.[111] Schumpeter set the tone of the session by noting that, 'Whatever the aspect or the approach, the name of Léon Walras towers above all others. Both in vision and achievement he was, without doubt, the greatest of economic theorists.'[112]

Marget specifically drew attention to the changed perspective on Walras. In the nineteenth century the only novelty in Walras's work was thought by many to be its attempt to justify what Jevons, ironically, called 'the obnoxious subject of mathematico-economic science' and even Edgeworth saw Walras as no more than a 'Helvetian Jevons' (a co-discoverer of marginal utility).[113] It was, Marget contended, only recently that economists had recognized his 'imperishable contribution' to economics – his theory of economic equilibrium.[114] Marget's papers sought to show that Walras could also claim novelty for his theory of monetary economics. After pointing out that Walras developed an equation of exchange long before Simon Newcomb and Fisher, a cash balance equation before Keynes, and the concept of forced saving, Marget claimed that the list of his achievements was as extensive as the one Keynes had attributed to Marshall.[115] Commenting on Jaffé and Marget, Fisher noted that, as a graduate student, he had been put on to Walras by one of his professors, William Graham Sumner, but that his enthusiasm for Walras had waned after the early 1890s. 'But', he said, 'I am now filled with a new enthusiasm' for Walras's analysis, suggesting that 'the truth planted by Walras is today growing into a rich harvest of econometrics' and that 'the work done by Walras and others in mathematical economics is now bearing more fruit than ever'.[116]

The centenary was also the occasion for a biographical essay by Hicks. In this memoir, Hicks challenged the conventional view which bracketed Walras with Jevons and Menger. 'The modern reader of Walras's *Éléments d'Économie Politique Pure*', he wrote, 'is struck by its affinity, not with the work of Jevons or Menger, but with that of Marshall'.[117] The difference was not so much technique but differences of interest: Walras sought general principles whilst Marshall sought an analytical instrument with which to tackle particular historical problems. Walras was the philosopher, Marshall the practical economist. After giving evidence for his view that there were strong affinities between Walras and Marshall, Hicks reached Walras's conclusion that the equations of supply and demand in *n* markets provided *n-1* independent equations and *n-1* unknowns, and that an equilibrium set of prices must therefore exist. He concluded, 'On our estimation of it our view of Walras's individual contribution to economics must largely depend'[118] Marking how the view of Walras had evolved over the decades, Hicks argued that Walras was to be judged not as a wide ranging economist, who had contributed to many fields, but for this one 'central achievement': the theory of general equilibrium.[119] Hicks expressed the opinion that though the equations were too complicated to be of practical use, 'Where they are supremely useful is in elucidating the general way the price system works, and in giving us a classification of those factors which may be relevant to any particular case'.[120]

The Centenary to *Value and Capital*

Several of the Walras citations in the years following the centenary come in reviews of Italian books, doing no more than using Walras to provide a context for the material under review. Others are focused on history, such as George Stigler writing about Menger and about production and distribution theories,[121] or in pieces the tributes published after the death of Schultz[122] and marking the centenary of Cournot's *Recherches*.[123] Newly published books by Walras, such as the *Abrégé* he had discussed with Moore twenty years earlier, or a proposed new edition of his works, were by then of historical interest.[124]

Often when Walras was mentioned it was without discussion, on the assumption that the meaning of phrases such as 'a Walrasian state of general equilibrium'[125] or 'the Walrasian equations'[126] or independence 'in the Walras–Marshall–Pareto sense'[127] was obvious to the reader. Walras was brought into discussions of the Keynesian system, as when Leontief referred to 'a classical Walrasian system,'[128] using Walras as the standard method for explicating the 'orthodox' theory under attack by Keynes. Lange, in an article on the rate of interest and the propensity to consume, which engaged extensively with Keynes, also drew heavily on Walras (in relation to both money and his methods) for his theoretical framework.[129] Though Waugh supported his case with a quotation from Walras, when he cited his doctrine of maximum satisfaction (an isolated reference to Walras's welfare economics) it was to point out what it did *not* imply.[130] There is a sense in which Walras's ideas are being taken for granted, as when Marschak called for Walrasian methods to be applied to durable goods and financial assets as well as to perishable goods.[131] He explained that this would help bring about a unification comparable with the unification of theories of energy in nineteenth-century physics.

However, though serious engagements with Walrasian ideas were much less frequent than the statistics in section 1 suggest, there remained economists for whom it was important to discuss his work. In the 'Annual Survey of Economic Theory' published in the 1936 volume of *Econometrica*, Walras's name cropped up repeatedly, and Åkerman pointed out that since Cassel's exposition, Walras's theory of general equilibrium was accessible to all students of economics.[132] Åkerman also coined the phrase 'neo-Walrasian', using it in the context of disputes over marginal productivity theory. Schultz discussed Walras's theory of the consumer, including his theory of money, necessary to discuss the value of money.[133] Leontief's input–output work, which began to appear from 1935 onwards, was explicitly a numerical implementation of a Walrasian system.[134]

One change is the appearance of technical criticisms, by mathematical economists, of Walras. In a talk at the December 1936 Econometric Society meeting, Gerhard Tintner, in the words of the secretary Dickson Leavens, 'referred to the remarkable work of a young Viennese mathematician, Dr. A. Wald, who has shown the conditions under which the Walrasian equations have one and only one solution'.[135] Wald had, however, made special assumptions about utility functions, and a solution of the more general case was not yet available. This implicitly questioned the claim, often made about Walras, that he had proved his system of equations to have a solution. Tintner had been even more critical of what Walrasian methods had achieved earlier in the year:

> In comparison with those achievements [the Marshallian school's use of partial equilibrium to analyze problems such as limited competition and price discrimination] the contribution of the Lausanne school with the methods of general equilibrium has been rather small. There has been a kind of unfortunate sterility about the great work of Walras and Pareto, which, so to say, was too good to be useful.[136]

A similarly critical stance towards Walrasian methods was taken by Tinbergen who, discussing work on achieving 'neutral money', challenged the use of Walrasian theory as a benchmark:

> [T]he identification of the optimum situation with a Walras situation is, in my view, very questionable ... My main objection is, then, that the realization of the Walrasian situation is impossible when we have a permanently changing situation in addition to some elements that make absolutely impossible an immediate reaction of all variables to any change in data. Elements such as the production period and the long duration of means of production make it impossible that a quick adaptation to new data should take place. Therefore, the Walrasian situation can only accidentally be realized. This is the reason why it seems better to discuss the desirability of a given stabilization policy without any connection with the Walrasian system.[137]

Tinbergen associated Walras with equilibrium and he thought that his system provided no guidance for what must be a disequilibrium system. Though expressed in different terms, Lorenz was also critical in pointing out that 'classical mathematical economics' was not based on 'statistical-numerical observation of economic processes'.[138] Similarly, though some economists, notably Schultz, thought it important to start from Walras, others simply cited him in a traditional manner, along with Jevons and Menger, as when Paul Samuelson sought to clear up the confusion in discussions of the concept of utility.[139]

Conclusions

Walras's name has never been absent from the pages of English-language journals, and those who cited his work did so, almost from the start, on the assumption that their readers would be familiar with it. At the turn of the century, Walras was one of the major authorities in economics to whom people would turn, or whose name they would invoke, along with others, in discussions of demand, economic equilibrium, money, population, productivity and factor pricing. He was thus cited along with not just Jevons and Menger, but also a wide range of his European contemporaries. Interestingly, when he was bracketed with Marshall the emphasis was on the similarity of their ideas – they had both proposed a theory of economic equilibrium and differences in the manner in which they had expounded it were generally seen as small. There was also great interest in his socialism and his work on bimetallism. However, citations of his work declined over the first two decades of the twentieth century.

There was then a revival of interest in Walras in the 1920s and 1930s, accompanied by a change in the way he was viewed. He came to be placed on a pedestal in relation to his contemporaries, as the one who had originated the theory of general equilibrium; where he was bracketed with others it was often with Cassel (whose simpler set of general equilibrium equations was very widely discussed) and above all Pareto (who had developed Walras's theory). This did not involve a rediscovery of Walras, for his work had never been unknown, but involved a focus on his contribution to general equilibrium theory at the expense of other aspects of his work. There was an increasing tendency to distinguish Walras from Marshall. No longer were they seen as two exponents of essentially the same theory; they were seen as rivals but as representing alternative conceptions of economic equilibrium. Paradoxically, when Marshall fell out of favour, an economist who had previously been seen as proposing a theory similar to Marshall's, came to be seen, instead, as offering an alternative to Marshall.

6 THE ENGLISH TRANSLATION OF LÉON WALRAS'S *ÉTUDES D'ÉCONOMIE SOCIALE*

Donald Walker and Jan van Daal

In this essay, we explain why we translated Léon Walras's *Études d'économie sociale (ÉÉS)*[1] into English, giving it the title *Studies in Social Economics (SSE)*, and how we edited it. On pp. 87–91, we describe briefly his social philosophy, and his social economics, in which he deals with the practical details of the distribution of social wealth. On pp. 91–2, we describe how *ÉÉS* came into being. On pp. 92–3, we explain why it was worthwhile to translate *ÉÉS* into English. On pp. 93–6, we indicate the respects in which we sought to improve its understandability. On pp. 96–9, we deal with some general issues in the translation of texts and with specific aspects of Walras's style of writing. Our concluding remarks follow on pp. 99–100.

A Short Summary of *SSE*

Walras's Social Philosophy

A primary concern of Walras's in his *SSE* was how to eliminate extreme poverty, an issue known as the Social Question. Observing the poverty and the misery of the workers and convinced that most of them were not able to improve their situation by their own efforts, he believed that 'the moral reform of [those] individuals, object of so many preachers and philanthropists, has as its necessary basis and point of departure *the economic reform of the very basis and natural milieu of all human individuality, namely society*' (*SSE*, p. 41; emphasis added).

Walras proceeded to present his social philosophy, including his theory of human behaviour and society, and his social economics, based upon that philosophy. Two facts that make man special, he argued, are his aptitude for the division of labour, and his moral personality (*SSE*, pp. 67ff.). The division of labour is the reason for human society. What each of us needs exceeds the goods and services that we can produce if we work in isolation, but as a member of a society where everybody has a specialization, we can largely satisfy our needs by exchange. Man's moral personality reveals itself in his sensibility, by unselfish emotions like sympathy, by his aesthetic sense, intelligence, understanding and reason, by his free will, and by his conscience. Art and science form the totality of man's sensory and intellectual relations with the world; industry and mores form man's economic and moral relations with nature and between persons. Beauty, truth, economic advantageousness and justice are the characteristics of these four categories of human facts; that is, of art, science, industry and mores. This leads to what Walras believed is a clear and comprehensive vision of society, from which he deduces rules for man's individual and collective behaviour. 'In summarizing', he wrote,

> we can say that the role of the individual is to achieve freely his destiny, and to feel, think, act, and work, alone or in association with other individuals, in agriculture, industry, or commerce, or as scholar, artist, or civil servant, in order to obtain a position justified by his efforts and merits. The state's role is to create the environment for the achievement of individual destinies, to assure exterior and interior safety, to enact, execute, and apply laws, to open means of communication, to promote the progress of science and the arts, and thereby to organize the conditions of existence of the society. The right of individuals is to act freely and to obtain different (unequal) positions. The right of the state is to act with authority and to establish equal conditions. *Liberty for the individual, authority of the state. Equality of* [social] *conditions, inequality of* [individual] *positions.* That is, in the last analysis, the highest law of the organization of society based upon order and justice (*SSE*, pp. 104–5; Walras's italics).

This means, according to Walras, that we must all be able to benefit equally from the resources of nature given to mankind. The social ideal involves the proper treatment of personal and impersonal property. He argued that a form of ill-treatment of the personal property of wage-earners, namely of their persons, is the unjust confiscation of a part of their wages by taxation. As for impersonal property, its major component is land. The implication of the prevailing point of view is that all value has its origin in labour. Therefore, land has no intrinsic value, and it is only bought and sold because labour and capital are in some way bound up in it. The value of a piece of land can be reduced to that of a quantity of labour, and this means that everything may be owned privately because a person is the owner of his own human capital and, therefore, of its products. Walras opposed that view. Land, he observed, is not produced by the activity of any individual; it is the endowment of a nation. Its owners benefit from an increase in its value that results not from their own doing, but from population growth and economic development. He was referring to land itself, not to improvements of land, which are investments in other types of capital goods.

Hence land should not be owned by individuals; it should belong to society. If society were a conventional free association, the parties contracting to establish it could decide to share the land in equal parts among themselves; however, since society is a natural and necessary fact, private ownership of land is against natural law, because it wrongs future generations. In legal terms, humanity is the owner, and the present generation has only the usufruct of the land.

Regarding taxation, Walras observed that it is simply impossible to find a just and rightful system of taxation because people do not benefit from public expenses in proportion to their income or progressively in relation to either their income or their capital. They all benefit equally, as equal members of the society. So far as the state is concerned, he wrote, the life, freedom and property of one particular individual have the same value as the life, freedom and property of any other individual. There is therefore no relation between the expenditures of the state for the protection, by means of the army, the police, and the judicial system, of an individual's life, freedom or property on the one hand, and the individual's wealth and income on the other. Hence, Walras provided this solution. 'For me', he wrote, 'the individual and the State are two equivalent social types'. The state makes its claim for a share of the national output on the same grounds as the individual. Here is how the distribution of wealth is to be carried out:

> [O]ne of the two natural types of social wealth – the personal faculties and their labour – is assigned according to natural law to individual property and enjoyment; the other natural type of social wealth – land and its products – is assigned according to natural law to common, collective enjoyment ... Then, the people of the society all unquestionably contribute an equal part to the costs of the state services, just as they definitely participate equally in these same services. This is how I understand the application of the principle of equal and compulsory contribution (*SSE*, p. 107).

In other words, individuals renounce any claim to landownership if the state leaves them undisturbed in the possession and enjoyment of what is rightfully theirs, and the state leaves the individuals undisturbed in the possession and enjoyment of what is rightfully theirs if the individuals renounce any claim to landownership. That ends Part 1 of the book.

The rest of the book deals with the economic interpretation and elaboration of the conclusions of Walras's social economics as set out above, namely with social wealth, landownership and taxation.

Social Wealth: Property and Exchange

In Part 2, Walras starts by defining wealth, following in the steps of his father. Wealth is constituted of three parts. First, there is capital: land, personal capital (man's body and mind) and artificial capital (buildings, machines, cattle, etc.); land and artificial capital together form impersonal capital. Second, there are these capitals' services: land services, labour and capital services. Third, there are the products resulting from combining these services. Above we have explained that natural law and economic analysis brought Walras (just like his father) to the conclusions that a man's personal capital is his unalienable property, that land should be the property of the State, and that artificial capital can be owned by individuals or by the State, depending on who produced it or paid for it. In this part of the book, Walras deals extensively with the property aspects of all kinds of social wealth in the past and in the present. Here, we will briefly discuss only what he said on the exchange of social wealth.

Where people specialize in one or only a couple of activities, it is clear that exchange is a necessary and essential phenomenon in the human society. The notion of property here plays an important role in the sense that, in free exchange, the exchangers' property rights always have to be respected. This brought him to observe that the individuals try to obtain by exchange the greatest possible satisfaction of their wants, given their initial endowments.

Walras rejected Gossen's criterion for the exchange of several goods for one another. According to this criterion, the outcome of the exchange should be such that the sum total of all the exchangers' utility be maximal. Then, however, it does not matter with what quantities of goods one enters into the exchange; only the total quantities brought in are of importance. Walras rejected this in his famous assertion: 'The economy is no picnic' (*SSE*, p. 140.)

The Distribution of Social Wealth

No one who gives *SSE* even a cursory reading would maintain that Walras was exclusively a theoretician. Part 3 of the book contains, and Part 4 is almost entirely, applied economics of a very high quality that Walras could well have put into his *Études d'économie politique appliquée* (*ÉÉPA*). Part 3 of *SSE* returns to Walras's point of departure, namely back to the Social Question. The solution to it will be found, according to Walras, in the achievement of the social ideal. He believed that, by his formulations on this issue, he achieved a vision of an equilibrated society, one in which individuals and the state respect each other's duties and rights. In that state of affairs, all persons would provide themselves with what they need for meeting their needs, using their own abilities and possessions. The state would buy land at current market prices, raising the revenue to do so by issuing bonds, and would eventually own it all. Similarly, the state would acquire natural monopolies and either lease out their operation or operate them directly.

Individuals would freely compete to rent land from the state, and would thus compete for its use, which would lead to its optimal utilization. The rent would be used to pay the state's expenses and eventually all taxes would be abolished. Inasmuch as the landowners would be paid the current price of their land determined in competitive markets, no injustice would be done to the landowners. The rent obtained by the state would merely suffice to pay the interest on the bonds if the rent increases at the rate expected at the time of purchase. For it to be possible to redeem the bonds without resorting to taxation, a price lower than the market value could be paid, but that is unacceptable to Walras. Instead, the state can take measures that accelerate economic progress and encourage the intensification of the use of land. Rent would then increase at an even higher rate. Economic progress would make the rent sufficient to finance the expenses of the state, and because the increased rent would not have been included in the purchase prices, it will also provide revenue for the bonds to be redeemed. Walras ends the chapter with some speculations on how the time will become ripe for this grandiose operation.

Taxation

In Part 4, Walras reviews a variety of taxes, although he preferred a situation in which there are no taxes at all. He comments on several kinds of taxes: multiple taxes versus proportional or progressive single taxes, indirect taxes on a number of different items, and direct taxes such as a tax on capital. He showed that, except for a tax on wages, all taxes have more than one final incidence, and, therefore, that their burden does not fall completely on a single tax payer. Furthermore, he emphasizes that a well-organized and well-maintained cadaster (land registry) is necessary for the proper allocation of taxes on landed property. The variety of taxes and their lack of logical bases, he concluded, are ample evidence that there is no uniquely correct type of tax.

The Genesis of *Études d'économie sociale*

For many years, Walras had the intention of publishing a comprehensive treatise on social economics, as he had done with respect to economic theory by writing his *Éléments d'économie pure* (*Éléments*). Ill health eventually forced him to abandon that idea, and, in November 1893, he decided instead to present a collection of his essays on social economics with the title *Études d'économie sociale*.[2] In preparing the first edition of the collection, he conceived of a number of successive plans for it, changing his choice of texts, altering their order, and even writing a few pages for the occasion. Walras's editorial work consisted of a preface in which he explained his motivation for his work on social economics and acknowledged the help of a number of his colleagues, and of some very short bibliographical notes. He had already completed the essays that he put into Part 1 of the collection and most of those in Part 4 when he arrived in Lausanne in 1870 to begin his career as a professor of economics. He wrote the rest of the essays between 1870 and 1896. With the exception of one chapter, all the essays had been published before. He had also presented some of them in public lectures, and he had altered most of them several times. Finally, *ÉÉS* was published toward the end of 1896. Subsequently, Walras indicated in a copy of the first edition the few changes he wanted incorporated into a second edition, finishing that small task by 1902.

After his death in 1910, Léon Walras's daughter and his adopted son Georges donated his personal library, his letters, his manuscripts and the manuscripts of Léon's father, Auguste Walras, to the University of Lausanne, with the stipulation that it initiate and sponsor the publication of the complete economic works of Léon and Auguste. Inasmuch as the University of Lausanne did not fulfill that condition, Aline began her efforts to bring about the publication of all of Walras's works, a project that was to be edited by Étienne Antonelli, a professor at the University of Lyon. For several reasons, including initially Antonelli's ill health and then his election as a deputy to the National Assembly, this project was not carried out. Nevertheless, in 1936, Aline succeeded, with the aid of Gaston Leduc, Professor of Economics at the University of Caen, in obtaining the publication of the second edition of *ÉÉS*. Leduc incorporated into it Walras's revisions. The only one of these of any significance was the addition of his 'Souvenirs de Lausanne' (ch. 10); apart from that, the first and second editions are essentially the same, and, indeed, have the same pagination up to the point at which that major addition was made. Inasmuch as Walras considered the prospective second edition to be the definitive version of the book, that is the edition we have translated, with the literally translated title *Studies in Social Economics* (*SSE*).

Why We Translated the Book

Léon Walras (1834–1910) is one of the four or five most important economists in the history of the science. He has had and continues to have an enormous influence on economics, so his writings are important for an understanding of how it developed. Walras set forth his economic theories in his *Éléments*. Most papers and books in English on Walras's work deal with the ideas he expressed in the fifth edition of that book, until recently the only book of Walras's that was translated into English.[3] Of course, this splendid and extremely important book may be fruitfully studied on its own, but it is most fully understood if it is considered in conjunction with his other important writings.

It is generally recognized by Anglophone economists that Walras was a great economic theorist. There is, however, almost total ignorance in the Anglophone community of the ideas he set forth in *ÉÉS* because until the publication of our translation, it was available only in French. However, to understand his reasoning, methodological approach and choice of subjects in his economic theory and applied economics, it is necessary to examine not only the books he devoted to them but also his social economics. The worldwide community of economists that reads English will find that our *SSE* presents essential parts of his system of thought, setting forth the philosophical foundations of his treatment of social science. For example, the passages in *SSE* concerning human nature and the motives of economic agents establish the rationale for the behaviour that he attributed to them in his models in *Éléments*. Walras's social economics relied upon the scientific foundations provided by his theories for the applications that he set forth in his *ÉÉPA*, translated into English in 2005. Thus all three of his books must be studied to achieve a full comprehension of any one of them, and hence of his system of thought as a whole. Consequently, in the absence of an English translation of *ÉÉS*, scholars that read English but not French have had a wide gap in their knowledge of Walras's work, and that has adversely affected their understanding not only of his social economics, but also of *Éléments* and *ÉÉPA*. To provide the means of eliminating that gap is why we translated and edited *ÉÉS*.

Editing the Book in Order to Improve its Understandability

SSE is a collection of essays, each of which was influenced in topic and treatment by Walras's interests, attitudes and economics abilities and understandings at the time it was written, so it is less well-organized and less complete than a treatise. Moreover, he did almost no editing or annotation of the text, and Gaston Leduc did none whatsoever. A good deal of editing was therefore required on our part to ensure a clear presentation and help in the task of understanding Walras's ideas conveyed in the translation. Our efforts took the following forms.

Annotation of the Text

We have explained the translation of certain words or phrases to help Anglophone readers to understand Walras's meaning. To this end, we introduced 230 notes at the end of the chapters, including the insertion into our translation, in some cases with modifications, of 43 notes made by Pierre Dockès in his superb French variorum edition of *ÉÉS*.[4]

Dealing with Walras's Terminology

Although language evolves and Walras wrote some parts of this book as long ago as the 1860s, from the literary point of view – that is, considering his grammar, literary vocabulary, turns of phrase, expressions, freedom from regionalisms, etc. – his texts give, with some exceptions, the impression of having been written recently. From the economics point of view, however, matters are different. In a few but important instances, the meaning of his economic terminology differs from the usage of the economists of his own times and from modern usage, as is the case with the terms 'rareté' and 'rente'. The reader will encounter Walras's idiosyncratic terminology throughout the book.

Fortunately, Walras explained the unusual definition that he wished to apply to one or another of his terms; for example, that 'rareté' means marginal utility and not scarcity and that 'rente' means the services of land and not rent. Unfortunately, however, he sometimes used his terms in ways that are inconsistent with the definition that he gave them. Walras simply tacitly assumed that the reader will mentally correct those defects of exposition. That being doubtful, in order to avoid any possible misunderstandings and to aid the reader in this matter, in the first part of an appendix to our introduction we have provided a table indicating Walras's words for the types of capital and their services and the English translation of the meaning he attached to them.

In the second part of the appendix, we discuss the table. For example, we consider his treatment of 'rente'. In normal French and English usage, the rent of land, paid at the beginning of the rental period, is the present money value of the services of land for that period. Walras, however, defined 'rente' as 'services foncières' or 'rente foncière', namely the in-kind services of land. His use of the word 'rente' is an example of his inconsistencies. Sometimes, instead of writing 'le prix de la rente' when he wanted to refer to the money price or value of the in-kind services, he wrote simply 'la rente'. For instance, in one place (p. 272 of the second edition; p. 183 of the English edition) among others, he wrote that the state purchases of the land would be paid for by 'la hausse de la rente foncière', i.e., by the increase in land services, whereas to be consistent with his definitions, and to make sense, he should have written 'la hausse des *fermages*' (in English, the increase of *rents*) or 'la hausse des prix des rentes' – the increase in money rents. Similarly, he wrote inconsistently (p. 396 of the second edition; p. 284 of the English edition) that taxes would fall on 'la rente foncière et sur les fermages'. That, according to his definition of 'la rente' and the normal definition of 'fermage', which he used, means 'on land services and on rents'. He should have written 'on the *value* of land services', and not added the duplicative words 'and on (money) rents'. On the other hand, Walras was consistent with his definitions when he wrote, many times, that in a progressive economy, 'le prix de la rente, ou le fermage, s'éléve sensiblement', meaning that the price (or value) of land services, in other words, *rent*, increases considerably.

Summaries of Ideas that Walras Presented in SSE

In the introduction, we briefly describe the contents of each chapter in order to enable the reader to decide which chapters to read, and to know the place of each of them within the framework of the book. Walras started the book by a presentation of his concept of an ideal society. He believed that his ideal and the policies to achieve it were based on his knowledge of human behaviour and of the functioning of the real economy. He undertook an in-depth study of the relation of reality and theory, and more particularly of the relation of economic reality and economic studies. He declared that the economy should be studied by the methods used in the natural sciences, namely, through sound positive economic theorizing, in contrast to what he called empiricism. Indeed, he believed, for a considerable part of his career, that economic theory is a natural science. Subsequently, he defined economics as a moral science, but, he argued, as a science, it nevertheless uses the methods of the natural sciences. Those methods, he specified, are the observation of facts, experiments, induction, abstraction, formation of hypotheses based on generalizations about the characteristics of the facts, the deduction of the consequences of the hypotheses using logic and mathematics, and the confirmation or the refutation of the hypotheses by means of empirical tests. He repeated time after time in *SSE* that theories are valid only if their elements are drawn from reality, if their structure and deductions are logical, and if their conclusions and predictions are verified by experience.

Walras reviewed contrasting socio-economic doctrines: socialism and liberalism, utilitarianism and moralism, communism and individualism, with the objectives of reconciling and synthesizing those different strains of thought to frame a new theory of society to serve in guiding the construction of a new society. Policies and private economic activities, he argued, should be examined to reveal their impact on both economic advantageousness and justice. These two outcomes are not necessarily in agreement, in which case justice should be the determining criterion of desirable policy.

A Clarified Presentation of the Contents

We have retained Walras's division of the book into four parts, and we have kept his order of the essays in each part. We gave chapter numbers to the essays. However, to improve the presentation of the extremely long *Recherche de l'idéal social*, we divided it into three chapters, giving them appropriate titles. To aid in providing an understanding of the course of the development of Walras's work, we have indicated when each chapter was written and when it was published for the first time, if that date differs considerably from the date of writing. We have provided this information at the end of our introduction in a bibliography of the essays. It also gives the publication details of all articles and books mentioned in our introduction.

We have placed numbers within bold brackets in the text of the translation that indicate the pagination of the second edition of *ÉÉS*. The text and notes indicate where, how and why the pagination of edition 2 is at variance with that of the first edition. We appended to our introduction a table of correspondences between the pagination of editions 1 and 2 of *ÉÉS* and the Dockès edition. This enables the reader to compare any passage of the translation with the corresponding passage in each of the French editions.

Walras presented two of his figures immediately after the pages on which he discussed them, and one plate with three figures at the end of the essay to which they appertain. In the translation, we made them an integral part of the text as close as possible to the passages to which they refer. They are reproductions of the original figures that were drawn by Walras himself. The figures were taken from a copy of the second edition of *ÉÉS*. We adapted, or inserted, the numbering of figures, formulas and tables.

We have provided two indexes. One is an index of subjects. The other is our translation, with numerous modifications, of Dockès's useful biographical index of persons mentioned by Walras in his *ÉÉS*. That index contains important facts about them that enrich the experience of reading the text. We are grateful to Dockès, and to Jean Pavlevski, director of the publishing house Économica, for their generous permission to use that biographical information and Dockès's above-mentioned notes.

Walras's Style

Expository and Polemical Powers Manifested in SSE

Walras's essays contain many striking passages, revealing expository and persuasive abilities, wit and force of intellect. We believe that we have conveyed the fine stylistic quality of his writing, and that we have done so by adhering to the letter and spirit of his text. An example of his powers of expression, of his acute perception of the realities of the political situation, and of his fairly accurate predictions about its future course, is provided by one of his comments on taxation:

> The state spends, gets into debt, and then declares that an increase of the rate of proportionality or progression is needed. This is called 'turning the press-screw tighter'. Now, such a turn of the screw is particularly easily done in the progressive system. The nation being then divided into two classes, those who have more than enough, or *the rich*, who are in the minority and pay most of the taxes, and those who have only the necessities, or *the poor*, who are in the majority and pay a small part of the taxes, why should not all tax increases be decided by majority vote? But this is not all. Given that the majority who vote on taxation pays little or nothing, why should it not use the result to its own benefit? After having introduced 'equity' into the receipts of the state, why not introduce the same thing into the expenditures? It will not take long before this will happen, and, if you doubt it, look at what is happening where progressive taxation already exists. You will see the proliferation of resolutions or propositions of equitable spending: excessive and badly organized public works that provide wages for the workers, profits to entrepreneurs or landowners, and votes to political candidates; state contributions to the premiums for insurance against accidents, unemployment, illness, old age; provision by the state of free medicine, medical care, bread, etc., etc., all provisions of private, not public interest. Thus, taxation tends to become an instrument to impoverish the rich and to enrich the poor (*SSE*, p. 331).

In those respects, Walras would have probably found striking similarities between his times and ours.

An example of his wittiness is provided by the following passage on taxation:

> The fact is that, when Mr. Maria Pastor became silent, the two direct and single taxes on income and capital began to engage in provocations mixed with flirtations. Please give a performance, the income tax said to the capital tax; I will appear on stage after-

wards ... [The delegates] must then be daring and sincere, must arrange the Congress as a show, and must organize its deliberations like the beginning of a ballet. One could have called it THE TRIUMPH OF THE SINGLE TAX. First, we would see the appearance of *Direct consumption taxes, Duties on imports,* and *Fiscal monopolies' duties,* only to be sent flying by a *Tax on capital* and a *Tax on income.* Then the *Tax on capital* and the *Tax on income* would perform some courteous dance-steps, unite and kiss each other, finally being carried heavenward in a grand apotheosis (*SSE,* pp. 279–80).

Walras demonstrated very considerable polemical powers in many passages. Two examples show that he could frame his argument in a persuasive way and simultaneously castigate his opponents with scathing sarcasm:

> The economists of Carey's school ... notice very well how capital enters the land in the form of seeds, husbandry, ameliorations, drainage, irrigation, etc., but they fail to see this capital come out in the form of corn, vegetables, and all kinds of fruit. This is, indeed, the little error made by these gentlemen: they are present when the farmer irrigates, works, sows, spreads manure, plants, or constructs, but they are absent or distracted when he mows, harvests, or picks the grapes. And these same economists, who revel in this phantasmagoria of an enormous, invisible, and impalpable mass of capital buried in the ground, are accusing us of living in an abstract world, taking the chimeras of our imagination as real facts, because, after having verified a hundred times the fact of the increase in value of the produce of land in a progressive society, we explain it by connecting it with the laws of exchange (*SSE,* p. 260, n. 7).

Similarly,

> There truly does not lack anything more for the direct and single tax, levied both on capital and income, the offspring of heaven only knows what promiscuity of empirical doctrines, than to be mated with fiscal beggary in order to give birth first to a tax on inheritances, and later on, if God so pleases, to duties on the occasion of a cheerful accession to the throne, royal duties, windfall duties, and all kinds of fiscal duties (*SSE,* p. 285).

Logical Constructions

Fine stylistic writing requires not only felicitous phrases but also precision and logical constructions. Walras's sentences and paragraphs are often long but nevertheless fulfill the requirements of precision and logical construction very well in most cases. In most instances, therefore, we have not broken them up into shorter units. Even in most of the rare cases in which they are not clearly structured, we have left them intact because to do otherwise would be to fail to present accurately his style of writing. The exceptions to that policy were made necessary by the differences between the grammatical structure of French and English. A sentence can be long, with a subject far removed from the object and its words from their antecedents, but it can, nevertheless, be clear in French because of the available ways of indicating features such as number, person, tense and gender, whereas English, not being an inflected language to the degree that French is, and using different ways to achieve clarity, must sometimes be expressed or punctuated in a different way to convey the meaning and to lead the reader skillfully. Going beyond the structure of Walras's sentences and paragraphs to the larger matter of the structure of his series of lectures on the social ideal and his arrangement of the other parts of the book, the reader will see that they are also logical.

Translating Walras's Meaning

Occasionally, however, Walras did not make his meaning clear, and sometimes, perhaps, his thoughts were not clear. The translators of some foreign language writings choose to write English sentences that have a clear meaning even though the foreign language text does not have a clear meaning to a native speaker of that language who has an expert knowledge of the subject matter. The result is an English sentence that does not state what the original states. Similarly, some translators choose on occasion not to convey certain stylistic features of their author's writing. They depart from his or her style, on the grounds that conveying it faithfully detracts from the clarity of the statements in English. Those choices produce inaccurate or inferior translations. A reader of a translation cannot undertake valid exegesis, criticism or praise of the author's ideas if their obscurity in the original language has been replaced in the translation by a clear statement that the author did not have in mind or did not write.

We have been careful not to distort what Walras wrote. If his meaning in French is obscure, or logically faulty, or understandable but expressed in words that do not strictly make sense, we have rendered it that way in English. We have then mentioned in a note the difficulties of translation that we have encountered, reproducing the original French text, and offering some speculations on what his meaning, not perfectly expressed by him or not clear to us, may have been. An example of a bad choice of words occurs when Walras referred to a passage of Frédéric Bastiat's in which needs are described as being greater or less than human faculties (see ch. 3, p. [103]). Human needs cannot be greater or less than human faculties; needs and faculties are incommensurable. They lack a common quality on which to make a comparison, as we remark in a note on the matter. An example of an unclear passage occurs in the third lesson of his *General Theory of Society* (ch. 2). Walras wrote: 'j'entends du spiritualisme pur et historique ... tel enfin que l'aura plus ou moins vécu l'humanité durant une période et pour des destinées à jamais glorieuses' (*ÉÉS*, p. 83). We translated this baffling passage without difficulty, but attach a note confessing our hesitancy to decide precisely what he meant (*SSE*, p. 54, n. xviii).

We offer here another example that gives some insight into the task of determining and accurately translating an author's meaning, and our approach to that task. In one sentence, Walras wrote: 'L'idée artistique consiste dans cette simulation, par des procédés de convention, des aspects divers du monde physique ou moral; elle se réalise dans une œuvre plastique, pittoresque ou littéraire' (*ÉÉS*, 2nd edn, p. 249). The sentence deals with three 'works', each qualified by an adjective: 'une œuvre plastique', 'une œuvre pittoresque' or 'une œuvre littéraire'. Our first approximation for translating 'une œuvre plastique' was the sentence: 'The artistic idea consists in the simulation, brought about by means of conventional procedures, of various aspects of the physical or moral world; the idea is expressed in works of sculpture, painting, or literature'. We decided, however, that we should not use the word 'sculpture' to translate 'une œuvre plastique', because the latter has a broader meaning than sculpture. It includes sculpture, and indeed that is the largest component of the category, but also, for example, furniture. Moreover, if Walras wanted to say 'sculpture', he would have used that word, as he did in an appropriate context, three sentences later in the same paragraph. We were also mindful of the fact that the 'œuvres plastiques' pertain to shaping or modelling, to works in a plastic medium, and are a subset of the '*arts* plastiques'. The latter include painting, choreography, engraving, etc., so the French 'arts plastique' and the English 'plastic arts' are false friends. In other words, the correct English translation of 'arts plastiques' is not 'plastic arts', but 'visual arts'. 'Plastic arts' is the correct English translation of '*œuvres* plastiques'.

The next matter is the meaning of 'une œuvre pittoresque'. When Walras wrote the essay, in the late 1860s, 'pittoresque' did not, in the context of the essay, have the modern meaning of the English 'picturesque', namely 'striking or interesting in an unusual way, suggesting or being worthy of a picture, quaintly attractive, etc'. It did not, in French, have the quality of a judgement about the subject. It described a category of artistic efforts, namely the design arts – decorative or artistic works such as drawings, engravings and paintings. As for literature, later in the same paragraph and elsewhere in the book Walras described literary works as art, by which he was referring to the creative activity of the writer and the experience of the reader. Literature is obviously not a plastic or design art, so he specified it separately. Taking all this into consideration, we determined that the correct translation of the end of the sentence in question is: 'expressed in the plastic arts, in the design arts, or in literature' (*SSE*, p. 166).

Concluding Remarks

Before undertaking this translation, we had a good knowledge of *ÉÉS*. We had read the book, studied some parts of it closely, and made reference to some of its contents in various publications. Of particular relevance is that we were sufficiently familiar with the book and with its essential role in Walras's system of thought to be convinced that its translation would be a very valuable addition to the economic literature in English. Then, as we began the work of translation, we realized immediately that it demanded and elicited a depth of understanding and analysis on our part that far exceeded the efforts that we had previously put into its study.

We made discoveries of weaknesses in Walras's reasoning or exposition that we would have never recognized without engaging in the work of translating his book. Mainly, however, what we discovered were strengths of reasoning and the workings of a powerful intellect, and the concerns of an enlightened, decent, civic-minded person, who was desirous, with no thought of personal gain, of improving the human condition. Far from being a narrowly focused mathematical economist, exclusively a formulator of abstract models, *SSE* reveals that Walras was a humanistic scholar, a highly literate person, a student of the social sciences, a philosopher and a historically minded thinker, conversant with past and contemporary cultures. We came to realize that his achievements in these fields of study were even greater than we had previously supposed. We therefore dedicated the translation: 'To the memory of the great economic theorist Léon Walras, who, in this book, revealed himself to have also been a great thinker on human nature, justice, mores, and the structure of scientific inquiry and knowledge'.

We hope that our translation and editorial work will enable the reader to benefit, as we have, but with a great deal less time and effort, from the richness of Walras's contribution to those subjects and to social economics in general.

7 PARETO: A POSSIBLE FORERUNNER OF THE STUDIES ON SOCIAL COMPLEXITY

Fiorenzo Mornati

In Pareto's thought, the idea of complexity, which he conceived as the need for an interdisciplinary study of social phenomena (starting from economics) with associated recourse to all available social sciences (and related methods), has been present since the beginning of his scientific production, as direct result of his methodology choices (see pp. 101–2). Having recalled that Pareto's interest for sociology arose much earlier than his Treatise on sociology (*The Mind and Society*) (pp. 102–3), we present an outline of the phenomenal interdependence in the Treatise (pp. 103–8), which apparently represents the reason why we might assume that Pareto is a forerunner of studies on social complexity. Having recalled the defence that Pareto made of his interdisciplinary approach (pp. 108–9), we end by illustrating an interesting interpretation of the phenomenal interdependence, according to Pareto, based on methods that are perhaps referred to the current school of complexity (pp. 109–10).

Methodological Choices

The starting point of the Paretian investigations on social complexity is surely the early Millian methodological choice, concerning the concrete deductive method, as well as that of the composition of causes, implying that social phenomena should, as a first step, be broken down into various aspects to summarize later on these partial studies. In a communication made to the Georgofili of Florence on 29 April 1877, Pareto in fact stated that nobody believes

> that events occurring in society are exclusively due to economics ... as wanted by the limited human science, phenomena of nature should be broken down into their components and these latter should be studied separately; synthesis is essential, but should be preceded by analysis.[1]

Further to the methodological Millian choice, it is necessary to take into account the early adhesion to the notion of interdependence of social phenomena, as supported by Herbert Spencer: most of the remarkable Pareto's commitment to the liberal and pacifist political activism, between the end of the 1880s and late 1890s, was based in fact on the Spencerian proposition, according to which, economic protectionism and militarism are strictly related.[2] (Pareto infers from this, *a contrario*, the need for an association between free trade and pacifism.)

Pareto's Sociological Interests before the 'Treatise'

So, it is not surprising that Pareto's interest has always been addressed to the whole spectrum of social phenomena. We believe that Pareto has begun from the study of economics only to theoretically refine his already quoted liberal militancy and above all, because the University of Lausanne had entrusted him, in the early stages of his academic career, with the teaching of political economy. The presence of extra-economic social interests in his previous writings at the start of his systematic study of sociology is easily documented: indeed, in his first course on applied economics, he referred also to the studies carried out on the societies of ants and their analogy, highly debated at that time, with the structure and evolution of human society,[3] although he considered that, 'in the current state of science' the study of animal societies' evolution cannot 'shed light on the study of economic facts of human societies'.[4]

Along the same line, Pareto also recounts the controversy between Cesare Lombroso and Napoleone Colajanni on the criminal man, underlining that even though both of them attributed crime to anthropologic and economic factors, the former believed that anthropological factors were predominant, while the latter supported the economic ones. Pareto shared with Colajanni the idea that safety of livelihood means and economic stability minimize crime, but at the same time he underlined that it was necessary to demonstrate that in order to achieve this latter result, as sustained by Colajanni, a greater equality in the distribution of wealth was also necessary.[5]

Lombroso was an important reference during this period, both positive and negative, for the Paretian reflections on sociology. Indeed Pareto attributed to him 'brilliant studies, new and sometimes profound ideas' but blamed him for lacking 'very often ... scientific rigour', having put together many remarks without verifying 'how much truth and how much error' they contained and drawing 'from a few and uncertain facts ... general conclusions' that oftentimes he would have even wanted to 'bulldoze and turn into rules'.[6] He challenged, for instance, Lombroso's assumption that in Italy, murders being more diffused among the Latin-Semitic 'race' regions than in Germanic-Slavic ones, murders could be more of a Latin-Semitic crime than a Germanic-Slavic one. One should in fact prove, as Lombroso rather did not do, that regions only differ by their race.[7] The original Lombroso's defect is thus highlighted by Pareto as his 'frenz[ied] attitude of oversimplifying social phenomena, which are indeed extraordinarily complex and locked in mutual dependence'.[8]

Moreover, Lombroso had, with his theory of the born criminal, 'the great merit' to have begun the study of relationships between 'material and mental qualities of man', thus supporting a more general theory that 'in the physical traits of men, who are part of society, he saw one of the non-neglectable factors of economic and social phenomena'.[9] Furthermore, the study of 'specific relationships that exist between that cause and those effects ... will be a lengthy and difficult work'.[10]

Finally, in a speech held on 23 October 1894 on the occasion of his taking office as Full Professor of Political Economy at the University of Lausanne, Pareto stated that political economy, dealing only with the property that goods have to satisfy consumers' desires, 'is just a part, and a small part of social science. It has a field of its own, where it is sovereign, but it should not spoof other sciences.'[11]

The Construction of Paretian Sociology or Paretian Study of Social Complexity

The vision Pareto had of the status of sociology (or social science), on the eve of his systematic studies on this subject matter, is shown in a passage of the *Cours d'économie politique*, where it is specified that the knowledge of interdependence[12] among phenomena progresses in stages: the first stage consists in knowing that the change in magnitude of a phenomenon causes the change in magnitude of other phenomena; the second stage consists in knowing the meaning (augmentative or diminutive) of the phenomenal variations caused; the third and last stage consists in knowing the extent of variations caused.[13]

While mechanics possesses the knowledge of the third stage and the General Economic Equilibrium notion has raised the level of knowledge of political economy to the second stage,[14] social science[15] is still fixed at the first stage.[16] Specifically, the knowledge offered by social science consists in highlighting 'the mutual dependence of physical, economic, intellectual and moral conditions of society, without in many cases, being able to specify the contents of this dependence'.[17]

Recognizing he was unable to give an answer, Pareto wondered whether the evolution of social science reaching the second stage of knowledge also depended, in addition to a higher amount of empirical knowledge, on the 'discovery of a new kind of logics' as 'mathematical logic seems very difficult to be applied to purely social issues'.[18] Anyhow, he added that comparisons between human society and a system of material points, at least gives us an idea of the social equilibrium and of the virtual movements of society (which indicate what might happen to society if it changed one of its fundamental aspects).[19]

The Foundation of Paretian Sociology: The Concept of Action

It was at the beginning of 1897, for educational needs, that Pareto had the opportunity to begin to systematically focus on sociology.

In his first lecture, having stated that the different human actions could be classified with at least two criteria (according to the first they can aim at material well-being, be indifferent to it or in some cases even contrary to it; according to the second they can pursue the achievement of a pleasant external object or the pleasure caused by the action *per se*, or imitate, or be repetitive[20]), he defined sociology as the study of 'these actions as a whole, taking into account their mutual influences, social institutions, or more in general, social regulations that stem from them'.[21]

Therefore, according to Pareto, sociology, the scientific sociology, should start by studying 'the fabric of society, the races it is formed of, diversities that are found'; he then went back to the study of basic actions (according to the second above-mentioned classification) and therefore investigated their combinations, as well as 'institutions and derived social habits; and only when we shall have gathered and combined all of these elements, we will give an idea of the complex body of society'.[22] Along with the study of what actually happens in society, Pareto confirmed that sociology should also study virtual movements, in other words, whether a slight shift of society from its equilibrium is able to change the well-being of the individual social classes.[23]

The original season of Pareto's sociological thinking started soon after, with the paper *Comment se pose le problème de l'économie politique pure* (dating back to the end of 1898) where Pareto established the foundations of both theory of choice (that is to say the theory of economic action) and of the more general theory of human and social action.[24] From that time on, Pareto also studied the economic theory within an explicit framework of social theory.

Speaking of action, Pareto meant from the start and definitely, the achievement that can be either logical or not, of an aim starting from data that can be experimental (that is to say actual) or imaginary. A taxonomy has been made of four types of actions: experimental and logical, experimental and non-logical, non-experimental and logical, non-experimental and non-logical.[25] In a biographically important letter written to Maffeo Pantaleoni on 17 May 1897,[26] Pareto stated that 'the principle of my sociology lies in separating logical actions from non logical ones and showing that for most men the second category is by far greater than the first'.

The Socio-Economic Equilibrium: The Core of a Paretian Notion of Social Complexity

After fifteen years of research, it is in the last two chapters of the Treatise (the twelfth and thirteenth chapters) that Pareto presents his final ideas on interdependence between economic and extra-economic social phenomena, that is to say, on the complexity of society.

The starting point is the idea that a social system 'is much more complicated' than the economic one and should be considered 'as composed of some molecules containing residues, some derivations, some interests, trends'.[27] Such molecules, subject to several ties, carry out logical and non-logical actions: in economics the assumption that men, in order to satisfy their tastes (not dictated by logics), carry out logical actions (that is to say characterized by conformity between aims and means) does not differ too much from reality, while in sociology this divide would be huge, precisely because non-logical actions, those considered by sociology, are performed under the pressure of residues (that is to say sentiments) and therefore they do not pursue compliance with aims and means. Moreover, men love to attribute to such non logical actions only apparently logical justifications, which Pareto called derivations, and through their analysis he identified residues[28] which are much more influential on social equilibrium than derivations.[29]

Human society furthermore is also heterogeneous in the sense that the need for uniformity of behaviour is not the same for all its members: society exists only because the number of its members who feel this need at a medium or high level is much higher than the number of those who barely feel this need or don't feel it at all.[30]

That being stated, social equilibrium could be established rigorously only as a solution for a system of equations gathering all variables indicated and their relationships expressed in quantitative terms. Naturally, the system would result in a solution if equations, the independent and compatible among them, were as many as the unknown factors.[31] Therefore, the assumption of interdependence requires, for its full cognitive development, the use of mathematical logics and can therefore be applied only to measurable phenomena, the extra-economic social ones not belonging to them. The assumption of interdependence in sociology is anyhow scientifically useful, because it gives us an image of phenomena that is less far away from reality than the one suggested by the completely erroneous causational logics.[32] It is furthermore possible to complete very interesting studies on social system variations around its point of equilibrium, having scrupulously specified that a society is in a state of equilibrium, if the artificial or accidental distancing from it leads to a reaction that brings back society to the pre-distancing state.[33]

Since we cannot resort to mathematical logic, the study of local deviations from the social equilibrium should be accomplished by presenting verbally the actions and the reactions among the above-mentioned categories of society's constitutive elements, that is to say residues (a), interests (b), derivations (c), social heterogeneity, which implies the divide of the society between the ruling class and the people (d).[34]

Among these categories the following combinations are logically possible:[35]

I: a acts on b, c, d;

II: b acts on a, c, d;

III: c acts on a, b, d;

IV: d acts on a, b, c.

Combination I 'gives a very important part of the social phenomenon', combinations II and IV follow in order of importance, while combination III 'is of lesser importance than all the others'.[36] Pareto states that 'actions and reactions follow each other indefinitely, as in a circle': for instance, in combination I, a acts on b, c, d (immediate effects), however in combination IV, d reacts in turn on a, giving rise to new variations of b, c, d, etc.[37]

Pareto furthermore, and above all, insists that 'the state of concrete equilibrium that is observed in a society is a consequence of all these effects, of all these actions and reactions', whereas, if we consider only some of these effects, only a theoretical equilibrium is achieved.[38]

The Fundamental Example of Interaction between Economic and Non-Economic Phenomena: Industrial Protectionism

Pareto suggested a long and special study of this system of actions and reactions, aiming at showing the assumption, as recalled above, that the economic effects stem from social phenomena; therefore a deeper knowledge of these effects can be acquired only by introducing political economy in a more general social science.[39]

Political economy, which is the science of interests (that is to say b), when studying customs protection (typically a b element) only deals with its direct effects, with low prices that are considered good by free traders (protective only of consumption) and bad by protectionists (protective only of production): however both approaches have 'from the scientific point of view ... little or no value' because, indeed, they originate from an incomplete analysis of protectionism.[40]

An important step towards the completion of the analysis consists in the demonstration, given by Pareto for the first time in the *Cours* (§§862 and following), that protectionism would result in the destruction of wealth:[41] but in order to be able to definitely state that protectionism is an evil, one should also 'look for indirect economic effects and social effects of protectionism'.[42]

Pareto's analysis focused on industrial protectionism (social element of b category) that in relation to:

a category has little effects because residues slowly change;[43]

c category promotes the creation of protectionist economic theories;[44]

d category accelerates social circulation, by fostering namely the social rise of those who possess the residues of combinations' instincts (industrialists who succeed and obtain protection measures from politicians).[45]

In turn, and this is true also in general, derivations (c category) act very little on residues (a category) and on interests (b category) and a little bit more on social heterogeneity (d category), 'because in all societies people able to praise the powerful, may enter the ruling class'.[46]

Finally, the effects of changes in social heterogeneity (d category) on residues (a category) are insignificant for the usual reason of substantial fixedness of these latter,[47] while the effects on interests (b category) are relevant because the arrival in the ruling class, thanks to industrial protectionism, of many individuals talented with the instinct of combinations pushes 'the whole nation towards economic activities, towards industrialism'.[48] If the production increase thus obtained is greater than the destruction of wealth, it occurs, 'but not necessarily, that economic prosperity of a country rises with the industrial protection',[49] contrary to the known free-trade proposition supported also by Pareto until the eve of the Manual of Political Economy.

Therefore, industrial protectionism can move society to a new equilibrium characterized by a higher production (b category) and by a different ruling class (d category).[50]

Moreover, considering that being able to govern requires both shrewdness (residues of class I, called the instinct of combinations) and strength (residues of class II, called the persistence of aggregates), Pareto remarks that if following the above-mentioned renewal of the elite produced by industrial protectionism, the residues of the first class prevail over those of the second, 'an unstable equilibrium and revolutions take place' through which the governed classes, traditionally rich in residues of class II, restore the appropriate equilibrium of residues in the elites by introducing, in fact, elements of class II.[51]

Since both shrewdness (that boils down to a patronage system of public expenditure) and strength (that boils down to expenses for the maintenance of army and police) bear a cost, it is necessary to know the economic effects of governance.[52]

In governments that resort primarily to strength, the residue of the persistence of aggregates predominates; this induces them to foster a slow circulation of elites. Therefore these are relatively inexpensive governments, which do not stimulate economic production, either because they are adverse to innovations or because they penalize the circulation of elites; they do not help the rise of those who have the instinct of economic combinations.[53]

By contrast, in governments that basically resort to shrewdness, especially in order to pursue the interests of their members, the instinct of combinations prevails. It induces them to foster a very fast circulation of elites: therefore, these are governments that cost a lot, but at the same time produce a lot 'and sometimes very much' create, in this way, the possibility of an overproduction compared to public spending, 'to the point that it ensures great prosperity to the country'.[54]

Among factors which enable the industrial cycle (that is, the system of socio-economic actions and reactions activated by industrial protectionism), Pareto believes that the presence of a wide class of savers is also crucial,[55] in order to satisfy the remarkable savings needs that among economically developed people, come from industry, trade and agriculture, as well as from the State.[56] But saving is much more fostered by residues of the persistence of aggregates than by instinct of combinations residues (those who follow the latter in fact save very little).[57]

It should also be noted that interests of savings' users (i.e. entrepreneurs and more generally speculators) and savings' producers (which are part of the more general category of the *rentiers*) are often 'different, sometimes opposed', entrepreneurs always being able to protect themselves from the increases of production costs by increasing their products' selling price (also to the advantage of their blue collars), an increase that savers can only suffer.[58]

Moreover, both 'the taste for an extravagant and adventurous life' (typical of someone who has the instinct of combinations) and 'the taste for a quiet life dedicated to saving' are 'largely the result of instincts and very little of reasoning':[59] it is therefore wrong to claim, as it has been done with the use of statistics, that saving is mainly a logical action caused by the interest rate.[60]

Pareto's Criticism of the 'Non-Complex' Authors

Pareto supports his complex approach to the study of social phenomena with direct and indirect criticisms of several contemporary authors, such as economists, sociologists and Marxists. We mention a few cases below.

The first target of his criticisms is Walras, to whom, summarizing the much wider methodological controversy that opposes him, Pareto attributed the 'generous impatience' of an early application of his pure economy to practical issues when indeed they belong 'almost always to economics and sociology'.[61]

From the point of view of social science, Pareto highlights that the positive side of sociological critique, consisting in pointing to neglected causes of social equilibrium, often degenerates into pure fiction when one assumes that such causes are instead the only ones to take into account, even individually. This is the case of both the theory of evolution, and its assumption of the survival of the fittest, and of the theory (supported by Georges Vacher de Lapouge) of the zoological race of mankind, as well as the assumption by Gustave Le Bon that social equilibrium can be explained only by means of religious beliefs.[62]

In the same vein there is the assertion of historical materialism, particularly in the keen formulation by Antonio Labriola, according to whom economic conditions only determine, although indirectly (through their influence on moral and religious feelings) 'fully social phenomena'.[63] Pareto criticizes Labriola by wondering whether 'this economic structure is, in some cases an effect in its own right, instead of being a cause' and whether 'sentiments, prejudices and passions of men are always derived phenomena and whether they could be in some cases primordial phenomena'.[64]

An Interpretation, in Terms of Complexity, of Pareto's Sociology

Among the many victims of the apparently irreversible divide between economics and sociology there are, of course, the interdisciplinary chapters of the Treatise on sociology that we mentioned above. It seems interesting to illustrate one of the very few reinterpretations of these made in the last decades by two American sociologists, Charles H. Powers and Robert Hanneman.

They attribute to Pareto a sociology theory, modelled on his previous analysis of economic cycle: social systems would thus be characterized by political and economic cycles (alternating élites characterized by the prevalence of instinct of combinations, leading to the decentralization of political power, and persistence of aggregates, with subsequent centralization of political power) and belief cycles (alternation between periods of fideism and scepticism) with the two first cycles, substantially synchronous, while the third one following with some delay.[65] There would be, in particular, synchrony between economic expansion and decentralization of political power, to be followed by a phase of scepticism: similarly, there would be synchrony between economic recession and centralization of political power, that it would be followed by fideism (or traditionalism).[66]

Although interacting, the three cycles are the result of an unexplainable alternation of residues of the combinations' instinct (that inspires innovation in economics, politics and social beliefs) and of residues of aggregates' persistence (that inspires conservation in economics, politics and social beliefs).[67]

Powers and Hanneman formalized their interpretation of the Paretian dynamic sociology into cluster of propositions (concerning the cyclical dynamics of political power, folk's beliefs, investments and productivity, the relationship between productivity and political power, productivity and popular beliefs, political power and popular beliefs).[68] According to them, it is the non-linear character of these relationships which produces both their cyclical nature (for example, in case of low levels of political power centralization, a small increase in this centralization shall not cause resistance but in case of high levels of centralization a small increase of centralization will be unbearable, giving rise to high levels of resistance that will start the decentralization of power) and their tendency to equilibrium.[69]

The relationships among centralization/decentralization of power and resistance to regulation/deregulation, anomie and traditionalism, investments and production, decentralization/centralization of political power and expansion/economic depression, etc. are formalized into a system of equations to the differences[70] that is resolved, by a simulation method, establishing the solutions, in various moments of time, starting from specifications (suggested by theory) of initial values of variables and parameters of equations.[71]

Simulations carried out starting from a situation of equilibrium (namely economic prosperity and decentralization of political power) enable the reproduction of Paretian sociologic theory, in particular synchrony between economic and political cycles and the slight delay of beliefs: the meaning of this experience, according to authors, is not the demonstration of Paretian theory's empirical validity, but rather a demonstration that Paretian dynamics are interrelated in a systematic way, which implies a synchronized cyclical oscillation.[72] Simulations carried out starting from a situation of lack of equilibrium (namely economic prosperity, political power centralization, high traditionalism and high anomie) show that the system tends to regain its equilibrium.[73]

Powers and Hanneman interpret the results of their simulations as reflecting a 'substantial correspondence between formal model and Pareto's discursive interpretation of socio-historical change'[74] and conclude that the scant attention paid to Pareto's socio-economic theory is due both to its 'complexity' and to the aversion of sociologists to the notion of equilibrium.[75]

Conclusions

In the social sciences, too, *nihil sub sole novum*: so the fundamental features of Pareto's sociology show that this author can be considered a forerunner of the recent literature on the complexity of social sciences.

Recalling that Pareto's social surveys have very specific methodological starting points in John Stuart Mill (for the deductive concrete method and the cause composition) and in Herbert Spencer (for the idea of interdependence of social phenomena), we have given some hints on the great number of references, in the Paretian texts before his Treatise on sociology, of interests on sociology themes. We therefore reconstructed the Paretian sociology. We dwelt on one of the most interesting attempts made by Pareto to describe the interdependence between economic and sociologic phenomena: the study of all actions and reactions produced by customs protectionism, which represents, in our opinion, a representative sample of the 'complex' way with which Pareto, after a very lengthy intellectual journey, was able to realize his social investigation.

Therefore, having been reminded that Pareto had defended on several occasions, and against remarkable antagonists (economists, sociologists and Marxists alike), his complex approach to the study of society, we have recalled an interesting reinterpretation of the theme of phenomenal interdependence (that is to say of the complexity) in the Paretian Treatise achieved in the 1980s by two American sociologists. Having summarized as propositions their interpretation of such an interdependence (actually seen by them as synchrony of economic, political and ideological cycles), Hanneman and Power resolve, by simulation, the corresponding system of equations to differences, being satisfied with the observation that their investigation reproduces the one carried out by Pareto. However, what is still missing is the empirical verification of the Treatise assumptions, which Pareto repeatedly called for in the latter part of his life.

8 SAMSONOFF ON RENT THEORY: OR, YET ANOTHER MEMBER OF THE LAUSANNE SCHOOL?

François Allisson

Basile Samsonoff is a minor member of the Lausanne School of Economics, author of a dissertation entitled 'Esquisse d'une théorie générale de la rente' (1912).[1] He was one of three students, the others being Marie Kolabinska and Pierre Boven, who obtained their doctoral degrees at the University of Lausanne under the supervision of Vilfredo Pareto. After obtaining his degree in Lausanne, Samsonoff went back home to Russia, where he continued his economic research and what already promised to be a brilliant academic career. In 1914, however, he was enrolled in World War I, and he died at the front in 1917, not yet 30 years old.

Samsonoff's dissertation was reviewed in the *American Economic Review* by Esther Lowenthal, who found that it looked more like a didactic essay, and in the *Political Science Quarterly* by Frank Fetter, who found that it should be read by every student of economic theory, especially by the tenants of the older theories.[2] In Russia, it was studied by Struve, who found it very stimulating and by Bilimovic, in the sole obituary of Samsonoff.[3]

Samsonoff is now almost forgotten. He has been mentioned by historians of the Lausanne School,[4] and in the Russian literature, he is listed by Paškov as a member of a Russian group of 'bourgeois' mathematical economists.[5] At the footnote level, Schumpeter, arguing in his *History of Economic Analysis* that he has no time to discuss in detail the theory of rent, gives among others a reference to Samsonoff's dissertation.[6]

Apart from these scarce mentions, Samsonoff is still an unknown member of the Lausanne School. Therefore, the aim of the present contribution is two-fold: first, to recount, with the help of new documents, as much as possible of Samsonoff's too brief and unknown life. Second, the aim is to evaluate to which degree his contribution to economic theory falls within the tradition of the Lausanne School.

Basile Samsonoff (1887–1917)

Basile Samsonoff (Vasilij Vasil'evič Samsonov) was born on 7 August 1887 (Julian Calendar; 19 August according to the Gregorian Calendar), probably in Yekaterinoslav in the Russian Empire (Dnipropetrovsk in today's Ukraine).[7] His family is from Yekaretinoslav. On his father's side, he is the nephew of the famous general of the Russian Imperial Army, Alexander Samsonov (1859–1914), who served during the Russo-Turkish War, the Russo-Japanese War, and during World War I. Samsonoff was schooled in Kiev.

After the 1905 Revolution, his family moved from Kiev to Lausanne. His father, Basile Samsonoff senior, was born in 1856 or 1857, and died early in Lausanne, aged fifty, on 16 January 1907. The official announcement of his death in the local newspaper described him as a Russian owner (*propriétaire*), and we learn that the family lived at avenue de Rumine 50, in Lausanne.[8] His mother, Sophie Samsonoff, was born in 1854 or 1855, and died in Lausanne in August 1930, aged seventy-five, after a long disease. She was buried on 21 August 1930, at the graveyard of Montoie, in Lausanne.[9]

Basile senior and Sophie Samsonoff had at least four children: Alexandre, Catherine, Nadine and Basile. Nothing is known of Alexandre Samsonoff, except that he was living in Bruxelles when his mother died.[10] Catherine Samsonoff attended the lectures at the science department of the University of Lausanne during the Winter 1905–6 term as a listener, but did not do this again afterwards. She married an Italian called Antonio Aruffo.[11] Nadine Samsonoff was born on 20 September 1888 in Yekaterinoslaw. She attended the Winter 1905–6 term as a listener at the arts department, and then, from Summer 1905–6 until Winter 1912–13 was regularly enrolled as a student at the medical department of the University of Lausanne, until she got her PhD in medicine with a dissertation entitled '*Etudes sur la cobraïsation*' (1913).[12] Apart from the fact that she got the *Certificat d'études de l'Union sténographique suisse* (speed above 60 words/minute) in 1922,[13] almost nothing is known about her life in Lausanne. She died on 21 April 1970, aged eighty-two, while living at rue de Cour in Lausanne, and was buried at the graveyard of Montoie.[14] The various admission files at the University of Lausanne allow us to follow the whole family, from 1905 to 1913, through the various places in which they lived in Lausanne: avenue de Rumine 38, then avenue Villamont 23, avenue de Rumine 64, avenue Druey 19, and Villa Emery on avenue Charles Secrétan.

Basile Samsonoff lived at his parents' places during his studies. He completed the admission form at the University of Lausanne, in the law department, on 20 October 1905. During the first term (Winter 1905–6), he was only conditionally enrolled as a student, and was then officially enrolled in the Summer 1905–6 term. During the course of his studies, from 1905 till 1911 (he was enrolled for ten terms), it is clear that his primary interest is political economy, as testified in the lecture registration forms (*Inscription aux cours; see example below*). He took a few lectures in French (*Diction, Littérature alpestre, Poésie alpestre*), many lectures in law, and followed the lectures in economics and sociology by the following members of the already well-known Lausanne School: Vilfredo Pareto, Pasquale Boninsegni and Maurice Millioud.

Samsonoff attended the following lectures by Vilfredo Pareto: *Économie politique* (Winter 1905–6➔W05–6), *Économie politique: production et consommation* (Summer 1905–6➔S05–6), *Conférence d'économie politique* (W05–6), *Économie politique: les systèmes socialistes* (W06–7), *Économie politique pure* (W07–8), and *Sociologie* (S05–6, W06–7, W07–8 and S08–9). From Boninsegni, he attended *Économie politique* (S05–6, S06–7, W07–8 and W10–11) and the *Conférence d'économie politique* (S05–6, W06–07, W07–8, S07–8 and W10–11). With Millioud, he had *Sociology* (W10–11) and *Séminaire de sociologie* (W10–11).

Samsonoff wrote a dissertation under the supervision of Vilfredo Pareto. At that time, Pareto had three students who were writing a dissertation with him, which were all published the same year: Pierre Boven's 'Les applications mathématiques à l'économie politique' (1912), Marie Kolabinska's 'La circulation des élites en France' (1912) and Basile Samsonoff's 'Esquisse d'une théorie générale de la rente' (1912). Samsonoff names both Pareto and Boninsegni as his professors in his dissertation, but we know that his personal relationship with Pareto was not perfect. Samsonoff thought that, because he authorized himself to criticize some aspects of Pareto's theory of rent, he was immediately condemned.[15] This must have been only partly true. Pareto explained in a letter to Pierre Boven that Samsonoff's theory was inconsistent with facts, while that of Guido Sensini on the same subject was consistent.[16] Pareto wanted Samsonoff to read Sensini's work.[17] Whatever the case may have been, the imprimatur of Samsonoff's dissertation was given on 11 May 1912 and the defense took place on 27 June 1912 in the second auditorium of the Palais de Rumine.[18]

On Samsonoff's life in Lausanne, it is only known that he played chess. He was a regular member of the *Club d'échecs de Lausanne*. He won the tenth tournament of the *club* in 1910.[19] And he was the organizer of the twenty-second Swiss Chess Championship, which was held in July 1912 in Lausanne. The Championship was 'well organized', and Samsonoff arrived at the fourth rank ex-aequo.[20]

Samsonoff decided to continue an academic career as an economist in Russia. He came back to Kiev. The holding of a foreign PhD did not prevent him from taking the *magister* exam. He enrolled at the St Vladimir University of Kiev. In 1913, he published a paper on the method of political economy in the *Bûlleten Kievskago Kommerčeskago Instituta (Heralds of the Kiev Commercial Institute)*. Then, as he was preparing for his exams, he prepared a work on the Physiocrats. A first part of this work was sent to Petr Struve, editor of the journal

Russkaâ Mysl (Russian Thought), for publication.[21] A second part of this work was eventually published in 1917, posthumously, in the *Izvestah RAN (News Bulletin of the Russian Academy of Science)* in 1917: the paper is entitled 'The Physiocrats' Theory of Net Income'.[22]

The family military tradition called Samsonoff back at the beginning of World War I. He voluntarily engaged in the Odessa artillery school in the summer of 1915. He was then sent to the front, in the West, and then in the South-West, as an officer. On 16 June 1917, he died on the battlefield.[23]

Basile Samsonoff was promised a bright academic future in Russia, as one of the few Russian specialists of the Lausanne School, with Dmitriev, Shaposhnikov and Yurovsky.[24] The Bolshevik Revolution could have interfered in his plans, but the war impeded them beforehand. He published in all three items (his dissertation and two papers), and left at least one lost manuscript.

Samsonoff's 'Esquisse d'une théorie générale de la rente' (1912)

In his dissertation, Samsonoff studies the phenomena of rent, defined by him as revealing itself 'under the form of *surplus* [plus-value, in French] enjoyed by some economic goods when they undergo successive stages of economic equilibrium'.[25]

In an essentially methodological introduction, Samsonoff outlines his conception of science, which owes much more to Pareto than to Walras. Samsonoff welcomes the emergence of a new scientific school, the Pantheon of which is already under construction,[26] which is based on 'the study of facts and the search for uniformities'.[27] This is seen by Samsonoff as a clear progress over past practices, composed by 'vulgar language' and 'metaphysics' (and in what obviously seems a direct attack against Walras, Samsonoff writes: 'Let us only remember the *value*!').

In addition, Samsonoff endorsed Pareto's logico-experimental methodology. Following his master, Samsonoff defines theories as follows: 'They can only be successive approximations of the truth, and that truth itself is modest'. He goes on to recall that theories are ontologically nonexistent:

> In particular, we must never forget that uniformities and scientific laws have no objective existence. They are all established by the abstract method by isolating a part of reality. They can be true only if the premises that led to their formulation are expressly maintained.[28]

Samsonoff recommends caution when moving from science to art, first because theories are necessarily imperfect, and second because it is difficult to strictly separate theory from ethics. Thus, Samsonoff sticks on the pure theory of rent, without immediate practical results: 'We will not bring any cure for the ills of the suffering humanity'[29] and by evoking the nationalization of land as a non-scientific subject, this is once again an affirmation of Samsonoff's remoteness from Walras.

UNIVERSITÉ DE LAUSANNE

Semestre d'hiver   1906 -1907.

INSCRIPTION DE COURS

Nom et prénom de l'étudiant *Basile Samsonoff*

Lieu d'origine *Russie, ...*

Domicile (adresse à Lausanne) *av. de Rumine, 64.*

Date de la naissance¹ (jour, mois, année) *⁷/₁₉ août 1887.*

Désire suivre les cours à titre d'¹*étudiant* .   et figurer dans la Faculté de *droit*

DÉSIGNATION DES COURS	PRIX *	NOMS DES PROFESSEURS
Économie Politique : Les systèmes	5	M. Pareto
Sociologie.	5	M. Pareto
Économie Politique	10	M. Beauregard
Droit criminel : partie spéciale	5	M. Maunier
Histoire du droit moderne	15	M. de Tourtoulon
Droit diplomatique	10	M. Fouvez
Droit civil comparé	10	M. Roguin
Droit international privé	10	M. Roguin
Conférence d'économie polit.	5	M. Beauregard
Les protestants ...	10	M. Oltramare
	95 +5	p. 11.10.06
Droit français	10	
	85	payé 10f. 15 XI
Droit commercial	10	à relire p. 10f. 2 XII 06
	95	

Lausanne, le *27 octobre,*   1906.

(Signature)
Basile Samsonoff

¹ Les auditeurs sont dispensés de donner la date de leur naissance.
² Inscrire dans cette ligne si les cours seront suivis à titre d'*étudiant immatriculé* ou à titre d'*auditeur*.
Messieurs les étudiants ou auditeurs sont priés d'indiquer dans ce formulaire *tous* les cours et exercices pratiques qu'ils désirent suivre durant le semestre, et de le rapporter au Bureau.

* Cette colonne sera remplie par le bureau.

T. S. V. P.

Figure 8.1: Samsonoff's *Inscription de cours* for the Winter 1906–7 term. Courtesy of the Service des Archives de l'Université de Lausanne.

- Introduction
- Part 1. Positive Part
  - Chapter 1. The Issue at Stake
  - Chapter 2. On Economic Equilibrium
  - Chapter 3. Statics and Dynamics: On Successive Equilibria
  - Chapter 4. On Rent of Capitals
- Part 2. Critical Part
  - Chapter 1. The Ricardian Theory
  - Chapter 2. Some Representatives of the Static Thesis: Thünen, Jevons, Launhardt
  - Chapter 3. Evolution of Rent Theories: Alfred Marshall and J. B. Clark
  - Chapter 4. Criticism of Static Theories of Rent
  - Chapter 5. Dynamic Theories of Rent: Hermann, Mangoldt and Schäffle
  - Chapter 6. Molinari and Vilfredo Pareto

Figure 8.2: Translation of the table of contents of 'Esquisse d'une théorie générale de la rente' (1912).

Samsonoff's dissertation consists of two parts of unequal length: a positive part of approximately 60 pages and a critical part of about 160 pages (see Figure 8.2). Both parts are governed by a strong thesis: the theory of rent was a chaotic affair during the whole nineteenth century because of an important confusion between the determination of prices and incomes, which is a *static* problem, and the determination of their variation, which is a *dynamic* problem. The rent, according to Samsonoff, is exclusively a dynamic problem.

Static vs Dynamic Rent in the History of Economic Thought

The critical part of the dissertation is a history of thought exposition of the distinction between the static and the dynamic theories of rent.

Ricardo is at the source of this confusion as it is possible to detect the two theories in his writings.[30] Ricardo's static theory of rent is a negation of the Physiocrats' claim, according to which the net product is a free gift of nature. For Ricardo, the rent is on the contrary the manifestation of the 'relative parsimony' of nature.[31] The static rent is presented alternatively by Ricardo as a residual and a differential income. The residual income, i.e. a consequence of the price but not the cause of the costs, is rejected by Samsonoff, quoting Walras's critique of the circularity of the argument. The static theory of rent as a differential income is accepted by Samsonoff, as an explanation of the rent of land through differential productivity. But Ricardo also had a dynamic theory.

Ricardo's dynamic theory of rent 'is about the establishment of a surplus on land in a progressive society'.[32] At first, land is free, and then it becomes costly, not because of improvements applied to land through labour and capital, but because of the new socio-economic conditions. The limited amount of land is the necessary and sufficient condition to explain the dynamic phenomena of rent, and not fertility.

The distinction between the static and the dynamic rent is the following: the static rent is *one* price; the dynamic rent is *the difference between two prices*. Subsequent economists often saw only one of these two theories. The main line (Thünen, Jevons, Marshall, etc.) saw only the static theory of rent, while the dynamic theory has been more neglected, with the exception of Hermann, Mangoldt, Schäffle, Molinari and Pareto. As far as Ricardo is concerned, both camps were wrong since he mixed both theories in 'his' theory of rent, which was a static-dynamic-historical one.

After this chapter on Ricardo, Samsonoff then studies, in two devoted chapters, the theories of some supporters of the static thesis. He turns essentially to mathematical-economists and gives detailed expositions of their doctrines, without much mathematics, but with sound explanations. The theories of Thünen, Jevons, Launhardt, Clark and Marshall are thus exposed. He then makes, in another chapter, a critique of these static theories, based on an idea dear to the founders of the Lausanne School: land income is no more a consequence or a cause of price than are the incomes of labour and of capital:

> We believe that we can demonstrate that the static theories of rent, although they may have been useful for the development of science, are, at the moment, overwhelmed by the general scientific trend: a synthetic general theory of the determination of all prices and incomes, taking into account the fundamental fact of the mutual dependence of economic quantities, replaced the former particular theories of the old economic science which turned its nose up at this dependency.[33]

The theory of general equilibrium, with its key concept of interdependence is here mobilized to the rescue. Then, relying on Wolkoff and Schumpeter, Samsonoff explains why static theories failed. The old theories were stuck on the concept of cost: what had value should 'cost' something: labour is a cost. Interest as abstinence is a cost. But land did not appear to them as a cost. But the fact is: land also has its own value.

Samsonoff then studies the various dynamic theories of rent. A chapter is devoted to three forgotten German economists who have developed this theory. Then, the last chapter of this critical part is devoted to Pareto on the same subject.[34] The German authors Hermann, Mangoldt and Schäffle are credited by Samsonoff as demonstrating brilliant intuitions. Their theories are vague, incomplete and sometimes still entangled in the original Ricardian confusion, but still, Samsonoff sees in them the essence of the modern dynamic theory of rent. They define rent as a difference between two prices, and recommend changing the name (from rent to surplus) in order to expend the phenomena of rent to other types of capital than land. Finally, they combine rent with social and economic change. They only miss a precise measure of the phenomena they described. When it comes to Pareto, Samsonoff emphasizes that his supervisor did not know the theories of his predecessors Hermann, Mangoldt and Schäffle.

In the *Cours d'économie politique*, Pareto gives a definition of the rent of capital as a surplus between successive stages of economic equilibrium, as a difference of prices between two equilibria. This rent has no singular cause, but depends on all economic variables. Samsonoff further explains that his own theory of rent directly follows Pareto, to which he essentially adds a few clarifications and amendments.

Samsonoff's Positive Theory of Rent

Samsonoff's positive theory is awkwardly presented *before* his critical part. It consists in an improvement of §89 (ch. 5) of Pareto's *Manual of Political Economy*. But on a conceptual level, the systematic distinction between the static and dynamic theory is Samsonoff's major contribution.

For Samsonoff, the distinction between statics and dynamics relies on two different ways of taking the time variable into account. The distinction of two prices distant in time, with equal economic conditions is given by the net present value and is a static problem. When the economic conditions change, the problem is dynamic. Samsonoff then returns to the definition of general equilibrium, 'one of the greatest and most definitive acquisitions of modern economic science'[35] that he contrasts with the Classical School and with the English and Austrian marginalist schools. According to him, Smith, Malthus, Ricardo and Mill were remarkable economists of their time, and they are not to be blamed for their works; unlike those who still defended them in Samsonoff's time. Samsonoff also attacks the naive empiricism of the historical school: for him, the Lausanne School, which is not to be confused with the whole mathematical school, is clearly the *avant-garde* in economic theory.

General equilibrium theory perfectly answers the issue of the determination of prices. But the question of the variation of prices, i.e. of successive equilibria, is still to be developed, according to Samsonoff. He excludes from his study temporary oscillations around equilibrium prices, as well as variations of all prices in the same proportion. He is only interested in changes in relative prices, whether the general price level remains the same or not.

He can thus give a definition of his rent: 'any positive or negative increase in value (price) of goods produced or existing in one economic state, and consumed or sold in another'.[36] The rent is therefore not a price (or a profit), but a difference between two prices, because of the changing economic conditions.

The rent, for Q units of good a, priced $\mathcal{P}_a$ at first period and $\mathcal{P}'_a$ at second period, given that all prices grew in $\frac{1}{m}$ proportion, is therefore $(\mathcal{P}'_a - \mathcal{P}_a \frac{m+1}{m})Q$. This formulation is Samsonoff's technical contribution to §89 of ch. 5 of Pareto's *Manual of Political Economy*, which had not taken into account the variation of the price level in his definition.

The existence of rent is explained by many factors: barriers to competition, technology of production, changes in means of transportation, mobility, crises, etc. From the moment an investment decision or the choice of an apprenticeship is made, and the moment these actions bear their fruits, the conditions have changed, and a rent appears. More generally: 'One could therefore define the rent as the positive or negative risk attached to property'.[37] Samsonoff also discusses the limits to the size of rent. There is no upper limit. The price may fall to zero, minus the raw materials included in the good.

The sphere of application of this theory of rent is general. It is not limited to perfect competition, but also applies to other social organizations. It concerns all economic goods, and not only land. By definition, only durable goods are concerned, i.e. only those goods that undergo successive equilibria: these are called capitals, in the sense given to them by the Lausanne School (Samsonoff quotes Boninsegni, who follows on this point Walras and Pareto), i.e. everything that is useful to production: land, human beings, houses, factories, tools, animals, raw materials, etc.

Samsonoff notes that it is interesting to show how, even under conditions of perfect competition, the rent can exist without external changes. He exposes the equations of capital formation, which give for the different types of capital (land, human capital and capital proper) an equal relation between net incomes (*fermage*, wage and interest) and their prices, which are all equal to the interest rate on savings. But, some capitals are not reproducible (land) and some are slowly reproducible (humans). Some are subject to competition (humans and capital) while others are not (land). Some are not mobile (land, plants) some only partially (human, some capitals) and only a few are perfectly mobile (circulating monetary capital). These differences imply that the equality between all yields, postulated in the theory, is not possible, or only possible at different adjustment rates. In the meanwhile, the rent exists.

To conclude, Samsonoff compliments Pierre Boven, who defined the rent as the difference in the adjustment in the prices of some assets;[38] Vilfredo Pareto, who wrote about rent as an index of the difficulties for savings to be transformed into some type of capital rather than some other; and Matthieu Wolkoff, who explained the difference between equilibrium and reality in the fiction of the equality between the rate of interest of all types of capital. In this perspective, the rent necessarily arises from a lack of competition for the establishment of the equality between all interest rates. The rent exists because the general equilibrium is not (yet) reached.

Instead of a Conclusion: Samsonoff and the Lausanne School

Samsonoff's dissertation contains no dramatic improvement on the theory of rent over its treatment by Pareto. At best, there is a more general mathematical formula in ch. 5, §89 of the *Manual of Political Economy*. In this, the positive part of the dissertation is not extraordinary. His key contribution to the debate, however, is his distinction between static and dynamic theories of rent.

The static theory belongs to a generation of economic theories that had separate explanations for each type of income (rent, interest, wage). Samsonoff reminds us that all prices and incomes should be determined at the same time, and within the same principle: that of general equilibrium. Samsonoff's rent, on the contrary, relies on dynamic general equilibrium theory, an issue that was *not* settled by Walras and Pareto. In doing so, Samsonoff furthers the criticism by theoreticians of the Lausanne School, of the Classical School, on a particular issue: the rent. In particular, his interpretation of Ricardo goes beyond those of Walras and of Pareto.

Léon Walras handles at least three times the notion of rent in his *économie politique et sociale*. The first time, he tries to show the feasibility of the nationalization of land by purchase, in the field of social economy. The second time, land and rent are treated as every *service producteur* and income in the theory of production (section 4 of the *Éléments d'économie politique pure*). The third time, he criticizes the English theory of the rent (section 7, lesson 39). It is to this seventh section of the *Éléments* that Samsonoff's work relates specifically, and in two ways. First, it is an extension and clarification of the criticisms to address to the English theory of rent (i.e. Ricardo's); and second, it is another attempt to explain the transition from a static to a dynamic analysis (lessons 35 and 36 on the *marché permanent* and the *société progressive*).

Vilfredo Pareto, on his side, handles the notion of rent at least twice: in a first approximation, and like Léon Walras, as a variable in the theory of general equilibrium, i.e. Samsonoff's static theory of rent. In a second approximation, the notion of rent is used to develop the dynamic theory, with the rent as a surplus between two economic equilibria. And it is to the distinction between these two rents that Samsonoff brings his contribution.

Eventually, Samsonoff, with his distinction between the static and dynamic theories of rent, contributes to the strengthening of the theory of general equilibrium, by a consolidation of the critiques addressed against the Classical School. In this, this is a positive contribution to the Lausanne School. But as for the constitution of a dynamic theory of rent, the latter supposes a *dynamic* theory of general equilibrium. This project was certainly too ambitious for Samsonoff. And not only for Samsonoff but also, probably, for anyone else...

9 ADMINISTRATION AND ŒCONOMIC GOVERNMENT IN QUESNAY'S POLITICAL ECONOMY

Philippe Steiner

Thus one can only evaluate the amount produced by taxes, the revenues of the nation and the condition of the population according to the capabilities and the management of those who are charged with administering the economic government of the kingdom.[1]

In Quesnay's writings there are many sentences in which government, administration, nation, State or kingdom are invoked to explain a particular point in his political economy. Quesnay's use of words pointing to the administration of economic affairs has to be examined in detail so that we might clarify the innovative nature of his vocabulary[2] during the formative period of the 'New Science' of political economy.[3] Such clarification will improve our understanding of the respective roles that this 'New Science' ascribed to government and administration at a time when there was increasing concern about administration.[4] Finally, this issue is of interest because historians of economic ideas should pay attention to the connections between political economy, with its due emphasis on the theoretical dimension of the subject, and the way and means through which political economy did have, or may have had, an impact upon society. I will therefore examine here the status of administration in the writings of Quesnay and other Physiocrats, as has recently been done in the case of industrial administration,[5] and also the with regard to commercial administration, examining the group formed around the work and administrative action of Vincent de Gournay.[6]

The first part of the essay considers the meaning of the above-mentioned terms as recorded in contemporary French dictionaries, subsequently considering the meaning of these and other related terms in the texts written by Quesnay during the Seven Years' War. The second part examines more specifically the role attributed to administration and to œconomic government. The third part considers the place of these ideas in proposals for reform of the taxation system contained in Marquis de Mirabeau's *Théorie de l'impôt* and Le Trosne's *De l'administration des finances provinciales et de la réforme de l'impôt.* The last part concludes this study by showing how the issue of administration and œconomic government is critical to an understanding of the Physiocratic view of the functioning of the economy.

Government, Administration, Management and Œconomy

Let us first consider the meaning given to words. The principal dictionaries of the period are the *Dictionnaire de l'Académie française* (first edition in 1694) and the *Dictionnaire de Trévoux* (first edition in 1708). For the sake of simplicity, I consider only the first edition of these two dictionaries, leaving out the small differences introduced in subsequent editions since it is generally believed that definitions given in dictionaries only become commonly accepted half a century later. Both dictionaries deliver the same message: to govern ('gouverner'), to administer ('administrer'), to manage ('mesnager') belong to the same semantic realm. Definitions are not strictly circular, but they are interconnected.[7] Two other words are also strongly connected to them: economy ('œconomie') and politics ('politique'); State is only loosely connected to them.

According to the *Dictionnaire de l'Académie française*, to administer means to govern, to steward, to govern wisely; this applies particularly to justice and finance (and to religion as well). The noun Minister ('Ministre') is linked with the verb, and conveys the idea that the minister in charge of the administration does his task on behalf of somebody else, notably the prince. To govern means to steward, to conduct with authority; the second sense is to administer something; it also means to manage with prudence. To manage means to administer oeconomically, to use wealth and make expenditures with prudence; it means also to direct judiciously; as a noun, 'mesnage' refers to the household, particularly the expenditures of a household. More specifically, it denotes œconomy in the administration of one's wealth. Politics relates to the government of a State, so that 'government' in this case becomes political government; politics is defined as an art, having need of subtle and shrewd people if they are to reach their goal; whereas œconomy relates to the rules followed in the conduct of a household, the government of a family; and figuratively, œconomy means the order within which a political body functions. As a noun ('œconome'), it means the person in charge of managing the expenditures of a household, the person who knows how to limit the amount of expenditure.

Published a decade later, the *Dictionnaire de Trévoux* does not significantly alter the meaning of these five words, and the semantic interconnection between them remains solid.[8] As with the *Dictionnaire de l'Académie française*, to administer, to govern and to manage are strongly interconnected; œconomy is also associated with the management of a household. The major shift relates to the continuing close connection between politics and management, whereas politics and œconomy are only connected indirectly through the noun government.

With these linguistic possibilities to hand, what does Quesnay do? For the sake of simplicity, I consider only those entries written for the *Encyclopédie* during the short period from 1756 (the entries 'Farmers' and 'Corn') to the end of 1757 (the entries 'Taxes' and 'Men', which remained unpublished). This period is a highly innovative one for Quesnay, and established the vocabulary that was used by the Physiocrats.

'To manage', 'œconomy', 'police' and 'politics' are not terms often found in Quesnay's vocabulary, whereas 'government' is quite common, with about thirty instances of its use in the entries written for the *Encyclopédie*. Government is used to emphasize the capacity to act upon society; it causes the 'resources of society to move' and 'creates general order [of society]'.[9] Government thus 'protects the activity of the farmers';[10] conversely, the government may be misled by private interests if merchants receive undue protection from the government at the cost of a 'good price' for corn, the price necessary to the wealth of the State.[11] The same difficulty arises with the distribution of the tax burden, a difficult task in which the government often errs.[12] Government is frequently associated with the State, a term which is quite common in Quesnay's vocabulary, with more than sixty instances. Importantly, however, the State is not opposed to the Nation: on the contrary, the word is used synonymously with Nation and kingdom. The State is often an abstraction to which Quesnay refers so that he might evaluate the consequences of a policy, or the behaviour of some constitutive section of the population – rich or poor farmers, merchants, and the like. It is common to find Quesnay using expressions such as the 'advantage', 'needs', 'wealth', 'revenues' or 'prosperity' of the State.[13] This holds true when issues of military strength or the power of the State are at stake, using expressions such as the 'strength' or the 'defense' of the State, which is after all not so surprising since these entries were written during the Seven Years' War. The abstract character of the State is particularly clear when Quesnay opposes the 'agricultural State' to the 'commercial State',[14] a most important point in the construction of his theory of economic policy, or the œconomic government necessary for the French kingdom.[15] Nevertheless, the most common use of the State is to be found with qualifying expressions such as 'useful', 'beneficial'; or, conversely, 'useless' and 'harmful' to the State. In these cases, the State is an abstract entity against which policies are evaluated according to Quesnay's form of utilitarianism, as can be seen in the following quotation:

> The more wealth men produce over and above their consumption, the more profitable they are to the State; but the more they spend over and above their incomes, or the more their consumption exceeds the degree to which their activities are profitable, the more they are a burden to the State.[16]

There is the same use of the expression in assessing the (weak) contribution of financiers: 'for men of fortune and of finance, and all those who are called men of business, one may evaluate their utility by comparing their gains with the value of their work for the prosperity of the State'.[17]

The term 'administration' is less common (about twelve occurrences), but of importance in understanding Quesnay's views regarding the changes needed to relieve the situation in which the kingdom finds itself. Administration is a menial part in the machinery of the government and, in this sense, it contrasts to government, as can be seen here: 'The government of the revenues of the nation must not be abandoned to the discretion or to the authority of a subaltern and particular administration'.[18] When Quesnay wants to give more weight to the subject, administration is described as 'general' administration.[19] What are the reasons behind such lack of confidence in low-level administration? Quesnay fears that poor decisions could be made by civil servants and clerks because they are badly prepared to resist particular interests,[20] notably the mercantile interest which is contrary to the good government of the nation, or to œconomic government. The limited importance of low-level administration can also be seen in the way that it is subordinate to and defined by the nature of the government, so if the government becomes despotic, the administration itself is unable to establish order.[21] However, administration may have a positive sense when associated with government, with good government or, to use the specific term created by Quesnay, œconomic government.

Quesnay and the Birth of the Œconomic Government

As illustrated in the opening quotation, œconomic government ('gouvernement œconomique') is Quesnay's major linguistic innovation. There are about fifteen occurrences of this expression in the entries written for the *Encyclopédie*; the first one associates œconomic government with the name of Sully and also with the core of the Physiocratic theory:

> this great minister had grasped the true principles of œconomic government of the kingdom, establishing the wealth of the king, the strength of the State, the happiness of the people, in the revenue of the land, that is to say in agriculture and the external commerce of its products.[22]

Of interest here is that it is where the name of Sully is invoked that the connection between administration and œconomic government is the strongest. In the passage following the one cited in the epigraph, Quesnay talks up the wisdom of Sully in the 'œconomic administration of the State'.[23] This passage is all the more significant since Quesnay stresses the fact that Sully was in the beginning of his career a man of war before he became a great minister. This was a change that opened up an enduring opposition to the politics of war, destruction and plunder, all of which latter politics Quesnay rejects in several places.[24]

In his subsequent use of this expression Quesnay clarifies the core policy of œconomic government – this policy changes somewhat depending upon the topic of the entry in question, but the theoretical foundations are the same. Œconomic government is devoted to the management of real wealth, the net product generated by the agricultural sector of the economy: 'Thus, œconomic government must take care of the growth and the perpetuity of this revenue, all the other advantages that depend upon it will develop and sustain themselves'.[25] In the entry on taxes, Quesnay gives a different twist to this statement when he points out that taxes should not encroach on farmers' capital: 'The most important and inviolable rule of œconomic government is thus to make sure that taxes do not endanger the progress of agriculture'.[26] In the entry on population, the same idea is maintained, noting the population necessary to the effective functioning of the agricultural sector:

> The condition of the population and of the employment of men are thus the principal objects of œconomic government in any State, because it is from the work and industry of men that the fertility of the land stems, the monetary value of its production, and the good use of monetary wealth. Here are the four sources of abundance; they each concur in their mutual growth, but they cannot do so without the general administration of men, of goods, of productions.[27]

Here, Quesnay provides much more than a definition of œconomic government: the sentence can be read as a definition of what is called political economy, an expression that he does not use apart from the subtitle given to the entries written for the *Encyclopédie*. This emphasis on the agricultural sector gives hand to the critique of the mercantile interest, or the 'mercantile system (*système des commerçants*)',[28] which was always prone to leading the government astray.[29]

The link between administration and œconomic government is particularly strong where the reform of the taxation system is at stake. Quesnay's theory of wealth and, consequently, his theory of value and price, follow from the question of who should pay taxes and how they should be paid. This is clearly stated by Quesnay himself:

> A long time ago, it was said that taxes in themselves do not ruin the State, but instead the way that they were imposed. This has been understood, but nobody has sought to prove or elaborate this truth ... As a matter of fact, it would be necessary to know in detail the sources of the annual wealth of the State in order to set a proportional tax upon the fortune of subjects.[30]

So while Quesnay's position on wealth and taxation is clearly in line with major political economists such as Pierre de Boisguilbert and Jean-Baptiste Say, Adam Smith and David Ricardo, it is important to stress that the administrative dimension of the issue is of significance to Quesnay, as he stated explicitly when commenting on Naveau's *Financier citoyen*:

> It is not so much the excessive gains of financiers, but the immense sum paid to the lower ranks of the administration, the injustices and trouble in commerce, that prevent the beneficial progress that the author imagines ... This multitude of clerks busy with levying taxes upon goods is, in itself, a loss of men to the State: all these men paid by the nation do not produce by their work any wealth for the State, thus this expenditure and these men are nothing but a sheer loss to the kingdom.[31]

However, Quesnay explains that the kingdom can improve if the administration does its proper job: 'thus, if bad administration of the kingdom can dramatically diminish the revenues of the King, [good administration] can increase these revenues dramatically'.[32] In that case, thanks to its contribution to œconomic government, the government belongs to the productive class, as is the case when landowners manage their property well:

> Landowners can be considered as men who produce through management and the improvement of their property; the sovereign himself and his ministers contribute directly and generally to the growth of wealth through the œconomic government of the State. Upon this depends the prosperity of the nation, but it is necessary that the administration does not lose sight of the true source of the revenues of the kingdom.[33]

The connection between administration and œconomic government makes it necessary for Quesnay and the Physiocrats to seek a possible solution to the issue, and to propose the way in which the taxation system should be properly administered. Later on, œconomic government became a central concept, establishing the connection between the economic domain proper and the political domain. Quesnay made this clear in his *Maximes générales du gouvernement économique d'un royaume agricole* published in 1767, the last important text that he wrote in this area before turning to his (unsuccessful) essays on mathematics.

Œconomic Government, the Administration and the New Taxation System

Taxes were obviously among the major issues considered by Quesnay in the series of papers that he planned to publish in the *Encyclopédie*. Tax was an issue in the entry 'Fermiers', then developed in 'Grains' and in 'Hommes'; however, the entry 'Impôt' was especially devoted to what was a highly controversial topic during the Seven Years' War.

The war was hugely expensive, the French monarchy being hampered by its relative lack of access to the international financial market as compared with the British. The domestic political situation was also difficult. Louis XV was facing political pressure from the *parlements*, which were necessary to legitimize government legislation. This was particularly true for the laws relating to the levying of new taxes – notably the various 'vingtièmes', or even the compilation of a general cadastral register. The fiscal issue was rendered even more complex because of its connection to a religious issue, since the *parlements* were at that time adamant in seeking the expulsion of the Jesuit Order from the French kingdom.[34] If we leave aside the religious issue and focus on the fiscal problem, the political struggle between the *parlements* and the fiscal administration of the kingdom had various ramifications, one of them being the supposedly loathsome behaviour of local fiscal administrations. According to the objections – the so-called 'remontrances' – sent to the king by *parlements* or the *Cours des Aides*, they considered that it was the king's duty to intervene and end the unfettered despotic power of fiscal administration, a claim particularly well articulated in Malesherbes's writings.[35] Another important issue was the taxation of the commercial and administrative classes, among which were members of the *parlements* themselves, joining their personal interest to the defense of the interest of citizens suffering from the burden of taxation. In such circumstances, how could Physiocratic reform make any headway? The answer to this conundrum is provided by the *Théorie de l'impôt*, a book published in 1760 under Mirabeau's name only, even if it is clear that Quesnay's ideas were vital to it.[36]

At the root of the Physiocratic proposal is the concept of net product, that is to say the difference between the value of agricultural production and its cost. The logical solution to taxation is therefore to levy a single tax directly upon the net product, which amounts to saying that commercial and financial revenues will be ignored by the new fiscal administration. This straightforward solution clarifies matters, since objections to inquisitive administrative practices become irrelevant. However, this net product raises a more difficult problem. Mirabeau follows Quesnay, and argues that it is unfair to tax two pieces of land producing output of the same value when their costs of production differ. The tithe system was the classical example of this, being levied more heavily on the net product obtained on the least productive land, as a result of which the tax system was both unjust and a further drag on the agricultural sector. The problem is therefore: how is it possible to know not the value produced on a piece of land, but the net product obtained on that piece of land, without however relying on local administration and its politically unacceptable behaviour? Mirabeau has an answer to this problem: there is no need to impose upon the people and seek access to the 'secrets of the households' to establish the exact amount of the net product; existing leases provides all the information that is needed:

> In a word, a lease is the only reliable basis for the government when assessment of the net product, that is to say the revenue of the country, is at stake. It is only from this revenue that the government can take its share; the total of the leases is the total amount of the revenues of the nation, and it is on this sum that the share of the State can be levied, according to the rule set by necessity; this is the only way to achieve an enlightened agreement between the king and the nation, the necessary basis for good administration in the domain of finance.[37]

The market agreement between the landowner and the farmer is the solution, since the agreement states explicitly the amount of rent to be paid by the farmer to the landowner. Is this solution a decisive step in ending the obstruction of administration? Is not Mirabeau naïve in believing that the actual leases will be accessible to fiscal administration?

Mirabeau makes clear to the reader that he is fully aware that leases were already the basis of fiscal administration when the 'vingtièmes' and the 'dixièmes' were levied.[38] And he knows that the real leases were hidden, and false ones given to the fiscal administration. Hence there were frauds on the one side, and disappointments on the other, since the amount of taxes accruing to the government was smaller than expected. This had prompted the need to delve into the 'secrets of households' in order to obtain the real leases, providing a source of complaint for the *parlements*. Nevertheless, Mirabeau claims that the single tax on the net product, assessed through the leases, offers a solution because it is in the direct interest of farmers practising 'grande culture', or the capitalist form of husbandry – furthermore, according to the Physiocratic theory of the incidence of taxation, it is also in the direct interest of the landowners. These capitalistic farmers, with whom Quesnay dealt in his entry 'Fermiers', would not jeopardize their wealth by using counterfeit leases; they would have no interest in cheating since the taxes would be paid by the landowner, and not by themselves: '[farmers] would not conceal the agreement, notably because they have no interest in the diminution of a tax which does not concern them in any sense'.[39]

Would the farmers be ready to cheat, and then share with the landlord a portion of the taxes due to the government? Mirabeau's answer is in the negative. Such a strategy of tax avoidance would imply a complex system in which a counterfeit lease would have to be written to diminish the rent paid to landowners and then their taxes, and a part of that sum – a third in Mirabeau's example – would be left in the hands of the farmer. In exchange for that, Mirabeau supposes that the concealed part of the lease would be paid in advance to the landowner, so that the latter would be sure to get his full share. Such a system would cost farmers too much capital and, consequently, Mirabeau claims that the leases used would be the real ones, thus providing an accurate basis for the single tax.

Later on this issue is considered in great detail in Gabriel-François Le Trosne's *De l'administration provinciale et de la réforme des impôts*, a massive book in two volumes. No claim to originality is made for this book, since Le Trosne makes clear that he follows the 'true principles of administration' discovered only fifteen or twenty years ago – that is to say, with the publication of the *Théorie de l'impôt* – to apply these principles.[40] Nevertheless, the author offers a synthesis of two different strands of the Physiocratic doctrine of taxation, administration and politics.[41]

Following Quesnay and Mirabeau, Le Trosne stresses the very great cost of the present system of taxation since, according to his calculation, indirect taxes cost the nation twice the amount received by the king.[42] This cost is a severe obstacle to the growth of the net product and to the strength of the nation. How is it possible to end the deficiencies of administration that have brought this situation about? In line with Quesnay's later views and the views advocated by Pierre-Paul Le Mercier de la Rivière,[43] Le Trosne mentions the positive role played by public opinion, which is the true legislator in the Physiocratic view of politics.[44] However, one cannot rely on this political force in the case of taxation: first, because public opinion is mainly Parisian, and people with an interest in the vagaries of the present inefficient administration are numerous in that city.[45] Second, it will take a long time before men of letters are inducted into the true principles of the administration of taxes, and thus it will take too long before public opinion is able to play its role fully.[46] Happily enough, there is a more straightforward solution: 'Nobody but an authority enlightened as to its true and well-calculated interest can intervene in private interests'.[47]

So in line with the Physiocratic theory of legal despotism, Le Trosne's solution is emphatically associated with an enlightened government and thus with an active role given to (economic) experts. However, this example of a top-down system of administration is associated with local administration, strongly advocated by Mirabeau since the beginning of his intellectual career.[48] Thus, Le Trosne suggests maintaining local administration in the Pays d'État, and to create an administration of this kind in the Pays d'Élection.[49] The role of that administration would be to distribute the tax burden among the landowners, whatever their social status (nobility, clergy or the third estate). Who will do this? The landowners themselves, and they will do it for free. Why? Le Trosne reassesses the Physiocratic credo according to which proper administration of the tax system will increase the revenue of the landowners, so that their interest is aligned with the proper administration of the tax system. This is stated in the eulogy that Le Trosne imagines he would like to hear from the landowners' mouth:

> Our interests are the same as Yours [the King's interests]; and this common interest consists in getting the largest output from the land … It is time to overhaul the present management system, which makes You poorer and which makes our efforts fruitless.[50]

This common interest explains why the landowners would do it for free; a further argument comes from the fact that provincial assemblies will decide how to use a part of the product of the taxes. Finally, Le Trosne also mentions the symbolic remuneration associated with the honour of being elected as a member of the provincial assembly and, potentially, as a delegate to the national council, which is composed of members of provincial assemblies who meet once a year to discuss, with the king or with the Contrôleur général, issues related to fiscal administration.[51] Following Quesnay's ideas, this administration would base the tax burden upon the leases agreed between landowners and farmers. These leases would be held by a trustee or a public notary, so that the progress of cultivation and the revenue accruing to the landowner would be known every nine years, when the leases were renegotiated.[52] The new structure of fiscal administration would not be costly, since landowners would work for free and the former local administration would simply be suppressed.[53] According to his calculations, the total cost would be about six millions French livres,[54] which means a massive reduction of the cost of levying taxes, compared to the 167 million livres that indirect taxes cost.

Le Trosne is adamant in making clear that his administrative system should stay entirely under the command of the central administration, or government: notably, provincial assemblies would not have the power to ratify either taxes or the rate of taxation.[55] In the same line of thinking, as it is important to proceed to a general and uniform change in fiscal administration, the reform must be made by the government, so that members of the provincial assemblies would have nothing to do but to implement the reform as designed by the government:

> provincial administrations will be in charge of implementation, no more. It is not enough to send them a general plan; it is necessary to send them all the details, with instructions and examples, in such a way that the planned reform and the way to implement it would be the same everywhere.[56]

Central expertise in the government therefore remains crucial, even when local administration is recruited to the reformation of the tax system.

Conclusion

This study of the role attributed to government, administration and œconomic government in Quesnay's first economic writings prompts some general remarks. I would like to single out two conclusive comments.

First, the study of the role played by the administration within the reforms proposed by Quesnay and the Physiocrats demonstrates that the two strands of Physiocratic political theory are strongly connected. As explained in a previous study,[57] the political theory of the Physiocrats emphasizes economic expertise at the level of central government, notably when Quesnay and Le Mercier de la Rivière explain how necessary and useful it would be if higher civil servants and magistrates were instructed in the 'new science of political economy', implementing an œconomic government which was much needed to relieve the problems of the French economy. In this line of thinking the constitutional aspect is most innovative, as it is the case with Le Mercier's proposal to create a body of magistrates charged with assessing the conformity of any law with the natural order. The local administrative dimension is then left out. This is not the case with the other strand of thought, upheld by Mirabeau, Le Trosne and Dupont de

Nemours, who developed reform plans in which provincial assemblies would play a major role, helping to resolve the complex fiscal and political problems in which the kingdom was trapped. However, these two strands were not in conflict with each other, as explained above; both were compatible, provided that the lead was given to the central government, because the current administration was not thought reliable by the Physiocrats, from Quesnay's first writings to Le Trosne's massive books.

Second, a further point can be made to strengthen the link between these two strands of political thinking. Self-interested behaviour, and in some cases self-interested market behaviour, is the link from the king and government to farmers, landowners and merchants. This is particularly the case with the emphasis placed on leases as a basis for a satisfactory distribution of the fiscal burden. In that case, interest means market interest, which I interpret along Foucauldian lines:[58] the market is a crucial political device providing food to the population when police is unable to do so, but the market is also a social sphere producing truth, a device for producing 'veridiction'.[59] This explains why Le Mercier is so adamant in stressing that interest – the common interest in the maximal value of the net product – is the source of political cohesion in the agricultural kingdom. Once the true common interest is found and made clear to all citizens, government and administration can be properly designed to make this common interest flourish. And the rest of the society will follow suit, because everyone is interested in making this common interest more profitable. It is not virtue, but interest that is the basis of the behaviour of the various classes in the society; it is not virtue, but interest that is the basis of good administration. In that sense, the Physiocratic view contrasts sharply with that advocated by Jacques Necker in the long preface opening his famous *De l'administration des finances de la France*.[60] This strong connection between self-interested behaviour and the government–administration nexus is thus a further illustration of what the theory of the legislator in eighteenth-century France means, within the terms of French 'Philosophie économique' from Boisguilbert to Say.[61] This is the case even if there are significant differences between them, notably because while Quesnay and the Physiocrats are seeking good administration, they do not suggest that the goal is to achieve a minimal State:

> Maxim XXVII: The government should be less preoccupied by saving, and more in the spending necessary to the prosperity of the kingdom ... Maxim XXVIII: The administration of finance, whether in the levying of taxes, or in the expenditures of government, should not bring about the creation of monetary fortunes.[62]

In their view, it is the administration of the tax system which is central, not the total sum of taxes gathered.

Appendix: The Semantic Nexus

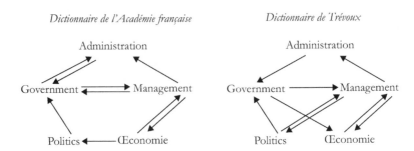

Figure 9.1: The semantic nexus.

An arrow between two words is present when an entry in the dictionary refers to one of the four other ones.

The density (45 per cent) of the two semantic networks is similar, with 9 arrows compared with 20 possible ones.

The aggregate score of Management ('Mesnager') is the highest (61 per cent, with 6 arrows sent and 5 received with 18 arrows possible); Government gets the next highest score (50 per cent, with 4 arrows sent and 5 arrows received). Management is maximally connected to Œconomy (four arrows of the four possible). Government and Œconomy are weakly connected (only one arrow of the four possible); in coining the expression 'œconomic government' Quesnay was decidedly innovative.

10 CONSTANT AS A READER OF SISMONDI

Francesca Sofia and Francesca Dal Degan[1]

I

Coppet's group – a 'cercle', as defined by Simone Balayé that 'ses membres n'ont à aucun moment tenté de baptiser'[2] – is an expression of informal sociability, cultural and intellectual interchange represents perhaps the only appropriate key to define it: 'un point de passage ou de cesure', as has been recently described, 'entre l'Europe du Midi et l'Europe du Nord, entre latinité et germanité, mais aussi entre les régimes des princes et les structures républicaines (patriciennes ou populaires)'.[3] Coppet's circle was not merely an academic or intellectual parlour, but for contemporary observers as well as for posterity it was an extraordinary vehicle for new ideas at an aesthetic, political and philosophical level. However, due to its informality, the group left only a few traces of the intense dialogue that took place among its protagonists.

In relation to the genesis of Benjamin Constant's two most important theoretical essays, *Principes de politique* and *Fragments d'un ouvrage abandonné sur la possibilité d'une constitution républicain dans un grand pays*, both written between 1800 and 1810 (a decade of intellectual splendour for Coppet's circle), and unpublished until the last century, it is relevant to recall the influence of the reading of *Des circonstances actuelles qui peuvent terminer la révolution et des principes qui doivent fonder la République en France* written by Mad. de Staël in 1798, which also remained a manuscript until its publication in 1906. Constant edited a partial copy of her writing and today it is considered to be one of the main elements for the development of his political reflection.[4] Recently a new book from Coppet's circle has become part of a list of those writings to be considered as cornerstones of the production of Constant's great political works: *Recherches sur les constitutions des peuples libres*, drafted by Sismondi during his exile in Pescia between 1798 and 1801, which Constant had in his possession between October 1801 and April 1802 in an unsuccessful bid to find a publisher.[5] Sismondi's writing seems to have provided a fundamental contribution to Constant's political reflection, that is, a critique of the General Will, as defined by Rousseau. Sismondi and Constant have different methods to approach and relate to the philosopher, who became the symbol of the revolution. Sismondi appears to be more dialogical and thus mindful of the role Rousseau played in Geneva's political debates, whereas Constant seems more critical, because of his personal history in the events of the revolution. Nevertheless, they both equate the concept of absolute sovereignty with unlimited authority and posit the primacy of individual rights over civil laws. Moreover, they draw a dividing line between the General Will and the Will of All and justify the rights of a majority to pragmatically overwhelm political minorities. By way of example, it is worth mentioning the following quotations by Sismondi and by Constant:

> Je regarde comme tyrannique l'usurpation faite par la communauté de tous les droits de ses membres. Et pour donner des exemples, je regarde comme tyrannique la vente de cinq mille citoyens Athéniens, privés de leur droits et réduits à l'esclavage sous l'administration de Périclès, parce qu'ils étaient nés d'une étrangère; décret atroce, qui en le supposant véritable, n'excède point le pouvoir que Rousseau abandonne à la société. Je regarde comme tyrannique plusieurs des institutions de Lycurgue, qui entravent la vie privée de chaque citoyen, je regarde come tyrannique la plupart des lois émanées dans l'Europe moderne du fatal système mercantile, et toutes les restrictions sur le commerce et l'industrie qui en sont la suite. Je regarde comme tyrannique, malgré sa futilité, jusqu'à la loi du Czar Pierre, pour forcer ses sujets à renoncer à leur barbe.[6]

> Lorsque cette autorité s'étend sur des objets hors de sa sphère, elle devient illégitime. Elle était tyrannique la vente de 5000 citoyens sous Périclès, parce qu'ils étaient nés d'une étrangère. Elles étaient tyranniques les institutions de Lycurgue sur la vie privée des citoyens. Elles sont tyrannique nos lois sur le système mercantile ... Elle était tyrannique la loi de Pierre Ier pour faire couper la barbe de ses sujets.[7]

This is not the only direct quotation, using almost the exact wording as his young friend. Further proof of profound intellectual esteem is evident in a letter from Constant to Sismondi dated 23 April 1803, when the latter was about to begin writing *Histoire des Républiques Italiennes* encouraged by Coppet's high regard:

> Je ne sais comment je m'ingère à vous donner des conseils, à vous qui a 30 ans avez déjà élevé un superbe édifice aux bons principes et réuni plus de connaissances qu'il n'en faut pour composer douze de nos publicistes les plus instruits.[8]

Reference to the contribution of Sismondi's writing to resolving some of the conceptual problems that were the focus of Constant's political reflection, such as the connection between liberalism and participation, appears very clear. In fact, Constant does not hesitate to define *principes* (just like the future title of his political essay) employing the theoretical structure provided by the young intellectual from Geneva.

Although the critique of Rousseau is certainly the most significant legacy of reading Sismondi's literature, Constant's first important political writings include other relevant references to Sismondi's works, to both the *Recherches* and the first volumes of *Histoire des Républiques* as a sort of *Additions* which should have been put in the essays in the final version developed by Constant in 1810.

A textual quotation from *Recherches* 'transmigrated' into many writings by Constant in a practice not uncommon to the intellectual from Lausanne. It is about the observation concerning the *Ordinamenti di giustizia* by Giano della Bella, assumed in Florence between 1293 and 1295, and considered in Sismondi's *Recherches* as a springboard for the anti-nobility legislation adopted by revolutionary France.[9] Constant resumes this analogy both in *Fragments*, in *Principes* and ultimately in the review of *Considérations sur la Révolution* by Mad. de Staël published in 1818 in 'Minerve française'.[10] What appeared to Sismondi as an unconsidered parallelism, as written in *Recherches*: 'Je sais que ces principes se trouvent opposés à ceux de nos législateurs durant la Révolution, mais il me paroissent résulter si évidement de tout l'ensemble de l'histoire d'Italie, que je n'ai pu les dissimuler',[11] becomes an indisputable observation in Constant's writing in 1818:

> A la fondation de la république française, on a eu pour but, comme dans les républiques italiennes du moyen âge, de repousser des conquérants plutôt que de donner des droits égaux à des citoyens, et l'on a de la sorte relevé momentanément la noblesse par une distinction nouvelle, la persécution. Forte de ce privilège, elle a combattu avec avantage les institutions qui l'opprimaient.[12]

Two other references to Sismondi's historical studies are found in one of the most original chapter of *Fragments*, the one concerning the connections between neutral power and executive and legislature powers. The first one, pertaining to the historic experience of the Otto di Guardia e di Balia of the Republic of Florence, probably taken from *Recherches*,[13] is negatively regarded by Constant:

> Il faut un pouvoir constitutionnel qui ait toujours ce que la ballia avait d'utile, et qui n'ait point celle qu'avait de dangereux, c'est-à-dire qui ne puisse ne condamner, ni incarcérer, ni dépouiller, ni proscrire, mais qui se borne à priver du pouvoir les hommes ou les assemblées qui ne sauraient plus longtemps le posséder sans péril.[14]

Whereas the second one, from *Histoire des Républiques*, regarding the right to dissolve the Council of Ten granted to the aristocracy of Venice when they refused to proceed with the periodic renewal of its members, is mentioned as a positive example. Almost paraphrasing Constant's words in his essay, Sismondi asserted:

> Il faut, comme on le pratiquait à Venise, que le premier attaque les fasse rentrer immédiatement dans le rang des citoyens, qu'on les dépouille du pouvoir de nuire, au lieu de penser de les punir. Qu'on les dépouille par un simple refus de suffrage, qui n'expose personne à leur vengeance, qui ne demande point le déploiement d'un grand courage civil.[15]

Two last quotations from *Histoire des Républiques* are worth some attention. The first one concerns the preference given by Constant in *Fragments* to exercising legislative power without remuneration. It is interesting to note that in his original writing Constant refers to the example of the English constitution, whereas in his later *Addition*, reminiscent of Sismondi, he refers to the city-state of Florence, explicitly promoting the advantages offered by a republican form of government. In fact, the section of Sismondi's writing referred to by Constant states:

> Dans une république, l'honneur de gouverner est une récompense suffisante, pour le travail du gouvernement; mais lorsque la bonne renommée est la seule rémunération des magistrats, aucun d'eux ne néglige de l'obtenir; s'ils reçoivent au contraire un salaire, leur but principal est atteint, pourvu qu'ils soient payés, et leur emploi ne leur paroît pas infructueux, encore qu'ils n'aient mérité ni l'amour du peuple, ni le respect de la postérité.[16]

In the title of his essay *Principes de politique*, Constant refers precisely to those principles described as 'applicables à tous les gouvernements'. Is it indifference in relation to forms of government that leads him to recall the Republic of Florence? Or perhaps Constant offers this quotation in order to refer to a specific form of 'republican government', entirely in line with his idea of liberalism. According to his view, placing an individual on a pedestal represents a basic condition for him to be seen as an ethical and political subject, capable of understanding institutions, of judging and possibly changing them; a scenario in which political participation extends further than the mere right to vote and plays an essential role. Similarly, liberty goes far beyond the atomistic existence of individuals competing against each other. Moreover, in a letter addressed to Sismondi, Constant seems to feel part of a re-emerging republican tradition, which was particularly important to his friend from Geneva: 'Vive la République de Consigal',[17] he wrote on 23 November 1807, 'il n'y a presque cet État au monde où il y ait encore du talent, de la noblesse et de l'energie'.[18] Praise for the ideal republic imagined by a twelve-year-old Sismondi, which outlines the main aspects of his political background in terms of classic republicanism, suggests that Constant shares that same political experience with his friend from Geneva.

Lastly, it is important to mention a long quotation by Sismondi added to the second chapter of Volume 16 of *Principes de politique*, regarding the 'première différence entre l'état social des anciens et celui des modernes'.[19] It concerns a little-known page by Sismondi written as a marginal comment on the oligarchic Republic of Venice, which merits an unabridged quotation:

> Deux choses cependant sont dignes de remarque dans ce despotisme républicain. La première, c'est la consolation que les citoyens peuvent trouver de la perte de leur liberté civile, dans l'acquisition ou le partage d'un grand pouvoir. Cette compensation n'existe que dans un Etat où les citoyens sont en petit nombre, et où, par conséquent,

la chance de parvenir au pouvoir suprême, est assez grande ou assez prochaine, pour adoucir le sacrifice journalier que chaque citoyen fait de ses droits à ce pouvoir. Ainsi, dans les républiques de l'antiquité, il n'existait aucune liberté civile; le citoyen s'était reconnu esclave de la nation dont il faisait partie; il s'abandonnait en entière aux décisions du souverain, sans contester au législateur le droit de contrôler toutes ses actions, de contraindre en tout ses volontés; mais, d'autre part, il était lui-même, à son tour, ce souverain et ce législateur. Il connaissait la valeur de son suffrage dans une nation assez petite pour que chaque citoyen fût une puissance, et il sentait que c'était à lui-même, comme souverain, qu'il sacrifiait, comme sujet, sa liberté civile.[20]

It is surprising how the difference between the Liberty of the Ancients and the Liberty of the Moderns described by Sismondi is outlined with the same terms used by Constant. As has been noted elsewhere,[21] on the one hand, the progressive historicization of the portrayal of the ancients, developed through the attendance of Gottingen School, leads Constant to consider the two Liberties as different though comparable, discarding any prejudice towards them. On the other hand, considering Sismondi, there is evidence of an accomplished historicization of the methods of political participation within the city-state that, again in *Recherches,* has been described as a viable path for contemporaneity.[22] As already written by Constant to Sismondi in 1803: 'L'histoire en ne vous permettant qu'une phrase après un fait vous trace des bornes qui préservent des divagations en même tems qu'elle sont utiles au talent, parce qu'elles forcent à la précision'.[23] Therefore, the study of history, whether it is the history of religions for Constant, or the history of the medieval republics for Sismondi, enabled both philosophers to adjust principles to each context in order to achieve a definition of some of their shared political beliefs. The praise for the historians of his generation, included in his final essay from *Mélanges de littérature et de politique* of 1829,[24] deserves to be considered as not only an implicit tribute to Sismondi (considering the fact that the first pages recall Constant's review of *Histoire des Républiques Italiennes*), but also as an intense dialogue that took place between the two intellectuals in the most prolific season in Coppet's circle.

There is plenty of evidence of a congruence with his friend from Geneva. He recalled this in his review of Charles Dunoyer in 1826, which was merged three years later into *Mélanges*, in which he describes the distinction expressed by the author 'entre la liberté des anciens et celle des modernes, et entre l'état industriel et l'état guerrier ... fort ingénieuse', although he admitted that it was not that original: 'Plusieurs écrivains, M. Sismondi notamment et l'auteur de cet Essai, avaient, il y a quatorze ans, dit les mêmes choses à peu près dans les mêmes mots'.[25] He had already pointed it out during a famous speech made in 1819 at the Athénée Royale, in which he concluded with almost the same words used by Sismondi in his caveat addressed to the rulers in the final pages of *Histoire* presented a year before.

> La liberté des anciens, comme leur philosophie – Sismondi wrote – avait pour but la vertu; la liberté des modernes, comme leur philosophie, ne se propose que le bonheur. La meilleure leçon à tirer de la comparaison de ces systèmes, serait d'apprendre à les combiner l'un avec l'autre ... Le législateur, désormais, ne doit plus perdre de vue la sécurité des citoyens, et les garanties que les modernes ont réduites en système; mais il doit se souvenir aussi qu'il faut chercher encore leur plus grand développement moral ... Et c'est en multipliant leurs droits, en les appelant au partage de la souveraineté; en redoublant leur intérêt pour la chose publique, qu'il leur apprendra aussi à connaître leurs devoirs, et qu'il leur donnera en même temps et le désir et la faculté de les remplir.[26]

And Constant on his behalf:

> Loin donc, Messieurs, de renoncer à aucune des deux espèces de liberté dont je vous ai parlé, il faut, je l'ai démontré, apprendre à les combiner l'une avec l'autre ... En respectant leurs droits individuels, en ménageant leur indépendance, en ne troublant point leurs occupations, elles doivent pourtant consacrer leur influence sur la chose publique, les appeler à concourir, par leurs déterminations et par leurs suffrages, à l'exercice du pouvoir, leur garantir un droit de contrôle et de surveillance par la manifestation de leurs opinions, et les formant de la sorte par la pratique à ces fonctions élevées, leur donner à la fois et le désir et la faculté de s'en acquitter.[27]

Both were confident that the ancients could provide the political debate with important elements for researching modernity. However, it is interesting to underline that, unlike Constant, Sismondi believed that the republics of the ancients, medieval communes above all, did not stand against the modern republics by giving priority to slavery over commerce. Sismondi sticks to the guidelines provided by Adam Smith, he does not see any contradiction between the economy of the moderns and republican liberty, both described as a result of a renewed urban life scenario. It is instead the great relevance that commerce has in the process to the definition of the liberty of the moderns by Constant that leads him to become a careful reader of another work by Sismondi: *De la richesse commerciale*.

II

Historical changes induced by revolution and by reaction[28] in Geneva influenced the genesis of Constant's *Principes de politique* and Sismondi's *De la richesse commerciale*. Revolutionary winds advocated egalitarianism which was anathema to the institutional organization of Genevan tradition. The reactionary phase (from 1795 onwards) and annexation by France after 1798 jeopardized the independence of civil society and reinforced executive power,[29] threatening to destroy Geneva's historical and cultural identity characterized by a long experience of 'sociability'. As Sismondi wrote in *Statistique du Départment du Leman* proposing 'une étude analytique et sociologique d'une région administrative',[30] and Constant echoed in his political writings, the invisible wealth of this region rested on immaterial 'capital' composed of civic values, public virtues, moral sentiments created within an articulated and dynamic social and institutional structure (*cércles*, public schools, press). Thus, this personal experience shaped Sismondi's and Constant's perception of the effects of arbitrary politics and became a pivotal element of all their intellectual research[31] also when considered in the economic dimension.

Sismondi's *Richesse commerciale*, with Adam Smith's *Wealth of Nations*, constitutes an important source of inspiration for Constant's reflections on economic subjects. In spite of Raynaud's affirmation: 'les principes *économiques* libéraux, chez les plus grands, ne constituent nullement un thème central',[32] economic themes absorb large parts of Constant's works. In his *Principes* three chapters are dedicated to economic arguments: X 'De l'action de l'autorité sociale sur la propriété', XI 'De l'impôt' and XII 'De la juridiction de l'autorité sur l'industrie et la population'. Economic themes were developed in the later works of Constant too, for example in the *Commentaires sur l'ouvrage de Filangeri* (1822), where the second part deals with 'impôts', 'commerce des grains', 'population'. The important role of economics in Constant's reasoning is demonstrated not only by the space it is allocated in his works, but also by the role Constant attributes to economic activity: it is one of the most important spaces of mediation within civil society enabling new forms of participation of the moderns in common life and ensuring that citizens are not dependent on decisions and power of others for subsistence.

The centrality of economy in building social order had been learned by Adam Smith and originally developed within Coppet's tradition of thought. Thus in Smith's footsteps, Sismondi wrote in *Richesse Commerciale*:

> Tenons-nous en à l'économie politique. Il ne devrait pas être difficile, ce me semble, de faire sentir aux hommes tout l'intérêt d'une science qui a pour but d'augmenter les richesses, ou, en d'autres termes, de multiplier les jouissances, de le mettre à la porté d'un plus grand nombre d'hommes et de les étendre plus loin ... tout aussi, en l'étudiant, lui verraient réfléchir la lumière sur l'objet le plus habituel de leur pensées et de leur désirs. Il n'est aucun des intérêts journaliers de chaque citoyen qui ne tienne par quelque côté à l'économie politique ... la rente des terres du cultivateur et du propriétaire, l'intérêt des fonds du capitaliste, les profits du commerce, les salaires des journaliers, les dépenses de tous les membres de la société et les jouissances qu'ils obtiennent en retour, tout se règle d'après les principes dont l'économie politique peut seule donner la clef.[33]

And Constant on his behalf attributed a fundamental role to work in creating morality and stability in social order:

> Ce qui rend le travail la cause la plus efficace de moralité, c'est l'indépendance où l'homme laborieux se trouve des autres hommes et la dépendance où il est de sa propre conduite et de l'ordre, de la suite, de la regularité qu'il met dans sa vie.[34]

Work, perceived in its double historical 'nature' as an exercise based on manual skills and intellectual acquisitions 'qui ont accrus les capacités sociales de prevoir à la subsistence', needs to be exercised in a social space of concrete liberty which, in Constant's thought, can be ensured by property.

> La propriété est au service du travail, de la division du travail base du perfectionne-ment de tous les arts et de toutes les sciences...La propriété foncière influe sur le caractère et la destinée de l'homme pour la nature même des soins qu'elle exige. Le cultivateur se livre à des occupations constantes et progressives. Il contracte ainsi la régularité dans ses habitudes. Le hasard qui est une grande source d'immoralité, parce qu'il bouleverse tous les calculs et par conséquent ceux de la morale, n'est jamais de rien dans la vie de l'agriculteur.[35]

This position echoes the message that Sismondi offered in *Essais sur les constitutions des peuples libres* and revisited in *Richesse Commerciale*:

> Qu'on se rappelle toujours que le Gouvernement de l'Amérique a été fait, pour un Peuple chez lequel on ne connait point de pauvre condamné à l'être toujours, point d'homme qui ait intérêt au désordre, ou qui soit indifférent à la chose publique, point d'homme qui fasse son métier, ou sa gloire de son oisiveté, et qu'on n'attribue point ces qualité à une éducation civique, cette éducation des Américains qui fait aussi partie de leur bonheur, naît ainsi que leur vertus (et je crois l'avoir prouvé) d'une autre cause, d'une cause plus éloignée, de la nature des propriété de ce Peuple; cause sur laquelle tous les efforts des philosophes politiques, ne peuvent acquérir qu'une bien légère influence.[36]

In particular, in the opinion of both authors, property rights are the basis for the circular and cumulative flow at the core of social progress: labour, property, leisure, education, liberty. In fact, property guarantees individuals mastery of the spatial and temporal dimension of life, ensuring control of the instruments of their subsistence (independence), and ensuring a space to mature and make visible their interests in the light of aspirations to the common good: 'Sous le régime de la liberté, l'intérêt personnel est l'allié le plus éclairé, le plus constant, le plus utile de l'intérêt général'.[37]

When conceived as a sort of positional right, in the words of Sismondi, property enables active participation in civic life through the expression of one's identity (mainly through work activities), and access to a space of plural rela-tionships (in particular the area of market exchange). Having a position from which to exercise direct participation in civil life is a condition necessary to attain knowledge and contribute to the production of social values – the *opinion publique* in Sismondi's and Constant's terms – through personal intellectual activity, and, at the same time, to control the economic process. The exercise of one's capabilities and relational attitudes is a necessary condition for gaining knowledge and participating in the identification of social values, as well as in the control of the economic process in its productive and distributional aspects.

If an individual is devoid of opinion and perspective, exclusion from social functions may occur.

When property is considered as an instrument to manage the temporal dimension of human activities, it reveals its main value as a way of guaranteeing stability to society by giving individual interests the possibility of maturing and enlightening, 'le loisir indispensable à l'acquisition des lumières, à la rectitude du jugement ... qualités propres à l'exercice du droit de cité'.[38]

Thus, property is the institution which enables the advantage of the necessary distance from the flow of time allowing availability for personal education and production of culture.

Following this reasoning, another element of Constant's economic perspective becomes clearer: the preference for land ownership in assessing the most effective resources and institutions for a peaceful social development.

Thus, Constant wrote: 'Une ferme est une patrie en diminutif ... (elle) parle à l'imagination, aux souvenirs, à la partie morale de l'homme'.[39]

Echoing Sismondi who, from *Ressources de la Toscane* to *Etudes*, never ceases to attribute to agricultural labour associated with land ownership (or shared ownership as in *metayage*) the most powerful way to ensure independence and moral development so that 'L'intérêt de la nation, celui du consommateur et celui de chaque capitaliste, exigent donc que les premiers capitaux disponibles soient employés à l'avancement de l'agriculture'.[40]

By contrast with the more instantaneous operations required by industrial labour, Constant and Sismondi underlined the superiority of agricultural labour in maturing individual interests and developing the moral and intellectual part of people without eliminating the possibility of attaining the same goals in commercial and manufacturing activities. In fact, if land ownership is more efficient in creating a stable social order, 'la propriété foncière garantit la stabilité ... la propriété industrielle assure l'indépendance des individus ... à travers la création pour la liberté, de l'industrie e du commerce du crédit'.[41]

The approach of Constant and the young Sismondi was defined schematically as Smithian and considered as based on the anthropological view of individuals motivated by their own interests and by the idea that social order and common good are the spontaneous and unintentional outcomes of the independent actions of self-interested human beings. However, social dynamics have to be rooted in individual interests but these interests have to be nourished by the physical presence and participation of citizens in intellectual and cultural life, and in slow processes of integration of their concrete existence in the historical process of 'civilization'.

Conceived as a space for modern participation in common life, property can reveal its conventional nature: in fact, in Sismondi's footsteps, Constant holds that property is not a 'natural right' but the outcome of social contract:

> Le lecteur a pu remarquer que, parmi les considérations que nous avons alléguées pour déterminer le rang éminent que doit occuper la propriété dans nos associations politiques, aucune n'a été puisée dans la nature métaphysique de la propriété même. Nous ne l'avons considérée que comme une convention sociale.[42]

Sismondi's and Constant's pragmatic idea of the social contract, by contrast with the 'métaphysique du contrat social' in Constant's words,[43] is conceived in order to identify and defend the integrity of civil spaces, such as labour spaces, from political interference. It serves to ensure the existence of the civil sphere in which liberty is perceived as infinitely renewable ways of being free and that is the basis of the perception and experience of personal development and concrete *Bonheur*.[44] In its economic dimension liberty has a sort of depth that largely corresponds to the possibility of activating human capabilities, a possibility contained within the acknowledgement of human rights. Government is called to operate in order to recognize and distribute equal rights to all citizens so as to allow free expression of capabilities in a way that makes this approach similar to the contemporary reflection of Amartya Sen. In fact, liberty becomes effective only when it is shared by all the social parties; it is attained only if every citizen can enjoy equal conditions of well-being.[45]

Therefore, in the nature of property, conceived as the right to use 'capabilities', the form of its sharing is written: 'C'est la circulation de la propriété qui garantit la justice de l'institution. Cette circulation est dans la nature des choses. Il suffit de ne pas l'entraver.'[46]

A large distribution of property among citizens was invoked by Constant as well by Sismondi in order to contribute to the establishment of an open-access economic space within society where every citizen could benefit from the free exercise of his skills, thus attaining independence. Moreover, the argument developed by Sismondi in Book 3 of *Richesse Commerciale* against monopolies, prohibition, companies and incentives, provides substantial material for Constant's reasoning on economic functioning. At this level, *Richesse commerciale* constitutes a matrix-text for Constant's *Principes de Politique*, for example when Constant observed 'Le commerce vit de liberté; mais le commerçant peut s'enrichir par les entraves dont il entoure ses compétiteurs',[47] revisiting the pivotal idea developed in *Richesse commerciale* that commerce is a place where liberty and well-being can be enjoyed and created, but only within some important institutional conditions and moral dynamics. The market is perceived as a public realm, a meeting place in which products of labour are displayed and personal contributions to the common good are recognized. The market is a civil area within which citizens meet and are exposed to each other's opinions. Moreover, through market exchange citizens can experience another kind of liberty: personal liberty which consists of non-submission of one's destiny to another's decisions and is possible only in the absence of slavery or of hierarchical relationships based on status. When government adjusts or decides to give a direction to individual and civil preferences, it unbalances the social order with the weight of its authority. This imbalance can only be avoided in a society based on a decentralized structure of power and an intense practice of shared participation in public life. In this sense the position taken by Constant and Sismondi against strong political intervention in economic and civil life become clearer. It does not respond to an explicit agreement with the liberal credo of *laissez faire* based on the substantial identification of human motivation with self-interest, but to the need to defend the fragile but powerful dynamics of common living within civil society which are grounded on richer and more complex human motivations:

> Voyez en Portugal le privilège de la Compagnie des vins occasionner d'abord des émeutes, nécessiter par ces émeutes des supplices barbares, décourager le commerce par le spectacle de ces supplices et porter enfin par une suite de contraintes et de cruautés une foule de propriétaires à arracher eux-mêmes leurs vignes et à détruire dans leur désespoir la source même de leurs richesses, pour qu'elles ne servissent plus de prétexte à tous les genres de vexations.[48]

This revisits Chapter 6 on 'Compagnies de commerce' in the third part of *Richesse Commerciale*.

State intervention, in this sense, becomes necessary when one social stakeholder threatens to overwhelm the others by accumulating power or wealth that obstructs the access of all citizens to common civil spaces such as markets. The negative effects produced are linked to the influence and the invisible action exercised by these interfering acts on motivations and moral dynamics. It is a question of attributing adequate conditions and legitimate spaces to human motivations recognizing their real subjects. In relation to economic values, Constant wrote:

> Il y a dans cette question une partie morale ; mais l'opinion seule peut prononcer sur cette partie morale et elle prononce sagement. Solon ne voulut point fixer à Athènes le taux de l'intérêt. Mais on y regardait comme infâmes ceux qui exigeaient des intérêts immodérés.[49]

And about incentives: 'Les encouragements de l'autorité portent une atteinte très grave à la moralité des classes industrielles. La morale se compose de la suite naturelle des causes et des effets. Déranger cette suite, c'est nuire à la morale.'[50]

In particular, incentives expose citizens to hazard, subverting the order established through slow a process of confrontation: 'Les encouragments pour l'industrie sont une espèce de jeu'.[51]

Incentives destroy the spirit of emulation and imagination in citizens' capacity to form economic motivations and, changing reality, make interests more complex and reactive. Instantaneous acts of the Legislator cannot replace the longer process of interest formation within social, horizontal relationships.

Following from Sismondi (chs 4–9 of Book 2, *Richesse Commerciale*) the argument in favour of imposing a reasonable level of taxes on citizens stems from the recognition that the real source of wealth is labour, *industrie*, and so it is reasonable to leave to 'industrie les moyens' to identify real needs in society and to organize an adequate productive response.

The complexity of this conception of liberty enables clarifying why it is simplistic to ascribe these authors to the liberal tradition based on the mere fact that they acted without compulsion and without external impositions. Such clarification fosters a better understanding of how their thinking may refer to values entrusted with the idea of a common good. Sismondi and Constant attempt to resolve the issue of conciliating different interests by marrying the Smithian vision of the role that interests play in supporting processes of economic and social development, with the ideas established in Coppet's circle, in which Rousseau's social contract theory was interpreted in favour of concrete participation in civil life. In particular, Coppet, like a 'magic lantern',[52] enabled a reinterpretation of the triptych of the French revolution, *liberté, égalité, fraternité* through the lens of Swiss cultural tradition, a culture with roots in an original conception of mediating instruments and spaces (institutions), that in the very fact of being 'shared', have the capacity to change society. Coppet's group was a place for 'forging politics of mediation'[53] focusing on the role of social institutions for the achievement of liberty and well-being. In so doing it marks the emergence of a modern perspective that, by creating 'systems of order that lay *outside* the political',[54] comes to challenge traditional authority. 'Society' and individual systems of choices and actions, among which commercial economy, are the main places to be considered for institutional germination and change. In this sense, Coppet's intellectual message corroborated the observation of Hirschman: 'In the Eighteenth Century the idea that social order could be an important factor for human happiness became central and this idea connected itself with the modern conscience that happiness could be engineered by changing the social order'.[55]

11 FRENCH LIBERAL ECONOMISTS AND THE 'LABOUR QUESTION' BEFORE AND DURING THE REVOLUTION OF 1848

Jean-Pierre Potier

Introduction

In France, during the 1840s, the 'labour question', as a main component of the 'social question', was discussed by a broad spectrum of people (economists, social reformers, paternalist entrepreneurs, social Catholics, socialists, and so forth), and so we find a wide range of suggestions for solving the problem. The 1840s is the period of the *Monarchie de Juillet*, and of the February Revolution of 1848, which ended with the (very short-lived) Second Republic. The economic depression began in 1847 and the French economy was in a depression until 1851. Textile industries, metallurgy and railroads were seriously affected, and unemployment strongly increased. Workers' misery was therefore one of the causes of the February Revolution of 1848.

This period is a very interesting test for studying the way in which the 'labour question' was tackled by the liberal economists. So, we will focus our attention on the so-called 'school' that emerges with the birth of the *Journal des économistes* in 1841 and the foundation of the *Société d'économie politique de Paris* in 1842. Rightly, Schumpeter said that this group had a 'too exclusive concentration upon economic policy' and 'lacked interest in purely scientific questions'.[1] Inside this group, broadly speaking, it is possible to distinguish two families:

the ultra-liberal economists: mainly Charles Dunoyer (1796–1862), Frédéric Bastiat (1801–50), Léon Faucher (1803–54), Joseph Garnier (1813–81) and Gustave de Molinari (1819–1912); these orthodox economists were the best supporters of the natural laws of political economy and the most uncompromising about the arbitrariness of the State.

the moderate liberal economists: mainly Adolphe-Jérôme Blanqui (1798–1854), Louis Wolowski (1810–76) and Michel Chevalier (1806–79); these economists were more interested in the 'labour question' and its solutions.

According to Charles Dunoyer, the industrial regime would improve the standard of living of all categories of the population thanks to free competition, which imposes itself in the long run, in spite of certain obstructions. One cannot charge the industrial regime for having caused pauperism,[2] whose causes are to be sought rather in several vices of the working class, in irresponsible individual behaviour, more precisely the idleness, improvidence and immorality, and also the 'bestial fertility' of the people in question.[3] Adolphe Blanqui, Louis Wolowski and Michel Chevalier do not support such a point of view. According to Blanqui, the cause of pauperism is mostly in the development of the manufacturing system, in the 'excessive competition', in the submission of workers to machines, but also in the industrial and commercial isolation, in protectionism which closes the markets and keeps the wages very low. According to Louis Wolowski and Michel Chevalier, the cause of pauperism is the insufficiency of production; it is not a problem of distribution of wealth. So industrialization, the increase of production thanks to mechanization, and the rise of wages will enable, in the long run, the solution of the labour question.[4]

During the 1840s, all these liberal economists denounced the utopian character of the ideas and programmes of the socialists. They criticized the ideas of the followers of Saint-Simon, Fourier, Cabet, but also of Pierre Leroux, Philippe Buchez and Louis Blanc. But this criticism reached a crisis point in 1848 when the liberal economists were fighting against the 'right to labour' and the propositions of the *Commission du Luxembourg* (see below).

The French liberal economists' points of view on the 'labour question' before and during the 1848 Revolution will be presented in three parts. The first part (pp. 148–51) deals with the question of liberty of work and of industrial legislation. The second part (pp. 151–3) deals with the question of the association and the 'organization of labour'. The third part (pp. 153–5) deals with the specific question of the 'right to labour'.

Liberty of Work and Industrial Legislation

The French liberal economists claimed the 'liberty of work' (*liberté du travail*). They referred to the *Édit* of 9 February 1776, related to the abolition of the corporative system (*jurandes* and *maîtrises*) in which Turgot supported the *droit de travailler*.[5] Therefore, according to them the *droit de travailler* consisted in the liberty of work, the liberty of industry, not to be confused with the right to labour (*droit au travail*) about which we will speak further.[6] Accordingly, the liberty of work marked the end of governmental regulation and of monopolies. The liberty of work was an integral part of the individual property rights. The individuals had their own industrial abilities (natural and acquired) and their application should not undergo any obstruction. The conception of the property rights defended by the French liberal economists was founded on natural law.[7] According to them, the property rights existed before society and are natural: this implies the inequality of condition. Consequently, any change by the State of the distribution of property would be dangerous.[8]

The liberty of work (*la liberté du travail*) must be accompanied by equal circumstances (*l'égalité dans le travail*) by means of free competition. So, the labour market must function with the play of supply and demand and with flexibility of wages, without any restriction. However, during the 1840s, this idea of the competitive labour market was the object of violent criticisms by the socialists, for example, by Louis Blanc in his book *Organization of Labour* [*Organisation du travail*] (first edn, 1839).

Concerning the labour market, the question of collective action of workers arises. In France, the law Le Chapelier (14–17 June 1791),[9] which prevents coalitions between masters but especially between workers, was reinforced by the law of twenty-second Germinal an XI (12 April 1803) on the 'police des manufactures' and further by the *Code pénal* – articles 410 to 416 (1810).[10] During the 1840s, collective action by workers was discussed among the liberal economists. In fact, they were very much divided on this question. Certain liberal economists, for example Charles Dunoyer, were entirely against the right of coalition. However, most liberal economists did not forget the points of view of Adam Smith and Jean-Baptiste Say, so they proclaimed the liberty of coalition and they wished to repress only its abuses (intimidation and violence). This is the situation in the case of, for example, Louis Wolowski and Michel Chevalier, but also in the case of Joseph Garnier, Frédéric Bastiat and Gustave de Molinari.

Joseph Garnier felt that the 'free and peaceful coalition' leading to strikes to obtain a wage increase was legitimate, because it 'results from the principle of property and that of liberty of work'.[11] The law should be restricted to punish violence. Gustave de Molinari shared the same opinion; according to him, the prohibition of coalitions draws the balance in favour of masters. In fact, coalitions are necessary because of the nature of the commodity traded on labour markets: labour, just like oranges, is a perishable good![12] And, in *Les Soirées de la Rue Saint-Lazare* (1849), Molinari proposed the creation of true *Bourses du travail* at regional and national levels, but also at international level.[13]

During the February Revolution of 1848, the liberty of association for workers was proclaimed and the law Le Chapelier suspended. But shortly afterwards, the laws of 15 March 1849 against coalitions and of 27 November 1849 against strikes would restore the content of the law Le Chapelier.[14] On 17 November 1849, when the National Assembly was voting the law against strikes, Frédéric Bastiat said:

> You recognize yourselves that under the influence of your legislation supply and
> demand are no more *à deux de jeu*, because the coalition of entrepreneurs cannot be
> asserted; and it is obvious: two, three entrepreneurs lunch together, make a coalition,
> anybody does not know anything of it. That of the workers will be always asserted
> because it is done openly. Since the ones escape your law and the others do not escape
> from it, it has as a necessary result to weigh on supply and not to weigh on demand,
> to alter, at least when it takes effect, the natural rate of wages, and in a systematic and
> permanent way.[15]

As regards working hours, the debates led to the distinction between two problems: the question of working hours for children and of working hours for adult
workers.

Concerning the first problem, the government of Louis-Philippe adopted the
law of 22 March 1841. This law regulated the work of children in the 'new industries', namely in factories with more than twenty workers, which was quite rare at
this time. According to this law, the work of children under 8 years was prohibited. Night work was prohibited until children were 13 years old. From 8 to 12
years, the daily working hours were limited to eight hours. From 12 to 16 years,
the daily duration of work could go up to twelve hours. Beyond 16 years, the child
was considered as an adult and could work beyond twelve hours.[16] As regards the
ultra-liberal economists, such as Charles Dunoyer and Frédéric Bastiat, the laws
which regulate the work of children or women were to be avoided. The legislation
was the worst solution. It is a good illustration of the 'perversity thesis' denounced
by A. O. Hirschman in *The Rhetoric of Reaction* (1991). However, the moderate
liberal economists had a perspective on the law of 1841 that was quite different.
According to Louis Wolowski, only industrial legislation is the 'organization of
labour' in the right sense of the term.[17] According to Adolphe Blanqui, State
intervention as regards the work by children was necessary because in this matter,
'private philanthropy is powerless'.[18] According to Michel Chevalier, the law of
1841 was undeniably a step forward, but it is insufficient:

> The law of 1841 on the work of children in factories is incomplete ... It does not
> deal with the workshops with less than twenty workers. There is only one ridiculous
> check: there are benevolent people who serve as inspectors nonpaid, and invested of
> with a temporary mandate only, who are reluctant to quarrel with the chiefs of indus-
> try they find at fault ... The inspection of factories should be entrusted to special civil
> servants, chosen among the most enlightened men, able to appreciate all the circum-
> stances, so that they will not make unproductive quarrels with the chiefs of industry.[19]

In reality, this law remained mainly a dead letter because the factory inspection
was entrusted to retired entrepreneurs or tradesmen and was not very effective.
In his study *Des classes ouvrières en France pendant l'année 1848*, Adolphe Blanqui noticed that the law is not applied in all the factories and that unfortunately
it does not concern the 'family workshops'.[20]

A second question emerged: was it necessary to reduce the daily working hours of adult workers? It was only during the Revolution of 1848 that an attempt was made in this direction. On 2 March, the provisional government, considering 'that manual work too long prolonged does not only ruin the health of the worker, but will prevent him from cultivating his intelligence, which undermines the dignity of the man', decreed that, in Paris, the daily working hours would fall from eleven to ten hours and outside of Paris from twelve to eleven hours. In fact, this decree introduced for the first time in France a national standard for adult working hours. Indeed, until this date, the working hours were neither limited, nor regulated.[21] This decree, approved by the *Commission du Luxembourg* (see below) was rejected by all the liberal economists. Thus, we find Léon Faucher, Louis Wolowski and also Michel Chevalier in the same camp.

Léon Faucher argued that the setting up of a reduced and single duration of work was to the advantage of the domestic industry, at the cost of the 'grande industrie'. So the manufacturers would be forced into mechanization and reduction of employment. They would not be able to adapt themselves to the fluctuations of demand; during the phases of prosperity the workers would not be able to work more and get more money. Finally, the foreign competition would win.[22] According to Michel Chevalier, the reduction of the working hours could be realized only in the long run, when the production strongly increased. In fact, 'undoubtedly a time will come where the daily working hours will be seriously shortened, not really because the worker will be more skilled and more attentive, but because a more considerable production will require less labour';[23] but today, it would only be necessary to respect the Sunday rest.[24]

But the decree about the working hours would have hardly any effect since it had already been repealed on 9 September 1848. With this law, the daily duration of work came back to twelve hours.

Association and 'Organization of Labour'

Let us recall first that the French liberal economists were supporters of free and voluntary association and not of imposed association, proposed by the socialists as a remedy for the disadvantages of competition. If several isolated people making use of their natural rights decided to join an association, they did that in a desire for security, or for insurance. One of the best advocates of this approach of association was Frédéric Bastiat. In his book *Harmonies économiques* (1850), he said that by far the greater part of mankind wants security and 'fixity', and felt an 'aversion for uncertainty'.[25] In fact, only a minority of men (the 'capitalists'), aspired to uncertainty. These voluntary associations could take the form of insurances, of mutual aid associations, and eventually, in the future, pension schemes. The wage system also belonged to this category because it provided a regular income, except during periods of industrial crisis: it was an insurance system against the risks that the capitalists agree to support. On the other hand, work could not be assured.[26]

According to Michel Chevalier, it was necessary to develop, in addition to the professional instruction, savings banks, mutual aid associations and pension schemes. In addition, he argued that a profit-sharing system would be useful in the long run. All these measures constituted the 'association', the 'organization of labour', in the broadest sense, but in the right sense of the term.[27] The liberal economists were much more reticent with respect to consumption and production associations; these developed during the Revolution of 1848.

Louis Blanc's book, *Organization of Labour* (first edn, 1839, ninth edn, 1850), raised an intense discussion in France on the question of association and organization of labour. Louis Blanc had a solution for the 'labour question': a social reform whose principle is association (union of men having hopes and sharing interests), which he opposed to the principle of individualism. The effect of this reform was to abolish, gradually, the proletariat. 'Social workshops' (*ateliers sociaux*) would be created in some of the most important branches of the economy by means of a special budget set up by a Ministry of labour (*Ministère du travail*). Only workers whose moral standards were high enough would be invited to work in these workshops. The State would establish the statutes of these workshops, confirmed by the National Assembly. The State would be the 'legislator' of the social workshops, but not their 'director', because its role would be limited to the monitoring of the observation of the statutes. Success and competition of these 'social workshops' with respect to the private sector would lead gradually to the extension of this system. This system allows a reconciliation of duties and self-interest (with a collective aspect) because each worker shared in profit. Concerning workers' wages, Louis Blanc's opinion fluctuated in the successive editions of *Organization of Labour*. First, he asserted that 'the inequalities in wages would be graduated on the scale of posts', at least temporarily (1840–5); then he supported equality of wages, in a context of a new education of people (1847–8). But in April 1848, in a famous speech, he changed his point of view. In the association system equality of wages would now be only transitory and the new motto in matters of justice would be: production according to the faculties, consumption according to the needs.[28]

The liberal economists deplored that the investigations on working-class conditions led eventually to the agenda of 'association' and of 'organization of labour'. Most of them saw in Louis Blanc's project a system that gave all the power to the State, which would become an unique entrepreneur and entrusted to provide for the needs of private consumption. According to Michel Chevalier, if Louis Blanc's ideas on equality of wages belonged to the 'classical' communist system, his new principle of distribution belonged to the 'fraternal' communist system; this new principle that introduced a split between duties and rights would put an end to personal responsibility, to self-interest and would drastically reduce the national production.[29]

Is Labour a Right?

During the Revolution of 1848, the question of the 'right to labour' was the subject of quarrels between economists and socialists. On the basis of their theory of property rights, the liberal economists fought against the 'right to labour' with a great obstinacy. They also saw in the 'right to labour' a means to restore privileges which had been abolished by the French Revolution.

According to Léon Faucher, who took up the argumentation of the lawyer Jules-Armand Dufaure, the 'right to labour' created a right and an obligation at the same time. It supposed a contract between the individual and the society, represented by the State. According to this contract, the State promised subsistence for each individual. However, speaking legally, we have here a non-synallagmatic contract, engaging only one of the parties. Indeed, the State must provide to the individuals, according to their demand, the means to work, but it cannot force them to work to find their current subsistence. Therefore, finally, the individual is the master, while the society (the State) is the servant and the State must necessarily be 'entrepreneur of all industries', to hold the monopoly of labour.[30]

Through these debates, the French liberal economists used the provocations of Proudhon to their profit. During a meeting of the *comité des finances* of the National Assembly, Proudhon said: 'Give me the right to labour and I give you the right of property'.[31] Joseph Garnier remarked on this subject: 'Mr. Proudhon was right: if one admits the right to labour, it is necessary to give up the right of property'. Indeed, the 'right to labour of the ones' is a 'right of property of the others', because to collect the capital to satisfy my right to labour, it is necessary to get taxes, therefore to levy taxes on the property of the others.[32]

The question of the 'right to labour' was at the centre of the debates during the 1848 Revolution. The decree of 25 February, written by Louis Blanc under the pressure of the crowd, proclaims the 'right to labour':

> The Provisional government of the French Republic commits itself to guarantee the subsistence of the workers by work. It is committed to guarantee work to all the citizens. It recognizes that the workers must associate themselves to enjoy the advantage of their labour.

But, like his colleagues, Louis Blanc was conscious that it was not a question of a mere economic claim and that this right had a much broader significance.[33]

Two days later, on 27 February, the *Ateliers nationaux* were set up under the control of the Ministry of public works (*Ministère des Travaux publics*) and an engineer, Pierre-Émile Thomas, was appointed as director. The *Ateliers nation-aux* were very far away from the project of the 'social workshops' of Louis Blanc, because mainly they constituted a kind of charity workshop.[34] If the creation of a *Ministère du Travail et du Progrès* was immediately rejected, on the other hand, the *Commission du gouvernement pour les travailleurs* (or *Commission du Luxembourg*) was set up on 28 February, with Louis Blanc as its head. With elected representatives of workers and entrepreneurs, this commission was insti-tuted to deal with the labour question. It is a kind of '*États généraux* of labour' to prepare some reforms submitted then to the National Assembly. However, this commission had no budget, no executive power. The *Commission du Lux-embourg* indeed proposed some reforms, and proclaimed the right to labour and the organization of labour.

Initially, in February 1848, the liberal economists believed that the social-ists would give up their main claims with a view to the economic situation and would agree to take part in the discussions. So, Joseph Garnier initially saw in the *Commission du Luxembourg* 'an act of wisdom creating a lightning conduc-tor'. But in April, the dissensions were numerous, for example, between Louis Wolowski and Louis Blanc. The economists brought together in a *Club de la liberté du travail* opposed the government policy, but they were not able to get an important position in the Constitutional Assembly (*Assemblée Constituante*). However, they intervene in the parliamentary committees (Bastiat, Wolowski, for example). One can say that the ultra-liberal economists (Joseph Garnier, Ambroise Clément, ...)[35] and moderate liberal economists (Adolphe Blanqui, Michel Chevalier, ...)[36] attacked equally violently the 'organization of labour' and the 'right to labour'. The *Ateliers nationaux* were even considered by Adolphe Blanqui and Michel Chevalier as instruments of a 'social war'.

In fact, the real constitutional work was not done in the *Palais du Lux-embourg*, but in a commission of Constitution, created on 17 May, whose composition was held secret. On the question of the 'right to labour', the posi-tion of this commission would move during the time. Just before the insurrection of June, the 'right to labour' was more or less admitted, under the condition of not comprising a reorganization of the society. This appeared in the first con-stitutional project of 19 June 1848, article 7. When the *Ateliers nationaux* were closed (20 June), the workers rebelled but they were put down by the National Guard under General Eugène Cavaignac. After the insurrection, the commission of constitution rejected the 'right to labour'. So, in the second constitution pro-ject (29 August), the 'right to labour' did not appear any more. The guarantee of liberty of work and industry appeared (*article 13*), but also the right to existence (*droit à l'existence*): '[The Republic] must, by a fraternal assistance, ensure the existence of the poor citizens, either by giving them work within the limits of its income, or, in the absence of a family, helping those who are unable to work' (*préambule, article VIII*).[37]

Léon Faucher, later *ministre de l'Intérieur* under Louis Napoléon Bonaparte, then asserted: 'The right to labour was struck down from the top of the tribune'.[38] But according to him, the 'right to existence' was, unfortunately, substituted for the 'right to labour': so it is a socialist victory! Louis Blanc is obviously not of this opinion:

> To admit the right to assistance and to deny the right to labour, it is to recognize to the man the right to live in an unproductive way, when one does refuse him the right to live in a productive way. In other words, to consider his existence as a charge, when one refuses to consider it as employment, which is obviously nonsensical.[39]

Consequently, the end of the Revolution from June 1848 onward, and the election in December of Louis-Napoléon Bonaparte as president thus brought a great relief to the liberal economists, but this was of short duration, because their relationship with the political power would be degraded soon with the *coup d'État* of 2 December 1851, which allowed Louis-Napoléon Bonaparte to become Emperor (Napoléon III).

Conclusion

Among the French liberal economists, the Revolution of 1848 caused a reduction of the possible differences of points of view about the 'labour question'. According to them, the true causes of the revolution do not lie in misery only, but also in the propagation of socialist ideas. According to Léon Faucher, 'socialism looks like the epidemics that save the robust constitutions and only hit the weak'.[40] According to him, it is not by chance that socialism prevails in the big cities. On 16 July 1848, General Eugène Cavaignac, *président du Conseil*, requests the members of the *Académie des sciences morales et politiques* to take part in the re-establishment of the 'moral order' and education of the public opinion by writing 'small treaties' intended to inculcate the respect of law and property.[41] In fact, the liberal economists had already begun this kind of work and during the second half of the nineteenth century they continued. The 'right to labour' would be regularly attacked, not only in booklets, but also in courses, in handbooks and in dictionaries of political economy. For example, we can read the entry 'Droit au travail', written by Léon Faucher in the *Dictionnaire de l'économie politique* edited by Charles Coquelin and Gilbert-Urbain Guillaumin (1852–3), and the entry 'Droit au travail', not signed, in the *Nouveau dictionnaire d'économie politique* edited by Léon Say and Chailley-Bert (1891–2).[42]

12 WHATEVER HAPPENED TO THE KEYNESIAN MULTIPLIER?

Maria Cristina Marcuzzo

Premise

The topic I have chosen for my contribution is the issue of the two-way link between economic thinking and facts. I will not attempt to address the complex issue of how theories are confirmed or falsified, here I wish only to explore the circumstances that prompt the return of ideas previously discarded or forgotten because they are believed to have been either disproved or surpassed by a better theory. The point has been nicely argued in a recent paper:

> Understanding in economics does not proceed cumulatively. We do not necessarily know more today than we did yesterday, tempting as it may be to believe otherwise. So-called 'lessons' are learnt, forgotten, re-learnt and forgotten again. Concepts rise to prominence and fall into oblivion before possibly resurrecting. They do so because the economic environment changes, sometimes slowly but profoundly, at other times suddenly and violently. But they do so also because the discipline is not immune to fashions and fads.[1]

In recent times facts are increasingly identified with empirical estimates of models which are believed to incorporate the progress made in the economic literature. These 'facts' are heavily dependent on the choice of the models and the methodology employed to find them. The relationship between facts and theory has become opaque and we may reasonably challenge the motives behind the discovery of 'facts', for they tend to be recognized or ignored according to the ebbs and flows of academic fashions.

Such is the case of the Keynesian multiplier, which has a story of alternate acceptance and rejection in the over seventy years of its existence. After more than twenty years of neglect and suspicion by the majority of the profession it has come back into favour. The history of this concept and its fortune with empirical testing provides an interesting illustration of the cyclical pattern of economic ideas.

A recent article in the *Financial Times* underlined how 'In the 1950s and 1960s, when Keynesianism was at its height, the multiplier was generally assumed to be about 2. Then in the 1990s and 2000s, these estimates gradually dropped, leaving the consensus range about 0.5–0.7 by 2009'. This is in striking contrast with the current figures of 0.9–1.7 presented in the latest *World Economic Outlook* by the International Monetary Fund (IMF).[2]

So the question arises whether we are witnessing a change in the structure of the economy or in the model chosen in the estimates, or indeed in the theory behind it. In the search for an answer, first, I sketch out the story of the multiplier up to the onset of the 2007–8 crisis (pp. 158–60), second, I look at the assumptions preventing the multiplier from being positive and greater than 1 in modern macroeconomics models (pp. 160–2), third, I trace out the resurgence of Keynesian thinking in the aftermath of the current recession (pp. 162–4) and, finally, I review the 'facts' for the explanation of which the multiplier appeared once again a useful tool (pp. 164–6). In the concluding section I claim that reasoning based on the multiplier remains valid and useful in our present times.

The History of the Multiplier

The concept of the multiplier was elaborated by Richard Kahn in the summer of 1930 – drafting began in August during a holiday in the Tyrol – to give support to Keynes's intuition that an inflow of investment in public works would bring about an increase in income greater than the initial expenditure.[3] In 1929 – in *Can Lloyd George Do It* – Keynes endorsed the idea of public spending as a way out of the crisis and set his 'favourite pupil' to work out the details.

The article containing the basics of the multiplier was published in the *Economic Journal* in June 1931[4] and although the idea might not have been entirely new,[5] it was in association with Keynes's *General Theory* that it became known and used in economic policies and forecasting. The importance of the multiplier essay lies in providing the terms for analysis of the conditions that see an increase either in the level of prices or in the quantities (or a combination of the two) in aggregate given an increase in demand (in this particular case public investments in road building).

Kahn set about studying the effects of an increase in investment on overall production in terms of the supply and demand of consumption goods in aggregate in short-period conditions. If the level of demand is high, then the productive capacity will already be made good use of, and greater use will entail an increase in costs and thus in prices. But if, on the other hand, the level of demand is low, then plant and equipment will be largely idle and production can therefore be stepped up without any appreciable increase in unit costs and prices.

The limitation of that as yet unripe formulation of this innovative approach was the failure to make clear the fundamental implication of the multiplier, namely the necessary equality of savings and investments. Kahn attributed this difficulty to the fact that the article – which also included the findings of Meade[6] – took as frame of reference the definitions of saving and income adopted in the *Treatise on Money*. Kahn himself made it clear: 'what we had done – but *failed completely to realize* – was ... to establish the identity of saving and investment'[7] and that it was rather with the article 'The Financing of Public Works', published in September 1932, that he finally abandoned the *Treatise* definition of savings (retained in the multiplier article). If, in fact, savings are defined 'in the ordinary sense of the aggregate of the excess of individuals' receipts over their expenditure on consumption[,] savings are *always and necessarily* equal to investment'.[8]

Some commentators hold that it was after reading the article by Jens Warming published in the *Economic Journal* in June 1932 that Keynes and his immediate entourage properly appreciated the role of the savings function in determining the equilibrium level of income. In fact it took Keynes a couple of years to incorporate the multiplier in his new theory based on the principle of effective demand, and only after publication of the *General Theory* did the multiplier acquire full visibility.[9] For many years afterwards – owing to the widespread interpretation through the IS–LM model – the multiplier was construed as a formula showing that any increase in autonomous expenditure guaranteed an increase in income greater than the amount originally spent, provided of course that conditions of less than full employment prevail. Deficit spending, i.e. government expenditure greater that tax revenue, became justifiable on two grounds: (a) it increases income; (b) it generates the savings (which are a function of income) necessary to finance it.

This 'Keynesian consensus' lasted for almost thirty years until it was seriously challenged by the Monetarist assault of the late 1960s. Building on his (and Franco Modigliani's) earlier work on the consumption function, Milton Friedman cast doubts on the efficacy of fiscal policy. Both the permanent income hypothesis and the life-cycle approach to consumption were shown to be empirically better supported than the decreasing marginal propensity to consume out of current income envisaged by Keynes, therefore leaving little room for the working of the multiplier.

The monetarist Counterrevolution was pushed further by Robert Lucas and the New Classical economists well into the 1990s, with feeble defence by the New Keynesians, who relegated the efficacy of the multiplier to the very short period when prices and wage rigidities prevented the system from getting into full employment equilibrium. Keynesian economics was put in mothballs, as Lucas recorded:

> One cannot find good, under-forty economists who identify themselves or their work as 'Keynesian'. Indeed, people even take offence if referred to as 'Keynesians'. At research seminars, people don't take Keynesian theorizing seriously anymore; the audience starts to whisper and giggle to one another.[10]

Well into the 2000s the profession remained converted to the new wisdom, and free market economics ruled the roost in the profession, while anti-government intervention sentiments remained strong in institutions like the World Bank and the IMF and in influential media such as the *Financial Times* and the *Economist*. The classical arguments against short-term policy interventions – the lags in making economic policy and further lags in the implementation and effects after the policy is enacted – coupled with Lucas's assumptions on the countering effects of expectations and actions of rational agents who observe the government's policy process had made it appear practically impossible for policymakers to time fiscal policy actions to stabilize the economy. So the author of a recent overview of the empirical studies on the multiplier could conclude that 'Before 2008, the topic of stimulus effects of fiscal policy was a backwater compared to research on monetary policy'.[11]

Behind the Rebuttal of the Multiplier

What are the forces said to prevent the multiplier from being positive and greater than 1 according to modern macroeconomics? There are two relevant assumptions made in modern theory (Dynamic Stochastic General Equilibrium or DSGE models) to justify rejection of the Keynesian multiplier:

(a) consumers are said to be forward-looking, taking into consideration permanent income and discounting future tax increase (wealth effect), so private demand offsets public expenditure; the credibility of fiscal policy may reinforce the wealth effect whenever consumers believe that the measures undertaken by the government are credible and permanent, rather than non-credible and temporary;

(b) in Real Business Cycle models prices and wages are fully flexible, competition is perfect and full employment is attained, so there is no scope for an induced increase in aggregate demand; in the New Keynesian models some frictions in goods, labour and financial markets are allowed, which account for some short-term output effect.

So the main drivers are rational expectations (or perfect foresight) guiding consumer choices, with perfect markets as a description of the working of the macroeconomic system. On the contrary, in the Kahn–Keynes approach perfect foresight and full rationality are not assumptions which can be applied in real economic systems and this in itself would prevent attainment of full market equilibrium, even if perfect competition and flexible prices and wages were the norm. The Keynes approach acknowledges the necessity to take on board the division of economics between 'the study of those economic activities in which our views of the future are ... reliable in all respects'[12] and the study of those in which 'our previous expectations are liable to disappointment and expectations concerning the future affect what we do to-day'.[13] The former allows for probability calculation, while the latter is dominated by the notion of uncertainty.[14]

The assumption of perfect foresight was discredited after the 2007–8 events, inducing some modifications in standard macro-models to incorporate limited rationality and a degree of rigidities in the goods, labour and financial markets. However, the exercise was conducted within a theoretical framework which excluded employment of the multiplier not only to measure the impact of government expenditure (or taxation) but as a tool to conceptualize the relevant forces at work in the economy. The 'remedies' generally proposed to overhaul the mainstream approach (behavioural economics, rejection of the efficient market hypothesis and extirpation of the DSGE macroeconomic model) have not fixed the problems with orthodox theory, which ultimately rest with the method and substance of neoclassical economics.

In fact Alberto Alesina readily admits:

> dynamic general equilibrium models ... are large models of the entire economy in which fiscal policy is one of the variables involved. As predictive tools, the results of these models very much depend on the assumptions that you make to begin with. If you assume large multipliers, then you will get out a certain effect of fiscal policy, and vice versa. They are very useful predictive models, but what they spit out is very much affected by what is put in as assumptions.[15]

A distinction was made by Keynes himself between the 'logical theory of the multiplier, which holds good continuously, without time-lag, at all moments of time, and the consequences of an expansion in the capital-goods industries which take gradual effect, subject to time-lag and only after an interval'.[16]

It has been aptly stated that the logical multiplier principle 'is a theory of the "order of events" in that it makes a distinction in macroeconomics between the expenditure that forms and the expenditure that disposes of national income'.[17]

Moreover, the whole point of the Keynesian argument is that demand derived from individual maximizing behaviour is notional and unless matched by a corresponding capacity to pay, is not actual expenditure or effective demand.

What has been the object of rebuttal in the forty years of Keynesian dissent is the logical theory of the multiplier, and the revival in interest in the concept since 2011 amounts to reluctant acceptance that the empirical estimates, in times of crisis and unemployment, yield a value well above 1.

This is the conclusion reached in a recent review article on the theories behind the multiplier:

Summing up, one can see that the different types of models will deliver fiscal multipliers of almost any magnitude. Moreover, even models of a particular class can deliver quite different multiplier values, depending on underlying parameter values, and assumptions regarding monetary policy reaction functions. As a consequence, one can only address the magnitude of multipliers by empirics.[18]

However, empirical estimates of the multiplier did not deliver the answer either. According to a recent summing up:

The range of the spending multiplier estimated using these various approaches is from .4 to 1.5, with some estimates even lower than .4 and some estimates larger than 1.5. However, most fall in the .4 to 1.5 range. This is a huge range because it includes 1.0.[19]

So the question remains unanswered, and the solution is hardly likely to come from exploiting econometric skills and ingenuity.

Triggers of the Mood Change towards the Multiplier

In fact it was the 2007–8 financial meltdown which triggered the mood change in the attitude towards Keynesian thinking; in academia and international economic institutions advocacy of a coordinated international intervention began to be voiced and heard.

Fiscal stimulus to keep the economy clear of the path to recession was back on the agenda. Action followed. China was in fact one of the first nations to launch a substantial fiscal stimulus package in March 2009 and similar, but more timid, actions were undertaken in the US and, to a lesser extent, Europe.

However, as Robert Hall noticed: 'Notwithstanding the highly publicized attempts of the Obama administration, government purchases sagged below their established growth path following the financial crisis in 2008. The same principle applies, on the average, among all the advanced economics of the OECD.'[20]

Mainstream economists strongly disagreed on the measures taken.

Robert Barro repeated that the multiplier affect was close to zero and that the extra employment generated by the stimulus was going to crowd out private investment;[21] J. Sachs was certain that the stimulus may work in the short term, but it was likely to cause more troubles in the future.[22] A manifesto sponsored by the Cato Institute was signed by 237 American economists (the most renowned among them being Michael Bordo, James Buchanan, John Cochrane, Eugene Fama, Steve Horwitz, Dreide McCloskey, Alan Meltzer, Edward Prescott, Robert Whaples and Larry White) who refused to endorse the statement made by President Obama on January 2009 that 'we need action by our government, a recovery plan that will help to jumpstart the economy'.[23]

These are just a few examples of the climate of opinion represented by academic economists, which remained in the main anti-Keynesian in the earlier stages of the crisis. In fact, the Keynesian resurgence in the aftermath of the 2007–8 crisis proved to be a phenomenon of politics and the media rather than academia.

The rhetoric calling for immediate fiscal tightening (especially in Europe but also in the US) gained momentum in 2010 (with the impending risk of sovereign debt defaults in several European countries) and hung around until early 2012. Among the economists in prestigious institutions, only Paul Krugman and Joseph Stiglitz in the US were vociferous opponents to the austerity wisdom, joined by a few other mostly heterodox economists in Europe. The twists and turns of the 'Return to Keynes' path, was ably described by Mario Seccareccia:

> For a short period during 2009 and 2010, there was a 'Keynes moment' when all governments internationally implemented fiscal stimulus packages largely on the basis of Keynesian demand-side ideas regarding the merits of running budget deficits in times of recession. These ideas defended by policy makers tended to be in strong conflict with the views of most academic economists who had been trained for decades to believe that budget deficits are destabilizing because they would ultimately lead to higher interest rates accompanying higher rates of inflation. Since early 2010, this new policy framework seems slowly to have been abandoned. On the one side, there has been significant pressure coming from conservative politicians who are alarmed at the large size of the public sector deficits because of fears of non sustainability of the public finances. At the same time, there has been pressure from mainstream neoclassical economists who fear that long-term deficits would be destabilizing for the economy, because ultimately, it is argued, governments face an inter-temporal budget constraint, whereby current fiscal expansion must be followed ineluctably by future fiscal contraction. Although this view has been severely criticized by heterodox economists, policy makers seem to have reverted back to the pre-2008 policy position on the need for an 'exit strategy' and a return to balanced budgets.[24]

Signs that the pendulum was swinging back in favour of an expansionary fiscal policy, with the tide bringing the multiplier ashore, became noticeable early in 2012. De Long and Summers made a timid overture:

> In a depressed economy, with short-term nominal interest rates at their zero lower bound, ample cyclical unemployment, and excess capacity, increased government purchases would be neither offset by the monetary authority raising interest rates nor neutralized by supply-side bottlenecks ... Thus, at the zero bound, where the central bank cannot or will not but in any event does not perform its full role in stabilization policy, fiscal policy has the stabilization policy mission that others have convincingly argued it lacks in normal times.[25]

Giancarlo Corsetti et al. put it in even stronger terms, asserting that 'Output and consumption multipliers [are] unusually high during times of financial crisis', thereby providing 'evidence in support of fiscal stimulus during financial crises'.[26]

Eventually both the IMF and the European Union in October 2012 followed suit:

our results indicate that multipliers have actually been in the 0.9 to 1.7 range since the Great Recession. This finding is consistent with research suggesting that in today's environment of substantial economic slack, monetary policy constrained by the zero lower bound, and synchronized fiscal adjustment across numerous economies, multipliers may be well above 1 ... More work on how fiscal multipliers depend on time and economic conditions is warranted.[27]

The *Report on Public Finances in EMU* stressed that:

> There is a growing understanding that fiscal multipliers are nonlinear and become larger in crisis periods due to uncertainty about aggregate demand and credit conditions, the presence of slack in the economy, the larger share of consumers that are liquidity constrained, and to the more accommodative stance of monetary policy. Given these findings, it is reasonable to suspect that in the present juncture the multipliers for composition-balanced permanent consolidations are higher than normal.[28]

So if 'empirically, estimated multipliers also depend on the methodology used to derive responses of economic activity to fiscal shocks'[29] and results are not conclusive as 'even differences in the sign of multipliers are observed',[30] it would be desirable for the discussion to be carried on to another level, involving examination of the competing theories rather than empirical findings. In fact, the discouraging discovery made in a recent scholarly review of the multiplier theory is that 'Despite the increase in the number of estimates, there is still no consensus on the mechanism by which government spending raises GDP'.[31]

The Impact of the Crisis

The main indicators of the crisis in the advanced economies measured with the rate of unemployment and the growth of real GDP, had brought the focus on the 'facts' for explanation of which the multiplier once again appeared a useful tool.

The IMF study showed that the actual value of the multiplier is twice or even three times that assumed in the growth estimates, namely in the range of 0.9 to 1.7 rather than 0.5. The recession had brought back values of the multiplier close to 1, from the average value of 0.5 for the advanced economies during the three decades leading up to 2009.

The reasons why the multiplier is well above 1 today are given as 'monetary policy constrained by the zero lower bound and synchronized fiscal adjustment across numerous economies'.[32]

The first reason is just a repetition of the 'old' argument that private investment is not 'crowded out' at zero lower bound interest rate.

The second argument is that synchronized fiscal contractions of the same extent do not impact on current accounts and therefore prevent real depreciation and current account improvement from occurring.

Both the arguments explain the multiplier effect of fiscal consolidation on output, taking into account the secondary effects (no crowding out and no trade expansion).

Others have argued 'that standard macroeconomic theory implies that private-sector spending is determined by the expected future path of short-term interest rates and not just the current level of the overnight rate', which is the only rate currently close to zero.[33] By stressing the role of expectations, news and credibility, the value of the multiplier can be made to stay below 1, also with zero bound interest rate. In fact, in modern macroeconomics the essential element is information, not needs, habits or distribution, which are the Keynesian forces behind the multiplier.

On the other hand it is argued that in the abnormal financial conditions of the crisis, credit constraints were more binding; so 'households could be expected to behave in a more "Keynesian" fashion, with less reference to "permanent income". This would tend to result in a larger multiplier'.[34]

In contrast, Shapiro makes a different analysis of the pattern of consumption in a financial constrained and debt-ridden economy:

> Debt-financed consumer spending is quite different from income-financed spending. The latter can continue as long as income is earned, whereas the debt financed spending cannot. Consumers have to pay interest on the debt they contract, and this interest can be paid in only one of two ways: out of their incomes or through incurring more debt. In either case, the interest payments on the debt will reduce purchasing power, and though the recipients of this interest may spend some of it on consumption, they are likely to be financial firms and wealthier households, neither of which spends much of their earnings.
>
> Most of the interest paid out of household income will go back into finance, used for the purposes of financial investments or speculations, so that while consumer credit can increase consumer spending in the short run, raising it above the level of household incomes, it cannot do so in the long run. Its long-run effects are ... the same as an increase in household saving: they reduce effective demand, worsening rather than ameliorating the employment problems of capitalist economies.[35]

The conclusion could then be that in these circumstances expansionary fiscal policy becomes effective: when economic agents are 'finance-constrained', unable to borrow as much as they would like in order to spend, their propensity to spend any additional income they may receive is high.

It seems to me that two different issues are at stake. The first is whether the multiplier properly defined, taking into consideration, with their appropriate signs, c (propensity to consume), t (marginal tax) and m (propensity to import), was lower before 2009 than afterwards. The second issue is whether we have to look at the factors affecting the autonomous component – I, X or G – to account for different output responses.

The literature is not in agreement on several of these points. The symmetric working of fiscal spending multipliers in business cycle upturns and downturns is questioned as being determined by the employment of linear estimation techniques for time series data which tend to underestimate fiscal spending;[36] another unsettled issue is whether inequality of income distribution can be regarded as a major factor accounting for aggregate consumption and saving.[37]

This state of affairs is behind the rather discouraged response by a renowned mainstream economist:

> It is very difficult to isolate the effects of fiscal policy. Therefore, the problem is inherently difficult. As economists, we should be more ready than we actually are in admitting that there are a lot of things that we do not know and be careful not to claim more than we actually know.[38]

Conclusions

Keynes dedicated three chapters (8, 9, 10) of the *General Theory* to the propensity to consume and to the multiplier. He listed the objective and the subjective factors underlying motives to spending, but concluded that expenditure in consumption 'depends in the main ... on the volume of output and employment'.[39] He always insisted that consumption and saving were not to be treated in the aggregate as in the case of the individual case. The paradox of saving is the best-known example of the fallacy of composition which occurs whenever the aggregate is thought to have same outcome as that deriving from individual behaviour, but the same holds true for consumption.

In commenting on Ohlin's article in 1937, Keynes wrote:

> prospective income as well as current income is relevant, but I have dealt with that, as I think one must in any formal treatment, in the function itself and not in the variable. That is to say, expectations of future income affect the propensity to spend out of current income ... this may be important to particular individuals, but [is] not likely to be important for the community as a whole.[40]

The basic thrust of the multiplier analysis is the induced effect on expenditure following an autonomous increase either of I, G or X as a consequence of variation in real income in the presence of unemployment of resources. The aggregate marginal propensity to consume out of a *given* income is assumed to be decreasing and stable, thus providing the parameter for the calculation of the multiplier. Once taxation and imports are taken into account the value is certainly lower, but the relation with real income remains the key determinant.

In the years of domination of the micro-foundations of macroeconomics this basic Keynesian lesson was forgotten. Consumption was modelled on individual maximizing behaviour, over an infinite time horizon and with perfect foresight, relegating real income as determinant of consumption to a negligible role. What has been lost and hopefully may be regained is the idea of the centrality of changes (with both positive and negative signs) in aggregate current income and its distribution in fuelling or dampening economic growth.

The story of alternate acceptance and rejection of the multiplier reasoning is another example of the nature of economics, where ideology mixed with academic training forge the path along which concepts are formed, theories are tested and the ground where disputes are won and lost. This recession sees the same plot acted out, but hopefully with a happier ending. Philip Mirowski's neat taxonomy is helpful here:

> we might divide the reactions of the economics profession to the crisis into three broad categories: one, *the orthodoxy was right all along* and nothing that has transpired in recent events impugns the fundamental soundness of basic theory; two, the orthodox have made some unfortunate conceptual choices in the recent past, but the crisis has sobered us up, and *we are working hard to rectify them*, while maintaining fealty to all that was legitimate, timeless and dependable in neoclassical economics; and three, the best response would be to renounce neoclassical economics altogether, *and start anew with some other tradition of economic thought.*[41]

The reader will by now have guessed to which category the present author belongs, in good company with Pascal Bridel, to whom this contribution is dedicated.

13 SUNDRY OBSERVATIONS AND NEW FINDINGS ON THE ANGLO-ITALIAN TRADITION OF ECONOMIC THOUGHT

Pier Luigi Porta

Introduction: The 'Cambridge Keynesians' vs the 'Sraffians'

The gist of Piero Sraffa's contribution to political economy lies in his criticism of the Neoclassical and Marginalist system *and* in his endeavour to establish an alternative approach to the discipline.[1] In this light there is a continuity of sorts within the Cambridge School of Economics taken in a long-run perspective, during almost a whole century from Marshall down to the 1970s, i.e. the time span which bears the imprint of a strong profile of the Cambridge identity.[2] Marshall, Keynes and Sraffa probably are the heroes of the School and they mark three very different ways of achieving the same objective: the criticism of the 'static' philosophy of the Neoclassical Marginalist School of economic analysis and thought.

Marshall pursued the objective by emphasizing the 'social economy' perspective. Keynes chose to lay the emphasis on the criticism of Say's Law in the context of a deeper analysis of the short-run dynamics of the system. Sraffa, despite his professed Ricardianism, had the surplus theory, or the basis of Marx's *Mehrwert*, in mind. Those are three completely different ways to go beyond the purely allocative horizon of political economy. Sraffa's case began with an analysis of the surplus, which soon turned into a research on problems of the definition and measure of the surplus in order to provide a secure basis for the approach itself.

In choosing Marx as his own starting point, Sraffa was unique in conceiving his own research programme as a non-Marginalist programme, designed to revert to a Classical (in Marx's sense) canon. At the same time Sraffa, who had started doing research with a positive and constructive aim in mind of a new approach to economics, through time felt obliged to retreat to what he called a 'prelude' to a critique of Marginalist economics. The *prelude* thus appears to have mainly concentrated on the *negative* task of proving the Marginalist approach untenable, and therefore to be abandoned, somewhat losing sight of the main aim (of which Sraffa continued to be conscious at all stages) of providing an alternative, a task explicitly left over to others (younger and better equipped, as Sraffa would say).

However, the *prelude* only makes sense if the prospective and constructive task is taken into account and, indeed, put at centre stage. For example, the very fact that Sraffa's prelude consists of a theory of surplus distribution with one degree of freedom, so that one of the distributive variables remains undetermined, is in itself *not* a Ricardian element at all.

That is the context which explains Pasinetti's approach. Two connected aspects of Pasinetti's approach are of interest in the present essay: his work as a historian of economic analysis and his analysis of economic dynamics. Both are prominent in Pasinetti.[3]

The legacy of the Cambridge School of Economics appears today to include at least two main strands, i.e. the 'Sraffians' on one side and the 'Cambridge Keynesians' on the other. Today Piero Sraffa is discussed, mostly if certainly *not* exclusively, by a restricted group of his self-styled acolytes, who call themselves the 'Sraffians'. This paper does not belong to that academic breed and it is based on the supposition (which of course cannot be proved) that, if Sraffa were alive today, he would say: 'I am not a Sraffian', paralleling Karl Marx when he declared 'Je ne suis pas Marxiste'.[4] The aim of this essay is to present a criticism of the 'Sraffians', who, in most cases, have made Piero Sraffa outmoded and incomprehensible. Much of the Sraffian literature today is conceived for use exclusively within the inner circle. The intellectual line of the 'Cambridge Keynesians', on the other hand, takes up Sraffa's legacy, published and unpublished, and discusses Sraffa in a constructive way, by looking backward and forging ahead, and is much more interesting and productive.[5]

The Cambridge Tradition after the Late War: The Building Blocks of the So-Called Anglo-Italian School

The majority of works concerning the Cambridge School of Economics and its relationships, both at the time of Keynes and in the years that followed, tend to highlight the influences that came to Italy from the outside. The intention in the present essay is to take the opposite direction and examine whether it can be claimed, or at least deemed plausible, that the Italian tradition had some influence in shaping and marking the development of the themes characteristic of the Cambridge School.

It is well-known that economic studies in post-war Italy were strongly influenced by the Cambridge School, in particular by the work of those direct pupils of Keynes who were in charge of the Economics and Politics Faculty at Cambridge from the immediate post-war period until approximately the mid-1970s: i.e. by the *Cambridge Keynesians* discussed and analysed in Luigi Pasinetti's recent work.[6]

The present contribution will focus primarily on three scientific personalities: Luigi Pasinetti, Nicholas Kaldor and Piero Sraffa. Even for those who took part in it or even for those who stood on the sidelines, thirty years is perhaps long enough ago to be able to revisit the Cambridge School phenomenon from a certain 'aesthetic distance' concerning the heated debates of the time, accompanied as they often were by excessive enthusiasm on either side.

Among the whole of the post-war Cambridge school, certainly both Sraffa and Kaldor belong, as Pasinetti puts it, to that 'unique group of scholars' in 'that unique intellectual environment that was the Cambridge in the late 1950s and early 1960s', basking in the unique blend of radicalism, traditional wisdom and social commitment that was the hallmark of the Keynes circle.[7] This is what we might call the nucleus of the vision we wish to focus on here, in all its historical, analytical and (I would add) intellectual sources. What transpires immediately from many studies is the towering, influential figure of Keynes himself. Yet themes also emerge in the Cambridge circle that were *outside Keynes's direct interests* and were not directly associated with the sources of his intellectual inspiration. We only have to think of the influence of Marx, which is of course essential to explain the special relevance s acquired by the issue of capital, or the influence of Ricardo which runs on parallel lines. Originally encouraged, in purely philological terms by Keynes himself (with the launching of the definitive critical edition of that great English economist), it was owing to the Cambridge School that Ricardo's influence underwent unpredictable and unimaginable developments, up to the point of marking an indelible and universal sign on the analytical history and records of the School itself and then, more generally, on Ricardianism as a movement. It is only natural that the various elements recorded here should have been – and still are – arguments of discussion, above all for what concerns perceivable theoretical connections. Many questions remain open. It may be useful to see whether, at least from the perspective of the sources, there are unifying elements in an environment and in a school that also shows, for numerous aspects, heterogeneous characteristics.

If we take the case of *Piero Sraffa*, the inquiry into the historical and analytical base of a possible temporal *unity* of Sraffa's research programme is as yet lacking sufficient explicit consideration of certain aspects belonging to the Italian tradition. It is in fact a characteristic of the studies made in Italy to have pointed, from the late 1800s to the early 1900s, to the path of a Marxian macroeconomy independent of value. Some of that Marxian influence is something that can be guessed from the extant papers, but the perspective receives fundamental confirmation from the study of the unpublished materials.

Let us see how the Italian tradition comes into the picture. A great interpreter and critical reviewer of Marx's theory of value, Antonio Graziadei, maintained that the economic system can be seen from a dual perspective that is as individual firms, which the system itself is made up of, or in accordance with the concept of all business as a whole. From the first aspect the conception of the economic system is dominated by the formation of exchange and markets: the needs that determine circulation act in such a way that the phenomena of production and distribution become almost inseparable from those of circulation. In contrast, the conception of business as a whole is not based on the analysis of the exchange ratio (that is, value) but on the concept of wealth. What interests the individual is how high the exchange value is, while society is interested in the general mass of use values. According to Graziadei it is 'the "superstition" of value' that 'has led the vast majority of economists to adopt exclusively, or almost exclusively, an individual firms' perspective', while the economist who has given the most complete and almost unique example of a systematic treatment for business as a whole is Quesnay in his famous 'Quadro economico', the Italian name of the *Tableau économique*. But that is not all: it was *Marx* who should have been able to restore to its just importance the outlook based (as we have mentioned) of business seen as a whole. Unfortunately his analysis, too firmly anchored in the explication of value, 'is suffocated and distorted by the constrictive framework of a vision based on individual firms'.[8]

The evidence obtained through archive papers shows how, in the mid-1920s, Sraffa had followed the negative strategy of *criticizing* in his published works the *false direction* taken by economic theory, especially by Marshall and his school, concerning the concept of cost. What we are arguing here is that, in the presence of an Italian tradition of socialist studies (Marxist contributions in particular), which were certainly not unknown to Piero Sraffa, the *positive* launch of a theory based on actual physical cost could only appear as the natural choice.[9]

Since the negative approach appears to be dominant in Sraffa's first *published* writings, it is evident that such an approach has to some extent distorted his public academic image, compared to what emerges from the unpublished writings. In reality, behind the scenes (i.e. in the unpublished notes and jottings of the same period), the author's ambition is quite different and much wider. This is the light in which the different sets of notes and, above all, the manuscript of the Lectures on the subject of *Advanced Theory of Value* should be seen. Sraffa's idea is precisely to take the opportunity of the *Lectures* to go back to Marx. My project – in Sraffa's own words – (unlike that of Marx, who wrote his *Capital* and then was unable to complete his *Storia delle dottrine*) is to begin with the *history*, which is in reality essential. This – he affirms – also involves proceeding from the known to the unknown, from Marshall to Marx, *from disutility to material cost*. After a long delay, undoubtedly, it would only be with his edition of Ricardo that Sraffa came to entrust the entire object of his ambition to the printed page.[10]

A possible return to the Italian school's studies as an indirect source of influence can be found in the parallel development of *Nicholas Kaldor*'s studies and the young *Luigi Pasinetti*'s. Luigi Pasinetti, who worked to a considerable extent under Kaldor's influence, is of particular interest here. A brief review of his production in order to grasp the significance of the relationship between Cambridge and the Italian school is now made easier by the recent publication of his *Keynes and the Cambridge Keynesians* (2007, Italian edn 2010). As I had occasion to emphasize in a joint paper with Roberto Scazzieri, Luigi Pasinetti's book puts forward a courageous, militant contribution, as indicated by the subtitle, 'A "Revolution in Economics" to be accomplished'.[11] A special undercurrent which emerges as a given characteristic of the Cambridge Keynesians lies at the junction of Piero Sraffa's and Nicholas Kaldor's work. Basic ingredients here included the analytical framework of structural analysis on the one hand, together with a sensitivity to the *dynamic nature* of the fundamental problems on the other, as well as an analysis of the *institutions* and with practical conditions to which the theory should apply.[12]

It is in that context that aspects emerge of an influence belonging to the Italian school. Among the many elements that have been highlighted and discussed in Pasinetti's work and which he calls the 'essential building blocks belonging to an alternative economic paradigm',[13] we would like to highlight two in particular here, as those that will draw more from the Italian tradition (even if that is not stressed by the author): the importance of a strong *ethical and social concern* that makes the theory more action-orientated and presented in such a way that makes the analysis 'natural' (while maintaining a strict separation of areas and levels of discourse) of institutions and, more generally, of the non-economic aspects on the one hand, and the direct and deep-rooted interest in *economic dynamics*, on the other.[14] These two aspects are linked with a specific interest in the *history of analysis*, in a sense that for the most part appears today to be broader and deeper than we had ever imagined. This is something that is, in fact, a living part of the experience of the Italian tradition of political economy, as well as the 'Cambridge School' in general and Luigi Pasinetti's approach in particular.

Any attempt to separate the legacy of the Cambridge School from these two factors actually betrays its spirit and stifles its ability to inspire and create. Moreover, it seems most unlikely that the role played by those two elements could be understood without some kind of reference to the Italian tradition in political economy. The role played by the Italian authors in the Cambridge School is therefore an active role, and not merely a receptive one.

It has been argued by several authors that economic thought in the Italian tradition is characterized precisely by the two factors just mentioned.[15] There is no doubt that we see them come together in an original way, mediated through the cultural world of post-Keynesian Cambridge, in Luigi Pasinetti's scheme of structural dynamics. These features are therefore one of the most significant and constructive expressions of synthesis contained in the Cambridge School. It is a live experience and in fact still in progress.

The change determined by the current economic crisis, which has begun to unleash its effects, will certainly contribute to a deep reflection about the tasks, scope and limits of economics as a science. It is a reflection that is likely to find many sectors of the profession largely unprepared – only superficially triumphant, and in actual fact victims of that 'pretence of knowledge' that takes by surprise especially those who consider themselves immune – while it certainly does not come unexpected to the best Anglo-Italian tradition which flourished at the University of Cambridge.

Pasinetti's Approach between the Cambridge Tradition and the Italian Tradition

In the opening sentences of his introduction to *Keynes and the Cambridge Keynesians*, Pasinetti describes his work as bending backwards while aiming forwards.[16] It is hardly surprising, then, that when this approach is brought to its ultimate consequences, one finds that in the most lively and constructive parts of the Cambridge School there resurface contents inspired by the Italian tradition. In this final section the objective is to illustrate the meaning – or at least discuss a possible interpretation – of what Luigi Pasinetti wrote at the beginning of his recent book.[17] It is a fact that the Keynesian revolution – Pasinetti argues in his Preface – did not manage to change the way of thinking of the majority of economic theorists. Keynes's pupils were themselves 'driven to pressing immediately for further developments of Keynes's ideas rather than for strengthening the foundations of the alternative paradigm behind them. Sraffa was the notable exception in this respect'. The theoretical foundations were, no doubt, set by Piero Sraffa, who had a superbly critical mind. However (Pasinetti continues) it is *not enough* to have a hyper-critical approach, no matter how penetrating it is.[18] And Sraffa was himself aware of the problem. It is this observation that allows us fully to understand the underlying motivation in Pasinetti's work. While proving to take stock of the criticisms addressed to the mainstream orthodoxy theory, Pasinetti's work also and above all intends to be the momentum for a constructive proposal of an alternative theory. The sense of looking at the past, aiming for the future then becomes clear,[19] but the need also arises for further discussion and deeper probing into those sources which allow Pasinetti to again launch the theme of reinterpreting the 'Cambridge School' with views and meanings largely rooted in the line taken by this author.

Today some go back to speaking specifically about 'civil economy'.[20] If the common image of the 'Cambridge School' seems far removed from the perspective of a civil economy, this is due to the *simplistic* criterion by which it was seen, especially in its relationship with Italy, which was too narrowly limited in space and time. In fact, the origins of that necessary 'connection' are to be found in the *classical period* and especially in the link between the Italian and the Scottish Enlightenment in the second half of the eighteenth century. The reference to the classical tradition is not surprising in the reconstruction of the 'Cambridge School'. It also takes on a more precise meaning, in fact, in the light of the line of thought developed by Pasinetti as time went by.

The idea of a *civil economy* emerges in the development of economics, first with the (trail-blazing) university course of 'Lectures of Commerce or Civil Economy' by Antonio Genovesi (1765–7). Economists travel straight from money, banking and finance (Mercantilism), to an emphasis on *productivity* based on production and circulation (Physiocracy), then to a logic of *creativity* based on learning and human capital (Italian schools first, and a little later Adam Smith). It is at this last stage that the theme of trust acquires new value together with a relational perspective and the link between the economy and the world of institutions. Here the contribution made by Italian schools is fundamental. Civil economy is a crucial aspect of the Italian Enlightenment.

The Italian intellectual environment, especially in Naples, was pervaded by an interest in the *social relationship* (today we would call this the social or the relational), including 'public trust' as a force capable of generating social order. The Milanese experience began with a practical application of empirical knowledge that aimed to provide the elements for a policy of reform. The contemporary experience of the generation of Verri and Beccaria must also be remembered. It was from the Milan experience that a practical application provided the inspiration and incentive for a broad conceptual elaboration that led to the fruitful conception of *public happiness*.

It is necessary to resort to these precedents and to understand the 'Revolution' lying in wait for political economy today. This is where the connection exists with the 'Cambridge School'. The intellectual experience of Pasinetti, in particular, makes clear the limits of a logic of surplus detached from its implications for economic dynamics and ill-prepared to provide meeting places for the study of institutions in civil society.

Especially where the study of institutions is concerned Luigi Pasinetti's basis of analysis resides in what he calls *a separation theorem*, through which (he writes) we must make it possible

> to disengage those investigations that concern the foundational bases of economic relations – to be detected at a strictly essential level of basic economic analysis – from those investigations that must be carried out at the level of the actual economic institutions.[21]

Investigations of the first type concern the fundamental economic relations defined and identified independently of specific behavioural models and institutional set-ups. This is the level of investigation that Pasinetti calls 'natural' and that allows the determination of economic variables 'at a level which is so fundamental as to allow us to investigate them independently of the rules of individual and social behaviour to be chosen in order to achieve them'.[22]

It is only natural to realize here that these observations cast Pasinetti's analysis beyond the horizon of the 'Cambridge School' taken by itself. In questions of analysis of the institutions we now find positions – in authors such as Douglass North – which seem to be moving towards that expressed by Pasinetti, though starting from different theoretical premises and contexts.[23] On the other hand, recent contributions, such as Daron Acemoglu's, still seem to be aiming to pursue the line of inquiry of much of the so-called 'political economics', turned popular in recent years, which boils down to enlarge the scope of the approach developed by the school of Buchanan's Public Choice, by massive injections of econometric analysis. This is a line of inquiry that makes the institutions themselves no longer a constraint to the 'rational' individual choices, but rather the *result* of these same rational individual choices, under whose rule the institutions themselves are made to fall back. On the contrary, precisely because of the 'separation theorem', Pasinetti's approach manages to embrace a whole series of new elements, including those that fall within the scope of the civil economy, of authors such as Bruni and Zamagni or Gui and Sugden.[24]

The structure of links of required compatibility expressed by the classical concept of a 'natural system' is associated – at a separate level of analysis – with the study of institutions (that is the 'rules of the game') necessary to address issues locally and historically specific to the working of the economic system. This approach fully corresponds with the logic of Verri and Smith (to quote two contiguous authors) on the *necessary* existence of a 'common price' (Verri) or 'natural price' (Smith), combined with the *variety* of specific institutional set-ups.

Among the recent studies on civil economy that appear significant in the perspective chosen for this essay, I would like to mention here some of the contributions of Alberto Quadrio Curzio, especially in the recent volume, which is particularly useful to illustrate the appearance of continuity of perspective of 'civil economy' throughout the entire tradition of Italian economic thought.[25] It is not surprising that Quadrio Curzio himself, dealing with the formative experience of Italian economists in the post-war period, recognizes significant elements of Italian tradition in the analysis and work of Luigi Pasinetti.[26] In particular, as an important ingredient of the meaning to be attributed to the concept-term of 'civil economy' in fact, we insist here that the *natural economic system* of Luigi Pasinetti excludes any claim or desire to make institutions endogenous, while granting that the natural system, as Pasinetti writes, does have the power to give indications for institutional blueprints. It has the power to clarify the aims pursued by the institutions and, in so doing, to set priorities in the institutions themselves.[27]

In a recent critical assessment of 'Sraffian schools' Mark Blaug has argued that it must be acknowledged that Luigi Pasinetti 'has veered away from the Sraffian camp with his own approach to the growth theory'.[28] This is both interesting and wrong at the same time: Luigi Pasinetti provides the link between Sraffa and Kaldor, if I may be allowed to express the problem in a way which, though not exhaustive at all, has the advantage of relying on the approach and the contributions focused upon in the present essay. So it is not a matter of veering away from the Sraffian camp: it is rather a matter of *making sense* of the Sraffian approach. Mark Blaug makes use of a wrong and misleading expression: it is not in fact a question of *abandoning* the Sraffian roots but it is, rather, that of making their creative potential evident, thus avoiding the risk of simply being turned into mere *epigoni* (the 'Sraffians') in the sense outlined above.

The contribution of Vivian Walsh also moves in this same direction. He treats structural dynamics not only as a child of the 'Cambridge School', but also as endowed with the specific features that are the basis of what he calls 'enriched classicism', with an explicit reference to an evident 'contamination' between Pasinetti's structural dynamics and Sen's studies on capabilities. This is – we add here – a perspective that, unlike other developments in the Cambridge School, is firmly rooted in the Enlightenment tradition, Italian on one side and Scottish on the other.

This is a line of inquiry which focuses on Adam Smith. The idea of the Classical School in economics from time to time has taken on different specific contents. On the one hand, this has sometimes been to prioritize the Smith–Ricardo–Marx line stressing the theory of distribution. From another perspective it is instead intended to give space to a Smith–Ricardo–Marshall/Walras–Pareto line, with emphasis on *allocation* and *equilibrium*. Of course, here we use a deliberately simplified representation, which should be carefully qualified: for example, to include debates developed over recent years on the contribution made by Marshall.[29]

However, it is useful to highlight how classical economics, which is both new and old, is probably the time and place today to revive a concept firmly constructed (as already mentioned above) on the modern theme of *growth*. As part of this vision the classical paradigm is a child of the Enlightenment and leads to everything you need to emphasize in terms of dynamic processes, learning, institutions, reasons for action. Here, I think, structural dynamics can find its natural collocation as the constructive branch of post-Keynesian Cambridge which is set to have a future.

The Legacy of the Italian Tradition at its Best

There are different notions of Classicism in Economics that have been discussed time and again by economists and historians of economic thought. In the present contribution I wish to take advantage of the historico-analytic perspective emphasized, among others, by Alberto Quadrio Curzio, particularly during the recent years, a perspective which is based on what he aptly called the *Lombard Paradigm* in political economy.[30] While the approach chosen here affords an opportunity for an analysis of the *Lombard Paradigm* in particular, it will also be appropriate to discuss the paradigm itself both within the context of the Italian tradition at large and also in connection with a more general discussion on the notion of Classicism in economics. Our analysis here completes, in a sense, Quadrio Curzio's treatment of 'paradigms [in the Italian tradition] between the 17th and the 20th century', as per the subtitle to Quadrio Curzio's *Economisti ed economia*.[31] For, indeed, Quadrio Curzio does not have a chapter or a section on Sraffa in his book: but much of what he says has to do with the sources and the future of Sraffian economics, especially as he deals with Pasinetti.

I have proposed in this essay to start from Piero Sraffa's notion of what the 'Classical School' or the 'Classical Economists' are meant to be. It is well-known that Sraffa's idea of Classicism puts the notion of *surplus* at centre stage. Sraffa's approach thus directly entails a radical criticism of the Neoclassical Marginalist approach.[32] To see this clearly, one must consider that the core issue of economics in the Neoclassical Marginalist sense is the theoretical idea, together with the practical aim, of achieving an efficient *allocation* of given resources. It coincides, in other words, with the notion of the 'nature and significance' of the discipline put forward by Lionel Robbins in his 'Classic' essay (here of course the word 'Classic' takes a different meaning). A 'Surplus approach' – without entering here and now a detailed discussion of its nature – is *not* focused on allocation in the first place. It is, instead, focused on the *accrual* of new resources, which is the more direct aim and, when fulfilled, the result of economic activity.

There are a number of ways of conceiving of a 'Surplus approach': the *Lombard Paradigm* contains the seed of one such conception. It is, in fact, based on learning and creativity as basic ingredients of a *dynamic* theory, meaning a theory which is designed to tackle the question of the growth or accrual in time of resources entering as inputs in the economy through all kinds of economic activities that take place in it.

It is in that line, of a Smithian-enriched Classicism, that it becomes easy to understand the spirit of Pasinetti's contribution. Structural dynamics can find its natural place as the main pillar of the constructive branch of post-Keynesian Cambridge, the side of the so-called Anglo-Italian School, which (as we have concluded in this essay) is set to have a future.[33]

14 FINANCIAL STABILITY: THE ROLE OF CENTRAL BANKS

Jean-Pierre Danthine[1]

Introduction

The recent financial crisis has highlighted the vulnerability of today's globally integrated financial system and the dismal consequences of financial instability for the broader economy. The deficiencies of the pre-crisis policy consensus on the way to deal most effectively with financial stability risks have also been laid bare.

An important first lesson of the recent experience is that price stability is not sufficient for preserving financial stability. Indeed, while monetary policy had been increasingly successful in containing inflation and reducing macroeconomic volatility during the 'Great Moderation',[2] it was not able to prevent a large-scale build-up of financial imbalances, which, subsequently, induced a severe global recession and potentially long-lasting welfare losses.

A second lesson is that the predominant microprudential approach to financial regulation focusing on the stability of individual financial institutions is not sufficient for system-wide stability.

The recent crisis has thus raised fundamental questions concerning the optimal macroeconomic policy framework – and the role of the central bank – as we move forward. Two issues stand out in particular: how can we improve our ability to contain systemic risks to financial stability knowing that, in case of adverse shocks, these risks can materialize with devastating consequences for the broader economy? And, more specifically, how and to what extent can central banks sustainably contribute to ensuring financial stability while pursuing price stability as their primary mandate?

This essay first argues that, because of the interconnectedness between monetary policy and financial stability central banks cannot shy away from assuming a major role in the pursuit of financial stability. The pre-crisis orthodoxy, focused on using monetary policy instruments predominantly to 'clean up the mess' after a financial boom busted, is unlikely to represent an optimal strategy, given the immense welfare cost of financial disruptions. At the same time, giving too big a role to interest rate policy in the pursuit of financial stability is also likely to be an inefficient way to deal with financial imbalances in all circumstances. Indeed, the negative consequences for the real economy of delivering a more than marginal reduction of financial imbalances through pure interest rate changes are probably unbearable. For this reason, pp. 184–6 of this essay stresses the necessity of using additional preventive instruments to counter the emergence of systemic financial instabilities more directly. That is, it underlines the case for a macroprudential approach to financial regulation and supervision. This approach should be seen as complementary to a well-designed microprudential regulation targeted at assuring the resilience of individual financial institutions and it should be conducted alongside a monetary policy remaining firmly focused on price stability. Against the background of tight interactions between macroprudential and monetary policies, pp. 186–8 argues that central banks have an important role to play in defining and implementing such macroprudential policies. The conclusion follows on pp. 188–9.

Monetary Policy and Financial Stability: A Tight Connection

It is undisputed that a monetary policy geared to securing medium- and long-term price stability provides significant economic benefits. High and volatile inflation rates are detrimental to productivity and growth. Uncertainty about future price trends leads to inefficient investment and consumer spending decisions. It is also well established that the optimal institutional setting to achieve this price stability objective is an operationally independent central bank mandated primarily to guarantee price stability.[3]

This insight does not mean that financial stability issues should be ignored by central banks. On the contrary, the traditional tasks of central banks are closely interlinked with various aspects of financial stability.

First and obviously, in their historical role as lender of last resort (LOLR), central banks bear a major responsibility in crisis management. During the recent crisis, central banks clearly demonstrated that they can fulfil this function to a previously unforeseen extent. Such crisis measures do not come for free, however. They should be seen solely as a last resort. In the longer term, they create distortions and can be the source of new instabilities in financial markets. In particular, there is a moral hazard issue. Banks that can rely on central banks' liquidity provision in a crisis have diminished incentives to manage their risks properly in good times.

Second, monetary policy affects financial stability through various channels.[4] Importantly, changes in the policy rate alter the tightness of borrowing constraints and the likelihood of borrowers' default. The policy rate also influences the risk perception and risk tolerance of intermediaries. For instance, low rates can create incentives for banks to leverage their balance sheets, increase their exposure to risky assets and reduce efforts in (and thus the cost of) screening borrowers. Moreover, interest rate changes may impose a negative externality on financial stability through their impact on asset prices and exchange rates. For instance, lowering interest rates can increase asset prices, which may trigger further increases in leverage and asset price booms, thus exacerbating the financial cycle.

Third and conversely, a stable, efficient financial system is an important prerequisite for the effective transmission of monetary policy signals to the broader economy. Developments observed during the recent financial crisis provide impressive evidence in this regard. As a recent example, balance-sheet strains led banks in the euro-area periphery to grant credit to the private sector only very parsimoniously and at high rates, despite record-low policy rates and unrestricted access to central bank liquidity.

Given all this, it comes as no surprise that many central banks' mandate includes an obligation to contribute to the stability of the financial system besides ensuring stable prices. In this regard, the crisis has brought an old question back into the limelight: to what extent should and can central banks proactively counteract the development of financial imbalances using monetary policy instruments?

Pre-Crisis Orthodoxy

Before the crisis, the consensus view on how to deal with financial stability risks was dominated by an attitude of restraint in addressing system-wide financial risk directly. This consensus was based on two key arguments.

First, it was largely assumed that securing the solidity of individual financial institutions would also grant system-wide stability and thus that regulation at the level of individual firms – microprudential regulation – would suffice. The crisis clearly proved this view to be untenable. Risk in a financial system can arise quasi endogenously, even if all or most individual financial institutions appear to be robust, as the imminent risk of a cascade of bank failures in the aftermath of the collapse of Lehman Brothers in September 2008 plainly showed.

Second, with respect to monetary policy, the predominant view was that it should not interfere with financial booms, as pricking an asset price bubble was thought to be generally more costly than cleaning up after the bubble has burst. In this view, monetary policy was supposed to remain firmly focused on (consumer price) inflation, using the short-term interest rate as its main tool. As a corollary, asset price developments were thought to be of significance only to the extent of their effect on inflation. The foundation of this doctrine resided in the difficulty of identifying ex ante when a bubble is forming. Specifically, it was argued that it is inherently difficult to disentangle situations where a credit or asset-price boom is justified by fundamentals from those where it is based on misplaced expectations and herding and thus is a threat to financial stability. As a result, an attempt to prick a bubble may lead to an intervention that puts a halt to 'a good boom' which could have pushed the economy towards a higher level of development. In this sense, stopping an asset price boom could well impose substantial economic costs in the form of foregone growth with no real associated benefit.

This arm's length approach in dealing with systemic financial risk was – seemingly – successful. It contributed to an extended period of macroeconomic stability as measured by low inflation, low interest rates, and a reduction in price and output volatility. This success fostered confidence in this policy approach and encouraged complacency both in academia and policymaking circles with respect to financial vulnerabilities. However, substantial financial risks were building up on the back of this superficial macroeconomic stability. Interest rates may have been optimal for achieving the price stability objective. Yet given the environment, they may ultimately have compromised financial stability by contributing to the vulnerabilities that, eventually, pushed the global economy to the brink of a financial depression. This argument is based on the presumed existence of a so-called risk-taking channel, that is, the notion that the low interest rates prevailing before the crisis provided fertile ground for miscalculation of financial risk and excessive risk-taking by financial intermediaries.[5]

Leaning against the Wind as an Alternative?

If, from this perspective, interest rates were indeed too low prior to the crisis, it may be conjectured that central banks – by keeping interest rates higher – could have helped avoid, or at least contain, the crisis. Indeed, raising interest rates seems like a natural response to a credit boom, as the higher market borrowing rates exert a dampening effect on credit demand and – eventually – on asset prices. When this calls for deviations from otherwise (that is, from a price stability point of view) optimal policy, one talks of 'leaning against the wind'. In economic upturns, this would involve central banks setting higher interest rates than would be necessary to achieve price stability alone. The objective would be to limit excessively risky behaviour on the part of financial intermediaries, avoid the overvaluation of assets and prevent bubbles from emerging, or at least constrain their size.

For various reasons, the policy interest rate is, however, a rather inefficient tool when used single-handedly for the purpose of dampening the financial cycle.

For one, even if price and financial stability goals call for an interest rate move in the same direction, empirical evidence suggests that containing an asset price-cum-credit boom may require very large interest rate movements, leading to commensurate output losses that may be difficult to justify given the prevailing uncertainties. For instance, Bean et al. estimate that a fairly aggressive 'leaning against the wind' policy by the Fed between 2003 and 2006 would, despite substantially higher policy rates,[6] have had only a limited impact on credit growth, while real house prices could have been some 7.5 per cent lower than they were at their peak. The simulated policy would also have prompted significant lower GDP growth rates, inducing a cumulative loss in output over the 2003–7 period estimated to be around 4 percentage points.

Second and related, sheer conflicts with the price stability mandate are possible. At times, monetary and financial stability assessments may require very different interest rate moves, sometimes even moves in opposite directions. For example, the economic outlook may justify lowering interest rates while a financial stability perspective would favour raising interest rates to counter potential imbalances. The current debate in Sweden is exemplary in this regard. During the recovery from the crisis, the central bank increased policy rates in several steps from mid-2010 to mid-2011. Monetary policy was thus substantially tighter than in most other advanced economies and it has remained so at least until 2013. This monetary policy stance was at least partially motivated by an attempt to dampen the dynamics in the domestic credit and housing markets.[7] The Governing Board of the Rijksbank has remained split on this policy, however. A vocal minority has consistently argued that this policy has led to a significant undershooting of the inflation target and entails substantial cost in terms of unemployment. These costs could be justified neither by the level of risk prevailing in the housing market nor by the presumably marginal impact of higher interest rates on household indebtedness.[8]

The situation prevailing in Switzerland since 2011 provides another case in point. Confronted with extreme safe haven pressures resulting in a massive overvaluation of the Swiss franc, the Swiss National Bank has been enforcing an exchange rate floor of CHF 1.20 per euro since September 2011. This policy move, aimed at fighting strong deflationary developments, has invalidated the interest rate as an instrument for dampening the strong growth in credit volumes.

Third, one may add that a 'leaning against the wind' policy could negatively affect monetary policy effectiveness in the longer run. Making use of the interest rate instrument for a variety of objectives may lead to confusion by the public as to the commitment of the central bank to the price stability goal, with the attendant risk of de-anchoring inflation expectations and undermining central banks' credibility.

To sum up, while interest rate policy may sometimes be enlisted in support of efforts to contain financial stability risks, it is unlikely to suffice as the sole, or even main instrument for doing so. At times, the interest rate may not be available as an instrument, at other times the rates required for monetary policy objectives may differ considerably from those appropriate to furthering financial stability policy objectives. Using the interest rate to contain asset price or credit growth would regularly lead to costly deviations from the interest rate path optimally justified by the pursuit of the price stability mandate. As a consequence, central banks would rapidly reach their limits if they were simply to put more emphasis on their financial stability mandate without simultaneously expanding their toolbox. The more objectives an instrument is expected to achieve, the greater the risk of wrong decisions and conflicting objectives. This is merely a restatement of the 'Tinbergen principle' according to which the optimal number of policy instruments equals the number of policy objectives.[9] Accordingly, additional instruments are needed to counter the emergence of financial instabilities. Instruments directly targeting the source of financial exuberance seem to be most appropriate.

A Macroprudential Approach to Financial Stability

In general, the goals pursued with targeted instruments should be, first, to enhance the resilience of the financial system to adverse shocks, and second – to the extent possible – to preventively contain the build-up of systemic risk, i.e. mitigate financial distortions ex ante. This is exactly the thrust of the macroprudential approach to financial regulation and supervision. Put simply, macroprudential supervision and regulation is concerned with the stability of the entire financial system, rather than that of individual institutions, the latter being the domain of microprudential supervision and regulation.

Macroprudential supervision and regulation involves, first, monitoring structural systemic risk. This is the risk that the default of a single bank – because of its size, market share or interconnectedness – could jeopardize certain functions that are vital for the economy, such as payment transactions or lending to the real economy. One way to address these risks is to impose progressive capital adequacy requirements. The greater a bank's systemic importance, the more equity capital it is required to hold. If capital adequacy requirements increase in step with systemic importance, banks have an incentive to stay smaller and less systemically important. If they do not, the extra capital at least makes them more resilient.

The second key dimension of macroprudential supervision and regulation is the build-up of systemic risk over time, and especially the risk induced by the procyclical behaviour of financial agents. Procyclicity can arise, for instance, from the tendency to underprice risk during booms and overprice it in downturns. Sometimes exacerbated by regulatory requirements, it causes agents to take similar actions in case of an adverse shock, for instance to dispose of risky assets when prices fall. While this behaviour may be individually rational, the outcome can be collectively devastating. Regulatory action can be taken to cushion against or hinder the growth of such risks over time – for instance, by imposing an obligation to build up additional capital, a countercyclical capital buffer, in phases of excessive credit growth. Another way of achieving the required countercyclical effect would take the form of tightening restrictions on loan-to-value ratios when signs emerge that a bubble could be forming in certain credit markets, such as the mortgage market.[10]

What is appealing in theory is not, however, always easy to implement in practice. The use of macroprudential instruments poses various challenges.

First, as mentioned earlier, identifying unsustainable developments in asset and credit markets is inherently difficult. Thus, the aim cannot, and should not, be to surgically prick bubbles or to fine-tune asset price or credit market developments. It is easier although not trivial to identify situations of intensified financial stability risk. In such cases, taking precautionary action is fully justified. The key question to focus on therefore is, 'How can we assess whether the build-up of risk is approaching a critical stage?' International evidence suggests a palette of quantitative early warning indicators that are reliable predictors of banking crises and financial instability. For instance, history shows that real estate boom/bust cycles are particularly damaging when associated with increased leverage in both the real and financial sectors.[11]

Second, so far, practical experience with macroprudential instruments has been fairly limited. Many issues have still to be settled, in particular regarding the effectiveness and optimal calibration of such instruments in the face of continuously changing economic conditions. The resulting scientific uncertainty increases the risk of policy errors and calls for prudent development and introduction of such new instruments.[12]

Third, as for any regulatory intrusion, macroprudential instruments do not come without costs. However, these collateral costs to the economy are plausibly lower than the stability benefits generated. In this regard, the Bank of International Settlements estimates that, by reducing the probability of a crisis, the benefit of higher capital buffers is, on average, significantly higher than their costs in terms of foregone real output.[13] On the downside, more targeted regulatory instruments may create stronger incentives and possibilities for circumvention. As the winners and losers are more apparent than in the case of broader-based policies, their usage can also be more politicized.

Despite these challenges, the case for a precautionary approach to financial stability risk is strong. Given the huge cost of inaction when imbalances develop in the asset and credit markets, it is imperative that policymakers be endowed with additional macroprudential instruments. This assessment is not only the product of careful application of the aforementioned 'Tinbergen principle'. On a deeper level, this conclusion is also based on the recognition that macroprudential instruments directly addressing the risks associated with credit and asset price booms should provoke smaller collateral damages than broad-based monetary policy tools. From a welfare perspective, applying instruments that target the root causes of the problems generated by excessive risk-taking in times of low interest rates should therefore dominate the exclusive use of a 'leaning against the wind' policy.

Implementing Macroprudential Policy:
A Key Role for Central Banks

Who should be in charge of macroprudential policies? And, in particular, what is the role of the central bank? In the absence of interactions between monetary, macroprudential and microprudential policies, each of these policies could be delegated to specific authorities acting independently. In reality, however, significant interactions exist. At the very least, this reality means that if different authorities are given responsibility for the different policies, strong coordinating mechanisms should be in place.

Tight Policy Interactions

The linkages discussed above between monetary policy and financial stability imply, in turn, a close interconnection between monetary and macroprudential policies. Monetary policy exerts an influence on the credit cycle and on asset prices and thus on the need for activating cyclical macroprudential instruments. Conversely, macroprudential policies aimed at credit markets influence monetary policy decisions. This is because macroprudential policies, at least in part, work through the same transmission channels as monetary policy – namely the bank lending and balance sheet channel. For instance, a targeted increase in capital requirements with respect to mortgage credits may increase the cost of borrowing in this specific segment of the credit market. Any kind of credit tightening triggered by this change in macroprudential policy could also affect real activity and inflation, thus interfering with the action of monetary policy.

The size of such interactions and feedbacks between monetary and macroprudential policies may vary, depending on circumstances. As an example, the impact of a change in interest rates on lending could vary as a function of the level of a bank's capital buffer. Moreover, we may observe either complementary, conflicting or independent effects on the effectiveness of each policy in achieving its own primary objective. The optimal mix and stance of both policies depends, not least, on the type of shock experienced by the economy. For instance, given a positive shock to aggregate demand (inducing an increase in both credit and inflation), the optimal response would be for both policies to tighten. Alternatively, a positive supply shock can give rise to policy conflicts since it may lead to rising asset prices and higher credit demand but dampen consumer price inflation. The ensuing tightening of macroprudential policy may require an easing of the monetary policy stance to achieve price stability.

Clearly, macroprudential policies interact not only with monetary policy, but also with microprudential policies. These interactions are particularly strong given that macroprudential and microprudential policies share a common fundamental goal – preserving financial stability – and given that they make use of the same instruments such as capital and liquidity requirements, at least to some extent. Here again, complementary or conflicting effects are conceivable. On the one hand, if macroprudential policy successfully contains systemic risk, the environment in which financial institutions operate will be less risky. This may facilitate the task of microprudential policy in promoting the safety and soundness of individual financial institutions. On the other hand, microprudential regulation, such as risk-weighted capital requirements aimed at ensuring the resilience of an individual bank, can have procyclical effects. However, it is precisely this procyclicity which macroprudential policies aim to counter.

Dealing with Policy Interactions

There are two distinct approaches to dealing with the coordination issues that arise as a consequence of the close interactions between monetary and microprudential policies, on the one hand, and macroprudential policy, on the other. The first is to place the responsibility of these three policies in the hands of a single institution. This is the approach chosen in the UK, with full responsibility for prudential regulation (both micro and macro) assigned to the Bank of England. Thus, coordination issues are *a priori* resolved at the cost of building a very powerful but complex institution which may prove politically vulnerable, given the scope of its action and the potential for policy mistakes.

Alternatively, and more traditionally, microprudential and monetary policy may be attributed to distinct institutions (the microregulator and the central bank, respectively), with macroprudential policy being a shared responsibility. This is the approach chosen in Switzerland, with the microregulator being fully responsible for the regulation and oversight of individual banks and the central bank mandated to conduct monetary policy, while macroprudential policy is implemented collaboratively. Clearly, such a 'shared-responsibilities' approach must be supplemented by sound coordination mechanisms. A clear definition of individual mandates and responsibilities, allocation of instruments among the authorities concerned, and the scope of information sharing between the authorities involved in fostering financial stability are all of utmost importance.

As far as the definition of primary responsibilities within macroprudential policy is concerned, a natural attribution of tasks emerges. In the case of the structural dimension of macroprudential policies – policies addressing systemic risk that arise from the systemic importance of individual financial institutions – the interactions are particularly tight between microprudential and macroprudential policies since individual and system-wide stability risks overlap. Here macroprudential policy relies first and foremost on the monitoring of single systemically important institutions, for which the authority in charge of individual institutions, the microregulator, has all the necessary competences. The microregulator is thus naturally best placed to take the lead. Being responsible for system-wide stability – and in its capacity as LOLR – the central bank must, however, be involved in identifying systemically important institutions and defining the regulatory requirements specific to these institutions.

It is in the case of macroprudential policies addressing the cyclical dimension of systemic risk that the interactions with monetary policy are the tightest and most delicate. It is also here that the specific analytical and forecasting skills of central banks can be most useful. It is precisely the expertise in analysing the overall economy and specific market segments, such as the real estate and credit markets, as well as the interlinkages between the financial system and the broader economy – a prerequisite for the conduct of monetary policy – that is relevant for devising cyclical macroprudential policies. It is thus natural that the central bank finds itself in the driving seat in this case. A different configuration is likely to inflict unwarranted constraints on central banks in fulfilling their core mandate, that is, securing price stability.

Conclusion

Contributing to financial stability is a fundamental element in the mandate held by central banks. The recent financial crisis has provided ample evidence that central banks have an effective set of instruments for crisis management, in other words, for mitigating the negative impact of financial crises. The key function of LOLR provides the foundation for this activity.

Yet despite extensive crisis management, the cost of a systemic financial crisis remains enormous. One central conclusion, therefore, is that more attention needs to be paid to crisis prevention. This applies to both the structural and the cyclical dimension of systemic risk. In the case of the latter, monetary policy is strongly challenged, since the interest rate is, at first sight, an obvious candidate instrument for addressing cyclical excesses in the credit and real estate markets. However, the effectiveness of the interest rate for this specific purpose is subject to strong limitations. Hence a complementary approach is needed, and the conditions must be created for the timely application of more suitable instruments which are targeted directly at the source of financial instability.

Placing more weight on macroprudential supervision and regulation is the way forward. Macroprudential policies should be seen as complementary to monetary policy and microprudential regulation in the pursuit of the twin goals of price *and* financial stability. When implemented credibly and effectively, macroprudential and monetary policies can reinforce each other. For instance, the introduction of additional instruments to deal directly with risks to financial stability renders more credible the commitment of central banks to price stability. Moreover, by containing the build-up of financial risks and helping buffer eventual shocks, well-calibrated macroprudential policies reduce the risk of overburdening monetary policy during periods of financial stress.

Implementing macroprudential policies is a shared responsibility among all authorities involved in fostering financial stability. The interactions are particularly strong and the required analytical competences particularly close in the case of monetary and cyclical macroprudential policies. Central banks thus have a natural role in the design and implementation of these policies.

An increased involvement of central banks in regulatory tasks is not without risks, however. As a result of their widened sphere of action, central banks may be exposed to increased political pressure that could endanger their independence. A loss of credibility would have substantial negative implications for the effective implementation of monetary policy and the pursuit of price stability. The fact that inflation expectations have remained firmly anchored has proven to be a considerable asset in the management of the most recent financial crisis. This asset, which builds on the clear mandate, the operational independence and the track record of central banks, must not be put at risk. Price stability is, and must remain, the principal objective of central banks.

15 THE FISHER RELATION IN THE GREAT DEPRESSION AND THE GREAT RECESSION

David Laidler

The so-called *Fisher relation* plays a central part in today's workhorse models of monetary policy and it often finds a place in general discussion of such issues far beyond the boundaries of the academic literature.[1] It had been making appearances in monetary debates long before the Great Depression began, indeed long before Irving Fisher himself discussed it with such skill and thoroughness in 1896 that his name became firmly and perpetually attached to it.[2] Even so, this idea's specific place in macroeconomics has changed considerably over the years. This essay explores the remarkable differences between the roles it played in the late 1920s and early 1930s on the one hand, and in the last decade or so, on the other. It also sketches an explanation for these differences in terms of the more general evolution of macroeconomics over the intervening years. In short, it presents a brief case study of the reciprocal interaction between the evolution of economic ideas and economic events which makes, or at least ought to make, its own history integral to the study of economic analysis.

The Fisher Relation

The phrase *Fisher relation* covers more than one idea. Nowadays, it is routinely used to denote a systematic tendency for variations in the expected inflation rate to be reflected – fully, it is usually assumed – in the difference between market rates of return expressed in units of current and constant purchasing power respectively. It is often set out in a simple equation

$$r = R + p(e) \qquad (1)$$

Here, r is the nominal interest rate in question, R is its real counterpart, often as a practical matter treated as a constant determined by the fundamental forces of productivity and thrift, and p(e) is the expected rate of price inflation.[3]

The idea embodied in this equation is, however, more helpfully labelled the *Fisher effect*. It expresses a rather complicated hypothesis about the economy's behaviour which requires both that agents form expectations about the future time path of prices, and that asset markets permit these expectations to be reflected fully in the difference between the nominal and real interest rates. Underlying this hypothesis is, of course, a less complicated idea, also sometimes referred to as the Fisher relation, but which is better called simply the *Fisher distinction* between nominal and real interest rates.[4] While the Fisher effect, depending as it does on expectations, is inherently forward looking, the Fisher distinction can be applied with equal ease when past, current or future values of inflation and interest rates are under discussion. In what follows, I shall try to be clear about these semantic matters, even at the risk of being a little ponderous from time to time, because they can be a source of confusion.

The Fisher Relation in the Great Depression

It is at first sight curious that the Fisher distinction, let alone the effect, seems to have played no significant part in the monetary policy discussions of 1929–33, academic and otherwise, even though both were already established in the literature of what we would now call macroeconomics. Meltzer sums the matter up as follows

> The minutes [of meetings of the Federal Reserve Board] of the period, statements by Federal Reserve officials, and outside commentary by economists and others do not distinguish between real and nominal interest rates. Surprisingly, even Irving Fisher did not insist on this distinction. Although Fisher pointed to the decline in demand deposits in conversation with [Governor Eugene] Meyer, his preferred explanation of the prolonged decline was the asymmetric effect of deflation on debtors.[5]

Just about everyone at the time who knew that prices were falling, ought to have known that this implied that real interest rates were high even though nominal rates were very low by historical standards, but no-one seems to have put matters this way.

Setting aside Fisher for the moment, to whose views we shall return in due course, Meltzer's basic point is well taken. A good example, recently documented by Romer and Romer,[6] of how even well-informed contemporary commentary stopped short of explicitly deploying the distinction is provided by *Business Week* magazine. Here, the observation that deflation was interacting with the nominal interest rates set by the Fed to create further deflation was clearly and often made, but to judge from the passages quoted by Romer and Romer, the corollary that this amounted to keeping *real rates high* is explicitly noted only by these modern authors, not by those who wrote those passages in the early 1930s.

I would suggest that the close-to-universal absence of such explicit references from the discourse of that time is accounted for by the fact that, by the late 1920s, discussion of the Fisher distinction had already become relatively uncommon, and was largely confined to discussions of the Fisher effect, notably those of Fisher himself. Furthermore, the literature of the time treated the latter mainly as a hypothesis about predominantly long-term relationships among price-level variations and interest rates, whose relevance by then had become subject to many doubts and qualifications. Such leading authorities as Ralph Hawtrey and John Maynard Keynes, both of them highly visible and influential in the US in these years, had long since either, in the first case, stopped deploying the effect altogether – compare Hawtrey (1919) with Hawtrey (1913) – or, in the second, had expressed serious doubts about its practical significance, cast in the following terms.

> Nevertheless in a period of rapidly changing prices, the money rate of interest seldom adjusts itself adequately or fast enough to prevent the real rate from becoming abnormal. For it is not the *fact* of a given rise of prices, but the *expectation* of a rise compounded of the various possible price movements and the estimated probability of each, which affects money rates.[7]

It is also worth noting that, because its exponents were from the outset reluctant to place any emphasis on such aggregate variables as the general price level, neither the Fisher distinction nor effect figured systematically in the then emerging and novel Austrian theory of the cycle which nevertheless focused on the interaction of bank lending rates and the expected rate of return on capital.

As to Fisher himself, he was perhaps already beginning to be regarded as something of a crank by the late 1920s, and his remaining public reputation would soon be thoroughly undermined by his very public failure to foresee the stock market crash of October 1929 or the seriousness of the real downturn that then ensued. More to the specific point, he had already himself ceased to claim anything more than marginal relevance for the effect that bears his name. *The Theory of Interest* (1930) included a lengthy chapter[8] that thoroughly updated his work on the topic, which he had begun in 1896 and carried further in 1907, and he summarized its overall lessons as follows.

> It should be noted that in so far as there exists any adjustment in the money rate of interest to changes in the purchasing power of money, it is for the most part (1) lagged and (2) indirect. The lag, distributed, has been shown to extend over several years. The indirectness of the effect of changed purchasing power of money comes largely through the intermediate steps which affect business profits and the volume of trade, which in turn affect the demand for loans and the rate of interest. There is very little direct and conscious adjustment through foresight. Where such foresight is conspicuous, as in the final period of German inflation, there is less lag in the effects.[9]

It is also worth recalling that, on the threshold of the Depression, discussions of monetary policy in the US had been conditioned by a prior six or seven years of price-level stability, and had centred on plans to give the Fed a binding legal mandate to continue to pursue it. Neither the Fisher effect nor the Fisher distinction had any direct role to play here, for obvious reasons.

It is indisputable that subsequent discussions would have been clearer, particularly to later readers in whose intellectual equipment the Fisher relation occupies a central place, had the real-nominal interest rate distinction been deployed in their course. But whether this want of clarity was crucial to the quality of anyone's decision making in the early years of the Depression is another matter. Even the Fisher distinction was not needed by anyone familiar with then common ways of thinking about monetary policy in order to assess the significance of the behaviour of interest rates under Fed control. These taught, among other things, that policy's tightness or looseness could be assessed by comparing the level of interest rates to expectations about what Henry Thornton had long before called the 'rate of mercantile profit',[10] and such a comparison could of course be made in either nominal or real terms, so long as consistency was observed. From this standpoint, the Fisher relation was an unnecessary extra embellishment.

This is why Hawtrey, for example, had been able to drop it from his analytic armory without any loss of substance, and write only about nominal interest rates and expected rates of return,[11] and why it made only occasional appearances in Knut Wicksell's later discussions.[12] To come to the Depression years themselves, it is also why contemporary commentators such as those associated with *Business Week* referred to above, were able to assess correctly the significance of falling prices as an indicator of the stance of monetary policy without explicitly invoking the Fisher distinction. In addition, as Frank Steindl has stressed, enough data, not least some related to the shrinking money supply, were available to judge the stance of policy along explicitly quantity-theoretic lines.[13] Many contemporary critics of the Fed, including Hawtrey[14] and his sometime assistant Lauchlin Currie,[15] not to mention Fisher himself on many occasions, derived policy advice from such data about the need to bring about vigorous money growth without referring to the real-nominal interest rate distinction. Perhaps then, the Fed's own neglect of it should not be listed high among the reasons for its unfortunate failure to heed such advice.

But though Fisher, like everyone else, had come to downplay the empirical significance of the Fisher *effect* by 1930, he nevertheless stood out from the crowd in emphasizing that the very fact of its empirical unimportance implied that the *distinction* between nominal and real interest rates was of great significance:

> In actual practice, for the very lack of this perfect theoretical adjustment, the appreciation or depreciation of the monetary standard does produce a real effect on the rate of interest, and that a most vicious one ... when the price level falls, the interest rate *nominally* falls slightly, but *really* rises greatly, and when the price level rises, the rate of interest *nominally* rises slightly, but *really* falls greatly.[16]

At first sight, then, his failure explicitly to stress the distinction subsequently, as claimed by Meltzer seems puzzling.[17] But only at first sight, because in fact Fisher did deploy the real-nominal distinction when dealing with what Meltzer refers to as the 'asymmetric effect of deflation on debtors'.[18] In the just quoted passage, Fisher is pointing to an example of the phenomenon that he had called 'The Money Illusion';[19] and the 'vicious effect' he invokes does not involve *perceived* rising real interest rates leading maximizing agents to reduce their expenditure plans. Rather, it involves agents' *failing to perceive* this rise – an error well documented by Fisher's own empirical studies of this matter – and hence making *ex ante* choices, about borrowing in nominal terms to buy real assets, whose market outcomes will *ex post* ruin them.

This is the phenomenon underlying Fisher's now celebrated, but then largely ignored, 'debt-deflation theory of great depressions' (1933), to which Meltzer obliquely refers. Fisher's original exposition of this theory in 1932 explicitly invoked money illusion and was cast in terms of the behaviour of 'nominal' and 'real' dollars in deflationary times. In one place it even offered its readers the following (not quite precisely formulated) advice, albeit in a passage enclosed in parentheses at the end of an appendix (number 5) rather than in the main text:

> To find the 'real' interest for a given period, take the percentage by which the dollar has increased and add to it the annual interest, raised by said percentage. For 1929 to 1932 the dollar increased by 53 per cent and to the third week of June 1932, by 62 per cent.[20]

In short, though the Fisher effect played no positive role in discussions of the behaviour of the economy during the early years of the Great Depression, the Fisher distinction in a straightforward backward looking application did, at least in Fisher's own account of matters, and precisely because his work had convinced him of the minor empirical irrelevance of the effect itself. As we shall see in due course, the Fisher effect's role in discussions at the time of the Great Recession that began in 2007 has been very different, but to understand how this change came about, we need to say something about its history in the intervening years.

The Fisher Relation between the Crises

Keynes, who had already expressed doubts about the Fisher effect's importance in 1923, set the dominant tone for much of its subsequent treatment during the years of the so-called Keynesian revolution in the *General Theory* (1936), albeit advancing arguments that were not quite so far removed from Fisher's own views on these matters as summarized in Fisher (1930), as he was inclined to claim.[21] True, Keynes denied any direct effect at all of expected inflation on nominal interest rates where Fisher had allowed for the possibility of a small one – 'The mistake lies in supposing that it is the rate of interest on which prospective changes in the value of money will directly react'[22] – but he was much closer to Fisher, though perhaps less definite, in accepting the possibility of an indirect causative channel, running through the influence of rising prices on the nominal value of what he called the marginal efficiency of capital, a concept, incidentally, that he himself agreed was identical to Fisher's own (1930) 'rate of return over cost'[23] – though Fisher, of course, habitually discussed the real variant of this variable.

> The stimulating effect of the expectation of higher prices is due, not to its raising the rate of interest (that would be a paradoxical way of stimulating output – in so far as the rate of interest rises, the stimulating effect is to that extent offset), but to its raising the marginal efficiency of a given stock of capital. *If* the rate of interest were to rise *pari passu* with the marginal efficiency of capital, there would be *no* stimulating effect from the expectations of rising prices. For the stimulus to output depends on the marginal efficiency of a given stock of capital rising *relatively* to the rate of interest.[24]

Keynes's disciple Sir Roy Harrod, one of the two authorities – the other being Sir John Hicks – who in 1959 informed the quintessentially 'Keynesian' Radcliffe Committee that the long-run equilibrium value of the long rate of interest was 3 per cent, was sticking firmly to this line as late as 1969[25] and indeed took it further, denying not just the empirical but the very logical possibility of expected inflation affecting the yield on bonds, on the ground that, like money itself, these were nominal assets. And though Hicks did not follow Harrod into the particular analytic error of ignoring the margin between nominal and real assets when dealing with this issue, he still wrote as follows as late as 1989:[26]

> it is commonly thought that these high rates of interest [since 1950] are a consequence of inflation: that if prices are rising at 4 per cent per annum, a nominal rate of interest of 8 per cent per annum is equivalent to a *real* rate of 4. It is true that inflation makes these high rates of interest bearable, so that their consequences are not so desperate as they would have been in the past. But to make these consequences into causes surely takes things the wrong way round.[27]

Even so, this quotation tells us quite clearly, and accurately too, that by the 1980s, the Fisher effect was back in play and 'commonly thought' to be true; and it also hints, again surely accurately, that this was in part the result of the so-called Great Inflation of that time and, by inference, of what Harry Johnson would call the Monetarist counter-revolution whose success this episode helped to promote.[28] But the idea's revival had nevertheless not been quite straightforward.

To be sure, the Fisher effect was explicitly expressed in eq. (9) of that counter-revolution's opening manifesto, Friedman's 'The Quantity Theory of Money, a Restatement', but with no citation of Fisher himself, and accompanied by the warning that 'differences of opinion [about expected inflation] cannot be neglected, so we cannot suppose (9) to hold; indeed, one of the most consistent features of inflation seems to be that it does not'.[29] What Friedman had to say about the Fisher effect in this seminal essay thus implied doubts about its empirical relevance not so far removed from those expressed, in the 1920s, not least by Keynes[30] as we have already noted, and of by course Fisher himself.

Twelve years later, in his famous AEA Presidential address (1968), Friedman's treatment of both the Fisher distinction and the Fisher effect was less hesitant. He cited their role in the theory of interest rates as the inspiration for his introduction of inflation expectations into the Phillips curve and he expressed no doubts about the effect's empirical significance or policy relevance when embedded in it. The main burden of Friedman's address was to promulgate the 'natural unemployment rate' hypothesis, whose validity required full adjustment of wage inflation to expectations about price inflation, but when it came to the parallel case of nominal interest rates, he rested content to point out that experience showed the adjustment of nominal interest rates to inflation to be 'slow to develop and slow to disappear'[31] and left the explicit question of its completeness unexamined. He was more definite in 'The Optimum Quantity of Money', however, as of course he had to be in a primarily theoretical study dealing with the monetary economics of fully anticipated inflation, but he still stressed that 'it takes a long time for people fully to adjust their anticipations to experience'.[32]

Empirical work on the expected inflation rate as a (negative) own rate of return on money, largely set in motion by Philip Cagan's paper in Friedman's 1956 volume,[33] was already well developed by the late 1960s, but explicit studies of its role in determining nominal interest rates were still rare. Only two papers from the 1960s directly dealing with US evidence on this matter are cited by Laidler and Parkin in their then comprehensive and widely read 'Inflation – A Survey': Gibson's 1970 paper and Yohe and Karnowsky's 1969 paper.[34] Still, these, along with the slightly later work of Feldstein and Chamberlain,[35] not only seemed to confirm the slowness of nominal rates to adjust to inflation, but also provided evidence that, albeit over periods that could be as long as one to three decades, it was essentially complete. Friedman's brief comments on this matter thus had an up-to-date empirical basis.[36]

The most important development of the 1960s, however, as far as the Fisher effect was concerned, was the growing acceptance that emerged at this time, mainly in theoretical work, that it should be treated as complete in the long run, and that decisions on the margin between real and nominal assets therefore should be modelled as free of money illusion. Thus, Martin Bailey and Robert Mundell introduced the effect into the then ubiquitous IS–LM model,[37] an essential step if the latter was to be deployed in analysing inflation – though it never really was with much success – but it would soon find a more comfortable home in the literature on the long-run equilibrium characteristics of a monetary economy, to which Friedman's already cited paper was a rather late but nevertheless distinguished contribution.[38]

This is not the place to digress into what this literature did or did not reveal about the possibilities for variations in a fully anticipated inflation rate to have long-run effects on real variables in general, and economic welfare in particular. These were many and various, and nowadays largely forgotten – interested readers are referred to Section 2 of Laidler and Parkin for further information[39] – but one approach to this issue, pioneered by Miguel Sidrauski would have a pervasive influence, long after his untimely death in 1968, and is important to our story.[40]

What made Sidrauski's paper seminal was his modelling of asset accumulation as the outcome of explicitly analysed forward-looking utility maximization rather than of the application of rules of thumb about propensities to save and the like. His deployment of a constant rate of time preference in formulating these decisions pinned down the real rate of interest to a constant as well, and ensured not only that the behaviour of real variables was independent of the inflation rate – a result that contradicted much contemporary wisdom, and which he emphasized – but also that the Fisher effect worked entirely on the nominal interest rate.

Obviously, from the viewpoint of analytic rigour, Sidrauski's model represented an enormous step forward.[41] Nevertheless, widely read though it immediately was, this paper appeared at a time when empirical evidence still trumped formal analysis when it came to getting ideas into general circulation, and its full impact had to await a change in economists' priorities in this regard. Thus, Laidler and Parkin noted it[42] but nevertheless expressed scepticism about there being any empirical basis for assuming that the real rate of interest was in fact invariant to monetary, or indeed any other, disturbances.[43] Their ambivalence here was symptomatic of the fact that, although the Fisher distinction and effect had come to play an increasingly important role in macroeconomic analysis as inflation gathered speed in the 1960s and into the 1970s, the literature dealing with inflation was still in a state of considerable flux, even confusion, in 1975.

The very idea that inflation was 'always and everywhere a monetary phenomenon' – to borrow Friedman's famous phrase – still generated heated controversy at this time, and so therefore did the question of how much the genesis of its then current manifestation owed to the neglect of earlier macroeconomic ideas – including the Fisher relation – in the wake of the Keynesian revolution. Furthermore, many of those who broadly accepted Friedman's view, and like Laidler and Parkin recognized the important role played by inflation expectations to its theoretical foundations, were nevertheless far from comfortable with questions about just how those expectations were formed and fitted into a bigger picture. Nothing illustrates this better than that their own main discussion of the Fisher effect itself occurs when they deal with 'The Redistributive Consequences of Inflation', not when 'The Quantity Theory and Perfectly Anticipated Inflation', 'Wage and Price Setting Behaviour and Expectations' or even '"Complete" Short-Run Models of Inflation, Output and Employment' are their topic. Furthermore, this discussion itself ends on a tentative note, by pointing out that the full adjustment period of 'one to three decades' implied by empirical results on the Fisher effect would appear to be inconsistent with the evidence [of much faster adjustment] generated in Phillips curve type studies ... However the relevant period over which expectations must be formed when setting interest rates on a long-term loan is much longer than that involved in striking a wage bargain. It is quite plausible that the same agents might adjust their expectations of inflation over the next twenty years at a much slower rate than their expectations of the next twelve months' inflation.[44]

Such indecisiveness would, of course, soon and quickly disappear from mainstream macroeconomics when formal treatments of monetarist ideas about inflation evolved into New Classical models, as they were already beginning to do by 1975, and analytic rigour came to be valued above all other virtues among the sub-discipline's practitioners. It was very difficult to write down an explicit model of an economy in which money-wage and price inflation rates responded fully and rapidly to inflation expectations but nominal interest rates did not, particularly when the idea of rational model-consistent expectations had become the foundation for modelling their formation and, crucially, also their simultaneous deployment across all markets.[45]

By the early 1980s, therefore, empirical uncertainty notwithstanding, the Fisher effect more or less as set out in equation 1, had become a routine and uncontroversial feature not only of long-run theoretical analysis of money's super-neutrality that Sidrauski had inspired, which by then had faded into the intellectual background, but also of short-run models of money, inflation and the cycle, which were nevertheless based, like his, on explicit forward-looking maximization. And in due course this effect would become equally well established in both the theory and practice of monetary policy.[46]

The Fisher Relation and the Great Recession

The Monetarism of the 1960s and early 1970s, and the New Classical economics that followed it, made major and long-lasting changes to macroeconomic theory and policy. Its interpretation of the essentially monetary nature of inflation, its claims about the likely futility of trying to engender improved real economic performance by pursuing a rising price level, and hence the desirability of making low and stable inflation the central goal of monetary policy, became widely accepted, and remain so today. However, New Classical economics' so-called 'monetary surprise' model of the cycle, which embodied the monetarist hypothesis about the prime importance of variations in the growth rate of the money supply in driving short-run macroeconomic behaviour, did not survive its encounters with empirical evidence,[47] while monetarism's preferred means of pursuing medium-term price stability – money growth targeting – would also prove fragile when actual policy was based upon it: one such scheme arguably served as a useful cover for the Volcker disinflation of the early 1980s, but the approach was otherwise soon judged impractical in the US, and similar regimes suffered the same fate in many other places too.

What then emerged on the policy front under these twin impulses, aided and abetted by Milton Friedman's spectacularly wrong forecast in 1983–4 that the rapid money growth then in progress would soon lead to a resurgence of inflation,[48] was a sort of 'Monetarism without money'.[49] The micro-foundations of this new approach were grounded in real business cycle theory, itself drawn from the same tradition in neoclassical growth theory to which Sidrauski had been a seminal contribution,[50] and on the policy front, it retained earlier emphasis on low and stable inflation as a goal and continued to stress the importance of inflation-expectations in models of how to attain it. Crucially, however, it replaced money growth with a nominal interest rate as the central bank's key instrument. Formal models of monetary policy with these features, whose classic exposition is that of Woodford where their descent from Sidrauski's work is explicitly acknowledged,[51] were well entrenched in the research departments of central banks by the turn of the millennium, and provided a background to the formal inflation targeting regimes that many of them had by then adopted. Much of the academic debate about monetary policy in the run-up to the crisis that began in 2007 was also cast in such terms.

Only the briefest reminder of these models' generic form is needed here. They have three components: an expectations augmented Phillips curve, which determines inflation as a deviation from expected inflation that is positively related to an 'output gap', the deviation of aggregate output from some long-run 'normal' level; a misnamed – here we shall let this pass – IS curve, whereby this output gap is inversely related to the real rate of interest, which in turn has a 'normal' 'neutral' or 'natural' value at which the output gap is zero, unemployment is at its natural rate, and inflation is therefore constant at its expected rate; and a policy reaction function, these days typically an explicit 'Taylor rule', according to which the central bank sets the *nominal* interest rate, and hence, through a Fisher effect, a *real* rate, so as to influence the output gap and keep inflation on some predetermined low and steady time path.

In strong contrast to its marginal place in the conventional monetary policy wisdom of the late 1920s, the Fisher relation, and more specifically the Fisher effect, was thus completely central to 'Monetarism without money', and in equally strong contrast to its virtual absence – Fisher's work excepted – from the debates that marked the Great Depression, it remained very much present even after 2007. Specifically, the relation was fundamental to discussions, set in motion by Lawrence Summers,[52] of the so-called *zero lower bound problem* posed by the possibility that, with a 'low' inflation target in place, the economy might encounter some shock in response to which a mechanical application of the Taylor rule would prescribe an impossible-to-achieve negative value for the nominal interest rate. And when, after 2007, this possibility became a reality, the Fisher effect also and necessarily figured prominently in arguments about the extent to which additional 'unorthodox' measures might, or might not, be needed to supplement what by then had become 'orthodox' interest-rate-based monetary policy. It also played a key part in the renewal of earlier rather low-keyed debates about whether price-level time path targeting (and more recently, nominal GDP growth targeting) might not in general be a superior alternative to inflation targeting in any event. The argument here is that when, in a recession, inflation falls and output slows down, these regimes, if credible, automatically give rise to an increase in the expected inflation rate, and hence lower the real rate of interest, even if the nominal rate is at its minimum, in a way that a simple inflation targeting regime in which bygones are bygones does not. Clearly the question of the policy regime's credibility, and the capacity of agents to penetrate its complexity so as to form accurate expectations, is crucial to Fisher-effect-based arguments along such lines.[53]

The Fisher effect was also in recent years an important component of the case that the Fed's policy rate had been set 'too low' in the years before 2007, and therefore contributed to – in some versions, notably that of John Taylor, caused[54] – the crisis that began in that year. There is a parallel of sorts between these criticisms of Fed policy before 2007 and some that were advanced with respect to its policies in the run-up to the Great Depression. In each case, it was argued that interest rates were kept too low for too long and fuelled speculative bubbles – mainly in the housing market before 2007 and mainly in the stock market before 1929 – whose collapse ushered in serious and cumulative dislocations of the financial system. The reasons given for these mistakes however, if mistakes indeed they were, are very different. In the late 1920s the Fed's alleged error was put down to its desire to help other countries, and particularly the UK, to cope with the stresses of returning to the gold standard at parities that in some cases were, to say the least, optimistic. More recently, the charge has been that the Taylor rule was ignored in the interests of sustaining the economy's recovery from the collapse of the preceding dot-com bubble.

In the late 1920s, Fed policy unambiguously did not lead to any general upsurge in inflation, so the Fisher relation is irrelevant to judging its appropriateness, even with benefit of eight decades of hindsight. In the mid-2000s, however, judgements about whether or not the Taylor rule, to whose deployment the Fisher relation is central, was violated hinge critically on how policy interest rates moved relative to inflation, and seem to depend, in part at least, upon how inflation is measured. To be more specific, between 2002 and 2008 CPI inflation in the US rose from a little under 2 per cent to over 4 per cent. As Taylor's work[55] has clearly shown, a policy model using this index would have called for a higher interest rate long before 2006, but over the same period, the Fed's preferred measure, core PCE inflation, remained firmly in a 'comfort zone' around 2 per cent per annum, and on this criterion, policy was about right.[56] The moral here is surely that when an important debate about the appropriate conduct of monetary policy hinges upon just which measure of the inflation rate agents are thought to form their expectations about, then the Fisher relation surely has become deeply embedded in the theory of monetary policy.

Be that as it may, the Taylor rule in general, and recent debates in particular about how it should have been applied, make most sense when cast in terms of a model in which private sector agents form their inflation expectations by observing, among other variables, the actual inflation rate, and then use this information, along with their understanding of the economy's structure and of the monetary policy regime, in making spending decisions. This idea underlies the requirement that, in implementing the rule, the monetary authorities should always raise (lower) their policy rate by more than any observed change in the rate of inflation, in order to ensure that their response results in a stabilizing increase (fall) in the real rate of interest that figures in the IS curve.

But the same class of model can yield very different policy implications if a more radically rational view of the formation of inflation expectations is embedded in the system alongside the assumption that the central bank is a completely credible inflation targeter so that policy announcements are in and of themselves sufficient to move expectations. In such systems, provided also that long-run equilibrium value of the real rate of interest is uniquely determined independently of monetary policy by the fundamentals of productivity and thrift and is constant, or at least very slow to move over time, and provided that markets work so as to keep the decisions of individual agents fully coordinated,– not assumptions that I would be any more willing to take for granted now than when contributing to Laidler and Parkin (1975) – the way for the central bank to lower (raise) the inflation rate is to lower (raise) the nominal interest rate.

This is because, in such a world, interest rate policy is interpreted by rational agents as embodying credible announcements on the central bank's part of its intentions concerning the future inflation rate, and the expectation that they engender then play a dominant role in the evolution of the equilibrium time path, and hence also the actual time path, of inflation. Given the premises, the conclusion follows. As Minneapolis Fed President Narayan Kocherlakota was a little while ago quoted as saying, 'Most of our monetary models tell us that, if the Fed maintains a constant nominal interest rate for ever, that will essentially determine the inflation rate, by way of the Fisher relation'.[57]

More specifically relevant to recent circumstances, these premises also imply that an economy can escape from stagnation accompanied by an essentially zero level of short-term nominal interest rates such as the US experienced after 2008, and the zero lower bound policy problems that go along with it, by having the central bank pre-announce a strategy of *raising* those rates. Stephanie Schmitt-Grohe and Martin Uribe have put the point as follows:

Perhaps the most problematic aspect of the analyzed exit strategy in regard to credibility is the need to communicate to the public that the increase in nominal interest rates is intended to raise inflationary expectations ... We believe that after observing falling inflation with near zero interest rates for a sufficiently large number of quarters the public will come to intuitively internalize the notion that the Fisher effect has become dominant and accept the monetary authority's argument of raising interest rates to fight deflationary pressures.[58]

In the light of such analysis, the logical coherence of which is not in question, but the empirical relevance of which depends critically on the perhaps implausible assumption that the economy always remains exactly on its equilibrium time path, as Peter Howitt demonstrated some time ago,[59] it is hard to avoid the conclusion that, although the absence of the Fisher effect and distinction from policy discussions during the Great Depression rendered these unnecessarily opaque to modern readers, the Fisher effect's central role in the debate about the Great Recession has in recent years sometimes led to a little too much clarity for comfort.[60]

Summing Up the Story

Over the century or so that our story of the Fisher relation's changing place in macroeconomics has spanned, the behaviour of the economy and of those making policy for it has changed quite radically, partly in response to changes in economic ideas. These ideas have in turn changed, again quite radically, in response to events, some of them policy induced. The evolution of the Fisher effects, and even of the simple Fisher distinctions, from something close to fringe ideas, through almost total neglect, into a core component of mainstream macroeconomics has been part of this broader process.

To be more specific: we have seen that the Fisher effect's position in the subdiscipline, already precarious in the 1920s for want of empirical support except in extreme inflationary conditions in remote times and places, was further weakened by the Keynesian revolution that the Great Depression helped bring about; that its revival came with the onset of serious inflation in major economies in 1960s and 1970s; and that this revival gathered further momentum from the emergence of an approach to macroeconomic theory that stressed logically rigorous and consistent analysis of forward-looking maximization as something to be valued above anything else. In today's intellectual environment, then, the Fisher relation, not only as a distinction but more particularly as an effect to which inflation expectations are central, cannot help but be at centre stage.

At first sight this looks very much like a Whiggish story of permanent scientific progress, but some of the recent deployments of the Fisher relation discussed at the end of the preceding section of this essay might just lead to overambitious policy developments that could at some future date turn our narrative into a cautionary tale of how particular economic ideas can after all come and go over time. Even the possibility that a few prominent central banks might adopt formal nominal GDP targeting, only to find that this scheme's purported advantages are too reliant for comfort on agents' sophistication in forming inflation expectations, could lead to such an outcome. Time will tell.

16 ENDOGENOUS MONEY IN AN ELEMENTARY SEARCH MODEL: INTRINSIC PROPERTIES VERSUS BOOTSTRAP[1]

Jean Cartelier

In the basic search-theoretic approach to money,[2] as in most sophisticated models which have followed, the quantity of money is given exogenously. That starting point is unsatisfactory and misleading. It is responsible for ascribing the existence of monetary equilibrium to *bootstrap effects* only. In fact, it turns out that some intrinsic properties of the economy, such as tastes and technology, are very important, and not merely beliefs. Moreover, assuming an exogenous quantity of money contradicts the now widely held opinion that monetary authorities do not have the power to *directly* determine the quantity of money but only to *indirectly* control it by manipulating some other variable, namely the rate of interest. Monetary models should account for the important 'stylized fact' that *money is issued at agents' request under the constraint of rules fixed by a non competitive authority*. The purpose of this essay is to propose an elementary version of such a model.

In our model, money is issued according to a very simple principle which is nothing but a generalization of the pure gold standard. In a pure metallic system, mintage consists of coining privately produced gold, making it useless for any purpose other than circulation. The gold producer has thus a choice between exchanging gold in the market or bringing it to the Mint. A condition of indifference between the two alternatives determines which quantity of gold is coined and which enters the market as a commodity.[3] Elements to be taken into account by gold producers are the cost of production, the cost of coinage (neglected here) and the seignorage earned by the monetary authority.

Let us generalize this view, assuming that the alternative offered to gold producers is now available to any producer. A producer now has to choose between two alternatives: either to enter the market with the hope of meeting someone and to exchange or to ask the monetary authority to transform, without delay, his good into a homogenous means of exchange at an additional cost s. Such a parable is not very far from what effectively happens in our economies where means of payment are issued by banks against a liability and possibly collateral. Debtors have to produce and sell something in order to pay back banks. In stationary equilibrium loans and repayments are equal. Repayment thus requires an activity of production (which implies a cost) and the payment of interest. Banks do not buy commodities, no more than the Mint buys the gold it coins, but production of gold or of a commodity is at the starting point of money issuance (in a more complete model money could be issued against a financial asset as well). Therefore, the fact that search models are not well-suited to accommodate credit must not worry us too much. Another story may be told where banks are easily located and monetization of commodities replaces credit. As a matter of fact, bank money obeys a logic which is not so much different from that of the gold standard, at least from the borrowers' point of view, once it has been understood that coins are distinct from gold and that cheques are distinct from capital.[4]

Metallic money is analysed in a search-theoretic model by Velde, Weber and Wright.[5] The concern of the authors is mainly historical. Their results are very interesting since they are able to endogenize the way coins circulate (by weight or by tale). But they do not address the question of the equilibrium quantity of money when every agent is able to monetize his production. Peterson has recently described a metallic system in the spirit of the gold standard.[6] His model is, however, restricted to a strict metallic money where gold (or money) may be consumed or sold abroad (his model is intended to study problems quite different from ours). Our purpose differs also from that of Li, who determines the conditions under which bank money can circulate, given a certain quantity of outside money.[7] The model presented here is very close to that of Kiyotaki and Wright[8] but with an endogenous procedure of issuing money. Such a model determines an equilibrium quantity of money and allows an embryonic study of monetary policy where the effects of variations of s on welfare are made explicit. Its main objective is to qualify the well-admitted proposition according to which a *bootstrap effect* is at the root of monetary equilibrium existence.

Two main results are the following:

There exist three barter equilibria in which *a zero quantity of money is associated with three different degrees of money acceptance.* The first is trivial: nobody resorts to the Mint when money is never accepted. But this may also be true when a positive fraction of agents accept money (second equilibrium) and it may even be still true when everybody is ready to sell his good for money (third equilibrium)! In other words, *an unanimous acceptance of money is not a sufficient condition for the existence of a monetary equilibrium,* contrary to what most search models with an exogenous quantity of money seem to suggest.

The existence of a monetary equilibrium depends, for a given s, *on the absolute level of specialization* and not only on a comparison between that level and the degree of money acceptation in the economy. Confidence in money, i.e. a positive degree of money acceptance, is a necessary condition for a monetary equilibrium but not a sufficient one. An additional condition must be satisfied which depends on the *intrinsic properties of the economy*, namely tastes and technology. Money is not mainly a *bootstrap effect*.

One has a complementary result for welfare and monetary policy. That monetary equilibrium dominates barter equilibrium can be proved without imposing the rather paradoxical condition that a same quantity of money exists in both cases, as in the Kiyotaki–Wright model; here the dominance of a monetary equilibrium depends on whether the quantities of money for which it would cease to be true can or cannot be reached through the endogenous money creation. The question of welfare becomes part of the (rudimentary) study of monetary policy.

The Model

The economy is described as is usual in search-models *à la* Kiyotaki–Wright with exogenous prices:

There is a continuum $[0, 1]$ of indivisible nondurable goods and of infinite-lived agents with a uniform rate of time preference r; each agent can produce only a unit of a fraction x of the goods and can consume only a unit of a fraction $y = x$ of the goods; agents never produce goods for their own consumption; production takes place at a uniform cost c and consumption provides a uniform utility u.

A monetary authority transforms at agents' request and at a cost $s \geq 0$ the produced good into a durable means of exchange[9] without any intrinsic utility; this means of exchange is called *money*; storage capacity of agents is limited to one unit of money; two versions of the model exist depending on whether money holders have an ability to produce (models S) or not (models K).[10]

Any agent may produce: (i) either for exchange (production takes places whenever an agent meets another with whom a transaction is possible) (ii) or for the Mint, in which case the agent becomes a money holder.

The equilibrium fraction of agents who accept money depends on the strategies chosen by others; it is endogenously determined.

Trade occurs in a bilateral random matching process, where agents meet according to a Poisson process with parameter α.

Let N be the proportion of agents who accept money and M that who bring their production to the Mint. At equilibrium $M \leq N$ must hold. Let V_m and V_0 be, respectively, the value of an agent holding a unit of money and producing for the market.

Bellman equations for model K in a stationary state are:

$$r V_m = \alpha N(1 - M)x(u + V_0 - V_m)$$
$$r V_0 = \alpha(1 - M)x^2(u - c) + max[0, \alpha M x(V_m - c - V_0)] \tag{1}$$

The first equation says that the flow return to a money holder is the probability of using money in exchange $\alpha N(1 - M)x$ (i.e. to meet a non-holder of money accepting money and producing a good suitable for consumption) *times* the gain in exchange. The second equation equates the flow return to a producer to a sum of two terms: the first one is the gain resulting from a barter $(u - c) > 0$ with another producer *times* the probability of such a meeting $\alpha (1 - M) x^2$, the second term is zero or the positive gain from accepting money and becoming a money holder *times* the probability of meeting a money holder interested in the good produced.

This system of equations, although usual in search models, is incomplete since it does not account for the choice producers have between going to the market or to the Mint. Producing for the Mint is interesting since money is immediately obtained (as it is proposed that Mint's location is common knowledge and it responds instantaneously) whereas in the market the probability of meeting a money holder with a single coincidence of want is $\alpha Mx < 1$, which implies a positive delay. But, such an advantage may be compensated by the cost of mintage and by the loss of the opportunity of a barter with a producer in case of a double coincidence meeting. In short, a producer will prefer to go to the Mint at any time if the following condition holds:

$$V_m - c - s \geq V_o \tag{2}$$

Thus, two decisions matter for producers: (i) whether to accept money or not in exchange which depends on the sign of $V_m - c - V_0$ (ii) whether to produce for exchange or for the Mint which depends on a comparison between $Vm - c - s$ and V_0.

From (1) and time normalization $\alpha x = 1$, condition $V_m - c - s \geq V_o$ may be written as:

$$\frac{(1-M)\ (u-c)\ (N-x) - rc}{r + N(1-M) + M} \geq s \tag{3}$$

Indifference between producing for exchange or for the Mint determines the equilibrium quantity of money:

$$M* = \frac{(u - c)(N - x) - rc - s(r + N)}{(u - c)(N - x) + s(1 - N)} \tag{4}$$

For $s = 0$, (3) reduces to the condition of money acceptance, a necessary but not sufficient condition for $M \geq 0$. Acceptance of money requires $(1 - M)(u - c)(N - x) - rc \geq 0$. It is $N = x + rc/(u - c)$ when a strict equality holds and $N = 1$ otherwise. Three cases are to be examined, according to the degree of money acceptance.

<1> When $V_m - V_0 - c < 0$, nobody would choose to go to the Mint since $V_m - c - s < V_0$ (note that $s \geq 0$). As a consequence $N^\circ = 0$ and $M^\circ = 0$ since no negative quantity of money is allowed. The economy is populated only by pro-

ducers who do not accept money. Their value is $V_0 = (\alpha\, x^2(u - c))/r$. This result holds for model K and model S.

<2> When $V_m - V_0 - c = 0$, $N^{oo} = x + rc/(u - c)$. Reporting this value in (4) gives a second barter equilibrium since $M^{oo} = 0$. That money is accepted by a positive fraction of agents does not prevent the existence of a barter equilibrium. When money is issued at the request of agents, money acceptance, although a necessary condition for going to the Mint, is not a sufficient one. *Barter and monetary equilibria differ less in the degree of money acceptance than in the degree of recourse to the Mint.* Barter equilibrium occurs when nobody has an incentive to go to the Mint $(M = 0)$, which is the case here despite the fact that $N^{oo} > 0$.

<3> When $V_m - V_0 - c > 0$, every agent is ready to accept money in exchange for his good: $N^{oo} = 1$. But, as we know, this does not mean that everybody has an interest in going to the Mint. When $N = 1$, (4) becomes:

$$M^{ooo} = 1 - \frac{rc}{(1 - x)(u - c)} - \frac{(1 + r)s}{(1 - x)(u - c)} \tag{5}$$

A fraction M^{ooo} of the agents chooses to resort to the Mint if a fraction $1 - M^{ooo}$ decides to produce for the market. Conversely, choosing to produce for the Mint is the best response for a fraction M^{ooo} to the strategy followed by the fraction $1 - M^{ooo}$. This non-symmetric pure strategy equilibrium is unique.[11]

$M^{ooo} \geq 0$ requires:

$$x \leq \bar{x} = \frac{u - (c + s)(1 + r)}{u - c} \tag{6}$$

Money effectively exists in equilibrium only if goods have a degree of liquidity, measured by x, inferior to a determinate threshold $\bar{x}$. Beyond a fixed level of specialization in tastes and technology $(x < \bar{x})$ the liquidity of goods is low enough to incite a positive fraction of agents to bring their production to the Mint. The critical level $\bar{x}$ beyond which no monetary equilibrium can exist does not depend on expectations or on confidence but uniquely on intrinsic properties of the economy such as preferences u and r or technology c. 'Confidence', if one decides to label so the condition of money acceptance, is necessary but not sufficient to push agents to resort to the monetary institution.

Besides, the maximum quantity of money is given for $s = 0$. It is equal to $\bar{M} = 1 - \frac{rc}{(1 - x)(u - c)}$ for both models K and S.

The equilibrium quantity of money is a decreasing function of both s, which may seem rather natural, and x.

By manipulating mintage conditions the monetary authority influences the equilibrium quantity of money. The relation between M and s is given by (5) and the equilibrium quantity of money is zero if the cost of mintage is sufficiently high. For $\bar{s} = \frac{(1 - x)(u - c) - rc}{1 + r}$, $M^{ooo} = 0$. There is thus a third barter equilibrium in this model if the cost of minting (or rate of interest) is equal to or above a determinate threshhold $\bar{s}$. In this case, all agents produce and have a value equal to $x(u - c)/r$, as in the other barter equilibria showed above.

The Monetary authority can get a once-and-for-all amount of utility sM which depends on s as (5) makes clear. A maximum gain is obtained for

$$\check{s} = \frac{(1 - x)(u - c) - rc}{2(1 + r)} \quad,$$

which corresponds to an equilibrium quantity $\check{M} = \frac{(1 - x)(u - c) - rc}{2(1 - x)(u - c)}$. This result will be used below.

Further examination of (5) shows that $M^{\circ\circ\circ}$ is also a decreasing function of x, since $\frac{dM^{\circ\circ}}{dx} = -\frac{(u - c)[rc + s(1 + r)]}{[(1 - x)(u - c)]^2}$.

For all values of x strictly inferior to $\bar{x} = \frac{u - (c + s)(1 + r)}{u - c}$, there exists a monetary equilibrium whereas only a barter equilibrium is possible otherwise.

Existence of a monetary equilibrium therefore depends on the *absolute degree of specialization* x and no longer, as it is the case in search models with an exogenous quantity of money, on a comparison between goods liquidity and the degree of money acceptance (parameter Π in the Kiyotaki–Wright model).

Barter equilibrium exists for $x \geq \bar{x} = \dfrac{u - (c + s)(1 + r)}{u - c}$

even though a positive fraction N of agents, possibly 1, accepts money. For

$$x < \bar{x} = \frac{u - (c + s)(1 + r)}{u - c} \quad,$$

a monetary equilibrium occurs and $M^{\circ\circ\circ} = \dfrac{(1 - x)(u - c) - rc - (1 + r)s}{(1 - x)(u - c)}$.

A recapitulation of equilibria is given for model K in Table 16.1:

Table 16.1: Equilibria for model K.

$V_m - V_o - c < 0$ $V_m - V_o - c = 0$	$N^o = 0, M^o = 0$
	$N^{\circ\circ} = \dfrac{x(u - c) + cr}{u - c}, M^{\circ\circ} = 0$
$V_m - V_o - c > 0, s < \bar{s}$	$N^{\circ\circ\circ} = 1, M^{\circ\circ\circ} = \dfrac{(1 - x)(u - c) - rc - (1 + r)s}{(1 - x)(u - c)}$
$V_m - V_o - c > 0, s \geq \bar{s}$ or $x \geq \bar{x}$	$N^{\circ\circ\circ} = 1, M^{\circ\circ\circ} = 0$

Welfare

In search models with an exogenously given quantity of money, comparison between barter and monetary equilibria, on the one hand, and study of the influence of the quantity of money on welfare, on the other, are distinct tasks. The first one, paradoxically enough, involves comparing a monetary economy with a barter one, endowed with a positive quantity of money but not using it. It generally concludes in the superiority of money over barter for a given quantity of money. The second one, independently, evaluates the extent to which the two effects of an increase in the quantity of money balance each other: a negative one due to eviction from production (only in model K) and a positive one due to the facilitation of transactions. It generally concludes in the existence of an optimal quantity of money for which the two effects exactly offset each other.

Similar conclusions apply here under some restrictive conditions. They result from a unique study comparing welfare associated to equilibria having a common acceptance of money, namely $N^{ooo} = 1$, but with different monetary policies or with different degrees of specialization (the two most interesting determinants of the equilibrium quantity of money).

Solving:

$$rV_m = N(1 - M)(u + V_0 - V_m)$$
$$rV_0 = (1 - M)x(u - c) + M(V_m - c - V_0) \tag{7}$$

Gives

$$V_0 = \frac{N(1 - M)(u - c)[(1 - M)x + M] + r(1 - M)x(u - c)\ \ Mrc}{r(r + M + N(1 - M))}$$

$$V_m = \frac{N(1 - M)}{r(r + M + N(1 - M))}[u(r + M(1 - x)) + x(u - c) - Mc(1 - x)] \tag{8}$$

Total value of the economy in model K is given by:

$$W = MV_m + (1 - M)V_0 = V_0(M) + M[V_m(M) - V_0(M)] \tag{9}$$

Substituting in (9) the values of V_0 and V_m given by (8) for $N = 1$, yields:

$$W(M^{ooo}) = \frac{1}{r}[-u(u - c)(1 - x)M^2 + (u - c)(1 - 2x)M + x(u - c)] \tag{10}$$

Two extreme values are $W(0) = x(u - c)/r > 0$ and $W(1) = 0.$[12] The derivative of W with respect to M is $W'(M) = 1/r[-2(u - c)(1 - x)M + (u - c)(1 - 2x)]$. It is positive for $M^{ooo} = 0$ and, more generally, for $M^{ooo} < \frac{1 - 2x}{2(1 - x)}$. $W'(M)$ is negative for greater values of M^{ooo}.

The optimal quantity of money therefore is $M^* = \frac{1 - 2x}{2(1 - x)}$ and is brought about by $s^* = \frac{x(u - c) - 2rc}{2(1 + r)}$.[13]

Let us come back to what has been said above on the possibility for the Mint to maximize total seignorage sM. Does such behaviour also maximize total welfare? A comparison between $\breve{M} = \frac{(1 - x)(u - c) - rc}{2(1 - x)(u - c)}$ and $M^* = \frac{1 - 2x}{2(1 - x)}$ will bring the answer. A simple calculation shows that:

$$\check{M} \lessgtr M^* \Leftrightarrow \frac{x(u-c)}{c} \lessgtr r \tag{12}$$

The same calculation applied to model S gives a non-ambiguous result since $\check{M} = \frac{(1-x)(u-c)-rc}{2(1-x)(u-c)} < \frac{1}{2}$ which boils down to $-rc < 0$.

In order to show that the monetary equilibria dominates barter, it must be proved that the quantities of money for which $W(M) < W(0) = x(u-c)/r$, cannot be true. From (10) $W(M) < W(0)$ holds in model K only if $M^{ooo} > 1 - x / (1-x)$. But it has been shown above that the maximum equilibrium quantity of money is $1 - rc / [(1-x)(u-c)]$. Condition $M^{ooo} > 1 - x / (1-x)$ is satisfied only if $\frac{x(u-c)}{c} \leq r$.

In model S the story is much simpler since $W(M) < W(0)$ holds only for $M > 1$ which is impossible.

17 *DIGRESSION* ON THE RELATIONS BETWEEN ANTHROPOLOGY AND ECONOMICS ON THE TOPIC OF 'PRIMITIVE' CURRENCIES: A PAGE IN THE HISTORY OF THOUGHT

Solène Morvant-Roux and Jean-Michel Servet

Introduction

More than a century separates the rise of political economics as a separate discipline in the mid-eighteenth century from that of anthropology, which became acknowledged as a distinct discipline from *belles-lettres* in the nineteenth century. This essay highlights some salient points on the interactions between the two disciplines, with a focus on the subject of so-called 'primitive moneys'. The authors first show that up until at least the mid-twentieth century, autonomous approaches were taken, after which analyses taking anthropology into account emerged at the heart of heterodox approaches to economics, notably in the work of the interdisciplinary study group that published *La monnaie souveraine* in 1998. The authors start out on the basis of observations they made in Mexico, while drawing on similar works from Guatemala, amongst others. They ultimately aim to show that this renewed approach to *La monnaie souveraine*, with its focus on the paradigm of debt, nevertheless excludes the potential contribution of an analysis of primitive currencies in terms of common goods. By taking this dimension into account, the possibility of a new paradigm based on sharing values is raised, allowing movement beyond outdated monetary orthodoxies for an understanding of finance and currency.[1]

Anthropologists and Economists: An Improbable Dialogue on Primitive Currencies

In 1949, two research works were published; one by an anthropologist and the other by an economist, both of which remain authorities as surveys in the literature on so-called 'primitive' currencies.[2] The first work, *A Survey of Primi-*

tive Money: The Beginnings of Currency, was a survey of primitive money by the anthropologist Mary Hingston Quiggin (1874–1971). She set out a culturalist and ethnographic approach to these currencies, classifying them according to continental areas. The second, *Primitive Money in its Ethnological, Historical and Economic Aspects* was written by the economist Paul Einzig (1897–1973) and focused on the functions of these monetary instruments. Up until then, he had devoted around forty studies to the contemporary aspects of money. These two publications showed that anthropologists and economists were taking highly autonomous approaches to primitive money in their studies. Einzig states: 'The present volume is, however, the first of substantial size that is devoted entirely to the subject of primitive money'.[3] Thus he seems to have been unaware of the work of A. Hingston Quiggin, who was working on largely the same materials and sources, at the same time and in the same city.

This apparent ignorance above all belies a fundamental disagreement as to the very definition of money. Alison Hingston Quiggin comments in the introduction to *A Survey of Primitive Money*: 'Everyone, except an economist, knows what money means, and even an economist can describe it in the course of a chapter or so, but it is impossible to define with rigid outlines'.[4] This short preamble to an encyclopaedic overview of so-called 'primitive' moneys highlights how, besides a few rare exceptions (J.-M. Keynes being one), most economists up to the 1990s were largely unaware of ethnographic works on money.

The difficulty of dialogue between economics and anthropology can be largely explained by economists' quasi negation, through the famous fable of barter, of the universality of monetary exchange, beginning from the discipline's founding texts such as those of Smith, Turgot and Beccaria.[5] This economist-created belief was so strong that it was put at the heart of how the very discipline was constructed.[6] The German historical schools, and Knies and Roscher in particular, set out various elements of the history and ethnography of money, particularly on the distinction between the internal and external uses of these supposed first currencies. These were then used by authors as different as Karl Marx and Carl Menger to set out a rational scheme of monetary evolution. Practically all economists studying the history of money then used this outline, implicitly or explicitly, without questioning its presumed tenets. In all, economists' interpretation of primitive money was based on evolutionist and functional logic: the belief in a time before money, which represented a first, original stage without money, and which was followed by the progressive elaboration of an ever more efficient tool for trading transactions. This pseudo-historical reconstruction belies the studies of other disciplines, which have demonstrated fiscal, religious and social uses of money, and which thus had no direct relationship to trade,[7] which most economists viewed as being of secondary importance. Economists did not lack the material to conceive money differently, but the logic of their discipline hindered their comprehension and thus the application of this new knowledge, which could be found not only through ethnologists, but also archaeologists, historians and travel writers.[8]

In this way, Stanley Jevons, in the first paragraph of the first chapter of *Money and the Principles of Exchange* (1876) uses the word 'barter'. While there was nothing original about discussing barter in a work on money, this co-founder of neoclassical economics gave an extraordinary testimony on indigenous practices while displaying a complete misunderstanding of a major characteristic of the historical use of money, namely the existence of compartmentalized spheres of exchange:

> Some years since, Mademoiselle Zélie, a singer of the Théâtre Lyrique at Paris, made a professional tour round the world, and gave a concert in the Society Islands. In exchange for an air from *Norma* and a few other songs, she was to receive a third part of the receipts. When counted, her share was found to consist of three pigs, twenty-three turkeys, forty-four chickens, five thousand cocoa-nuts, besides considerable quantities of bananas, lemons, and oranges. At the Halle in Paris, as the prima donna remarks in her lively letter, printed by M. Wolowski, this amount of live stock and vegetables might have brought four thousand francs, which would have been good remuneration for five songs. In the Society Islands, however, pieces of money were very scarce; and as Mademoiselle could not consume any considerable portion of the receipts herself, it became necessary in the mean time to feed the pigs and poultry with the fruit.[9]

It is interesting to compare the above description of compartmentalized uses of money (which anthropologists mostly began to study from the 1960s, notably with the publication of *Markets in Africa* by Paul Bohannan), with the reaction a Melanesian gave to an anthropologist a hundred years later as to the idea of giving monetary value to the various gifts necessary for a wedding:

> The people of Sivepe expressed real horror as to the idea that one could calculate the value of a bride to be $200. For them, the gift of pigs, bark cloth, food or traditional goods is a particular kind of offering that cannot be translated into money. I then asked an informant if he didn't think that this evaluation was a distortion brought by modernity and he answered: 'Not modern, but stupid'.[10]

Incomprehension of these 'archaic' monetary practices by the economists who observed them was largely due to the opposition they projected onto all societies between status and contract; money is understood as a specific element of a contract between two people who make an exchange, who are assumed to be equal in this relation, other than in a monopoly situation. This way of thinking can be summed up as a vision of money as an intermediary of a transaction, even if for Knapp this was a non-trading obligation, as it was a fiscal one. Money is a means for acquitting or paying, or even to evaluate what is being paid for.

In an almost caricaturized way, one can say that the individual of economic theory only exists though his capacity of ownership and exchange. If he produces something, it is with the goal of reproducing his existence as an individual directly through self-consumption, and above all indirectly by transferring production or the rights he has to a form of wealth by acquiring another kind of wealth. Money is the essential vector of the acknowledgement of this ability to buy and sell, thanks to which, through belief in unlimited commodification, the use of money can extend almost infinitely, up as far as moral restrictions will permit (as with the abolition of the slave trade, for instance).

This transactional perspective on money is well illustrated by the 1924 publication in the *Economic Journal*, under the impetus of Keynes, of Armstrong's discoveries from Rossel Island to the south-east of New Guinea. The holders of these moneys are equated to a 'London bill broker'.[11] Similarly, Boas had made an analogy between New York stock exchange transactions and the aggressive gift exchanges of the famous Potlach of the north-west American coast.[12]

We can counter this view by pointing out that monetary flows are not limited to a relationship between two things, or between an individual and an object and another individual and another object, but that money is essentially a social relationship involving status considerations and social bonds. Beyond the bilateral relationship between one who gives and one who receives,[13] it is necessary to situate this relationship within an ensemble of elements which must be understood as interdependent, i.e. where money creates or, more precisely, is a bond.[14] Moreover, a symbolic object is accepted in a transaction because the person accepting the transaction is aware that the object is acknowledged as conferring rights over other elements within a community of payments. Methodical trust in the circulation of money can only work if there is a vertical and hierarchical trust in a collective entity. There is a collective debt in a group vis-à-vis the holder of the monetary instrument. The issuing institution can only function in the name of the group, which will acknowledge it as its own.

Breaking away from the approach of modern economics, some economists have, in the analysis of primitive money, applied the discoveries and analyses of anthropologists, beginning with Melanesia. This is the case of Gregory, Servet and, subsequently, Rospabé. These economists, by training, have more or less quickly adopted an essentially anthropological or socio-economic perspective in their work, while having little influence on mainstream economics on the topic.

These economists, in rereading the anthropological literature, have been greeted as 'heterodox' or have even been rejected as non-economists. It was not until the publication of *La monnaie souveraine*[15] in 1998 that a progressive shift of paradigm emerged through a change in the relationship between the different schools of the two disciplines over this question. Its publication marked a clear reciprocal step forward in terms of dialogue between the disciplines.[16]

A Heterodox Reconciliation between Disciplines through the Understanding of Money as Debt

The central elements of the new definition of so-called 'sovereign' currency can be summarized in three terms: debt, sovereignty and trust, which follows in order the titles of the three parts of the book.[17] This project principally opened a dialogue between economics and anthropology, history[18] and psychology[19] on these three key concepts.[20] These economists recognize the gaps within standard economic works on currency. Moreover, they show that economic knowledge cannot construct an analysis of money without introducing foundational extra-economic elements. Thus in *La monnaie souveraine*, money is not analysed using a traditional instrumental approach according to the function of payment, account and reserve. It is understood on the basis of membership of a community sealed by dependency on shared gods, ancestors and sovereigns, and *in fine* to a social Whole which these incarnate; hence the importance the authors place on debt when defining currency differently to the reduction of it by economists to a simple medium of exchange.[21] Not only does money allow the establishment of private and public debts, but it also ensures their perpetuation and transmission, including on an intergenerational basis.

It should, however, be pointed out that despite making an important epistemological break from standard economic analysis, most of the most recent works on monetary practice follow on from the reflections of *La monnaie souveraine* to essentially highlight its circulatory properties, whether for gifts, debts, trade or the market, while substantially overshadowing another essential property of sharing and its usage.[22] This is probably because the function or uses of reserve that money allows are often considered as secondary to other monetary functions and usages (account and payment), because they depend on the latter to manifest themselves.[23] This is a position already defended by such thinkers as Aristotle and Marx. Polanyi's analysis of 'treasury' and 'precious goods',[24] however, returns an entirely different meaning to these practices of money conservation as a form of treasury, namely as a means of domination to reproduce the social order. This is notably the case for events where there are displays of ostentation or where deposits are made for essential moments of social reproduction. The circulatory properties of money via debt, in particular, have been widely studied and even accorded excessive attention.

We would like to focus on a far less recognized dimension of money which archaic monetary practices reveal, and which has been given all the less attention because it opposes the neo-liberal conception of economic relationships and its reduction of social relationships to a vast market on every level.

A Possible Progression by Hypothesizing Finance and Money as a Common Good

To look beyond the circulatory perception of money, as is also central to the approach to debt proposed in *La monnaie souveraine*, has two implications. First, one must consider the subject–object distinction at the heart of the representation of money as a circuit. Equally, one must reassess the real capacity of a subject to alienate a good, focusing not on the capacity of alienation (an individual or group having the exclusive use of a good) that property confers, but on the capacity of utilization (possession) that makes money a common good with a limited capacity of alienation, defined by the social group.

Thus a new perspective emerges if the monetary relationship is considered as a whole. This relationship reveals a hierarchical link between the people observed in the transfer. Should we objectively favour the bilateral operation as being what separates and opposes two partners? Or is it better to focus on what links them, and what goes beyond the individual through the role of money? At stake is an end to thinking about *individuals* (basic units which standard economic analysis aggregate through its conception of economic relations) but of *people* (whose definition depends on the relations between one other as a group with mutual recognition of membership). One could probably object that the market, in its modernity, can only be conceived and represented as a sum of bilateral relations. If one thinks that the development of market relations and financialization have made all the members of the market exchange community interdependent through the market, and that money is the link between them, this objection cannot stand. It is a question of the difference between a market which has expanded to cover all potential goods (without compartmentalization, as with the utopia of proponents of free exchange) and of societies where such types of relationships are only sporadic. Besides, many observations have shown that in certain cases, the particular subject–object relation is reversed. This is the case of land ownership, when a population says: 'land does not belong to us, we belong to the land'; the population feels an obligation to look after the land, to watch over it and take care of it. This necessarily brings us back to the collective, because in the somehow reversed relationship conceived, we can only belong to the land if we form a collective towards it, we are somehow the daughters and sons of a same land.

The problem is that in order to understand this, we need to make a distinction between property, possession, ownership, and having something at one's disposal and control.[25] In fact, possession implies recognition of subordinated rights of use, while property (exclusive appropriation, if only by the group) is predicated on an acknowledged owner's capacity to exclude others from using a good; hence the capacity to alienate this good, and to concede it to a new owner who can then enjoy the same rights as the previous owner. Money here displays its supposed capacity to permit the acquisition of all other goods, and its desirability as the ultimate form of liquidity, and as the form of wealth which best embodies property rights. Thanks to its supposed universality of usage, currency makes this capacity of alienation possible.

Ultimately, if we look at currency beyond the necessity to circulate wealth in the form of gifts, withdrawal-distribution, recognition of debt, and sale purchase (without of course denying the existence of these practices and logics), currencies can be understood not as counterparties or evaluations of counterparties (goods or services) but rather as the witnesses of the elements of recognition of a relation, like the memory of an obligation, and not to be confused with a security or a guarantee, which would restrict us to the terms of counterparty and a catallactic vision (see the function of the Greek goddess of memory, or of Juno who warns).

This allows us to approach money in terms of, and for, the circulation of inalienable currencies, an approach incomprehensible to standard economic theory. These can then be the object of a deposit, which has wrongly been taken as a security or a guarantee, a contribution to deferred transfer over time in the form of a loan or a gift exchange (the best-known example being shells on Rossel Island in the works of Amstrong and later John Liep). These moneys allow alliances to be made. They allow the recognition of filiations through the composite identities of individuals.[26]

To explain our distinction between circulation and sharing where money is concerned, we will now turn to practices observed in Amerindian societies. These have widely been interpreted as forms of gift exchanges (and hence only from the perspective of circulation). Objects which circulate have monetary dimensions in that they are made as obligatory gifts, are favoured in certain ceremonies and/or generally serve as a form of savings for those who hold them with respect to these obligations. They therefore serve part of the functions traditionally devolved to money. This analysis should help to explain the shared usage rights previously highlighted with the goal of understanding money differently.

This analytical framework allows us to reinterpret the underlying logic of certain debt links identified in the indigenous rural zones of South Mexico.[27] These are complemented by Agnès Bergeret's similar observations in the context of Maya communities in Guatemala.[28] They allow us to see behind debt ties not the logic of the circulation of goods, but one of sharing certain indispensable goods for the socio-economic reproduction of the villages. We can argue that these goods participate in the currency because they create links within the communities. This also shows how the currency (moreover present in the form of coins, bills and even accounts) can manifest in these societies in a somewhat disparate fashion, instead of within a single object concentrating all the characteristics of money.

In the villages of south-west Mexico one can observe how food products, building material (bricks, limestone) and animals are made available for use (or put to shared use). These goods, which play a central role in the social, political, demographic and economic reproduction of the villages, thus tend to be loaned out by those who possess them, rather than immediately used.

The duration of the transfer of the rights of use is not fixed in advance, and varies from a few weeks to several years; this all depends on the needs of those who have made the loan and the person using the goods. We can say that the object has been entrusted, in the sense that there is trust between the two protagonists.

Of the objects entrusted, a turkey is a particular example with a central position in the ritual life of the Zapotec localities of southern Mexico. Life-cycle events are marked by organized celebrations which could not take place if turkeys were not killed, this being not only a question of prestige but also of prosperity, as the health of the family and the fertility of the couple getting married depend on it. The number of turkeys killed at a wedding varies greatly, but is often as high as thirty to fifty. This is a large amount if one takes into account that a male is worth approximately US$30, and a female half that amount. Family mothers thus plan well ahead so as not to be caught out. Turkeys can be shared in two ways. The first relates to the need to accumulate turkeys over the long term, which can exceed the lifespan of a turkey. As soon as a woman gives birth to a boy, she knows that her son's wedding will entail a great expense in turkeys, and that it will be difficult to meet this need without planning ahead. She will therefore begin to raise turkeys to accumulate a large enough stock for the wedding. She makes adult turkeys available to those of her women neighbours and family members who are in immediate need of them, and they commit to give turkeys of the same sex and weight to the woman in return if she needs them. This shared usage allows the women to best conserve a good for which they have no immediate use: 'We loan them, so they are kept. If we sell them, we don't have them any more' (we can't count on them any more). In other words, they give up the turkeys while keeping them; this is a different logic to a gift exchange. This analysis is supported by how usage is immediate, and one would not entrust the animal one has received to anyone else. This system backs up the concept of sharing rather than circulation. If it were a matter of a gift, there could be wider circulation.

The second mode of shared usage relates to animal (turkey or pig) breeding. Males or females are loaned to another woman in order for them to breed. The length of the loan varies from one to several litters, which are divided in two.

It is out of the question to withdraw usage rights or dispossess an individual too quickly, without sufficient warning to plan ahead. Many women thus sometimes find themselves having to seek help from other individuals in their social network because the resource they have is with a third party. Many women told us when we met them that quite a few turkeys are lent to other women who are still owed them.[29]

To conclude this point, let us highlight that as soon as someone obtains some money, they do not use it over the short or medium term, because they are asked to put this liquidity to the service of others who are in immediate need of it. There is no distinction between savings and mutual assistance, and the two practices are intimately linked. The analysis of the provision of turkeys thus applies to money in the narrow and commonly used sense of the term.

We saw that this management takes place within a close social network of neighbours and relatives, domestic or political, but that the financial flows can reach more distant social relations. This finding confirms Olivier Favereau's analysis of African economies, the examples of which suggest that, in contrast to its *market* form, *domestic* liquidity corresponds to the maintenance of a network of community relationships, which through solidarity organizes liquidity 'on the basis of collective rather than individual resource holdings'.[30] The maintenance of social relations, particularly through these forms of mutual assistance through goods or money, express a feeling of interdependence that persists in these villages. There is no question here of painting an idealized picture of how they work: the shared usage of certain goods or animals does not rule out power relations or certain forms of socio-economic inequalities, dependence and domination. The shared usages these monetary practices reveal are not about redistributing wealth, but about manifesting social relations and maintaining links of interdependence.

Comparing this example to other cases, particularly in Latin America, helps us to see possession in terms of a variably developed and autonomous capacity of usage, and the rights to use something as hierarchical. This explains how loans are made and that loans or concessions can be compulsory. No one can directly refuse to concede a good; to do so, he or she would lie by claiming that they have a prior engagement to someone else who asked first. Certain popular myths warn of the risks of refusing the use or concession of a good one possesses to someone else.[31]

It is interesting to observe that these practices apply to money coming from outside the village, such as transfers from migration and microcredit. In the case of Oaxaca in Mexico, part of the money received as a transfer is in fact most often loaned to neighbours, parents or the migrant's close family. The principles of its distribution are agreed with the migrant. In general, the family mother uses one part as a kind of income to cover various household expenses. Another part, by contrast, is loaned on a variably long-term basis to people within the social network and serves as savings for the migrant. Large sums are loaned out of these transfers, and most often an interest rate is applied, which varies from 3 to 5 per cent monthly.

It is likely, as Zanotelli argues, that external money reaches the village through money loaned from migration, or that money is appropriated according to locally shared social values.[32] This is a thesis shared by Greenberg, who claims that 'horizontal' credit or collective survival strategies allow local populations (in this case the Mixe ethnicity of Oaxaca) to resist outside domination, and thus serve as a means of identity affirmation.[33]

Conclusion

Returning to the question of an analytical framework for reinterpreting the opposition between circulation and sharing in the context of money, and moving beyond *a priori* exotic examples, we can draw on Elinor Ostrom's analysis of common goods to apply the elements of an originally ecological and environmental analysis of water, air and forestry resources to finance and money.[34]

Unlike a freely available public good which does not decline in quantity or quality as it is used, notably on account of its perfect reproducibility (running water used by a mill upstream is thought to be one, unlike water used for irrigation or for polluting industrial processes), and unlike a good which is immediately shared by everyone without the possibility of exclusive access (peace, for example),[35] consumption of a common good by a member of a community restricts the possibility of it being used by others. Its very rarity creates rivalry and its use by a few people for their own benefit can lead to the resource becoming exhausted or depleted.[36] If everyone is to be included, the rights of everyone in sharing usage must be set out. So-called 'primitive' moneys offer many examples of this kind of sharing in the use of a resource within these communities. Credit and money can be treated as common goods, as common 'natural' resources are, but to follow Elinor Ostrom's work, such a theoretical renewal necessitates the adoption of a truly interdisciplinary approach through the comparison of the hypotheses of each discipline or its schools, leading to a deconstruction-reconstruction of the objects studied, according to whether these hypotheses prove compatible or not.[37]

18 THE ECONOMICS OF ETHICS AND THE ETHICS OF ECONOMICS IN ADAM SMITH

Amos Witztum

Introduction

What is unique about Smith's approach to ethics and economics is that in his case, both theories are social theories derived from the same starting point. Most ethical theories are engaged with the question of how we judge whether something is morally good (or just) but few, if any, make the judgement depending on our character, social experience and interaction. This, in turn, allows a better insight into Mandeville's famous private vice–public good conundrum. From the moral point of view, Mandeville's assertion requires resolution. Either the private vices are moderated by the public good to a degree in which they cease to be vices, or, the public good is not really morally acceptable. It is difficult to imagine how moral principles condemning the behaviour of agents who produce public good, can be sustained over time.

There has been a considerable amount of work devoted to the exploration of Smith's moral views.[1] Most of it is predominantly engaged in enumerating those things which Smith believed to be good or just. Subsequently, ethical behaviour is deemed to be a precondition for the economic working of natural liberty to succeed. Jeffrey Young is one of the few who tries to examine the interrelationship between Smith's ethics and economics.[2] He finds in the notion of the natural price a focal point in which ethics and economics meet and where each one of them affects the other. While I agree with Young about the significance of the natural rates for the question of the ethics–economics relationship in Smith, I believe that there is even a more fundamental concept in Smith's analysis of the relationship between ethics and economics which lies in the way in which he conceives both ethics and economics.

In my view, one of the reasons that we find Smith's text both rich and, sometimes, confusing is that Smith was, perhaps, the first social theorist who offered a method of analysis which combines evolutionary empiricism with deductive reasoning. This means that, on the one hand, Smith did not shy away from the idea of universal premises upon which we can construct a theory. The most obvious candidates, though only apparent, are the principles of sympathy in the *Theory of Moral Sentiments* (hereafter *TMS*) and that of the tendency to barter and exchange in the *Wealth of Nations* (hereafter *WN*). Both follow Smith's own notions on rhetoric where he seems clearly to employ what he calls the Newtonian Method.[3]

On the other hand, while the principles are clearly universal, their content is not. For instance, our ability to sympathize – or feel as others would, had we been in their place – depends to a great extent on the context. Sentiments and experiences need to be familiar to the observer for him or her to be able to exercise sympathy. As Smith himself admits, with growing distance, our ability to sympathize diminishes. But this distance does not have to be physical proximity. It could easily also be cultural or other social differences.

But it is not only the distance which matters. It is also the character of the observer. As Smith clearly suggests, the character of the observer always interferes in the process of sympathy and will, inevitably, affect the degree to which a person may feel sympathy with another. Therefore, one's moral judgement becomes relative rather than absolute.

As for the tendency to barter and exchange, this too depends on the state of development of society. The origin of the tendency to barter and exchange is, of course, the desire to be socially approved. This, more than anything else, is bound to be dependent on the state of social development.

Thus, even in a relatively superficial way, one can see that Smith could not have been committed to any specific implication of his ethical model. In turn, this may help one to understand the many occasions where Smith, the observer, is commenting disapprovingly on what he observes. But this should not guide us away from the model.

In what follows I intend to develop the following argument. First, I will argue that the collective of Smith's apparent principles are derived from a single idea: the pleasure of harmony. I will argue that it is this pleasure which connects our search for knowledge (in the *Essays on Philosophical Subjects*, hereafter *EPS*), our search for beauty (in *Essays on Rhetoric and Belle Lettres*, hereafter *ERBL*), our tendency to sympathize and our desire to be socially approved. While this may draw some attention to the potential identification of Smith with utility theory, I should say from the outset that this is not the case, first, because it is not necessarily a motive to action and, second, as will soon become apparent, it is not, in itself, the criterion of moral evaluation.

Second, I will show that when understood in this way, that which drives the economic organization is not very different from that which underlies our sense of morality. Consequently, the way we interact in the economic scene is closely related to the way we form moral opinions and the former would not have been possible without the latter. We are unlikely to act in the economic world in a way which is inconsistent with our beliefs about what is good or just.

However, this does not mean that the economic system is inevitably good or just. It may mean that people think that the system is good or just, but this is not the whole story. Exactly in the same way that people may think that self-interested-based natural liberty is efficient even though it is not (due to, say, incomplete markets), so it is in Smith's moral system where people can wrongly believe something to be morally good. While it is based on what people do and the way they form opinion, it has a logical – almost Kantian – benchmark and final arbitrator: the impartial spectator.

If we see the 'impartial spectator' as the average individual then there is no way in which Smith the observer could be so disapproving of individuals' practice: see, for instance, merit in wealth accumulation. Therefore, I believe that the impartial spectator is the logical limit of what people actually do. In other words, like in economic analysis where we know that perfect competition is the logical limit of decentralized systems while reality falls well short of it, so it is in Smith's ethics. There is the logical limit of the well-informed rational observer and there is the practice of the ill-informed flawed human character. In both cases, the foundation of the theory is an observation (or introspection) with regard to how people behave but there is a difference between their reality and their logical limit.

Having said this, it is important to emphasize that this logical limit is not an absolute ethical judgement as the impartial spectator acts as an informed character for a given social state. He is not forming a judgement on the principle of the best of all possible worlds.

In the next section (pp. 226–33), I will discuss Smith's methodology to demonstrate that the search for a unifying principle is consistent with Smith's view of science. I will enumerate the conditions which would make such a principle valid and I will also discuss the difference between the scholastic use of universals and Smith's use of it. I will show that in Smith's work, universals are not the substance which typifies that scholastic and purely rationalistic approach but rather a tool which needs to be filled with content that is time and circumstances sensitive. This, in turn, allows Smith's theory to be both empirical and rational.

The following section (pp. 233–40) applies this methodology to Smith's analysis of economics and ethics and identifies the interest-in-the-others as the common principle underlying both the economic and ethical analysis. I will show how the universal principle becomes relative and sensitive to the character of individuals and to the circumstances in which they operate. The role of the impartial spectator will then be identified and discussed.

In the section which follows (pp. 240–4), we will explore the ineffectiveness of the common approach which applies ethics to economics in a way that focuses on the morality of characters or the beneficence of the outcome. Such an approach ignores the commonality of the origin of economic behaviour and ethics and therefore falls in the trap according to which it is possible for a self-interested community of people to believe that their system is morally good while the impartial spectator would not go along with it.

To see this last point clearly, in the subsequent section (pp. 244–57) we analyse Smith's theory of human and economic interaction. We find those principles which govern the judgement of actions and reward and we discuss the meaning of justice in Smith within the context of acting and being acted upon. We then examine the system of self-interested individuals and we find that while it is indeed possible for a system based on self-interest to believe in its moral goodness, it is, in fact, the beneficence of the outcome, the unintended consequences, which ensure that the system will not be considered morally good.

In the final section (pp. 257–63), we reflect on some institutional consequences of the theory with regard to the question of whether there are groups in society who are being acted upon given a system of interdependence. We also look at the role of ownership in the moral evaluation of the system.

A Note on Smith's Methodology

Moral philosophy, for Smith, was not much different from any other natural philosophy (what we would nowadays call science). 'Philosophy', he said, 'is the science of connecting principles of nature ... [It], by representing the invisible chains which bind together all disjointed objects, endeavour[s] to introduce order in this chaos'.[4]

In that respect he was following the tradition of the eighteenth century. There, science and philosophy were frequently interchanged when referring to an effort to understand nature in general, and human nature in particular. Therefore it would be useful to begin our analysis of his moral theory (or system might be a better term for it) with some notes on his methodology.

There are mainly two sources for that inquiry. First, his article on the different forms of discourse ('Lectures on Rhetoric and Belles Lettres', hereafter LRBL) allows us to deduce his scientific method from his form of presentation. The other is a collection of three articles, the title of each of beginning with: 'The Principles which Lead and Direct Philosophical Enquiries Illustrated By...'.

In these articles, as their titles indicate, Smith presents and illustrates some of his ideas on methodology. In spite of them being incomplete and unpublished papers they nonetheless constitute a good source for the understanding of Smith's scientific method. For various reasons most writers on Smith's methodology have taken into account only the most complete of these articles: the one in which the principles of philosophical enquiries are illustrated by the 'History of Astronomy' (hereafter HA).[5] I will maintain that some of the ideas presented in the other articles are as valid as those in HA. I will also argue that these ideas are particularly relevant to his social and economic theories.

Let us begin with the LRBL, where methods of inquiry are reflected in the forms of discourse. The basic distinction Smith makes in this article is between what he calls 'historical narrative' and what he names 'rhetoric'.

The 'historical narrative' discourse proposes:

> barely to relate some facts ... to put before us the arguments on both sides of the ques-
> tion in their true light, giving each its proper degree of influence, and has it in view to
> persuade no further than the arguments themselves appear convincing.[6]

On the other hand there is the 'rhetoric' discourse that proposes 'to prove some proposition ... [and] endeavour by all means to persuade us'.[7]

It is quite obvious that any sort of philosophical or scientific system will fall under the category of 'rhetoric' discourses. In fact it is the other way around. All discourses that are presented in that 'rhetorical' fashion reflect an attempt to construct a philosophical (scientific) system, or theory. Indeed, the relevant writings of Smith do fall in this category and thus we are able to look upon them as scientific theories.

The 'rhetorical' discourse itself is subdivided into two methods, producing a much clearer picture of his form of presentation. First, we have the 'Newtonian method' where 'we lay down one or a very few principles by which we explain the several rules or phenomena, connecting one with the other in a natural order'.[8]

Second, we have what Smith calls the 'Aristotelian method' where 'we begin with telling that we are to explain such and such things, and for each advance a principle either different or the same with those which went before'.[9]

It seems to me that the 'Newtonian method' of discourse is the more prevalent one in Smith's works. The *TMS* is a distinct example of it. First we have an exposition of the principle behind the whole system: the principle of 'sympathy'. Then it is used to connect certain phenomena like, for instance, moral opinions, class structure, self-interested behaviour, and so forth. The *WN* also follows that line of presentation. Again the principle behind the system, the division of labour, is presented at the beginning and together with what motivates it (the propensity to barter and exchange), the rules connecting different phenomena are being displayed. Even the three articles illustrating the principles of philosophical enquiries are constructed in the same manner. The system which is being investigated there, is the system of scientific inquiries.

We may conclude now that even from the mere form of discourse it seems that both his economic as well as moral systems are scientific systems and thus there exist a common ground to investigate their interrelationship. The next step will be to explore the nature of scientific systems.

There are three illustrations of philosophical enquiries; first in the 'History of Astronomy', second in the 'History of Ancient Physics' and third in the 'History of Logics and Metaphysics'.[10] In each one of them the first part is devoted to some general remarks that are made by Smith himself about the task of scientific inquiry. It is his conception of science that is portrayed at the outset of each article and only then he goes on to show how it reflects on the history of science. Indeed, it is in the first illustration, the one on astronomy, where Smith gives the introduction to the general problem (or phenomenon) of scientific inquiry. But this does not mean that the points made in the other two illustrations are less significant. In both the 'History of Ancient Physics' and the 'History of Logics and Metaphysics', Smith advances the historical account with his own remarks on methodology. Some of them are elaborations of ideas presented in the HA, and some 'new' ideas that arise due to different degrees of complexity, which emerge as the subject matter of our investigation 'descends' from the investigation of heaven to the investigation of earth.

Thinking on the trio as a whole, one can very clearly draw the logic of their arrangement. They are arranged according to the degree of the complexity of the subject under investigation. But this might have been just a coincidence. Even though the heavens have just a few objects (hence, in Smith's view, a lower degree of complexity), their influence over the faculties in human beings which promote philosophical investigation (admiration, wonder and surprise) are stronger.[11]

Nevertheless, though it is clear that in Smith's view the effects of heaven were stronger on motivation, human inquiry has descended to earth only to find that it is a much more complex task.

> From arranging and methodizing the System of the Heavens, philosophy descended to the consideration of the inferior parts of Nature, of the Earth ... [But] [i]f the imagination, therefore, when it considered the appearances in the Heavens, was often perplexed, and driven out of its natural career; it would be much more exposed to the same embarrassment when it directed its attention to the objects which the Earth presented it.[12]

In the HA, Smith presents us with some basics of what he considered to be a scientific theory:

a. It must have a principle which will unify all those apparently irregular phenomena.
b. It must be a simple system that would put our mind at ease.
c. It must be based on familiar qualities.[13]

The need to deduce familiar qualities, operations and laws of succession is already presented in the HA. However, the search for familiar qualities was a negligible part of 'methodizing the Heavens' as there were only few objects involved. Consequently, finding the familiar qualities was not an issue of great importance that can be illustrated by the HA. But it does have an important role in 'methodizing the Earth' as on the earth, according to Smith, the number of objects exceeds significantly those which are in the heavens.

The principles and characteristics of such an inquiry where the subject matter is complex are the more relevant ones to his *TMS* and *WN*. They are, however, more carefully analysed in Smith's other two illustrations of methods of scientific inquiries; the 'History of Ancient Physics' and the 'History of Ancient Logic and Metaphysics'.

The reason that these articles were neglected probably has something to do with Smith's performance as a historian. Even though his account on astronomy leaves something to be desired, it is still far better than those presented in his other articles.[14] But, from the point of view of studying Smith's methodology, it is completely irrelevant whether his historical accounts are correct or not. What is important is what he called the principles of enquiry. It does not matter whether they are demonstrated in a true or false story. What counts is what is being demonstrated. Therefore, one cannot be satisfied with what is deduced on Smith's methodology from his article on astronomy alone. One must also take into account, when analysing 'earthy' phenomena, what Smith thought of scientific methods in this context.

There is a significant addition to his methodology in the other two articles. This addition that is derived from the complexity of the system of earth is worth quoting at some length.

> In every body, therefore, whether simple or mixed, there were evidently two principles, whose combination constituted the whole nature of a particular body. The first was the Stuff, or subject matter, out of which it was made; the second was the Species, the Specific Essence, the Essential, or, as the schoolmen have called it, the substantial form of the Body ... In every case therefore, Species or Universals, and not individual, are the object of Philosophy ... As it was the business of Physics, or Natural Philosophy, to determine wherein consisted the Nature and Essence of every particular Species of things, in order to connect together all the different events that occur in the material world; so there were two other sciences, which, though they had originally arisen out of that system of Natural philosophy I have just been describing, were, however, apprehended to go before it, in the order in which knowledge of Nature OUGHT to be communicated. The first of these, Metaphysics, considered the general nature of Universals ... The second of these, Logics.[15]

This argument appears to be in complete accordance with what is suggested in the HA,[16] namely, that there is a need to classify matter according to familiar qualities. The only addition here is that we must analyse these qualities separately. Metaphysics, for Smith the theory of universals, is a theory, the domain of which is not the matter itself but its classification. This does not mean that there is no connection between the different theories or that the universals are based on some *a priori* notion. Even in Hume we can find assertions of the following type: 'I must distinguish in the imagination betwixt the principles which are permanent, irresistible, and universal ... And the principles that are changeable, weak and irregular'.[17] That is to say that we have, in fact, two distinct levels of analysis. In each of them there are principles, the role of which is to connect the different phenomena. The rules that are derived from them may be permanent in character, or temporary.

From Smith's point of view, therefore, a scientific investigation of everything, and in particular, earthy matters, is conducted at two different levels. One, the level of the subject matter – the level of the nature of things – where the rules might be changing, and the other is the level of the universals; namely, that familiar quality that is common to all the subject matter that is under investigation.

In his economic system one may consider the notion of natural price as part of the universals analysis (and I do not refer here to the natural price in its 'long-run equilibrium' interpretation), while market price may reflect the analysis of the subject matter.

In his moral analysis this distinction is even clearer. The level of the subject matter is the level of the observed behaviour of human beings. Namely, it is people's actual moral opinion that is based on their actual disposition to 'sympathize'. The universal, however, the familiar quality that is common to all mankind in different degrees, is the emotional meaning of sympathy. In other words, what it is in human beings that determines how much effort they are willing to put into trying and seeing the other from a true 'impartial spectator's' point of view.

The investigation of its permanent rules constitutes what Smith called Metaphysics, or 'nature of sentiments'. In the account of Smith's life given by D. Steward, who was helped by one of Smith's students, J. Millar, he describes the convention of moral philosophy at that time: 'The science of Ethics has been divided by modern writers into two parts; the one comprehending the theory of Morals, and the other its practical doctrines'.[18] It seems as if this distinction falls very clearly under the one just made; that is, the part of the moral system which is theory, is the one that is at the level of 'universals': the level of the permanent, while practice falls under the category of the changeable relations, the rules of matter.

What we learn from all that is that though Smith was, in principle, an 'empiricist' in the sense that the subject matter of any investigation was to be known to us through observation, he nevertheless adhered to some semi-rationalistic ideas.[19] Universals are not necessarily 'rational' even though one can always argue that at the level of analysing human beings one cannot think of a universal which is observable. But what makes Smith's approach semi-rationalistic is the fact that he is willing to treat those universals as subject matter in themselves. This was precisely the essence of the scholastic approach.

The main question is, however, whether or not we can observe these distinctions in Smith's work. The answer, in my view, is yes. Not only that the distinctions exist, they are almost the only means by which one can explain the apparent contradictions in his writings.

The 'principles' in human nature upon which Smith bases his two theories are 'sympathy' and the 'propensity to exchange and barter',[20] or, the 'principle of persuasion'.[21] Both these 'principles' are strongly dependent and correlated with a person's attitude towards the others. 'Sympathy' is his disposition to put himself in another person's place and the propensity to exchange reflects a person's drive, or need, to trade with another.[22] His ability to bargain depends on how well he can persuade the other.

I maintain that both these 'principles' are a reflection of the same fundamental in human nature. I call this fundamental 'the Interest in Others' that people have regardless of the particular constitution of their characters. 'Sympathy' is clearly a reflection of people's interest in others. It is, however, a reflection of it and not the interest in others itself. This can be seen by the existence of different degrees of 'sympathy' which, I believe, is a reflection of the different form that this fundamental takes in different people. I will show later on that Smith was aware of two important modifications. The first modification is that people's particular character interferes in their 'sympathy'. In other words, when an individual is trying to be the 'impartial spectator' his effort depends on his personality. It is not an effortless process to reach true 'impartiality' and, therefore, a person with little interest in others will be less inclined to put into the imaginary change of places the required effort for 'impartiality'. It is the difference between asking the question 'what would I have felt (and done) had I been the other person in his predicament' and asking oneself, 'what would I have felt (and done) had I been in his predicament'.

The second modification is concerned with the role of utility in forming people's opinions. Sometimes, Smith argues, people tend to confuse aesthetics with morality. They are so impressed by the beauty of, say, a system, that they believe that it must be morally good.[23] The same tension exists in Smith's *Lectures on Jurisprudence* (*LJ*) where he discusses people's social sense (acceptance of authority). There seems to be a substitution between 'utility' and 'sympathy' (the origin of authority). The more one has from the one, the less he has from the other.[24] When 'sympathy' is dominant the social organization will tend to be authoritative, when 'utility' dominates, a less authoritative organization can subsist.[25]

Given that 'utility' is an effortless method of forming a moral opinion it is not inconceivable that people with low interest in others will tend to form their moral opinion by utility. Hence, 'sympathy' is not the interest in others itself but an expression of the particular form that this fundamental (universal) takes in each individual.

The propensity to exchange and barter and the 'principle of persuasion' which is behind it are also a reflection of the interest people have in others. The brewer and the baker provide their service from self-love. They have no interest in the other apart from being a source of commodities and services to them. But they succeed in their bargaining because the one persuades the other that the deal is one where you 'give me what I want, and I shall give you what you want'.[26] But if the two individuals had different characters they might not have reached agreement on similar terms of trade. If an individual has a positive interest in others he might be persuaded to exchange for the 'cost of production'. For instance, in the Deer and Beaver case where there is no capital accumulation Smith argues that the only acceptable rule of exchange is according to labour inputs (effort).[27] But for that norm of behaviour to prevail and to have persuasive power we must establish whether and why it became a social norm. The mere idea of persuasion depends on conventions and other side products of social organization. People's acceptance of these conventions is a crucial input to the process of bargaining and in itself, depends on people's disposition towards others (and the social organization).

As I said before the mere analysis through universals is by no means a reflection of 'rationalism'. It is the treatment of it as substance which takes us away from pure 'empiricism'. In the case of Smith this treatment appears in the form of the 'moral instructor' who deduces his prescriptions from an abstraction of the 'impartial spectator'. This abstraction is an analysis of an 'imaginary change of places' that is performed by an imaginary human being who has only the interest of the others at heart. 'Interest in others' as an independent quality generates, through its impartiality, Smith's benchmark for moral analysis. It explains then what the grounds are for Smith's criticism of the individual's actual judgement. It is, simply, that his moral theory is not a 'naturalistic-positive' one. Rather, it is a delicate combination of 'empiricism' and 'semi-rationalistic' ideas. It thus makes his theory much more rich and interesting.

It also helps to explain the meaning of the 'labour theory of value' in Adam Smith. It is by no means based on the assumption that labour is the universal of commodities and therefore, commodities relate to each other, as a matter of fact, according to labour ratios. Rather it is through the universal of 'interest in others' that in a pre-capital-accumulation stage the social convention of the 'impartial spectator' will be that it is right to exchange commodities according to their labour ratios. The labour theory of value, therefore, is not a positive theory of exchange values. It is, rather, a normative, or conventional, theory of exchange.[28] Of course one needs to explore what happens when capital accumulation begins. Whether labour values can still play the role of the normative benchmark without a metaphysical conception of commodities the intrinsic value of which is comprised of past and present labour.

The idea of a universal in Smith's perception of human nature can also be supported for two other reasons. One is the influence of Newton on Smith's perception of the world and in particular, his influence on Smith's belief in the unity of nature. The universal in such a case helps to relate the various aspects of human nature that are being examined by his various theories. There is also Smith's discussion of the problem of describing human characters. In the next two sections I will explore the consequences of the 'rationalistic' aspects of Smith's theory on the moral values of self-interest and natural liberty. The universal (the unity of human nature) and the manifestation of 'rationalism' in the idea of the 'impartial spectator' will here play a significant role.

On the Interest in the Other as the Foundation of Smith's Social Theory

From the opening statement of the *TMS*, where Smith presents us with the 'principle' of his theory, it is quite clear that the part in human nature that dominates his moral theory is the interest people have in the fortunes of others: 'there are evidently some principles in [man's] nature, which interest him in the fortune of others'.[29] It also means that it is by means of this particular interest that Smith describes human nature. It is a quality that prevails in all human beings (otherwise it could not have served as a principle), and people are distinguished by the different degrees of this quality. Some characters may reflect a high positive interest in the fortune of others and some, a highly negative one. Some, indeed, may reflect very little interest altogether.

The quality of Interest in Others (IIO) may have two different expressions. It may manifest itself through sentiments as such (sympathy), or in actions (motives). The interest in others as manifested through action, is reflected by the intention, or motive to action ('by [the] disposition either to hurt or to benefit').[30] Thus a high positive interest means the want to benefit (benevolence) while the high negative interest means the want to hurt (malevolence). In between, there exists a point where Interest in Others is at zero, which means, no-interest-in-the others whatsoever: neither the want to benefit nor the wish to harm. In other words, the only interest that such a character reflects is self-interest.

Let me now explore in more detail the other aspect of interest in others: the side of sentiments and sympathy. The IIO as expressed through sentiments, in Smith's analysis, is the tendency to identify with the sentiments of the other. 'That we often derive sorrow from the sorrow of others, is a matter of fact too obvious to require any instances to prove it.'[31] But 'As we have no immediate experience of what other men feel', we do so by an imaginary change of places with the person we observe. We consider ourselves in his position and we try to experience through our own senses what he might be feeling. We realize harmony if our sentiments coincides with his (and this is what Smith called 'sympathy' and I will call 'technical harmony'), and dissonance if they don't.

However, the effects of harmony (or dissonance) that are being felt by the person who observes depend, to some extent, on his own natural constitution. 'The imaginary change of situation ... is but momentary. The thought of their [the observers'] own safety ... continually intrudes itself upon them'.[32] That is to say that a person's experience of the imaginary process is not at all independent of his own disposition. And in particular, it depends on his disposition towards (interest in) the fortunes of the other. Hence whether or not the harmony we discover with the sentiment of the other is agreeable to us depends on the nature of that sentiment as well as on our disposition towards the fact that the other is experiencing it. For instance, whether or not we feel harmonious (in the sense that the harmony is agreeable to us) with the other's sorrow or joy depends on the existence, or absence, of envy. 'If there is any envy in the case ... our propensity to sympathize with sorrow must be very strong, and our inclination to sympathize with joy very weak'.[33] When we observe the sorrow of another person and we try to experience it through our own emotions (the imaginary change of places), it is painful to us. But if the observer has a negative interest in the fortunes of the other (where envy is more likely to prevail), the realization that this pain has befallen his 'rival' gives rise to a great pleasure. Thus, though the observer feels that he would have felt the same as the person who is being observed ('technical harmony'), his direct sentiments towards the other contradict the pain that he derives from the imaginary process. Because the former are much more real sentiments than those that are being experienced through imagination, they are also the more dominant ones. Consequently, the envious person (or the one that has a negative IIO) will find the sorrow of another, when rightly felt (in the sense that the observer would have felt the same had he been in his place), more pleasant than painful. Thus, he will find it easier to 'sympathize' with sorrow.

If, on the other hand, the observer has a positive interest in the fortunes of others (the case of no-envy), the realization that the pain he experiences has befallen his fellow man gives rise to a terrible distress. Thus, his direct feelings are in complete harmony with those that he derives from the imaginary process. Consequently, the non-envious person will find sorrow, when rightly felt, most unpleasant. He will therefore find it more difficult to 'sympathize' with it. But there is another case of non-envy which is significantly different. The case of no-interest-in-the-fortunes of others (or, self-interest). When the observer has a positive IIO, his direct emotions enhances the pain he experiences through the imaginary change of places. When he has no such positive interest (but also no negative interest), the fact that the other is experiencing this pain will be of no significance. From the observer's point of view he is quite indifferent to the sorrow (or joy) of another. Thus, the pain that is being transferred in the imaginary process does not seem to get a hold on any of the direct sentiments of the observer. It will hence dissolve rather quickly and will hardly be felt by the observer. Of course, one may also ask whether such a person will bother at all to exert himself to an imaginary change of places in the first place. At present, however, we assume that he does but I shall deal with this point later on.

On this tendency to identify with the sentiments of the other Smith constructed his moral theory. We morally approve, or disapprove, of anything according to whether it invokes harmony of sentiments, or dissonance. But it is not upon the mere harmony (or dissonance) that we morally approve or disapprove. It is upon the pleasure we have in finding such a coincidence of sentiments with someone else. However, these pleasant, or unpleasant, feelings, as I have shown above, do not reflect the simple sense of pleasure like the one derived from utility. It is a much more complex notion of pleasure. In fact, it is comprised of two different sorts of pleasures. First, the pleasure we derive from realizing that we would have felt the same as another, had we been in his place: 'nothing pleases us more than to observe in other men a fellow-feeling with all the emotions of our own breast; nor are we ever so much shocked as by the appearance of the contrary'.[34] And the important feature of this sort of pleasure is that it is independent of the nature of sentiment in question. Namely, that the pleasure we gain from realizing that we would have felt the same as the subject of approbation in case of a pleasant sentiment, is the same as the one we would have experienced in the case of an unpleasant sentiment.

The second sort of pleasure, on the other hand, depends on the nature of sentiment in question as well as on the observer's disposition towards the other. Thus the other's sorrow, or joy, gives rise to pleasure or pain according to whether or not we have a positive or negative interest in their fortune.

Therefore, if we find 't. harmony' in sentiments that are a natural cause of pleasure to us (the other's happiness, or joy, in the case of 'no-envy' and his sorrow in the case of 'envy'), we shall obviously approve of the actions and circumstances that have brought them about. We are experiencing what I shall call 'pleasant harmony'; a harmony within ourselves. That is, a consistent composition of the pleasures that are being derived from the imaginary process.

If, however, we find 't. harmony' in sentiments that are a natural cause of unhappiness, we are, in fact experiencing within ourselves an 'unpleasant harmony'. The pleasure derived from 't. harmony' is being contrasted by the pain derived from the sentiment in question. This, in turn, means that within ourselves we experience 'dissonance'. We cannot approve of the actions and circumstances that have brought those justified (in the sense that we would have felt the same) unpleasant feelings.

In the same way, if we find 't. dissonance' with sentiments that are a natural cause of unpleasantness we approve of the circumstances that brought them about. (If, for instance, there is no envy, we would approve of the circumstances that have brought about sorrow with which we experience 't. dissonance'. Namely, we are dismissive of sorrow that we would not have felt had we been in place of the subject of approbation). So 'unpleasant dissonance', which means 'harmony' within ourselves (between the two components of pleasure that are involved in the process), gives rise to moral approval.

If, on the other hand, we felt 't. dissonance' with the pleasant sentiments, we would disapprove of the circumstances that have brought them about. (If, again, there is no envy, we would disapprove of the circumstances that have brought about happiness that we would not have felt had we been in place of the subject of approbation). The 'pleasant dissonance' means a 'dissonance' within ourselves and, thus, moral disapproval.

So moral approval, in Smith's system, depends on the consistency between the pleasure gained from observing the other experiencing the particular sentiment and the pleasure gained from experiencing 'technical harmony' (see Table 18.1):

Table 18.1: The machinery of moral approbation.

		The effects of the other's experience as perceived from the point of view of the observer	
The result of the imaginary change of places		Pleasant	Unpleasant
	Technical harmony	Moral approbation (harmony)	Moral disapproval (dissonance)
	Technical dissonance	Moral disapproval (dissonance)	Moral approbation (harmony)

We have now seen that at least the pleasure that is derived from observing the other experience a particular sort of sentiment, depends on the nature of the observer's character. Hence, we can already conclude that the actual moral judgement, in Smith's theory, also depends on it. But it is not only this aspect of moral judgement that depends on human nature. Whether or not we realize 't. harmony', and derive pleasure from it, also depends on the nature of the characters involved.

Generally speaking any person will find it easier to feel 't. harmony' with a person of a similar character. When a benevolent person comes to judge any other person's behaviour he would most likely have felt and acted the same if the other person was benevolent too. If, on the other hand, the observed person is malevolently disposed, it is most unlikely that the benevolent observer would have felt, or acted, the same. The further the observed person's character is from that of the observer's character (on the malevolent–benevolent sequence), the less likely it becomes for the observer to find 't. harmony' with the observed person.

Consider now a society which is comprised of self-interested people. Also, suppose that it is as beneficent as indicated by the *WN*. Everyone in this society is constantly improving his conditions. Consequently, everyone's happiness increases continuously.

The self-interested observer, and indeed each member of that society, will consider this situation as morally good, simply because he would have felt and acted the same as any other member of society had he been in their position. However, this would have been his moral verdict even if the outcome of this state was harmful. For the self-interested observer, or member of society, this is also the highest level of moral approbation that he is capable of. As a self-interested person derives nothing from seeing others happy or sad, his complete moral judgement depends on the degree of 't. harmony' that he experiences. Regardless of the consequences, he will most likely experience the highest level of 't. harmony' when observing another self-interested person.

For a benevolent observer, on the other hand, this state of affairs will not invoke the highest level of moral approbation. His moral approbation is based on an accumulated sense of pleasure. The higher that pleasure, the higher the degree of moral approbation.

Obviously, he will feel some pleasure from seeing other people enjoy themselves as a result of the cumulative activity of society. However, he will find no 't. harmony' (or 't. dissonance', for that matter) with the self-interested subjects of approbation. He will thus experience less pleasure than, say, if members of society were benevolent as well. In other words, in the scale of morals of a benevolent person, the self-interested person who unintentionally causes beneficence has a moral value which still falls short from what one may call the moral good.

The question that immediately arises is whether or not the moral judgement of the benevolent person is more valid than that of the self-interested person. The answer to this question is indeed a complicated one. It involves the question of whether or not there is any meaning, in Smith's system, to a 'proper' (or ideal) way of moral judgement. Or, that his system is entirely 'naturalistic' in the sense that moral judgement is determined by instincts (or sentiments) rather than by rational dictates. We saw already in the previous section that 'rational' considerations were not unrelated to Smith's work. We will see in a later section how the 'rationalistic' nature of his work is interpreted in his model of the 'impartial spectator'. At present I will only say that even without this question it is rather clear that as a matter of fact people's judgement will depend on their character.

It is also possible to show that in Smith's view it is the judgement of the benevolent person which is the proper one. To begin with, the moral judgement of the self-interested person suffers from a serious problem of consistency as far as an objective observer is concerned. If an objective observer looks at the actions of a self-interested person he can only see whether it produced harm or beneficence.

Surely he would expect the moral judgement of actions that have produced pain and misery to be different from those which have produced beneficence. However, the self-interested person will judge only according to whether or not he finds 't. harmony' with the actor. The outcome is entirely insignificant. He will mark the self-interested person's action as morally good whether it produced harm or beneficence. This, very clearly, is against what Smith considered moral judgement to be based on.

> The sentiment or affection of the heart from which any action proceeds, and upon which its whole virtue or vice *must ultimately* depend, may be considered ... in two different relations; first, in relation to the cause which excites it ... and *secondly, in relation to the end which it proposes, or the effects which it tends to produce.*[35]

But it does not seem reasonable to suppose that anyone, as selfish as may be, will be so indifferent to the actual outcome of actions when he comes to assess them morally.

One may argue, however, that this is only the result of applying to the self-interested person a practice of moral judgement which he does not actually use. The self-interested person, who has no interest in others, may not judge by an imaginary change of places (the process of 'sympathy') altogether. After all, for anyone to judge from the 'impartial spectator's' point of view, he must have some interest in what happens to the other. For the 'impartial' imaginary change of places to take place, one must exert oneself to see the subject of approbation's point of view. Why would someone with no interest in others whatsoever bother at all and exert himself to an imaginary change of places?

So it seems as if the character of a person affects not only his moral judgement as such (as discussed above), but also the way he actually forms his moral opinion. Those who have some kind of interest in the fortunes of others will be more inclined to judge by the imaginary change of places ('sympathy'), those who don't will probably judge in a different fashion. This other fashion is 'utility', or the 'beauty of the system'.

Whatever is the nature of Smith's ethics one thing seems to be quite clear – that practical moral judgement depends on some sense of pleasure. So far we have mentioned two sorts of pleasure. One, the pleasure from 't. harmony', and the other, the pleasure from seeing another person's happiness (or misfortune). But Smith devotes a whole section in *TMS* to another sense of pleasure – utility.

It would be interesting to note that in another place, where Smith discusses the formation of societies, he writes: 'There are two principles which induce men to enter into civil society ... the principles of authority and utility'. Both these principles, in Smith's view, explain the social existence because they explain people's obedience to different sorts of authority. Obviously, they are complementary. The principle of 'authority' 'arises from our sympathy with our superiors

... we admire their happy situation, enter into it with pleasure, and endeavour to promote it'.[36] Namely, people's readiness to accept authority is based on their disposition to 'sympathize' with it. The principle of utility, on the other hand, explains obedience because of the 'love of systems'. That is, 'we take pleasure in beholding the perfection of so beautiful and grand system, and we are uneasy till we remove any obstruction that can in the least disturb or encumber the regularity of its motions'.[37] In other words, it is the pleasure we gain from the beauty of the system that is the source of our loyalty and obedience. Precisely as is the pleasure we gain from 'sympathizing' with our 'superior'.

Now, as these two faculties of pleasure are substitutes, the greater the one becomes, the less we have from the other. If a person has a high interest in others, he will (a) be more inclined to feel 'sympathy' with other members of society; (b) be less inclined to be impressed by systems as a whole. The fortunes of individuals will have a greater effect on him than the 'contrivance and beauty of the system'. A person who has no interest in others will reflect precisely the opposite. Figure 18.1 illustrates this relationship. The character of an individual – depicted in the benevolent–malevolent sequence – determines the composition of his dispositions to derive pleasure from 'sympathy' and from 'utility'.[38]

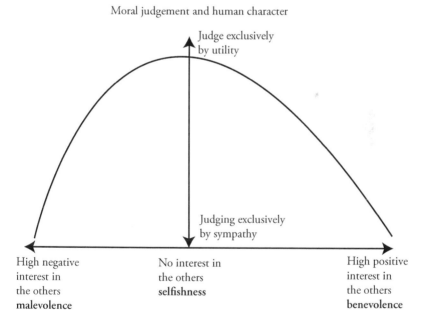

Figure 18.1: Moral judgement and human character.

The extremely benevolent person will have a greater capacity to 'sympathy' and will hardly be impressed by the mere 'beauty of the system'. The extremely malevolent person will have the same constitution though with reversed signs. The selfish person will have little patience to contemplate others' points of view and he will therefore be more impressed by the 'beauty of the system'. Others will have bits of both. They will be able to 'sympathize' and they will judge through an imaginary change of places but their judgement might be affected (to some extent) by the 'contrivance of nature'.

The fact that utility may sometimes take the place of 'sympathy' in determining moral opinion is very clearly considered by Smith:

> From a certain spirit of system ... from a certain love of art and contrivance, we sometimes seem to value the means more than the end, and to be eager to promote the happiness of our fellow-creatures, rather from a view to perfect and improve a certain beautiful and orderly system, than from any immediate sense or feeling of what they either suffer or enjoy'.[39]

However, though he is aware of the existence of the two principles in human nature, he is also very clear in arguing that utility ought not to be the source of our moral opinion. He writes, 'it seems impossible that the approbation of virtue should be a sentiment of the same kind with that by which we approve of a convenient and well contrived building'.[40]

Nevertheless, in our analysis it seems as if the self-interested person will indeed refer to this particular kind of pleasure as a moral guide. He will consider the system explored in the *WN* as the moral good because of its extremely appealing beauty. A benevolent observer, on the other hand, will determine its moral value far below what he considers as the ultimate moral good.

Thus, when a self-interested person hails the system of natural liberty that is based on self-interest, he does so for the wrong reasons. In Smith's view, his sense of morality is corrupt.

On Character-Based Moral Judgement of the Economic System

The Inadequacy of the Moral Exoneration of the Self-Interested Character

Much of the debate surrounding the moral significance of natural liberty in Adam Smith has been focused either on the legitimacy of 'self-interest' as a motive to action or, on the beneficent consequences proposed by its free reign. If 'self-interest' is a morally approved motive and the consequences of its applications are beneficial to society, it is difficult to imagine on what grounds one can question the morality of such a system.

Yet, as Griswold puts it: 'Smith forces the reader to put commercial liberal society into question even as he elucidates it and argues for its virtues'.[41] Indeed, Smith's reservations about the moral dimensions of commercial society are well documented[42] and have been a cause of many disputations. These, ultimately, have been confined to the general debate stemming from *Das Adam Smith Problem* with regard to the human character,[43] and, to a lesser extent, to the fate of the moral/social stock (i.e. long-term social benefits) with regard to the consequences of natural liberty.[44]

The subsequent resolution of *Das Adam Smith Problem* led scholars to consider the fuller *character* of the self-interested person as opposed to the mere *sentiment* of self-preservation. Thus, the 'other regarding' dimension of individuals' character became an important component of human nature which – in its entirety – is given free rein in natural liberty. This led some to argue that in Smith 'human beings are equally motivated by selfish, unsocial and social passions'[45] and subsequently, that '[a] system of economic liberty and natural jurisprudence can provide the best kind of political economy'.[46] Others conclude that the free expression of the inherently flawed human nature can only produce a system of 'second-best' morality.[47] And, that 'only in a world of ethical beings can the coordination of markets function smoothly'.[48] In 'A Study into Smith's Conception of the Human Character: Das Adam Smith Problem Revisited', I argued that the consistency of human nature implies that even if we take on board the 'other-regarding' faculties in human nature, but we distinguish between motives and mere emotional capacities, the character behind the *WN* would not be very different from Smith's own definition of selfishness; a character which is clearly morally rejected.[49] While this sits comfortably with the assertion of a 'second best' morality, it is inconsistent with the presumption according to which if people were ethically minded (i.e. self-interested with well-developed 'other-regarding' faculties), the system of natural liberty will indeed be the one which is depicted in the *WN*.

Either way, it became apparent that there are serious qualifications with regard to the moral acceptability of the 'self-interested' character. Consequently, the morality of the system of natural liberty which is based on it, must also be questioned. Moreover, although in the eyes of many, the social benefits of natural liberty are obvious, some debates have cast some doubt even on this question. The West–Rosenberg debate about the long-term effects of competition has raised the possibility, that not only are the motives behind the system morally dubious, their free reign will not really produce the promised 'public good'.

In parallel to this retreat from a received view according to which Adam Smith provided a moral advocacy of 'self-interest' based natural liberty,[50] there was an attempt to narrow down the moral dimension of the debate. The question that was implicitly set is this: do all these reservations amount to an injustice? In other words, is the system of natural liberty which is based on the 'self-interested' character, at least, a just system?

Obviously, the significance of the question depends on what we mean by 'justice'. Smith is clearly aware of the different usages of the word[51] and if indeed we consider both Grotius's definitions of *justitia expletrix* and *justitia attributrix*, asking whether the system is just or not is not very different from the general search for the moral significance of natural liberty. However, the objective of the 'justice' approach was very different indeed. Instead of struggling with the more elusive problem of whether natural liberty is a *good* system, the focus of attention has shifted to the claim that it is a just system where justice is taken to be individual freedom and 'adventitious but perfect rights to property'.[52]

In part, the shift towards the 'just' and away from the ideal of the 'good' is a reflection of the state of moral theory in the latter part of the twentieth century and subject to the influence of Rawls.[53] But there are two obvious difficulties with this approach. First, while Smith's ethics is clearly not utilitarian, it is by no means deontological. As will be demonstrated below, there is only one process of moral evaluation in Smith. The distinction which is subsequently drawn between justice and moral goodness is really a question of degree rather than a question of substance. Second, and not unrelated, it is far from obvious that one can restrict Smith's notion of justice to individual freedom and property right construed as the right to what is one's own (*ius in re*).

There is an important anomaly, in my view, which is underlying the debate about the moral significance of natural liberty. It is the implicit presumption that the morality of the system can be determined by the mere examination of its two extreme ends: that which motivates people and the nature of the outcome. In some respects, this seems to be a reflection of a very modern perspective. Much of what is currently said about economic justice is confined to either the initial distribution with the voluntary nature of exchange, or to the final distribution. Little, if any, is being said about the procedures of economic interactions. This is partly due to the dominance of general equilibrium analysis where the simultaneity of the system prevents us from being able to ascribe any clear causality between intentions, or actions, of individuals and specific outcomes.

But an economic system is really a system of *interactions* where agents act and are being acted upon. Whether or not all of this happens simultaneously is an important question but we shall not be able to understand its significance without focusing on the basic cycle of action and counter action. The absence of the analysis of actions is particularly surprising as almost a third of *TMS* is devoted to it.

Young attempted to deal with the morality of natural liberty from the point of view of interaction by examining the moral significance of exchange.[54] This is clearly a step in the right direction. However, his reference point was not the analysis of actions but the judgement of an 'impartial spectator' with a *social conscience* who is concerned with the good of society. This again leaves us with a somewhat general conclusion which is not altogether different from the view which sanctions natural liberty for its proposed unintended benefits.

The Complications Presented by the Analysis of Actions

In the economic set-up, people act and are being acted upon. This means that the question of the application of moral judgement cannot be confined to either motives (character) or outcomes alone. While this complicates a lot the implementation of the idea of the harmony of sentiments, it also provides a unique opportunity for the role of the 'impartial spectator': he needs to know some economics (!)

Smith's analysis of the action cycle is where he generates the principles for the moral evaluation of actions in general and economic interactions in particular. This will produce three types of moral assessments. First, we have the actions where there is propriety in motives, appropriate choice of action and *proportional* benefits to the person who had been acted upon. This is an action where an 'impartial spectator' would expect the person who had been acted upon to act on his sense of gratitude and reward the original actor. Second, there are those actions where the sentiments of either gratitude or resentment are not shared by the 'impartial spectator' and which therefore, do not require any redistribution. Nevertheless, the dissonance between the 'impartial spectator' and the sentiments experienced by those who had been acted upon, suggest that the moral value of the action is inferior to the one which was generated by the first type of action even if redistribution did not occur in either case. The third type of action is where resentment is approved of by the 'impartial spectator'. This means that punishment (or possible redistribution) should be administered. This category of actions clearly fit the category of commutative justice.

The significance of this last type of action cannot be overstated. The received view with regard to what constitutes justice in Smith is that only the violation of the rights which people have as people, are within the domain of commutative justice. Hence, there is no role for distribution in the analysis of justice. This interpretation has been questioned recently[55] from the point of view of the analysis of property rights. This last type of action opens the door to a different justification for matters of distribution to become part of commutative justice.

In many respects, Smith's analysis follows that of Aristotle although this is not clear from his own account. Aristotle distinguishes between 'distributive' and 'rectificatory' justice. The former is concerned with 'the distribution of honour or money or such other assets as are divisible among the members of the community', and the latter 'rectifies the conditions of transaction'.[56] Distribution, argues Aristotle, should be based on merit and this may be derived from the political culture of society and does not seem to depend on specific actions. Smith too, follows a similar line. He writes,

> man is by Nature directed to correct, in some measure, the distribution of things which [nature] herself would otherwise have made ... The industrious knave cultivates the soil; the indolent good man leaves it uncultivated. Who ought to reap the harvest?

Who starves and who lives in plenty? The natural course of things decides in favour of the knave; the natural sentiments of mankind in favour of the man of virtue.[57]

But rectificatory justice is the concept most relevant to economic analysis as it treats all agents as equal and solely focuses on their actions. In terms of the later distinction between commutative and distributive justice, it is clear that both Aristotle's definitions of distributive and rectificatory justice are present in both concepts of commutative and distributive justice. Given that the first two parts of the *TMS* are devoted to what Aristotle calls 'rectificatory' justice, it is particularly unclear on what grounds have distributional matters been excluded from the question of justice.

The Moral Analysis of Actions

Smith's theory of actions and their moral evaluation is spelled out in the first two parts of *TMS*. The lengthy and sometime complex analysis of how to properly evaluate the cause and effects of an action may hide the very simple foundation upon which Smith conducts his analysis. It is nevertheless revealed explicitly towards the end of his analysis:

> Whatever praise or blame can be due to any action, must belong either, first, to the intention or affection of the heart, from which it proceeds; or, secondly, to the external action or movement of the body, which this affection gives occasion to; or, lastly, to the good or bad consequences, which actually, and in fact, proceed from it. These three different things constitute the whole nature and circumstances of the action, and must be the foundation of whatever quality can belong to it.[58]

Let me begin by presenting Smith's idea of an action through this proposed decomposition of it. A certain person 1, acts A. He does so because of various reasons. Let us denote those reasons by α. Action A is therefore the result of sentiments (or emotions) in 1 that were invoked by circumstances α.

While performing A, a second person, 2, is affected by it. 2 has sentiments which are invoked by action A, and by his own particular circumstances which we shall denote by β. These sentiments, in 2, are also the motive behind the desert which emanates from the action and we mark it by D.

This produces the basic, and quite obvious, structure of an action cycle:

$$S^1(\alpha) \text{------>} A \text{-------->} S^2(\beta, A)$$
$$\text{<----------} D \text{----------|}$$

Read: sentiments $S^1(\alpha)$, invoked by α, initiated action A, which affected 2 in such a manner that aroused sentiments $S^2(\beta, A)$. The sentiments in 2 invoke him, or her, to want to reward or punish the actors (action D). Ultimately, the moral judgement of the action would rest with the 'impartial spectator's' approval of the sentiments invoked in the person who had been acted upon.

Propriety

The first stage of the cycle, $(S^1(\alpha) \text{----} > A)$, is the subject of what Smith calls *propriety*.[59] Namely, the question of approval of the relation between: (a) circumstances, (b) motives (sentiments) and (c) the subsequent action.

> The sentiment or affection of the heart from which any action proceeds, and upon which its whole virtue or vice must ultimately depend, may be considered under two different aspects, or in two different relations; first, in relation to the cause which excites it, or the motive which gives occasion to it; and second, in relation to the end which it proposes, or the effect which it tends to produce.
>
> In the suitableness or unsuitableness, in the proportion or disproportion which the affection seems to bear to the cause or object which excites it, consist the propriety or impropriety, the decency or ungratefulness of the consequent action.[60]

To make more general sense of the above we note that as far as actions are concerned we are interested in motives inasmuch as they affect the others.[61] Hence, to make the analysis meaningful we shall look at motives in terms of what they propose for to others, i.e. they will range from benevolence to malevolence.[62] The self-interested motive (to distinguish it from the self-interested character), on such a scale, means that the actor intends nothing for the other. Equally, actions too are defined in terms of their consequence to the others. That is to say, they range from the beneficent to the harmful.

The key word in propriety is 'suitability', namely, whether the sentiment (S^1) that was invoked by circumstances α, stands in some relation to these circumstances. To establish this, we must bring ourselves to a position of an 'impartial spectator'. Then we can see whether we would have felt the same had we been in place of the subject of approbation. If there is a coincidence of sentiments between the 'impartial spectator' and the subject of approbation, then there is 'suitability'. In other words, a sentiment is suitable to the circumstances that invoked it only if everyone, in that position, would have felt the same.[63] But this is not the only 'suitability' that is required by propriety.

Once it is established that a person's feelings were reasonable in relation to the circumstances that had invoked them, we must also ask whether an 'impartial spectator' would have *acted* in the same way. This corresponds to what Smith's refers to as 'the external action or movement of the body'[64] as one of the three determinants of an action's moral value. We must examine whether the choice of action was suitable to the sentiments which drove the person to act *and* to its proposed consequences. In other words, we must again ask ourselves whether if we, or anyone else, had been in place of the subject of approbation, we would have acted (not just felt) in the same way.

The importance of *design* and *intent* in Smith's analysis of the morality of actions cannot be overstated.[65] This, of course, may shed some light on the real significance of unintended consequences as Smith, the observer, is acutely aware of the tendency which people have to attribute good fortune or harm to the immediate objects which tend to generate them. However:

> Before any thing, therefore, can be the complete and proper object of either grati-
> tude or resentment, it must possess three different qualifications. First, it must be the
> cause of pleasure in the one case and of pain in the other. Secondly, it must be capa-
> ble of feeling those sensations. And, thirdly, it must not only have produced those
> sensations, but it must have produced them from design, and from a design that is
> approved of in the one case, and disapproved of in the other.[66]

But what exactly is meant by the approval of design? Evidently, Smith is referring here to the 'impartial spectator' who would not only have felt the same as the subject of approbation but would have transformed these feelings into the same kind of actions. But while it is quite easy to comprehend the approval of an 'impartial spectator' with sentiments and motives, it is less obvious with regard to actions.

In the case of the design of action it must mean that the observer has some knowledge of the proposed consequences of various possible actions.[67] This knowledge, in turn, is inevitably comprised of two elements. First, the observer must be able to establish whether the action that was chosen had a reasonable chance to bring about a proper manifestation of the sentiments which invoked it. In such a case, when a good intention turns harmful we can attribute it to fortune rather than a mistaken choice of action. Second, the observer must also be conscious of what might be the likely consequences to society if this kind of action *habitually* followed these kinds of sentiments.

For instance, we may on many occasions feel that we could sympathize with the anger of another person. We would approve of such sentiments in relation to the circumstances that invoked them. However, anger, when transformed into action, may result in harming someone – the cause of that anger. Naturally, the 'impartial observer' must first consider whether the choice of action (in terms of its proposed consequences) stands in some proportion to the sentiment from which it sprang.[68] We must be quite sure that, say, shaming that person in pub-lic will indeed harm him according to our intent or, that it may snowball into such a state in which the whole family is affected and the person must leave town. But in the case of transforming sentiments into actions there seems to be another proviso. The 'impartial observer' must examine whether allowing a free transformation of such sentiments into such actions may prove dangerous to society as a whole.[69] For instance, in the case of resentment and hate, Smith believes that an 'impartial spectator' may feel 'sympathy' with the subject of approbation. (i.e. everyone would have felt the same). Nevertheless, as far as transforming this hate, or resentment, into a harming action is concerned, Smith is quite adamant. 'There can be no proper motive for hurting our neighbour ...

which mankind can go along with'.[70] Although we may approve of someone's feelings in certain circumstances, we confront, all of a sudden, a sort of a Kantian 'categorical imperative'. It is a kind of 'categorical imperative' because the reason Smith believes that an 'impartial spectator' will never consider a harmful action as suitable to the approved resentment, is its 'universal test'. 'Society', writes Smith, 'cannot subsist among those who are at all times ready to hurt and injure one another'.[71] Obviously the reason for rejecting the harmful action is not the absence of suitability between it and the resentment or hate behind it, but rather, its *global significance*. If everyone would act in such a way *habitually* (at all times), society could not subsist.

In other words, in Smith's system, the 'suitability' of an action to the sentiment that invoked it is examined at two different levels. One is, whether or not the particular action has a high probability of successfully implementing the sentiment behind it. The other is, the global significance of such an action; the effect on society if all individuals acted similarly in response to certain sentiments.

Merit and Demerit

> In the beneficial or hurtful nature of the effects which the affection aims at, or tends to produce, consists the merit and demerit of the action, the qualities by which it is entitled to reward, or is deserving of punishment.[72]

The second stage of the action cycle, $(S^2(\beta,A)\text{---}D\text{--->})$, is the subject of the theory of *desert (or merit and demerit)*. Namely, it is the analysis of the *propriety* of the sentiments that are felt by the person who *had been acted upon*. As such, it is where the final judgement on the action is proclaimed.

As we said earlier both intention (motives) and outcomes are measured in terms of what they propose to the other. The sentiments of the actor range from benevolence to malevolence and the outcomes to the person who had been acted upon range from beneficence to harm: 'and that upon the beneficial or hurtful effects which the affection proposes or tends to produce, depends the merit or demerit, the good or ill desert of the action to which it gives occasion'.[73]

However, according to Smith there are only two types of sentiments invoked in the person who had been acted upon. They are *gratitude* and *resentment*. These sentiments are in themselves, the 'motives' for the sub-action of desert. And as the sentiments are so narrowly defined, so are the actions that comprise desert. They are either reward, punishment, or no action at all. In broader terms, whenever there is a sanctioning of either reward or punishment, there is a call for redistribution. When neither reward nor punishment is approved, the natural distribution of things should be left untouched.

Gratitude is a feeling that will be felt by the person who had been acted upon when the outcome of the action was beneficial to him. Resentment is the feeling when the outcome was hurtful.[74] Desert, therefore, is: 'To be the proper and approved object either of gratitude or resentment, which naturally seems proper, and is approved of ... when the heart of every impartial spectator entirely sympathises with them'.[75]

However, whether gratitude, or resentment, is *duly* felt depends primarily on whether or not the action that has brought about those outcomes was 'proper'. Namely, whether the sentiments that invoked it were 'suitable' to their circumstances (α) and, whether the choice of action was appropriate.

> It is to be observed that, how beneficial soever on the one hand, or how hurtful soever on the other, the actions or intentions of the person who acts may have been to the person who is, if I may say so, acted upon, yet if in the one case there appears to have been no propriety in the motives of the agent, if we cannot enter into the affections which influenced his conduct, we have little sympathy with the gratitude of the person who receives the benefit; or if, in the other case, there appears to have been no impropriety in the motives of the agent, if, on the contrary, the affections which influenced his conduct are such as we must necessarily enter into, we can have no sort of sympathy with the resentment of the person who suffers.[76]

Hence, to understand desert and thus, the moral evaluation of the action, we have to consider the cycle of action in full. Let us therefore, recap:

$$S^1(\alpha) \text{-----> A =======> } S^2(\beta,A)$$
$$\text{<}^{****************}$$

Propriety is the moral analysis (or judgement) of suitability in the triangle: circumstances-sentiments/motives-action (i.e. $S^1(\alpha)$----> A). Merit and demerit is the analysis of the circumstances-sentiments/motives-reaction of the person that was 'acted upon':

$$S^2(\beta,A)^{***********}\text{>}.$$

$S^2(\beta,A)$ may have two values: Gratitude or Resentment. But the values of $S^2(\beta,A)$ are determined by the consequences of the action A. Desert, therefore, may have three values: Reward, Punishment or No-change.

We are now confronted with four possibilities:

(a) $S^1(\alpha)$----> approved & $S^2(\beta,A) = G =>$G is approved.
(b) $S^1(\alpha)$----> disapproved & $S^2(\beta,A) = G =>$G is disapproved.
(c) $S^1(\alpha)$----> approved & $S^2(\beta,A) = R =>$R is disapproved.
(d) $S^1(\alpha)$----> disapproved & $S^2(\beta,A) = R =>$R is approved.

G and R represent Gratitude and Resentment respectively. The approval or disapproval of G and R are somewhat more complex. They represent the 'impartial spectator's' approval (or disapproval) of the second person's response *in* action. The 'impartial spectator' may feel that he would have felt the same as the person who was acted upon due to this person's own circumstances. However, given the nature of the action and the objective nature of the outcome he might not approve of the second person's acting on his sentiments.

Also, we know that:

$$\text{Desert} = \begin{cases} \text{Reward} & \text{if } S^2(\beta,A) = G \text{ } and \text{ approved.} \\ \text{Punishment} & \text{if } S^2(\beta,A) = R \text{ } and \text{ approved.} \\ \text{No-change} & \text{otherwise.} \end{cases}$$

These three values of desert generate, in principle, three moral categories. These correspond nicely to Smith's own distinction between the three possible social states:

> It is thus that man, who can subsist only in society, was fitted by nature to that situation for which he was made. All the members of human society stand in need of each other's assistance, and are likewise exposed to mutual injuries. Where the necessary assistance is reciprocally afforded from love, from gratitude, from friendship, and esteem, the society flourishes and is happy ... But though the necessary assistance should not be afforded from such generous and disinterested motives, though among the different members of the society there should be no mutual love and affection, the society, though *less happy* and agreeable, will not necessarily be dissolved. Society may subsist among different men, as among different merchants, from a sense of its utility, without any mutual love or affection ... Society, however, can not subsist among those who are at all times ready to hurt and injure one another.[77]

Naturally, there is a distinction between the evaluation of a single action and the analysis of a social state. While the outcome of a single action may be accidental, the social state is about the habitual practice of agents in terms of their motives to action, their choice of actions, the effects on others and the others' response. I use this social ranking benchmark merely to confirm that in my formulation of the action cycle I have not departed from the principles which guide Smith's analysis. However, the insight we can derive from the analysis of actions is much greater. We shall now examine in more detail how each of the general states of society can emerge.

The Good Action and the Good Social State

In the good social state 'the necessary assistance is reciprocally afforded from love, from gratitude, from friendship, and esteem'. Consequently, society flourishes. The actions which would dominate such a social state must be of the following characteristics:

(a) $S^1(\alpha)$-----$>A$, approved & $S^2(\beta,A) = G$ approved.

That is to say that the sentiment and choice of action were approved, and the latter successfully implemented the actor's intentions (hence the sentiment of gratitude which rose in the person who had been acted upon). This action is fully approved and the 'impartial spectator' would have therefore gone along with the sense of gratitude felt by the person who was acted upon. As such, one may say that such an action reached the peak of approval and therefore, commands the highest moral value of, say, a '*good*' act.

However, Smith does not leave the story at this. As the person who had been acted upon experienced gratitude which is approved by an 'impartial spectator', there is an expectation that the person who had been acted upon should now act on his own sentiments and reward his, or her, benefactor.

It is true that Smith makes clear that failing to reward one's benefactor turns one into an 'object of hatred' but not of resentment.[78] It is also true that Smith believes that such an appropriate response could not be extracted by force. However, Smith does qualify this for the relationship amongst equals: 'Even the most ordinary degree of kindness or beneficence, however, cannot, *among equals*, be extorted by force'.[79] But this is not the same when people are not equal.[80] 'The civil magistrate', writes Smith,

> is entrusted with the power not only of preserving the public peace by restraining injustice, but of promoting the prosperity of the commonwealth ... he may prescribe rules, therefore, which not only prohibit mutual injuries among fellow-citizens, but command mutual good-offices to a certain degree.[81]

This means two different things. First, it means that the duty of someone in power is to ensure that in some cases and to a certain degree, reward should be as compulsory as punishment in the case of injury. In other words, even among equals the duty of recompense may be enshrined in law if there is someone who may be able to force it.[82]

Second, there is an implicit admission here that when there is inequality between the two agents, the duties of the one with greater power are greater than those who are without it. This, I will later show, becomes an important issue when we come to investigate economic interactions in the presence of property rights.

So will the good social state remain good irrespective of whether the good action generated reward? Naturally, if the beneficial action was intended to generate reward it would lack propriety and thus would not fall into the category of the good state. But if there was propriety and reward did not follow, it means that some agents are the object of hate and as such, this cannot constitute a state of harmony and good fellow-feeling. Indeed, Smith quite clearly claims that the good state is that of gratitude as a motive to action and reciprocity. The call for a higher authority – with power – to enforce reward seems to be in line with the centrality of reciprocity for the good social state to emerge. In other words, a good social state is where there is propriety of actions and appropriate reciprocity (i.e. redistribution).

The Subsisting Social State: The State of Acceptable Actions

In this state,

> though the necessary assistance should not be afforded from such generous and dis-
> interested motives, though among the different members of the society there should
> be no mutual love and affection, the society, though *less happy* and *agreeable*, will not
> necessarily be dissolved.

We saw already that even a good action, where there was no reward, may cause hatred and unhappy feelings. This means that even a benevolent action may slip into Smith's second state of unhappy subsistence. In this sense, what distinguishes the good social state from the subsisting state is that in the former, due reward is distributed while in the latter it is not. Failing to act on the demand for reciprocity is a lower moral state to the one where the impartial spectator approves of the behaviours of both those who act and those who are being acted upon.

Recall that the difference between the discussion of a single action and a social state is that while an action is an ad-hoc event, when we refer to a social state, we refer to the habitual nature of actions. In the socially good state, people usually act out of proper motives (thus there is propriety in most actions) and choose actions which reflect these motives. They generate intended beneficence such that most people who had been acted upon, act on their sense of gratitude and reciprocate.

When a good action slips into the subsisting state it is, again, because of the habitual refusal by those who benefit to reward their benefactor. This creates a continuous state of disharmony between most members of society. But there are other cases where there is no reward (or punishment), a situation which is typical of the subsisting state. Unlike the previous case of failing to reciprocate when reward was due, in these cases desert (either reward or punishment) has not been sanctioned by an 'impartial spectator'. There are two such cases. First, we have the case where gratitude is not sanctioned:

(b) $S^1(\alpha)$-----$>$A, disapproved & $S^2(\beta,A) = G$ disapproved.

This is a somewhat delicate and complex case. As was described above, Smith's terminology here is a bit imprecise. At first, Smith talks about propriety as the ability of the 'impartial spectator' to sympathize with the motives of the actor. But he does recognize that the outcome of actions may not be intended and therefore, implicitly he extends the idea of propriety to the design. In the action described above the 'impartial spectator' disapproves of the first element in the action cycle (i.e. the relationship between circumstances, sentiments and choice of action). As we saw earlier, this means either that the motive to action was not appropriate to the circumstances which invoked it, or that the choice of action was inappropriate to the intention. The action chosen generated much more beneficence than was intended and therefore, according to Smith, gratitude is not sanctioned. In part 2, section 3 of the *TMS*, Smith conducts a lengthy discussion about the influence of fortune on the sense of merit and demerit. His conclusion is that for something to be the object of desert 'it must not only have produced those sensations [of pleasure or pain], but it must have produced them from design'.[83] In other words, for a beneficial outcome to generate approved gratitude, the beneficial outcome must stand in some proportion to the intention behind it.

Thus, when we say that the first part of the action cycle is disapproved this does not necessarily mean that the motives behind the actions were inappropriate. It could be simply that the kind of action which serves the approved motive generates an unintended benefit. As it was not intended, the sense of gratitude is not approved and there should be no reward. We may call such an action *appropriate* or *proper* but in spite of the possible propriety of the sentiments which invoked the action, its moral position is inferior to that of the good action.

It is conceivable that many actions which are appropriate for a particular end may generate unintended consequences. If the pursuit of those ends is habitual, we may end up with a social state where beneficence is generated yet no reward – no redistribution – is sanctioned.

Equally, a clear case of impropriety is also possible. In such a case, the motive to action may be disapproved of by an 'impartial spectator' and so would the choice of action. But such an action can accidentally generate benefits. Naturally, the sense of gratitude would not be approved. The outcome of both cases is the same but the difference between them is that the previous case is more typical of a habitual state than the case of an accident. If a malevolent intention accidentally produced beneficence, it is unlikely to happen again. Such an action will not habitually fall into this category.

The second case of disapproved desert is when the outcome of the action was hurtful:

$$\text{(c) } S^1(\alpha)\text{-----}>A, \text{ approved } \& \ S^2(\beta,A) = R \text{ disapproved.}$$

The sentiment and choice of action were approved but they appeared to be unsuccessful. Because the choice of action was approved, it means that the reason for failure must be accidental, thus the action, again, is *appropriate* or *proper* but it cannot gain 'full approbation' as it invoked resentment in the person who had been acted upon. The propriety of the first part of the action cycle suggests that acting on the resentment felt by the person who had been acted upon will not be justified.

Another possible explanation is that a person may feel resentment even if the approved action was successful. The reason, then, for the resentment, is due to the second person's circumstances, β. In such a case, the 'impartial spectator' may approve of the actual resentment in the sense that he might have felt the same. However, he will not approve of person 2's acting on it.

The habitual practice of such actions is unlikely to leave us in the same position. If the harm was created by fortune, habitual practice of actions with propriety will normally be beneficial and thus command reciprocity. In such a case, it will fall into the category of the good actions.

The Bad Action and the Unjust State

The two previous cases represented the forms of social interaction which, according to Smith, may subsist for a long period of time in spite of being characterized by actions which command different degrees of morality. The good state was that in which there was a considerable amount of harmony between agents who approve – through the idea of the 'impartial spectator' – of the behaviour of both actors and those who had been acted upon. The morally inferior state is the one where society may subsist but at a considerable lower level of harmony either because there is a universal disapproval of the failure of agents to reciprocate or because of the absence of proportionality between design and outcome (unintended consequences).

The unjust case is that case where the actions of individuals threaten the existence of society:

$$(d)\ S^1(\alpha)\text{-----}>A,\ \text{disapproved}\ \&\ S^2(\beta,A) = R\ \text{approved}.$$

As before, the disapproval of the first element in the action cycle may be due to either impropriety of intentions or to the failure in the choice of action. Naturally, if there is impropriety in the sense that there was an intention to harm the other, the resentment which is felt by the person who had been acted upon would be approved. This means that an 'impartial spectator' would allow the person who had been acted upon, to act on his resentment and punish the actor.

Both the good and the bad actions have something in common. In both cases, the 'impartial spectator' expects and sanctions the response of the person who had been acted upon. The apparent difference between the two is that in the case of the good action, the reciprocity appears to be optional while in the case of the bad action it seems to be compulsory. The reason for this is quite obvious. Failing to reciprocate on approved benevolence would be a source of unhappiness but will not endanger society. Failing to punish acts of malice might endanger society as there will be no deterrent from wanting to harm others. 'Resentment', writes Smith, 'seems to have been given to us by nature for defence, and for defence only'.[84]

Smith's analysis of actions produced four types of actions which seem to fit well into his three possible moral states of society. What typifies the different social states from the point of view of actions is the value of the reward. The good social state was the one in which rewarding the benefactors is sanctioned. The inferior yet viable second state is the one where desert is not sanctioned and the bad state is the one where punishment is sanctioned. The need to activate desert is essential. Without punishments in the bad case, society may not exist and without reward in the good state, society may not flourish.

The Self-Interested Action

Of all the sentiments and motives considered in Smith's analysis, self-interest is perhaps the most important one. It is so, because it seems that Smith assumed it to be a prime sentiment,[85] and it is clearly the subject of investigation in the *WN*. Inasmuch as the invisible hand of the *WN* depicts the spirit of Smith's analysis, it is all about how through natural liberty, self-interest may be transmitted into public good.

As I said at the beginning of this chapter, much of the debate surrounding the morality of natural liberty was focused on the evaluation of self-interest. Clearly, if self-interest is a morally good character, the unintended consequence of its free reign is just an extra bonus. But if the self-interested character is morally condemned, the morality of the system seems to rely entirely on its unintended outcomes. From the previous discussion this does not seem consistent with Smith's own analysis. Unintended beneficial consequences are the reason for rejecting a sense of gratitude which might have been invoked in the person who had been acted upon. Thus a happy and flourishing society will fail to emerge. This does not really sound like a wholehearted endorsement of natural liberty.

The problem is that there is a great deal of confusion with regard to what exactly one means by 'self-interest'. Is it a particular sentiment or motive? Or is it a characterization of overall human behaviour? In our case, however, none of this matters. We are not concerned here with the abstract analysis of a community of self-interested individuals who are allowed to freely pursue their interests. Instead, we are interested in a system which is characterized by a set of actions.

Evidently, if we take the broader view according to which self-interest is a characterization of how people moderately seek to preserve themselves (i.e. prudence) while at the same time being capable of 'other-regarding' benevolent feelings,[86] the total sum of social actions will be comprised of mixed motives. Some actions will reflect that which Smith calls the selfish motive, while other actions may be motivated by the social motive. While this may indeed be a correct description of society, the subject matter of the *WN* is the cumulative effects of the pursuit of one's own interest. It does not matter whether or not this is so because self-interest is the strongest motives or because of a conscious decision to limit the scope of the investigation. Either way, Smith was clearly delineating economics as the investigation of the self-interested activities even though this does not mean that he thought that such a study can be conducted in isolation from other aspects of social life.

Therefore, from the point of view of the theory of action, the system of the *WN* is a set of actions dominated by a *habitual* practice of self-interest.

Like any other action, the moral significance of a self-interested action depends on its propriety as well as its consequences. Self-interest, as a motive, means that the actor is seeking to benefit himself while intending nothing at all for the others. Hence, a successful implementation of this intention would mean exactly this: that the actor benefited himself while producing neither benefit nor harm for the others.

On the face of it there seems to be a paradox here. If we approve of the motive to preserve one's self and it is executed in complete accordance with its intentions, this must be a good action. From the point of view of propriety one can easily imagine the circumstances where a person feels that he wants to do only for himself and nothing for the others. After all, according to Smith this is one of the strongest natural urges. It is therefore quite plausible that an 'impartial spectator' would have felt the same in such circumstances. As for the other part of propriety – the appropriate choice of action – it too, indicates propriety. When the outcome was neither beneficial nor harmful to the others, the choice of action is proportionate to the proposed outcome and thus, reflects well the motive (intentions).

There is, however, one obvious difference between what we consider as morally 'good' and this particular action. The self-interested action seems to raise neither gratitude nor resentment. Hence, to some extent, such an action has *no moral dimension* at all, as it has not affected anyone but the actor himself.[87]

However, apart from the lack of any sense of gratitude or resentment in the system there is the question of whether the successful implementation of the self-interested motives depended on what others were doing. It is not inconceivable that a successful implementation of a self-interested motive depends on, say, others being self-interested as well. It is clear that the idea of natural liberty as a harmonious machine is precisely the general interdependence between members of society. In such a case, we cannot really think of the successful implementation of one's intention in an isolated manner.

If all individuals are self-interested in a similar manner then we might say that each of them acknowledges the others' contribution to their success in implementing their own intentions. However, as there was no intention to help the other, any sense of gratitude would have been dismissed by an 'impartial spectator'. Thus, a 'self-interested' action that satisfies one's expectations but does not produce any benefit for the others, will, at best, be considered merely as a *proper* action in the sense that there is propriety but gratitude, such as there is, could not be sanctioned. Therefore, the *habitual* practice of self-interest which does not produce any benefit for the others will not take society beyond its viable stage and into the happy and flourishing one.

Quite often the argument about the morality of a self-interested system is focused on the unintended benefits that are generated by its free reign. However, paradoxically, in Smith's theory, it is precisely such benefits which undermine the morality of the self-interested system. If the pursuit of self-interest is manifested through an action that has a high probability of benefiting the others, its proposed outcome stands in no proportion to the motive. As the beneficence of the outcome cannot be attributed to the intention, any sense of gratitude felt by those who had been acted upon would not be approved by an 'impartial spectator'.

There are, therefore, three possible situations which may arise when the sentiment of self-interest is approved by any 'impartial spectator'. The difference between them lies in the proposed consequences of the choice of actions:

(i) there is unintended beneficence in the outcome;
(ii) there is unintended harm in the outcome;
(iii) there are no effects on the other.

In the case of (iii) it seems that there is no moral dimension to the problem, as people act upon themselves. If we do allow the implicit assistance of other people's behaviour then the gratitude is felt by the actor and not by those who had been acted upon. As no one intended to generate this gratitude, it would not be approved by an 'impartial spectator' and the action fails to become a good action.

In case of (i) the unintended beneficence will raise gratitude in those who had been acted upon (directly or indirectly) but the lack of intention will cause the 'impartial spectator' to disapprove of such sentiments. The overall reduced level of harmony suggests that such actions will only yield the socially unhappy state of mercenary exchange of the necessary assistance which we all require in a world of interdependence.

In case of (ii) the outcome of the self-interested action was harmful to the others. Evidently, as the pursuit of one's own interest in a moderate fashion is a motive with which an 'impartial spectator' would approve, the harmful outcome must be accidental. The harm was not intended and the resentment raised in the person who had been acted upon is not sanctioned by an 'impartial spectator'.

However, as we are focused on a *habitual* practice of self-interest, both benefits and harm are potentially a regular unintended side effect of such an activity. An action may have a whole host of side effects which are obviously unintentional. If, for instance, there is only one way of pursuing one's own interest but the side effect is beneficial, the fact that we repeatedly act in the same way does not mean that we begin to intend the side effects. Consequently, the gratitude of unintended consequences, according to Smith, will never be sanctioned. But what about a harmful side effect?

In principle, the analysis should be symmetrical in the sense that repetitive use of a successful measure to serve one's own interest which generates a harmful side effect does not mean that at some stage, the actor begins to mean that harm. But, according to Smith, while society may subsist even when gratitude is not sanctioned, it may not subsist with the regular generation of harm. Thus, in such a case, while there may be only one course of action to fulfil the pursuit of self-interest, if it habitually generates a harmful side effect (even unintended) there is no more propriety in the action and the action sinks into the status of a bad action in an unjust social state.

Hence, the nearest to the morally good action that a self-interested motivated action can get is when it does not produce any beneficial outcome to anyone except the actor himself. In such a system there will be complete harmony of sentiments as the impartial spectator would approve the action and there will be no discord associated with disapproval of false sense of gratitude.

When there is an unintended consequence which is beneficial to the others, the disapproval of the 'impartial spectator' of the sense of gratitude felt by the others turn this action to the one which was typical of the unhappy, yet viable, social state.

When harm is the unintended consequence of the regular pursuit of self-interest, the action falls into the domain of the unjust even though the moderate wish to pursue one's own interest may be a sentiment with which an 'impartial' spectator could identify.

Spillover and the Beneficence of Natural Distributions

When we move to investigate the moral significance of a set of actions comprising the economic system we must carefully identify (if possible) those who act and those who had been acted upon. The Walraisian system of contemporaneous simultaneity implies that all agents act and are being acted upon at the same time. Moreover, as all of them are equally rational utility maximizers, there is complete symmetry in the position of agents in the system. No action of a particular agent is the cause of the outcome to another and therefore, there can be no real debate about morality within the interactions of the Walrasian system. Outcomes are determined by exogenous variables and that is why discussions of ethics in modern economics have been confined almost exclusively to the two ends of the system: initial allocation and final distribution. In Smith, I claim, the story is very different indeed.

Let us begin by specifying what we mean by *economic* actions that could become the subject of moral assessment. The first two things that come into mind are exchange and production. But while relationships between the different agents (or social classes) that are involved in the process of production seem to be a natural (or perhaps traditional) subject of moral debate, exchange as such seems to have been more difficult to analyse. Can we really say that in an action of exchange there is a person who acts and another who is being acted upon?

According to Viner there is not much point in a moral analysis of exchange in the framework of Smith's analysis.[88] The reason is that exchange is a very impersonal action. The 'social distance' between the participants is so great that none of them will feel 'sympathy' with the other. Neither of the bargaining sides will have the tendency to feel like the other had he been in his place. Hence, as moral judgement depends on 'sympathy', no moral opinion will be formed. Young, on the other hand, argues against Viner's assertion. In his view, even when the 'social distance' is large, 'sympathy' may still be felt by strangers provided that they meet face to face.[89] Consequently, a sense of moral approval or disapproval will emerge at both ends of the deal. In my view, however, there is a stronger case for morally assessing exchange even though the 'social distance' may be great. The 'impartial spectator' is an ideal as much as it is a description of how people actually form a moral opinion. It is a model of how to form a 'proper' moral judgement about anything at all. As such it may very well be applied to situations where people do not have an immediate sense of 'sympathy' or, morality. Viner's argument is that there is no moral value in exchange because the actual participants don't employ 'sympathy'. This, however, does not mean that we cannot conceive an 'impartial spectator' who would pass a judgement on both sides of the bargain. When a burglar breaks into a house he probably has no idea of who lives there. Does this mean that because of his social distance from the people who, as it were, are being acted upon his action is now value-free?

Beneficence

A person, say the capitalist, from self-interest, advances materials to the action of production. Another person, the labourer, again from self-interest, brings his labour to the process of production. Both of them act and are acted upon at the same time, and the outcome of their interaction is a certain level of wealth.

Suppose now, that they produced wheat, does the mere extraction of wheat from the land indicate a beneficial outcome to their action? Surely not; not even in terms of nature's plan for the preservation of the species. The first thing about which we should inquire is whether this quantity is more or less than it takes to reproduce it. Surely when we began the action, we must have had some quantity of the product; otherwise we could not have produced it.[90]

If the quantity that came out of the act of production is less than what is needed for its reproduction, the action cannot be considered as beneficial. In this particular action the amount of seeds and subsistence of the next period cannot remain the same. If we do not cut subsistence then we must reduce the seeds, hence, the next period will yield even less output. At some stage we shall have to give up some of our food as well. In the long run, if the trend continues, neither the capitalist, nor the worker would be able to maintain the same level of consumption, thus, though wheat is still extracted from the land, the action of its production cannot be considered beneficial in its outcome. From nature's point of view (the multiplication of the species) it is disastrous as well. With less wealth than earlier, the species would disappear.

When the quantity produced is exactly equivalent to what is needed for its reproduction (including the subsistence of the labourer and capitalist), we may say that the action has had no effect.[91] From nature's point of view, this action will preserve the species but will not multiply it.

Only when surplus is produced, it is guaranteed that the species will advance in quantity. However, from the moral point of view the question of whether the action can be considered as beneficial is not yet settled. For that we need to explore more carefully the question of who acts and who is acted upon.

Ownership and the Distinction between Acting and being Acted upon

If a surplus has been produced, the person who initiated the action, the capitalist (who, for reasons that are not under consideration at present, owns the outcome) can decide to consume the whole surplus himself. He will, obviously, be able to increase his family and advance the race but the other person, the labourer, will remain in the same state as before (he might even be worse off, according to the capitalist's whim, if he was above subsistence in the previous period). Hence, the action will certainly raise the feelings of gratitude in the capitalist and, at the same time, it might even raise the resentment of the labourer if his level of consumption decreased.[92]

On the face of it, the situation seems undetermined. However, we must look again into the description of the action in order to solve this problem. If indeed we had two persons who act and are being acted upon at the same time, the question of who owns, or who ought to have received, nature's remuneration (i.e. the total produce), should have been left open or, at least discussed more carefully. However, we have an exogenous constraint that dictates that the produce of the action 'belongs' to the initiator of the interaction (the capitalist). The distribution of it becomes a separated action; an action where the person who acts is clearly the capitalist, and the person who is acted upon is clearly the labourer. In other words, the capitalist's benefits are mainly due to the work of nature, which is not an object of morals. Those of the labourer depend on nature as well as on the decisions of those who command the produce of nature. Therefore, whether an action of production, of which the 'action' of distribution is an integral part, is beneficent or not depends on the labourer's feelings. As he is the one who is ultimately acted upon, it is his sense of gratitude which indicates a beneficent outcome. As the complete produce goes through the capitalist, it is unlikely that he will bestow benefits on the labourer, while harming himself. Hence, the beneficence of the worker necessarily implies the beneficence of the capitalist, but it does not hold the other way around.

We may return now to the question of whether an action where the capitalist (the initiator of the action), who was rewarded by *nature* for his dexterity and, who leaves the wages of his labourer at their previous (or even, subsistence) level, is beneficent or not. The answer, I feel, depends on the use that the capitalist will make of his surplus. He might not share it with his labourer, the one that participated in the production of his surplus, but, at the same time, as his stomach is not larger than that of the poor person, he is bound to share the surplus with another labourer whose services he might require.[93] Does this mean that the outcome is beneficent?

To begin with, we must acknowledge that the analysis of the relationship between those who are involved directly in the action is insufficient to determine the real effect of the action. If the capitalist does not share his surplus with the person who was involved in producing it, there must be another action involved: the action in which he exchanges the surplus for some sort of labour, which Smith named as unproductive labour. Obviously, the outcomes of both actions (the production and exchange of surplus) are interdependent. Therefore, we shall have to extend the framework of analysis so that we can measure the complete effect of the actions of production and exchange.[94]

In short, as the beneficence of a single action may spill over beyond the direct participants in the original process, we have to consider these effects as well. On the one hand, we have the initiators of actions, those who own the benefits that are bestowed by nature. On the other hand, we have the labourers (of all kinds) who are engaged in either mere exchange (in the case of the unproductive labour) or, in a complex action of production and remuneration. Now, as we consider the complete system, the question is whether or not the process of the invisible hand guarantees a beneficent outcome to the production of surplus.

Consider the following case. In an economy there are twenty capitalists, and eighty labourers, and the sole product is wheat. A unit of wheat is produced by 0.1 units of labour, and 0.5 units of wheat. In order to subsist through one period of production, a person needs 1 unit of wheat. In the initial state, the economy was producing 200 units of wheat. This means that twenty labourers are productive and sixty are unproductive, if employed at all. From the point of view of reproduction, to maintain the same level of output, the capitalists will have to put aside 100 units of wheat, as seeds, and 20 units of wheat as subsistence for the required labour input. Adding to it their own subsistence, (20) the surplus that remains is 60 units of wheat. If the capitalists will use their surplus for 'luxurious' consumption, they can employ sixty unproductive labourers. Note however, that no one can subsist on 'luxurious' consumption. Indeed, though wealth is unequally distributed (eighty people in the economy have only the level of subsistence, and twenty have, in terms of wheat, their subsistence + other trivial convenience), necessities of life (subsistence) are equally distributed (everyone , at the end of the process of production and exchange, has only 1 unit of wheat). This economy will not be able to maintain more people in these circumstances. This economy can subsist for a long period of time assuming that productivity remains unchanged.

This picture is an outcome of a set of repeated actions where agents act and are being acted upon simultaneously. As we assume that all acted out of self-interest, we shall assume that there is propriety in all the actions. Is the outcome benefi-cent? Is there any sense of gratitude in the system? At first sight, the only reason for gratitude on the part of the labourers is that they are alive and have something to eat. However, as time passes, in this stationary state, there is no room for any more gratitude. The first set of actions (the functioning of the system at the first period) raised gratitude because it *changed* the labourers' position from hunger to subsistence. But, once they have reached subsistence, there seems to be no reason for gratitude, as the system merely reproduces itself in each period.

Furthermore, one can argue that even the initial provision of subsistence through the offer of their labour should not generate gratitude among the workers. To see this we must ask ourselves what would have been their lot in a different form of social organization. If, for instance, the alternative to the current commercial stage were a state of autarky, the workers would have been clearly better off. If every member of society had 2 units of wheat (equal distri-bution of *wealth*), he would be able to produce, as an independent producer, 2 units. Though he only works 0.2 of his time, he needs for subsistence 1 unit of wheat as well as 1 unit of wheat as seeds (half of 2). Hence, he is being left with no surplus. From the point of view of those who were labourers in the previous situation this must be a much better state of affairs. Under equal distribution of wealth with no division of labour (autarky) they will receive the same net income (subsistence) as before but with much less work on their part.[95] While they gain in working hours, workers cannot earn more than what they were used to earn under the previous arrangement. So it is clear that under equal distribu-tion of wealth and autarky, those who became workers in the commercial stage were either as well off or even better off than they became under the interde-pendent commercial stage.

From the point of view of the ex-capitalists, they are now clearly worse off. Though they still have their subsistence as before, they simply cannot have any extra convenience. Luxury consumption and unproductive labour would not be available.

Thus, it is clear that against the alternative of autarky, the workers are not bet-ter off in this stage of interdependence. Hence, there is no obvious reason why they should feel gratitude by being offered the opportunity to subsist through employment by the capital owner. To summarize this point: in the stationary state described above, workers will not feel gratitude because their wages remain constant at subsistence level as well as because their lot would have been the same or better under a different form of economic organization.

To see clearly that the moral fate of the system must rest with the sense of gratitude felt by the workers, consider the effect on the system of a decision by the capitalist to invest. Recall that in our example the surplus of 60 units went as subsistence to the unproductive labourers. Thus, eighty workers had been employed. If, instead, the capitalists would want to invest it in order to increase output for the next period, they would need some of the surplus to be used as circulating capital (raw material: seeds). Consequently, there would not be enough subsistence left for all the labourers in the economy.

If, say, they wish to increase output by 80 units of wheat, they will need 40 as seeds and eight workers who should get subsistence of 8. Thus 48 units of the surplus are taken by the investment leaving 12 for unproductive workers. Thus, the total demand for workers shrinks from eighty to $28 + 12 = 40$. If there is one labour market, the wage rate would fall below subsistence and some of the workers may be unable to find subsistence. Whether this means that they themselves might die or that they would be unable to raise a family, they are bound to feel resentment. Moreover, it is evident that this outcome is entirely due to the action taken by the capital owners. Hence, in spite of the apparent symmetry in the sense that all agents are equally self-interested, the institutional set-up may give extra power to some agents. This means that in terms of the entire picture, some agents clearly act while others are clearly acted upon.

Naturally, we must acknowledge that the above decision by the capital owners would, in the end, benefit everyone as it would increase output in the next period and thus, increase the surplus and the demand for workers. However, I was trying to demonstrate how the fate of the workers depends on the decision by the capital owner in a way which is not symmetrical. We could have equally described a case where the capital owner uses a greater proportion of his surplus in an unproductive way. This, in the following period, will cause a collapse of output and inevitably lead to a fall in wages.

It is true that workers, by propagating, may affect the wage levels in the economy but this, in the end, affect them more than it affects (in Smith) the decision of the capital owner with regard to the use of his surplus.[96]

From all this we may conclude that the mere production of surplus (wealth) is by no means in itself a beneficent outcome. The fact that it may distribute subsistence in an equal manner is completely insignificant to the question of beneficence which is dynamic in nature. Thus, the self- interested economic action may create harm even though it was not intended. If the decisions by the capital owners with regard to the use of their surplus are repeatedly harming the workers and raising their resentment, there should no longer be propriety in the actions of the capital owners. Their motive (self-interest) may be approved by an 'impartial spectator' but their choice of action (their decisions regarding the allocation of surplus between productive and unproductive labourers) is rejected. In such a case, even a surplus-generating economic system (i.e. a growing system) may produce a social state which is unjust in the sense that the impropriety of actions together with the resentment felt by those who had been acted upon should call for reprisal.

There is no doubt that in the *TMS*, Smith is trying to make the case for the beneficence of the invisible-hand mechanism. However, this case is being reviewed and modified in the *WN* where he very simply argues that the beneficence of the system is possible, but it does not lie in the mere creation of surplus (or by the mere division of labour). Indeed, we can find an intriguing correspondence between the three social states in the *TMS* and the three economic states in the *WN*. In the former society may flourish and be happy, may subsist but be unhappy or may become unjust and cease to be viable. In the *WN* we have the corresponding state of progress, the stationary and the regressive state.

It is quite significant to note that what distinguishes these three economic states, according to Smith, is the fate of the workers. It is all based on a presumption, made by Smith in the *WN*, which is perfectly consistent with what we have established through the analysis of actions. In the *WN*, Smith reiterates the significance of the workers' disposition to the evaluation of society.

> Servants, labourers and workmen of different kinds, make up the far greater part of every great political society. But what improves the circumstances of the greater part can never be regarded as an inconvenience to the whole. No society can surely be flourishing and happy, of which the far greater part of the members are poor and miserable.[97]

Again, perceiving beneficence as a dynamic concept, Smith notes that '[i]t is not the actual greatness of national wealth, but its continual increase, which occasions a rise in the wages of labour'.[98] He then goes on to discuss with great detail how the rise in demand for labour (determined by the decisions of the capital owners) allows workers to propagate and live a long life while in the stationary state, there is nothing for them to be grateful about as wages remain at their subsistence level. In a decaying state, Smith quite clearly points at famine and death which would be an obvious cause for resentment.

Conclusion

Most moral philosophers ponder the question of how we recognize good and just things, and by implication, what makes things good or just. Smith, I claim in this essay, went one step further by building a framework – a model, if you wish – for moral judgement which is sufficiently universal to allow both the relativity of ethics and the potential for ethical self-delusion.

After identifying the fundamental principle which governs the sociality of mankind, we saw how that which governs our judgement may depend on our character and the circumstances in which we operate. This means that a self-interested character may judge things differently from a benevolent one. The impartial spectator, however, would properly judge like the benevolent person simply because such a person will have enough genuine interest in the other to properly experience fellow feelings with that person. In turn, this leads to the possibility that the deception of nature has worked so well that people's ability to properly judge the outcomes of their system are completely blurred.

To be sure that such a conclusion does not rest only on the commonality of that which governs the economic system and that which provides the grounding for our moral judgement, we expand the analysis to examine the ethical evaluation of a system of actions and interactions.

The traditional way of looking at the morality of natural liberty – which seems more becoming modern economic analysis than classical economics – is focused on the two ends of the economic cycle: motives and outcomes. In modern economics this is so, in part, because of the simultaneous nature of interdependence where it seems difficult to assign specific outcomes to specific actions. But in Smith this is not the case.

While Smith clearly recognizes the notion of interdependence and perhaps even the simultaneity of individuals' action, he has clearly not abandoned the thread of causality. This can easily be seen through his elaborate study of the moral evaluation of actions. Here, the ideas of proportionality and reciprocity – very much in line with Aristotle's rectificatory justice – are pivotal to his ethical discussion.

We discovered that there are basically four types of actions and three moral states. What distinguished one moral state from the other was the approval, or disapproval, by the 'impartial spectator' of the sentiments raised in the person who had been acted upon. When there is intended beneficence, gratitude is approved and the 'impartial spectator' expects reciprocity (i.e. reward). When reward is administered, society will flourish and be happy (according to Smith's conception of the three social states in the *TMS*).

When there is no correspondence between intention and outcome (including unintended benefits) the 'impartial spectator' disapproves of the sense of gratitude or resentment which was raised in the person who had been acted upon. This disharmonious situation corresponds to the second social state where society may subsist, but in an unhappy state. The third situation is where the 'impartial spectator' approves of the resentment felt by the person acted upon due to the malicious intentions of the actor. The habitual practice of such actions will bring a social demise and corresponds to the third, unjust and unviable, social state.

We then looked at the implications of this for the moral evaluation of a self-interested-based system of natural liberty. We noted that an economic system is characterized by a set of actions rather than by a set of characters. Even if all agents are motivated by self-interest and act simultaneously it is possible to establish who acts and who is being acted upon. This is due to the particular ownership structure and the legal arrangements according to which it is capital which hires labour.

We have shown that, paradoxically, self-interested actions will be consistent with the moral good only if there is no unintended beneficence. Once we consider such beneficence, the self-interested action become merely proper. These three categories of moral value of actions were found to be consistent with Smith's explicit moral ranking of the three social states in the *TMS*.

While considering the question of a *system* of actions where all agents may be equally driven by self interest, I have tried to show that the notion of interdependence does not blur the distinction between those who act and those who are being acted upon. The key definers of these relationships are the distribution of ownership and the legal system (i.e is capital hiring labour or the other way around). We saw that in the Smithian system where capital hires labour, the workers are those who, in the end, are being acted upon. Consequently their resentment due to their pay conditions which may be the result of the rational behaviour of the capitalists, deems the capitalists' actions as unjust. In this way, it becomes apparent that distributional matters are within the domain of justice and that justice is not the only moral issue in the analysis of natural liberty.

There is an interesting anecdote I wish to note in conclusion. Samuelson's (1977) 'vindication' of Smith's economic model ensures that in the long run, at the stationary state, the economy will reach the state in which no beneficence will occur and the habitual practice of self-interest will become 'suitable' to its outcome.[99] If indeed this is true, then the Smithian dynamic is such that it will bring efficiency and morality together. But whether or not Samuelson has managed to capture the essence of Smith's economic and social systems, is another matter altogether.

19 WHY DO ECONOMISTS AND PHILOSOPHERS RESORT TO THE HISTORY OF THEIR DISCIPLINE?

Pierre Livet

Two Roles of History and Two Ways to Compare History of Economics and History of Philosophy

History of economics is not considered as the core of economics, which is supposed to be the theory of general equilibrium and game theory (one can add the theory of social or collective choice). Econometrics is in the second circle, providing theory with empirical data, and experimental economics and neuro-economics are newborn marginal fields, a bit heterodox in their inspiration. History of economics is supposed to be an ancillary discipline, but can be taken either as a way of criticizing the mainstream, or from the orthodox point of view. In the second case, the historian uses methods of history and history of science in order to show through which steps economics has been developed until it comes to its supposed acme (the combination of general equilibrium and game theory). In the first one, the historian pays attention to ways of thinking that have been left aside in this development and evaluates the theoretical cost of such giving up – mainly, the inadequacy of economics with real social interactions.

Pascal Bridel knows very well the details and limits of the theory of the general equilibrium. At the same time, he uses the methods of history to examine what were the real contents and aims of the works of such prominent economists like Walras and Pareto. But in the end, he takes the stance of criticizing history when he denounces the simplifications of Ricardo, or the excessive use of Adam Smith's metaphor of the invisible hand, and their relations with the turn from political economics to mainstream theoretical economics, or recalls the Paretian suspicion about the indifference of theorists to the ways of functioning of the real economy, or Sismondi's attention to the relation between sentiments and rationality. In this sense, his work gives us paradigmatic cases for studying the relation between economics and its history.

By contrast, history of philosophy is not an ancillary part of philosophy, neither institutionally nor in a conceptual perspective. Most of the members of the academic population of philosophers are historians of philosophy. Even analytic philosophers, who are often accused of neglecting the philosophers of the past by the continental historians of philosophy, make reference to Plato, Aristotle, Descartes, Leibniz, Kant, and the medieval philosophers. Innovative philosophers in the past have always had a double stance towards more ancient philosophers: they criticized their theses and arguments, but at the same time acknowledged their authority and considered as necessary to refer to them in an argumentative relation (even if Descartes claims that he dismisses the medieval scholastic, he uses a lot of its conceptual distinctions).

We can try to draw a parallel between the roles of history of economics and of history of philosophy, just for a first examination. Theoretically innovative researchers in the theory of economics – in the previous century – can do without reference to the history of economics. From their perspective, they are making science, and for them the role of the history of economics is reduced to the one that any history of science made by scientists (for example, history of physics made by physicists) has: to give information about the success and failures of the past research in the discipline. Innovative philosophers in the same period keep on referring to philosophers of the past, and take them as sources of inspiration. Paying better attention to the history of economics has often been a stance adopted by people who wanted to criticize the mainstream, but who were not necessarily innovative on the theoretical and formal field. Criticizing the claims of past philosophers was an obligatory step for an innovative philosopher who wants to develop an own perspective (and want to be considered as a great philosopher).

We should not forget that the main theorists (and not only the historians) in economics also criticize the limits of the works of their predecessors. But in this case criticisms that matter take as their targets the limits and drawbacks of the formalism: they are internal criticisms. On the contrary, the criticisms coming from the historians are mostly external ones – for example the denunciation of the social lack of realism of the economical theory. The criticisms of the innovative philosophers are both internal and external. By contrast, the historians of philosophy do not take the liberty to make external criticisms. They reduce internal criticisms – like the detection of possible incoherence in some reasoning – to temporary interpretative tools, used to raise challenges for the interpretation. But historians of philosophy intend to let them aside once a philosophical solution has been found. This solution is either internal, giving a cleverer interpretation of the doctrine. Or it is external, and it reconstructs the argumentative or rhetorical strategies of the examined author, strategies that historians show to be biased by the constraints of the interactions with other philosophers and with political or religious authorities (see Leo Strauss).

If we simplify a bit, external criticism is forbidden or marginal in the history of philosophy and usual in the history of economics. Innovative theorists in economics limit their criticisms to internal ones, while innovative philosophers make use of both the inconsistencies revealed by their internal criticism and the deficiencies revealed by their external criticisms. The uses of the history of the discipline in economics and in philosophy seem at cross-purposes.

Another kind of comparison is possible if we do not reduce history of economics or philosophy to a dual perspective. On the one side, we have the pure description of the evolution of ideas in these domains, on the other, history as criticism. We can focus instead on the conceptual dynamics of the successive evaluations of the theoretical steps of this evolution. This dynamical perspective is not to be confused with 'judged history'. In this kind of history, the historian takes as benchmark and end point the present state of the discipline and makes a retrospective evaluation that depends only on the present trends, the perspective of which is applied to any previous state. On the contrary, we focus on the change between successive trends, the successive revisions of the orientation of the discipline and their relations with each other. At each step, theorists make a change in their perspective. We have to analyse in each case in which respect this implies also a change in the evaluation of previous perspectives, including the changes in the previous interpretations of the past changes. Of course, these changes in evaluation may also imply changes in the status of the discipline.

We want to focus on some examples in which these changes and revision of evaluation and status are related, in economics and philosophy. These relations present a double aspect. On the one hand, the previous attempts to reach a stable state or even an absolute one are demonstrated to fail. On the other, there is a shift from the absolute to relativity and relatedness – not to relativism, but to the implication of previously assumed stable elements into an evolving network of relations. In the end, adopting this dynamical and relational perspective will make us more sensitive to the importance of the relation between vagueness and uncertainty. Both are often neglected companions of the theoretical effort, but are nevertheless at the core of both economics and philosophy.

Equilibrium, Emotions and Systematization

We will make reference to two examples in economics that Bridel has analysed: the general equilibrium and the possible role of emotions and sentiments. Corresponding examples in philosophy are the attempts to systematize philosophy by linking it with mathematics, logics, formalization or only organizing it as a system, and the philosophical treatment of passions and emotions. We cannot get into detailed analyses, and our study will be similar to what Bergson called 'an overview of the history of systems'.

Adam Smith's *Theory of Moral Sentiments* combines these two kinds of examples, as it is a conjunction of philosophy and of problems that are at the roots of economics. Smith proposes not to focus at first on particular categories of emotions or sentiments, but to build a process by which the relation between sentiments and evaluative judgements – including the categorization of different sentiments – will enable a stable structure of evaluations to emerge. Roughly, this process is the following: we share the emotions of other people, but in a less intense and more distant way (this is what Smith calls 'sympathy', that differs in this respect from our 'empathy'). When considering two people in interaction, we partly share their two emotions, even if they are opposite. Our manner of balancing them is a first step towards a comparative evaluation: we will share more intense emotion with the victim of an injustice than with the pleasure of the author of injustice (if there is such a pleasure). These ways of balancing emotions can be shared by other observers, and we learn in this way about the evaluative balance that can resist conflicting evaluations coming from other people. This evaluation has a name: it is the perspective of the 'ideal observer', and we internalize this perspective as the one of our moral self.

This impressive theoretical construction avoids the problem of defining in a fixed way the elementary emotional components and finding a unique systematic way of assembling them (a problem for the conceptual constructions of Descartes, Spinoza or Malebranche). It is, then, remarkable that the famous 'invisible hand' of *An Inquiry into the Nature and the Causes of the Wealth of Nations* is also the indication of a process that allows Adam Smith to avoid having to define from above and in a fixed structure the economical system of a nation, leaving it to the interactions of the people who take care of their own interests. The two works seem to have as a common inspiration the acknowledgment of the failure of top-down systematicity and the sensitivity to the role of comparisons, relations and interactions. As Bridel has noticed, it is a pity that the invisible hand has been taken as the ancestor of the demonstration of a formal equilibrium, and combined with the idea that the existence of such a fixed point in a free market could justify the claim that the market is always the right judge. Paradoxically, Smith has given us in the *Theory of Moral Sentiments* a process that could lead to intersubjectively stable judgements (relatively stable, of course, and presumably not with a unique solution), while the fixed point of the equilibrium of the market cannot be related to a formalized process that can guarantee to reach it even from a neighbouring but not very close state: even in this neighbourhood, instability is still possible, as demonstrated by Debreu and Scarf.[1] This kind of equilibrium can be compared to the one of a pencil that is put on its tip: surely not stable in the usual sense.

History of philosophy and history of economics are mixed in the works of Adam Smith. In each domain, the dynamics that we are interested in – the steps of revision of the conceptualizations – are similar. The philosophical project of building the unique systematic structure of the passions, the project of Descartes, Spinoza and Malebranche, has not given convincing results. They aim to find a systematic and combinatorial order between components (e.g. good and bad) of emotions of passions taken as natural kinds with absolute definitions – for example in Spinoza's *Ethics*. But it leads them to give to some passions a content that does not correspond to the phenomenal and cultural experience (for example, admiration in Descartes's *Treatise of Passions*). It implies normative choices that can bias the description of emotions. The failure of such systematic and substantive conceptions triggers a conceptual revision that leads Adam Smith to adopt a relational and comparative perspective. Our sentiments of sympathy cannot be defined as combination of good or bad, for us and for others, for the past, the present and the future (as in Descartes and Spinoza). It emerges from the process of balancing between two kinds of emotions. The first is the emotion triggered in a third observer by the situation of one people. The second one the emotion triggered in the same observer by the situation of the partner of this people in the observed interaction. In this way the whole interaction is considered from a third perspective, a perspective that can be shared with other third parties. The failure of conceptions that aim at being systematic and absolute – 'more geometrico' – gives rise, after revision, to a relational and dynamical perspective.

Conceptual Dynamics in Philosophy

Can we see the conceptual dynamics presented by the history of economics and the history of philosophy as a succession of attempts at systematicity and absoluteness of definitions, of failures of these attempts, followed by revisions that lead to more relational and complex perspectives? Yes, if we apply also this dynamics of revision to the systematicity of this dynamical schema itself! First, each step of the dynamics is *both* the result of a revision and a new attempt at systematicity. Second, we cannot in advance, when we belong to one period of this dynamics, predict in what way the new present attempt will fail. Third, our retrospective reconstruction of the differences between the steps is itself an attempt to systematicity that can fail and be revised. But this very failure and revision will corroborate the general schema.

The application of the schema to itself has a consequence: the difference between the systematic and absolute tendency and the relational one is not absolute, but itself relational. The relational perspective is not reserved for the modern thinkers and the absolute to the ancient ones. For example, in economics the systematic quest for a general equilibrium implies that the notion of value (the exchange value) can no longer be taken as an absolute one, but is necessarily relative to the exchange relation and its possible disparities – for example, when the supply is bigger than the demand. The absolute is here a relational one.

If we look back to Plato, everybody knows that this innovative philosopher proposes to anchor the thought on Ideas that are supposed to be absolute (kat'auto). But Ideas are relational, as established in the dialog 'The Sophist', in which a prominent place is given to the concept of 'Other'. In the same dual way, Plato has also supported an esoteric doctrine of Ideal Numbers, that gives a systematic and mathematical structure to the fundamental reality, but at the same time he has suggested in Timaeus some ways by which these numbers might be related to the structure of the physical world and not only reserved to ideas in our minds.

Aristotle has criticized this combination of absoluteness and relational structure for its absoluteness. He has argued convincingly that the relation of participation between absolute Ideas and the world of our senses failed to solve the problem of the link between the two. He has himself insisted on the epistemic process that could not always grasp the essence but might just catch a glimpse of it, and he has tried to structure this process as relational, by extracting the essence from a dialectical inquiry that compares the different theses and induces the false ones to eliminate each other. At the same time, he has defined systematic rules of reasoning that we have to follow, once we have some grasp of the essence, in order not to introduce falsity when we start from true propositions.

It has taken a very long time for logicians to criticize this dependence of reasoning on essence (still an absolute) and to anchor it on mathematical structures. Frege could have hoped to reach some absolute of logic in this new relation, but the result has been that a logic has become relative to the choice of a variety of mathematical structures (instead of giving a foundation to mathematics, a Hilbertian's hope that Gödel has demonstrated to be a failure).

In a similar way, the Kantian Critic was an attempt to take our knowledge as relative to the constraints of our perceptive and epistemic processes, and it has been criticized as taken these constraints as absolute (*a priori* forms of sensitivity and understanding).

The Hegelian construction was an attempt to include every possible relation between concepts in a unique system – an absolute, but made up of interrelatedness, including oppositions and conflicts. The failure was a result of the claim to uniqueness, as his system was relative to particular choices of specific oppositions. But maybe the profound cause of this failure was that Hegel has tried to include in his system the very means of detecting the failure and triggering the revision: the conflict between theses and their consequences. A particular system cannot be the unique source of its own revision. The test that leads to revision has to come not only from the previous theory but also from other perspectives and the development of a new kind of relativity has to be innovative.

We cannot hope to escape this constraint of revision by admitting once and for all a relativistic perspective: it will have the same defect, but for opposite reasons, as the Hegelian system: relativism does not offer a hold to change the conceptual perspective. To take another example, the combination of attachment to formal structure and tolerance about the choice of a particular logic adopted eventually by Carnap, which could appear as a reasonable balance between systematicity and relativity, is subjected to a similar criticism: tolerance is not a good thing insofar as it could be used to immunize a system against revision.

The Double Test of Systematization and Revision

One could argue that this succession of failures and revisions shows that the attempt to systematize and to formalize, in economics and in philosophical logic, is a useless step, as it is doomed to failure. This is not true. If the economists and philosophers did not sharpen the distinctions and make explicit the relations between concepts – formalization is the best way to do so, systematization being the second best one – it would be difficult to detect failures: the discrepancies with the evidences could be smoothed out by small changes of the interpretation, changes that would not be salient enough to be considered as negative tests for the theory. Our intuitive interpretations have been built as flexible enough to cope with the small changes of context that often occurs in our practical tasks, and we react mainly to the changes that require alertness because they endanger the success of our everyday practice. As theory goes further than these intuitions, it has to go deeper than them, and it needs more restrictive testing conditions.

Of course, we cannot give a meaning to a failure in a test if we have no idea of how to change our theory in a sensible way. Test and revision require not to be separated. Revision is itself another kind of test: are we able to build a new conceptual framework that makes the failure understandable? Of course, we cannot hope to find the revision that will cope with every problem once and for all. In the same way as systematization and formalization, the construction that the revision consists of implies a restriction in its domain of application, because formalization, but also systematization, require strict conditions in order to work. These restrictions make the theory more sensitive to the possible discrepancies with the results of experiments, and prepare it again for the first kind of test, the confrontation with experimental and empirical evidence. Systematization paves the way for revision and the test of revision is a new systematization that paves the way for the following revision. The two kinds of test are the two inseparable sides of the coin of scientific research.

Vagueness and Uncertainty in Economics and Philosophy

This is not to say that scientific research grows in a realm perfectly defined by strict conditions and with no relation at all with what is the contrary of a crisp definition, the vagueness inherent to the flexibility of our intuitions and to our everyday relation with the world. The problems and questions that are the driving forces of the scientific quest come from the inadequacy of the restricted and strictly formalized realm with the undefined complexity of our environment, which implies both the vagueness of our intuitive conceptualizations together with their flexibility, and the uncertainty of their efficiency.

Economists in the real world have to deal with uncertainty. Most of the time, they reduce it in their theory to risk, which is uncertainty controlled by probabilities (even if Knight has stressed the importance of the difference between risk and uncertainty). Probabilities imply to define a partition of all the possible states of the world relative to the considered problem. As such, they paradoxically imply more fine-grained information about the world than the one that is at our disposal. Vagueness is reduced in this case to the overlap between two parts (or more) of the partition induced by our uncertain knowledge. We have only a subjective probability of identifying the right part. Economists deal with uncertainty by having recourse to this kind of higher order probability (probability between different probabilistic partitions). The process of the Bayesian learning is used in order to refine and ascertain the subjective probability.

Economists justify these theoretical choices by the social demand on their discipline: they are requested to predict and control the economical phenomena. But economists admit at the same time that prediction is very difficult in their domain. In their actual decisions, economic agents do not escape from variations in the weight of probabilities (we overestimate the importance of small probabilities and of certainty). Non-additive probabilities are used in order to deal with this problem. But in the end, uncertainty is not confronted with itself, neither is its relation to vagueness. For example, one of the formal devices used to deal with vagueness, fuzzy logic, uses a graduate notion of membership, requiring one to start from a very fine-grained gradation, the contrary of a vague one.

Philosophers have another way to consider uncertainty and vagueness. They do not try to control them. Philosophers who acknowledge their importance use them as the main sources of sceptical arguments, directed against systematic and dogmatic doctrines. But scepticism is not by itself a sufficient driving force for revising a philosophical theory, as most sceptics do not suggest theoretic innovations (Hume is an exception in this respect). Philosophical revision is triggered by the combination of sceptic attacks of a doctrine (internal attacks) and detections of incoherence between the consequences of the doctrine and the evolution of values and social demands (external undermining).

Economics is also moved by such discrepancies, and not only by the discovery of logical or mathematical dead ends, for example, impossibility theorems about social choice, or the absence of guarantee that an effective procedure of 'tâtonnement' could reach the general equilibrium. More recently, experimental psychology and now experimental economics, as well as their neuro-economic extension, have tried to adjust the theory to the actual behaviour of human people. But here again the variability of such behaviour and its dependence on the differences of context introduces resisting vagueness.

Philosophy is not directly sensitive to experiments, but its revisions can be triggered when the conceptual framework assumed to be the background of the philosophical discussions is questioned by scientific discoveries (for example the relations between space and time in the theory of relativity). 'Experimental philosophy' admits that experiments in psychology or in economics can have the same kind of impact. If the sceptic arguments are not really source of innovations, their relation with uncertainty and vagueness became such a source when they are related to the recognition of the complexity of real dynamics. Such a complexity is invoked in the works of Bergson or Nietzsche. This notion has also been renewed in relation to scientific innovations like the analysis of chaotic trajectories (e.g. Popper) or quantum mechanics (e.g. Van Frassen). Experimental measurements appear in this last domain as temporary reductions of the rich complexity of a system of possible states correlated with each other. Here again, the conceptual revision induced by the theoretical interpretations of these results leads to take into account a richer and more extended system of relations.

Conclusion

What can we conclude from this comparison of the history of the dynamics of concepts – understood as the conditions of conceptual revision and innovation – in economics and in philosophy? The two disciplines present a conceptual dynamics of revision and innovation, both associated with an evolution from fixity to relatedness. Up to this time, economics has been more engaged in controlling uncertainty and reducing vagueness than philosophy, which takes them either as the source of sceptical arguments or as an incentive to be sensitive to dynamics and their complexity. One could think that philosophy has to take uncertainty and vagueness as a more central theme, and is the right discipline to do so – as pure scientific disciplines are trying only to reduce them. At the very least, philosophy is led by its conceptual history and dynamics to warn economists against the temptation of taking uncertainty and vagueness as already reduced, at least in the purely theoretical realm. The conceptual history of economics leads it to converge with extensions of economical theory that imply a new kind of relatedness (not relativism). Theoretical economics begins to take into account the complexity of the collective dynamics, its irreducibility to a simple kind of equilibrium, the contextual or path dependency of human decisions, and even the variety of social interactions. At the same time, philosophy becomes more involved in the task of making explicit how the different theoretical perspectives about concepts and values are related to the experimentally observed limitations and peculiarities of actual human interactions. Could we hope for a new kind of convergence between the two histories of philosophy and economics, almost three centuries after the convergence between the two disciplines in the works of Adam Smith?

20 INTEREST-BASED PREDICTION AND MUTUAL EXPECTATIONS: REFLECTIONS ON THE NORMATIVE VALUE OF HOBBESIAN METHODOLOGY

Emmanuel Picavet

Introduction

Interest-based individual action is both a predictive resource in social science and a tool for the normative assessment of social life and collective institutions.[1] This association, I will argue, helps to clarify why the liberal and non-liberal doctrines about politics and economics can find a common ground in the kind of political methodology Hobbes promoted. Liberalism old and new is obviously not a theory of freedom alone: it is also a theory of coercion. Among the classical thinkers of man-made legitimate coercion, Hobbes stands out as an all-time intellectual model. Taking a look at some aspects of his intellectual legacy may help us understand the complex association of freedom and coercion we find at the heart of liberalism.

The fact that Hobbes's political theory remains an important reference point for present-day liberalism and economic conceptions of liberalism[2] is understandable because this theory endeavoured to justify exactly what stands to be monitored from a present-day neoliberal standpoint, namely, the Sovereign's power, as historically embodied in national-State power (by now the object of consistent attacks which come from the neoliberal fringe of conservative thinking and also from anti-capitalist circles). But there are other, slightly less obvious reasons to believe in the importance of this connection. In particular, I would like to draw attention to the common problems which lie in the analysis of social interaction, when it is structured, as well as threatened, by the individual pursuit of self-interest. Indeed, Hobbes's intellectual enterprise comprised an exploration of the problems associated with this kind of interaction.

First of all, given the versatility and the strategic dimension of human interests, if the social order is to be grounded in free agreement between individuals, and the power to enter into contracts, how is individual rationality to be reconciled with the validity of enforceable mutual agreements? And how does individual interest connect with the capacity to contract, that is to say, the capacity to exchange rights? These questions are still with us (see pp. 278–84) because influential views about political and economic freedom, and more particularly the alliance of both, find their justification in an analysis of the extent to which individuals are left free to contract with one another.

Notwithstanding the good reasons to assess the value of social states of affairs by referring to individual interest, the same kind of reference is also instrumental in the characterization of the limits of an interest-based, spontaneous social order. I'll try to highlight the persisting relevance of the Hobbesian problematic in the current-day pattern of possible approaches dealing with the necessity of restrictions on individual action capacities within a social order which nevertheless treats individual freedom to choose as its own foundation (see pp. 284–90).

Individual Interest and the Assessment of
Spontaneous Social Interaction

From Interest-Based Expectations to Economic Equilibrium

Modern and contemporary liberal thinkers have usually been far more optimistic than Hobbes ever was, concerning the achievements of decentralized social interaction in the human species. It can even be said that optimism in this respect is a major identifying trait of 'liberalism' and hence it comes as no surprise that many liberals (in the sense of classical, so-called 'political' liberalism) take a keen interest in the kind of spontaneously reached 'equilibrium' economists hold to be a plausible outcome of spontaneous interaction among social agents who are equipped with resource endowments, interests and capacities of trade and production.[3]

In a less ambitious understanding of the methodological meaning of the notion, 'equilibrium' will only be an interesting and somehow 'natural' reference point for the assessment of social proceedings and institutional frameworks, given the structure of individual interests. The interest we will presuppose in discussions of 'self-interest' will not be restrictively identified with an egoistic view of the world on the agent's part. By 'interest' we shall refer to the complex of behavioural goals, tendencies or preferences which help one articulate the object of one's wishes, once it is decided not to rely on sources of valuation which are external to the individual agents themselves. This complex provides a basis for liberal-minded analysts who prefer not to rely on more particular, presumed connections between interests of a given sort and such notions as happiness, virtue, social harmony and other notions of things of value. Some authors insist that we should separately consider a 'narrow' meaning of 'self-interest' to capture the kind of interest which is 'important to one's role in the price system', given that 'in price system agendas individuals are often required to play a role to which the term "self-interest" was once commonly applied to distinguish it from a role marked by broader identifications, sometimes called altruistic'.[4] This kind of restriction, in turn, prompts doubts about the validity of a fairly strange dual-motive view of the human person, accompanied by normative claims which are grounded in an economic view of the world.[5]

Hirschman,[6] as pointed out by P. Bridel,[7] held Hobbes's contribution to be the key step in the development of the Machiavellian notion of the pursuit of individual interest as a necessary and sufficient force when it comes to counterweighting the deleterious effects of human passions, including the religious and political ones. The intellectual task in this kind of research programme would amount, then, to considering a society made of individuals who are moved by their interest rather than by the pursuit of vainglory; this kind of society, with its distinctive merits on the scores of stability and coordination, would make a lot of advantages available to humankind; in short, this would amount to agents's behaviour being made infinitely more accessible to expectations-fulfilment, and more 'civilized'.[8]

Whether this intellectual transition can be equated with a 'research programme' in the Lakatosian sense or not is unclear, if only because the pro-tagonists of the project were so few. The resulting shift in the study of human motivation, however, is quite clear. As Bridel lucidly noted, there was a marked transition from the typical study of *affectus* as constrained according to the prin-ciple of countervailing passions, to the study of interest, particular interests, increasingly viewed as tamers of passions. According to Hobbes –Bridel further argues – such (beneficial) consequences clearly follow from the crucial hypoth-esis according to which the agent's pursuit of his own interest – rather than his passions – is a *rational* objective, which is amenable to *computatio* and, therefore, to fulfilled mutual expectations among agents.[9] Interest-based action is indeed an important tool of normative social analysis.

Following Hirschman's initial historical insight, Bridel was able to identify in the seventeenth century (rather than the eighteenth century) the unveiling of the rich potentialities of a spontaneous order. Later on, Bridel argued, Mandeville and Smith would be able to suggest in a 'natural' manner that the spontaneous order, which follows from the pursuit of individual interest on the part of indi-vidual agents, results in unforeseen *and* socially beneficial outcomes – an idea which was called to a brilliant career in posterior economic thinking up to now. Interestingly, this major trend in economic thought has typically been associated with attempts at normative assessment of the rationality or efficiency of mar-ket interaction, as exemplified by the 'theorems' of welfare economics which are companions to the Arrow–Debreu proof of the notional existence of an equilib-rium in a stylized competitive economy.

According to this kind of historical reconstruction, the Hobbesian moment is important because it testifies to the potentialities of a theory which focuses on the structure and outcomes of social interaction (rather than a detailed understanding of the particulars of individual psychology and collective history). Some kind of psychology is needed but it remains rough and stylized. Even though Hobbes is best remembered for his pessimistic picture of human nature and his rather authoritarian political conclusions, his contribution also impresses by the novelty, and enduring impact of a treatment of the social world in which individual actions are strongly polarized – or even constrained – by social interaction, while the latter is structured by hypothesized, stylized interests.

The Hobbesian approach is an invitation to look for correct decision making and institutional settings, starting from the examination of the foreseeable outcomes of social interaction, and this kind of methodology has normative value because it provides benchmarks for the defence or criticism of hands-off strategies. In addition, it provides a common reference point in interdisciplinary dialogue about the value of normative statements. Hobbes built a theory of representation in which inter-individual relationships are irreducible to matters of property rights.[10] But his philosophy is not alien to the concerns of economists and other social scientists who pay serious attention to the association and co-evolution of individual interests and predictable social patterns (eventually giving rise to fears about an excessively restrictive view of democratic social patterns).[11]

Rationality, Justice and Interest

The use of interest-based action for the purposes of normative assessment has a rich background in the history of philosophy. Classically, it has been involved in discussions of the possibility of a willingness to be treated unjustly. The Hobbesian thesis of a universal desire to advance one's good through valid contracts can usefully be compared with the Aristotelian thesis according to which nobody ever bears injustice in a voluntary manner because it would amount to suffering evils voluntarily. In Aristotelian ethics, two questions came up together: may we voluntarily suffer injustice? May we voluntarily suffer some harm (or inflict harm on ourselves)?

In the very detailed developments of the Aristotelian treaty *Magna Moralia*[12] and in the *Nicomachean Ethics*,[13] the focus was on exposure to harm: can it be voluntary? The first, quick answer was negative: nobody ever suffers what is a source of harm to him, and is therefore an evil, in a voluntary manner. But then, a difficulty had to be faced: how are we to deal with those cases in which somebody renounces a right he is entitled to by virtue of equal treatment, and gives it up to someone else? The proposed answer was framed in terms of exchange: those who renounce their entitlement to something do so in exchange for something else.

Another source of perplexity was the lack of self-control of an akratic individual. Through the bad choice of actions, this individual is at risk of harming himself; is it not the case, then, that he does injustice to himself? The answer follows from the fact that suffering injustice (which involves suffering some harm) cannot be voluntarily wanted by a deliberating agent. This draws attention to the chosen definition of an action which is unjustly done: it had been equated with the fact of voluntary harming somebody.[14] This treatise was very explicit about a desirable refinement: the problem is with harming somebody in full knowledge of the harmed person, of the instrument and manner, but also in contradiction with the well-considered wishes of the considered person.[15]

Whenever we consider a man who lacks self-control (and therefore well-considered wishes), we should abstain from saying that he voluntarily harms himself. In sum, even though it is true that we may voluntarily suffer some harm because we aim at a good, it should be acknowledged that nobody ever takes as a goal in itself something which goes against one's well-considered wishes. Clearly enough, renouncing a valuable thing which is an object of entitlement would exemplify such a paradoxical goal. Suffering injustice and giving up one's claims to objects of entitlement are social notions and they are intermingled with the analysis of the pursuit of self-interest.

A quick comparison with Hobbes helps us bring to salience the simplified nature of the latter's distinctive thesis: in the state of nature, nobody has an interest to renounce a right to anything whatsoever. Starting from the premises of Hobbes's well-known 'state of nature' premises in *Leviathan*, this would amount to harming oneself in a voluntary manner, since anything can prove useful to safeguard life or the comforts of life in some circumstances. Matters of justice are separately dealt with, in a rather strict conventionalist perspective. Thus, it cannot immediately be considered that individual interest as such has normative content for society (in terms of collective rationality or justice or goodness) beyond the association with everyone's strictly individual 'natural right' to life and the comforts of life.

These core consequentialist components of Hobbes's theory are crucial to the characterization of the state of nature's internal problems in Chapter 13 of *Leviathan*: they make it possible to hold that some covenants are void (do not really exist). Alternatively, they help characterize as 'without force' some conventions which must be held valid since one of the parties has performed whatever was expected, thus proving a manifest will.[16] 'Void' as they are in the state of nature, conventions cannot be fully binding ('valid' in the sense which is familiar to us) in such a state of affairs. The criterion is the incompatibility with the agent's interest.

This description gives a key role to the effective accomplishment of actions, as it can be observed, or (if the agreement is simply a notional one) as it can be safely predicted, given the involved interests. But the fact that actions are carried out, and how they are carried out, depend on social interdependence. Following Hobbes, the valid conventions, which have sufficient 'force', involve the accomplishment of the specified action by one of the parties, and thus the fact that this party's interests are met in so doing, and the strategic side of the issue is not ignored.[17] Their being forceful (valid) involves the fact that the link they create, should it be broken, would then be associated with disadvantages – and this feature is missing in the state of nature.

The agents's interest is thus an important reference point but its use is not such that normative validity is, so to say, swallowed by interest, as in the innumerable variants (up to our days) of Thrasymachus's speculations about justice in the first book of Plato's *Republic*. If the first step involved in the contents of a convention has been honoured by one the parties, the other party is under a valid obligation to carry out the second step – in accordance with the third 'law of nature' – no matter how individual interests look like, contrary to the classical conclusions of Cicero.[18] The difficult part of the theory is the contrast between normativity and empirical prediction: from a predictive point of view, so long as punishment cannot be guaranteed in case of a missing second-step action, the expectation is clearly established, and it does not coincide with the convention's enforcement.

In the background, the Hobbesian mention of everyone's pursuit of a personal good is psychological (insofar as individual motives are concerned) as well as methodological in character. It is grounded in the hypothesized structure of human action and interaction. This, it must be allowed, provides indications for a comparison with the posterior developments in political theory and the social sciences, especially economics. Indeed, this use of the notion of everyone's interest is much in line with the psychological interpretations of the 'rational choice' methodology in our time, which emphasize the centrality and the primacy, in social explanation, of the presupposition of a consistent pursuit, by everyone, of the kind of good one takes as an objective in social interaction.

This amounted to the autonomous development of the study of the interplay of interests, in the beginnings of modern philosophy. It paved the way for theorists who, contrary to Hobbes, would later concentrate on the potentialities of social self-regulation, starting from the interplay of interests as they are. Leaving aside the conjectures about the role of Hobbes in the rise of 'possessive individualism' in modern history, it can be emphasized that Hobbes's theoretical work provided the general model of the way interests can be treated as benchmarks for the prediction of actions and the determination of social outcomes. This could be done apart from positive or negative judgements about the morality of actions. Also in accordance with important aspects of the typical normative exercises in our time, the desirable or less desirable features of social outcomes were studied separately, and the conclusions yielded restrictions on individual acceptable behaviour.

Interest-Based Reasons and Interest-Based Action: Lessons from Hobbes

The Hobbesian model of a civil pact highlights the resources of threat and force for overcoming the dilemmas of social cooperation which originate in individual interests. Viewed as a contribution to the study of the patterns of cooperation among intelligent agents, it is still the classic reference point for analysts who are interested in showing the benefits of organized coercion, given the sad limits of spontaneous mutual agreements. Coercion and force, in spite of their more sinister instantiations and predictable abuse in the real world, are thus easily portrayed as constitutive of a second-best approach to human cooperation, as in James Buchanan's justly famous *The Limits of Liberty* (aptly subtitled *Between Anarchy and Leviathan*). For all the 'pessimism' of Hobbesian anthropology, the doctrine's legacy has yielded a fairly benign view of the use of coercion among human beings, in a kind of problem-solving approach. Only recently (in the face of evidence of extreme abuse of organized control and violence in totalitarian regimes) have the facts about malevolent (or sadistic) dispositions and administrative routine operations come to the forefront of moral and political analysts, with the result that nothing like a problem-solution approach can be considered sufficient when it comes to describing or justifying the use of organized threat and violence.

Hobbes's contribution, however, does rely on individual reasons, not just the mechanistic kind of comparison between well-working and ill-working schemes of organization. A key insight of classical contractarianism is that the rational individual should opt, on the basis of good reasons, for the threats and machinery of coercion rather than anarchy, making it possible to implement the correct patterns of behaviour which are couched in the 'laws of nature'. In contrast with other theories which deal with the connection between social order and individual interest, especially eighteenth-century elaborations about the benefits of civilized exchange and cooperation (following useful social conventions), Hobbes's theory isn't as immediately convincing from the point of view of individual interest as it is in the real world. The path which leads to the institution of sovereign power is thorny, if we start from Hobbesian premises about individual interest; its practicability is still discussed in philosophy and the plausibility of Hobbes's inferences has been a source of perplexity from the seventeenth century onwards. The convincing power of Hobbes's answer to *Leviathan*'s Fool is unclear, to say the least, even though the clarification of the objections stemming from the Fool's egoistic, utility-maximizing standpoint was indisputably a major achievement.

In the social-contract framework of Hobbes's theory, correct interest-based reasons do not always translate into correct interest-based actions. Thus, the kind of duty we must associate with the laws of nature is a reflection of the best reasons we have, but it has no direct correspondence with the correct choice of action for an individual who lives in the state of nature. The correlation between the good reasons and the right course of action is, of necessity, an institutional one, because its implementation presupposes the institution of power and threat, thus making the theory deeply 'political'. This is an invitation not to look at it simply as an exploration of interest-based predictable behaviour among reasoning, interest-driven individuals – indeed, such individuals might well get trapped in their cooperation dilemmas with no way out.

Moreover, the Hobbesian version of the social contract gives a modest role to individual interest (compared with structural order) in the following sense. The comparison of the dire straits of a 'state of nature' and the more felicitous life in a civil state doesn't involve the notion that everyone is better off from the general conformity to a standard of behaviour, which should simply be selected. If we look at the laws-of-nature standards of behaviour from the state of nature, it is clear that they convey a notion of universal advantage but, at the same time, nobody has an *individual* interest to act in accordance with them.[19] Hence the institution of power proves essential to the alignment of general reasons (pertaining to what would be good for us to do generally speaking) and situated good reasons for a given individual's action. Correlatively, the use of self-interest for the assessment of collectively binding rules of behaviour is normative at core: it has to do with the quest after the kind of rules we should try to turn into reality by institutional means, not simply by acting upon interest-driven motives in ordinary life.

The economic approach to human behaviour has been predominantly concerned with the interplay of social order (as it gradually emerges) and individual, interest-related reasons. Public behaviour is amenable to economic explanations but standard economic theorizing deals with it as ordinary, businesslike behaviour. The institution of sovereign power (as Hobbes thought of it) is a very special kind of action indeed and the contrast between classical political theory and economic theory remains striking in this respect, even though philosophers have proposed analyses of the interplay of individual interests and evolving rules (following Hume and Montesquieu), while a number of economists have made the tools of economic analysis available for the abstract assessment of alternative political rules (as in contemporary 'constitutional economics'). Classical political theory, as exemplified by Hobbes's doctrine, is an essential enrichment in this respect.

Rights and the Limitation of Action Capacities

Individual Rationality and Restrictions on Rights

Given the importance of property and markets in contemporary social life, the free exchange of rights is an integral part of economic behaviour and, clearly enough, a component of the explanations of the emergence of norms and institutions which give primacy to economic motives. The market economy is objectively grounded in rights and transaction on rights, and the credibility of the social explanations (or justifications) which start from self-interest, understood as in mainstream economic discourse, depends on the quality of the theoretical link which is established by analysts between interests and rights, and between the pursuit of self-interest and transactions on rights. Such a link, however, involves more than freedom of choice, even though the parlance of 'rights' is evocative of individual freedom. It also involves external constraint on behaviour, since the enjoyment of capacities for unhindered action and the freedom to exchange rights are secured through coercion.

The contrast between the possibilities of a spontaneous order and the necessity of a designed order is clearly important in typical contemporary neoliberal doctrines which mingle classical free-exchange views with variants of political liberalism. Such doctrines deal with the relationships between the spontaneous organization of social life on the one hand, and other kinds of organizations, which rely on both human will (in the design) and man-made coercion devices, on the other. The kind of social order which is based on the decentralized exercise of rights must somehow rely on consent to a restriction of rights. This essential dialectic is rightly understood by those lucid economists who have decided to study economic freedom and coercion as two faces of the same coin.[20] Here again political theory can be understood as a complement, when contemplated from the standpoint of the economic tradition, because it puts forward a number of reasons why individuals, starting from their own legitimate wishes (as in standard economic analysis), are interested in being subject to coercion in the background of free choices.

Provided that organized coercion is considered an answer to the problems of social interaction (rather than a goal in itself as presupposed in so many political and religious doctrines), the legitimacy of coercion can be characterized as a solution to otherwise unsolved problems of social interaction. Absent from any endogenous or spontaneously emerging solution to the practical problems of men, the 'mortal God', in Hobbes's phrase, is welcome. This kind of argument, while leading to authoritarian conclusions in Hobbes's own contribution, is also a model for those more optimistic explanations of problems and solutions which follow from the interplay of individual-interest driven intentional behaviour (the kind of self-centred behaviour favoured in familiar interpretations of economic models). Such alternative explanations usually leave room for self-organization or a kind of spontaneous order, as exemplified in the economics of norms and institutions. Thus, there is some plausibility to the association of Hobbes with a roughly 'economic' perspective in social theory.

Liberals, as it turns out, do not always sympathize with the model of a social pact which induces us to forget about the past and its legacy of well-established traditions, smoothly working institutions, and time-honoured maxims of practical wisdom. Hobbesian theorizing still strikes contemporary readers as radical or deeply theoretical in character, with its near-cartesian *tabula rasa* outlook, which stands in sharp contrast to the larger part of political theorizing, which deals with the development and desirable evolution of political institutions, starting from our own position in the course of history.

Nevertheless, liberals are indebted to Hobbes because the philosopher was able to identify in a rigorous way the reasons which call for political organization in order to secure effective individual liberty, thus building a bridge between the study of human action and the political discussion of freedom, at a basic level. This was a great originality in intellectual history, with the possible exception of Glauco's well-known hypothetical-deductive reasoning about spontaneous human interaction in Plato's second book of *The Republic*. Paradoxically, this major intellectual achievement was enshrined in a political system which is also a defense of strong and centralized, sovereign power-exercising, not liberalism in any plausible understanding of the word.

The Hobbesian approach to political power makes it clear that, starting from premises which pertain to the life of individuals, convincing reasons can be put forward in order to justify the use (or threat) of coercion on the basis of problems which stem from the structure of social interaction. Granted the indispensability of a certain kind of coercion, the associated implementation mechanisms are another subject of inquiry and, here again, the proximity of economics and politics is obvious. Contractarianism on its Hobbesian 'conventionalist' side made it possible to deal with the allocation of protection through coercion with the desirable generality (thus putting aside the mythological connections between man and object – the beliefs about a natural right to the ownership of particular things).

Hobbes's theory drew attention to the fact that 'justice', in the basic sense of securing to everyone what he is entitled to, must be defined through the exercise of authority. This way to look at justice matters has always lacked popularity and there is no denying its lack of completeness, but it rightly conveys the notion that the allotment of effective protection is a social mechanism which involves the limitation of action capacities for various people. The coercive side of individual freedom cannot be ignored. Hobbes's theory is a reminder that the free exchange of rights always presupposes a tacit consent to the conventional limitation of rights.

Liberal theorists, however, have always been interested in decentralized rights-allocation mechanisms which rely on mutual agreement, given the antecedent definition of coercively and socially protected property rights (or other similar rights which consist in use, control and access prerogatives). A natural question for liberals of all schools is then: how may we extend the logic of individual consent to the abandonment of the direct and individual faculty to exercise one's rights? Obviously, this inquiry is an integral part of the contractarian heritage from *Leviathan* onwards, which provides meaningful and convincing explanations of the reasons why individuals might agree on such terms in a fully rational way, given the expected benefits or (in more idealistic versions) for the sake of protecting and honouring the humanity in each of us. At root, this inevitably involves an examination of the reasons why we could voluntarily accept the abandonment or transfer of rights. Here again, the basic issues of liberalism are aligned with the basic questions raised by Hobbes's theory about interest-based action and the justification of collective institutional arrangements.

How Can it be Rational to Relinquish Rights?

Although Hobbes can be credited with essential insights, readers of *Leviathan* have long been reluctant to consider as fully rational an individual's decision to relinquish the entire domain of his rights on things. Whereas Hobbes's original problem started from the *jus in omnia* premise for everyone, liberal doctrines usually deal with the more familiar problem of relinquishing existing rights for the sake of securing another set of limited rights. In many cases, initial and posterior entitlements alike can be portrayed as 'just' or 'equitable' in some way or other: on grounds of need or merit, for instance. Procedural features associated with freedom of choice or the fair terms of exchange can also be mentioned. This is not to say, however, that the old Hobbesian, interest-based perspective on the validity and real content of conventions (putting matters of justice aside) is indifferent for justification purposes.

Indeed, when rights are relinquished in favour of other rights – possibly more effectively protected ones, thanks to the institution of some authority or common agency – it is of interest to know whether the agreements are binding. Practically speaking, even well-established liberal democracies do have worries with the regular compliance of citizens with rules and authoritative decisions as they are. Quite often, legitimate authorities lack real power, understood as the capacity to bring about the desired changes in the world in accordance with the formal distribution of action capacities to the various social actors. This, of course, secondarily threatens the freely chosen exercise or exchange of existing, recognized rights.

As it turns out, matters of deeply felt (or religion-based) procedural fairness and substantive social justice often interfere with due obedience to legitimate rulings by recognized political authorities. Liberalism can never be confined to libertarian claims which are based on the supreme value of free choice. Selecting and securing the prerogatives which come along with a restricted set of claims is essential to both the political order at large and to the sequences of free exchanges of rights which follow from our freely chosen mutual agreements (including those of production, trade and consumption). For this reason, liberalism must, of necessity, be a doctrine of social order, taking good notice of individual interests.[21] Some way or other, liberal argument about the value of free exchange must have a foundation in the justification of coercion (or constraint) but it must meet individual interests at some level (how else could it be used with credibility?).[22]

All this gives a lasting relevance to the Hobbesian problematic of an interest-based assessment of the validity of those agreements by means of which we transfer rights, relinquish rights and establish authoritative agencies (not just in the grand social-pact intellectual exercise but also on more mundane occasions in everyday institutional and economic life). The enduring prestige of Hobbes's political theory, which is by no means reducible to historical curiosity, is a good reminder of the fact that, putting matters of social (or natural, or divine) justice aside, effectively secured rights can only be established or transformed by valid agreements, so that their enjoyment is grounded in the interplay of interests, not just the generic availability of coercion at some level. At this level of analysis, it is apparent again that interest-based action, just because it is the kind of action which is predictable on the basis of individual interest, has normative significance for the normative assessment of collective arrangements (such as individual rights and their evolution).

Should We Trust in Coercion?

A major difference to be found in our contemporary inquiries, compared with Hobbes's perspective, is the more limited trust we have in coercion. First of all, we know better about the abuse thereof (owing to the experience of extreme State terror in the twentieth and twenty-first centuries). In addition, we know better about the way reputation, communication and games of institutional (or political) support can be put to use in order to induce rightful behaviour on the part of social agents, as exemplified – among other social mechanisms – by the impact of media image on corporate interests, and by the powerful trends in (voluntarily endorsed) corporate social and environmental responsibility. Coercion is not always the last word but the classical philosophical developments about coercion are a good reminder of how important the alignment of interests is, when it comes to matters of rights and freedom, notwithstanding the (no less) classical opposition between interest-bound calculus and the quest for political and economic freedom.

Some rights, in good Hobbesian logic, must be relinquished for the sake of secure rights exercising: liberals have to come to terms with this reality. This is not to say, however, that they should wholeheartedly embrace Hobbes's concept of a complete transfer of rights. Here again, the economic logic of the interplay of interests can help. So long as we contemplate a plurality of individuals in the abstract, the general transfer of rights might appear to be the only way to secure the advancement of common interests, given the difficulties revealed by Hobbes (or more benign ones if we start from different premises about human motives and behaviour). When individual preferences are brought in, the picture is different. By exploiting the complementarities between their preferences, individual agents may distance themselves from the immediate rights-exercising choices which would follow from their preferences; on the basis of subgroup agreements, they can do better, as illustrated by the following example, proposed by Allan Gibbard.[23]

Consider the set S of possible states of the world, which consists of possible states x, y and z:

x: Edwin marries Angelina;

y: The judge marries Angelina and Edwin remains single;

z: Angelina and Edwin remain single.

Edwin would rather remain single but is ready to marry Angelina so that she does not marry the judge. The judge wants what Angelina wants. Angelina would like to marry Edwin but she would accept a marriage with the judge as a second choice. For the purposes of description, we associate sets of persons with sets of possible states of the world: acting in a certain way, those people can see to it that the state of the world which will eventually prevail is to be found among these possible states of affairs. The system of rights in the example can be described as: (Edwin, {y,z}); (Edwin, S); (Angelina, {y}) ; (Angelina, {z}); (Angelina, S); (Edwin, Angelina, {x}).

If Edwin remains single, he forces the state of affairs to belong to {y, z}. Absent of any agreement with the judge, this is in accordance with a limited view of Edwin's interests, but not with a more complete view, because Angelina would then marry the judge. As this example illustrates, individual agents can look for agreements on a decentralized basis, thus voluntarily limiting their capacity to act or choose as they like. When it is not advantageous to exercise rights directly and unilaterally in accordance with one's own preferences, it is clear that transferring rights in a limited manner is a valuable way to get better results in the end. Thus, the use of coercion is not inevitable in all cases, any more than a general transfer of rights to a central authority who would redistribute the capacities to act in the first place. When fears of power abuse are serious, interest-based reasoning of this sort yields some reasons to favour a decentralized system for the evolving allocation of rights.

The story may also be interpreted as an indication that the cost of relinquishing rights is not always a high price after all; it can even be beneficial. But this depends on the ability of agents to find out the beneficial subgroup agreements, which is a cause of uncertainty. Here, interest-based argument should be supplemented by cognitive details. In addition, existing agreements put constraints on subsequent opportunities for other agreements[24] and this brings interpersonal problems into the picture. These problems, however, do not annihilate the possibility of mutual gains agents might achieve through their abstaining from direct action in accordance with their own preferences.

Conclusion

Hobbes provided the model for a certain kind of inquiry which remains essential to liberal argument, notwithstanding the distance in the substantive conclusions. This intellectual endeavour relates the investigation of rules or institutions to the purpose of assessing their appropriateness to the structure of human interaction. The latter is supposed to be governed by the interplay of individual interests. Normative conclusions about social life (or institutions) are reached in a manner which involves the nature of predictable, interest-based individual action. I have argued that this general approach is still relevant today for a variety of reasons.

Should Hobbes's political theory be considered a major reference when it comes to understanding the development of economic thinking as we think of it and, more particularly, the development of the economic approach to social rules, institutions (with their gradual emergence, destruction, replacement or consolidation)? This would be justified to a certain extent. Hobbes has provided the pattern for a style of social and political theorizing in which expectations based on the structure of individual interests are taken seriously, both as key components of the strategic understanding of human cooperation, coordination and conflict, and as foundations for valid normative arrangements. All this remains central to contemporary economics and game-theory inspired political theory. Furthermore, it must be observed that the version of contractarianism we find in Hobbes is such that it provides a common ground for interdisciplinary dialogue.

Taking a second look, however, we have noted that the kind of rationality explored by Hobbes, although similar in many respects to the underpinnings of contemporary game theory, has little to do with the association of causally influential reasons, best practical argument and actual behaviour favoured by the psychological, intentional-action interpretations of formal economic models. Some of the crucial good reasons we have, although practical in nature, are not to be converted into actions by a rational agent; rather, they call for institutional solutions. This clearly emerges if we look at the kind of rational agreement which can be mentioned in support of the practical endorsement of Hobbes's 'laws of nature' (a conditional rationality, so to speak – what it would be rational to act upon provided we have sufficient guarantee that everyone else does the same).

21 TEMPESTS OF THE BUSINESS WORLD: WEATHER METAPHORS FOR CRISES IN THE NINETEENTH CENTURY

Daniele Besomi[1]

This is a world of storms, and all of life's atmospheres are liable to be clouded by tempest – the commercial horizon, the political horizon, and the domestic horizon.[2]

Introduction

Capitalistic crises, as distinct from the previous purely financial or agricultural crises, started to become a theoretical problem early in the nineteenth century. Their occurrence, and then recurrence, raised the question why the accumulation of capital and the flow of exchanges were on occasion abruptly interrupted. The problem was perceived to be an eminently practical one, as the ultimate aim of the quest was finding a remedy; in the mechanical approach prevalent at the time, the solution required the removal of the cause (or causes), and therefore their preliminary identification. The literature is immense, but mostly in the form of pamphlets and other topical contributions often published immediately after each crisis, written by bankers, merchants, politicians and occasionally operatives, only rarely by theorists.[3] The style was often loose, teeming with rhetoric (their purpose was, after all, to convince the addressee) and often made use of metaphors.

In these debates on a phenomenon that was slowly taking shape before the witnesses' eyes, and for which there was scarcely a theoretical foundation, concepts and interpretations emerged as the discussion unfolded. In a discipline so much in the making, metaphors were often used not much to embellish the text, but as an aid to discovery and/or as a means for communicating ideas. Metaphors (and analogies and similes) are based on a (perceived) partial isomorphism between the object or phenomenon into which one is inquiring and some other object or phenomenon, about which more is known. The properties of the unknown object are studied *as if* it behaved as the better-known object (the metaphor is thus a transfer of properties), or the latter object is used as a means to explain to the reader the conclusion one reaches about the object of inquiry. Examining metaphors in this perspective helps to characterize the fundamental features of crises as they were perceived by these writers. Occasionally, the insight offered by the use of metaphors is deeper than what is revealed by arguments expounded in full, for they lie at the core of the essential interpretation of phenomena.

Writers in the nineteenth century used a number of families of metaphors to account for crises, the main ones being medical, geological, naturalistic, behavioural, oceanic, mechanical, astronomical and meteorological. In this chapter I will focus on weather metaphors,[4] one of the most popular choices. Writers relied on the familiarity of all readers with the vagaries of the elements, either trivially by using expressions such as 'financial storm' or more revealingly when comparing in detail some role or feature of crises to that of meteorological perturbations. There are no complicated meteorological theories involved in the metaphorical usage surveyed here: crises were mostly compared with the damages caused by storms, or with the cleaning of the atmosphere that follows them. Only occasionally do we find references to some well-known basic principles such as the saturation and condensation of vapour or the electric nature of storms. But even the most intuitive perception of meteorological phenomena can originate a vast number of possible analogies, as the nuances of the weather (that can vary in different parts of the world)[5] offer the chance of selecting among a vast array of properties that can be transferred to crises in several combinations. Yet the actual choices by writers of the nineteenth century reflect only two of the interpretations of crises in their relationship to the 'normal' working of the economic system (arguably the most fundamental level of understanding) prevailing at the time.[6]

Gradually in the course of the first half of the nineteenth century a subtle but important change in perspective took place in the approach to economic crises. In the early decades of the century, most commentators considered crises as sudden and unexpected disturbances to the normal state of trade, caused by anomalous circumstances perturbing the accustomed flow of exchanges. The sources of disruption were ascribed to entrepreneurial miscalculation or failures to adapt quickly to changed markets, to trade flowing into the wrong channels (in these cases, overproduction in some parts of the economy would have as a complement underproduction in other parts), but more often to political interference, in particular due to protectionism or other legislature preventing the system from self-adjusting. In this view – which I shall call 'crisis approach' – crises are unrelated and abnormal accidents; they can be remedied by eliminating the disturbing cause, after which competition brings the system back to a healthy, normal state of affairs.

This perspective came under attack (without, however, disappearing altogether) when the repetition of crises along similar patterns and at more or less regular intervals suggested that they are not independent events but are somehow related to each other, and have a common agent. Such a cause was identified by an increasing number of writers in the excesses that take place during prosperity: when trade is brisk, every business opportunity is seized, including the most implausible ones; credit is easily available, as confidence is strong and, so far as trade keeps increasing, debts are regularly paid back. But speculative and doubtful businesses are also stimulated, and the increase in prices accompanying the increasing volume of trade further feeds speculation. When anything shatters confidence, the entire construction collapses under its own weight. The cause of the crisis is thus rooted in the conditions that make prosperity possible; human nature being what it is, crises are the price to pay for growth. They are undesirable, but are necessary for the elimination of bad debts and misdirected business. After these are liquidated, trade can resume towards a new prosperity. This is taken to be its normal state, and therefore does not need an explanation. Accordingly, in this perspective – which I shall denote as 'recurring crises approach' – there is no account of how the economy recovers after the trough, and indeed there is not even a name for the 'recovery': the attempts at describing the phases of this process included an odd number of phases, centered around the crisis. The object of these writers was to explain how the crisis comes about during prosperity, and how it is resolved, while the resumption of trade along its 'normal' path after its conditions were re-established by the elimination of excesses was taken as a matter of course.

The references to crises in terms of weather phenomena fit well into one or the other of these approaches. The purpose of this essay is to show how crises are characterized in each of these two ways by means of meteorological analogies, first in the 'crises' perspective (pp. 293–8) and then in the 'recurring crises' approach (pp. 299–307). The last section (pp. 307–8) sums up and draws some conclusions.

Crises as Perturbations to the Normal State of Trade

In the 'crisis' perspective, crises are seen as the result of impediments disturbing the normal flow of trade. While the 'natural' state of trade is associated with prosperity and progress, perturbations bring ruin and distress.[7] They do not perform any useful function in the working of the capitalist system, and are a pure anomaly. Accordingly, they do not have any place in a theoretical discussion, except being depicted as short-lived aberrations that will last only until their cause, external to the proper working of the system, is removed.

Among these features, the one more widely represented by means of weather metaphors is surely the destructive character of crises, described by means of violent atmospheric disturbances. Financial or commercial storms, tornadoes, hurricanes, flurries, cyclones and tempests are self-explanatory and recurred so frequently (both in the daily press and in the writings of essayists) as to be considered expressions that are part of common usage: as stated by the correspondent of the *New-York Daily Tribune* a few months after the outbreak of the 1857 panic, such 'an event in the history of finance and trade' was 'so remarkable in its sudden development and so devastating in its immediate effects as to be distinguished by such names as a financial "tornado", a "whirlwind", and a "hurricane"'.[8] A few other examples will suffice. The same crisis was described by Homans as 'the financial hurricane, that has devastated almost the whole commercial world during the past four months';[9] Lamb later described the same events as follows:

> the financial skies were suddenly clouded. Wall Street was the first to suddenly feel the effects of the storm, which rapidly spread with devastating fury over the entire country. Enterprises of every description came to a standstill, industries were paralyzed, the working classes were throw into a state of extreme destitution, to which a severe winter added fresh terrors, and the avalanche of discredit brought down merchants, bankers, and moneyed corporations without distinction.[10]

Later West wrote of 'the financial storm which is sweeping over the whole civilized globe and compelling the nations to exercise all their skill and ingenuity in resisting its destructive influence'.[11] An anonymous writer described the vicissitudes of the dramatis persona of his story as follows:

> The great financial storm of [1857] burst upon the State unheralded. Like a thief in the night the one fatal word passed over the wires that shut the door of every bank, and made the boldest turn pale. Suspension was followed by panic, panic by ruin and dismay. Yankee Jim was only an atom swallowed up in the general and overwhelming disaster of that day.[12]

These descriptions, general as they are, introduce two further characterizations of crises in the 'crises approach'. The first is that they are rather catholic in their consequences, affecting the prudent and the injudicious traders alike; the second is that they come suddenly and unexpectedly.

The issue of the universality of the damage wrought by crises emerges better in comparison with its denial by the writers in the tradition of thought stressing the recurrence of crises, and will therefore be taken up in the next section, below. For the time being, a few examples will suffice. Revisiting the *History of England*, half a century after the facts Craik and MacFarlane noted that

> Many of the houses that came down in this commercial storm of the spring and summer of 1793 were of old standing and great eminence; and their liabilities were of an amount proportioned to the extent to which their business had been carried on, and the confidence that had been universally reposed in their wealth and stability.[13]

Similarly, in his book on the banks of New York during the 1857 panic, Gibbons reported that

> House after house, of high commercial repute, succumbed to the panic, and several heavy banking firms were added to the list of failures ... Commercial business was everywhere suspended. The avalanche of discredit swept down merchants, bankers, moneyed corporations, and manufacturing companies, without distinction. Old houses, of accumulated capital, which had withstood the violence of all former panics, were prostrated in a day; and when they believed themselves to be perfectly safe against misfortune. The bank suspension of New York and New England, in the middle of October, was the climax of this commercial hurricane. Such is the outline of the most extraordinary, violent, and destructive financial panic ever experienced in this country.[14]

Like Gibbons, other writers conceded that solid houses (the building metaphor is here called upon to complement the natural disasters metaphors) could better resist the adverse conditions, but were eventually wiped out. The correspondent of the *Nashville Union and American*, for instance, pointed out that during 'the great financial storm [that] swept over the Union, and over Europe also' in 1857, 'the weak and rotten concerns tumbled down during the first weeks of its fury, others which possessed a better basis resisted for a time, and were only forced down by the pressure of ruin'.[15] Another writer, again stressing the unexpected character of the crisis, also pointed out that the credit screw affected everybody:

> This financial cyclone came upon us suddenly, and, to a certain extent, unexpectedly, as a storm from an unclouded sky. It came in the midst of what appeared to be a time of unparalleled prosperity in all branches of business. Trade was active, manufacturing establishments were working to their full capacity, agriculture was broadening its acres, railroads were extending their lines, and substantial progress was apparent in every direction. Suddenly every interest was threatened with disaster for the want of money, which could not be obtained: deposits were rapidly withdrawn from the banks, and urgent applications for loans were of necessity refused or but partially responded to. All men seemed anxious to borrow and none to lend, and confusion and uncertainty seemed to possess the minds of the community.[16]

Laveleye also rounded up both themes, developing the weather analogy in some detail but crucially stopping right before drawing the conclusion that will be reached instead by the writers belonging to the 'recurring crises' tradition. His passage is precious, as it makes explicit (by commission or by omission) the singling out of the specific features of the crisis that one wants to highlight and those one ignores. He wrote:

> [Monetary and commercial crises] are the tempests of the business world. They remind us of those frightful hurricanes, of the cyclones which, in tropical areas, break loose all of a sudden and tear down trees, crash ships and knock down houses, scattering land and water with wreckage. Similarly to such dreadful convulsions of the elements, crises bring devastation in the sphere of exchange. They topple the soundest

commercial houses, bring down the most solid banks, make the rich poor, kill the poor, and cover the ground with remains. The tempests of the financial world and those of the physical words originate and spread more or less in the same way. After a number of days of good weather, the earth becomes warm, the atmosphere is charged with electricity, the forces of nature are strained as if preparing for a struggle. Soon the sky is covered with clouds, the hurricane is in the making, it approaches and finally rages across counties, where it wreaks havoc in its ruinous path. Similarly, in the economic domain, there is at first a time when everything conjures to favour all kinds of enterprises; confidence is unlimited, gold flows copiously; the prices of public funds and assets increase; the rates of interest fall; well-being and prosperity pervade everything. Suddenly, a black point appears in the blue sky, the dark cloud grows, expands and becomes menacing. Mistrust spreads, credit tightens, the stock exchange is suspended, money disappears, and eventually the crisis explodes and moves from a country to the next, marking everything with the ruinous tracks of its passage.[17]

The first part of the quotation takes up the theme of universal destruction, more or less along the lines of the other writers cited so far. The second part is more interesting. Laveleye's comparison of economic and physical tempests begins very promisingly with the description of the mechanism preparing, and eventually bringing to maturation, a storm. It presuppose a few days of good weather, during which the air grows warmer, the atmosphere becomes overcharged with electricity, the tension continues to increase until a point is reached when it can no longer be contained, and the storm is finally released. The description of the economic crisis begins with a description of the expansion of prosperity. There is, however, no mechanism analogous to the cumulation of tension: the black cloud suddenly appears out of the blue, with no warning sign. The outbreak of the crisis is described in its unfolding: the cloud grows and becomes menacing, but its origin remains unexplained. The astonishment of merchants and bankers, who are hit by an event that seems to them completely extraneous, is paralleled by the surprise of the economist and the chronicler, who also perceive the crisis as caused by something alien to the normal working of the economic system.

The storm metaphor is suitable to represent the bewilderment of the chronicler. Freedley, for instance, observed that 'a gale may burst out of a clear sky, like the Panic of 1857, and dissipate the accumulations of years as the dew of the morning'.[18]

Another recurring theme within the 'crises' tradition of thought is the contrast between crises as an abnormal condition and the normal state of the system. This opposition was often brought out by means of the health versus disease metaphor,[19] but the storm metaphor is also very suited to the purpose. Blanqui, for instance, compared crises to 'thunderstorms temporarily perturbing the good weather of industrial horizons, after which – notwithstanding some devastation – business resumes its usual course'.[20] Note the emphasis on the temporary character of crises, and the description of normality as 'the usual course' of business. Similarly, de Molinari refers to the good weather to which business is accustomed:

the sun has barely dissipated some of the thick clouds that made the commercial and financial horizon of Britain gloomy. Nevertheless, the sky is still overcast and not at all likely to find any time soon its accustomed clearness. The perturbations of the economic world do not subside any faster than those taking place in the physical world.[21]

The reporter for the *Memphis Daily Appeal* insisted explicitly on the abnormal yet temporary character of the 1873 panic in America:

> The fact that the failures among the mercantile and trading classes of the country have not been more numerous than during the preceding year, is sufficient to show the totally abnormal character of the furious financial typhoon which swept through Wall Street in September and October, leaving numerous wrecks among the bankers and brokers. Though the legitimate business of the country was not seriously injured, the fury of the financial storm was followed by a brief inactivity, thus involving temporary hardships, not only among business men, but among the artisan and laboring classed of many sections. Happily, however, trade and industry are already assuming their normal condition, and if the speculative classes have been taught by sharp experience the valuable lesson of conducting affairs upon a better basis, the panic will not have been without compensating influences.[22]

The *Daily Globe* expounded the contrast right in the title of an article: 'After the storm. The financial flurry over, the markets settling down to regular business.'[23] The *National Republican* reported that

> The late panic is already beginning to be forgotten, business is flowing in its accustomed channels, the markets are becoming steadier, and in a few weeks at the very farthest we shall be sailing on the same smooth seas, and with all the favoring breezes, that we knew before the financial hurricane of last month.[24]

The *Anderson Intelligencer* contrasted the flowing of trade through the customary channels with the artificial stagnation of business and locking of the wheels of commerce by means of the use of the passive voice of verbs:

> The effect of the great panic in New York has been felt throughout the country. In all the principal towns and cities, business has been stagnated, and the wheels of commerce effectually locked. In the South, the banks and business men have generally agreed to sustain each other by temperate and prudent action during the crisis. The cotton markets show plainly the effect of the financial storm. The lack of currency suspends the purchase of cotton in the interior markets, and the crop is moving slowly, as a matter of course. In due time, the money will be forthcoming to buy cotton, and the Southern planter can rely upon it that there will be a demand for the staple in a few weeks, and we trust a corresponding advance in prices. The general aspect of the financial situation indicates an early resumption of business. The heaviest failures have already taken place, and when the sky is cleared, with the debris of the storm removed from sight, the legitimate channels of trade and commerce will resume their accustomed appearance.[25]

The clearest illustration is perhaps de Broglie's description of the natural state of the economy undisturbed by political intervention, as contrasted with the stormy alternation of overexcitement and crises that would result from protective legislation:

> Each country has received from providence a natural use for its activities and its talents. When pursuing the path indicated by nature, public prosperity follows a regular course; it progresses without storms, it expands without interruption. Everything retains its place. Everything is predisposed for a foreknown movement, in some way predestined, which is carried out effortlessly.[26]

The interpretation of crises as originating outside the normal working of the economic system was sometimes represented geographically in terms of crises being initiated elsewhere – thus in no need of a specific explanation – and spreading across countries or regions. It is represented in terms of travelling storms, shockwaves, waves and tidal waves, all metaphors which, contrary to the reference to epidemics and contagion,[27] do without a specific diffusion agent and leaves the international diffusion of crises largely unexplained. In a document incorporated in the proceedings of the Committee to Investigate Bank of the United States, for instance, it is stated that 'the very same storm which thus broke on England, passed over this country a few weeks before: it was on the eve of producing precisely the same results'.[28]

To sum up, the depiction of crises by means of the selective usage of the weather analogy described in this section enabled writers to stress some features of crises compatible with an interpretation of the phenomenon as essentially extraneous to the normal working of the economic system. This view, which was mainstream in the first decades of the nineteenth century and gradually lost its appeal, was rarely theorized in full or expounded in detail. More often than not, it was expressed in fragments; the frequent references to the storm image, however, offers one of the possible unifying threads by means of which the fragments can be recombined into a recognizable pattern. Crises are thus seen as essentially destructive events, affecting the entire economy – new enterprises and old, solid houses alike. Being anomalies, they do not admit an explanation within the theoretical system explaining the normal course of trade, and their appearance is thus sudden and unexpected – not in the sense that one never knows when crises strike, but in the sense that one has no theoretical reason to expect that crises should occur.

By selecting different properties of weather phenomena on which to base the analogical reasoning, one can come to (or, *ex post*, support or expound) an altogether different interpretation of the phenomenon.

Crises as the Expurgation of Cumulated Excesses

Laveleye's description of the making of a storm based on the gradual accumulation of tension that is at some point released (see pp. 295–6) is curiously at odds with the lack of a corresponding explanation of the making and breaking out of a crisis, at a time when a number of writers had already invoked similar explanations of the causes of these phenomena. Writers within the 'recurrent crises' tradition saw crises as the result of the production and trading processes gradually abandoning the conditions for an orderly and harmonious growth, leading to the cumulation of excesses which, after a while and often rather suddenly, become unsustainable. The black clouds announcing the crises do not emerge out of nowhere but build up for some time and are visible from a distance, not only because crises are roughly periodical and can be foreseen but also because the increasing extravagance of the businesses carried on during the apparently prosperous phase, or the flimsiness of the credit base, lead to growing suspicion that the situation is unsustainable. When crises finally break out, they are instrumental in eliminating those excesses and bring the economic system back to its accustomed track, from where the process can resume until it goes out of gear again.

The first phase of this view is analytically translated in some kind of cumulative mechanism, the most common of which was the credit-overtrading speculation process, the illustration of which occasionally relied on the analogy with some natural process: the 'overcharging of the atmosphere' when crises were compared to storms, the accumulation of igniting materials leading to an explosion or a fire, or the piling up of snow eventually precipitating an avalanche. Sometimes the comparison was rather accurate, working out the details of the analogy, other times it was fairly superficial yet sufficient to capture the difference with the competing approaches.

As an illustration of the latter case, the 'recurring crises' view could distance itself from the 'crises' approach in stressing that crises do not come like tempests out of the blue sky: in this view, storms 'gather'. The first instance of this usage of the weather metaphor goes back to the end of the eighteenth century. Patrick Colquhoun described the course of events leading up to the panic of 1793. When the general state of confidence was good, manufacturers and merchants could trust the banks for credit. But the failure of two banks in London, 'of themselves of little consequence in a national point of view', caused an alarm, created distrust which grew cumulatively among merchants and country banks, to the point where national banks perceived 'the gathering storm',[29] shut down credit altogether, and distrust became universal. Similarly, Thomas Joplin noted that 'By the middle of November [1825], the shadow of the approaching storm was upon us. It was yet to burst – but the gloom was palpable.'[30] Later we find similar statements in the press. A *New York Herald* article titled 'symptoms of the coming crash', for instance, foresaw the 1857 'tornado ... gathering on the horizon',[31] and the *Daily Globe* caught sight of a 'Financial storm gathering in Montreal',[32] witnessing that the omens of a crisis can be detected some time in advance. Such events are thus expected, and can be seen forming a long time before, as in the following example from the *New-York Day Book*:

> The clouds are gathering rapidly overhead just now, and it would seem as though the great financial tornado was about to burst upon the country in all its terrible fury. We, as yet, have escaped. Once or twice in the past six months, the commercial and financial atmosphere has betokened the great crash which, sooner or later, must come; but the evil has been, for the time, arrested, and a glimmer of blue sky momentarily appearing, has dispelled the fears of the benighted fools in Congress, whose evil doings are hastening this impending calamity. But at this moment, they are again awake to the terrible doom which has so long threatened them; and the leading spirits are pausing in their mad career, and casting their eyes to the threatening heavens above them. The mutterings of the discordant elements, which, in time, will break out in the wild roar of the tempest are now heard, and the miserable creatures are again quaking with fear.[33]

The *New York Sun* had already noted a few months earlier that

> the signs of the coming financial storm are steadily growing more ominous. The comparative dullness of business, the downward tendency of prices, the increasing number of failures, and the uneasiness manifested in nearly every department of trade, are sure harbingers of a general financial crash. Every shrewd observer has been convinced, for a long time, that a monetary crisis is inevitable, and that its coming is only a question of time. The financial atmosphere has been closely watched.[34]

The surprising part, therefore, is not the bursting out of the storm but its destructive power: 'The storm had long been gathering; but was never expected to possess such destructive and devastating powers'.[35]

This image of the 'gathering' of the storm translates the view that during prosperity, tension accumulates. The most popular explanation, based on the 'overtrading' process, suggested that credit allows trade to expand beyond its 'legitimate' boundaries – that is, beyond the limit of one's capital. As this takes place when the prosperous phase is already under way, overtrading causes an increase of the general price level, which in turn induces speculation. Loanable capital is abundant, but the real possibilities of investing it in 'proper' productive activities are limited. Speculation either further feeds inflation in the value of stocks or goods, or is misdirected towards fictitious enterprises. This was widely seen, by both popularizers and the essayists, as introducing 'impurities' into the system, which, as we shall see below, storms are in charge of eliminating.

The mechanism of cumulative tension was transferred, well before Laveleye, from atmospheric to economic conditions by other writers. The first example is slightly off our focus as it does not necessarily involve crises; it is, however, very precise in its formulation. It concerns the fluctuations of the quantity of money necessary for the needs of the economy:

> it depends on the volume and the strength of business, which never settles to a constant degree of activity or extension. This works like the water absorbed by the atmosphere; the warmer the temperature, the more can be dissolved and incorporated. At the slightest cooling down, the air can no longer retain it, and it releases it in the form of rain.[36]

The mechanism described in this passage can give rise to gentle rain or to devastating storms, depending on the quantity of humidity gradually accumulated in the atmosphere and the temperature gradient. It is taken up in much more detail by John Laing, who also emphasized the suddenness of the outbreak of the storm and its seemingly trivial originating cause:

> Mutual indebtedness always exists as an unknown quantity, and a state of excessive engagements may unexpectedly be disclosed. When business is in such a condition, some cause, in itself trivial, often serves to alter the entire aspect of affairs. With the air barely above dew point, the sky may be perfectly clear, but in an instant, by some unlooked-for cold cross-current, it becomes covered with dense black clouds; so with excessive obligations pending, the apparently clear commercial atmosphere in a few days, even hours, is agitated with storms, the rate forced to panic point, ruining many who entered into engagements heedless of the warning, plain though inarticulate, usually afforded by a persistent drop of the industrial weather glass, in other words by a continuous outflow of bullion from the coffers of the Bank of England.[37]

A contributor for *The Victoria Herald* was less specific, but encompassed under the same mechanism storms, volcanoes, political revolutions and economic crises: they all are the consequence of the cumulating of forces which are liberated at once, and produce disastrous results in proportion to the power that is stored in the preparatory phase; during these cataclysms, their respective systems tend towards their 'natural' or 'perfect' states:

> Every now and then the commercial world is disturbed by vast convulsions, which rend great houses and private firms, and produce the most disastrous consequences. Philosophers tell us that storms are necessary to clear the atmosphere, and that the devastations they occasion are but the necessary results of the vast power which must be exerted to secure it. They also inform us that earthquakes and volcanoes are the natural consequences of the progress and development of those natural operations by which the earth is advancing to its ripened condition. The philosophic historian will not fail to mark the recurrence of cycles of political revolution and anarchy, which are the necessary struggles of national life towards that perfect state of freedom and prosperity which no nation has as yet attained. So the political economist, or the financier, reminds us that commercial life, like all other kinds of life, must have its crises; and that they are to the world of money what the storms and the earthquakes and the revolutions are to their respective spheres. It is an undoubted fact that they do

transpire, and that their cause can be equally defined by the operation of well-known laws; but, although like the storms and earthquakes, they may be foreseen and foretold, they often pursue their own wild erratic career and burst upon the attention of the world in a way men looked not for them.[38]

The perspective that crises are the means to eliminate the excesses of credit, trading and speculation cumulated during prosperity and to restore the normal conditions for prosperous trade is well illustrated by one of the features of storms these writers appreciated most: their effect of clearing the air. Interestingly, this metaphor changed its meaning gradually. At first the elimination of insolvent businesses was seen merely as a silver lining. A Boston merchant, for instance, wrote to the editor of the *Niles Weekly Register* that 'The effect of these occasional periods of pressure is salutary – they keep the currency sound, and purify the commercial atmosphere'.[39] He was pressed by another reader of the magazine, who wondered whether the atmosphere had 'become so corrupt or infected in Boston' as he 'had always thought the commercial atmosphere of Boston was pure; that it did not require the healing process of bankruptcy to make it salutary. But, when a Boston merchant avows the contrary, it is time for the nation to be on its guard against the causes of its pollution, as well as to prevent its becoming contagious'.[40] The merchant explained that

> By 'purifying the commercial atmosphere', I certainly mean the removal, by failure, of insolvent commercial houses – a pressure for money tends to expose the weakness and cause the stoppage of such houses. This effect is salutary and such was its effect with us. Not a single failure took place where the parties were not *deeply insolvent*.[41]

There is no hint that the insolvent houses were in any way responsible for, or related to, the pressure; it is to be noted, however, that the crisis struck selectively rather than universally, a feature that was also frequently stressed by writers in this tradition, as we shall see in more detail below.

We find the purification metaphor also on the other side of the Atlantic, tinged with a similar sense of relief at the realization that the panic of 1825 had not brought only severe distress. The Chancellor of the Exchequer, in fact, stated in Parliament 'that the violence of the storm has passed away; that the clouds which impended over us have begun to disperse; and that, by very conflict of the elements, the atmosphere has, to a certain degree, been cleared and purified'.[42] This passage was taken up by several newspapers, but the idea must have already circulated before. The press, in fact, reported that Alexander Baring criticized this view a few months earlier before a meeting of merchants:

> It would be well if those who coolly utter such phrases as that the commercial storm would purify the air, would bear in mind that the prudent and the imprudent, the solvent and the insolvent, are sacrificed in this process of purification.[43]

A few years later, the New York Bank Commissioners estimated that

> The general effects produced by the panic of last winter have, on the whole, probably been rather salutary than otherwise. It is true, great sacrifices have been sustained by individuals, and much individual suffering has grown out of it; but yet the storm has purified the commercial atmosphere, and a more healthful state of business has undoubtedly succeeded it. The revulsion which has overthrown so many extensive establishments both in city and country, would in all probability have occurred at a later period, and with increased severity.[44]

After the next crisis, in 1837, there was a first hint that the purification was connected with the previous cumulating of 'evil elements', in an article significantly titled 'the moral of the crisis':

> The storm has now expended itself, and has begun rapidly to abate; the clouds are breaking up the heavy pall which for a time seemed to enshroud the whole heavens in a portentous darkness, and their black masses are already beginning to roll away; the atmosphere has been purified of the evil elements with which it had gradually become surcharged.[45]

With the following crisis, in 1847, the purifying effect of storms was invoked more often, no longer as an accidentally beneficial side effect occurring at a specific stage of an individual instance but as a systematic accompaniment of crises. The transition is marked by the explicit comparison of storms and crises in general. The *Friend of India*, for instance, maintained that 'A periodical storm in the commercial world, is just as beneficial as a storm in the heavens. It clears the commercial atmosphere, of noisome and noxious vapours.'[46] Matthew Begbie was even more explicit:

> In the natural world, a tempest frequently is of material benefit, by clearing the atmosphere, and distributing the elementary phenomena, which, when congregated, might produce disease in the animal creation, or throw blight upon the vegetable productions with which the teeming soil fructifies, and by which life is sustained. In like manner, in the world of business, a strong convulsion such as we have lately witnessed, and the effects of which, even yet, agitate our commercial system, may not be without its use. Great as have been, and are, the evils which the 'panic' has brought in its train, they may be even more than counterbalanced by great advantages, if principles of action be introduced of a more healthy nature than those which have guided, or rather *misguided*, us for the last thirty years.[47]

With the following crisis (1857) the purification was upgraded to a *necessary* process to restore suitable conditions for the resumption of business. The first examples are found in the periodical press.[48] The *Morning Chronicle* argued that

> These periodical convulsions to which the community is subjected, are in one respect healthy – they are the natural process by which, after a period of expansion, prices

return to their true value, and by which real capital and industry are vindicated against undue speculation. As the storm purifies the atmosphere, so we believe the recent explosions will relieve the legitimate transactions of trade from a pernicious influence which has absorbed an immense amount of capital, and diverted it to the Stock Exchange in wholesale operations of a very questionable character.[49]

The *New York Observer* blamed panics on fraud and corruption, and maintained similarly that 'a plentiful crop of roguery is being provided for the next generation, and [that] some such visitation as this is needed to purify the commercial atmosphere of the country',[50] and the *Harbinger* analogously argued that

> Storms clear the air, and revolutions give breath to liberty. Panics also appear to be useful, and like most mighty powers have their law. We seem to need one every ten years, to clear our commercial atmosphere; at all events we have one about that time.[51]

The usage of this simile spread with the diffusion of the 'recurring crises' view, with the further specification that the purification of the atmosphere brings back to the normal state of trade – and at this point it was often coupled with the metaphor of 'health'. Morier Evans, for instance, wrote that

> This remarkable reaction [the revulsion of 1857] was as necessary as a thunder-storm in a mephitic and unhealthy tropical atmosphere. It purified the commercial and financial elements, and tended to restore vitality and health, alike conducive to regular trade, sound progress, and permanent prosperity.[52]

Likewise, after noting that 'There seems to be a periodicity about these panics', which is unavoidable in that 'Trade is fluctuating in its nature, and prosperity is its own destruction', Samuel Jubb stressed that

> Even as in the physical world, the thunder storm purifies the atmosphere, and refreshes the air; so in the commercial world, revulsions purify the trading atmosphere, and restore it to a normal and healthful condition. They are, therefore, not without their uses; but if the disease did not exist, there would be no need for a painful remedy.[53]

Finally, Roscher pushed the metaphor one step further. He took up Marx's discussion of the 1825 and 1836 crises not as

> single economic phenomena – such as the depreciation of precious metals in the sixteenth and seventeenth centuries ... or the depreciation of paper currency during the eighteenth century and the beginning of the nineteenth – but of big storms on the world market, in which the antagonism of all elements in the bourgeois process of production explodes.[54]

He added that this was 'the reason why one can fertilize the soil and purify the air'.[55] While clearing the air simply eliminates old impurities, fertilizing the soil actively helps the subsequent recovery. The idea was taken up by Max Wirth.

While in the first edition of his history of commercial crises in 1858 he compared crises to storms born out of the accumulation of hazardous elements which, thanks to lightening, thunders and rain clean the atmosphere of the evil vapours,[56] in the 1890 edition he added that the rain fertilizes the ground:

> The crises should be compared to a terrible thunderstorm, with lightning and thunder and torrential rain, during which people are killed, storage magazines burned down, meadows in bloom flooded, with devastating losses to livestock and crops – but which in the end sends to the region a fertilizing rain. The crisis generates monstrous losses, which destroy many institutions, ruin lives, not a few of which are driven to suicide by desperation! The impact is felt deeply by all classes of the population, and yet it must be said: when overspeculation – comparable to a thoroughbred racer with the bit between his teeth – has ignored all the cautionary warnings, exceeded all limits and brought the catastrophe, the latter must be considered as a healing process of purification and equilibrating process, which separates the pure metal from the slag and bring the feverish state of markets to the normal condition of health.[57]

The passage was eventually taken up by Tugan-Baranovsky, who wrote that 'the old theorists of crises (doubtlessly apologists of capitalistic economic order, like J.-B. Say) used to compare crises to storms, which smash trees but purify the atmosphere and refresh the countryside'[58] – or, in another version, 'compared with favourable thunderstorms, which break a few trees, but at the same time purify the atmosphere and invigorate the ground'.[59]

These impurities to be eliminated are an inevitable consequence of prosperity and, in the view of most writers in the 'recurring crises' approach, are intrinsically inherent to human nature. The purification, then, passes through the elimination of those who have indulged into excesses: the crisis is selective, not universal in its effects. It is beneficial, rather than merely harmful as believed by the holders of the 'crisis' view. This is explicitly stated in some of the examples cited above, but a few more instances will make it clearer.

The *Observer* pointed out that after the 1857 panic,

> The trader who has kept within moderate limits, and has not launched into extravagant expenditures, will find his position sensibly improved, and notwithstanding the pressure has been severe, and prejudicial to the interests of many respectable houses, the large amount of good effected by the clearance of the commercial atmosphere will be experienced before long.[60]

Similarly, the *Daily News* maintained not only that prudent traders survive the storm, but that the elimination of the unscrupulous businesses is necessary and beneficial:

> [at] the commencement of 1867 ... it was generally supposed that, according to a well-used metaphor, the storm of 1866 had cleared the air, and, by sweeping away the unsound companies which had brought so much loss and discredit on the mercantile

community, legitimate businesses would be at once the gainer ... Mercantile crises have, unhappily, not been infrequent in England; but while pressing sharply and heavily for the time on those traders who united prudence with enterprise, the latter benefited in the long run. Nothing is more destructive to fair and honest speculation than the recklessness of bankrupt firms who contrive to get credit and use it to carry on operations which they know full well can only result in loss. Sooner or later the end must come; but in the meanwhile the careful merchant finds that, from dishonest unscrupulousness, he is undersold in half the markets of the world. A panic, therefore, has been always held to have the beneficial, though indirect effect of hastening the inevitable crash, and thus of getting summarily rid of a constantly recurring evil in English commerce. In one sense the storm of 1866 has cleared the atmosphere, since it removed a number of insolvent companies, of which the longer continuance would have caused a proportionately greater loss.[61]

Other writers, instead of stressing the euthanasia of unsound business as the means for clearing the atmosphere, suggest instead that improvement is brought about by restoring confidence and inducing better business practices. A correspondent of the *Pittsburg Dispatch*, in an article significantly headed 'A Financial Storm Brings Disaster to a Chosen Few, but its Very Violence will Soon Clear the Atmosphere', reported that

Wall street had a wave to-day which is likened to several others that have passed over the street in the last 20 years. It was disastrous to a few individuals, but there is scarcely a doubt that the general effects will be beneficial and help the street toward restored confidence.[62]

Another writer maintained instead that

The recent failures, some of them for a very large amount, have naturally enough disturbed business generally to a considerable extent. They have unsettled the public mind, and have, to a considerable extent, shaken confidence. Confidence is one of the essentials of business. In its absence, doubts, hesitations and halting will result, and business generally is restricted and curtailed. If what has happened serves to clear the business sky, making business men more prudent and cautious hereafter, good results will follow.[63]

Whether by elimination of unsound business or by teaching prudence, the crisis restores the conditions for prosperous trade, thus bringing the economy back to normality. The trite 'calm after the storm' was sometimes evoked, not without a word of caution. While Michie noted that 'the commercial atmosphere having been cleared by the monetary hurricane of 1857, a period of comparative tranquility ensued',[64] a piece in the *New-York Daily Tribune* warned:

It takes time to clear away the wreck of such a revulsion and get under easy sail again. Are we hard at work clearing away? Or are we waiting a favorable gale to waft us into port dismantled and water-logged? Let every one answer for himself. – There will of course be a revival of Trade and apparent Prosperity, for 'after a storm, comes a calm'. Shall it be a real, well-grounded, lasting revival, or a mere bridge of fog, raised suddenly by some financial enchantment, to vanish in the next clear sunshine? Men who look and sigh for the return of good times, be sure you know what you mean![65]

Conclusion

Specific references to one or another feature of meteorological phenomena bring to light (and on occasion provide a foundation for) the differences between the 'crises' and the 'recurring crises' interpretations of such events. These views could not be more distant. 'Crisis' theorists emphasized the universally destructive character of tempests, while 'recurring crises' writers stressed the selective and regenerative nature of storms, which only eliminate unsound trading houses and thereby clean the atmosphere and set the conditions for a recovery of business life. In the 'crisis' approach storms originate outside the system and materialize out of the blue, while in the 'recurring crises' view storms gather due to accumulation of impurities in the atmosphere. On the one hand storms are understood as anomalies, on the other they are seen as the system's reaction to excessive strains; in both cases, after the storm the system returns to its natural state: but on the one hand, the tempest was seen as a temporary disturbance, while on the other the storm is a response to a disturbance.

Of course writers in this field have also used different analogies. Several metaphors, like the meteorological ones, are suited to different usages that can fit one or the other interpretation of crises. Earthquakes, for instances, help to stress universal devastation but also selective destruction of buildings not erected on solid foundations. Explosions and avalanches allow writers to emphasize their sudden and unforeseen character, but also to draw attention to the previous accretion of igniting materials or the cumulation of snow on a slope. Reference to the opposition between health and disease enables writers to stress either the abnormal character of crises or, on the contrary, the feverish state of the previous prosperity. Some metaphors are more suited than others to express any specific argument; to some extent, however, the choice also depends on the preferences and the culture of the writer. At any rate, the point here is not to discuss which metaphor would have best served the scope, but how people who have actually employed weather metaphors used them (usually rather carefully) to bring to light their interpretation of crises.

The function played by the metaphor is to transfer some known properties of a phenomenon familiar to the reader and to the author to another phenomenon that was not yet fully understood and even less theorized. Metaphors, of course, are no substitute for argument and theoretical reflection; indeed, excessive reliance on metaphors often denounces the lack of a theoretical argument. In the examples quoted in this chapter metaphors are very rarely called to supply an analytical mechanism explaining one or another aspect of crises (proper theoretical explanations of crises were rare in the nineteenth century as compared to the volume of writings on the subject, and when they were formulated they did not need metaphors to support them). Metaphors were used instead to expound or illustrate a very broad interpretation of the phenomena at hand. Their heuristic value consists precisely in their stressing the main features of the very different understanding of the role of crises in the working of capitalist economies. The metaphors illustrated in this chapter capture two of these basic views.

These two approaches to the problem of crises coexisted through most of the nineteenth century: the 'crises' view was predominant in the early decades, while later – under the pressure of the almost periodical outbreak of crises – the 'recurrent crises' approach gained more and more consensus until towards the end of the century, when a new shift in perspective, focusing on cycles, gained large acceptance.[66] By that time, economics was well on the way to professionalization, and the treatment of crises and cycles was formulated more and more in the language and the analytical concepts of theoretical economics. The (mathematical) pendulum, instead of the storm, became the founding metaphor of economic dynamics.[67] Yet storms have hardly disappeared from both common and scientific language.[68] This may be no accident: the problems affecting our economic system have surely become more complicated but remain essentially similar to what they were a century ago; and the language of economics has become more technical, but the interpretations of crises and of their role in the working of the economic system have not changed that much.

22 SAMUELSON AND THE NON-SUBSTITUTION THEOREM: SOME METHODOLOGICAL REMARKS

Amanar Akhabbar

The world takes people too much at their words.[1]

When dealing with the Pareto-Walrasian general equilibrium theory, Pascal Bridel repeatedly underlined that from one generation of economists to another, the methodology ruling this theory has been continuously changing:[2] from Léon Walras's idealism to Vilfredo Pareto's positivism; from Paul A. Samuelson's operationism[3] to Robert E. Lucas's instrumentalism; and so forth.[4] In this regard, one major methodological turn was the move from cardinalist utility functions, resting on psychological foundations, to ordinalist ones. Samuelson's contribution, both methodological (introducing operationism in economics) and theoretical (the well-known revealed preference theory), is probably the most important,[5] although recent works in economics increasingly reintroduce psychological elements in economic theory.[6] In our essay we attempt at drawing a parallel between Samuelson's operationalization-of-consumer theory through revealed preference theory, and his works in production theory from the late 1940s on, in particular the non-substitution theorem (NST).

In 1949, the NST was first demonstrated simultaneously and independently by Samuelson and Georgescu-Roegen for a so-called (static)[7] 'generalized model of Leontief'. The theorem raised the question as to whether substitutions among factors of production could not occur even if possible. Samuelson and Georgescu-Roegen showed that, although possible, in certain conditions if the structure of final demand changes, the structure of production remains unchanged and no factor substitution occurs. These special conditions are, in particular, that the economy admits (i) at most one primary factor, i.e., one non-produced factor of production like land; and (ii) no joint production, i.e., each technology produces only one outcome. The dual interpretation (in the mathematical sense) of the NST asserts that 'under certain specified conditions an economy will have one particular price structure for each admissible value of the profit rate, regardless of the pattern of the final demand'.[8]

As a matter of fact, such specific conditions are verified in the '*simple* models of Leontief', the famous input-output Leontief models.[9] Therefore, in such a model, it is relevant to assume, like in Walras's 'theory of production' in the *Éléments d'économie politique pure*,[10] constancy of technical coefficients and thus to rule out the substitutions phenomenon. However, in a '*generalized* model of Leontief',[11] one assumes multiple primary factors and joint products, and thus factor substitution occurs and, as a consequence, marginal productivity theory is verified. To Samuelson, classical political economy falls under the specific (restrictive) assumptions of the NST, while Pareto-Walrasian general equilibrium theory falls under the generalized system. Furthermore, according to Samuelson, the generalized model is the relevant one to describe real economies:

> Ricardo and Smith would probably have admitted that the relative prices of joint products – of venison and skin, for example – would have to be determined by a demand theory and not from labor and land costs alone. One wonders why they did not worry about this 'jointness', which every student of Walrasian equilibrium knows to be an intrinsic part of the actual pricing relations among diverse factors and goods.[12]

In a nutshell, from a theoretical point of view, non-substitution then 'is here to remind us that it is not easy to escape the imperialism of the general equilibrium theory'.[13] The NST has eventually become one of the cornerstones of post-Walrasian general equilibrium theory of production.[14]

Our essay deals only with Samuelson's NST. We do not discuss the theoretical relevance of the NST for political economy. Instead, we are interested in the possible relationship between, on the one hand, Samuelson's well-known operationist methodology[15] that he developed about consumer theory, in particular the revealed preference theory,[16] and, on the other hand, in the realm of production theory, his demonstration of the NST. We ask the following question: given Samuelson's operationist epistemology, is the NST an operational theorem? We argue in favour of a positive answer.

'A Theorem Concerning Substitutability in Open Leontief Models'

The NST was first demonstrated[17] for a so-called 'generalized open model of Leontief',[18] which is an n-industries full-employment general equilibrium model with exogenous final demand.[19] In order to 'generalize' Leontief's model,[20] Samuelson took the same set of assumptions as Leontief except for the constancy of technical coefficients: the generalized-production function allows substitutions among factors of production. This is a *generalized model of Leontief*.

Let X_i be the total output of industry i, for all $i = 1 \ldots n$; x_{ij} the output of the i-*th* industry used by industry j; a_{ij} is the quantity of input i used to produce one unity of output j; and C_i the final demand ('final output') addressed to the i-th industry. For each industry, equilibrium quantity is distributed such as:

$$X_i = \sum_{j=1}^{n} x_{ij} + C_i.$$

Labour is the $n+1^{th}$ commodity and is the only primary factor. The final demand for labour is assumed equal to zero ($C_{n+1} = 0$), and $C_k = (F_k(X) - \sum x_{kj})$.

Production of each good depends on a homogenous production function $F_i(.)$ of first degree (constant returns to scale). There is no joint production, thus this is a one-commodity-per-industry economy: $X_i = F_i(x_1, x_2, ..., x_{n+1i})$. Since factor substitution is assumed, technical coefficients are not constant, and we deduce from the production function the following simple relation: $F_i(a_1, a_2, ..., a_{ni}) = 1$.

Given technical constraints and the available quantity of labour, and given the final demand for other industries, equilibrium is determined for each industry k in such a way that the final demand for industry k (C_k) is maximized. Each

$$\begin{cases} Max\ C_k = X_k - \sum_{j=1}^{n} {}_{k \neq j} x_{kj} \\ X_k = F_k(x_{1k}, x_{2k}, ..., x_{n+1\kappa}) \\ F_i(x_{1i}, x_{2i}, ..., x_{n+1i}) - \sum_{j=1}^{n} x_{ij} = C_i \quad \forall i = 1, ..., n\ et\ i \neq k \\ X_{n+1} = 0 + \sum_{j=1}^{n} x_{n+1\ j} \end{cases}$$

industry k, is ruled by the following optimization programme:
The solution to the programme is found using the Langrange multipliers. One shows easily that technical coefficients are *independent* of the C_i (final demands) of the prices and of X_{n+1} (the available quantity of labour). As a consequence, even if factor substitution is possible, i.e., technical coefficients are not constant in such specific conditions (one primary factor, no joint production), the technical coefficient will not change whatever change occurs in final demand, prices, and availability of the primary factor. Hence, constancy of technical coefficients is a particular case of the general case where joint production and multiple primary factors allow changes in the structure of production.

According to Samuelson, the NST reconciles the model of Leontief (constant technical coefficients and the value-added distribution is given) with the theory of general equilibrium (variable technical coefficients and the theory of marginal productivity rules income distribution). For Samuelson, 'actually all his [Leontief's] theory in its present form is compatible with the more general case of substitutability'.[21] In other words, the situation described by the model of Leontief isn't contradictory with and not exclusive of the theory of general equilibrium: it is a particular case of the Walrasian theory of general equilibrium. Indeed, Samuelson's NST means that under certain circumstances 'all desirable substitutions have already been made by the competitive market, and no variation in the composition of final output or in the total quantity of labour will give rise to price change or substitution';[22] otherwise, whether the factors of production are substitutable, a change in final demand, relative prices, or in available labour, substitutions between factors occur and technical coefficients change. In a nutshell, the theorem raises the question of the validity of a price-quantity equilibrium independent of consumers' tastes and of the structure of demand.

From an epistemological point of view, the NST is powerful because it makes an initially postulated assumption (the constancy of technical coefficients) the *consequence* of a set of reduced assumptions. Indeed, while Leontief assumed the constancy of technical coefficients, Samuelson showed that in a generalized model of Leontief the constancy is true under precise conditions (only one primary factor, no joint production, etc.). In other words, in the generalized model of Leontief, the constancy is the result of a deduction from fundamental assumptions. From a logical point of view, the status of the theoretical proposition concerning the constancy of technical coefficients changes in the generalized model: this is no more an initial assumption but the result of a deduction (a theorem). We will show now that this theorem is an 'operational' theorem according to Samuelson's operationism definition.

Deductive Methodology and Operationism: A Cambridge Methodology

From the point of view of theoretical political economy, Samuelson's NST is a strategic piece of the hegemonic ambitions of the general equilibrium theory. Now, we aim at examining the NST's epistemological status.

Samuelson's methodology is well-known. The methodological criterion he chose to change the scientific vocabulary of economics was an operational one.[23] However, Samuelson wasn't alone in using the operational criterion. The term 'operational' was common in Cambridge and especially in Harvard. Indeed, while empirical and experimental studies had been developing in social sciences since the end of the nineteenth century, there were very different ways to articulate theory and observations, even under the influence of the Vienna circle: the operational methodology is one of them.

In economics, Henry Schultz was the first to allude to an *operational* methodology.[24] According to Schultz, his demand-estimation method was 'an illustration of what ... Bridgman ... has called "the operational procedure" for determining the meaning of a concept [in this case the meaning of demand]'.[25] Indeed, the physicist Percy W. Bridgman, from Harvard University, developed in his book *Logic of Modern Physics*[26] the philosophical doctrine he called *operationalism*.[27] This doctrine states that the meaning of a scientific concept is synonymous with the set of operations entering its definition.[28] In other words, the meaning of a concept is given by an explicit definition of this concept stating experimental or mental operations of measure. This is the experimental version (and not the *mentalist* one) of Bridgman's operationalism that was successfully exported in social sciences, psychology and philosophy.[29]

One particularity of operationism is that it proposes a strong relationship (synonymy) between theoretical terms and observational terms (direct observations or sense data), without distinction between induction and deduction. Nevertheless, in contrast to induction, operationism considers theory as necessary *and* requires theoretical terms to be operational, that is to say to be empirically meaningful (while induction is suspicious about theory). In the philosophy of science, Rudolf Carnap[30] showed that operationism was actually the strong version of neopositivist verificationism. Carnap stated at the same time that operationism was impracticable. For the philosophy of science, Carnap's article ended the operational programme, although Carl Gustav Hempel, Karl Popper and Nelson Goodman continued to criticize and to discuss operationism during the 1940s and the 1950s. It also put an end to the until-then-flourishing verificationist programme. This led to the creation of what Carnap called *logical empiricism*.[31] Despite the doom of operationism in pure philosophy of science, the very spirit of Bridgman's methodology became very fashionable in American sciences. In Cambridge (MA) again, first Samuelson,[32] a student of Leontief at Harvard and then working at the MIT, and later Leontief,[33] at Harvard, alluded to the operational criterion.

Samuelson's Operational Theorems

Samuelson first studied the neoclassical theory of demand and utility and raised the question: if one denies to the 'hedonistic, introspective, psychological elements' explanatory value, 'does not the whole utility analysis become meaningless in the *operational* sense of modern science?'.[34] The *Foundations of Economic Analysis*[35] aimed at being a translation of economic theory into the operational language of science. For Samuelson, 'A meaningless theory according to this criterion is one which has no empirical implications by which it could be *refuted* under ideal empirical conditions';[36] and again, 'It is the purpose here to demonstrate that the utility analysis in its ordinary form does contain empirically meaningful implications by which it could be refuted'.[37]

The definition Samuelson gave of his operational criteria was stable in time and he didn't remove it. In 1998, Samuelson stated the following: 'My approach looked backward in summarizing "economically" (in the Mach-Vienna Circle sense) the "meaningful" (testable and, in principle, refutable) core of constrained-budget demand theory'.[38]

Samuelson's project was to eliminate from 'the theory of consumer behaviour' any 'vestigial traces of the utility concept', consequently stripping consumption theory "to its bare implications for empirical realism"'.[39] According to Samuelson, this is that method that permits to state *operational theorems*.

Now, it is important to underline that the definition Samuelson gave of the operational meaning of a theory is different from both Bridgman's definition and Carnap's version of operationism. Compared to Carnap and Bridgman's approaches, it is controversial to state whether the methodology Samuelson adopted was based on a *meaning* criterion or a *falsification* criterion.[40] Blaug[41] argued that Samuelson's operationalism was a mixture of empiricism and falsificationism.[42] Although commentators agree about the radical difference between Bridgman's and Samuelson's operationism, there is no consensus about the falsificationist nature of the latter: for instance, Cohen[43] rejected Blaug's position. To reject the falsificationist interpretation of Samuelson's operationist methodology, Cohen argues that Popper's book *Die Logik der Forschung* (The Logic of Scientific Discovery), published in 1934, was translated in English late in the 1950s,[44] and he assumes that Samuelson didn't read it. Now, on a pure epistemological stage, Samuelson's definition is clearly not the one of operational methodology, but is a version of falsificationism: according to such a methodology, theory doesn't need direct correspondence with data, but only indirect empirical implications, in order to be (possibly) refuted.

To our demonstration about the operationality of the NST, it is not important to determine or choose one or another interpretation of Samuelson's epistemology. This will not affect our result. From now, we will consider that operationism is in the first place the methodology Samuelson practically implemented in revealed preference theory (RPT), and we will show that the same methodology was implemented in the NST.

Operational Theorems: From Revealed Preference Theory to NST

Samuelson first applied his so-called operationist methodology to (neoclassical) consumer theory. To bring empirical implications to the theory of consumer, Samuelson chose to start his analyses with the data consumers reveal in the marketplace. The utility function is then the one maximized that corresponds to the revealed preference. This function is a transitive and complete ordinal utility function, which satisfies the weak axiom of revealed preference. Ordinal utility is then purged from introspection and gets an operational meaning, according to Samuelson: the function is defined 'as that which is maximized by means of *revealing preferences* in the market place'.[45]

This is clearly the same principle employed in the theory of revealed preference and the NST: given prices-assumed to be 'parameters not subject to influence by the individual' noticed Samuelson[46] – the explanation of empirical data, namely actual technical coefficients (or *consumed quantities*) is expressed as an optimization programme[47] of a derivable mathematical function, namely final net output (or *utility function*) under constraints, here the production function and the quantities equilibrium (or *budgetary constraint*). Let's note that in the NST, the production function actually appears in the objective function since, for each industry k, one maximizes consumption C_k where $C_k = (F_k (X) - \sum x_{kj}$, $F(-)$ being the production function. Therefore, in the NST, like in revealed preference theory, the unknown objective function is to be found. In both optimization problems, to solve the programme, the method of Lagrangean multipliers is used.

On the one hand, the NST shows that a production function with substitution exists that induces under certain circumstances constant technical coefficients (one *observes* constant technical coefficients) and that induces under other circumstances variable technical coefficients (one *observes* the variation of technical coefficients). On the other hand, in the same way as the production function obtains an operational meaning by its references to variations of measurable technical coefficients, the utility function gains empirical significance once getting rid of introspection.[48]

In microeconomics textbook language, Samuelson's analysis starts with an observable point, namely bundles of goods. In the entirety of this paragraph, we assume given prices. In the realm of production theory, the problem is as follows: given observable bundles of inputs, what is the corresponding operational production function? In the realm of consumer theory, the problem is as follows: given observable bundles of goods, what is the corresponding operational utility function? Indeed, given prices, on a two-axis diagram one represents quantities of input A and of input B required to produce x units of commodity X; this point gives a measure of one technical coefficient of the production function of commodity X. One may represent the isoquant passing by this observable point. The isoquant is not observable in reality while the technical coefficient may be measured. Given assumptions on the production function and given a series of observable input vectors (A,B), one deduces the (derivable) production function, $x=F(A,B)$. This is the operational analysis of the production function. In the same way, when one deals with consumer acts, given prices, one observes and measures the consumed quantities of commodities X and Y. On a two-axis diagram, one represents consumed quantities of X and consumed quantities of Y. One may represent the indifference curve passing by this observable point (X,Y).

The indifference curve is not observable in reality while the consumed bundle of goods X and Y is observable. Given assumptions on the utility function and given a series of observable bundles of goods (X,Y), one deduces the (derivable) utility function, $u=G(X,Y)$.

These functions (the production function and the utility function) are operational by means of indirect references to observation: this is the deductive method and not the canonical operational method of Carnap and Bridgman. Indeed, Carnap's operational methodology requires direct correspondences between concepts and observation: to gain an operational meaning the mathematical function must be defined by synonymous measure operations ... which is not the case.[49] But the mathematical functions obtained by Samuelson are operational according to Samuelson's operational criterion. Samuelson's methodology lies on two stages: (1) enunciation of minimal ('economical') assumptions under which rest deduction and calculation and (2) expression of the explanation of the problem as an optimization programme. Ultimately, then, the NST is operational according to Samuelson's definition of the operational meaning of a theory, but this definition is completely different from the one Carnap proposed. On the other hand, Samuelson's criterion is falsificationist (close to Popper) and corresponds to the one proposed by Koopmans[50] at the *Cowles Commission*: the empirical content (and not operational meaning) of a hypothetic-deductive theory comes from the singular statements (observable) deduced from the general assumptions.

Conclusion: Samuelson and a Symmetric Operationist Theory of Value? Operational Theorems for Consumption Theory and Production Theory

In this essay we have shown that Samuelson applied the same methodological approach to both the economic theory of consumption and the economic theory of production: he intended to offer operational concepts to build economic theory on new and operational foundations. On the consumer theory side, Samuelson produced the revealed preference theory as the operational theory of ordinalist utility analysis. As such, he aimed at getting rid of the psychological basis of utility theory: the utility function was nothing more than an artefact reproducing the observable consumed bundles of goods. On the production theory side, Samuelson grounded controversial-factor substitutability on (expectedly) uncontroversial operational-production functions: the opposition between, on the one hand, classical and Marxian political economy (rejecting substitutability and assuming complementary factors), and so-called neoclassical theories was expected to vanish under the effect of operational theorems of production, beginning with the NST. True or false, the NST is operational.

23 *HOMO ŒCONOMICUS* AND *HOMO SOCIOLOGICUS* AS CONTRASTED IDEAL-TYPES

Jacques Coenen-Huther

No social science can pretend to understand and explain the behaviour of the real human being in the totality of his life. This holds true, of course, for economic science and for sociology. Both disciplines conduct their analyses on the basis of an ideal-type of man shaped by their independent and dependent variables.[1] In the domain of natural sciences, the discrepancy between empirical reality and scientific constructs is taken for granted and does not surprise anybody. As Ralf Dahrendorf put it, 'we do not much care that the table, the roast, and the wine of the scientist are paradoxically different from the table, the roast, and the wine of our everyday experience'.[2] Indeed, for all practical purposes, scientific reasoning does not play much of a role in the world of everyday life. A table is quite a convenient support if we want to lean on it and a physicist would not change our perception by observing that it is in fact 'a most unsolid beehive of nuclear particles'.[3]

Two Ideal-Types

As soon as we deal with human affairs, on the contrary, scientific constructs do interfere with our beliefs and our actions. Economists' and sociologists' interpretations of human attitudes and behaviours have a potential influence on social life by affecting decision making. Decisions made on false premises lead unavoidably to wrong expectations and to unintended consequences. It has long been usual to name *Homo Œconomicus* the individual conceptualized by economic science although Pascal Bridel does not seem to hold him in high regard when he writes that 'every action of the economic agent is linked to his environment including his experiences, his beliefs and, of course, a particular type of rationality'.[4] In an effort to distance themselves from that ideal-type, sociologists took upon themselves to elaborate another model of man as most of them see him and to christen him *Homo Sociologicus*. Both *Homo Œconomicus* and *Homo Sociologicus* are the products of processes of reduction of complexity quite common in intellectual endeavours as different as, say, history and physics. Both make decisions but not on the same basis and not according to the same criteria.

Homo Œconomicus is the individual dealing with the problem of scarcity – scarcity of resources as well as scarcity of goods and services – and with the necessity to make choices in his capacity of producer, distributor or consumer of goods and services deemed useful. As a producer, he has to juggle with the various factors of production and to combine them in the most efficient way. As a distributor, he has to choose the best strategy according to the structure of the market. As a consumer, he has to establish a hierarchy of preferences and decide what his priorities are. Regardless of his specific position on the market as producer, distributor or consumer, *Homo Œconomicus* is a calculating being. His guiding principle is his interest and he always behaves so as to maximize his benefits and minimize his costs. To either produce, to distribute or to consume goods and services, he has to allocate available resources – which are always limited – in a coherent way: a way he would describe as rational although his rationality can be deemed narrowly utilitarian and often very cruel. Indeed, the world of *Homo Œconomicus* is a rather abstract one, structured by supply and demand treated as abstract quantities. However, production, distribution and consumption, organized in such a restrictively defined 'rational' way, entail much human suffering when these operations are translated in terms of employment, wages, work environment and retail prices. A certain indifference to the human costs of economic activities has led to the denigration of *Homo Œconomicus* seen as a quintessential egoist whose preferences are specified on a pure individual basis. In the durkheimian criticism, cognitive and normative arguments blend together when man conceptualized by economists is labelled an amoral being.[5]

On the other hand, *Homo Sociologicus* – even when he has to make choices – is confronted with the normative influences of his social environment and reacts to them by assuming social roles. These roles can be related to a professional activity: the role of the professor, the role of the physician, the role of the waiter; to a special function: judge, solicitor, member of the Parliament; or to a position in the course of life: the role of the parents, the role of the spouses. Every role bearer is subjected to role expectations and the interplay between roles and role expectations holds society together when discrepancies between both categories are not too great. Roles and roles expectations define what can be normally expected from an individual in a given interaction sequence. This anticipation of normality, however, is a major source of ambiguity in daily life. Normality in the statistical sense of the word becomes a norm of behaviour. In other words, what people usually do becomes quickly what they ought to do. Failure to meet expectations can provoke astonishment or annoyance but can also be a source of scandal. The character of the norm reflects the strength of the expectations and the importance of the need to prevent possible transgressions. Some expectations are imperative and supported by formal sanctions involving various kinds of coercive measures. Others are only preferential and transgressions are met by milder forms of disapproval. Less important expectations are merely optional: failure to meet them is sanctioned by expressions of bad mood in informal settings. Needless to say, role expectations do not determine roles: they interact permanently with them in a dynamic process. The role bearer can submit obediently to expectations but can also rebel against them. Ultimately, there is always the possibility of stepping out of a role, even if the price to pay for such show of dissent can be high.

Compared with each other, *Homo Œconomicus* and *Homo Sociologicus* can be pictured by way of caricatures as two different characters. The first one appears as a lonely figure, spending the best part of his time in a kind of solipsist bubble, ruminating and weighing options. In a Cartesian way, his very existence depends on his ability to think properly and to behave accordingly. A social environment is not part of the picture. As for the second one, on the contrary, it seems impossible to imagine him alone. We see him in the middle of a crowd, arguing, seeking advice, hesitating, changing his mind. Various people try to pressure him into selecting their preferred course of action. He seems torn between several possibilities and the tension is palpable. Can these two cousins – the one-track-mind obsessed by efficiency and the versatile fellow unsure about his preferences – be brought to a kind of cooperation? Put in another way, is there a possibility to contemplate a model of man combining the characteristics of these two ideal-types? The focus of *Homo Œconomicus'* thinking is not on the reasons of his behaviour but on its distinctive features. He is in a problem-solving mood and wonders whether his actions are the most appropriate. This brings about the notion of rationality as a matter of debates. Economic science relies implicitly on the concept of human nature and produces lines of reasoning supposed to be universal in scope. *Homo Sociologicus*, on the other hand, tends to question the very idea of a human nature implying universal rules of action. Sociological propositions concerning human activity are always relative to a particular environment. The focus here is not on the characteristics of behaviour – rational or not – but on the various influences bearing on it. This leads to one central question: why do we act the way we do?

Both disciplines answer that question differently. Economic analysis has traditionally considered supply and demand on the market as independent variables which can explain all the facts under consideration. Indeed, the principle of supply and demand obviously plays a part in explaining the level and composition of the production, the way factors of production are used and the modalities of distribution of goods and services between various groups or individuals. In Keynesian analysis, independent variables are the propensity to consume, the marginal efficacy of the capital, depending on expectations of profit, and the rate of interest, function of the supply of money and the demand for liquidities.

But these variables may be subsumed under broader categories of supply and demand. Turning to sociology, the first impression is of an irreducible multiplicity of potential independent variables. Sociologists, however, give the preference to structural variables, i.e. the variables resulting from belonging to a category or a group, the variables locating an individual within a structure and the variables indicating the characteristics of these structures.

Various Rationalities

If one tries to combine economic and sociological perspectives on human behaviour in an integrated approach, *Homo Œconomicus* becomes a subspecies of *Homo Sociologicus* who has to be considered in economic roles, that is in behaviours aiming at the same time at facing the problem of scarcity and the normative expectations of his environment. At first glance, normative expectations will reduce the options of an individual who wishes to behave rationally. From a pure instrumental point of view, snatching the purse of an old woman can be a convenient way to supplement scarce resources. However, this practical solution to the problem of scarcity is not congruent with mainstream norms of behaviour; it is only in marginal groups that purse snatching can be a source of pride. On the other hand, sociological reasoning, for better or for worse, is prone to relativism. The specific contribution of sociological analysis in its relation to economic knowledge seems to be a diversification of the notion of rationality to the point of equating it with coherence. It can be argued – as many sociologists do – that rationality is a relative concept: relative to the formal aspects of the situation and relative to the characteristics of the actor. Very broadly speaking, a behaviour is deemed rational by the sociologist when a certain adequacy can be detected between motivations and actions. The motivation can originate in the promotion of interests – which are not always of an economic kind – or in the disinterested respect of a value. And the value-oriented behaviour can be seen as lofty but inadequate to protect the legitimate interests of the actor. Rationality, or coherence, is also relative to the socio-cultural context. From one historical period to another, from one culture to the other, the common-sense notion of rational behaviour can change a great deal.

The story of Manuela, the young Mexican girl whose life story was told by Peter Berger, illustrates that diversity. To escape the poverty of her village, she manages to go first to the nearby town and then to cross the border illegally into California. For the first time in her life, she finds herself able to save money and to plan for her future life. She can build up on her experience in the US and go to commercial school to become a bilingual secretary. But members of her extended family never stop asking for her help: financial contribution to a wedding, lawyer's expenses for a jailed cousin, funds for the grandfather's medical treatment, investment in a small business... For Manuela, the choice is clear: either to loosen herself from family ties and make her way to a new life, or keep in touch with the family system that will eat up all her savings. As Peter Berger put it, 'the choice is not between two courses of action, but between two moralities. The first course is dictated by the morality of collective solidarity, the second by the morality of personal autonomy and advancement.'[6] This dilemma does not oppose the attitude of *Homo Œconomicus* to that of *Homo Sociologicus*: it combines both. Manuela is aware of her personal interest as defined by her Californian acquaintances but she is not indifferent to the voices coming from her village, making appeals to her generosity. To follow the course of personal autonomy, 'she must, literally, hack off all those hands that would hold her back'.[7] Her choice will be a choice 'under constraints', as contemporary economic theory would have it, but in such a case the constraints are internalized norms and those are the most imperious.

Very often, norms of behaviour alien to the world of *Homo Œconomicus* tend to reduce the devotion to strict economic efficiency. Fifty years ago, in a kibbutz of Galilea, decisions regarding the crops to be cultivated were made collectively by the general assembly of the members, like in all *kibbutzim* of that time,[8] Some crops were more profitable than others and decisions were made accordingly, with the view of balancing the budget. Advantages and disadvantages of growing oranges, avocados, bananas, etc. were discussed extensively. At one point, the culture of mushrooms came under scrutiny. It appeared that it had never been a profitable business for the kibbutz. But, to quote the Russian writer Vladimir Doudintsev, 'Man lives not by bread alone'; the idea of discontinuing its production never gained traction. One respected member of the community had long identified himself with that culture and enjoyed it. For the majority of the assembly, it was sufficient reason to keep that branch of activity going. In a move which would seem surprising in our time of exacerbated economic competition, the principle of efficiency was clearly supplanted by the principle of pleasure. Contrasting modernity to tradition, Marcel Mauss once wrote that it is only recently that Western societies 'made an economic animal out of man'.[9] Kibbutz members were obviously prepared to make a financial sacrifice just to keep one of them happy. However, they did not act out of nostalgia for pre-modern times as the Maussian statement would suggest; they were consciously promoting a value they judged of higher order than economic value. From an entrepreneurial point of view, such decisions can very easily be considered irrational and it has to be acknowledged that the term 'irrational' tends to be used as a sign of disapproval. Yet, conflicting values implying various logics irreducible to each other are here at stake. The actors themselves were torn between instrumental and axiological orientations. The result was a mitigated instrumental attitude: in most of the problems at issue, the economic calculus prevailed but there was room for exceptions.

Irrationality as a Misguided Diagnosis

The diagnosis of irrationality appears frequently in the field of aid to development. In their contacts with traditional societies, Westerners tend to think of themselves as representatives of rational thinking and to consider objections by natives as the result of ignorance or irrational fear of innovation. A classical example of such misunderstanding is offered by a birth control programme in India, quoted extensively by Peter Berger[10] and by Raymond Boudon.[11] In the 1960s, a birth control experiment was carried out with funds of the Rockefeller Foundation in a group of villages in the Punjab. Contraceptive tablets were distributed in some villages while others were used as a control group. The results of the programme were very disappointing to its promoters. From the beginning of the experiment to the follow-up study, no variation in the birth rate could be attributed to the use of the contraceptive tablets and no significant difference between experimental and control groups could be registered. For the people involved in the project, there was no doubt that birth control was in the best interest of the villagers and that promoting contraceptive practice was the rational thing to do. With fewer children, families would be better off. The villagers themselves were of the opposite opinion; they were convinced that numerous offspring was an advantage to every household. Being dismissed as irrational, these objections of the local population were not taken seriously. Renewed efforts were made to convince the villagers of the benefit to be expected from a lowering of the birth rate. Finally, the villagers gave up any attempt to make themselves understood, took the tablets, but never used them. For Western commentators, this was one more case of 'resistance to development'. The fact is that the villagers' attitude was as rational as the attitude of the advocates of birth control. In the context of an agricultural production based on rudimentary technology, children, soon able to help their parents, are a 'rational economic investment' for a peasant family: the cost of each child is negligible, compared with the increase in income they bring about.[12] From a national viewpoint, birth control was advisable. From the point of view of the rural population, the opposite was true.

Ironically, although Berger and Boudon describe and analyse quite convincingly the resistance of the rural population to a logic imported from outside, they stick to the notion of economic rationality and they explain the attitude of the peasants by contrasting two different conceptions of their economic interest. They are obliged to do so because they both are looking for *reasons* to behave in a certain way. The fact is that most people are not motivated by specific reasons but by a feeling that the way they act is the normal thing to do. And that feeling is the product of socialization and immersion in a particular culture. In traditional societies where a marriage without children is compared to 'a tree without fruit', a man gifted with many children is held in high esteem regardless of the practical advantages of this situation. When he reaches old age, he can rely on the assistance of his children since he is widely respected. Let us mention in passing that the responsibility for the sterility of a marital union is always placed on the woman. As long as the social order is stable, it is taken for granted that numerous offspring are desirable. It goes without saying and it is not a matter of discussion. When doubt is casted on that conventional wisdom, the economic advantage is brought to the fore but only as a reaction to the challenge. To make use of the Paretian conceptualization, the argument can be seen as a *derivation* masking a *residue*, in this case a residue of 'persistence of aggregates'. The 'one child' policy forcibly implemented by the Chinese government when the current rhythm of economic growth was not yet anticipated is one more example of the disruption that can be brought to a traditional social system by an intervention from the outside. Chinese parents are worrying more than ever about the future of their only child and that child feels the burden of a frightening responsibility towards them. As a Chinese mother recently said in an interview, 'I've only got one [child], so I have to make sure that one takes care of me when we get old'. But when she urges her daughter to keep studying to be able to support her parents later, the daughter replies: 'That's too much pressure. I don't want to think about all that responsibility.'[13]

Symbolic Gratifications versus Self-Interest

In the various examples of population planning, a traditional way of life is analysed from an economic point of view, even when outside observers are sociologists. Some of these observers will find a behaviour economically detrimental, others will detect in the same context very logical attitudes, quite defensible in the eyes of an economist. The father of numerous children can be seen as a *Homo Sociologicus* disguised in *Homo Œconomicus*: the calculating fornicator! In other instances, there is no coincidence to be seen between the two points of views. The kibbutz mentioned above was an important producer of bananas. In the 1970s, the research institute of the Kibbutz Federation in Tel Aviv undertook to reorganize the harvest of the fruit with a view to increasing productivity. The old *hagalot* or trailers used to carry the bananas away from the plantation were to be replaced by smaller vehicles easier to move and to load. The new system was clearly progressive, especially for the workers in the field. Nevertheless, these very workers – including the writer of these lines – did their best to convince their colleagues that the old way to handle the loading was preferable. This was another case of resistance to change, although less legitimate. The reason behind the lack of goodwill from the potential beneficiaries of the reform was paradoxically that the old trailers were more difficult and tiring to load; the bunches had to be stacked up in the form of a seven-levels pyramid and this operation required both physical strength and manual dexterity. Since the work ethic was still strong in the old-fashioned *kibbutzim*, the worker able to build a neat pyramid withstanding the shocks of the transport on dirt roads was admired by his comrades and was proud of his achievements. In spite of the prevailing egalitarianism of the kibbutz, a hidden stratification of the workforce was built on the basis of such skills in the banana plantation. The workers reaching the highest position in this informal hierarchy were clearly unconvinced by the entrepreneurial logic of looking for a better organization of the production in economic terms. It is fair to say that they were unconvinced because they did not want to be convinced: they enjoyed the moral gratifications deriving from their hard work whereas the new system clearly had an equalizing effect. Eventually *Homo Sociologicus* had to give up the fight and *Homo Œconomicus* prevailed. Of course, there are other settings in which symbolic rewards have precedence over material advantages. The academic world is one of them, although neither physical strength nor manual dexterity is involved; university professors write books yielding honours but very little money and most of them are happy that way even if a few of them envy the royalties amassed by the authors of detective stories.

Coherence versus Rationality

At this point it becomes necessary to take a closer look at the concept of rationality. It has often been said that economists are inclined to define rationality too narrowly, describing for example some movements on the financial markets as irrational reactions of the investors. This has long been a point of contention with sociologists. Indeed, if rationality were to be equated with instrumental rationality geared to the optimization of material gratifications, a lot of meaningful activities would fall outside the scope of rational behaviour. Even for sociologists, however, the attribution of rationality has become a matter of debate. And it can be argued that for sociologists and for economists alike, it is not *that* important to decide whether a particular line of action is rational or not. Rationality is not only a matter of empirical verification, it is also a matter of presupposition. The social scientist – economist or sociologist – may believe that a postulate of rationality is required to understand the behaviour of the actor. The validity of this postulate can be preserved by a diversification into instrumental rationality, axiologic rationality, cognitive rationality, bounded rationality, etc. One wonders, however, whether the actor is not supposed to exhibit a certain form of rationality because the social scientist tries to analyse his behaviour in a rational way. The presumed rationality of the actor would then mirror the rationality of the scientist. In other words, the observer would presuppose a kind of rationality because it seems the only way to understand the observed. But it is absolutely not necessary to adhere to an elaborate version of the Paretian distinction between logical and non-logical actions. It can be argued that the so-called 'non-logical actions' have their own logic that can only be labelled 'non-logic' from a particular point of view. The relativity of rationality could be a reason to look for a broader concept of coherence and to substitute a concept of coherence to a postulate of rationality.[14] This is also a way to avoid the very common habit of using the adjective 'irrational' as a derogatory term to disqualify a particular way of behaving. The behaviour of the investor is deemed 'irrational' when it collides with the economic policy of his government and the decisions of the authorities – or the actions of the trade unions for that matter – are labelled 'irrational' when they hamper business activity. There are good reasons, however, to consider all these decisions and actions coherent and to apply rational understanding to them.

As sociologists see it, the rational understanding of a behaviour is a reconstruction of the actor's logic of action, based on reasons which seem obvious to the observer. These reasons can coincide with motivations or justifications that could be stated by the actor himself but not necessarily. A set of reasons that the researcher takes for granted is being projected on the actor's behaviour. Data have to be interpreted in order to give them meaning. In the rationalist line of thought, the actor is supposed to be driven by reasons and these reasons are the independent variables which serve to explain his behaviour. However, the focus on a particular set of variables depends on a preceding intellectual choice which has to be made if we want to avoid a regression *ad infinitum* from the one cause to another. If another choice was made and if the explanation did not stop at the reasons attributed selectively to the actor, his reasons would no longer be independent variables and would become intermediate variables in any sequence of research. And this is the point where *Homo Œconomicus* and *Homo Sociologicus* can enter into discussion. The independent variables of economic thinking can be considered intermediate variables in the sociological perspective. Individual preference are the product of social processes; they can be skilfully induced by marketing techniques, some of them reminiscent of those described by Emile Zola in *Au bonheur des dames*. Even the very trivial example of the cake versus the cup of tea acquires more complexity. The actor is reasonably entitled to an additional cup of tea but his longing for tea is not to be taken for granted. The preferences have always to be accounted for. In extreme situations, some individuals have astonishingly relinquished badly needed food since they were craving a cigarette. An urge to engage in a particular activity can always be translated into reasons. But there should be something behind the reasons, something contributing to explain them. That 'something' could be predefined norms of understandable behaviour. Or it could be a whole process of socialization involving a variety of 'significant others' and a variety of means of influence. It is what Bourdieu called *habitus*. For sociologists and for economists alike, attributing a decisive role to socialization and/or to social norms means that the behaviour under scrutiny would fall outside the scope of rational behaviour as it is usually defined. The notion of rationality would lose part of its fruitfulness but one could still relate on a postulate of coherence.

The analytical process of rational understanding deriving from the Weberian *Verstehen* presupposes a continuity between common-sense knowledge and scientific knowledge, the latter being derived from the first, which is: derived from common experience. And here both economists and sociologists are on shaky ground although they do not often realize it. However, *Homo Œconomicus*, being a doer, seems more inclined to adhere to common-sense assumptions than his dreamy colleague, *Homo Sociologicus*. In South Africa, under apartheid, mineworkers lived away from their families for most of the year, in hostels reminiscent of barracks that lacked the conveniences deemed indispensable nowadays. They had very few pastimes except for alcohol and women. Later on, in the post-apartheid era, thanks to the action of the trade unions, these workers were paid 'living out allowances' enabling them to rent more comfortable accommodation. The common-sense assumption was that they would make use of this opportunity to let their families join them. From an economic point of view, this was indeed a reasonable option: to invest the bonus, as was expected, in 'decent housing' and a normal family life. But the allowance became 'a case study in unintended consequences'. The great majority of the mineworkers considered the allowance as just a salary rise. They moved from the hostels 'into cheap shacks', sent a little extra home but used the rest in an apparent selfish way 'to defray the costs of a girlfriend'.[15] A sociologist trained to take cultural differences into account would probably have been more prudent in his expectations. He would have realized that the allowance was coming too late. The apartheid system had already perturbed the life of those workers and they had adjusted to their particular conditions in their own way.

Towards An Integrated Approach?

Some social scientists, including economists and sociologists, are eager to look for an integrated approach of social life in all its aspects. Others are reluctant to move in this direction since they fear missing the specificity of their own disciplinary viewpoint. In the practice of research, however, each discipline studies human behaviour in a particular perspective and sets itself a limit to its explanatory possibilities. Beyond this limit, any cognitive problem is passed to other disciplines: neurosciences are currently likely candidates for the reception of the 'hot potato'. As far as economic explanations are concerned, their limits have long been defined rather precisely. They seem to rest on two methodological artifices: the first is the presupposition of optimization of the balance cost-benefits, the second is the distinction between variables and given conditions to be taken as such. Roughly speaking, the given facts of economic analysis were traditionally seen as the pattern of consumers' needs, the volume of natural resources, the social and juridical organization and the state of technical knowledge. At the moment, however, it becomes difficult to consider all these categories as just 'given' and there is truly a 'displacement of the borders' in this respect. The natural resources are scarce and increasingly taken as a commodity, consumers' needs are manipulated – even created – by the supply side, even in the field of health, the social and juridical organization is at stake in the ongoing debate between advocates and adversaries of economic regulations; finally, there is a greater awareness of the relevance of education systems in the orientation of technical development. It is widely understood that the state of technical knowledge is not just a given fact but a function of the nature and scale of the investment in education. Given the built-in tendency to relativism in sociological thinking, this shift in the data of economic analysis is a boon for sociologists. The intervention of sociological research could become useful – even welcome – not only on the methodological presupposition of the economic science but also on the heterogeneous data of economic analysis. This is certainly not to suggest that it should be tampered with economic models to make room for a sociological narrative. These models would lose a great deal of their operational value in the process. If we want *Homo Œconomicus* and *Homo Sociologicus* to cooperate successfully, sociological analysis should make itself instrumental in narrowing the sphere of application of each of these models. In other words, sociologists could suggest additional variables where everything has seemed to be taken for granted so far.

24 SOCIAL SCIENCES IN FRONT OF 'BROAD QUESTIONS'

Jean Pierre Gaudin

Introduction

Interdisciplinarity is an intricate question, involving at the same time scientific concern and societal rules. On one hand, it has to do with structures of scientific knowledge and with the multiple aspects of cumulative learning.[1] But interdisciplinarity also faces the ranking of universities and research centres, assessment of results, pertinence of academic specializations and norms ... And if we consider the whole set of scientific disciplines, today we get a very wide range, from exact sciences to social sciences. Even if restricted to social sciences, the scope is still rather wide. Because of the inherent complexity of society itself, it is always a challenge to give a place across academic disciplines to the relationships between various factors and explanations. So the issue with interdisciplinarity in social sciences is to go beyond reductionism and to cope with interactions between elements or dynamics. And at the same time to face new transversal questions emerging and challenging the classical disciplines and division of knowledge: as for example in the near past, in biochemistry or biomedical science in technical sciences, and in environment, urban affairs or international development in social sciences.

In institutional academic terms, interdisciplinarity is a rather new issue. The first introduction of interdisciplinary university learning programmes in the US, for example, was quickly accompanied by new academic organizations.[2] Some international organizations and specific research institutes (New Texas, Arizona) followed during the 2000s. But many obstacles arose, professional (disciplined scholarly journals are still giving academic legitimacy) as well as cultural or organizational ones (especially when there are budgetary retractions as channel resources are organized by disciplines). The attempt of interdisciplinarity to become an academic discipline was also often considered as a battle against established disciplines.

From a critical point of view, it is true that interdisciplinarity may present risks such as forgetting central disciplinary paradigms, and avoiding confrontations with one's peers or challenging the intellectual core of each science discipline.[3] But is it not a 'nostalgic' and conservative position? In favour of interdisciplinarity, on the contrary, it can be argued that if the approach is sometimes risky ... it also opens strongly to broad perspectives and synthesis approaches. Interdisciplinarity may facilitate the study of subjects with large social coherence (environment, social care, climate and so on) that cannot be understood from a single disciplinary perspective. It may also be a heuristic mean to develop comparatist perspectives, in order to analyse the impact of similarities and differences within various contexts. More than this, it is a way to analyse the history and development of disciplines, i.e. to follow circulation of intellectual references, and to study conditions for transfers of concepts from one discipline field to another. This is a kind of epistemological approach of interdisciplinarity, attentive not only to a theory of knowledge but also to different steps of research history and to plurality of sciences.

This kind of debate between advantage and inconvenience is not really new. In the past, bridges between knowledges were already tried through new disciplines or federations of disciplines. For example, two global labels have been competing from the end of the nineteenth to the beginning of the twentieth centuries to design new research fields: *Social Science* (singular) and social sciences (plurality). In fact, one can observe various names and forms, confronting one author to another, or one country to another, with hesitant uses. The singular label seems to be initially preferred, in relation to social philosophy. And the plural label has been more readily adopted by Anglo-Saxon pragmatism. But there are exceptions. The plural label is in the title of a survey book published for the International Exhibition of Paris in 1937. On the contrary, the SSRC (Social Science Research Council), founded in 1923 in the US for interdisciplinary purposes, still uses the singular in its name.

But words (alone) do not create reality. From a sociological point of view we prefer a semantic and historical rather than a nominalist approach: behind labels, the use of singular (THE Social Science) may be taken as a regret for unity of knowledge. From Renaissance humanism to A Comte evolutionism, the hope existed for a synthesis of human knowledge that could embrace all aspects of experience, from liberal arts to mathematics, from philosophy to the techniques of engineers. But let us be realistic. Science is now divided in specific fields of various development and at the same time is a shared social issue mainly connected with technics and economic development in every country. Interdisciplinarity, multi-discipline, trans-disciplinarity: these are now more and more official attempts to define new spaces confronting classical discipline barriers (such as higher education programmes, scholar journals and research assessments).

Today, interdisciplinarity is a fight against growing divisions of knowledge into academic disciplines ... which still react, resist and try to recolonize the emerging fields of learning. In this essay, I shall also argue that interdisciplinarity has to do with the way knowledge is elaborated within society.

So in this chapter, we shall first consider how interdisciplinarity takes place in a long-term strategic game between social sciences disciplines: which one will 'govern' the others, be the referent, spread the dominant paradigma, try to be a kind of social science of its own (see pp. 331–3).

But, nowadays (after 1970), there have been growing official incentives to mobilize and federate different disciplines in front of 'broad questions' within society, with an emphasizing social demand for 'problem-focused research'. But does this new 'interdisciplinarity' only mean a kind of domination by funding? (See pp. 333–4.)

Or will it give also way to new intellectual perspectives? We shall propose a shade answer in this essay, considering two contrasted 'broad questions' that emerged across disciplinarity: the cases of the *Sustainable Urban Development programme* in France and of the European Union *Multilevel Governance* researches (see pp. 335–41).

Interdisciplinarity and Academic Competition

To be at the centre of social sciences, to be THE Social Science, as a synthesis or as a central paradigm, has been a periodic dream affecting one discipline or another. But may we say there is a constant strategy linking intellectual unity and academic domination at the same time? Interdisciplinarity itself might be understood as an attempt to keep the unity of disciplines through one 'general' unified knowledge or by reunification of previously separated disciplines. In all cases, it is supposed to be the end of 'inter-' or of 'multi-' and the assumption of a transversal and global way of thinking and analysing. But it may be also a strategy of hegemony from one discipline over the others, in order to control funding as well as values and social norms in the academic field.

In the past of academic institutionalization, there have been such historic battlefields initiated by one discipline: law and the sustainable social role of lawyers in Germany, or regional geography (P. Vidal de la Blache) allied with colonial expansion in order to confront first construction of sociology in France (E. Durkheim). An interdisciplinary necessity was then claimed but from a point of view controlled by one discipline. So intellectual pride was often mixed with domination strategy at the very moment when the university institution was structured by main national states in different countries of Europe. These attempts came after former endeavours of the early nineteenth century (A. Comte, trying to elaborate a general theory on historical evolutions of society;

or F. Le Play, willing to build a global knowledge on popular ways of life). This was more an emergence of trans-disciplinarity than interdisciplinarity. But we should not forget the initial endeavour of what were called in ancient times philosophy and theology, as global knowledge embraces also psychological, social, natural and physical aspects. Neither history, considered over centuries as a global understanding of societies and powers structures. Or, more recently, statistics and probabilities being a common basis to near all social behaviours, such as demography, psychology, marketing, political ballots, security, acceptability analysis and so on. And today, within this kind of path dependency, the 'queen discipline' seems now to be economy, influencing all the others, diffusing its paradigma as a new trans-disciplinarity ...

But economy as an influent way of thinking is not quite new. France, for example, is not only a delightful country of theoretical schools that the US cherish so much, like structuralism, marxism, psychoanalysis, semiotics, structuralism, stimulating trans-disciplinarity or even transversal knowledge. During the period 1970–90, we noticed also the launching of a very pragmatic, so-called 'socio-economical' approach, as a kind of interdiscipline bridging various knowledges, in order to officially favour more 'reasoned public decisions'. Socio-economy targeted a wedding between economy, psychology and sociology, under the statist blessing of planist administration. Many government research programmes then operated by technical administrations (such as transports, health or culture departments) and planning agencies have consequently sustained the organization of specific new scholar teams in this field. They were gathered under the leadership of economists or sociologists, generally speaking young academics (without tenure or private advisers) at the margin of the university or the French National Centre for Research. The issue of these socio-economic interdisciplinary programmes consisted of more applied research and a growing dialogue with policymakers, in order to 'resolve conflicts' and contribute to the education of 'informed' leaders and citizens.

Nowadays, a new point has been reached. Economy as a whole appears as a new total knowledge. It governs decisions, and is today the main political and social subject, the true heart of international relationships. But, also within the academic field, an international diffusion of microeconomic paradigm into a very large set of social sciences (sociology, political science, history, geography, psychology, archeology, anthropology, ...) is noticeable. Economy is not only the main concern in present society, it is the imperial way to think of social relations. And this centrality, some say hegemony, depends in fact on worldwide diffused concepts that are very coherent with individualism and utilitarism. Among these concepts, let us think of the impact through a large set of other disciplines of, for example, decision theory, rational choice, games theory, or principal/agent contract asymetry ... Present standard economy becomes a kind of trans-disciplinarity reference, offers bridges between disciplines, works for a kind of multidiscipline built around its paradigm. Such a theorical pregnancy is linked with neo-liberal explanations of global market rationality, international trade regulation, bankable activities, and so on. It is an expression of the 'Empire', as a paradigma theorized by Negri and Hardt.[4]

Market economy as a rational and as a public management does not only become a new trans-disciplinary academic reference. It has impact on academic policy. For at the same time it suggests more and more cost/benefit rationality as a good allocation of public fundings for university research. Grants, research funds and programmes are benchmarked according to rankings based on reputation and 'research products' assessments. Evaluation of research is part of an economic approach of return on public and private spending in this field. So, with economy today as with philosophy or law in the past, could we assert that domination is the real face of trans-disciplinarity or interdisciplinarity?

Interdisciplinarity and Emergence of 'Broad Questions'

Interdisciplinary and trans-disciplinary academic institutions may be seen as a new trend emerging during the 1970s. In fact, there were previous attempts. But they used to be generally initiated by one discipline trying to gather and control other disciplines (see pp. 331–3). In the 1970s, the interdisciplinary purpose seems to become less hegemonic and more federative. But beginnings are difficult in front of academic barriers. Some international organizations are founded to increase visibility, for example the International Network of Inter and Trans-Disciplinarity; some research institutes are specifically devoted to the theory and practice of interdisciplinarity.[5]

Why this trend during this period? Was it for scholars the discovery of a new knowledge synthesis or a fresh way to avoid duress of 'disciplinary discipline'? In fact, this trend may be seen as a component of a constant search for interdisciplinarity, but with a focus on the post-war period. This is a consequence of 'problem-focused researches', depending on public funds and demands from the policymakers which were managing a growing Social State and wishing more 'reasoned decision'. For it is true that government actors usually don't care very much about disciplines, specializations and academic organization. And they prefer to get a quick overview on a breaking issue rather than a deeper but narrower one and to wait for segmented analysis. These reasons make sense in a certain way. But let's not forget the role of emerging new 'large' questions, supplied by industrialization spread, social state and urbanization after World War II and with huge developments in Europe. So it was a time when environmental challenges, urban planning and transport management or health issues, in particular, became more and more prominent on the public policy agenda.[6]

In fact, not every European country has been so statist as France, with its economic national planning and its public agencies monopolizing research funding (CNRS with its interdisciplinary *Recherches Coopératives sur Programmes* of the 1970s about 'questions de société', and the *Délégation Générale Recherche Scientifique et Technique* with its 'socio-economic research'). But, early on, many of them developed focused research programmes, and not only about military questions. The main purpose was to accompany economic growth with social and economic researches. Then, in a second step, the involvement of public authorities within governance of scientific research tends to be mainly influenced by another priority, facing public funding retrenchments, then financial crisis: the quick return on (research) funds became more and more the issue. At the same time, neo-liberal ideas pleaded in favour of market-oriented public priorities. From that time, focused research has been amplified and funding connected to economic competition and innovation, with a growing contrast between financing of higher education still allocated on a discipline basis, and research funds distributed through focused calls and growing interdisciplinary programmes (at national as well as European levels, see Frame Programmes of Development Research, p. 340).

But there was not only a shift in terms of public financing. The recent interdisciplinary turn also had to do with interest for new 'broad questions' linked to emerging public policies. Sooner, in the context of first town planning attempts for example, some scholars, like P. Geddes or M. Poete at the beginning of the twentieth century, thought of analysing growing cities as global 'organisms'. So they tried to transfer such biological notions, in order to conceptualize the growth of urban settlements and define the 'laws' of cities' evolution. It was mainly elaborated on a metaphoric basis but it helped anyhow to refresh classical historic analysis of city expansion and to consider planning in a more dynamic way.

Interdisciplinary transfers try nowadays to renew questions or to challenge very broad subjects, especially those facing information from multiple fields. Broad questions can be defined as mobilizing a plurality of disciplines and/ or involving a set of public policies. The issue is how to synthesize broad perspectives. How do we account for the interactions between phenomena and interconnections between social processes? How do we formalize 'complexity' beyond empirical observations? One may argue all this is more an epistemologic than an interdisciplinarity scope preparing 'reasoned decisions'. But nowadays, these two purposes are in fact often imbricated. After cities or socio-economic development, climate changes, health risks and sustainable development are the main subjects presently able to closely mix these two scopes. In such a context of demand and of epistemic evolutions, are academic disciplines going to compete or to cooperate together, that is to say to help transfers from one field to another, to find bridges, or not?

Interdisciplinarity, Social Sciences and Complexity

In order to have a precise understanding of what is presently at stake with interdisciplinarity, we shall consider how broad questions have been recently put on research agenda through public incentives. We shall compare two different cases of interdisciplinary programmes initiated by institutions and concentrate on the social sciences field because we assume society is for scholars one of the best examples of complexity: impossible to reduce to one dimension of explanation, but difficult to study in a synthetic view without confronting the epistemic difficulties of interdisciplinarity. So, social sciences could be seen above all as sciences of complexity. But what kind of bridges between knowledges does this imply, and according to which synthetic theory, or with what kind of methodological choices, in order not to be too reductionist?

The two cases that we are going to compare take place during the same period at the end of the twentieth century, when incitement to interdisciplinarity was growing and wishes for 'reasoned decisions' became more intense. But they differ in terms of institutional support, period of effectiveness and consequences. They are not 'representative' in a statistic way, of course, but express the role of contexts as well as the impact of the theoretical construction issue.

The 'Sustainable Urban Development' (SUD) Research Programme in France

At the start of the 2000s, 'sustainable development' was confirmed as an important theme on the international public policy agenda. After the Brundland's report (1987) and some UN conferences it becomes a global 'public problem', with large rhetorical government concern in every developed country. In 2003, according to this *Zeitgeist*, the French government started a large interdisciplinary academic programme under the co-responsibility of the Ministry of Research and CNRS, and in financing partnership with some other ministries (environment, housing, town-planning and public transport, amongst others). This programme has been scheduled for four years, and includes national calls for research proposals launched each year. As a whole, roughly sixty projects have been selected and achieved. The general purpose is to analyse various cases, at local, national and international levels, of experiments as well as theorizations of what could be targeted as 'Sustainable Urban Development' (SUD). Each team was supposed to be composed of scholars of two or more different disciplines and to answer the call on an interdisciplinary basis.

What was the SUD research programme's initial concern? It was officially said to be the transfer and application at the urbanization development level of the general 'doctrine' of sustainability: to leave to other generations a legacy as good as we had. This supposes at the same time less polluting economic activity, ecology protection without absolutism, and also care for 'social justice' and 'citizen participation'. But everyone knows putting together these three kind of norms is a very difficult issue. And we may see it is a complex stake too for professionals and policymakers, because these three pillars of sustainability, if they should cooperate, are also going to compete in terms of professional routines, political struggles and social interests. In order not to be too reductionist or idealist, how to think of these pillars without being linked together by numerous retroactions, locks and monitoring bias? And how do we take care and synthesize the multiple aspects of sustainability, across barriers of knowledge and differentiated disciplines fields without an interdisciplinary framework? Of course, interdisciplinarity was here a requisite. Such incitement was given by the SUD research programme in different ways: combination of long- and short-term analysis (through, for example, a disciplinary mix of history, geography, political science or economy); combination of actors and institutions factors (through sociology and psychology); combination of interests and values analysis (through cooperation between economy, philosophy, sociology, and so on).

The SUD programme was of course more oriented towards interdisciplinary studies (i.e. subjects with large coherence that cannot be understood from a single disciplinary perspective) rather than studies of interdisciplinarity (nature and history of disciplines, self-consciousness questions about how interdisciplinarity works). But in fact it had to cope with these two kinds of challenges and difficulties at the same time, with limited success.

On one hand, interdisciplinarity or multi-disciplinarity in practice was not easy to promote and to organize at that time. Interdisciplinary labs or teams were not numerous in France at this point. It was also not easy to mobilize or create teams in this kind of field involving at the same time many social sciences and also some technical and engineers sciences. In fact, it was noticed that many multidisciplinary teams were formed especially to answer the SUD programme calls, without much previous experience of such collaborative work. And it happened that the range of interdisciplinarity was often limited to two or three closely neighbouring disciplines only. So barriers to interdisciplinarity lie in professional specializations and existing disciplinary assessments, and in the organization of labs and universities, generally speaking in rooted cultural habits. It also became obvious that to build a new scholar and research environment a much longer time than four or five years was necessary. An interdisciplinarity policy needs a persevering will, a lot of collective learning processes and long-lasting financial incentives, in fact huge means that were not available in this programme.

On the other hand, one could observe a cross combined effect between terms of the research calls, finally issued from negotiations between the different funding actors (less academic than technical ministries), and the improvised ad-hoc composition of answering research teams. It drove projects and selected researches towards rather operational feelings and technical concerns. Away from epistemic and theoretical questions, the financed research generally focused on decision-friendly aspects and on professional stakes. That is why many researches financed and diffused by the SUD programme so often targeted new participation in town planning, energy saving within the housing sector or transport, and environmental protection itself. So, despite their specific interesting results, they inherited and more confirmed the sectorial public policies questions and approaches (until definition of 'best practices' or prescriptions) than work on the borderlines of classical policies as well as of organized disciplines.

Therefore SUD research perspectives was deeply involved with complexity, according to its very broad field of concern and its supposed interactions between three dimensions, economic, ecological and social. In order to enlighten and explain effective complex processes through this incentive programme, some very important investigation perspectives should have not been so much kept aside, mainly:

(a) Analysing loops and retroaction systems between the three 'official' sustainable development priorities. How may economy, ecology and social justice interact? Precisely what is 'social justice', fund redistribution or citizen participation? And how may public policy decisions be analysed in a realistic way through 'uncertainty analysis'?[7]

(b) Combining quantitative (ecological or economic factors, for example) and qualitative (political, for example) formalizations and explanations. Researches formalizing 'agent-based models' have brought some answers, especially in analysing planning and environment policies (owing to sets of 'participative boxes'). Can 'acceptability analysis' be of the same interest? This last perspective is mostly interesting but difficult to manage: how do we not reduce interactions and negotiations processes to psychological dimensions, that is to say, how do we avoid micro-politics by reintroducing society at large within reflexivity and participation models?

(c) In trying to link more structures and actors, how do we go beyond bottom-up classical micro-macro analysis (very present in physics and biology)? Micro (or local) levels are not necessarily the basis of macro (or global) ones in social analysis. Things may structure interactively without a previous hierarchy of levels. Regarding society problems, agenda and public policies, for example, how do we pay more attention to go-between scaffoldings and 'meso' organizational and institutional levels? Are there kinds of 'multilevel analysis' that may take in account the diversity of continuous retroactions between macro and micro without the kind of 'bottom-up fundamentalism' we often meet in interdisciplinarity? And may a kind of 'complex theory' help to formalize systemic retroactions (positive and negative) within society problems and politics?

European Union and the Multilevel Governance

The same kind of questions are on the research agenda regarding another subject we shall now consider, the building and development of the European Union (EU) during the last fifty years. But we shall argue that these questions get better interdisciplinary answers than in the case we introduced before (the SUD programme).

As One Considers the European Union, the First (and Apparently Basic) Question to Begin with is: What is it Really and How do We Define it?

But it is not so easy to answer, even for specialists! The EU appears mainly as a long process and an uncertain construction, which challenges classical categories, especially those of international jurists and legal experts. Since 1957, even more, the dimensions of EU have broadened considerably, from six to twenty-eight state members. And its political powers and decision processes have changed a lot. Today, one may consider it as not really a super state, neither a federation nor an international organization. There is, therefore, still a juridical and political controversy. It is generally said to be a *sui generis* construction, and clearly a hybrid between all these categories. But the important issue, indeed, is not names or classifications but the reality behind it. Presently it is obvious that the identity of EU is still much debated and, even without periodic crisis, the processes of its development is not easy to formalize and to understand.

Empirical facts to remember are, on the contrary, rather easy to summarize. During the first steps of the initial treaties, relationships were mainly organized between two nodes of actors, the State members and the EU bodies (Commission, Parliament). After successive enlargements and further treaties (Unique Act 1988; Maastricht treaty 1992), new interaction actors and levels have been dramatically multiplied around the former ones. They are mainly citizens forums or NGOs groups, as well as corporations lobbies and business networks, and also European Regions (with a representation institutionalized in a specific assembly). So, the general feeling now is that what has to be explored and explained is mainly networks of coordinations and interdependences between these actors all through EU. We shall see this perspective is, for Europe, both a way to explain how it really works and to legitimize itself as a specific political and institutional system.

EU Funding (Research Programmes, Grants, Universities) and the 'Governance Turn'

A first rendezvous between scholars and EU institutions took place in the context of growing interest for the idea of governance during the 1990s and the beginning of the 2000s. The research publications on the governance idea (at large) then focused on coordination processes, especially coordinations through social networks and also through institutionalization of cooperations between public policy levels. So this pluralistic paradigm of governance was also supposed to lighten up the role of private sector policymakers in Europe and of generalized negotiation processes between public and private. Such a view on EU-negotiated decision has been explored through three main rationales, covering relationships between EU institutions but also its regions, European programmes and private actors (business and social).

First, 'Governance in the EU'[8] analysed horizontal networks within EU public policy involving mainly business actors. A parallel analysis by R. Mayntz insisted further on negotiation networks regarding NGOs and 'civil society'.

Second, the concept of 'regulatory state'[9] was developed to formalize production of public rules on market competition within a neo-liberal context. The EU might appear as a good example of this policy regulation style, and trying at the same time to get more legitimacy through agencies efficiency. Benz and Eberlein[10] added to this the study of regulation sets between different levels, European, national, regional, in a large problematic confronting decentralization (*subsidiarity* principle) and recentralization processes (role of European Councils) within the EU.

Third, the scaling dimension of those evolutions was more elaborated by the notion of 'multilevel governance'.[11] Mainly from 1993 to 2003, they formalized the EU core as a system of interdependencies and compromises without any steady rule of governing (type principal/agent) of one level on the others. Operating at different scales, motors of the multilevel governance appeared to be mainly the Open Coordination Method (set for example by EU for social policy, water resource management, health and climate issues), and the cross monitoring of structural funds by national and regional levels together. Their analysis shows that if sub-national power stays modest within institutional design of a majority of unitary States in Europe, the regional bodies get more and more territorial initiative through the negotiated monitoring of European rules and funds.

Those three rationales that are trying to understand EU integration and at the same time sketching an original institutional design, more sophisticated than a *sui generis* one, are not a pure accident or good luck. They are in fact linked with a kind of 'academic policy' the EU has set during this same period. For those research rationales have to be set into a context of incentives and facilitating factors.

Created in 1976 by six countries, then enlarged afterwards to twenty through co-financing, the European University Institute of Florence has become more influent after 1990 owing to its Robert Schuman Centre for Advanced Studies. Operating through 'Jean Monnet grants', visiting professors, research projects, scholar publishing and chairs, it had a large impact and orientation on academic activities with European concern. F. Scharpf, G. Majone, P. Schmitter and

S. Bartolini, who have all published much in English about European governance, have belonged to its academic staff.[12]

On the other hand, the EU has created and funded an Atlantic Network
of Universities after 1998 with the US, in order to stimulate research on European matters. The project was sustained by Sciences Po and by the Max Planck
Institute. But the head of this network has always been University of North
Carolina. This was also the university of G. Marks and L. Hooghe, as they built
the concept of European multilevel governance (before coming afterwards to
Amsterdam University)!

Finally, one has to think of a third very important mean of EU academic
policy, the Frame Programmes of Research Development, especially the sixth
(2002) and the seventh (2007) ones, which had a specific focus on European
governance. They deal with non-public actors in local governance, citizens and
businessmen. A lot of money on each project is supposed to help building interdisciplinary and international teams on subjects and rationales considered as
pertinent by juries where academics are mixed with EU policymakers (and decisions taken by the last ones).

So European governance is a scholarly interdisciplinary construction, involving sociology, economy and political science, which has been rather encouraged
and piloted. Anyway, European integration has become more explicit owing to
such interdisciplinary studies. Behind the episodic political and economical crisis, very sudden compromises and finally a surprising European resilience, it has
been possible to understand something more consistent than the mediatic scene
and the usual quarrels about diplomacy show offs. In terms of regulation and
multilevel governance, EU resilience appeared to lie deeply within an important
role of actor-oriented networks and in flexibility of norms, directly linking the
EU and regions with positive retroactions on states relations. Between regions
and EU, states level becomes a kind of meso level. This can be observed especially
in the multilevel monitoring of structural funds, programming massive European investments every seven years (and, complementarily, through EU-specific
programmes connecting different territorial scales). The so-called 'periphery'
of the regions therefore appears full of mediations and initiatives. It appears to
be a key lobby to promote and mobilize euro funding through networking and
mediation between the EU and local bodies. It becomes also an ally for the EU
in funds negotiations with member states and sometimes an ally for the states in
norms negotiations with the EU.

Shifting the EU Understanding towards Public Policy Analysis

So the EU today appears easier to understand through public policy analysis,
including mainly regulatory state and multilevel governance theory, than in the
traditional legal one trapped in administrative and political institutions. This
is the output of a progressively interdisciplinary approach, mainly combining

political science, economy and sociology in its developments for fifty years. Cross-fertilization came from circulation of notions and analysis. For example, the initial 'public problem' approach was enriched by political-agenda-setting sociology; 'decision taking' was revisited by bounded rationality theory of economists and sociologists; studies of 'policy monitoring' were much deepened by analysis of political mobilizations; and 'evaluation' methods of public policies were re-examined by the political theory of legitimacy.

Regarding the EU integration process and present dynamic, an important contribution has been the concept of multilevel governance, in order to formalize scale interdependencies which link the monitoring of European policies without a linear top-down hierarchy. In many scholarly approaches (and not only from lawyers) the hierarchical paradigm is still very much present, as it is in collective imaginary, even if it was then not entirely new in the social sciences field. For relations between national state and local authorities had already been analysed in a systemic way by sociologists and political scientists. Especially in France, despite a long statist and centralist tradition, it had been possible to characterize political and administrative interactions centre/periphery as a non-hierarchical scheme. Soon before French decentralization, Worms,[13] then Grémion with its 'pouvoir périphérique'[14] and Thoenig argued for the important role of cross regulations and systemic regulations between the French centre (state administrations) and its 'periphery' (local elected authorities) where each one depends on the other for practical and symbolic resources. Centralism appeared to be in fact a 'système politico-administratif local', full of retroactions and cross-regulations complicating legal hierarchies. They engaged their field studies with help from concepts of 'organization sociology', such as information, uncertainty, and the relation between the organization and its environment. These concepts were transferred from initial researches about business decisions based on the general paradigm of 'bounded rationality (Simon, March, Olsen, Crozier). So it was already in that period a good example of a cross-discipline approach with transfers of notions and cooperations between scholars in different research fields.

Conclusion

Social sciences is today a very large field of knowledge with growing specializations, far from the global knowledge dreamed or experienced in the past. This produces segmentation of researches and barriers between disciplines. The problem is getting more accurate, with policymakers' demands to answer more and more mediatic broad questions. There is a need for breaking partitions of knowledge and gaining a better understanding of interactions between processes. Considering social sciences at large, should we better speak now of a need for interdisciplinarity or for a general systemic theory?

More than a hope for a synthesis of social sciences, it seems important to look for bridging knowledges and researches. System theory and analysis may be in practice, as we have seen with EU integration, a hyper-language, or a bridge, to connect the different dimensions of society; i.e. formalize transversal inter-dependencies and retroactions linking different actors and levels. And positive and negative loops may allow us to characterize changes of a social system within its environment. In order to focus on dynamics of systems, a future perspective on cross-disciplinary analysis could rely, then, on a complexity approach, where network of components, through their interactions, transform the network in a continuous way.

25 SOCIOLOGY: AN INFIRM SCIENCE?

Giovanni Busino

By Way of Introduction

A discipline with mythical origins, an almost legendary genesis, with indefinite and undefinable boundaries, with uncertain and controversial results, sociology has always claimed for itself the right to be the science of society, the only scientific discipline entrusted with the study of the entire set of intersubjective relationships and the magnetic field they constitute.

The term sociology was first used in 1838 by Auguste Comte with the intention of designating 'the science of the observation of social phenomena'. Since then, the term has been used to characterize empirical analyses and theories having social facts as their object, or all types and species of intersubjective relationships.

Now, the term sociology has two connotations-denotations. The first refer to the systematic study of the laws governing the social entirety in all its complexity; the second covers the analytical study of social groups and phenomena, which allows the formulation of general statements.

Both systematic study and analytical study are usually founded on assertions of a philosophical nature which we think to dodge by using various subterfuges, the most important of which is, still today, formalization. Sociology aspires to solve social problems. Its conceptual options give us the vocabulary to present such problems as well as the tools to solve them. The first and most fundamental of its options is this: the raison d'être of a society is not found in an exterior reality. It is the result of human interactions. Consequently, any social phenomenon can and must be explained as the product of these same interactions. This is also true for social order, for institutions and for tradition. Of course, the rhythms of development and historical heritage impose fragmented and discordant explanations at present. However, that cannot last for long.[1]

At the 'Probable' Origins of the Discipline

Sociology made its appearance at the moment in which the societies of the old order were in jeopardy. At the outset, it aspired to giving an account of modernity, to explain the emergence of new social relationships, as well as the functioning of societies and their social evolution. It also wanted to create the conditions for establishing a rational social life, namely, to shape the emerging social world, to endow it with efficient, harmonious and enlightened institutions, in short, with a stable and sure moral authority.

The proto-sociologists considered themselves authentic scholars but also social reformers, prophets of the 'true social order'. Thus, from the beginning of its history, sociology manifested a strong ambivalence: science and prophecy, empiricism and reform. Such a situation forced the sociologists to question themselves as to the 'scientificity' of the discipline, on its epistemological autonomy, on its independence and on its singularity with regard to other fields of research, notably that of philosophy.

In the new society, with former balances ruined, with destabilized living and working conditions, with social rapports and practices overturned by the technological changes arising from the Industrial Revolution – in this society appeared new value systems and new forms of organization that soon provoked questions and perplexities.

In *L'Esprit des Lois*[2] Montesquieu worked out a synthetic interpretation of society. It would be governed by 'climate, religion, laws, maxims of government, examples from the past, mores, manners; from which is formed a general spirit resulting from it'.[3] Adam Ferguson (1723–1801) in *The Origin of the Distinction of Rank*[4] states that society is an integral part of the natural world. It can thus be explained in terms of causal and hypothetical-deductive relationships.

Beginning with phenomena such as the family, the group, self interest, authority, etc., Ferguson induced the existence of natural laws governing society. The dependence of the individual on the group, the social functions of conflict, the role of property, social stratification, functional differentiation, division of labour and anomy were described and explained using the laws of mechanics.[5] As for Millar, he discovered a functional interdependence between commerce, industry and political, juridical and military institutions. Technological, economic and environmental determinisms led him to manipulate factorial analysis, to hunt down social causality, to seek the 'univocal' relation between rapports of property and the various forms of power.[6]

All these approaches were an open break with philosophy. What this latter discipline had said on society, in ethics (or in the philosophy of practice) and in politics was now obliterated. The 'new scholars', those 'social scientists', believed they could explain better than the philosophers the changes engendered by industrial society, foresee the transformations and control the implications and consequences. They were certain that they could finally give modern man a truly scientific doctrine of social life. Such a claim was soon attacked by the traditional disciplines and in a particularly radical way by philosophy,[7] which easily showed the specious sides of the reasonings of sociologists, the fragility of their theoretical constructions, the logical and practical difficulties found by social studies to rise to the level of formal or experimental sciences.

We know the answer of the sociologists: there is a specificity of the 'social' that renders the sociological process irreducible to that of other disciplines. Now, this specificity is the result of a series of interferences and of contaminations, analogies, metaphors and borrowings from the 'concrete' sciences. If geology, for example, has furnished models for social stratification, botany and zoology, the systems of classification, it is nonetheless physics that has for a long time given us the essential of our paradigms.

The Mechanists Model

The extraordinary progress made in the seventeenth century by physics and mathematics (Newton, Galileo, Copernicus, Leibnitz, Pascal, Kepler, Bacon and others) encouraged researchers in human sciences to consider social phenomena as the equivalents of physical phenomena explained by mechanics. Hobbes or Spinoza, Descartes or Leibnitz no longer approached the study of man and society in terms of teleology, teleonomy, morals or hierarchy. They tried to discover the laws governing the functioning and production of social data. Society was a machine, an automaton, and had to be studied with tools perfected by physics and, more precisely, mechanics, the properties brought to light by statics, kinematics and dynamics also being at work in society. The law of universal attraction governs individuals and society, and there is a sociological weight similar to physical weight.

This approach allowed the study of social phenomena as systems of relationships between connected elements, whose rapports can be measured and transcribed into mathematical terms. Only this latter science would be appropriate to guarantee analyses and coherence of sociological syntheses, thus elevating them to the dignity of a 'true science'.

Sociology, conceived thereafter as social mechanics, would thus borrow all its theoretic constructions and part of its conceptual schema from the physicists. Naturally, in most cases it made a more or less metaphorical use of them, but the supreme reference remained physics and methodology. The most classic example, relative to space, is that in which all movements must be verified. Let us also take the idea of status (the situation of the individual, a group, their level in society, the roles that fall to them, their social functions); it is the exact copy of the notion of position in physical space. The system of reference (abscissa, ordinate) made a correspondence with a system of social coordinates (sex, age, occupation) determining the position of individuals and groups in society.[8] In mechanics, movement is explained through inertia and gravitation. In sociology, all social processes are clarified beginning with the same principles that then become social attraction and social repulsion. In mechanics they are a function of time and space. This is why sociologists place *status* in social space and time. The *graphs* would then illustrate the social processes. Even individual biographies would be represented by means of graphs, as though it were a matter of descending objects. In mechanic physics, equilibrium is an essential property of all systems; in sociology society is only a system of centrifugal and centripetal social forces in equilibrium. Consequently we confide the study of social equilibrium to social statics, the laws of coexistence, while movement, evolution and the laws of succession are the object of social dynamics.

Quantification

The mechanics model forced the proto-sociologists to refer to mathematical formalization and statistical techniques.

William Petty (1623–87), Hermann Conring (1606–82) and Gottfried Achenwald (1719–72) were, with others, the initiators. They applied quantification to all the aspects of social phenomena.[9] Claude-Henri de Saint-Simon (1760–1825) was in this lineage that applied the law of universal gravitation to social phenomena and the mechanics principles of Newton to society.

Saint-Simonism strongly conditioned the later developments of sociological knowledge. Was it not the former secretary of Saint-Simon, Auguste Comte, who proclaimed loud and clear the need to construct 'social physics'? If he gave up this label and opted for the term 'sociology', it was to mark his distance with regard to the social physics of the Belgian astronomer Adolphe Quételet (1796–1874), to his 'bad habit' of probabilities and the law of large numbers to social data, which according to Comte denied man's liberty and freedom of choice.

The adoption of the mechanics model and formalization barely conceals an insoluble difficulty that later developments in sociological efforts never succeeded in eliminating. Sociology believed it had taken on the dignity of science by adopting the processes that had made physics the queen of the sciences. In spite of that, its products appeared as an incongruous medley of practical information and definitively would hardly be more than an art at the service of a prince, a social group or an institution.

Antisociologism

A discipline producing such meager fruit could only awaken the most severe and spiteful criticism. Philosophy did not hide its scorn of the 'infirm science', for the doctrines of 'incurable infirmities'. Literature observed a stubborn and persistent aversion to it and saw in the sociological description of reality a danger for artistic and literary effort, a biased form of competition in shaping the sensitivity and opinion of the public. Beyond scientific projects literature glimpsed an unacceptable ambition in sociology, that of telling the truth about the world, establishing social values and finalities, giving modern society ultimate orientations.

Dickens, Stendhal, Balzac, Flaubert, Zola, Gogol, Pushkin, Dostoyevsky and many others, up to Stefan Georg, Thomas Mann, E. R. Curtius and T. S. Eliot, barely hid their deep hostility to sociology. They claimed the privilege of formulating the 'truth', 'values', 'ends' and 'meaning' of the world for artists alone. Science is powerless; it cannot speak 'true' of society. Writers affirmed that social novels describe society and problems such as socialism, anarchism, poverty, prostitution, the dissolution of mores and so on, better than the 'infirm Science'. From this point of view they expressed the same opinion as Karl Marx and Friedrich Engels.[10]

Thus literature saw itself alone qualified to speak of values, from the moment that sociology succeeded in only exposing its impotence and stray impulses.

This dispute – at times virulent, still quite alive today, and of which Lepenies has scrupulously given the historical account[11] – proved highly prejudicial to the development of sociological knowledge.[12] Among other things, it deprived us of the contribution of cognitive aesthetics and certain modes of knowledge, fragmentary but useful in the logic of discovery.[13]

Moreover, this dispute helped to further enclose us within a rigidly marked territory where we could only work for the defense and consolidation of our professional integrity as scholars, convinced like all the others of the unity of all sciences.

The Organicist Model

The borrowings from mechanics physics are still preponderant today. They have undergone various adjustments, sometimes metamorphoses, but we have never denied or rejected them, in spite of the meager results obtained. The great sociologists were able to 'play around' with them, manipulate them, adapt them, combine them in an ambiguous way, without however going too far from them.[14] On this subject, Pareto's case remains paradigmatic.

The sociologist from Lausanne constantly held physics as the 'queen of the sciences', it alone being able to keep us from the snares of tautology. But he regularly united it to organicism and other epistemological models borrowed from biology.[15] Organicism has fascinated sociologists and continues to have a powerful influence, even when it widely borrows from linguistics and law. In fact, it allows a better treatment of problems posed by immanent forces, such as intentionality and the metamorphosis of the social system, than mechanization. Spencer made it the basis of sociology. Organicism continued to prosper through the different forms of evolutionism[16] and today, thanks to Edward O. Wilson and the doctrines of the 'biocultural revolution'.[17] Organicism has allowed a conception of society as a biological organism, as a relatively closed system, having a preponderant finality: survive and grow. To realize this end, society must adapt to the environment and set up complex strategies so as to produce and reproduce. The various types of societies (hunting and gathering, pastoral, horticultural, agricultural and industrial) correspond to the stages of development of the living organism. Changes are brought about by the natural laws of development. They rarely happen by chance; they are slow, continuous, progressive, linear, necessary and endogenous. Primitive societies are those in which evolution is only beginning or has been blocked. From this come the analogies, even used by Jean Piaget, between children and primitives. Biological analogies allow the identification in primitive societies of growth factors in modern societies, at an earlier stage of their evolution. They are the presuppositions of most of our theories of change, development and modernization. The borrowings from biology have accustomed the sociologist to come to terms with circular logical constructions and to believe that explanation is possible by means of a reduction of complexity. The strength of sociological borrowings from physics and biology has been such that when it was necessary to turn to economics or other disciplines, we have only done so in order to find in them our basic models, coming from physics.

Sociologism

This continual flow of conceptual borrowings, these analogical and metaphorical uses of theoretical constructions worked out within the formal and experimental sciences result in sociology still being a discipline with uncertain boundaries, a nebulous identity and cognitive results that are more or less contestable.

Among the founding fathers (Pareto, Max Weber and Simmel) only Durkheim considered himself exclusively as a sociologist;[18] he alone acted so as to obtain the academic institutionalization of the discipline, to make it completely legitimate as a university science. He was the only founding father to believe that sociology indubitably possessed all the characteristics of an autonomous discipline. He was also the only one to presume the existence of a sociological method. However, Durkheim never succeeded in detaching himself from the charms and ease of the mechanistic and organistic approach, nor to rid himself of the belief that there is no other way in the study of societies than that furnished by rules, procedures and deductive and inductive reasoning through the models of rationality of the physical sciences.[19] In *Les règles de la méthode sociologique* Durkheim does no more than resume the epistemological statements of Henri Poincaré and Ernst Mach. He tells us no more than what physicists were saying at the time.

He gives us no indication on the subject of research procedures proper to sociology. He says and repeats that social data are objects[20] that have nothing to do with psychology.[21] At no point does Durkheim succeed in setting up a truly autonomous theory with regard to economic utilitarianism, biological organicism, Gestalt psychology, the philosophy of the history of Marxism or the preponderant model of physics. They are scientific models, often transformed into very elaborate metaphors, which are the substance of his bookish sociology. Nevertheless, his sociology allowed the establishment of an academic space, a social identity, and created conditions propitious to the birth of the 'profession of sociology'.

The New Sociology

In the early 1940s Talcott Parsons tried to unite all the many epistemological presuppositions and contradictory statements into a unified, unitary and compact social theory. He set up a rigorously constructed paradigm in a language of dazzling abstraction and hermetism.

In reading *The Structure of Social Action* sociologists discovered that they are the heirs of a great intellectual tradition; that of Alfred Marshall, Vilfredo Pareto, Emile Durkheim and Max Weber, recognized descendants of Hobbes, Locke, Malthus and Marx, of utilitarianism, evolutionism, positivism, that had given sociology all the analytical diagrams allowing the elaboration of a unified theory of the social structure, systems of action, a theory capable of giving an account of all the logics of the social. By systemizing and generalizing everything that had until then been scattered among the founding fathers, Parsons settled down to the construction of the great theory presented in *The Social System*.[22]

The basis of this theory is social action, which covers biological, psychical, social and cultural activities, organized into subsystems and together making up the system. Relations between the whole and its parts make up the social organization. Stable elements form its structures (roles, collectivities, norms, values) while the dynamic element is provided by the functions in charge of maintaining social equilibrium. The social system is a four-dimensional space characterized by a general equilibrium and partial equilibriums, real and/or potential. Thanks to Parsons, the physical model finds its most complete and sophisticated formulation.

This model, refined and clothed in fabrics taken from the closet of the founding fathers, was the fundamental paradigm in sociology until recently. Neither Marxism nor culturalism succeeded in drawing us away from the ascendency and fascination of the Parsonian construction, an undisputed and dominant sociological paradigm, in the US but also in Europe, where even the sociologies of action and reproduction were contaminated, to a greater or lesser degree. Since Parsons, all sociologists have been conscious of the existence of a sociological tradition and the importance of the heritage of the founding fathers, without, however, accepting the idea that the history of sociology can exert the same influence on sociological research as that which the history of philosophy exerts on the philosopher.

Parsons's paradigm, called structural-functional, has required an incalculable number of borrowings from mathematics and statistics and has favoured the development of a mathematical sociology, a quantitative sociological methodology and techniques of social research which for many years have favoured the means of expression to the detriment of the pertinence of the problematics.[23]

The Mathematization of Social Data

The often illusory or tautological results of quantification in psychology and sociology were analysed, harshly but plausibly, by Pitirim Sorokin.[24] The implicit assimilation of the social world to the physical world and the faith in the explanatory power of the tools of the 'queen of the sciences' have made us transpose into the psycho-social sciences everything that had produced results in the 'noble' or 'concrete' disciplines. So it is that topology has been used to account for social conflicts; the analysis of concomitant variations to explain suicides; ecological, contextual and dimensional analyses to arrange the orders of preference.

Without going into the lengthy developments, it is certain that we have assured the passage of qualitative facts (the most numerous) to quantification by means of the irrational acceptance of certain formulas that arise from the basest empiricism, especially by a tacit manipulation of the tools of quantification and formal terms. Just one example will suffice to illustrate my statement: the construction of the sociological sample, whose formula is given us by statistics. It is written this way:

$$n = \frac{\left(\dfrac{t\,S}{d}\right)^{2}}{1 - \dfrac{1}{N}\left(\dfrac{t\,S}{d}\right)^{2}}$$

where n is the number of subjects in the sample to be determined, N the number of subjects in the field, d the error we decide to accept, t the interval of reliability, S^{2} the variance of the variable x which we do not know. To establish the size of the sample, we must know the field of variance to be measured. If the variance of the variable x is large, n must also be large; if the variance is small must be small. Now S in sociology is always an estimation, and it is on an estimation that we are obliged to base *n*. In other words, we fix the size of the sample beginning with an estimation made on the basis of the hypothesis, never verified, that the distribution is normal. Then we must ignore the fact that there are several variables which the estimation of S must take into account. Most often we consider these variables separately while recognizing that they have two or more dimensions, which is important for the fixation of *n*. On the other hand, the theory states that the persons interrogated be chosen by chance. Now this is revealed to be almost always impossible in sociological research. To have representative samples, we must correct the random choices by reasoned choices. It is well known that the theory of estimation through the interval of reliability is only valid in the case of a random survey, while all our surveys are empirical. In addition, our sampling by reasoned choice rests on the hypothesis that the variables of control are statistically distributed as variables to be analysed. Such a hypothesis assumes the strict correlation between the variables of control (age, sex, socio-professional categories, milieu, religion, etc.) and the kind of answer given. It is practically impossible to control such a hypothesis. Therefore, we have no means to evaluate the variability in the estimation.

Thanks to a borrowing from statistics, we have here an important tool, but as far as sociology is concerned, one that is deprived of all theoretical validity and thus of practical legitimacy. I could also mention the determinist models for the analysis of social processes; simulated models as physical realizations of mathematical models, as well as applications to psycho-sociology or socio-demography of the simulated models without a direct mathematical equivalent, but that would add nothing to my thesis. Since there is no isomorphism between the physical world and the social world, all borrowings by sociology from other disciplines must undergo changes, be transformed into metaphors or analogies. After that, they no longer produce the same results as in their original disciplines.

The relentless antagonism opposing sociologists favouring nomothetic explanations to the partisans of ideographic interpretations and the supporters of the quantitative method (participating observation, clinical method, etc.) has its origin in the faith in the validity of statistics in sociology. Even when analyses with multiple variables are possible, can we say that the analysis of discrete variables helps us grasp the entire systems? The collection of the causes into a system obscures the genesis (as well as its boundaries and structures) because it is more the sum of the parts and specific causal relations.

In the present situation, the study of events whose frequency is at the same time variable and measurable does not guarantee sociologists the certainty of identifying the variables whose regularity would authorize their codification into laws and then the elaboration of a theory from them.

Stagnation and Conflicts of Today

Thus sociological tradition, borrowings from other sciences, acquired experience and the restrictions arising from the institutionalization of the discipline result in sociology continuing to believe that the imitation of the natural sciences will inevitably earn it the dignity of science. This is why it treats the social, culture and sentiments as though it were a matter of a 'natural history' of societies. And the best way to analyse them comes straight from the adoption of quantitative methods, the only means to identify the structures of the phenomena and laws of movement in modern society.

The insistence on imitating natural sciences, to put sociology in the place of metaphysics and religion, cold Reason in that of faith and passions, like the distinction between ends and means, facts and opinions, as well as the opposition between the objective world and the sensorial world of feelings – all this has plunged us into the present stagnation and conflicts.

Convinced that the logic of demonstration remains the only way to produce knowledge and to construct a general conception of the world, a rational substitute for religion, sociologists are now calmly and agreeably installed in universities, teach more or less abstruse specializations, are neither listened to nor influential, are barely tolerated by the specialists in other disciplines, and produce fragments of practical knowledge, consultations and expertise that are quickly forgotten or received with general indifference.

Waiting to rise to the level of the exact sciences, attracted by reflexivity, interpretation and hermeneutics, today's sociologists continue to borrow more than ever from the most disparate disciplines and the most varied techniques (for example, the theory of games, the general theory of systems, cybernetics, etc.). At times we call upon literary and philosophical disciplines when the meaning of life and the logic of a society escape us; at times we find a safe refuge in the imitation of transposition of the attainments of the concrete sciences, and among them our preferences are always on the side of physics, mathematics and biology.

In one case as in another, sociology can continue to cultivate its age-old mythology: to be a science but also a practical activity; to theorize but animate action; explain social behaviour but also evaluate it; give an account of social passion and daily life with 'participating' objectivity. In short, today's sociology continues to take from elsewhere its theoretic and non-theoretic constructions, which give it the illusion of explaining behaviour in terms of finalities or causes where it can find them. It continues to remain a polyparadigmatic science. Functionalism and experimental empiricism that stress controlled deductions and comparisons, explanations through causal laws, that organize the universe of experiences into formal structures, are the most convincing examples of this situation. However, for several years we have begun to notice openings toward and some borrowings from history, economics, linguistics, philosophy and other disciplines. I am going to list them quickly, without pretending to be exhaustive.

History

Sociologists have always considered that history could furnish the social sciences with an objective knowledge of some isolated events but deprived of solid explanatory elements on the how and why of their unfolding in time.[25] If the study of socio-cultural structures, their structuration and their destructuration, relationships between social facts and the biophysical environment is of great importance for understanding the modalities of production and reproduction in the social system, it remains nonetheless anchored, according to sociologists, at the level of the ideographic interpretation of unique situations, particular groups governed by singular rules, motives and intentions. Alex Inkeles resumes the problematic in this way:

> The historian takes pride in the clarity and precision of the details that characterize his discipline. The sociologist is more inclined to make reality abstract, to categorize and generalize; he is interested in what is true, not only the particular history of a people but also the histories of different peoples.[26]

However, faced with the failure of development and modernization, it has been necessary to borrow from history the techniques to treat (and also identify) the temporal texture of all human experience, as well as the contexts of situation and the transitions from one kind of society to another.[27] The borrowings allowed a sociological treatment of former questions (anomy, generation, the formation of states, the twilight of cultures, emergence and decline of the different forms of welfare state, etc.) and especially to favour the birth of a new sub-discipline: historical sociology.[28]

Economics

As in the past, sociologists call on economics because of its conceptual proximity to natural sciences. Some of them, fascinated by the progress made by economic science, think that the adoption of the economics method will bring sociology out of the impasse where it has always found itself. Since then, they borrow from neoclassical economics its basic postulate: society is composed of individuals in juxtaposition seeking their interests in a rational way. They enter into contact with each other through the intermediary of the market in order to maximalize their interests. An order is thus created due to the automatic mechanisms of adjustment to the market. Agents seek to attain their own position of equilibrium. Each agent is endowed with will-liberty and capacity-efficacity, qualities that are indispensable for reaching their objectives.

Sociologists extend this paradigm of the market to non-marketing areas, in short, to all the aspects of social life. Gary S. Becker says,

> In fact, the economics theory is perhaps well on the way to furnishing a unified framework for each behaviour that puts to work rare resources, non-marketing, non-monetary as well as monetary, within a restricted group, as well as concurrent ones.[29]

Elsewhere he says, 'All human behaviour may be conceived as putting into play participants who maximalize their usefulness beginning with a stable group of preferences and who accumulate the optimal quantity of information on a variety of markets'.[30] What do Becker and the sociologists who are partisans of the economic model want to obtain? The constitution of all the human sciences in a generalized economy of human behaviour, from marriage to criminality, from adultery to justice, from non-profit organizations to the religious market, from the electoral vote to assistance to developing countries. Each individual finds meaning in his actions only by maximalizing his usefulness. Producing these utilities in an efficient way is the only, ultimate stake of his choices that have an impact on time, the only truly rare asset.

An example taken from Becker's *A Theory of Marriage* will serve to illustrate these ideas.

According to this author, to analyse the family we must borrow from the economic theory of business, because the family is nothing other than a 'small factory'. It is organized exactly like a business. The marriage contract is the result of a process of trial and error on the marriage market. The ultimate goal – the choice of a mate – will concretize the maximalization of the joint investments of two individuals. In the family, individuals produce final satisfactions, objects of a function of family investment contributing to the transformation of all consumption into production. So it is easy to formalize the production of these investments and state that the function of domestic production introduces time as a rare asset. In a situation of maximalization of investments with restrictions (budget and time) how will the members of a family act? By sharing their time between production of revenue, a salaried job and the production of satisfactions of non-marketable origin. Certainly, such borrowings allow the treatment of the family as though it were a matter of a business; however, it forces us to consider time in the family as the equivalent of the time of salaried work, to mix the private with the public, to dodge the fact that in domestic work there is a part that cannot be measured, because socially it is invisible, to ignore that exchanges cannot all be transcribed into monetary terms. Behind all that there is, of course, a representation of society as an automatic mechanism of regulation, as a natural order, as physical or organic systems.

These borrowings have brought about an important intellectual current that today is called 'theory of rational action' (Rational Action, RAT or Rational

Choice). It groups different tendencies, such as 'logic of collective action', 'methodological rationalism', 'methodological actionalism' and 'methodological individualism'.[31] All the supporters of this current borrow from neo-classic economy the hypothesis that social actors behave in terms of their preferences and thus behave in a rational way. However, the pure economist tendency excludes solidarity, power and prestige from its rationality; that of rationalism, behaviour governed by rules; that of actionalism, beliefs and preferences; that of individualism, totalities. These tendencies do not all produce the same results. For example, methodological individualism can reverse or eliminate its initial economism[32] while economic rationalism must break with methodological individualism in order to remain faithful to its corollaries (acting egoistically, exclusively for material interest, being content with 'satisfying', various factors affecting the function of service, information is always correct and the environment of the action is always constant and given). Whatever the case, borrowings by sociology from economics have up until now not helped our discipline to give itself a specific identity and limit its province.

Linguistics

This science has intrigued sociologists, especially since the beginning of the century. Pareto, Durkheim and Mead gave an important place in their sociological studies to language as the keystone of culture and thus of society. But for half a century we have also been aware that this system of expression and communication can define social action.

Three sociological schools developed from this realization: symbolic interactionism, ethno-methodology and structuralism. By applying several analytical formulas to sociology, especially those of diachrony/synchrony, form/substance, language/work, logic/language, meaning/sign, sociologists hope to show the systems of rules that govern society, its functioning here and now, to discover the mode of production of meanings as well as the modalities of construction of social reality. Nonetheless, they do not succeed in characterizing the specificity of language through opposition to the social constructions it is able to elaborate. If language organizes and conditions our way of conceiving the world, our social behaviour, our symbolic systems, must we then affirm that the social order is language? Must we also say that the knowledge we have of society comes from language? It is impossible to answer these questions, since neither language nor society has a transcendental ontological status, since neither general linguistics nor sociology has concrete units that can be immediately recognized. But linguistic borrowings, transformed into metaphors and heuristic canons, have allowed Blumer and Goffmann, Garfinkel and Cicourel to show how the operations of designation by which social objects and the social system are constructed are put into place. The conversational analysis of Sacks and Schegloff, the argumentative logics of Toulmin and Grize have opened up fine perspectives for us on the persuasion and non-demonstrative logics of communication and, in general, on the connotative representations of the everyday world.[33]

Sociology has drawn two major hypotheses from linguistic research: (a) spoken language is one system of signs among others; (b) any sign system has a hermetic and auto-referential character. The use that Lévi-Strauss has made of these two hypotheses to analyse the rules of marriage and parenthood, as well as mythologies, is well known. The analysis of verbal and non-verbal sign systems has made sociologists take an interest in hermeneutics, interpretation, the reading of cultural systems, decoding the individual and social behaviour governed by rules, actions set up in terms of these rules and governed by the coherence that characterizes any system of rules. It is precisely from that slant that sociology has rediscovered philosophy and its great tradition.

Philosophy

The discovery, or better, rediscovery of the philosophical tradition is too recent to give even a short inventory of it here. Sociologists try at present to familiarize themselves with the techniques used in the history of philosophy and hermeneutics. Thanks to what philosophers have written on self-awareness, intention and the reciprocity of perspectives, we have learned that social action is structured by three kinds of awareness: that of the actors living a situation; that of actors anticipating future actions; and that of the researcher himself. Thus sociologists have begun to realize the importance of reflexivity. Today, some of them hope that the profession will turn away somewhat from empirical research to the profit of the development of reflexive sociology.[34]

To Conclude

After more than two centuries of research and speculation, sociology continues to inquire about its field of study, its specificity, its methodology, its chances for finally setting up a veritable store of knowledge. While the 'concrete' or exact sciences bring up fundamental epistemological problems and treat order and disorder, chance and necessity, self-organization and complexity with originality, sociology is still wondering about its own identity and its scientific and social functions, meditating on the rapport between descriptions and the world of norms and values, between science and action.

At the moment in which the 'concrete' sciences take into their charge the dynamic complexity of phenomena, at the moment in which they boldly go beyond chance and discontinuity and seek the system that can give a meaning to the universe, what is contemporary sociology doing? It continues its self-satisfied musing. The old themes of subjectivity and objectivity, universality and relativity, qualitative analysis and quantitative methods, society as a system of action, the actor as product of structures that determine him, of intermediary thanks to which the rules of functioning and reproduction are expressed, or of subject able to make choices – all these old themes continue to attract sociologists and make them work with calmness, sobriety and method, without getting carried away, determined and meticulous.

The freedom of the subject ? An illusion. It is up to society to speak and act. No accidental creativity. Morphogenesis comes from a hidden teleological order that the sociologist will be able to reveal. Values and meanings? Purely impersonal significants. The social transforms values into facts, facts into legitimate power relationships and consequently the cultural arbitrary into subordination and hierarchy. All social rapports are a totality in which society is massively reflected. Intelligibility is, then, only disengagement from a concealed order, verification of the existence of determinisms. Thus we believe that we have re-established the social in its ontological pre-eminence and its causal self-sufficiency.

Can this *Homo sociologicus*, based on empirical subjects, prisoners of time and society, escape the appearance of all that he is living? Can he really remove himself from the experience of his particular society and its characteristic existence? Can he really conceive the other and the elsewhere?

The history of sociology reveals its principal difficulty: it searches a universal truth in a particular society, identity in diversity, analogy in otherness. This knowledge elaborated within a society, that of generalized exchanges through the industrial system, will only succeed in giving an account of certain functionings of modern society as opposed to other, earlier societies. And yet it claims the right to universality. Sociology hierarchizes societies with regard to a primordial, original state. The distance in regard to the original state characterizes the progressive order in the following.

Societies near the origin are primitive societies; they are the object of study of the ethnologists. The study of societies in time, societies passing from one stage to another, is left to the historians. Present society, a veritable conclusive consubstantiation of human society, belongs to the sociologist. It is to them that is confided the construction of the science of society. Beginning with a particular society, they hope to give us a social theory with a general validity, a universal and general claim.

Such a conception of modernity has two important omissions: it is given as an absolute novelty, detached from genealogy and chronology, therefore without duration and history; it is conceived as a system of functioning, without genesis but still reproductive. It is time that sociology dropped history and claimed its autonomy and disciplinary specificity, its experience of universal meaning.

Now, the present is the product of the past, whose permanence assures the configuration of the present, makes it what it is. This permanence of the past in the present is the framework of our consciousness, our social identity, institutions, values, norms; it constitutes the armature of social structures, indeed, the process of social structurations.

Men create a world of objects, meanings, restrictions in duration. They assure its stabilization and permanence with institutions. These gradually become subjects that transform their creators into objects. We create rules, values, signs; we act through them. Institutions condense and sometimes crystalize social experiences. The almost automatic recourse to these experiences facilitates individual and collective action, orders social life, makes interaction easier, fixes the field of the possible, preserves energies and stimulates motivations and orientations.

This constructed world presents itself to us, throughout the years, as a world independent of us, implacable in its own autonomy, with a destiny at times different from that of individual subjects. From this comes the duality of social action; it is choice and obligation at the same time, but in time. That means that action depends on historical situations with which the subject is confronted. Our historical condition gives us the framework of our experiences, shapes our conduct and facilitates certain behaviours. Our actions and all that we can construct or destroy happen in time and with time. The rapport between the social structure and social action is tied to temporality. Between the individual-actor and society conceived as a restrictive environment of laws, norms and values, there is reciprocity. Even this reciprocity has a history and remains the history of the present. It is useless to separate sociology from history. The disciplines make up the two faces of the same coin. They are occupied with the same realities; they must give an account of the same process, in other words, the reasons for which men live together, produce meanings, give sense to things that otherwise would have none, create the mechanics for legitimizing and validating arbitrary choices, perpetuate them, change them, exchange them, to give an order where there was only insignificance, indifferentiation, inconsistency and contingency.

Even though it is constitutionally impossible to extract sociology from history, what brought about the separation and competitive evolution of these disciplines? Assuredly, the vision of a radically new society, the mirage of modernity and the illusion of indefinite progress. The latest stage is a long evolution, and modern societies have become universal and exclusive paragons.

As long as sociology only had to produce information to renew existing meanings, broaden and complete them, account for classes, class struggle, bureaucratization, its weakness was not immediately perceived. Sociological studies served to nourish arguments, give the varnish of rationality and scientificity, even the technical nature of its projects, choices and decisions often purely superfluous. The sociology of education or modernization, that of mass communication or work spoke in vain; all these efforts, in their agreeable insignificance, have admirably confirmed the observation Henri Michaux made in a different context: 'The philosophers of a nation of hairdressers' assistants are more profoundly hairdressers' assistants than philosophers'. Then came the crisis and the illusions were quickly swept away. After having been a shaman, the sociologist was considered as a creator of smoke. Since then our inability to escape wordiness is made fun of and our work is ridiculed as a derisory effort to finally demonstrate what the world already knows.

Such a shock could be healthy. In fact, it forces us to ask real questions, to come closer to history, to make sociology a historical discipline, to get around the difficulties of throwing the observer off centre with regard to his own society, to become aware of the historical character of our categories. There is still much work to be done, but there are already pioneers: Elias, Abrams, Tilly and many others. However, among the most urgent tasks to be accomplished, the reflection on the history of sociology, at the same time sociological history and sociology of sociology as well as historical sociology of knowledge is imperative.

Only the study of the history of sociology can make us understand the reasons for the considerable difficulties already present when Auguste Comte gave a name to our discipline. Since 1830, sociologists have attacked each other on the finalities of their science, on the role of the sociologist. They persisted in asking if it was first of all necessary to do empirical social research, produce information, reveal what is dissembled or analyse words and objects and leave to social actors the possibility to draw lessons from them and make the desired social use of them. What can we offer that is solid to the social actors when in sociology there are no universal procedures, conventionally accepted, allowing the validation through proof of the true and the false?

Of course, the founding fathers foresaw that sociology essentially treats meanings and that these are almost always manifested in words. Some of the founding fathers understood that language determines the classification of ideas and things, from which comes the careful attention given to questions of taxonomy and classification. But they hesitated to admit that the words of sociology rarely correspond to real objects, to relations objectively observable by all in space or in time. The cognitive model borrowed from the exact sciences kept them from recognizing that the knowledge produced came from adopted conceptual divisions, that they exist due to the 'arbitrary' cutting carried out on reality and that it is exactly this cutting that is the basis of sociological knowledge. Social reality has no other existence than that attributed to it by words. The sociologist can never refer to things to express signs. It is the cutting that guarantees the existence of the thing, never will the thing succeed in validating the sign.

All these original contradictions make us understand why there is always disagreement with regard to the birthdate of sociology. For those who considered that sociology is a reflection on the principles of life in society, the discipline identifies with social philosophy, with social theory and with social doctrines. It was born with the Greek philosophers. On the other hand, sociologists who attribute to sociology the task of making positive and empirical research on the organization and functioning of society, place its origin shortly after the Industrial Revolution, when new phenomena were calling for prerogatives and the concession of new meanings.

The disagreement on the origin of sociology is also fed by contrasting social practices. Some sociologists reflect on the phases of life in society, on social order, on what life in common should be, and this without any other concern than to understand, explain and grasp the nucleus of things the way artists do. On the contrary, other sociologists are exclusively concerned with the modalities of observation, question of verification and control, procedures of generalization and everything they think could found a store of knowledge with the dignity of science.

Philosophical and literary sociology seeks its precursors in Aristotle and Balzac; scientific sociology in Achenwall, Conring or Quételet. Macro-sociology prefers Ferguson, Montesquieu, Comte or Saint-Simon. Micro-sociology refers to the political arithmeticians, to the caméralistes, to Villermé or Le Play. The history of sociology thus allows us to understand many of our own problems and to see, beyond methodological credos, how sociologists have produced knowledge, in what way they axiomatize it and construct theories, from what point of view they have succeeded in putting paradigms of 'scientific' knowledge into place, making possible the socialization of the newcomers and the institutionalization of a social practice in a profession and professional roles, in a system of power, in a subculture.

In addition, the study of the history of sociology allows us to relativize our claims and prepare ourselves to work with historical material. Contrary to what happens in economics, where we distinguish the history of economic doctrines from the history of economic analysis and history of economic thought, in sociology the history of sociology integrates in itself the sociology of sociology, sociology of knowledge and social history. Why? Because sociological practices are simply sociological practices.

The study of the history of sociology, reflection on the sociologies of the past, has yet another function, that of allowing us to construct new knowledge with the aid of the practices of translation, combination and repetition. The sociologies and sociologists of the past have much to teach us about the societies that they have represented conceptually, and still more about the unsaid, the empty places, about suspended time, about differences, about ambiguity and the intangible shadows of the present.

The history of sociology offering us the only possibility of decentering with regard to our knowledge and our society, the only means of relativizing our scientific beliefs, frees us from the present and makes us understand why the classic values of identity, order, organization, centrality are giving way before those of difference, disorder, fragment, periphery. The history of sociology invites us to live the present as history and history as genealogy, duration, structuration of differences.

To the degree in which we are able to recognize the permanence of the past in the present, we reject as inauspicious the distinction between history and sociology, between sociology and anthropology, and we will be able to elaborate true knowledge about man.

The reaffirmation of our identity as researchers in human sciences passes through a return to memory and history. Sociology will take on its cultural importance if the sociologist admits that history is at the same time our memory, our tradition and our one and only reality.

Lacking such a reconversion, sociology will not come out unscathed from the crisis that is severely shaking the human sciences of our era.

26 IMAGINATIVE INTELLIGENCE: COGNITION IN THE VISUAL ARTS VERSUS RATIONALITY IN ECONOMICS

Bruna Ingrao

Olympian Rationality, Adaptive Routines and Bounded Rationality

Markets work through networks of information flows, thanks to which people define contracts of exchanges and implement allocative choices. Understanding the way markets work means conceiving the cognitive capabilities which people use when they cooperate or compete in production and exchange. Both intellectual and relational capabilities are required, including attitudes pertaining to the sphere of behaviour related to 'sympathy'. In considering cognitive aspects in economic activity, a minimum requirement should be to look at the multiple sides of intelligence explored by scholars in psychology.[1] In economic theory the focus was primarily on intellectual capabilities in 'rational choice'. Since the nineteenth century, in economics 'rationality' was conceived along three modelling strategies, which we broadly distinguish under the labels of perfect rationality, adaptive rationality and bounded rationality. They embody different views of how the mind works, when people deal with economic affairs, though they may partially overlap, calling into question the complexity or consistency of the architecture of cognition, which different economists propose.

The label 'perfect' rationality is here adopted to indicate the highest normative standard of rationality, also named 'substantive' rationality, or 'Olympian' rationality in Simon's definition. Perfect rationality postulates the best cognitive abilities in conceiving stable and coherent preference orderings, and in computing optimal solutions, applying well-defined optimizing procedures within given constraints, and on comprehensive data sets. It postulates the capability to perform algorithmic procedures and derive logical inference from given sets of axioms, and the related capability of recognizing fallacies in logical reasoning according to coherent sets of logical rules. These postulates have been dominant in economic theory in the twentieth century, being at the core of equilibrium models of different brands based on the theory of optimal choice on given opportunity sets under constraints. In common interpretation perfect rationality as a normative standard in rational choice admits of no violations of basic axioms on the coherence of preferences in choice, and no resource constraints in the agent's computational abilities as a rational maximizer.[2] The notion of perfect rationality seems to imply that the ideal rational agent in economics fully masters the theory of statistical inference and optimization, as it was developed in the last 200 years in statistics, econometrics and decision theory.[3] 'Puzzles', 'biases' or 'failures' in rational choice are discovered, when people do not conform their choices or procedures for choice to these normative standards. Although diversity of cognitive abilities and asymmetric information were at the core of controversies in game theory, macroeconomics and industrial organization, in models where markets are theoretically conceived as the interplay of free optimizing agents, symmetry in cognition is generally postulated, in line with the idea of rationality assumed as the normative standard. The idea of Nash equilibrium is based on the perfect symmetry in cognitive abilities of the rational agents, their unlimited computational abilities and resources, and the transparency of common information on the rules of the market game.

Since the nineteenth century, however, a number of economists explored the evolutionary reading of human choices, with nuances depending on the biological model of the mind and the architecture of cognition they endorsed. Marshall built a complex model of the mind with mechanist and biological components, including both routines and creativity.[4] Schumpeter, who underlined relational abilities for success in innovative business, noted that routines transmitted by 'inheritance, teaching, upbringing, pressure of environment' are effective to deal with established tasks in economic life.[5] Hayek explored both the evolutionary, biological bases of the mind and the cumulative heritage of norms in cultural transmission.[6] These economists dealt with evolutionary routines within complex visions of the mind, a merit of their research that is often forgotten in contemporary debate.

The second strategy, here labelled 'adaptive' rationality, focuses on preset frames and simplified procedures in problem solving, which arise from adaptive processes of biological evolution in the interaction of humans with their environment. In the bioevolutionary reading of intelligence, the focus is on adaptive rules of behaviour, in opposition to the logical or computing abilities postulated in the perfect rationality approach. To build manageable mathematical models, contemporary literature in behavioural and cognitive economics defines routines as mechanist, adaptive reactions in sequential choices, or as easy algorithms to reach reasonable inference under the pressure of time, or in case of missing information. Routines are alternatively conceived as sub-optimal, second best, procedures, which lead to mistakes in judgement, or as rules of thumb permitting the efficient adaptation of human agents to the environment in conditions of scarce resources. In the latter interpretation, in contrast with the approach of mainstream currents in behavioural economics, agents adopt heuristics matched to their particular environment, and are able to be 'ecologically rational' agents with 'fast and frugal' decisions.[7]

The strategy of perfect rationality was subjected to radical criticism from inside the economic profession well before the attacks launched by Herbert Simon or, later on, by researchers in experimental economics. Early criticisms called into question the distinction between risk and uncertainty and the frail foundations of forecasts about radically uncertain events; the impossible requirements in terms of computing abilities and access to data by economic agents; the division of knowledge.[8] The 'bounded rationality' approach was defined by Simon in the 1950s; it was developed along different lines in Simon's own writings and in contemporary behavioural economics. There is an open and continuing controversy regarding the proper definition of 'bounded rationality'.[9] Simon underlined sequential problem solving in conditions of scarce information and limited computing capabilities.[10] Notwithstanding his criticism of 'absolute' or 'Olympian' rationality, his definition of 'bounded rationality' highlights cognitive abilities in terms of coherent algorithmic procedures, though in sequential choice. His rationalistic view of the mind was inspired by the Artificial Intelligence programme – the idea that all cognitive processes in the mind may be simulated by sequential steps in computer programming.[11] It is controversial whether Simon denied the primacy of the first best approach in terms of exact computation and optimization, or if a standard of normative rationality, though procedural and sequential, is at the core of his idea of bounded rationality.[12] In contemporary literature, 'bounded rationality' is most often conceived as a sub-optimal shortcut or a second best path to solving problems, which would best be solved in conditions of complete information and unlimited computing abilities.[13] It is, thus, conceived as the defective set of inferential instruments adopted by poorly rational or hasty agents, which induce systematic deviations from the best available techniques, as they would be adopted by fully learned and thoughtful agents.[14] In mainstream behavioural economics, both economists and psychologists postulate as the normative model of human rationality *tout court*, the mastery of the complex set of statistical and optimizing procedures, which results from specialized disciplines, such as statistical theory, econometrics, operational research, decision theory or game theory.

In line with the old tradition of thought at the junction between philosophy and economics, our purpose is to suggest a richer vision of human intelligence, as compared to the three strategies briefly summarized above.

Reasoning and Intuitive Judgement

Kahneman, who researched jointly with Tversky the systematic mistakes which people are prone to commit in judgements under uncertainty, proposed a comprehensive vision of the mind, underlying both the role of intuition and the role of reasoning. He described the salient characteristics of the rational economic agent in terms of two modes of thinking and decision, under the labels of Intuition (System 1) and Reasoning (System 2). In Kahneman's research, the emphasis is on the biases[15] induced by the reliance of System 1 on intuitive judgements and the poor monitoring of intuitive judgements by reasoning.

> The rational agent of economic theory would be described, in the language of the present treatment, as endowed with a single cognitive system that has the logical ability of a flawless System 2 and the low computing costs of System 1. Theories in behavioural economics have generally retained the basic architecture of the rational model, adding assumptions about cognitive limitations designed to account for specific anomalies ... The central characteristic of agents is not that they reason poorly, but that they often act intuitively. And the behaviour of these agents is not guided by what they are able to compute, but by what they happen to see at a given moment.[16]

The literature on biases in intuitive judgement mentions visual illusions to underline context-dependence, reference-dependence or preset framing. Kanheman and other scholars developed the theory of framing having in mind frames in visual perceptions, which induce errors in evaluating relative size or other properties of the observed images. Framing is a distorting way to look at, both literally in vision and conceptually, when a compulsive mental model induces systematic mistakes in problem solving. In common parlance, we would say, 'to have blinders on'. In his Nobel lecture, Kanheman explicitly illustrated the way intuitive judgement works by analogy with visual biases, which induce false evaluation on relative size or distance, or in decoding images.[17] He presented four examples to illustrate by visual analogies biases in intuitive judgement due to differential accessibility, context dependence, or preset framing. The figures of standing and laying blocks illustrate the property of differential accessibility, accessibility being defined as 'the ease with which mental contents come to mind'.[18] The height of the blocks' tower is easily accessible in the figure, where the blocks are standing, while the area covered by the blocks is easily accessible, if they appear laid out on the flat surface.[19] The effect of context on accessibility is in question in the figure, where the identical graphic sign is, alternatively, seen as a letter or as a cipher, depending on the sequence in which it is placed (B in a list of letters, 13 in a list of numbers). The example is meant to illustrate the 'complete suppression of ambiguity in conscious perception' of graphic signs because of context dependence.[20] 'Reference-dependence' in visual perception is shown in the figure where the differential perception of the size of two identical squares depends on their relative brightness, due to the darker or lighter colour of the background.[21] The picture with two rocking horses of identical size in the background and in the foreground illustrates deception in evaluating relative size as 'an illusion of attribute substitution', 'attribute substitution' being a heuristic procedure to reduce complex tasks to simpler operations, at the cost of possible mistakes in judgement.

In his Nobel Lecture Kahneman was cautious in his conclusions. He underlined that differential accessibility in visual perception improves through experience and training; heuristics may be useful; intuitive judgements are reasonably successful in many cases, and are highly improved by acquired skills.[22] The architecture of cognition that Kahneman presents is, thus, open to richer interpretations than the dominant reading in terms of cognitive biases. However, in the book he devoted to communicate the message of his lifelong research, Kahneman placed almost exclusive emphasis on the 'biases of intuition', although declaring that the focus on errors was not meant to denigrate human intelligence.[23]

The balance between biases in intuitive judgement and poor learning or poor training remains a critical point in contemporary behavioural economics. The body of knowledge that is assumed as the normative standard of rationality is a set of scientific disciplines and mathematical techniques of optimization, which evolved in history as the product of specialized learning. J. von Neumann defined the axioms of expected utility in the 1940s, a result reached by a trained scientist with mental effort, notwithstanding his genius. Operational research was developed in research for military logistics; it requires university training in mathematics and statistics to be effectively applied in problem solving. Good performance in the algorithmic procedures defined in these disciplines results from education and training, as does the ability to play chess or to compute a three-digit division. In optimization, inference and optimal forecasting, much as in integral calculus or elementary arithmetic, people use the procedures which they have learnt to use.[24] Training in basic accountancy was not widespread among illiterate rural populations in European societies just three centuries ago, for lack of access to schooling. Managerial resources are still scarce in many societies and their increase requires investment in human capital, or is the result of historical processes involving institutions and incentives.

As Hayek underlined, Reason with a capital R does not exist in one mind; it is the process of sharing and exchanging the specialized knowledge with which each agent is endowed.[25] A principle of division of labour is at work in financial choices and economic forecasting, as in other fields with increasing returns to specialization. Time is the scarcest resource in human life. People may not care to learn econometrics or sophisticated optimizing procedures, much as they do not care to learn dentistry or the best techniques in bakery. They buy the services of financial consultants, brokers, insurance and estate agents, as they buy the services of dentists, or buy pastries at the shop around the corner. More or less frequently, they get intoxicated, or have the wrong tooth extracted, according to the quality of the services available in their societies.

Our plea for a richer vision of human intelligence is not meant to deny the achievements of psychological research on economic choices; it is meant to focus attention on the core function of human intelligence, which the ideas of perfect rationality, adaptive or bounded rationality leave in the shadow. We aim at reaching a deeper understanding of how in human minds rational procedures work in fruitful combination with intuition and imagination. The visual arts will offer the starting point to explore these richer nexuses. The reference to the visual arts has a further motivation. We shall compare the biased perceptions read as examples of 'differential accessibility', 'reference dependence' or 'framing' with the optical tricks practised in the visual arts. In artistic work, optical illusions are intentionally manipulated by artists, and enjoyed by lovers of artworks. In the skilful hands of artists, far from being compulsory perceptions, which admit of no double reading, visual illusions are plastic instruments of emotional expression, which invite multiple reading by observers open to new experience in sympathetic arousal.

Imaginative Intelligence in the Arts and in Economic Life

The three ideas of rationality mentioned above leave out of sight the aspect of human thought that we label imaginative intelligence, also absent in Kahneman's opposition of intuition and reasoning. The divergence from the paradigm of perfect rationality having been argued mainly from the pessimistic side, the effectiveness of imaginative intelligence was forgotten. The controversy on rational choice overlooked the ability of the mind to perform creative tasks through the plastic power of imagination. Imaginative intelligence works through the visionary capability of human thought; it acts through the faculty of imagination. We explore the working of imaginative intelligence as constructive rationality with specific reference to artistic work, and notably to the visual arts; but imaginative intelligence is crucial for good performance in a wide spectrum of economic activities.

Imagination, as here defined, is the capability to mentally design in the mind symbolic entities, be those geometric forms, patterns in 3D space, concepts or ideas expressed according to linguistic codes, stories or characters in fiction, and so on and so forth. They are mentally designed and seen as single entities or in their interaction in sequences and in complex situations. Imagination is the capability of the human mind to mentally build and explore parallel worlds, composed of images or concepts, or of any forms, which may be drawn from perceptive experience or conceived by purely mental creation. The ability of the mind to create and see mentally symbolic objects and their interactions is the proper mark of human thought.[26] Even the conscious perception of a unified self, and thus the very possibility to speak of a maximizing, problem-solving 'agent', is rooted in the imagination, which builds personal identity through life memories, a personal life story, and projections of the imagined self in future life.[27]

Symbolic forms are born in the mind as merely mental entities (e.g. the plot of a story in the mind of the writer); but they take life, after being conceived, as symbolic products (e.g. a written narration). In operational activities, imaginative intelligence is supported by constructive abilities, including trained routines and rational principles to monitor the coherence in the building blocks of the symbolic vision. Symbolic forms are rooted in imagination; but imaginative intelligence requires procedures to test feasibility by the joint cross-fertilization of education, training and experience. Tacit knowledge, as embodied in the mind and the bodily experience, inspires the conception and enriches the realization. Constructive rationality is the practice of imaginative intelligence covering the two cognitive systems underlined by Kahneman, working at their junction and through their fruitful interaction. Though substantiated by trained routines and reasoning procedures, it is not just a set of routines or logical procedures.[28] It cannot work exclusively through adaptive rules or algorithmic sequential steps. The imaginative faculty provides the core strength to human reason in performing rational, operational tasks; imaginative intelligence fuels the process of discovering new opportunities, both in highly creative enterprise and in more daily business.

Architectural work well illustrates imaginative intelligence and its practice as constructive rationality. The idea of a building is initially a mental vision, an image in the mind. A drawing, according to symbolic conventions in shared languages of visual communication, gives it blood and flesh. A twofold relation links the image intuitively coming to the mind and the mastery of the linguistic code, in which it will be sketched, since the code helps to conceive a clear image in the mind. Visual intuition is rooted in the heritage of symbolic forms which nurture the mind, as they were acquired through learning and life experience, or deeply assimilated in tacit knowledge. When drawings turn into the plans of a project, the learned training the architects have acquired in education and experience monitors feasibility and structural coherence in the planned construction. Interactions go from vision to feasibility and from feasibility to vision. Constraints help to structure the imagined plan, or focus the symbolic vision. The imaginative faculty is at the core of each step in this cognitive sequence.

In experimental economics, rationality is often tested having in view specific tasks, such as selecting a secretary in a random sequence of persons, or checking the performance of people in logical tests. An ambitious adjective as 'rational' is applied to check the conformity of sequential choices to the axioms of revealed preferences, instead of being applied to qualify the structural properties of the

Divina Commedia or *Die Kunst der Fuge*, remarkable products of the human mind, which required the mastery of complex procedures in conformity with formal rules. Both poetry and music have been produced for centuries building symbolic frames according to sets of principles, by procedures of variation and coherence. The violation of received codes, as practised for enrichment and innovation, generates new frames and constraints. Cognitive processes in artwork illustrate the multiple interactions involving intuitive imagination, technical procedures acquired by learning, skills by the practice of the craft, cultural transmission of symbolic forms, emotional resonance. Artists operate with techniques and know-how codified in established professions and crafts, and imaginative intelligence is the ability to solve complex problems with innovative solutions, starting from a symbolic content in imagination that is translated into a feasible plan of action. Cultural transmission and social interaction are crucial in creative work; constructive rationality works with socially constructed capabilities. Shared frames nurture the imagination; capabilities are learnt in formal education, training or cultural exchange.

Intuition and tacit knowledge are at the heart of the imaginative conception; but complex decision processes are required in artistic work, which do not belong to the sphere of the irrational or the purely intuitive. Nurturing and enriching visual imagination requires hard technical training, acquiring a body of conscious, systematic knowledge, assimilating techniques involving bodily attitudes, training intuitive judgement and visual framing. In artistic work imaginative intelligence as constructive rationality draws from repertories of symbolic culture, which are transmitted through generations. In the history of art, the repertories of symbolic forms have been extensively studied, since an artwork, even when most innovative in conception, is structured into codes of representation and expression. It is built through innovative borrowing from previous works, or the creative assimilation of subjects, images and forms.[29] The portrait *Femme Fleur* by Picasso is still a portrait, a definite genre in painting. Genres admit of infinite variations within some structural scheme, such as landscape, still life, portrait and nude. Historian of art Kenneth Clark, studying the nude in the history of art, analysed its expressive functions, and the structural properties of the images.[30] Examples may be drawn from other genres.[31]

This digression on imaginative intelligence in the visual arts may seem displaced in discussing rationality in economic theory. Do people who are involved in financial choices and business, in consumption or investment, act according to cognitive processes, which recall those discussed so far?[32] Without denying obvious differences, we conjecture that imaginative intelligence and constructive rationality, as defined above, are at the core of successful economy activities, notably in management, in investment projects, in banking for finance of investment projects, in technological innovation and marketing, in all industries where success depend on design, and even in economic policies. Imaginative intelligence, notably, creates technological innovation – 'the lever of riches' that spurs major advances in economic progress along history.[33] All successful innovation, all ideas of new opportunities, are based on the visionary faculty of imagination. They require, literally, the free wandering into the mental space of some imagined world. As in the arts, the conception is refined and brought to life in this world through rational procedures to monitor feasibility and structural coherence in the imagined project. In economic life, as in the visual arts, trained routines give an operational skeleton to innovative choice. As Schumpeter described them in *The Theory of Economic Development*, routine and innovation are radically different cognitive processes. On the contrary, trained routines are a powerful instrument in constructive rationality, the more so if they have been assimilated as tacit knowledge in deep intuition. In the visual arts, no extraordinarily creative personality failed to have deep technical control on the heritage of symbolic forms, or the instruments and tricks of the craft, thanks to training and the constant habit of exercise. The creative agents, who have access to a wealth of ideas through education or experience, may freely recombine them in innovative directions.

The most dramatic failures in economic rationality are not the biases in performing logical tests, but the failures of imaginative intelligence as constructive rationality, for lack of vision or adequate training or for poor incentives in exploring feasible opportunities for innovation and change. Even the design of appropriate economic policies is not the computation of optimal solutions in various families of dynamic mathematical models, as it is assumed in theoretical economics. It is the visionary capability to conceive and promote sustainable processes of innovative change, involving social actors and institutions in some historical environment. Many tragedies of failed growth are recorded in developing countries due to poor constructive rationality in dealing with the complexities of social and economic change.

Perceptive Illusions in the Visual Arts

Distorting framing, or to have blinders on, is a widespread phenomenon in human behaviour; but framing also plays a constructive role in cognition. Multiple decoding and framing through preset cognitive structures are part of the complex control system in the sight that works both at the level of perceptions' decoding in the brain and in conscious thought. Visual signals are filtered in the mind through stable codes to reach an understanding of the external world, translating sensory impulses into recognizable perceptions and conceptual learning.[34] People suffering from diseases or impaired in their ability to see are usually able to diagnose their defective vision, and do not trust as reality the unusual perceptions they experience.[35] A frequently mentioned example of framing in visual perception is the difficulty and almost the impossibility to perceive the concave side of a mask representing a human face as indeed concave. We normally perceive the concave mask as convex since our inner cognitive framing tells us that human noses jut out.[36] The cognitive framing from previous experience includes the global system of perceptions (the five senses); it controls the interpretation of sensory signals, separating reality from illusion, normality from distortions within the cognitive canons shared with other human fellows. Along the centuries visual artists had recourse to the conscious manipulation of optical devices based on the physiology of sight. They refined their techniques in combination with advances in other disciplines, having in view the visual effects they meant to achieve for stylistic or emotional purposes. These techniques belong to the toolbox of painters, designers, architects and professional people in the graphic arts. The trained artist may or may not take advantage of this repertoire of optical devices, according to expressive purpose or the task at hand.

Painting is the representation of light and matter on a flat surface, with the aim of creating optical illusions capturing the sight of the observer.[37] The representation of 3D visual objects on a flat surface requires techniques to create visual illusions. They include *chiaroscuro*, the relative whiteness in the greyscale or the relative brightness in colour signalling 3D volumes by the way lights and shadows define form; *tonal contrast* signalling the source of light and the incidence of shadows; *geometrical perspective* simulating distance by the declining size of objects according to distance from the focal point of vision; *aerial perspective* simulating distance by the fuzziness of more distant objects; *occlusion*, the visual object partially covering other objects signalling that they are behind it; *grain of texture* creating the illusion of different materials; *theory of colours*; *relative height* stressing proportions and emphasizing small size or stateliness; *contours*, suggesting the decoding of flat lines and silhouettes according to inner or acquired codes.

Let us look at the previous examples of biases from perceptive illusions in this different perspective. The picture with two identical rocking horses appearing as of different size is a visual deception arising from the accommodation the sight naturally applies to more distant objects. Since in natural sight more distant objects are seen as smaller, the mind is trained to approximately decode distance from size, among other parameters. This natural ability is most useful, though approximate, and the possible source of mistakes in exact computation. A proper pictorial representation of the rocking horses, not intended to cheat the observer as the experiment meant, would have proportionally reduced the distant object with the technique of geometrical perspective. In the picture the size of the horse in the back is overvalued also because of its vicinity to the chair that suggests a proportion as in natural sight, since the perception of size is also by comparison with objects whose height or extension the mind knows from experience or other sources of knowledge. To play with the relational evaluation of size is a technique of optical illusion in the visual arts; the artist transmits the height of an object by contrasting it with its environment, other objects or the human body. In Dutch paintings, the height of vaults and columns in painted cathedrals was emphasized by introducing human silhouettes, which by contrast conveyed the sense of hugeness and solemnity in the building. The disproportionately large representation of some characters in comparison with other human images or the environment has been systematically used in some styles of paintings for emotional purposes.

Let us look at the reference-dependence effect in the perception of identical geometrical figures due to their relative brightness and the spatial idea, which the darker or lighter colour of the background conveys. In his *Trattato della Pittura* Leonardo da Vinci clearly underlined the differential perception of brightness, proposing the variable perception of the whiteness of snow as an example. He dealt with the point in various passages.[38] Relative brightness with its effect on spatial perceptions is dealt with in the theory of colours. Brightness in the perception of colours is due to the juxtaposition of primary colours (red, yellow, blue) and their complementary ones in the colour wheel. Red, for example, is exalted near green. Artists creatively played with brightness effects, as in the contrast of blue and orange in the *Tondo Doni* by Michelangelo. The contrast of light and darkness, exalting white or bright tones against a dark surface, has been systematically used in painting. It is a powerful instrument of emotional expression in the fresco illustrating the deliverance of Saint Peter by the Angel in the Vatican *Stanze* painted by Rafael, much as in Caravaggio's paintings, in Goya's etchings on bullfights, and in so many masterpieces. It carries with it a compelling emotional effect. The light-dark contrast may be so strong to almost conceal to the sight the objects in the dark areas, a natural phenomenon, which the artist may simulate. The painting *A Man Seated Reading in a Lofty Room* by a follower of Rembrandt shows the dramatic impression created by tonal contrast; the height of the room is stressed by contrast with the sitting figure and the profile of the shadows projected by the window.[39]

The images of standing or laying blocks illustrated by visual analogy the property of differential accessibility. Kahneman underlined that accessibility is a continuum, varying by degrees, and mentioned the factors, which improve accessibility of some properties in visual perception, recognizing the role of experience and training.[40] In the figures the blocks were drawn with the technique of axonometry, or parallel perspective. In natural sight, to literally see the straight lines of an axonometric drawing on the flat sheet as 3D objects requires appropriate visual decoding by the observer; the eye of the trained professional will quickly decode relational properties, which the untrained eye is unable to see. A standard technique to draw objects in the 3D space on a 2D flat surface, axonometry is a sophisticated symbolic language used in technical drawing, architecture, artistic drawing, to summarize the skeleton of 3D forms, decomposing them into simpler solids. Axonometry does not correct for the reduction in height of more distant objects in natural sight; it is thus less faithful to natural sight than the images built with techniques of linear perspective. Axonometric forms are faithful in measurement, this being their specific function in architecture, engineering or design. They may be generated by sophisticated software programmes according to measurement parameters. Axonometric representation is not meant to permit the intuitive computation, at first sight, of height or extension. Its purpose is to visually study the geometrical skeleton and aesthetical appearance of the planned 3D structure. Axonometry is a sophisticated language of constructive rationality to draw on flat surfaces the images of 3D structures, turning them into feasible plans for construction.

Kahneman, illustrating the effect of context on accessibility in the figure where a sign in a sequence may be read as a letter or a cipher, asserts that the viewers reach the total suppression of ambiguity in perception; they 'see' the object that is most likely in the context. Ambiguity and uncertainty are suppressed in intuitive judgement, as well as in perception.[41] On the contrary, in the visual arts the human mind enjoys playing with the ambiguity of graphic signs; the artist is perfectly at ease in amusing the observer with the more or less accessible perceptions, which they evoke. Historically, the graphic elaboration of letters and ciphers has been developed to a high degree of aesthetic perfection in many civilizations. In medieval illuminated manuscripts, single letters were embellished with miniature paintings, with visual effects both revealing and concealing the storied initials. In Japanese culture, the exquisite graphic design of ideograms is a specific artwork; calligraphy as an art requires aesthetical sensibility, and long training of the hand. In ancient Hebrew, letters and numbers share the same graphic signs. The symbolic resonance of graphic signs goes well beyond the ornamentation of written words and the inventive manipulation of graphic signs is alive in contemporary artworks. Both in contemporary art and in old paintings playing with concealed letters, suggesting effects of ambiguity and double reading is an important aspect of *trompe-l'oeil* artworks. The *trompe-l'oeil* painting by artist J. Poirier, *Artnica*,[42] is a complex composition, where words may be read in vertical and horizontal lines as in a crossword, but the letters are concealed in the casual disposition of disparate objects (a pipe, scissors, a compass, etc.) in wooden boxes. The artist ironically invites the viewer to decode the words, jointly with the secret meanings of such a heap of curious objects. Playing with letters as graphic signs, or concealing letters in images, is an ancient artistic tradition; innovation in art is rooted in the old reputation of genres.

Emotional intelligence involves the ability to play with optical illusions, enjoying them as artists or observers; constructive rationality requires trained capabilities to flexibly encode and decode symbolic signs. Why do these properties of supple, imaginative intelligence disappear from the realm of rationality in the literature relying on perceptive illusions in analogy with biased intuitive judgement? Why do optical illusions never appear as powerful cognitive instruments in the system of rational cognition?

Seeing-In in Painting

The reference to visual analogies in behavioural economics ignored the debate on visual illusions, recognition of images and pictorial representation that went on in the history and philosophy of visual arts along more than two millennia, since it goes back to Plato.[43] In the last century, this debate had important developments, and was enriched by exchanges with psychologists. The historian of art, R. Wollheim, distinguishes three basic perceptual capacities by observers on which the artist relies: seeing-in, expressive perception, and visual delight.[44] He quotes the passage by Leonardo da Vinci, where the painter suggests to a younger artist to look at the stains over the surface of a wall.

> Seeing-in is a distinct kind of perception, and it is triggered by the presence within the field of vision of a differentiated surface ... The distinctive phenomenological feature I call 'twofoldness', because when seeing-in occurs, two things happen: I am visually aware of the surface I look at, and I discern something standing out in front of, or (in certain cases) receding behind, something else ... In virtue of this experience I can be said to see the boy in the wall, the dancers in the frosty glass.[45]

Woollheim notices that the two aspects of seeing-in (discerning the surface and something else on it) 'are distinguishable but also inseparable'. The boy or the dancer the observer sees on the wall or on the glass, looking at the stains or at the frost, are experienced jointly with the perception of the surface; alternatively the observer may concentrate on the surface as such, or on the images. If twofoldness is lost, and just one aspect of the visual experience comes to the forefront, then seeing-in is lost.[46] Much of the pleasure enjoyed in seeing paintings is connected to twofoldness that permits one to freely perceive both the texture of materials, the lines and the strokes, and the images, which appear by optical illusion on the flat surface.[47] A philosophical debate went on regarding the possibility of seeing-in or seeing as (in Wittengstein's terminology), and the nature of illusion in art.[48] The visual illusion perceived in the enjoyment of artworks (the 'seeing-in' described by Wollheim) should not be confused with '*trompe-l'oeil*' effects, where the observer is, if for a second, deceived by the visual illusion. The artist need not deceive the observer to believe the images are real, although the viewer sees the evoked images in the pictorial surface and echoes to them in sympathy with emotional reactions. Observers appreciate they are the artful effect of optical devices manipulated by the painter, laying powders or inks on paper, wood or rough canvas. The art of painting cannot exist but for perceptive illusions of 'seeing-in', manipulated according to the style of expression or the optical technologies known to the artist. Optical illusions, codified in framing conventions, have been adopted for millennia in the visual arts. The empathic power of images has been dealt with in extensive literature, and it is explored from the perspective of neurology in neuroaesthetics.[49]

The schematization of forms by contours defined on a flat pictorial space (*campiture piane*), such as in Palaeolithic art or in Matisse's dancing nudes, supposes the shared capacity of both painter and observer to recognize objects from contours, seeing-in through patterns with no relief traced on surfaces. Monochrome chiaroscuro, such as in drawings or etchings, presupposes the shared capacity of both painter and observer to recognize visual objects from spots of light and darkness, in techniques that simulate light and darkness by spaces of blank on paper and by spots, stains or lines of black ink. Chiaroscuro in etchings and drawings uses complex techniques of optical illusion, taking advantage of the artful use of graphic signs. Curve lines and hatching evocate direction of movement, plasticity and density.[50] The trend of lines and the grain of black spots, the graphic texture traced by lines or cross-hatching, have the power to arouse strong emotional reactions in the observer, by way of resonance and intuitive association. Virtuosity in painting shadows creates a rich variety of optical illusions, with worlds of emotional echoes.[51] Fleming and Dutch painting developed elegant techniques of visual illusion for rendering palpable, through light effects, the qualities of the matter of which objects are made (porcelain, glass, metal, damask, velvet). Along the centuries, *trompe-l'oeil* techniques aimed at deceiving the observer on the tactile nature of the portrayed images, imitating to perfection wood, paper, the softness of a mature fruit, a broken glass covering the canvas.[52]

Techniques of optical illusion developed in combination with the progress of scientific disciplines were codified in writings and transmitted through technical training. Geometrical perspective was born as a sophisticated mathematical discipline based on the codified language of geometry in 3D space. The calculated convergence of straight lines towards one or more vanishing points on the line of horizon simulates on the plain surface the effects of distance in natural sight, with complex computations. Based on the rational analysis of sight in the human eye and applied with the help of scientific instruments, geometrical perspective is an abstract representation of human vision not fully coincident with natural vision.[53] Aerial or atmospheric perspective, as defined by Leonardo da Vinci, uses the optical device of attributing a lower degree of clearness to images receding in distance, which are rendered by a softer outline ('sfumato'); shapes far away lack details. It is another code of perceptive illusion to evocate spatiality on the flat surface. It seems that Dutch painters in the seventeenth century used 'camera obscura'; their techniques developed in contact with the progress of optical instruments and theories.[54]

Through techniques of perceptive illusions, painters are able to create multiple cross-references to the perceptions of different sensorial systems or complex sensorial experiences, such as appetizing food or sensual attraction.[55] The aim of the visual arts is to convey emotional resonance by images; through the images, a world of sensations, feelings, and ideas is brought to light. Visual illusions stir global sensorial cognition. Seeing a painting may convey the impression of silence, the smell of a woman in bed, the creamy taste of milk, a sensorial atmosphere with its mental echoes. Berenson spoke of 'tactile values' in painting. Merleau-Ponty affirmed the power of painting to access sensorial experience in its totality, making visible what in ordinary experience is not perceived as visible.[56] In his watercolours illustrating *Robinson Crusoe*, T. Pericoli effectively created the impression of the first shot from Robinson's rifle in the air of the desert island, where never before a shot had resonated.[57] In his essay on the drawing of portraits, he compared the human face to a landscape as seen on a wall, with echoes of the global perception of reality from the seeing-in, much as from the landscape metaphor.[58] In the Cappella Sansevero in Naples, the statues are sculpted to create the impression of bodies wrapped in veils or nets, with extraordinary effects of tactile illusions. The *Veiled Christ* sculpted in 1753 by G. Sanmartino is the marble image of Christ wrapped in a shroud; the optical illusion of the shroud sculpted into the marble emphasizes the frail, excruciated corpse, transmitting a compelling emotion. The observer is not deceived about the matter being hard stone instead of frail tissue or tender flesh, nor was it the artist's intention to deceive.[59] Even in *trompe-l'oeil* painting, painter and observer consciously participate in the imaginative play. It is a game of cross-references, back and forth from the consciousness of the artificial nature of the object creating optical impression to the emotional resonance the image arouses. Far from being captured by a compelling perception dictated by contest, the mind enjoys the fascination while appreciating the artist's skill, thanks to the imaginative faculty in the observer's mind, much as in the artist's mind.

Techniques of controlled optical illusion elaborated by Greeks architects aimed at approximating ideal proportions or pure geometrical forms in natural sight. Greek temples were built applying devices of controlled visual illusion, to prevent the distortions in sight due to sunlight, horizontal lines or distance. These included the 'swelling' (*entasis*) of columns distorted from the perfect cylinder, their inclination and size according to position, the overall curvature of the building.[60] In the Renaissance, the size of a statue was adapted in conformity with the niche, where it should be placed, calculating distance from the soil or angle of view. The trained artist had to be able to evaluate the visual effect considering the relative position of artwork and observer. In painting, the technique of foreshortening builds compelling visual illusions manipulating the divergence from realistic proportions with dramatic effects, as in *Dead Christ* painted by

Mantegna. In Byzantine art a figure's height signals the place in hierarchy or the divine nature of the character portrayed; silhouettes against the flat, golden background impress themselves on the observer at first sight. The statues in clay in the *Mourning of the Marys over the Dead Christ* by Niccolò dell'Arca stir up emotional 'sympathy' to the tragedy of Crucifixion and the depth of human sorrows; the optical illusion of movement is at the core of the commotion the mourning women in agitation evoke in the viewer's mind.

The aim of the artist is to emotionally share the ideas which the imaginative faculty generates, whether they are images born by *mimesis*, fancied creatures or a creative combination of both. Manipulated optical illusions are instruments of symbolic imagination, which convey meaning and create emotional resonance to artworks.

Imaginative Intelligence in the Visual Arts and Beyond

Optical illusion may be manipulated to achieve a different aim, when the artist creates parallel worlds going beyond what the cognitive faculties know about the laws of the physical world, or when the seeing-in creates double reading in the images. Optical illusion art is a specific discipline, creating perceptive illusions about impossible phenomena or ambiguous images, which convey feelings of two-facedness, undergoing transformation, a parallel reality.[61] Contemporary techniques by computer software have enhanced the instruments to create graphic optical illusions.[62] The best-know optical illusion artist is Escher; Arcimboldo and Magritte may be mentioned in different epochs and with different styles; Dali is on the list with many other 'masters of deception'.[63] The images in illusion art do not suppress ambiguities. The purpose of the illusion artist is to keep alive the two-faced nature of the images to the eye of the observer, and make their ambiguous nature unavoidable for the cognitive system of the viewer, who is 'deceived' by them. When looking at these paintings or drawings, ambiguity is not suppressed in intuitive judgement; the artist conveys meanings of multiplicity, metamorphosis, never-ending loops, infinity, being upside down, which invite the viewer to be surprised and perplexed in looking at the world outside or at our inner worlds. The meanings conveyed may be abstract views of a philosophical nature and/or emotional states of mind. In the fruition of pieces of illusion art, the effect of context on accessibility works in the direction of opening the mind to imaginary worlds, both theoretically and in immediate perception. Illusion art is a symbolic language to express complex mental representations, enriching our inner world and cognitive capabilities.

To sum up, who appreciates a drawing, a water colour, a painting, a sculpture is able to experience a degree of sensory illusion that is the vehicle of symbolic communication and emotional resonance, while appreciating the nature of the manufacture from which the mental impression springs. The fruitful imaginative deception works through the seeing-in effect and the whole complex of feelings it stirs up; but the viewer does not lose the distinction between image and reality, being perfectly able to perceive the surface creating the seeing-in illusion. Even a *trompe-l'oeil* painting that at some distance provokes a compelling perception of reality, mimicking the sensory impressions conveyed by real objects, invites the viewer to make the humorous discovery of the fading borders between appearance and substance.[64] It is a philosophical form of art; irony and surprise are among its basic features.[65] The encoding and decoding of visual perceptions are creative instruments in symbolic languages. The symbolic representation of 3D forms, noting crucial characteristics in black and white on a plane surface according to geometric codes, is a cognitive instrument with enormous potential for constructive purposes in applied fields or theoretical disciplines. Procedures for mapping 3D images onto the plane are codified communication languages with a variety of reading codes, including the sophisticated software to simulate the figure of the Ice Man Ötzi, the hunter dead in the Alps sometime before 3000 BC.

Controlled optical illusions in symbolic languages are applied in less emotional fields than art. In science and technology, as in the visual arts, imaginative intelligence works as constructive rationality adopting a rich toolbox for rationally encoding and decoding visual perceptions. CAD programmes are software to generate 3D models in industrial design, specifically built to visualize the salient characteristics, which are of interest for the task at hand. The same cognitive processes mentioned above are at work. Imaginative intelligence conceives the piece to be designed. Imagination working as constructive rationality focuses the solution best adapted to the function to perform, thanks to the trained capabilities to draw the fancied 3D object on sheet or screen, creating optical illusion within a shared code of technical communication. Training in decoding the visual signals permits us to summarize the salient characteristics; who draws or sees them recognizes their patterns as symbolic forms within shared codes of communication. Visual perceptions, which admit of multiple reading, are decoded according to the task at hand, as it happens in the perception of hollows and swells in reading drawings traced by black and white spots on a sheet. Optical illusions codified in framing conventions are systematically used in design, in engineering, in architecture, in all the applied fields which use techniques of visual representation. In all techniques of notation, the ability to mentally evaluate the characteristics of the imagined object is fortified by exercise and training. The exact decoding of the perceived visual patterns is professionally acquired, training the ability to convert the inner world of mental images into codified visual signs and give them meaning. The trained architect literally 'sees' the building decoding the axonometric representation or the plane projection, with a capability for creative imagination that the untrained person cannot reach.

This capability is systematically trained to the effect in architectural schools, also by the active exercise in drawing. In all professions using visual languages as their instruments (e.g. a CAD professional or a geographer), people are trained to fortify the ability to creatively manipulate visual signals in symbolic languages, as they are codified in framing patterns. The human mind freely walks into the world of codified 'optical illusions', and out of it.

A whole range of possibilities in manipulating and encoding visual perceptions for expressive, theoretical or practical purposes has been recalled so far. Our focus was on the toolbox at the disposal of artists along centuries to produce artworks, which were at the core of civilization all over the world; but manipulating visual signals is an important procedure in human knowledge at large. Visual illusions' tricks are powerful instruments in artistic expression for emotional purposes, much as in performing a rich array of creative tasks by imaginative intelligence. The multiple reading of images and their decoding according to shared languages of communication are fundamental procedures in creative cognitive processes. They enrich cognition and we should not overlook the enormous creative potential due to our capability of freely playing with mental images, reinterpreting them in multiple directions, decoding them in a variety of interpretations. Framing should not to be conceived exclusively as distorting lenses or 'blinders'. Mental frames include the cultural heritage of symbolic forms, which may be recombined or literally seen anew in different perspectives to create new symbolic products. Musical forms (concert, sonata, fugue, etc.) have the role of creative framing, admitting of infinite variations and radical innovation, but imposing shared rules of communication to both trained musicians and audience. In architecture, constructive frames, as both ideal forms and standard technical solutions, were adopted for millennia, transmitted by tradition and craft or codified in learned treatises (e.g. the architectural orders in ancient Greek architecture or in the Renaissance).[66] The cultural heritage of symbolic forms offers patterns to the creative wandering of imaginative intelligence; it suggests paths along which the creative mind explores innovative solutions.

It would be especially interesting to study the mental process of listening to some piece of music in the mind by reading the notes written as graphic signs on a sheet of paper. The capability to hear a piece music in one's head reading a score, or conversely to translate the music heard into musical signs according to some code of transcription, is a specific ability of the educated musician. The score is a piece of blank paper crossed by black lines and tainted by black spots; yet when the signs are seen by the musician, they translate into mental melodies, though these are not real vibrations in the external world. The mental reading of music has, in some sense, the nature of a sensory distortion. All written musical production is based on these imaginative, sensory perceptions and with it the whole communication of musical works in concert halls and opera theatres, the training of professional musicians and the enjoyment of so many lovers and practitioners of music.

The human mind inhabits the worlds of imagination living the double life of the real and the imagined worlds. We cross the strictures of immediate perceptions travelling deep into symbolic imageries; perhaps, we are able to perceive reality only because we are able to live in the islands of imagination. The symbolic world, which is essential to human cognition and is the specific mark of it, is at the core of emotional resonance and sympathy and thus at the very heart of human relations. Imaginative intelligence and its practice as constructive rationality offer extraordinary enrichment to human cognition and creative innovation.

27 REALISM AND REALITY: THE ARGUMENTS OF CINEMA

Maria Tortajada

The question of the definition of reality within a larger reflection on 'realism' involves several fields of knowledge and disciplines, in science as well as in human sciences.[1] These matters are prevalent in the domain of aesthetics, whether they touch on literature, art or cinema. A positivistic nineteenth century outlined its own version of reality as given, as being-there, available for both experimentation and representation. Still, when confronted with one another, the variants of realism modulate this very proposition. The emergence of cinema at the turn of the century has largely been thought from the question of reality: it outdid photography – or so people claimed. In any case, cinema was a scientific tool before it became a media: Etienne-Jules Marey first defined the chronophotographic method with his invention of chronophotographic cameras and projectors to perform the analysis of movement in animal locomotion. Cinema thus developed in the crucible of the scientific experimentation of a real phenomenon, movement. At the crossroads between science and spectacle, it raised the issue of the representation of reality from the specificity of its photographic medium, which could record the 'truth' (a term always in need of a definition) of the reality of the world.

Throughout the twentieth century, the variants of realism had to respond to a 'positivistic' definition of reality, adding complexity to it and modelling it. They brought up the inherently aesthetic question: how can art represent 'reality as it is', since it relies on human intervention, precisely, on the transformation, transposition, translation of a 'given'. This is the fundamental paradox of realism, which produces different strands according to the discourses that formulate and unfold it endlessly. Approaching these questions from a theory of representation, it is possible to try and come up with a definition of reality, not as an essence, a given, a domain of pure experience; nor as a discursive production unmoored from the world of experience, demonstrated or taken apart through the instruments of logic alone; but as a construction depending on the place occupied by the notion of reality in a play of conceptual relations. The theory

of representation makes it possible to define reality in the relation that develops
between representation and spectator in the construction of realist discourse.

This essay does not aim for a general theory. Rather, using a case study, it puts
some topoi of realism to the test, bringing out attempts at a theory of representation and highlighting a historically situated line of argument in the process. I
would like to start from a few texts in the context of film criticism, texts which
were articulated to a growing debate in the years following World War II, at a time
when several national cinemas were confronted with the 'representation of reality', Italian Neorealism being the inescapable model. A figure was then beginning
to emerge and was to become a reference in the film profession. In the history
of cinema, André Bazin, a critic at *Cahiers du cinéma*, which he also headed in
the 1950s, holds a canonical position founded on his critical and theoretical
standpoints as well as on his commitment to film at various institutional levels
(pedagogical, cultural). He is the representative of realist discourse in France, the
unavoidable reference in cinephilic and aesthetic discourse, and enjoys international recognition.[2] The selection of his critical texts in the four-volume anthology
Qu'est-ce que le cinéma? has contributed to the reconstruction of the theoretical
form of his discourse,[3] to the extent that his status as 'author' and the focus on his
own positions obscures a complex network of discourses and ideas on the issue of
realism in French film criticism after World War II.[4] Yet what is most interesting
in realist discourse is its variability. It varies throughout history, whether we think
back to the Renaissance in the aesthetic domain, with the reflection on perspecti-
val representation in painting, to the realist century by excellence, the nineteenth
century, or to the different realist schools in the twentieth century, in cinema, art
or literature. Realist discourse also varies across the dominant debates of a period.
However, aesthetic realism, that which questions representation in its capacity to
represent reality within an artistic set of problems, is founded on a criterion systematically repeated with ever-different actualizations. Indeed, realist discourse
is governed by a paradoxical centre which creators, theoreticians and critics keep
facing. What I call the fundamental paradox of realism forces a tension within
any realist aesthetic: between the will to show the real 'as it is', erasing or denying
as much as possible the formal and discursive reality of the passage to representation, and the will to art, which assumes the creative intervention of the artist, and
consequently a mediation that precisely calls into question the idea that reality
appears 'as it is' within representation.

A Phenomenological Idealism

In 1948, *La Revue du cinéma* published a debate on realism. Jean Desternes[5]
then wrote an introduction that directly explained this tension, offering a particular interpretation of it:

In aesthetics, the term realism indicates a will to translate reality as strictly as possible. As it happens, direct translation is impossible, since this reality has to be conveyed in words, sounds, colors and, in the domain of film, in images and sequences – which is to say that the real has to be distorted.

I already want to write: first proof that realism does not exist.[6]

According to Desternes, the first proposition in the fundamental paradox of realism is untenable, as it supposes an economy that cannot sustain artistic creation and even goes as far as to negate the creative act:

> If we lay down the equation Reality + Art = Realism, the terms are not quantitative but – that is the crux of the matter – qualitative.
>
> Conscious realism will try and reduce the coefficient Art to be richer in Reality and would even suppress it if that did not simultaneously mean suppressing itself. Cruel failure: serving as the record-keeper of the real, opening the cine-eye, recording as mechanically as possible life as it is …
>
> Then what? All that is left to do is the presentation, as artistically as possible, of these elements of the real thus obtained, and leave it to art to forge afterwards what had been warded off from it beforehand.[7]

The artistic character of representation has to be assumed. For Desternes, this is encapsulated in a word, 'style', a classical defining element for art that involves the claim to a singular mark and the power of mediation on the part of the author. First transcription, then translation: the sequence works well, apart from the fact that representation is already a reformulation. With the idea of 'transcription', the reasoning goes through a recurring argument in discourses on cinema since the 1910s, a time when the status of cinema as art was being debated. The theme of automaticity in the reproduction of reality supposes that, since the apparatus of cinema is a 'machine', the constitution of the copy does not involve human intervention. But without man, no art. The same arguments had been advanced in the 1880s and 1890s in discussions on the status of photography as art. This evidently shows to what extent certain themes keep reappearing in the debate on realism; but also how deeply intertwined this debate is with the very existence of cinema as a photographic medium.

The whole reflection focuses on the relation between representation and the world. To better understand the outlines of a theory of representation here, it is necessary to move away from the aesthetic formula 'Reality + Art = Realism', which is akin to a recipe, a sum of essential elements needed in an aesthetic compound. One possibility is to centre on the schema that supports this line of argument. To define realism, the following should be accounted for.

Representation — Reality

We thus need to leave behind the metaphor of addition to privilege this schema, which implies that we define representation, reality and their relation at the same time. Relation is central to the operations of representation. Mimesis as imitation may, for instance, be considered as a copy. Theoretical modernity opened this to other formulations, with representation 'standing in for' reality. Representation does not imitate in the sense of resembling, but it represents, it 'is the sign for'. Realism focuses the discussion on the 'referentiality' of representation. What does Desternes have to say about this?

> In art, realism thus consists in recreating the real with as much verisimilitude as possible. Indeed, let us not forget that the goal is persuasion, and that the true becomes believable only insofar as its alteration by art makes it plausible to us.[8]

The interpretation of this relation ('standing in for') rests on two points: the first is an explicit return to a theory of verisimilitude, from which realist theories usually differentiate themselves. While it is a version of reality in which one may believe because it is 'possible', verisimilitude does not refer to reality in the sense of a given (no matter what this given is), of an outside positivity indifferent to man's evaluation, but to an acceptable, conventional, consensual reality. Verisimilitude is the value of the seventeenth century, the touchstone of classicism dismissed by nineteenth-century realisms as they placed 'reality itself' at the forefront of the referential horizon. Here we are broaching a borderline proposition in the context of realist theories, a proposition which to some extent lies beyond realism.[9] Verisimilitude is thus reintroduced with the corollary that representation should recreate the real. No copy, but an almost demiurgic act to manufacture reality: this conception brings the artist closer to the divine. Most importantly, it is a way to make the relation between representation and reality more specific while weakening it.

> In art, then, nothing is true, or rather, everything is. Indeed, from the moment when this reality is translated into words and images, only its expression undoubtedly exists, as fake (realistically speaking), fanciful and fantastic as it may be. And this reality to the power of two then becomes more true than prime reality since, 'fixing' it in the chosen artistic medium, the artist gives it a chance to last. Take Mona Lisa: a few grams of colour applied on a canvas by a fifty-something with little inclination for realism constitute a more solid reality than the smile of the model, long reduced to dust. Or take the mutiny of the Potemkin: where did Eisenstein need the stamp of a 'certified copy'?[10]

Resemblance becomes secondary, which adversely affects imitation, understood as a copy of reality. What matters is recreated reality, reality 'to the power of two', 'fixed' in the medium of representation and which comes to coexist with the other, better than the other, a 'given' subject to time and death. Art puts reality on the side of eternity. The reality of things is in itself little defined in this critical-theoretical text: it is a smile, a rebellion, it may be just about anything. What matters is to evacuate its vividness, the most important thing being this new reality, which defines representation itself rather well. Still, there remains the idea of 'translating' the reality of the given into words and images. Positive reality resists its expulsion and maintains itself in the system. We then reach the first outline of a theory of representation:

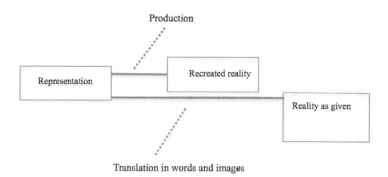

In this balance between an idealism and a phenomenology, the creator's sensation and perception temper the return to classical values:

> In the simple operation that consists in saying again what one believes to have heard, in showing what one believes to have seen, in reconstructing what one believes to be the real, multiple factors of illusion come into play. But in the case of a work of art, with the material of 'testimony' needing further elaboration (if only through editing or writing), faith alone can save.[11]

This reality in which 'one may believe' is still dependent on the relativity of the point of view or point of audition, 'illusions' which interfere in the artist's perceptive act. Desternes's article approaches this in a roundabout manner, yet it is an essential aspect that resituates this discourse in the realist debate on positivity: reality exists (for us) only insofar as it is seen. Kracauer considered this definition as inherent to twentieth-century realist discourses, but it is intrinsically linked to a realist questioning in the face of reality as given.[12]

What does recreated reality represent, in the end? If direct imitation of reality in its likeness is minimized while an emphasis is maintained on the process of perception of this reality as given, then a genuine questioning becomes possible on the representational status of perception or the place of 'the image' in perception – mental image or matter-image, as with Bergson, for instance. Desternes's brief text cannot deal with this vast subject other than through a mere mention of the problem. However, the problem is still presupposed in this kind of theoretical outline, since producing recreated reality out of multiple perceptive 'illusions', of perceptions blurred by the senses, amounts to implying a representational relation in the creative act – an imitation of the perceived, in which the link between the idea that has been formed of reality and reality as given depends on the uncertainties of perception. It could be said, then, following Jacques Derrida, that to produce recreated reality is to imitate the idea 'inside me', 'la copie en moi'. This is tantamount to the confirmation of a form of idealism.[13] For Desternes, however, the subject is phenomenological, not Cartesian: the idea imitated by artists is elaborated in themselves through their perception.

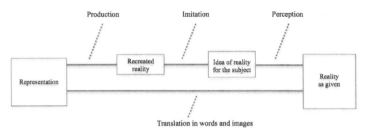

Translation in words and images

What still surprises in Desternes's discourse is his insistence on the co-presence of two realities. Representation becomes a new reality, different from the first, 'truer' even in that it is no longer randomly affected by time. In the order of values, it substitutes for the first reality because it is paradoxically a 'more solid' reality. There is little difference, then, between this and a representation considered in its materiality, as an element of reality itself. The author stops short of making this assertion: to refer to representation as an object in the world would mean moving too unequivocally toward a reappraisal of positive reality – and attribute its nature and value to representation. The discourse would be too 'frontally' realist; instead, the text stays within the boundaries of an idealist theory of artistic creation, with an attachment to verisimilitude and a form of phenomenologization of the idea.

Although this theory is approached from the perspective of creation, the issue of spectatorship, without which a theory of representation can only proceed halfway through, is raised. Spectators should be grasped within their relation to this ensemble: reality, representation, or both. Faced with so many uncertainties and perceptive illusions in the mediation performed by the creator, 'faith' is a necessary avenue, according to Desternes. The relation put forward here is that of confidence in this recreated world, the product of perceptive illusions and belief in 'testimony'[14] – a word that requires quotation marks as soon as reality as a given is considered from a distance. The term is essential in the discourses of realism, where it raises the question of the document – or, in the context of cinema, of 'documentary' as a genre. Film critics disagree on this point: either 'testimony' is rejected as insufficiently artistic, as raw material that makes the whole issue of realism irrelevant, in the absence of a creative act;[15] or it is postulated as the very example of the realist approach, joining in that respect the tradition of naturalism and its historical representative Zola. Desternes advances the term while simultaneously marking it off.

Realism of Commitment: Reality between Reflection and Analysis

Within explicitly representational approaches of realism, another version substantiates the notion of reality as 'given'. In 1949, Raymond Barkan wrote a film review of Louis Daquin's *Le Point du jour* for the periodical *Europe*.[16] The script for the film, which told the story of a mining village, was written by Vladimir Pozner. Barkan elevated the two men to the rank of a collective author. The film shows the world of work and miners and was highly praised by Barkan, whose writing was informed by a Marxist critique. From the late 1940s on, critics clashed on questions related to the representation of reality from ideological positions marked by the increasing international polarity crystallizing in the Cold War. The choice of a definition of reality is therefore decisive in determining the position of each discourse on the ideological spectrum. For Barkan, what makes the quality of a film is its capacity to go particularly far in 'the analysis of the real world':

> Starting from the existence of miners and their families, the authors attempted to lay bare all the elements shaping that existence with their camera. To the probable exception of a few Soviet and Italian productions, *Le Point du jour* is thus the first film conveying to us the kaleidoscopic dimension of reality. Yet these elements are not autonomous or isolated from one another. They intersect. They have an effect on one another.[17]

Reality pertains to the 'given' here, but unlike Desterne's proposition, Barkan's directly specifies it: a plural, compound and composite reality, it is arranged as a kaleidoscopic image. The detail of the film's presentation thus accounts for what different characters crossing paths will become, and describes particular situations having nothing to do with the typical hero of film drama but bearing witness to a social issue beyond them. Marxist terminology allows to articulate the form of this reality, where the collective is the raison d'être:

> Their dramas have nothing exceptional to them. Still, their emotional resonance is contagious and they are full of significance. Indeed, under the guise of different sensibilities, each of these dramas goes far beyond the individual, reflecting a large swath of the contradictions of reality.[18]

> In *Le Point du jour*, the miner is not simply a worker tiring himself out extracting coal, sleeping like a log, getting up at dawn to repeat the same gestures as the day before, with alcoholic drinks as his only relaxation on Sundays at the local tavern. He is no longer a slave with the summary psychology of naturalism and populism. The miner

is a worker with a consciousness, a living consciousness modelled by a living reality. Some of his problems crop up because of his trade. Others are related to the fact that he belongs to a family collectivity, to a mining collectivity, to a proletarian collectivity, to a national collectivity.[19]

Contradictions in a kaleidoscopic reality, problems tied to concrete aspects of work, where the individual is understood on the basis of his relation to the collective: here is what representation retains of reality.

Reality is not approached in its phenomenological nature but in its social dimension. The smile of a character as Desternes presented it – Mona Lisa rather than miners – does not matter if it does not come within a network of relations between elements that can give an account of the social position of the characters. Barkan can therefore dismiss as secondary typical arguments of the realist critical discourse that found the authenticity of the film on the faithfulness to the very locales where the action takes place: 'The natural setting is a means, not the condition for realism'.[20] In his view, realism is fundamentally political indeed, which echoes the propositions put forward in the debate of the 1930s.

To describe what representation 'does', two ways are available. They are opposed in some regards; the excerpts quoted here articulate them together. Representation either reflects or analyses. The first option, which recurs throughout discourses on socialist realism, stands on the side of the historical metaphor of the mirror held out by the artist to reality, a metaphor which also points to techniques of perspective and the nineteenth-century novel. Reality is given, it self-depicts on the representation: this is the ideal cultivated by the myth of the 'transparent' representation, to convey 'reality as it is'.[21] It is in this sense that the camera should bear witness, with the representation functioning as a document.[22]

The second option implies an act that organizes reality. While Barkan is opposed to a formal, purely aesthetic realism, stressing out the importance of the subject dealt with, which carries the weight of reality,[23] he tempers the theory of the reflection with the compositional process being implemented:

> In practical terms, Daquin's construction has allowed the image to explore the mine as would have the pen of a writer. Destinies come close to one another, cross paths and join in a mosaic of meticulously planned sequences. A synthetic view, where each element is in its place, emerges from their juxtaposition.[24]

The mosaic as a form responds to the kaleidoscopic quality of reality. The principle of composition is that of the juxtaposition of destinies and individual stories. This passage from imitation to reformulation through representation clearly appears in another article written by Barkan for his film column in *Europe*:

> Some see in our wish for these essential themes drawn from everyday life a progression toward who-knows-what elementary cinema excluding the analysis of individual

behaviours and high ethical problems, banning any subtlety in style. Admittedly, these people instinctively identify quality in art with aesthetic refinement and intellectual Byzantinism. Whereas realism, on the contrary, is the projection of the multiple facets of life, the analysis of movement teeming with intricacies, the nuances of beings and things transposed in their full complexity.[25]

As the development of the sentence shows, the author goes from the idea of a 'projection' of reality in representation – which should be understood as a synonym for reflection[26] – to the 'analysis' performed by representation, which is itself 'transposition'.

The representational position is stressed out, but on the basis of an extreme emphasis on reality which is the most interesting aspect of Barkan's article: in short, representation is this apparently contradictory object, a reorganized reflection. This process of giving form concerns the subject, the themes, the creative work in its organization of the content imitated from reality. In a semiological formulation borrowed from Hjelmslev, the work could be said to bear on 'the form of content'.[27] As for spectators, they are on the side of reason and comprehension: as 'attentive spectators', addressees of a 'message',[28] they should be able to see this reality in its contradictions. Their position is implied by this realism. The relation will be communicational, in the service of commitment.

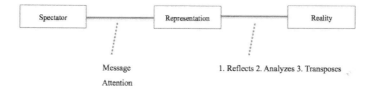

Message   1. Reflects 2. Analyzes 3. Transposes
Attention

An Ontological Realism

'The cinematic esthetic will be social, or else will do without an esthetic', Bazin wrote in 1943.[29] This categorical statement, which may partly explain all the energy spent by Bazin in defense of Italian neorealism, is not what he has been remembered for in the history of film criticism. This probably owes to the fact that, as far as social critique went, his approach – steeped in the Catholic Left – did not go as far politically as the positions advocated in the 1950s by *Positif* or by Italian critic Guido Aristarco, who headed the review *Cinema Nuovo* and with whom Bazin was engaged in an ongoing debate.[30] It may also be that the reference theoretical articles of Bazinian realism reprinted in *What Is Cinema?* ('Ontology of the Photographic Image', 1944–58, and 'The Myth of Total Cinema', 1946–58) did not deal with reality from the standpoint of social truth, implicitly approaching it as a phenomenological, Bergsonian alloy. 'On Realism', published in 1944, goes along the same lines.[31]

For Bazin, realism is the idea shared by humankind from its origins, at least since its involvement in representation, from its primary religious formulation to its modern, artistic version. Humans are tempted by the copy of the real; they are driven by the desire to perfect this imitation. This psychological premise determines the rewriting by Bazin of art history in order to include means of mechanical reproduction. After photography, cinema has fulfilled this tendency. It is itself driven by the guiding myth which, according to Bazin, conditioned its invention and has determined later improvements of its technique (color, three-dimensionality, etc.):

> The guiding myth, then, inspiring the invention of cinema, is the accomplishment of that which dominated in a more or less vague fashion all the techniques of the mechanical reproduction of reality in the nineteenth century, from photography to the phonograph, namely an integral realism, a recreation of the world in its own image, an image unburdened by the freedom of interpretation of the artist or the irreversibility of time.[32]

The fundamental paradox of realism is expressed here. Cinema is putatively freed from the weight of the artist's mark, from creation, becoming available for a direct representation of reality. The Bazinian version is founded on a line of argument linked to the photographic and cinematographic medium:

> Again, the essential factor in the transition from the baroque to photography is not the perfecting of a physical process ... rather does it lie in a psychological fact, to wit, in completely satisfying our appetite for illusion by a mechanical reproduction in the making of which man plays no part. The solution is not to be found in the result achieved but in the way of achieving it.[33]

The explanation does not pertain to the aesthetic debate but to the making of the material image, its genesis, and therefore what determines the medium prior to putting anything into form artistically.[34] The first argument stems from the automatic nature of the technical phenomenon of cinema. Even as this has been traditionally contested through the emphasis on framing choices or the writing involved in editing, the cinematographic 'machine' excludes the creative act. A theme already present in Desternes's text thus returns, but Bazin treats it very differently: while he shows interest in style and the creative act in countless articles, Bazin still develops an ideal of realism using a mechanical figure from which human action is excluded. On photography, for instance, he writes:

> The personality of the photographer enters into the proceedings only in his selection of the object to be photographed and by way of the purpose he has in mind. Although the final result may reflect something of his personality, this does not play the same role as is played by that of the painter. All the arts are based on the presence of man, only photography derives an advantage from his absence.[35]

The twin argument to mechanicalness is the indexicality of the photographic image: a trace produced by light on the sensitive emulsion coating the film, the photographic image is determined by the process of its making, which also gives rise to its imagination. Here Bazin proceeds through comparisons: 'The photograph as such and the object in itself share a common being, after the fashion of a fingerprint'.[36] He also draws a parallel between photographic genesis and the 'molding of death masks ... which likewise involves a certain automatic process': 'One might consider photography in this sense as a molding, the taking of an impression, by the manipulation of light'.[37]

With cinema, this moulding is temporal – that is, reality being defined by duration, the continuity of the temporal flow, any account of it will have to respect its essence and as a consequence avoid a certain type of editing.[38] This consideration pertains to the second level of realism, however, whereas our present concern is the genesis of the image. Here Bazin adopts a Bergsonian position suitable for a phenomenological definition of reality:

> Viewed in this perspective, the cinema is objectivity in time. The film is no longer content to preserve the object, enshrouded as it were in an instant, as the bodies of insects are preserved intact, out of the distant past, in amber. The film delivers baroque art from its convulsive catalepsy. Now, for the first time, the image of things is likewise the image of their duration, change mummified as it were.[39]

Bazin does not go through semiology (the index) to describe what happens between reality and representation: in his view, this relationship is immediate. What Bazin has in mind is a kind of direct contact. Representation attracts a part of reality in itself. The process is described as a 'transference of reality from the thing to its reproduction',[40] with Bergson's theory of images (and its notion of representation as a piece of matter) as its implicit model. On photography, Bazin goes on:

> Only a photographic lens can give us the kind of image of the object that is capable of satisfying the deep need man has to substitute for it something more than a mere approximation, a kind of decal or transfer. The photographic image is the object itself, the object freed from the conditions of time and space that govern it. No matter how fuzzy, distorted, or discolored, no matter how lacking in documentary value the image may be, it shares, by virtue of the very process of its becoming, the being of the model of which it is the reproduction; it is the model.[41]

The relation disappears in the copula, in the radical identity between model and representation. If the real is in fact revealed, it is because it is made present. The question is no longer about copy or imitation, for it does not matter how resemblance may be adversely affected by possible distortions of the image. At the time of the ontological formulation, we are far from the ideal of transparence implicit in the metaphor of the window pane, akin to that of the mirror, and which stands for two modes of representational relation: either the glass becomes invisible and is forgotten, in which case a complete illusion is at work and the representational relation of imitation is concealed; or the transparence of the pane is brought out at the same time as the world being observed, with the result of a mixed illusion where both access to reality as it is and the mediation of the pane are pointed out. Neither option functions in the model produced by Bazin. What he has in mind is the 're-presentation' of the object of the world, its being-there in representation. This differentiates his position from Desternes's, which referred to a recreated reality. For Bazin, the representation is reality itself. The schema can then be written as follows:

Representation = reality

Accordingly, representation is an object in the world, of which it is a part, phenomenologically speaking: 'Every image is to be seen as an object and every object as an image'.[42] Bazin also writes: 'photography actually contributes something to the order of natural creation instead of providing a substitute for it'.[43] Already, at the beginning of his piece, he states that 'Photography affects us like a phenomenon in nature, like a flower or a snowflake whose vegetable or earthly origins are an inseparable part of their beauty'.[44]

What Desternes did not suggest – relinquishing the structural relation of mimesis, that between representation and reality – Bazin lays down as the foundation of a realist ontology. It does not consist in an idealization of reality or in a view of representation itself as recreation, but in an idealization of the mimetic relation. As a consequence, the documentary function finds itself raised to a higher power. Thus formulated, the ontology provides a justification for the defense of a realism founded on the notion of document, natural setting, non-professional actors, etc. Quite logically, and unlike Desternes or Doniol-Valcroze, Bazin makes it a decisive element in his aesthetic choices.

Still, what is the place of the spectator in this theory of representation? Admittedly, the representation-reality depends on the spectator's belief – not in a 'perfect' imitation, but in an event pertaining to faith: 'In spite of any objections our critical spirit may offer, we are forced to accept as real the existence of the object reproduced, actually re-presented, set before us, that is to say, in time and space'.[45]

The ideal of realism is to reach this limit where reality and representation form one body, where the mediation of the given has ceased to be an issue, with the solution originating in the mechanical and genetic justification of the image's making. Yet this ideal requires belief in the form of faith: what is involved here is an 'embodiment'.[46] This theory of representation draws from a Christian conception that structures Bazin's theoretical stance as well as his critical positions. Realism is a path to salvation.[47] Belief has nothing to do with the issue of illusion, which operates within deception or the ambiguous play of the representational link. The faith to which Bazin invites the spectator is not a belief underpinned by illusion, for the ontology is given as true – not out of naiveté, but as a challenge to the representational order of mimesis. Non-believers (such as the theoreticians that we are) can always resituate this belief within the play of variables in the mimetic relation.

The resulting scheme is quite different from those explained so far. It may be summarized as follows:

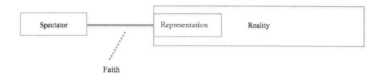

The force of Bazin's proposal lies in how radically it collapses the representational relation and defines ontology as identity between representation and reality. The critic put this forward clearly in the years 1944–5. Evidently, he was not the only one to outline a strongly articulated realist theory in film criticism in the 1940s. Like others, he expressed himself on a highly topical issue related to the representation of reality. I have chosen to take seriously several of these discourses contemporary with Bazin's theorization, before he became the chosen representative of the thought of ontological realism on cinema in France. All in all, we have the texts of three authors – only – here, whose theoretical importance was sometimes limited by the material place of film criticism or the debate they framed within a review, but whose coherent propositions provide different perspectives to the thought on realism in cinema in the post-war period. Indeed, these propositions generate new questions. Within the discourse of realism, several ways in which representational relations operate are highlighted. The definitions of reality are initially explicit: reality as given, social reality as kaleidoscopic and plural, recreated reality or representation-reality. Juxtaposing these definitions is not enough, however. Each may be grasped only as part of the relations that involve it within a theory of representation. In short, to know what reality is, it is necessary to know what representation 'does' with it.

To be sure, this empirical method leaves aside essential aspects of the theory of representation: the part played by codes and aesthetic traditions in the definition of reality, which E. H. Gombrich's approach on illusion or Roman Jakobson's on the historicization of realist discourses could help relativize. Besides, concerning the representational relation, Nelson Goodman's analytical theory would lead to a more specific description of the nature and directionality of the relations involved.[48] I have chosen to limit the scope of this study to the terms of these critics and not go at length over points that call for complementary developments. Rather, my ambition has been to show that the theory of representation plays out in journalistic practice on a daily basis, that it structures ideological positioning as well as aesthetic choices and that, accordingly, it is important to understand its nature to better identify what is at stake in the field of cinema around the question of realism. A history of film criticism cannot be separated from an analysis of the theorization produced by such criticism, through the voice of its authors and considering the discursive sites that periodicals are.

28 A REFLECTION ON THE SOCIAL UTILITY OF MODERN MACROECONOMICS

Michel De Vroey

Introduction

The question I wish to address in this essay surely makes sense in the context of the time we are living in. For the last four years our economies have been experiencing a deep recession, and, right or wrong, this experience has spilled over into the general judgement made about macroeconomics. In a nutshell, its reputation is at a low ebb. Is this judgement justified? On a broader level, what can civil society expect from macroeconomic theory? Is the discussion triggered by this last question ridden with ambiguities and misunderstandings, and, if yes, of which nature? These are the questions that I want tackle. To do the job, I shall follow a historical thread starting with the rise of macroeconomics to end up with real business cycle macroeconomics.

The Rise of Macroeconomics

The sub-discipline of macroeconomics studies aggregate economic variables such as employment, output, the general price level, the interest rate, etc. It saw the light of day in the wake of World War II. Actually, it did not arise from scratch. Previously, it existed under the name of monetary theory, and its concern was the study of how money, in particular the supply of money, had an impact on 'real' economic outcomes as studied by pure economics.

The piece that, rightly enough, is considered its starting point is John Maynard Keynes's 1936 book, *The General Theory of Employment, Money and Interest*, in short the *General Theory*. Before writing it, Keynes was already a towering figure in the economic profession and a widely recognized expert on monetary matters. His main concern was practical policy until the outburst of the Great Depression with its mass unemployment, peaking above 20 per cent in several countries. This dramatic event triggered Keynes to become concerned with high theory as he felt that the economic theory of the time, mainly Marshallian neoclassical theory, proved unable to come to grips with it. The 1930s were also a time where Russia was witnessing strong economic results with the effect that a possible electoral victory of parties leaning towards communism (or their taking power in more unorthodox ways) was a possibility that could not be discarded. In short, capitalism was in peril, both economically and politically, and Keynes realized that its survival implied important changes in its functioning. While these elements, beautifully expressed in the concluding chapter of the *General Theory*, were looming in the back of Keynes's mind, his endeavour was mainly theoretical. To him, the economic theory of the time was wanting and the policy conclusions that they reached were exactly the opposite of what should be done. This was the state of affairs he wanted to change. As aptly noted by Skidelsky, Keynes's biographer, this venture intertwined theory and persuasion: 'Keynes understood that his theory had to be usable for politicians and administrators: easily applied, offering political dividends. But he also understood that, before he could win the political argument, he had to win the intellectual argument.'[1]

The main diagnosis about the crisis available to economists at the time was of 'Austrian' inspiration. The crisis, the story run, signalled a situation of overinvestment and misallocation of resources, a state of affairs that required a process of 'liquidation' for its solution, a real wage deflation on the one hand, and elimination of the firms that had engaged in wrong investment decisions on the other. Flexibility was thus the motto. The more flexible prices and wages were, the faster the liquidation process would come to an end and conditions for prosperity would be re-established. However, when the depression kept its course without wages deflation failing to exert its proclaimed effect, economists started to waver about the virtues of laissez faire and to wonder whether, the laissez-faire doctrine notwithstanding, the state should engage more actively in the economy. Thus, economists were torn between the policy conclusions following from accepted theory and their gut feeling that another policy should be taken. Keynes's aim was to remove this contradiction by providing a theoretical argument in favour of the gut feeling. He did not mean a total overhaul of standard economic theory, but rather its emendation. The task he set himself was to demonstrate that the economy could be stuck in a state of equilibrium while also featuring the presence of involuntary unemployment, a notion that had no place in the lexicon of accepted economic theory. In a nutshell, his explanation was to state that involuntary unemployment resulted from a deficiency in aggregate demand, itself the result of insufficient investment. To chase the economy away from its involuntary unemployment equilibrium a policy of autonomous demand activation was needed.

Keynes's book got an enthusiastic reception, especially from young economists. Dissatisfied with the existing situation, they were crying for a new theory that would justify the abandonment of the laissez-faire doctrine. In this respect, Keynes's work delivered beautifully. As Axel Leijonhufvud said, it was received as a 'liberating revelation'.[2] Nevertheless, confusion over the central message of Keynes's book was great, even amongst his admirers. In effect, the *General Theory* was a complex book, hard to read and intertwining different types of arguments, and developed at distinct levels of abstraction, the compatibility of which was hardly obvious.

Progress came when Hicks succeeded in transforming Keynes's cryptic analysis into a simple system of three simultaneous equations. This is the renowned IS–LM model, the starting point of what can be called Keynesian macro, a paradigm that reigned over the profession for the twenty five years that followed the end of World War II.

The IS–LM started as an abstract model, but under the stewardship of another great Keynesian economist, Lawrence Klein, it became transformed into an empirically testable model. The Klen–Goldberger model (1955) marked the start of a long chain of macroeconometric models to be used for making predictions as well as for assessing alternative policies.

These are the three stages – the *General Theory*, the IS–LM model and the birth of Keynesian econometric models – through which macroeconomics came into existence as a new sub-discipline of economics. It soon thrived. The offspring of the Great Depression, its prominent aim was to highlight market failures and to vindicate that they could be remedied upon by state interventions. So, from the onset, it had a reformist flavour. From the 1950s onwards, Keynesian macroeconomics established itself as a new sub-discipline of economics. It was taken up both in universities and public institutions such as central banks.

Characterizing Keynesian Macroeconomics

Let me now try to describe to you the main features of Keynesian macroeconomics in its theoretical rather than its empirical dimension. To this end, I shall use the following seven benchmarks: (1) macroeconomics overarching *explanandum*; (2) the place and role of the notions of equilibrium and disequilibrium; (3) the relative importance of supply and demand; (4) the main methodological rule; (5) the micro/macro relationship; (6) theory's accessibility to laymen; (7) the underpinning ideology.

1. The *overarching object of study* of Keynesian macro is departures of the economy from full employment. Although this was not the line that Keynes had favoured, underemployment is viewed as the result of some sluggishness in the adjustment of wages. State interventions aiming at activating demand through fiscal policy or monetary activation are the remedy to such occurrences.

2. Keynesian theory mixes the notion of *equilibrium and disequilibrium*. The result that it strives for is one where the economy is in equilibrium, in the 'state of rest' sense of the term, this going along with excess supply of labour, i.e. involuntary unemployment. That is, some agents are in a state

of individual disequilibrium – they are unable to make their optimizing plan come through.

3. *Supply of and the demand for labor.* According to the Keynesian approach, variations in employment result from changes in aggregate demand. The underlying picture is that labour suppliers are passive, employment decisions being made unilaterally by firms. Moreover, this approach tends to consider the supply of labour and the labour force as the same thing, to consider it a fixed magnitude.

4. *The central methodological principle* of Keynesian macro is external consistency. That is, theory consists of propositions aiming at explaining reality. Models are good if they realistic. The prevailing intellectual mood is pragmatism. That several of the basic notions – involuntary unemployment, full employment, rigidity and sluggishness – are defined in a loose way, that the analysis focuses on the short period cut off from the long period, that expectations receive little attention and are conceived of as backwards-looking, all this is hardly considered harmful. Empirical models, the construction of which was often due to engineers rather than economists, are more data- than theory-constrained.

5. *Relationship between micro and macro.* Little attention is given to the process through which agents make their decisions. It is not that Keynesian economists were against what is now called microfoundations, i.e. the need to start the analysis of aggregate magnitudes from individual agents' optimal choices. Rather, they treaded Marshall's footsteps by considering that goal-oriented behaviour is a matter of intention, not of performance, and by seeing no harm in starting the analysis from market functions without explicitly deriving these from individual decision making. To paint with broad strokes, macroeconomists were lagging behind microeconomists in terms of the rigour of their analysis.

As far as the relationship between the scientific communities of microeconomists and macroeconomists was concerned, it took the form of a partition of territory. Each of these two scientific communities had their own field of research and good practice was not to look in the neighbour's garden. Keynesian theory was concerned with the study of the economy in the short period, where it supposedly featured market nonclearing and individual disequilibrium. In turn, the study of the long period, where the economy was supposed to experiment market clearing and individual equilibrium, was neoclassical theory's domain. This consensus was called the *neoclassical synthesis* (i.e. the Keynesian/neoclassical synthesis) – actually, a rather inappropriate appellation since it designates the view that it is better to have the two fields developing separately rather than try to integrate them.

At the time, neither microeconomists nor macroeconomists complained about this division within economics broadly understood. Two reasons may explain this. First, it is true that Keynesian macro was premised on the view that the market system could be prone to market failures, and hence that laissez faire was the wrong policy to be taken. But this view was congruent with the general mood of the time about the role of government in society, a mood probably shared by microeconomists, and due to the lasting impact of the Great Depression in people's minds. The second factor was that that the fine-tuning recipe associated with Keynesian theory seemed to be working and to have played an important role in the unprecedented economic prosperity of the time.

6. *Accessibility to laymen.* The result of this pragmatic attitude is that Keynesian macro theory was and remains simple to understand, even for non-economists. Its level of technicity was low. It used a terminology close to that of newspapers and political discourses – for example, the idea that employment is decided unilaterally by firms, and that excess supply of labour is a directly observable occurrence.

7. *Associated ideology.* Macroeconomics is normative because its concern is the ideal way of organizing the economy in terms of efficiency and welfare. This is a subject about which people often hold prior judgements. Therefore, the field bears an ideological dimension, the 'ideology' term not being taken in a pejorative way. It just designates a given vision about economic governance. The vision most congenial to Keynesian macro can be branded 'mitigated liberalism'.[3] It defends the market system as being superior to a planning system without going to the full extent of advocating laissez faire.

Such are, in my mind, the central features of Keynesian macro. As I said, it reigned for a quarter of century after which it lost its grip over the profession. First, some macroeconomists ceased to adhere to the earlier partition of territory between micro and macro. Taking micro principles more in earnest than their predecessors, they started to critically investigate the foundations of macro to discover that they were shaky. Second, the arising of stagflation in the 1970s was a phenomenon absent from the Keynesian radar. It was taken by many as the sign that demand activation failed to work; instead, it was argued, it generated a cumulative inflationary process. Third, as the remembrance of the Great Depression faded away, the defenders of a higher pitch of liberalism found themselves under more favourable winds.

The New Classical Revolution

Milton Friedman was an important character in the transformation of macro. When thinking of critics of Keynesian theory, it is his name that first comes to mind. However, while it is true that he blazed the trail, the direction that was eventually taken was different from what he envisaged. In effect, Friedman's dislike of Keynesian theory was more due to a matter of disagreement about policy conclusions than methodology. In contrast, the economists treading his footsteps, Robert Lucas, Thomas Sargent and Robert Barro, were after a more radical breach from Keynesian macro. As Lucas was the leading figure in this move, I shall be concerned with him only.

Lucas and his companions started their career as applied macroeconomists. Their microeconomic background was stronger than that of most of their macroeconomist colleagues, which led them to become aware of several weaknesses in the Keynesian paradigm. It also led them to refuse the neoclassical synthesis, the view that macro theory could be exempted from abiding by the microfoundations requirement that prevailed in microeconomics. In a surprisingly short span of time, they were able to formulate and impose a new conception about engaging in macroeconomic research. They called it 'new classical macro' to honour the tradition that Keynes wanted to dismiss.

This transition deserves to be called a 'scientific revolution' in the sense proposed by Thomas Kuhn, referring to episodes in the history of a discipline where a series of unsolved puzzles pile up, disturbing its normal development. This situation of unrest, of dissatisfaction with existing theory then triggers a drive to change the agenda, the conceptual toolbox and the research methods in radical ways. All this is often accompanied by thundering declarations of war, a confrontation between younger and older generations of researchers, the rise of new stars in the profession, and the eclipse of the previous ones.

Like all scientific revolution, the new classical transformation was two-legged, with a criticism of the existing paradigm, on the one hand, and the construction of a new one, on the other. Lacking time to enter into the critical aspect, let me just say (a) that Lucas argued that Keynes did not deserve the 'great economist' stature usually ascribed to him; his main contribution, he claimed, was ideological and political and consisted of having helped to preserve capitalist economies from the socialist temptation; as far as theory was concerned, his contributions were minor; (b) that the central concepts presented by Keynes in the *General Theory*, involuntary unemployment and full employment in particular, were hollow; (c) that adaptive expectations were an ill-footed way of representing expectations; (d) that, as the result of their lack of microfoundations, Keynesian econometric models were of no help for comparing alternative policy measures (the famous 'Lucas critique').

I shall come to Lucas's positive programme presently. However, since one of the distinctive features of the new classical revolution is that consisted in a shift from the Marshallian towards the Walrasian approach, a preliminary task is to clarify the content of the Marshall–Walras divide.

The Marshall–Walras Divide

Alfred Marshall and Léon Walras are the two towering historical figures of neo-classical theory. Most economists, though aware that these authors differed in purpose and methodology, think that these differences are small fry compared to what they have in common. I, for one, believe that, on the contrary, these differences are sufficiently important to warrant the conclusion that the Marshallian and the Walrasian approaches are alternative, not complementary, research programmes within the broader neoclassical family.

Marshall wanted economic theory to solve practical and well-defined issues – e.g. what is the impact of a change in the demand for fish on its price and quantity traded? To him, the economy was such a complex reality that studying it as whole was a desperate enterprise. Hence his partial equilibrium research strategy of studying problems under the *ceteris paribus* clause. It was also important for him to start the analysis of any problem well armed with observed facts. In his mind, definitions and distinctions should not be fixed all and for all. Rather, they should be dictated by the specific problem one is dealing with. Theory had to espouse the contours of reality as much as possible. In view of the complex character of reality, Marshall was sceptical about building formal models. Although trained as a mathematician, he was of the opinion that mathematical considerations should not take a dominant role in economics. Their proper place was in the appendices of theoretical works. An additional factor for this viewpoint was that he intended to be read by a large audience and knew that most of his readers would be repelled by formal arguments.

In contrast, Walras was interested in matters of principle, in questions of a more philosophical nature – in particular, the issue of the logical existence and the efficiency of the equilibrium of a decentralized economy, a query that can be traced back to Adam Smith's attempt to elucidate the mechanism behind the invisible hand metaphor: can a decentralized economy with no authority in charge be an efficient system of resource allocation? However, Walras addressed this issue at an incomparably higher level of abstraction than Smith. Although, unlike Marshall, he had little mathematical training, he was convinced that economic theory needed to be mathematical and built on the model of physics. Of course, he was also aware that an economy was a complex reality, but his strategy for tackling this problem was to start the examination with the study of the most conceivable simple economy (a two-good exchange economy) instead of foregoing the study of the economy as a whole. Thus, in his *Elements of Pure Economics*, he began with assessing the mechanism of equilibrium determination in this simplified framework. This done, he extended the results there obtained to more complex economies. To him, internal consistency was the primary criterion for good theoretical construction, which he viewed as a step-by-step process leaving no conceptual issue unsettled.

Walras was fully aware that his theory was about fictive construction. The role of theory *vis-à-vis* reality was to be a foil, possibly an ideal to be attained, not a description of reality. He once wrote that 'pure theory requires no confirmation from reality'.[4] To him, doing theory amounted to constructing a conceptual benchmark helping to reflect upon the market system and its functioning. Therefore, Walras's work can be conceived as belonging to political philosophy, for that matter analytical political philosophy, doing for the economic sphere what Rawls would later be doing for justice. Small wonder then, that Walras was poles apart from Marshall as far as the target audience was concerned. In his eyes, the price to be paid for rigorous thinking was that theory could no longer be understandable to the non-initiated.

I cannot enter into the description of Walrasian theory content-wise. What ought to be noticed, however, is that the trade technology, the institutional set-up making up for the formation of equilibrium, is devised in such a way that equilibrium is always achieved, equilibrium being understood as a result where all agents' optimizing plans have been made compatible or, in other words, were all agents are in a position of individual equilibrium. Thus, the idea that agents might find themselves non-participating in a given exchange against their will (the gist of the involuntary unemployment notion), that firms might find themselves with unsold good or non-used production capacities against their will, has no room in this framework. What at first sight could be viewed as excess supply is nothing else than the manifestation of the optimal decision not to participate in exchange, prices being what they are.

To summarize, Marshallian theory focuses on external consistency, Walrasian on internal consistency. When Marshall pronounces a theoretical proposition, it pertains to reality. In contrast, Walras's propositions pertain to the fictive economy that he has created, not to reality. Moreover, while a Marshallian proposition is matter-of-fact, a Walrasian proposition is the result of a mathematical demonstration.

At first, everybody will favour the Marshallian methodology strategy striving at a direct explanation of observed phenomena even if bears the price of some sloppiness and of explaining behaviour in terms of rules of thumb rather than optimal choice. However, this is a short-period judgement. The Walrasian strategy, consisting of admitting no loose ends in the reasoning, should not be discarded too fast in so far as it cannot be excluded that, for all its outwardly benign character, the Marshallian lack of rigour may end up blocking cumulative theoretical development, in which case the Walrasian strategy would prove to be more productive eventually.

The background clarified, I now return to the main thread of my argumentation to expose the distinctive features of new classical macro. To this end, I shall use the same benchmarks I used for describing Keynesian macro.

New Classical Macro

1. *Overarching aim.* The first point to be stressed is the change in the research agenda that occurred. The central object of study of Keynesian macroeconomics was unemployment – and, in a wider sense, the search for the malfunctioning of markets. In the span of a few years, the unemployment theme ceased to be an important preoccupation of macroeconomists and was sent back to labour economists. The issue of explaining business cycles took its place at the top of the agenda. Of course, variations in economic activity (and hence in employment) are a central item in the study of economic fluctuations, but in the new paradigm they are accounted for in terms of hours worked without consideration of the split between the employed and the unemployed.

   Keynes had been unable to construct a theory of the business cycle, contenting himself with addressing the task of trying to demonstrate the existence of involuntary unemployment at one point in time, a task that in itself was already daunting. Lucas's opinion was that the profession was now ready to address the topic that Keynes had left aside. He also wanted its study to be part of the Walrasian approach. We have seen that Walrasian theory is an equilibrium theory, hence the 'equilibrium theory of the business cycle' label. Such an attempt was audacious because, before, it was believed that constructing a mathematical model of business fluctuations inspired by Walras was an impossible task. The merit of Lucas, and later of Kydland and Prescott and Plosser and Long, is to have invalidated this opinion.

2. *Equilibrium/disequilibrium.* We are in a Walrasian world. Thus the discussion bears on a fictive model economy. It is constructed in such a way as to be always in equilibrium in the Walrasian sense of the term. Lucas uses the expression of 'equilibrium discipline' understood as a rule that one imposes on oneself to achieve a certain activity. Perhaps some readers know of the French writer Georges Perec. Among other things, he wrote a book entitled *La disparition*. It tells a normal story except that the letter *e* is absent from the whole book. This was the discipline Perec imposed on himself; in his case it was a purely gratuitous one. As far as macro is

concerned, the exercise is made on the presumption that it can be theoretically productive to picture agents and the economy in this extreme way.

The result is that a totally different picture of the business cycle emerges. Earlier, it was viewed as the disequilibrium phenomenon *par excellence*, the manifestation of a market failure. The mere assertion of its existence was seen as an invitation for the state to take steps to make it disappear. In the new approach, the business cycle expresses the optimizing reactions of agents to outside shocks affecting the economy. In other words, business fluctuations are no longer viewed as market failures, and governments should refrain from trying to prevent their occurrence.

3. *Supply and demand.* Lucas's hunch (first presented in a paper co-authored with Rapping) was that changes in the supply of labour, viewed as a result of optimizing decision making, play a central role in explaining fluctuations. This insight was further developed in a paper published in 1972, entitled 'Expectations and the Neutrality of Money', in which Lucas aimed to give a stronger foundation to Friedman's natural rate of unemployment notion.[5] Market clearing, rational expectations (the assumption that agents' subjective expectations about any coming event coincide with the model builder's objective expectations) were the three cornerstones of the paper. Lucas's take in the paper, borrowed from capital theory, was that the decision to participate in the labour market or to produce on a self-employed basis is a matter of allocating leisure (and hence labour) both within a given period of time and over time. Economic agents ought to be depicted as comparing the wage rate at one point in time with the wage rate they expect to prevail later in time, say today and tomorrow. If the former is higher than the latter, they will decide to work more today and less tomorrow.

This intertemporal substitution phenomenon, Lucas contended, is decisive in explaining variations in the level of activity over time. Using this insight, he constructed a model of the business cycle where variations in activity over time are due to two factors: exogenous monetary shocks, on the one hand, and agents' imperfect information, on the other. In this model, agents receive one signal incorporating two distinct pieces of information. Taken separately, these two pieces of information would trigger opposite reactions, changing or not changing the total hours worked. Needing to engage in signal extracting, the optimal solution agents will adopt is to mix the two opposite reactions in some weighted way. Hence the hours worked departs from what they would have been with perfect information. Here, Lucas claimed, rests the explanation of the variations in hours worked over the business cycle. Monetary shocks have real effects but, as argued by Friedman, the government cannot exploit them since they occur only when the changes in money supply are unanticipated.

4. *Main methodological principle.* Lucas wants macro to abide by the Walrasian methodological principles that I have evoked earlier. That is, internal consistency is the alpha and the omega of theoretical construction.

5. *Micro/macro relation.* New classicists want to get rid of the neoclassical synthesis. The neo-Walrasian conception of equilibrium having been adopted, there is no longer any reason for trying to build a synthesis between Keynesian disequilibrium theory and Walrasian equilibrium theory because the latter can perfectly take on board that part of the *explanandum* that earlier on was assigned to Keynesian theory. This marks the end of the Keynesian exception. In Lucas's words:

> The most interesting recent developments in macroeconomic theory seems to me describable as the reincorporation of aggregative problems such as inflation and the business cycle within the general framework of 'microeconomic' theory. If these developments succeed, the term 'macroeconomic' will simply disappear from use and the modifier 'micro' will become superfluous. We will simply speak, as did Smith, Ricardo, Marshall and Walras of *economic* theory.[6]

6. *Accessibility to laymen.* A dynamic study of the economy requires using new tools, resorting to new difficult mathematical techniques such as optimal control, dynamic programming, etc. As a result, the level of mathematics used in new classical macro bears no comparison to what was the case earlier. A high barrier to entry needs to be overcome in order to have just a mere understanding of what is going on.

7. *Ideology.* Keynesian theory was geared toward bringing out market malfunctioning. Here we have the opposite, a Panglossian view of the economy, to use Keynes's nice reference to Voltaire's *Candid* in the *General Theory*.

> The celebrated *optimism* of traditional economic theory, which has led to economics being looked upon as Candides, who, having, left this word for the cultivation of their gardens, teach that all is for the best in the best of all possible words provided we will let go along.[7]

Fluctuations in employment reflect rational and optimal reactions by economic agents to changing conditions. If there is no pathology, there is also no need for the state to intervene. Table 28.1 summarizes the result of my confrontation between Keynesian and new classical macro. Two points emerge from the comparison. The first is that these visions of macroeconomics are poles apart. The second is their respective roots ought to be traced back to Marshall and Walras respectively.

Table 28.1: A confrontation of Keynesian and new classical macro.

Criteria	Keynesian macro	New classical macro
1 Overarching *explanandum*:	underemployment	business fluctuations
2 Equilibrium/disequilibrium:	disequilibrium	equilibrium
3 Labour supply/demand:	focus on demand	focus on supply
4 Main method criterion:	external consistency	internal consistency
5 Micro/macro relationship:	neoclassical synthesis	hegemony of micro
6 Accessibility to laymen:	easy	high barrier to entry
7 Underpinning ideology:	mitigated liberalism	laissez faire

RBC Macroeconomics

The 'new classical macroeconomics' term applies only to the works of Lucas and his fellow travellers. Soon, the paradigm that they had inaugurated underwent an inner evolution led by Kydland and Prescott that resulted in the emergence of real business cycle (RBC) modelling. A further transformation that I shall not discuss led to the emergence of dynamic stochastic general equilibrium (DSGE) modelling. These three modelling strategies should be considered as phases within the same research programme, the main features of which were present from the beginning.

From the start, Lucas had expressed the view that the task ahead in business cycle theory was to write a FORTRAN programme, 'a fully articulate artificial economy which behaves through time so as to imitate closely the time series behavior of actual economies'.[8] He himself, however, did not contribute much to the implementation of this programme. Those who did it were Kydland and Prescott whose 1982 paper, 'Time to Build and Aggregate Fluctuations', started RBC modelling.[9]

Kydland and Prescott's model is neo-Walrasian, like Lucas's. The equilibrium discipline, rational expectations, a dynamic-stochastic environment, and inter-temporal substitution are the basic ingredients of their model, as in Lucas's. But there are also striking differences. First, Kydland and Prescott abandoned Lucas's insight that the shocks triggering the business cycle were monetary. Instead their hunch was that technology shocks were the right suspect. Second, they abandoned the imperfect information line of research. Third and most important, Kydland and Prescott's work was quantitative while Lucas's model was qualitative. In short, they brought macro to the computer.

The aim of Kydland and Prescott's 1982 model, like that of Lucas, was to show that economic fluctuations could be explained as a consequence of economic agents' optimizing adjustment to exogenous technological shocks. To the outside observer, what is striking in their endeavour is the contrast between the model they use – a stochastic version of the Ramsey model, close to a Robinson

Crusoe economy – and its purpose, to shed light on the development of the US economy from 1950 to 1975. The task that Kydland and Prescott set themselves was colossal. Several steps needed to be taken for such research, each of which involved solving a lot of tricky mathematical, computational and empirical work. The empirical validation of the model proceeded through comparing the volatility, correlation and auto-correlation of output, investment, consumption, hours worked and productivity, as characterizing the US economy, with the equivalent moments from the model economy, the success of the model consisting of having the simulation of the model mimic the empirical observations. Kydland and Prescott's model achieved this aim to a rather large extent.

While their paper was first met with scepticism, it gradually became the accepted view that it marked a methodological breakthrough. Several ways were proposed to overcome the objections that were levelled against the inaugural model, other shocks than technology were conceived, and several other extensions were undertaken. From the mid-1980s to the mid-1990s, RBC modelling witnessed a tremendous internal progress, to an extent that few would have predicted at the time Kydland and Prescott published their paper.

For lack of space, I cannot enter into more details. Nor can I recount the different ways in which economists with a Keynesian inclination endeavoured to retort to Lucas's attack against Keynesian theory. Nor have I the time to speak of how, starting in the mid-1990s and somewhat surprisingly, a consensus arose between so-called new Keynesian economists and RBC economists on using a model borrowing its basic elements from the two approaches, sometimes labelled the 'new neoclassical synthesis'. Fortunately, for my purpose of answering the question that makes the title of this essay, it is unnecessary to delve in these developments.

Let me thus go at once to the assessment part of my discussion. How should we judge the developments that took place in macro, namely the dethroning of Keynesian macro and its replacement by new classical/ real business cycle macro (or to use another label, DSGE macro)?

Is it progress or regress?

An Assessment

The question in everybody's mind is which of the two approaches I have described (the 'old' Keynesian macro or the new non-Keynesian macro) is the best one. Lipsey, an old-Keynesian, wrote that what happened was the 'replacement of messy truth by precise error'.[10] His point is that Keynesian theory has a strong truth-value; it constitutes a good representation of reality even if the argumentation can be loose. The opposite would be the case for new classical theory.

Lipsey's standpoint is clever and there are good chances that it may seduce many. In my eyes, however, it is wanting. Why would Keynesian theory have a higher truth-value than new classical theory? Both are fictive constructions differing just because they start from different premises. It is just that one looks more realistic than the other. Keynesian theory, I claim, is based on propositions that seem obvious – for example, that there exist two types of unemployment, frictional and involuntary unemployment, or that the existence of something called 'excess supply' can be assessed right away by observing reality or real-world statistics but cease to be so upon closer scrutiny. The blind spot of Keynesian economists is that they are unaware that the Marshallian supply and demand apparatus is almost as inadequate as the Walrasian one for tackling the unemployment phenomenon. Neither of them is useful for such a task – and until the advent of search theory in the 1980s no adequate apparatus existed. The difference between the Marshallian and the Walrasian framework is that, since in the former the reasoning is looser, it is easier to force an outwardly fine (but at bottom defective) explanation of unemployment into it while in the Walrasian framework the contrived character of such an import would be blatant.

If this view is accepted, the conclusion must be drawn that Lucas did a good job in bringing out the conceptual defects of Keynesian macro. In terms of logical consistency, the replacement of Keynesian macro with Walrasian macro was certainly a progress.

Does this mean that NC/RBC macro is without defect? Surely not. A first reason is that Lucas, Kydland and Prescott may well proudly declare themselves neo-Walrasian economists, but most great names of neo-Walrasian theory have qualms in considering them part of the family. The reason is that traditional neo-Walrasian economists accept the limitations of their approach while thinking that Lucas and company transgress them in their attempt to bring Walrasian theory to the empirical test. By doing so, their judgement runs, they try to marry two incompatible bedfellows, Lausanne and Chicago. Let me illustrate the point with two quotations.

> Lucas was in the Chicago tradition and was very concerned about empirical testing – whatever the hell that means – something that I have little sympathy for and very little interest in, to be perfectly honest ... I am still of the opinion that theory is more a way of organizing your thoughts, how you would think about the world. And it's strongest in providing counterexamples when people confidently claim that something is true in general.[11]

To Hahn, the role of the Arrow–Debreu model, the emblematic neo-Walrasian model, is to provide a benchmark.

> The Arrow–Debreu model serves a function similar to that which a perfectly healthy body might serve a clinical diagnostician when he looks at an actual body. Now one

of the mysteries which future historians of thought will surely wish to unravel is how it came about that the Arrow–Debreu model came to be taken descriptively; that is, as sufficient in itself for the study and perhaps control of actual economies ... If ever a theory was straightforwardly falsified it is the theory of the American economy in Arrow–Debreu equilibrium. But it was never meant to be so obviously falsified; it was designed as both a reference point and a starting point.[12]

A second critical observation is that, in equilibrium models of the BC, the policy conclusions are embedded in the premises of the models (this is also the case for Keynesian macro but there the premises are less spelled out). As a result, theorists should refrain from peddling them to politicians. The conclusions of the models cannot be exploited politically. It is to Lucas's credit that this is something he has been aware of:

> There is something wrong, and necessarily transient, with this easy translation of a technical contribution to economic theory into a platform for economic policy ... There can be no simple connection between what appears on the scratch pads of professional economists, however original, and important conclusions about the way our society ought to operate.[13]

Unfortunately, it is far from sure that all modern macroeconomists share Lucas's lucidity.

My third and final remark is about the equilibrium discipline, the glasses through which Walras, new classical and RBC economists decide to look at reality. I have already underscored its ideological underpinning. But here I want to draw the attention to another drawback, again one that Lucas was clever enough to perceive without being followed by Prescott. At stake is whether RBC modelling should limit itself to the explanation of mild, normal business fluctuations while admitting its inability to address more dramatic episodes such as the Great Depression (or for that matter, the 2008 recession). Lucas is of the opinion that RBC modelling is valid only for phases of plain sailing.

> One may thus think of the model not as a positive theory suited to all historical time periods but as a normative benchmark providing a good approximation to events when monetary policy is conducted well and a bad approximation when it is not.[14]

Lucas is right, I believe, but the consequences are more far-reaching than what he was aware of, as an another quotation, this time from Obstfed and Rogoff, makes clear: 'A theory of business cycles that has nothing to say about the Great Depression is like a theory of earthquakes that explains only small tremors'.[15]

These remarks bring me to my final conclusions. Although I have much sympathy for Keynes and Keynesian economists, I am of the opinion – *horresco referens* – that the dismissal of Keynesian macro has been a theoretical progress. Moreover, the evolution that took place has brought to the forefront a tension that is proper to the macro field. As stated, the latter is supposedly about policy and models end up with policy conclusions.

A second conclusive remark is that the judgement made about present-day macro cannot be based only on its theoretical content. The meta-theoretical comments made about the theory also matter. In this respect, economists engaged in the same type of theorizing may fare very differently. To wit, as seen, Lucas is well aware of the methodological limits of the theory he inaugurated while, in contrast, Prescott seem to take pleasure in crossing these thresholds, in my eyes, to the disservice of his theoretical contribution.

My final remark is that the path taken by macroeconomics, which in itself has much going for it, has also led to a widening of the gap between the production of economic science and economic policy as an art. With macro becoming more like hard science, academic economists lose the ability that earlier economists, like Keynes, for example, had of going back and forth between the roles of a good scientist and a good statesman. Therefore, to return to my basic question, the progress of macro hardly allows civil society to expect more from it on the matter of choosing the right policy with which to engage. The public should not have wrong expectations about what present-day macro theory can deliver and macroeconomists should avoid the pitfall of believing that they have an edge on policy matters.

29 FAILING TO CONTROL: ACCOUNTABILITY IN HISTORICAL PERSPECTIVE

Biancamaria Fontana

For Pascal, a few sceptical remarks

An Old Problem

The belief that no human agent is entirely dependable, that humans – taken both individually and *en masse* – are prone to error and vice, that, in short, nobody can be trusted, is one of the few certainties (if a disheartening one) around which Western political theory has confidently built its precepts since classical antiquity. For all their differences, Greek and Roman authors as well as the writers in the Christian tradition converged on this simple assumption: because human agents are unreliable and people represent a threat for one another, the primary task of any political authority is to ensure the safety of its subjects from the hazardous behaviour of their peers.[1]

In Thomas Hobbes's *Leviathan*,[2] for example, the establishment of absolute power was justified precisely by this necessity of mutual protection. It was because individuals feared and mistrusted one another that they agreed to submit to the rule of a 'common reason' – represented by the absolute monarch or by some ruling body invested with similar prerogatives – thus preferring the certain evils of repressive authority, to the far worse uncertainties of anarchy. Whenever the sovereign failed in its task to grant safety and protection, the compact that constrained the subjects to obey its diktats would be dissolved, and the subjects themselves would be restored to the hazardous freedom of the state of nature.[3]

But if ordinary individuals could prove mutually dangerous, so as to call for the kind of impersonal superpower imagined by Hobbes, this capacity to cause damage was bound to be greatly enhanced in those persons who were placed in a position of authority. In the state of nature individuals could be regarded as equal, on average, in strength and abilities, so that the outcome of any war of all against all was likely to prove uncertain. But whoever held, even temporarily, some public authority, could add to his natural faculties the artificial powers of the state: their limited physical strength would be supplemented by the assistance of armed guards, their decisions would carry the authority of the law, and in all matters of public concern they had limitless opportunities to deceive, corrupt and manipulate.[4]

Even when those who governed were honest and well-meaning, they could still prove feeble and incompetent, or they may be misled by bad advisers and false principles, causing their subjects to suffer from the consequences of their miscalculations. Hereditary monarchies and aristocracies were exposed to the genetic hazards that may deliver power into the hands of inept or rapacious individuals; elective systems had to contend with the volatility of public favour and the dangerous influence of demagogues. In short, the power exercised by the few over the many could never be expected to guarantee the latter from its prevarications.

Those observers who witnessed the struggle of modern nation states to assert their rule, in a world wrecked by the dissolution of feudal authority and by the religious wars were, perhaps understandably, more responsive to the hazards of civil war and anarchy than to the abuses of power. On the contrary, democratic doctrines, both ancient and modern, have always been characterized by an acute anxiety over the responsibility of governors: from their viewpoint the possibility that the citizens might resort to rebellion or engage in mutual aggression has seemed on the whole less immediately alarming, than the chance that they might become the victims of the errors and vices of their rulers. In particular the anatomy of the lies, frauds and depredations to which politicians are naturally addicted, at the expense of those who elected them, represents a direct historical link between the forensic rhetoric of classical antiquity, with its famous tribunes and orators, and the contemporary world of political scandals and tabloids.

Given that the democratic tradition is especially concerned with the responsibility of rulers towards the general will, it is natural to imagine that democracies, broadly described,[5] should be better equipped than any other kind of regime to ensure vertical accountability, in other words to guarantee that the people will retain a high degree of control over those citizens who are raised to the position of governors. For the tradition of monarchical absolutism, the accountability of rulers was clearly a rather remote and uncertain prospect: the concern for social order was altogether paramount, and the eventuality that the sovereign might prove a liability and a danger was regarded as very extreme, and very exceptional indeed. All considered it was only *ex post* that the illegitimate character of political authority could be confirmed, once, for example, a successful revolution or a dynastic change had sanctioned the removal of the existing sovereign, and the advent of a new regime.[6]

In a democratic system, the nature of the compact upon which political society is founded is entirely different, so that the conditions for vertical accountability may seem *a priori* far more favourable. To begin with, in democracies governors and governed are alike: in principle no special group or caste has a monopoly over political authority; rulers are chosen by the people from amongst the people themselves, for a limited period of time. They are temporarily entrusted with some specific powers and tasks and – though while in office they are free to follow their own line of action – they are ultimately answerable for their conduct to those who selected them. If the people are dissatisfied with their performance – because, say, they have proved incompetent or did not fulfil their promises – they can decide not to choose them again; if they suspect them of abusing their prerogatives, they can demand their resignation and even their punishment. Under absolute monarchies, secrecy was the privilege of the sovereign, and one of the essential prerogatives of power; under democracy the public has (always in theory) the right to be informed about the conduct of elected officials, who are bound to guarantee the transparency of their actions.

Yet, in spite of this formidable array of conditions, all designed to establish the responsibility of public agents under democratic rule, the mechanisms of vertical accountability have always proved, even in this context, altogether inadequate to the task. This is apparent in the practice of contemporary democracies, but it was already clear in the experience of ancient city-states or in that of early modern republics: in the hierarchical relation between electors and elected, governed and governors, it is apparently always the latter who seem to have the advantage.

Politics as a Profession

There are a number of factors that account for this failure of control from below, but on the whole such factors are all connected with the same feature: the natural tendency of politics to turn into a profession, a distinct activity requiring specific skills and dictating its own particular rules. Because democracy means government by the people, democratic regimes are constructed around the presupposition that governed and governors are basically the same, and that their aims and interests are, in the last instance, identical, since the rulers of today are the subjects of tomorrow and vice versa. As the Roman writer Marcus Tullius Cicero explained in his famous dialogue *De legibus*:

> In fact the whole character of a republic is determined by its arrangements in regard to magistrates. Not only must we inform them of the limits of their administrative authority; we must also instruct the citizens as to the extent of their obligation to obey them. For the man who rules efficiently must have obeyed others in the past, and the man who obeys dutifully appears fit at some later time to be a ruler. Thus he who obeys ought to expect to be a ruler in the future, and he who rules should remember that in a short time he will have to obey.[7]

This presupposition was already largely fictional in Cicero's own time, during the terminal phase of the Roman republic (Cicero himself was, after all, a career politician), and it is very far from reality in the context of the large democratic states of today. The institutions of ancients republics were in fact originally designed to preserve as far as possible the occasional, amateurish character of political activity: thus the resort to balloting instead of election as a means to select public officials, the interdiction to serve several times on the same council, and the short tenure of most magistracies, were all instrumental to the objective of making political participation accessible to the widest possible number of citizens. But notwithstanding these precautions, it proved very difficult to prevent ambitious would-be leaders or prominent citizens from monopolizing the relevant institutions and imposing their influence, if necessary hiding behind obscure clients or front figures to circumvent the rules.

In modern democracies the division of labour between citizens and representatives is taken for granted;[8] generally we expect our representatives to serve full time (the Swiss Confederation being a notable exception)[9] for several years on end, so as to master the technicalities of government, and we see it as an advantage, that they should possess particular qualifications as, say, economists, administrators or jurists. While in these regimes anyone in principle can become a member of the political class, in practice, short of having some extraordinary advantages (like being a millionaire or belonging to the higher ranks of the civil service), the aspiring politician will have to plan a substantial part of her future around this particular ambition and, if she succeeds, she will spend most of her adult life associating and competing with people who share the same obsession.

Why is the transformation of politics into a separate activity exercised by professionals a problem for accountability? Because in so far as rulers constitute a distinct occupational group, rather than a random selection of the population, they are bound to have interests and objectives that in some respects differ very sharply from those of the mass of the citizens. The most important respect in which under democratic rule, the interest of the governors conflicts with that of the governed is that, once elected, representatives will strive to stay in office as long as they can, regardless of whether they are in fact best capable of performing their task. The need to please the electors at all costs, persuading them to confirm their mandate, may seem the best possible guarantee of good behaviour on the part of politicians, the very essence of vertical accountability, but in practice it does result in a number of perverse effects, that have been familiar to political observers for centuries, and that modern democratic institutions have done little to correct. As a general rule politicians will naturally try to stretch the limits of their authority so as to govern with as little opposition as possible, and carry out their plans with minimal resistance on the part of everyone else. In some cases they will also multiply their interventions to prove their own importance and efficiency. As Benjamin Constant observed in his *Principes de Politique*:

Every time you give a man a special task he will tend to do more rather than less. Those who are charged with arresting vagrants on the main road are inclined to pick a quarrel with any travellers. When spies fail to discover anything, they invent. It is sufficient to create in a country a ministry that watches over conspirators, to hear incessant talk of conspiracy. Legislators share out amongst themselves human existence, by right of conquest, in the same way as Alexander's generals shared out the world.[10]

Such attitudes do not necessarily betray a sinister craving for power: they may simply originate in the sincere desire to run things more smoothly and effectively, to obtain more rapidly some beneficial results, or achieve a more impressive performance. Even so, fulfilling one's electoral programme may take too long, or prove impossible, and of course there is a strong chance that the electors will not like it in the end, whatever they thought before. The delayed impact of most legislative measures, means that politicians will often be punished or rewarded by the electors for initiatives taken by others before them. Negative effects – such as those resulting from the fluctuations of international markets – are also frequently ascribed to political groups who were in no way responsible for them in the first place. On the whole in some contexts refraining from taking any action may seem the best option: those in office will concentrate on strengthening their personal position, building networks of patronage or promoting popular measures with a short-term impact.[11] In any case transparency will seldom be to the advantage of representatives, who have a vested interest in hiding behind the technicalities of government, and providing a partial and distorted picture of their activities.

While in modern democracies the level of education is generally higher, and the circulation of information wider and faster than ever before, the strategies of manipulation of public opinion have also developed accordingly, so as to ensure that the gap in knowledge existing between rulers and citizens remains in favour of the former. If politicians are necessarily in competition for power and popularity, the fact that they are all subjected to the same occupational hazards creates amongst them, across party divides, strong bonds of solidarity and complicity, once again at the expense of the electors. Since in democracy most political bodies are collegial, this practice of 'honour amongst thieves' continues to make it difficult to assign to a single individual or group the legal responsibility for acts of abuse or mismanagement.

Checks and Balances?

This sketchy overview of the limits of vertical accountability shows clearly enough why the mechanisms of horizontal control have often seemed a more promising way of ensuring the correct functioning of political systems.[12] This alternative approach to accountability can be described as 'bureaucratic': historically it is associated with the great European monarchies of the Ancien Regime, but also, before that, with the administration of, for example, the Roman and Chinese empires. At a later stage it was embodied in the constitutional structure of representative governments, and from there it passed into the institutions of modern democracies.

In the tradition of bureaucratic control it was generally taken for granted that the people should not be entrusted with the surveillance of government, both because they did not know how to go about it, and because to allow them any say in the matter would only invite disobedience and rebellion. This left as the only alternative the choice of entrusting the control of government to the governors themselves. But how could this possibly work? The general idea was that the administration of the state should be managed by a particular class of people, who would serve in virtue of their specific character and competences. These civil servants may belong to a blood aristocracy, and inherit their posts as one inherits a title; they may (in countries where this was the current practice, such as France) buy their position as a means to social promotion, or simply be recruited in virtue of their loyalties and abilities. The administration of the Roman Empire was largely in the hands of educated slaves or freedmen; in the European monarchies of the Old Regime some impressive ministerial careers were made by commoners.

Whether or not they belonged to the aristocracy, bureaucrats would derive their importance from their function, from being members of a professional body, not from the usual aristocratic solidarities of clan and faction. In theory they could be trusted because providing good government was what they were trained to do, and the only focus of their ambitions. Clearly a non-elective administrative caste would be largely indifferent to considerations of popularity and to electoral strategies. Moreover, when their posts did not depend directly on royal patronage (as was the case with venal offices), they could also provide an effective barrier against the abuses of monarchy. In France, for example, the courts called *parlements* had the subordinated task of rubberstamping and registering the orders of the sovereign: they could not deliberate, initiate legislation, veto laws, or propose measures of reform. And yet institutions of this kind had a great potential for passive resistance: they could quibble over the interpretation of a law, redraft documents, raise conflicts of competence amongst superior instances, and generally delay the enforcement of any measure. In some cases their reluctance to endorse royal injunctions resulted in open revolt and armed resistance.[13]

It is less clear why such bodies should be expected to check their own actions: competence is not incompatible with dishonesty, and as a rule *parlements* were more effective in resisting against the monarch, than in reforming their own, often corrupt, practices. To guarantee accountability, the autonomy of these bureaucratic elites had to be combined with other constitutional mechanisms. In his work *De l'Esprit des Lois*,[14] Montesquieu, himself the member of one of those courts, outlined what still remains the most influential theory of inbuilt horizontal control.[15] For him the necessary condition for any moderate (as opposed to despotic) regime, was the articulation of the activity of government in separate functions, and the allocation of these functions to different bodies. This breaking down of the exercise of political authority offered a double advantage: first, the different departments of government would operate in competition with one another, each limiting and controlling the other's scope of action; second, the necessity to gain the approval of different authorities would delay the enforcement of legislation from above, and allow more opportunities to monitor each initiative, and to detect abuses.[16]

Montesquieu's theory is generally known as the theory of the separation of powers, but it would be more accurate in this context to use the phrase 'checks and balances'. The relevant point in fact is not simply the existence of boundaries separating the different powers of the state (a separation that in any case can only be partial),[17] but the fact that such powers should behave as dynamic forces, acting in friction against one another. In this way the natural tendency of every authority to expand and overstep its competences could contribute to a correct and equitable administration, by becoming part of a system of guarantees.[18]

Significantly, though originally conceived to limit the power of monarchical absolutism, the separation of powers was enthusiastically adopted by the theorists of modern representative government, when they realized that any ruling body elected by the people was as capable of abuses as one resting upon hereditary authority.[19] The dynamic dimension of the division of powers is still apparent in contemporary democracies in the conflicting relation that opposes the judiciary and the political class. Whenever the latter proves unable to keep in check the corrupt practices of its own members, the judiciary steps into the breach, and predictably, political leaders seize every opportunity of getting their own back, by stretching the competences of the executive and legislative powers to exercise some control over the magistracy.

A different example of horizontal control associated with representative government is offered by the role of political parties as it took shape in the context of the parliamentary regimes of Britain and of the US during the eighteenth century. The presence of political factions was traditionally regarded as one of the main obstacles to accountability in representative governments, the instrument of partisan interests and corruption, and the very symbol of the separate identity of the political class. As David Hume observed in his essay on 'The Independency of Parliament',[20] men were generally more honest in their private than in their public behaviour: the same partisans who may hesitate to break the law for personal gain, would be happy to justify any irregularity committed for the sake of their own cause. However, parties – Hume stressed – offered two important advantages: their visibility and their competitive nature. Political movements with a transparent identity, openly organized, would be an improvement over secret associations and cabals, and over the murky exercise of patronage; as public institutions their membership, propaganda and financial arrangements would become open to scrutiny.[21] As the future American president James Madison explained, in his contributions to the *Federalist Papers*,[22] while the causes of faction could not be removed, without forcing people to renounce their interests and their opinions, it was at least possible to control their effects. If corruption and complicities were inevitable, the necessity to compete for popular favour, and the distribution of interests across the country, would guarantee at least some degree of mutual vigilance.[23]

Today parties are seen again, by a substantial part of the electorate in different democratic states, as the instrument of privilege and corruption, and as an obstacle (rather than the means) of democratic participation. And yet recent experiences of 'non-party' movements (such as the *Movimento 5 Stelle* in Italy) seem to confirm Hume's analysis of the crucial role of parties in ensuring the visibility of political decisions and actions. In the absence of a party structure and party leadership, the conduct of representatives tends to become confused and opaque; the lack of transparency on the nature of their mandate and their strategy is a major obstacle to their declared objective of 'answering to the people' at every step of their action.[24]

People's Tribunals, Ancient and Modern

A distinctive approach to accountability, one that combines the idea of vertical democratic control with that of the horizontal separation of powers, is offered by the institutions known as 'people's tribunals'. Accountability from below did not work, because the citizens were helpless in the face of the abuses committed by those in power, except, to a very limited extent, on the infrequent occasion of elections; even then they were generally ill-informed about the activities of their rulers and could easily be misled or manipulated by them. But things could be different if the people were given extraordinary powers to appeal against the initiatives of governors, investigate their conduct and eventually reverse their decisions. These powers could be exercised by means of special institutions that would operate at the same level of other existing legislative or judiciary bodies.

The most important historical examples of this kind of procedure can be found in the Athenian People's Court (*dikasterion*) and, to a lesser degree, in the Roman tribunate of the plebs. In Athens the People's Court was a tribunal formed by a random selection of citizens, who were called upon to judge controversies of public relevance, and in particular the legitimacy of the decisions of the legislative body, the People's Assembly (*ekklesia*). According to the importance of the case to be judged, the size of the Court could vary from a few hundred to over two thousand men; jurors were chosen by lot and were picked twice: first to be part of a panel of 6,000 on duty for a year, then to serve on a particular trial on a given day. They had to be at least thirty years old (a selectively mature age by the standards of the time), they were bound to swear a solemn oath (which was not required to vote in the Assembly) and were entitled to deliberate by a secret ballot, not by show of hands as in the Assembly itself. By the fourth century BC the large majority of the cases brought in front of the Court were political, and aimed at overturning a decision of the Assembly (*graphe paranomon*); but the procedure was accusatory, as in a proper tribunal: appeals took the form of a charge brought by a particular individual against a named person (for example the proponent of a measure of law that was being contested, or someone who had openly supported it in the Assembly); people were expected to argue their own case, and the employment of professional speakers or advisors was strictly forbidden.[25]

In the Roman republic the *ius provocationis* (the right of the citizen to appeal to the tribunes of the plebs against a magistrate) was regarded as the cornerstone of Roman *libertas*: throughout the second and first centuries BC the growing control of the aristocracy over the tribunate of the plebs and over the citizens' assemblies (*comitia*), gradually reduced its political significance, but could not entirely suppress its symbolic appeal.[26] In both examples the people's courts had a double nature: they provided a form of democratic surveillance 'from below' and were also a means of 'lateral' control, as they became autonomous bodies that checked and limited the action of the legislative.[27] They also anticipated an ambiguity that is still present in modern approaches to accountability, namely the tendency to confuse the accusation of acting against the law, and that of acting against public interest, or, in other words, the penal and political responsibilities of representatives.

The fact that we have a limited knowledge of the actual functioning of these ancient institutions, has not prevented them from exercising a strong appeal upon modern imagination. In 2006, during her unsuccessful presidential campaign, Ségolène Royal famously evoked the possibility of ensuring 'popular surveillance' by introducing 'citizens' juries selected by ballot'. Though widely criticized at the time as vague and demagogic, the candidate's suggestion was in tune with the new tendencies in the definition of democratic practices. In recent years the frustration experienced by citizens in the face of the elusiveness and impunity of representatives, has in fact generated a series of militant projects for popular participation. These combine old instruments (such as popular juries and balloting), with new technologies (electronic consultation, streaming, etc.). While thus far practical applications are very limited, the pursuit of new forms of citizens participation is clearly bound to grow, both as an object of reflection for democratic theory, and as a set of demands for the future organization of political systems.[28]

A Mutual Dissatisfaction

In conclusion: what (if anything) can we learn from this survey of past and present reflections on accountability? The first observation concerns the heterogeneous character of the instruments of political control on which we still rely today. These are in no sense specifically 'democratic': they derive indifferently from autocratic, aristocratic or popular regimes; they are passed down from secular bureaucratic routines, reflect relatively archaic constitutional devices or imitate remote experiences of citizen participation. A second consideration is the absence of any decisive turning point, any radical qualitative improvement in the secular exercise of controlling rulers. The size and complexity of modern states makes the efficacy of popular surveillance rather problematic, in spite of the extraordinary development of the technology of information. It is significant in this respect, that one of the modern responses to the problem should still be the old republican remedy of reducing the scale of government, shifting power from the centre to peripheral authorities. The demand for local autonomies and federalism is to some extent a demand for greater accountability, for keeping political power within the grasp and under the eyes of the citizenry (though in fact historical experience shows well enough that enhanced responsibility is not necessarily the outcome of fragmented political authority).[29]

If there is an obvious continuity between ancient and modern attempts to enforce democratic accountability, the same continuity exists in those factors that, today as in the past, make it very hard to achieve it.

The recent phenomenon of an increasing personalization of politics, though apparently favouring a greater transparency, in practice provides the public with an excess of information on what are often marginal aspects of the conduct of representatives (looks, personal life, frequentations) and very little else. No doubt such attention may confirm suspicions about the marital or financial integrity of politicians; it does however provide a limited knowledge of the substance of their performance. As Germaine de Staël observed in 1796, the constant attention that the press in modern societies lavished on public personalities was very effective in reducing their prestige, by revealing the most insignificant of their faults; but in the end the only purpose it served was to satisfy the democratic passion for equality, by diminishing anyone who was raised above the masses; it did not help to determine any real shift in power.[30]

The administration of modern states is run by large and intricate bureaucratic organizations, that have never been (were never *meant* to be) answerable to the sovereign people. To some extent the upper reaches of these bureaucracies are of course dependent on the political class – on elective ministerial personnel. But in practice their inertial qualities and their capacity to resist political change are virtually unlimited, witness a long history of failed attempts to 'reform' public administration in different European countries. Moreover, some sections of this administrative apparatus have now become detached altogether from individual nation states, turning into totally independent units, with considerable powers to condition political decisions: central banks, national research boards, organisms of monetary or commercial regulation, and so on.

The paradox in this state of affairs is that institutions which started off as instruments of control, barriers erected against the arbitrary initiatives of absolute rulers, now appear to the general public as being themselves capriciously despotic, an insult to the principles of democratic government and probably the expression of sinister interests. After all are the judges who prosecute corrupt politicians the defenders of the people or, as some prefer to think, a dangerous clique of disaffected clerics? Do you really believe what remote expert agencies tell you about nuclear power, epidemics or foodstuff? And do you feel safer being governed by politicians or by bankers?

In fact the dissatisfaction is mutual: the people feel that they are not in control of political decisions and institutions that, in principle at least, should be subjected to their sovereign will; those who govern on the other hand witness with dismay the multiplication of agencies of power and centres of decision, that escape from any kind of vertical authority, and lament somewhat undemocratically the loss of order and hierarchy.[31] Both of course are right: as Benjamin Constant observed commenting on Jean-Jacques Rousseau's idea of democracy, the people may well be sovereign in one respect and subject in another, but in practice these two relations are always confused, and no political system can entirely eliminate the dangers embodied in this confusion.[32]

30 DOES TRANSPARENCY ENGENDER THE CONFIDENCE OF THE GOVERNED? A CONTRIBUTION TO POLITICAL THOUGHT

Sandrine Baume

Introduction

Over the past few decades, transparency[1] in the handling of public affairs has become an increasing requirement. It is nowadays considered simultaneously a basic feature of good governance and a protection against misrule. This coincides with greater expectations from the public regarding the availability, accessibility and diffusion of information. Such great enthusiasm for transparency – which comes not only from public opinion and the media but also from entrepreneurs in civil and political life – is in fact multidimensional; many hopes have been associated with the requirement of transparency in public affairs. Among these hopes are an improvement of the moralization of politics, greater confidence and consent of the governed, and a capacity for the public to form its judgement in a more enlightened way.[2] Among these factors that speak to the application of the principle of transparency, the confidence of the governed has played a very decisive role in political thought. In this essay, I will focus on the question of trust as a major argument for those who promote the principle of transparency. This essay will be developed along these two temporal axes: first, I would like to come back to the period of the emergence of representative government (late eighteenth to the early nineteenth century), where writers such as Jeremy Bentham and Benjamin Constant showed how transparency could engender the trust of the governed. Second, I would like to come back to the contemporary arguments that viewed this relationship between transparency and trust of the governed in various and less optimistic ways. In this contribution, I have adopted Hardin's definition of trust:

> Usually, to say that I trust you in some context simply means that I think you will be trustworthy toward me in that context. Hence to ask any question about trust is implicitly to ask about the reasons for thinking the relevant party to be trustworthy.[3]

Transparency at the Time of the Emergence of Representative Governments

Transparency establishes its legitimacy in Europe during the second half of the eighteenth century. It is at this particular point in time that an important step is taken, diverging from previous theories of the state, which were until then upheld by the idea of secrecy: both the birth of modern states and their development were underpinned by the practice of secrecy. It is only when representative governments begin to emerge in Europe that a discourse articulated around the norm of transparency is truly developed. At this period, the notion of publicity is much more in use for qualifying open-door policies. The word transparency is more an exception, present notably by Bentham.[4] It is the contemporary literature that has largely diffused the word transparency, often used as an equivalent for the notion of publicity.[5]

If several pleas for transparency developed at that time, it's not due to a historical coincidence. For philosophers such as Jean-Jacques Rousseau, Immanuel Kant, Jeremy Bentham and Benjamin Constant, the principle of publicity becomes a protection against bad administration or misrule, especially through the power of surveillance that it allows. Marc Richir reminds us that 'it is the whole "revolutionary" thought that is animated by a belief in the transparency of society towards itself'.[6] According to Richir, the failures of past revolutions can be assessed by their incapacity to achieve transparency. In 'The Eye of Power', Michel Foucault persuasively describes the dread that opacity instilled at the time:

> A fear haunted the latter half of the eighteenth century: the fear of darkened spaces, of the pall of gloom which prevents the full visibility of things, men and truths. It sought to break up the patches of darkness that blocked the light, eliminate the shadowy areas of society, demolish the unlit chambers where arbitrary political acts, monarchical caprice, religious superstitions, tyrannical and priestly plots, epidemics and the illusions of ignorance were fomented.[7]

In the course of the eighteenth century, as Jean Starobinski notes, the rejection of opacity coincides with the denunciation of appearance, lies and social masks: 'In the theatre and the Church, in novels and in newspapers, sham, convention, hypocrisy, and masks were denounced in a variety of ways'.[8] Such a stigmatization of the mask, the appearance of the 'costume', marks a new turn from the culture of court society, a 'society of representation where everyone had to keep his place, [... it] was the ideal stage for this kind of role-play'.[9] Finally, the necessity of transparency as an emerging value coincides fundamentally with a questioning of and an objection to absolute authority, whose strength lay in part in state secrets – *arcana imperii*. As Jürgen Habermas noted, the rejection of state secrets goes hand in hand with a requirement of general and abstract norms.[10] This emerging and growing enthusiasm for transparency doesn't mean that there wasn't any 'doctrinal' resistance against the diffusion of public information. Critiques of transparency existed in Bentham's time and emanated most of the time from the counterrevolutionary movement. They did not relativize transparency as a means, as is more often the case today,[11] but disputed its legitimacy as an end; the *raison d'état* tradition challenged the appropriateness of transparency in the conduct of public affairs. In the twentieth century, Carl Schmitt can be considered a follower of this tradition.[12]

Transparency and Confidence in the Classical Age

As mentioned in my preliminary words, one of the major reasons that classic authors set out for advocating the principle of publicity is related to (dis)trust: publicity would secure the people's confidence and the consent of the governed. But on this topic and more generally in advocating the public advantages of the principle of publicity, Jeremy Bentham offers the largest and most systematic contribution on the advantages of publicity. His plea for publicity related to trust can be broken down into several arguments, all expressing the optimism of their author.

First and according to Bentham, secrecy engenders suspicion, and, consequently, policy clarity ('free policy') prevents false accusations. Politics 'shrouded' in mystery causes distrust even in upright governments. According to the English philosopher, mystery is a fertile ground for calumny. Obscurity or the impression of mystery is never beneficial to reputation:

> Suspicion always attaches to mystery. It thinks it sees a crime where it beholds an affectation of secrecy; and it is rarely deceived. For why should we hide ourselves if we do not dread being seen? In proportion as it is desirable for improbity to shroud itself in darkness, in the same proportion is it desirable for innocence to walk in open day, for fear of being mistaken for her adversary ... The best project prepared in darkness, would excite more alarm than the worst, undertaken under the auspices of publicity.[13]

Rather than detracting from honour – a frequent grievance voiced about open policy – publicity often preserves it. The principle of publicity helps to establish the truth about the merits of a case, and to recognize honourable behaviour, thereby raising esteem. For Bentham, this applies of course to the reputation of representatives but also to the reputation of judges.[14] And should publicity generate unfounded judgements in public opinion, Bentham contends that unjust accusations will of their own accord soon become exhausted. The function of publicity is to get merits correctly assessed by showing acts as they are. According to Bentham, a broad application of the principle of publicity removes from public opinion the weapon of distrust.[15]

Bentham enumerates the information that the public, in order to have solid opinions, should have access to with regard to acts of an assembly; one of these is the need to publish the respective number of the voters on each side, hence he denounces the objection that displaying the numbers for and against – which involves exposing the dissensus – weakens submission to the law. The argument that Bentham develops here is based on the same premise as before: that it is better to expose the real facts, including the fact of dissension, than to fuel suspicions that shrivel public confidence:

> Do you expect that you will obtain greater submission by concealing from the public the different numbers of the votes? You will be mistaken. The public, reduced to conjecture, will turn this mystery against you. It will be very easily misled by false reports. A small minority may represent itself as nearly equal to the majority, and may make use of a thousand insidious arts to deceive the public as to its real force.[16]

If in 'Of Publicity', Bentham admits that policy secrecy could be convenient in the short term for officeholders; in the long term he considers that publicity strengthens the government:

> That a secret policy saves itself from some inconveniences I will not deny; but I believe, that in the long run it creates more than it avoids; and that of two governments, one of which should be conducted secretly and the other openly, the latter would possess a strength, a hardihood, and a reputation which would render it superior to all the dissimulations of the other.[17]

These arguments in favour of the principle of publicity largely developed by Bentham are also expressed by Benjamin Constant with a similar argumentation. In *Principles of Politics*, Constant notes that ministers' honour can be guaranteed by public opinion only when the life of the state appears clearly. The opacity or vagueness that surrounds state operations leads to suspicion, doubt and mistrust:

> The honour of ministers, far from requiring that any accusation directed against them should be shrouded in mystery, on the contrary imperiously demands that its examination should be made in broad daylight. A minister vindicated in secret has never been fully vindicated. Accusations will not have remained unknown. The impetus that dictates them inevitably leads those who formulate them to reveal them. But revealed in this way, in vague conversation, they are bound to assume all the gravity that passion seeks to give them. Truth has no opportunity to refute them. You will not prevent the accuser from speaking, you will only prevent him from being answered. The minister's enemies take advantage of the veil of secrecy covering the case to make any untruthful accusation they wish. A full, public explanation, in which the representative bodies of the nation enlightened the entire nation on the conduct of the accused ministers, would prove perhaps both their moderation and his innocence. A secret discussion would leave hanging over him the accusations, which has been rejected only by some mysterious inquiry, and weighing upon them an appearance of connivance, weakness of complicity.[18]

According to Constant, libel and unfounded accusations do not make very solid arguments against the legitimacy of the publicity principle:

> Thoughtless declamations, unfounded accusations, wear themselves out; they discredit themselves and finally cease by the mere effect of that opinion which judges and withers them. They are dangerous only under despotism, or in demagogies with no constitutional counterweight. Under despotism, in spite of what they continue to circulate, they are taken up by everyone in opposition; in demagogies because, all powers being united and confused, as in a despotism, whoever dominates them by subjugating the crowd with his oratory, is the absolute master. It is despotism under another name. But when the powers are balanced and they restrain one another, words cannot have such a rapid and immoderate effect.[19]

Constant is in complete agreement with Bentham on the idea that opacity and mystery are never profitable for reputation, for they encourage suspicion and lead to calumny. Publicity, rather than damaging honour, more often preserves it; open procedures prevent false accusations.

Second, in *Political Tactics* Bentham exposes another argument, which is more original than the first. He believes that the free expression of the opposition and of adversaries' arguments give occasion to the government to counter-argue or to counter-attack publicly adversarial arguments. Supposing that the government is 'victorious' – Bentham seems to suppose it in most cases – this would strengthen the legitimacy of the government:

> Consider, in particular, how much public deliberations respecting the laws, the measures, the taxes, the conduct of official persons, ought to operate upon the general spirit of a nation in favour of its government. Objections have been refuted – false reports confounded; the necessity for the sacrifices required of the people has been clearly proved. Opposition with all its efforts, far from having been injurious to authority, will have essentially assisted it. It is in the sense that it has been well said, that he who resists, strengthens: for the government is much more assured of the general success of a measure, and of the public approbation, after it has been discussed by two parties, whilst the whole nation has been spectators.[20]

Third, in 'Of Publicity' Bentham finishes this discussion with another quite unusual argument. He defends the idea that the quality of the discussion – always presupposed by the English philosopher – will elevate the 'national spirit'. This kind of new order created by regular and high-level public discussion, he assumed, will moderate the public opinion and prevent it from the temptations of quick judgements, which are fertile grounds for suspicion:

> Among a people who have been long accustomed to public assemblies, the general feeling will be raised to a higher tone – sound opinions will be more common – hurtful prejudices, publicly combated, not by rhetoricians but by statesmen, will have less dominion. The multitude will be more secure from the tricks of demagogues, and the cheats of impostors; they will most highly esteem great talents, and the frivolities of

wit will be reduced to their just value. A habit of reasoning and discussion will penetrate all classes of society. The passions, accustomed to a public struggle, will learn reciprocally to restrain themselves; they will lose that morbid sensibility, which among nations without liberty and without experience, renders them the sport of every alarm and every suspicion. Even in circumstances when discontent most strikingly exhibits itself, the signs of uneasiness will not be signs of revolt; the nation will rely upon those trustworthy individuals whom long use has taught them to know; and legal opposition to every unpopular measure, will prevent even the idea of illegal resistance.[21]

In presenting Bentham as a major defender of the principle of publicity, it would be erroneous to pretend that Bentham's faith in publicity did not have limits or exceptions. As a utilitarian, he could not make this principle an absolute law, but always assessed things in terms of the (collective) consequences that are entailed. In 'Of Publicity', he noted some exceptions to the application of the principle, especially when publicity would 'favour the projects of an enemy', i.e., endanger the nation's security; when it would '[u]nnecessarily ... injure innocent persons'; or when it would 'inflict too severe a punishment upon the guilty'.[22] As an example, in 'Rationale of Judicial Evidence, Specially Applied to English Practice', Bentham noted that in legal proceedings we cannot damage the honour of an individual or of a family, including by revealing harmful information.[23] Nevertheless, in his enthusiastic case for transparency, Bentham introduced some considerations of proportionality, and he was not insensitive to possible negative effects.

Finally, one superficial paradox has to be revealed here regarding Bentham's argument. On the one hand, he believes that political institutions are founded on distrust,[24] and on the other, he puts the question of the rehabilitation of trust toward officeholders in the center of his own political argument favouring the principle of publicity. This superficial paradox could be in my opinion resolved by considering that in Bentham's idea, trust is always built on a primary distrust that has to be contested and dissolved by the proofs given thanks to the available information. To put it another way, trust doesn't have any affective, but rather cognitive, components for Bentham. As developed in the next section, the cognitive component of the feeling of confidence is qualified nowadays.

Trust and Transparency Today

In contemporary literature, trust is seen as a very fashionable topic. Matthew R. Cleary and Susan C. Stokes affirm that 'social scientists have become obsessed with trust'.[25] Moreover, the contemporary literature tends to consider confidence from the governed as constituting an essential feature of democracy. Thus, a decline in this confidence is often seen as compromising the health of our democracies.[26] Paradoxically, Luhmann noted thirty-five years ago in *Trust and Power* that trust has become obsolete due to the complexity of 'modern differentiated social orders'.[27] Consequently but surprisingly – considering Cleary's and Stokes's words – Luhmann adds: the 'old theme of political trust, which played a large role, especially in the period after the end of the religious wars, has virtually disappeared from contemporary political theory'.[28] If Luhmann is clearly not prophetic in his affirmation of trust's obsolescence, he could be useful today in understanding why an increasing amount of information (or of transparency) doesn't engender a feeling of confidence by the governed and how this is due to the complexity of the modern world. I feel that this helps to qualify the Benthamian assumption that presupposes that a great amount of information engenders, quasi-mechanically, trust – notably by the governed. In other words, and reasoning along Benthamian lines, there would be an alleged correlation between increased transparency of officeholders and increased public trust of them. However, in the contemporary literature, many contributions have minimized or even contested this optimistic causal relationship. Let's look at these arguments.

The first problem with this assumed relationship between transparency and trust is that it presupposes that information is actually disseminated, that it is received, and thereby effectively contributes to the formation of public opinion. This is obviously not the case. If transparency is a prerequisite, it is not a guarantee for that access. According to Naurin,[29] three factors explain the gap between transparency and effective publicity: the absence of opinion-making agents (in case, for instance, of lack of media coverage); rational ignorance (on behalf of the public or even of the media) according to which one won't invest in information-seeking (which entails costs) if one is not strongly interested in an issue; and, in addition to this rational type of choice, cognitive limits such as incompetence.

Moreover, we can question whether the quantity of information available is really a (sufficient) condition for creating a feeling of trust. As Stephan Grimmelkhuijsen convincingly demonstrates, trust is connected not only with cognitive elements but also with affective components. His conclusions are partly built on Robert Zajonc's theory of 'primacy affect'.[30] People don't 'make trust decisions based on their cognition ... Individuals are influenced by a general positive or negative feeling with regard to a mental object'.[31] It seems that a citizen's pre-existing global perceptions of the government are much more prevalent than the effect of a particular experience of transparency.[32]

The conclusions drawn by Grimmelkhuijsen regarding the impact of transparency on trust by the governed are made even less optimistic by authors who not only believe that transparency isn't a sufficient condition for increasing transparency, but even worse, that transparency can deteriorate the feeling of trust in two ways: first, transparency generates confusion and, second, transparency engenders cynicism. Let's look at the first argument, notably developed by Onora O'Neill. In *A Question of Trust*, she exposes the negative impact of excess information provided to the public, which is likely to generate confusion about the pieces of information that can and cannot be trusted as well as doubts as to whether officials are trustworthy or not.[33] Facing such an excess of sometimes contradictory information, people have no indications to decide in which cases they can reasonably place trust:

> As the quantity of (mis)information available rises, as the number of bodies with self-conferred credentials and missions and active publicity machines increases, as the difficulty of knowing whether a well-publicised claim is a credible claim increases, it is simply harder to place trust reasonably.[34]

Second, this supply of (excess) information may also generate a kind of cynicism in the public, knowing that the public will be often be exposed, through the media, to the misconduct of officeholders. This can dramatically undermine the level of trust that the public puts in its officials and ultimately leads them to the excessive conclusion that the incumbents never deserve trust.[35] The increasing mediatization of politics plays here an essential and negative role. In fact, the commercial media are more tempted to exhibit sensationalist elements, for example, of the private life of officeholders, than to proceed to careful inquiries bringing less explosive conclusions.[36] This trend seems to be confirmed by studies showing that in different countries the substance of the news became more critical of politicians.[37] The disillusion, disappointment and even cynicism of the public seem to be a natural consequence of being continuously exposed to denigration or defamation:

> [T]he present system disseminates an oversupply of oxygen for cynicism through the visibility of manipulative publicity efforts and the increased flow of negative messages. A related product is a highly pejorative, oversimplified and, in many cases, probably unfair stereotype of the standard politician as someone who cares only for power and personal advancement, is not bothered about problems that matter to ordinary people and is constitutionally incapable of talking straight. Audience disillusionment with political leaders and their utterances is a natural outcome of such a bombardment. Credit is not given to government even when it deserves it.[38]

The quantity of information available – necessarily not convergent – is not the only reason for distrust; the content, as well as the specific quality of information – tending to be more pejorative according, for example, to Dalton and Papadopoulos – can be considered a contributor to distrust.

Finally, it may be erroneously assumed that the public processes the information available with pure intentions or with rectitude. In order for transparency to play its role as a counter-power, those who process political information should be incorruptible. Bentham assumed purity of intentions on behalf of the public opinion 'tribunal' when he emphasized the positive role of publicity. According to Foucault's critique, Bentham shared with several thinkers of his time an idealized view of public opinion:

It's the illusion of almost all of the eighteenth-century reformers who credited opinion with considerable potential force. Since opinion could only be good, being the immediate consciousness of the whole social body, they thought people would become virtuous by the simple fact of being observed.[39]

These hopes are today largely disappointed. Public opinion is neither crystalline, crystal clear nor homogeneous. It is taken in economic and political mechanisms and then loses the autonomy that Bentham optimistically assumed – an autonomy that would have allowed the public to make incorruptible, independent judgements and to pursue moral and political sanctions.

Conclusion

As Onora O'Neill suggested, if confidence were correlated with the current supply of information – considering the new technology of information simultaneously easy to use and inexpensive – we would be today in a 'trusting society'.[40] This is obviously not the case. It seems that the increasing flow of information has either little to do with trust by the governed or, even worse, deteriorates the public's feelings of confidence. The relationship between trust and transparency assumed notably by Bentham is based on the idea that distrust is generated by a deficit of information. This assumption is clearly contested by some of the literature. To decrease distrust, we have to work more on the feeling of being deceived, which is not mechanically correlated with the information at our disposal.[41] O'Neill and Grimmelikhuijsen share the conclusion that the feeling of confidence is more related to affective components than cognitive ones.

The general, rather pessimistic, tone of the contemporary literature can also confirm Rosanvallon's assumption, which presupposes that the history of democracy is deeply impregnated by the continuous dissociation between legitimacy and trust,[42] engendering a long tradition of distrust, which Bentham recognized as well, in a way, when he affirmed that 'the political institution is founded upon distrust'.[43] It seems that, for Bentham, the feeling of confidence, which he tried to reinforce through publicity, is built on a firm basis of distrust, which still belongs to the institutions of representative government today.

31 THE ENTERPRISE FACE TO THE ENVIRONMENTAL CHALLENGE: STRADDLING THE FENCE BETWEEN SOCIAL RESPONSIBILITY AND PENAL RESPONSIBILITY

Nathalie Dongois and Sophie Swaton

Introduction

The modern ecological critique appeared mainly in the 1960s, along with the new social movements.[1] But it is since the 2000s that the damage (or negative externalities, in economic terms) caused by companies to the environment have been most publicized. Now, with the web, image issues are so crucial that no company can afford to ignore them.[2] NGOs therefore have a powerful tool at their disposal and they could use it as a credible threat against groups that tried to pursue a type of growth undermining the environment. However, NGOs are claiming for further guarantees: if they can indeed get results – getting harmful operations to be discontinued, for example – it is through their actions, their denunciations but also and especially thanks to the media exposure they manage to get, mostly via social networks. Should we settle for such a system?

This question lies at the heart of debates about corporate social responsibility (CSR).[3] Translated from the American concept of 'Corporate Social Responsibility', CSR was defined in 2001 by the European Commission's 'Green Paper'[4] as the 'companies' voluntary integration of social and environmental concerns in their business operations and their relationships with stakeholders'. At the 2002 Earth Summit in Johannesburg, CSR was one of the main topics. Large companies active in the fields of the environment and energy participated.[5] Their responsibility was unambiguously questioned:

> We agree that, in the course of its legitimate activities, the private sector as a whole, that is to say both large and small companies, have the duty to contribute to the emergence of equitable and sustainable companies and societies.[6]

However, environmental responsibility and sustainability have not been clearly defined.[7] Moreover, companies have been accused by some NGOs of taking advantage of their presence at the summit to get free communication and publicity. More generally, it is true that, when the environmental stake is taken into account by enterprises, it is mainly in response to pressure from civil society or sometimes upstream, under a marketing approach meant to provide the company with a 'respectable image'. As stated in the definition of CSR, it is a 'voluntary integration' of societal concerns, including the environment. Thus, the European Commission's Green Book addresses the issue of companies' CSR through societal recommendations: therefore, the principles outlined in it are not legally binding for business. The approach is only intended as an incentive one, which is denounced besides by a number of environmentalist associations and NGOs that are internationally active in ecological matters.[8]

How do companies perceive their environmental responsibility and what clout does the law have to force them to honour their commitment? In some cases of offenses against the environment, some sanctions are possible: in Switzerland, the Law on Environmental Protection (EPA), for example, provides for the imposition of criminal sanctions against the perpetrator who violates a number of behaviours, but it is strictly confined to a particular type of offense, committed by an individual – not a business – in a specific area. The polluter-pays principle[9] makes it possible, meanwhile, to compel a company responsible for an act of pollution to repair the damage; this principle aims to enforce incurring the company's civil liability, not its criminal one.[10]

This contribution aims to analyse how to incur companies' criminal liability when they violate environmental protection globally. In Switzerland, companies' criminal liability has already been provided for to fight against money laundering (Article 102 CP). Could a similar liability be incurred, in Switzerland, for companies that infringe environmental protection? This is what our contribution is all about. Since the company is at the heart of our subject, the point is to see to what extent criminal liability could be transposed to cases of violation by companies of the environmental principles promoted by the CSR concept. Companies are actually the ones that are likely to cause environmental damage in the course of their economic operations; therefore, steps should be taken to make them directly liable. CSR, in turn, aims to expand the purpose of enterprises: next to the pursuit of profit, meeting environmental and other societal stakes should also be imposed. Given this context, it becomes relevant to ask whether the scope of companies' criminal liability as provided for in Article 102 CP could be expanded so that it should serve CSR.

Would imposing a legal obligation on companies to apply the principles of firms' environmental responsibility included in the concept of CSR make it more effective? Would it be possible – and if so appropriate – to make a company criminally liable if, having committed itself to CSR, one of its operations seriously damaged the environment? These are the questions we try to answer in this essay, showing the limits of existing legal mechanisms for the protection of the environment and the exploitation of these devices by companies. Given these limitations, we wonder whether the environmental issue could be a binding target for companies, by means of criminal law.

Environmental Protection: It is Instrumentalized by Companies

The state has two main levers as guiding principles for companies: taxes and rules. The first may be imposed through the polluter-pays principle developed by liberal economist Arthur Cecil Pigou in the early 1920s, or even be paid back in the form of premiums to companies that proved responsible, including when they have tried to upgrade their facilities with cleaner equipment. The second action lever relates to policies that are implemented, and CSR could become one of them. This raises the issue of control. Nevertheless, in both cases, the limits of these levers are visible: they can be manipulated by companies that can hardly be subject to the concept of responsibility.

The 'Polluter-Pays' Principle

A Legal Principle ...

The polluter-pays principle has two meanings, which gives it a very varied scope, depending on the case. In its broadest sense, this principle aims to charge the polluter with the social cost of the pollution it creates and results in an accountability mechanism covering all the effects of pollution, not only on goods and people, but also on nature itself. Based on this broad definition, the polluter-pays principle may be invoked to justify the adoption of strict liability regimes in environmental matters, that is to say, based on merely finding damaging results, regardless of any fault on the part of the company. Still, in most cases, it justifies the implementation of a civil liability regime, but does not aim to define the conditions for its application, so that its implementation usually requires evidence of misconduct imputable to the company.

But determining misconduct, as well as the person (or entity) responsible for it, is probably the major obstacle to obtaining redress where environmental damage is concerned. The issue of identifying the polluter has been raised by the OECD when it came to know who some pollution subsidies should be assigned to. Thus, determining who the polluter is requires attempting to discover who really holds the technical and economic powers in order to influence the pollution.[11] As for identifying the polluter responsible for environmental damage, doubts remain as to whether this definition is still relevant because reporting a natural person is awkward most of the time (how can one know with accuracy and certainty who did what), when blame may most often – at least partly – be apportioned to another person ...

Therefore, some claim that finding objective liability is best suited to the polluter-pays principle because it results in optimal effect.[12] Indeed, it eliminates the need to establish misconduct. Also, in order to avoid having to charge a person or another, it might be more appropriate – though not so fair – to make the company criminally liable as a legal person.

In a more limited sense, the polluter-pays principle can be analysed as a partial internalization of the costs incurred to fight against pollution by companies likely to pollute, as it makes it possible to impose taxes or fees on polluters without the entire community having to bear the burden of pollution remediation. In such a system, it is paradoxical to admit that the state could give subsidies to polluters in order to help them finance pollution control investments. Yet this is one of the exceptions that may be allowed during transition periods, to the extent it does not lead to significant distortions of competition. Similarly, it might be worth considering supporting industries that faced insurmountable difficulties due to the enforcement of that principle. The point here is to make environmental improvements faster and easier during transitional periods.

Based on this principle, on the one hand standards might be developed that require the polluter to use less, or even non-polluting methods, or setting standards for maximum emission rates, the average quality of the receiving environment or the characteristics of the finished product; on the other hand, the state may collect fees from polluters in proportion to the amount of pollution they cause, or even provide affixing labels to products. From that point of view, this could provide greater scope to the polluter-pays principle applied to businesses, encouraging them to upgrade their facilities rather than look for an interpretation of the principle in terms of 'right to pollute' or optimum pollution. The latter interpretation prevails today. Indeed, this principle has been hijacked by economic theory.

.... Hijacked by Economic Theory

In economic theory, the polluter-pays principle as it was taken up following Pigou's work, primarily means that external social costs accompanying industrial production (including the costs resulting from pollution) should be taken into account by economic agents in their production costs. Thus, businesses' external costs should include both prevention costs, such as antipollution investments, and costs related to compensation for damage to third parties and the environment.

However, the first problem that arises concerns the resulting overhead: who will pay? There is a serious risk the cost might be passed on to consumers. Furthermore, it could also penalize exports. In such a context, companies might refuse to follow Pigou's principle in order not to make their sales decrease. Nevertheless, if fees are too low, large businesses might seize the opportunity to purchase a 'right to pollute'.

A second set of issues relates to costs assessment. How do we assess the economic costs of environmental degradation? In addition, the environmental cost may exceed the polluter's capabilities to pay. How, then, can the person responsible for it be identified, as demonstrated by the cases of past oil spills, where the tanker captain, the owner and the charterer kept passing the buck from one to the other? In this case, other mechanisms such as insurance or national solidarity must stand in for the polluter. However, compensation mechanisms are an admission of failure, because the plundering of scarce resources and the destruction of some species cannot be offset, whatever the financial compensation.

Finally, there is no empirical study on the effectiveness of the polluter-pays principle. The media has often highlighted that its preventive results are disappointing, and apparently some companies are willing to bear the costs of pollution in case they are prosecuted[13] – which boils down to the possibility of buying a 'right to pollute'.

Actually, if companies have come to terms with the polluter-pays principle, it is primarily based on strategic calculation; it is a partly speculative one since – in addition to taking into account antipollution investment costs – they merely anticipate the assessment of legal damages in the event of damage to third parties or to property or then again to the environment, caused by the company in connection with its business operation. So the polluter-pays principle sounds simple at first glance: it is pregnant with several problems, both economic and legal ones. Therefore it is rarely applied and legitimizes environmentally questionable behaviour. Yet when companies consider the polluter-pays principle as a 'right to pollute', it creates problems in terms of liability: will it be possible to take legal action against a company that has paid the fee? What about that from a criminal point of view? The OECD, for its part, advocates combining fees and standards.

However, an evolution meant to facilitate its implementation has been noticed: the latest European decisions concerning the application of the polluter-pays principle seems to promote broader interpretation of the principle, in particular by not requiring to establish proof of misconduct, by not imposing to prove either the existence of negligence or that of fraudulent intent, but assuming instead that presumption of guilt is sufficient.[14] With this in mind, should we not make reference to companies' liability? According to the European Commission's Green Book, attitudes are changing and consumers' expectations evolving, to the point that this would be a paradigm change, perceptible in the concept of social and environmental responsibility. What this concept means for business and how it is translated into law is a different matter altogether.

Corporate Social Responsibility

Priority to Profits at Economic Level ...

The term 'responsibility' is a difficult one for a company to interpret at philosophical and economic levels. When it emerged in the 1950s, the CSR concept equated the company's responsibility with the current manager's. It was only in the 1960s, with the rise of new social movements (the political environmentalist movement in particular), that business leaders began to be deemed accountable to the society in which they operated, in that they were economic entities with duties towards society. But these perspectives were criticized in the next decade by authors supporting the dominant ideology prioritizing profits. In economic theory, the assumption of profit maximization is fundamental. It is the bedrock of the liberal paradigm[15] that, according to some dominant interpretations, considers individuals as selfish agents only preoccupied with maximizing their expected utility.

In this context, the only responsibility that might be incurred to business is increasing its own economic capital rather than preserve the limited and natural capital of the planet. That is why on 13 September 1970 Friedman gave the following definition of it in an article published in the *New York Times*, the title of which spoke volumes: 'The Social Responsibility of Business is to Increase Profits'. The tone was set: CSR is not an objective in itself but merely a means to increase profits (*business case*). At economic level, the environment is an inescapable fact to generate profit (*business case*). In the production function, it is understood as an additional resource, next to labour and capital. Its exploitation by companies is both necessary and legitimate.

Therefore, commitment to CSR, which a company can currently make only on a voluntary basis – such as setting up a fund for the 'reforestation' of the Amazon or signing a so-called 'ethics' charter – are initiatives that are part of a specific logic of active profit-seeking. Large groups' CEOs make no secret of it, for that matter.[16] The Chairman of the Nestlé Board of Directors unequivocally asserted that joining CSR pertains to the group's business strategy, not at all an idea imposed from the outside, an integral part of Nestlé's principles of conducting business. What matters for the group is to 'create value for society in the long term', given that our consumers 'feel an emotional connection when purchasing our products, and would not have a good feeling when purchasing our goods if they thought we were an "evil" company'.

Note that the terms 'good' or 'evil' used by large groups to defend their sudden inclusion of the environment belong to an ethical approach to business called Business Ethics, which emerged in Europe in the late 1980s. Unlike the previous decade, the 1980s were set in a context of extending responsibilities to everyone connected with the company, whether employees, customers or suppliers, beyond the sole shareholders' interests. Yet, when the term responsibility is raised to describe a company's conduct in environmental matters particularly, this responsibility is primarily an economic one. In his formalized ethical approach, Carroll[17] distinguished four responsibilities: the economic, legal, ethical and philanthropic ones. However, the foundation of it all still is economic responsibility.

Today, the environment is not – yet – seen as a resource to be defended in itself[18] but used in the name of companies' best interest, and they have no qualms about communicating on the subject and on how well-behaved they prove to be in the matter. Moreover, they are often accused of greenwashing or of green marketing, which betrays the gap between rhetoric and practice, as apparent in Total's initiative to set up a foundation promoting sustainable development while still investing heavily in the consumption of non-renewable energies. In this context, business ethics is a case in point of how the ethical charter is a middle ground agreed on by business and government: as in the case of CSR, the regulation results from the firm's voluntary approach.[19]

... facilitated by the Priority Given to Recommendations at Legal Level

Several initiatives to guide companies' behaviour are worth mentioning at international organizations level.[20] These principles have served as a framework for the development of different standards or labels, including ISO 26000 or ISO 14000 for environmental protection. Ensuring the existence of an international consensus on the need for companies to take into account environmental concerns was a prerequisite to preparing labels – reflecting states' political will to commit themselves in this way. The need for labelling and certification[21] was the main achievement of the 1992 Rio Summit. Any company can apply for such and such a label, provided it meets defined conditions, particularly in terms of compliance with a number of economic, social and environmental commitments, as set out in particular by CSR[22] – which obliges it, upstream, to comply with the label's requirements. In this sense, labelling can be deemed a binding measure.

However, commitment to labelling remains a choice for businesses, not an obligation. From this point of view, it is an incentive approach. Though it cannot be imposed on businesses, there is no denying that the concept of eco-efficiency[23] is making headway and has become part and parcel of an environmental management approach companies are keen to adopt. Therefore, the economic interest that may be served through labelling or getting the 'eco-efficient business' label is a key determinant in companies' choice of respecting CSR principles. Still, the company must pay for the external audit allowing access – often in gradual stages – to its certification.[24] In this context, the more resources a company owns, the more likely it is to acquire high-quality labelling. Consequently, labelling risks becoming no more than a luxury that only companies with substantial resources can afford.

Therefore, is there not a cause here again for speaking up and voicing our concerns against possible instrumentalization? If labelling is perceived by consumers as a sign of abiding with some principles and/or as a guarantee of quality, is it not time we asked what are the means of control implemented to ensure the long-term quality and continued compliance with the contracted guarantees? The objectives of environmental protection are made public and validated by accredited organizations. Is it enough? If not, would it be, for all that, desirable – or even possible – to threaten a company that has committed to a number of environmental protection principles with inflicting criminal penalties for violating these commitments?

Though the duty to protect the environment has indeed emerged, CSR does not provide the means to go further than fostering corporate awareness of environmental concerns. However, legally, a company's criminal responsibility as a legal person has been provided for by the legislator in Article 102 CP. It meets the demands from a particular context, but is enough to show that the concept does exist. At a time when CSR is gaining clout at economic level, could companies' criminal liability, applied to the field of environmental protection, become the strong arm of the law? This question needs to be asked all the more as it remains widely accepted that if, one day, a company's profits happen to collapse, concern for the environment will suffer. For example, look at the case of Suez, when the media laughed at them with the following quip: 'Suez, le développement durable qui ne dure pas!'[25]

Environmental Protection: A Binding Objective for Companies by Means of Criminal Law?

Towards Implementing Companies' Criminal Liability in Case of Breach of Environmental Principles as Promoted by CSR?

Companies' criminal liability was laid down in Article 102 CP, making this new legal person subject to criminal law.[26] The company is understood in a broad sense here, based on an economic approach; indeed, based on any unit (it can be composed of several natural or legal persons) engaged in commercial activities, i.e. selling goods or providing services against remuneration.[27] This definition of the enterprise is the approach adopted by economists' CSR concept.

Companies' criminal liability is based on an organization's failure. Therefore, Article 102 CP may be analysed as an imputation standard[28] and establishes a new form of criminal offense, in addition to intent and neglect – the organization's failure. It provides for two forms of companies' criminal liability, a subsidiary one, and the other: a primary one. We will analyse them in turn, in order to see to what extent they are transferable to any violation by the company of the environmental principles promoted by the CSR.

Companies' Subsidiary Criminal Liability as a Way to Foster Compliance with Environmental Principles Included in the Concept of CSR: Poor Usefulness and Feasibility

According to the first paragraph of Article 102 CP, when a person (including a manager)[29] can be held criminally liable for committing an offense within the company and due to a lack of organization, the company as a legal person goes unpunished, thus enshrining companies' subsidiary liability. Priority is thus given to an individual's criminality. However, when this is not possible, then the company may – under certain conditions – be punishable by law. Indeed, it is necessary for an offense to have been committed within the company and in the course of its business consistent with its purposes, without any specific individual being possibly held liable for the organization's failure,[30] thus making it impossible to charge the offense to a specific individual. The requirement of this causal link is a reminder that the legislator has expressed his will to punish an agent rather than the company as a legal person, which moves away from some stakeholders' desire to make the company criminally liable directly, considering that the enterprise is first and foremost responsible for implementing the environmental principles promoted in the context of CSR.

Regarding the first condition – the commission of an offense – CSR is based only on recommendations and is therefore not binding. Therefore, it would be worth ensuring political determination to allow the legislature to establish violations of these recommendations as criminal offenses did exist. This would imply that these principles become mandatory (and no longer be mere guidelines). The switch in the status of recommendations into binding measures, violations of which are criminalized is the *sine qua non* condition of the possible transposition of the company's subsidiary criminal liability. However, fines are excluded from the scope of Article 102 CP,[31] so – unless a change on this point is contemplated – it should be ensured that transposing environmental guidelines attached to CSR into criminal offenses do take the form of offenses or crimes. This can be problematic because, while offenses enabling or facilitating money laundering are all deemed serious ones (and therefore correspond to felonies or crimes), this is not necessarily so with regard to any new offenses against the protection of the environment.[32] Indeed, environmental law is primarily a preventive form of law, so such offenses might mainly be considered as violations of precautionary rules.

Once the political will to turn the violation of environmental principles promoted by CSR into major offenses or crimes has been remedied, it would still be necessary to ensure that the offense was committed in the course of commercial activities consistent with the purposes of enterprises.[33] This condition should not pose a problem to the extent that CSR provides principles that companies have an incentive – and in future may be forced – to comply with, in particular in the course of selling their products or providing services. We have in mind here the guarantees provided in products manufacturing or production methods ...

The Primary Criminal Liability of the Enterprise in Furthering Compliance with Environmental Principles Included in the Concept of CSR: Difficult to Apply to Negligence Offense

The second paragraph of Article 102 CP provides primary responsibility, i.e. independent from an individual's, if some offenses are committed through the company. Targeted offenses are exhaustively listed and meet a clear political will: the fight against money laundering. This is the only objective underlying Article 102 CP.

With regard to conditions of application, a lack of organization on the company's part must be charged to the company concerned. Such failure must be the cause of committing the offense. In other words, it is because the company has failed in its duty as an organization that the offense was committed. The company is then criticized as a legal person, for not having taken all necessary and reasonable measures to prevent the commission of the offense. It is therefore not sufficient for the company to have taken a few measures only: it must have implemented them all, provided they are necessary – that is to say, used to prevent commission of offenses – and reasonable, in that we can blame the company for not having taken the measures it could and should have implemented. While no one is bound to achieve the impossible, the conditions laid down in the second paragraph of Article 102 CP refer to 'diligence of the whole company'.[34] That way, an obligation rests on the company to take, as a preventive measure, all necessary steps to avoid these specified offenses being committed while conducting its business and in accordance with its purposes.

To ensure this provision is applicable to companies that violated environmental principles specific to CSR – criminalized – a paragraph 2a should be provided in connection with these offenses. However, the offenses listed in paragraph 2 of Article 102 PC, are all intentional crimes. Violations of CSR environmental principles by companies targeted for transposing this provision should thus be constitutive of intentional offenses (serious offenses or crimes). Indeed, due diligence (the firm is bound to it), which specifically refers to compliance with rules of conduct and standards accepted in a given industry, is simultaneously one among negligence offenses. It would not make sense if the organizations' failure was both the cause of the commission of the offense and the offense itself. Yet, to effectively fight against damage to the environment, criminal liability should be provided for regarding companies that, in the course of their business, negligently violate the required precautions.[35] Seeking intent would then be an obstacle to the effectiveness of the fight against environmental damage by applying a hypothetical extended section 102 CP. From this point of view, negligence offenses are problematic.

In view of these drawbacks, expanding the scope of Article 102 CP establishing companies' criminal liability does not seem to be the appropriate solution. Still, from an economic point of view, a paradigm shift is about to occur. Should we be content with it – considering that it will suffice to guide corporate behaviour differently towards greater respect for environmental concerns – or contemplate resorting again to criminal law in order to anchor this paradigm shift?

A Much Disputed Paradigm Shift

If contemporary approaches to accountability in economics identify a new responsibility under the term 'global responsibility', they also confirm an analysis in terms of preponderance of economic responsibility. However, within the broad definition of CSR adopted by the European Commission, corporate social responsibility must go beyond shareholder value and seeking profit for the sole stockholders. The environment is a fully fledged component in its own right. For this reason, some companies, such as those participating in the lineage of the social economy could take it more into account because they implement responsibility of a global kind[36] – in principle and not out of strategic anticipation.

But what about other companies? For the latter, as for economic theory for that matter, Friedman's injunctions are not so obsolete. The dominant economic theory based on agents' selfish preferences not only considers that only capitalist enterprises are effective, but prove unable to explain the existence of a social or environmental objective for companies other than through the thesis of survival.[37]

It is under pressure from civil society that companies must now adapt themselves and, paradoxically, take the environment into account, beyond the strictly economic perspective. While, for some, that explanation of adaptation is only based on 'survival of the fittest' and can be interpreted as a mere extension of standard economic theory – hence still based on the assumption of purely selfish preferences – others see it as a considerable reduction of it. The company is not an entity composed of selfish preferences, but it also incorporates a minimum of partially altruistic behaviours, not motivated solely by profit-seeking.

According to Borzaga and Tortia, though companies do have a 'coping behaviour', their goal is not necessarily profit, 'but more generally the creation of an economic and social surplus'.[38] Specifically, this potential to create a surplus also depends on factors other than profit and exclusive concern for stockholders. According to these authors, 'the latest trend' in for-profit companies is 'to increase their level of social responsibility'.[39] Hence, the latter's support to CSR. Beyond the socio-economic perspective previously underpinned in the theory of the adaptation of capitalism to the new constraints[40] it might be legitimate now to talk of a paradigm shift.[41] Clearly, a new paradigm cannot prevail overnight. We talked about corporate responsibility but, in parallel, we must mention consumers, whose responsibility is also at stake. However, according to research in the field,[42] there is a gap between consumers' intentions, allegedly willing to consume in sustainable ways, and their actual practices. The price-effect does play a great part and can indeed hardly be disputed, either as regards low-income households or at the broader theoretical level. Similarly, consumers demand guarantees, and are civil society stakeholders who have played a great part in CSR's media and academic success, by threatening to boycott companies that acted against the environment.

Consequently, if one wants to support the paradigm shift, then responsibilities should probably be framed more strictly, beginning with large groups, since pollution and resources consumption are mainly due to industrial operations. According to Capron and Quairel-Lanoizelée,[43] by acknowledging CSR and making it mandatory for companies, the concept is endowed with a legal nature, which ultimately warrants the institutionalization of the concept. In practice, such institutionalization should incite consumers – or rather '*consum'actors*', as the current buzzword puts it[44] to also align their practices and make them more sustainable. If consumers stopped looking only for the cheapest products and included as prime determinant of their choices the company's commitment to a number of societal concerns, whether environmental or otherwise, then constraint would need play no part in guiding corporate behaviour.

Now, to do this, consumers also need to identify the legal constraints on business. Consequently, the law is seen as an intermediary, knowing that companies develop coping skills to suit consumers' expectations. For now, economic constraint seems more effective than any other sort, be it criminal. However, the situation may change: for consumers to adopt responsible ways of consumption it is necessary to send them a signal the law can embody. In this sense, criminal sanction could be useful.

Conclusion

Henceforth, protecting the environment requires making companies criminally liable, but current tools have proved rather inadequate, whether because they are insufficient or inapplicable. To be effective, the law, criminal law especially, must enjoy legitimacy: it must be perceived as useful to society. If it seems at odds with inherent economic activity in its classic approach, namely seeking profit and profitability, then it will carry no weight.

Therefore, a paradigm shift including the environment as part of the equation in its own right, and not as an additional variable in the production function, would endow criminal law with renewed usefulness. Still, the appropriate tool is yet to be found. This issue is being investigated, as evidenced by lawyer Polly Higgins's proposition to turn damage to the environment into so-called 'ecocidal' offenses;[45] witness also the recent efforts to establish an international climate court.

In any event, damage to the environment must be clearly defined; principles and rules to be followed in the modes of production of goods and provision of specific services should be determined, so as to provide appropriate criminal sanctions, should they be infringed by companies. This would make it possible to impose criminal penalties on clearly defined behaviours, whether intentional or resulting from negligence[46] and make enterprises criminally liable as legal persons.

32 LAW AS A SYSTEM OF NORMATIVE PRODUCTION: LAW AND SEMIOTICS

Pierre Moor

The Law as Objectivation of the Form and Substance of Power

There is in a certain way a vulgate of legal theory in which the legal system is defined as a set of norms.[1] I say Vulgate: a theory circulating widely enough to be considered the official theory, which is composed in a fairly undifferentiated way of a few doctrines put together (mainly Kelsenian and post-Kelsenian normativism, realistic theories and logical formalization approaches).

Thus, the definition of the law immediately refers to that of the norms, as they are its constitutive components. According to the Vulgate, these are requirements, or behavioural models – accompanied, should they be breached, with the threat of sanctions. This definition raises a problem, which is primarily theoretical: what is the distinguishing criterion of the legal norm, given that there are other prescriptive systems? (I just said 'theoretical', which is not, or not immediately pejorative: I'll wax theoretical myself, while nevertheless incorporating the *practice* of law into the theory by showing that work done *on* the norms is as important as the norms themselves.)[2]

The classic illustration of this distinguishing criterion issue is provided by the well-known comparison of two situations: the first is that of a bandit extorting his victims of their jewellery, the second that of a bailiff seizing goods from a recalcitrant debtor. Why should the order of the second be 'juridical' and not that of the first? Kelsen's response is that the bailiff is empowered by a norm pertaining to positive law, itself based on the assumption of a logico-transcendental fundamental norm; Hart's is that it is a legal issue in accordance with a positive law recognized as such by all authorities. These statements hardly give the question a satisfactory answer. Finally, a band of robbers – in more modern terms, organized crime – is also institutionalized as a hierarchy and its members are subject to rules whose violation is accompanied by threat of sanctions. Granted, the state has a monopoly over so-called legitimate constraint, or at least it claims it does, but in the final analysis, this power also rests on a mere fact of life, whose legitimacy has been the subject of endless philosophical debate.

What seems more crucial to make a difference pertains to the analysis of the modalities within which coercion action is exercised. In the context of a robbery, two purely subjective wills are at loggerheads, which have no other source but themselves and are not related – as wills – to anything other than themselves. The bailiff's situation is another matter altogether: he does not exercise his own subjective will, nor does the judge whose court order he implements, and nor, finally, does the legislator whose decision is grounded upon the law. Each in their own ways, they all act in accordance with an order that is superior to all of them and over which they have no control (and it is superior to the debtor, as shall be seen in a moment): they cannot change it as they please, as their actions have got to comply with it. And such compliance is not only the one they owe to the rules governing their respective formal skills, their empowerment, it is as much about integrating to *substantive* rules the content of the acts they decide to undertake. And the meaning of their compliance is altogether different from what compels a band of robbers to obedience: it aims to embody the objective rationality of authority acts, that is to say, a transfiguration of *de facto* power (always subjective) into the power of reason. Legal determination can exist only insofar as what the authority decides is integrated into a set of rules, which, since these are beyond the decision maker's control, warrant that his own will becomes irrelevant – insofar as possible. I call this transfiguration a 'general rationality requirement', and it is the complex institutional system that guarantees this requirement is met. That complex is the essence of law. We might as well say it straight away: the legal norm is not what defines the law; quite to the contrary, any prescription can only become legal to the sole extent that it belongs to the law, as a system that has been so organized.

I should mention here it is true that, for Kelsen as well, the authority's intention becomes objective will: but only insofar as it is – formally – authorized. However, I believe this is not good enough to characterize the law: it is also necessary that objectivity be ensured in its substance.

One point needs developing at this juncture: it is not only the state power's will that is objectified: the individual's will also is, embodied in the legal person as subject of law. By integrating individuals via this figure, the law recognizes them as persons, that is to say, gets them to carry the burden of this general rationality requirement. The subject of law, thereby transfigured, is as much bound by the legal system as a whole (and therefore, but only therefore, by the norms herein) as the authority itself: it is bound to it, but also benefits from it in that, as a subject of law, he can enter into any legal relationship, whether as debtor or creditor, and is protected by it in these positions. Moreover, as such, he is entitled to that double compliance highlighted above – the formal and material integration to the legal order; we could even say this, perhaps: that, ultimately, is what properly defines him. That is why he is not only a 'subject' ruled by a government, or even one 'subjected to the administration', or finally, a 'person subject to the law' – since all these terms are passive! The rationality requirement thus includes the legal persons who are such – as much as are authorities on their part – only because they are made so by the legal system, because it institutionalizes the rationality requirement. That *common reference* to the legal order as a system, without which no government or legal subjects could exist, is what is totally foreign to the relationship between a band of robbers and their victims.

The introduction, in the definition of law, of the rationality requirement has a number of theoretical implications. I mean, it must be said outright: this is a *requirement*, not a reality, in that nothing is ever granted. But I am merely pointing to an avenue of research that would lead to presenting checking institutions and correcting instruments (namely, for example, the good faith principle, or the concept of gap).

Legal Epistemology as the Core of the Theory of Law

If the rationality requirement of law is the very essence of law, it means that any theory of law must include an argumentation approach: an analysis of the process the law undergoes before being formulated, a path through which any assertion can be said to be purely legal – that is to say *integrated* into the legal system. While this is also a jurisdiction issue, it is not only that. No legal expert will be satisfied with the competent judge's assertion that virginity on the wedding night is (or is not) a bride's essential quality (to take an example that has hit the press): the first and foremost focus is the argumentative chain by which the judge reached this conclusion. Evidence of it is that the judgement may be appealed, not because its quality as an individual norm issued by a competent judge could be challenged, but rather because the *material* implementation of this norm in the legal system is questionable. The purpose of the appeal is the appropriateness – the epistemic validity – of the argumentative chain in favour of which the lower court held that the norm it is about to issue actually fits into the legal order.

It is therefore the object of legal theory that is involved here: how to define law. Law may be considered as established through a collection of norms. But in doing so, it completely ignores what the law is in terms of work to be done: it is a theory of law that law experts in their daily activities, in their practice, are entirely absent from: law devoid of the practice of it. Now, they spend their time writing, reading, speaking, listening, in short, arguing. Arguing to put forward that the rationality requirement has indeed been met, because there is no norm – at least in the modern times legal system claim they are grounded on – that can dispense with showing its credentials – even the one enacted by the Supreme Court.

This bears out that legal theory must begin with its epistemology: that is to say, by analysing the mode of legal normative production, because it is precisely this mode of production that distinguishes it from other normative systems. I will do that here only in part, by focusing on the dynamics of institutional actors in the system.

To take up again the example I have just given: under Article 180 al. 2 of the French Civil Code, 'should there have been an error about the person, or concerning the person's essential qualities, the other spouse may demand nullity of marriage'. The legal question asked in the instant case is whether the bride's non-virginity is an essential quality, an issue whose solution will be given in the particular/individual norm ending the dispute. As for the legal problem, it is a matter of finding relevant arguments making it possible to move from the text of section 180 to the individual norm, a move that is no logical evidence, by far, witness two conflicting judgements on the same issue.

However, though that shift is not logical evidence, how should is it to be conducted so that it can be described as legal, i.e. considered legally valid? Besides, what are its impacts on the legal system?

Two Modes of Legal Imperativeness

In terms of theoretical analysis, the answer obviously depends on the initial choice of the problems approach assigned to the theory of law.

Arguably, it is sufficient that the individual norm has been decided by the competent authority. This is the answer I mentioned above. The implications of this position are reflected in the concept of the sources of law: the law is what emerges at some point from an authorized source. What happens before it surges, as much as what happens afterwards, is concealed. Evidence of it is the wavering of the theory as to the characterization of jurisprudence as the source of law, and its refusal to regard the doctrine as such.

However, despite what I called concealment, it is perfectly true that a norm adopted in accordance with the rules of jurisdiction is considered valid, at least until another authority competent to do so has decided otherwise. In terms of specific/individual norms, the *res judicata* principle applies. In terms of legislation, the problem is the institutionalization of the control of their constitutionality. Once the force of *res judicata* has been acquired, the norm becomes undeniable: it is imperative by itself. I call this mode of imperativeness an *institutional* one, since it depends on the institutional arrangement of jurisdictions.

It should be noted that the force of the *res judicata* principle affects the pronouncement and it alone. The grounds themselves remain questionable. The cancelled wedding is cancelled once and for all, once the judgement becomes final, whatever opinion one may have of its motivation. Yet, if no appeal had been lodged against this judgement, nothing would have prevented specialists of marriage law to carry on discussing the grounds that founded it – hence turning it into a *legal* discussion, since it would have covered the definition of what is considered, within the meaning of Article 180 of the civil Code, as an 'essential quality'. Similarly, indeed, the argument followed by the Appeals Judge may be challenged. What would have been involved in either one of these discussions, which I would dub doctrinal, is the *material* integration of the particular/individual norm in terms of the legal rationality requirement. The persuasiveness of this precedent would have been challenged in favour of another argumentative chain, which would have led to a different norm. And the purpose of this discussion would have been what I call the *epistemic* imperativeness, i.e. the compliance, of a *material* nature, of the solution brought to the legal system.

It is true that neither the doubts one may have afterwards on the merits of a final judgement, nor even the certainty you might have afterwards of its lack of merit, result in any implication as to its institutional imperativeness (excluding exceptional grounds for review). That does not mean, however, that they have no effect on the epistemic dynamics of the legal system. On the contrary! But demonstrating it requires an analysis of the epistemology of interpretation and application.

Interpretation and Application of the Law: From the Normative Text to the General Norm

We distinguish between interpretation and application. Interpretation means determining the meaning of a text for its own sake, while remaining at the same level of abstraction: for example, if a text contains the words 'the French', are these to be interpreted in an epicene way, that is to say, including both sexes, or does it refer only to French males? As for the application, it is a matter of determining in the concrete case what the particular/individual norm is that, with reference to the general rule applied, will solve the legal situation: for example, in such an accident, might any wrongdoing cause the author's responsibility to be involved? That question begs another: what are the duties of the author of the tort in the concrete circumstances in which he acted?

All too often, legal methodology is confined to exploring methods for interpreting texts; it neglects law application – as indeed it neglects the problem of finding the facts (probably because legal theorists read supreme courts' decisions, not the first instance or appeal judgements!). At best – as does Kelsen – it isolates the problems approach for exporting it, by attributing it to the so-called 'judicial policy'; on one hand, such a strategy comes as no surprise since, for Kelsen, the validity of the individual norm does not depend on its material compliance with the superior norm. On the other hand, it is surprising, since, as I have already noted, a considerable part of legal experts' daily work is dedicated to establishing the facts and enforcing the law. But the reason why we should pay attention to it goes beyond the realistic concern of taking into account the actual practice of the law. The legal authority – that is to say, the power of definitively addressing a situation – lies in its essence in conferring meaning to concrete facts by *determining* what the general norm states only as an abstraction, i.e. as indeterminacy: do such and such clues allow one to conclude that the facts that have been presented are true? (For example, has the defendant had an intimate relationship with another person? Was the ground slippery?), and are these facts likely to be given the characterization ensuing from the general rule? (May the act be considered as a fault? Is this monument worthy to be placed under protection?). Indeed, the uncertainty inherent in any abstraction relative to the historical peculiarities of any individual situation (idiosyncrasies) must be resolved by a choice between all the solutions indeterminacy makes possible. It is in this opportunity for choice that legal authority lies (and its micro-political dimension) – and it is a considerable power, because it is the power of *giving a name* to the things: facts become, and in imperatively binding manner, something other than what they are in themselves; they enter another world, a symbolic one: 'adultery', 'negligence', 'essential quality' – in it, they are transfigured, and compellingly indisputable.

However, there is a profound difference between the logic of interpretation and of application (I leave aside the issue of finding facts). The first regards definition, logic that (in accordance with Umberto Eco) I call dictionary logic: it is a matter of replacing one or more terms with other terms that will be considered as their exact equivalent. This is what happens when the norm emerges as the 'true' meaning of a text; actually, we only substitute another text for the original one; the text of the norm is redrafted (e.g. 'French men and women' instead of 'the French').

The application logic is that of the encyclopaedia. The particular/individual norm arising through application (or concretization) is a special *case* of the general norm – one among many others, hence not at all identifiable to the general norm. If I say, regarding a dispute to settle, that the pharmacist, who, by profession, knows the dangers of it, should take all necessary precautions for storing toxic drugs in a place inaccessible to children and that storing them on a shelf is not good enough, I develop a particular norm, which is one *case* of the notion of wrongdoing; yet, I might as well reach a particular norm that is the reverse, noting that, to access that shelf, he necessarily had to climb on a stool – this norm is also a case of the notion of wrongdoing (non-cases are also 'cases' of the norm).

However, the cases of the notion of wrongdoing are endless, and occur in the most varied and most unexpected situations. To take another example, it is certain that, when it was adopted, in most constitutional laws, the guarantee of personal liberty did not know that cases could refer to the current legal issues related to data protection, artificial insemination, etc., and we do not yet know what situations techno-scientific developments will create – and the judge will have to assess them in connection with this guarantee. Therefore, the specific norms constituting the encyclopaedia of indeterminate legal concepts such as 'wrongful act', 'personal freedom', etc., are also countless and unexpected; the encyclopaedia is permanently and essentially always *open* to being enriched with new cases.

A major consequence results from it all. The general norm cannot simply be the meaning of the text that formulates it. It is also the encyclopaedia of the specific norms that were decided by reference to that text. In other words, the general rule known as Article 1382 of the French Civil Code or as § 823 of the German *Bürgerliches Gesetzbuch* is not only the 'dictionnaristic' meaning of these texts, but also *the whole encyclopaedia* of all particular norms issued to solve concrete cases of civil liability – a whole set that is always open to future developments.

This set is an organized and structured whole, worked out to become the system of the norm, with Article 1382 being the original text. It cannot be formulated in all its complexity; no textual formulation is able to account for all the internal differentiations brought into the norm by practice, i.e. into the richness and fertility of its encyclopaedia. Moreover, should this general norm be formulated – in a ruling, or by the doctrine – as soon as it was being written, such formulation would immediately cease to be the norm itself, as it would in its turn become just one *text* among all possible ones. *Any* text *formulates*; therefore it merely fills *the role* of the norm; it is only that by which we can *speak of* the norm – it is even impossible to talk about it otherwise –, but it never will be, whatever its complexity, the norm itself. Besides, the original text has no other scope than to serve as the identical reference to all the discourses bearing on the norm – a reference that ensures that the former are about the same thing. Thus the general norm can perform itself throughout its history, whose episodes it keeps in mind to constantly organize and reorganize them.

Therefore, any norm exists as a complex *idea*, which resides in the collective memory of the legal community, beyond all textuality, but can only be understood within the world of texts which speak of it as their reference. It is complex because it organizes the 'tradition' – to borrow a term from hermeneutics. The tradition began with the adoption of the original text (often even before: Article 1382 of the Civil Code did not come out of the blue in 1804) and continued with case-law casuistry. It has been, and is, permanently developed and organized, reworked and reorganized, not only by case law but by the doctrine, which reflects it, i.e. works on it, systematizing and sometimes even anticipating it.

Argumentative Paths

Any lawyer knows that only rarely can a specific legal issue receive an immediate solution. In most cases, there are several possible argumentative paths, leading to different normative solutions. While clear texts do exist, they are most often clear only in one aspect. For example, maximum speed in urban areas is 50 km/h; but the rule applies *generally*, which means that, depending on specific situations, it might be less applicable, since 'speed must always be suited to circumstances' (according to a Swiss legal provision; its equivalents are bound to be found in other highway codes). Then again, clarity is only apparent: for example, if there is a provision that 'inside railway station buildings, dogs must be leashed', what about monkeys or snakes? The general norm will have to be formulated in a second text providing that 'animals presenting a risk must be controlled adequately'.

It is therefore necessary, since the text and the norm fail to achieve perfect clarity as formulated by interpretation, to argue until the validity of the normative solution is established. Arguing means showing that the solution about to be chosen is the one that fits into the legal system better than others, and is the one the text itself would also have permitted. Normative indeterminacy exists from the start; therefore, it is necessary to make a choice by adopting a particular/individual norm – what I earlier called the 'power of naming things'. The need to make a choice, which creates the micro-political dimension of law, constitutes the limit of the rationality requirement, because, as it can never be fully met, it always leaves some room for subjective determination – that which decides which the most relevant argument is.

Two points are worth careful attention here, before a semiotic theory of interpretation and application is outlined, and before it is shown how it can account for the way information flows between society and the legal system.

The first point concerns the relationship that allows giving meaning to the norm, either by interpreting or applying the text. Legal language is written in ordinary language, whose signs it uses: the signifiers of the former are made up with signs of the second (/dog/, which is the signifier in the normative text, is the word *dog* found in common language). Yet, if, in ordinary language, the relationship between the signifier /dog/ and the signified, 'dog' is arbitrary (there is no reason to attribute to the signified that particular signifier rather than another), the same can't be said of the legal language: in other words, the relationship between the legal signifier and its signified is not arbitrary, it is *motivated*. However, as part of the legal code (not of the linguistic code), it can be *demotivated*, that is to say, distanced from its meaning in ordinary language ('dog'), precisely according to its code. The interpretation and application can therefore use all polysemous possibilities and ambiguities of ordinary language, which form the semantic framework (all encyclopaedic potential meanings) within which the reading of the text evolves; it can even use figures of speech – e.g. metonymy, in the case of the legal signifier /dog/. However, demotivation from the linguistic code and ordinary meaning of its signs requires remotivation explaining the reasons (rationality) of this distortion of meaning. It is at this point that classical interpretation methods take place, with a heuristic function (as in the example of /dog/, the purposive (teleological) approach); they are used to suggest directions for other possible meanings, but they obviously do not directly provide the *reasons, motives, rationality* of such diversion. This is why, incidentally, there exists no methodology for methods of interpretation. This could be summarized as follows: any reader – as a matter of law – must be able to *understand* the normative text using the vocabulary and syntax of ordinary language, including the *surprises* embodied by diversions of meaning.

These reasons, contrary to what one might think, do not only have endogenous origins. Indeed, the legal argument not only contains reasons already known to be legal (*internal* argumentative schemes), but also the arguments it takes from its socio-cultural environment – arguments that, by taking them up again, gets them to become legal (external schemes). We are now addressing the second point here.

First, let us take an example. For a long time, on the basis of a text dating back to the nineteenth century, Swiss private international law used to recognize the divorce of foreign spouses living in Switzerland, provided their state of origin recognized that divorce; for spouses of different nationalities, the text was interpreted as requiring recognition by both states of origin. In 1968, at a time when Italy did not recognize divorce, the Federal Court proceeded to a reversal of precedent and admitted that only the law effective in the state of the requesting spouse was critical; the plaintiff was a French woman and the defendant was Italian (significantly, the Court, composed of five judges, ruled by a majority of three against two). Here is an excerpt of the reasons:

> If the judge cannot base his judgements on considerations of desirable law, he must nevertheless strive [to interpret] the law in a manner as consistent as possible with the situation and the current mentality. To this end, he will often be led to abandon a traditional interpretation, which was probably justified when the law was drafted, but that is no longer sustainable because of changing circumstances or even due to the way ideas have evolved ... The cumulative application of each spouse's national laws is indefensible if the principle is openly laid down that divorce should remain an exceptional mode of marriage dissolution. Such a statement is inconsistent with reality, both in Switzerland and in most neighbouring countries.

What we see in this judgement, is the intervention in the argumentative path – assuming that the original text of the norm is drafted so as to allow both interpretations – of reasons relating to 'change in circumstances' and the 'evolution of ideas', in short, to 'reality'. So these are facts, not legal ones, which are considered critical: since the adoption of the text, divorce has become common practice, an institution socially recognized for being ordinary, that has somehow fully become an everyday feature of life; therefore an interpretation restricting the possibility of divorce must be rejected, and the norm reformulated otherwise than previously. We see here that the assessment of a social fact – a culture, social knowledge – is taken up again by the court and, as such, will enter the legal order as a legal rationality reason.

The same goes for the case of the pharmacist, mentioned above, who stored a drug in a place where, by climbing on a stool, a child was able to grab and gulp it down it as if it was a sweet. The judge will have to decide between pharmacists' ethical duties (was the precaution he took good enough?). What about the duty of parental supervision (should they have watched their offspring's behaviour more carefully?). To do so, the law, in the current state of its encyclopaedia, might prove of no avail (if we hypothetically assume that there is no case law and no specific legal provisions on one point or another): he will then have to resort to such patterns of behaviour that are considered as received in the customs, habits and manners of the society in which he lives and that, finally, the particular norm he will select is designed for – which presupposes it will have to be such as being socially acceptable.

There is therefore a constant information exchange between the law and society: on one hand, from the former to the latter, by providing knowledge, models, etc., and on the other, the latter reinstates the former in normative form.

Conclusion

There are three conclusions actually, to gather all of the above, which may appear heterogeneous.

First, institutional imperativeness – that of *res judicata* – is only one part of the legal order. What constitutes, organizes and systematizes it, allowing its coherence and development, thus ensuring the general rationality requirement, is working on epistemic imperativeness.

Second: norms are the result of production work. This work is accomplished through texts – the original text, the texts of the specific norms, those of the doctrinal systematizations. It is communication work: in other words, a constant exchange of discourses. All these discourses always give themselves the same reference, namely the original text, which ensures the unity of their object (which is the norm, their common *referent*, as we would say in semiotics); but this object is permanently found and recovered in enriching the encyclopaedia of knowledge that is being developed on this topic. A more rational encyclopaedia, as consistent as possible, so that it can project itself into the future, when it will have to include new specific norms, as they will be required to accommodate all of the unexpected situations that are sure to arise in future.

Third: norms result from the work of all legal institutions, not only the legislator but also the judges – past, present and future – as well as doctrine. The law is not only a static reserve of texts (or of norms), but also a set of institutions that produce norms by working on texts. A *set of people* – the legal community – in whose operations not only memory, but also its actors' imagination, guaranteed by judicial independence and freedom of expression, play a crucial role. Or, more precisely than a whole set, it is a *system*; by that I mean an organization that has three characteristics. First, its identity lies in the way its elements relate to each other and at the same time – in second place – it, within itself, confers to each of them their own identity, by differentiating their functions; third, this differentiation enables the system to maintain its own relations with its sociopolitical environment. And, speaking of the environment, we must specifically include, among the actors of the legal system, an essential category we sometimes tend to forget: the subjects of law, who, as such, are *inside* the system, but who, as individuals, remain *outside* – it is, factually, this dual nature as both a legal concept and a social reality that opens a channel of communication between the legal system and its environment. Indeed, the practices, knowledge, ideologies that prevail in society make up a secular legal culture, in a somehow inchoate way, awaiting consecration; a culture whose priestly caste – legal experts – keep fuelling its argumentative paths during the normative invention process. A dual nature, moreover, that also affects the judge's position, as he is both and at the same time a function as well as (he, too) an individual.

Conclusion of conclusions: a definition of the norm can hardly be given, let alone defining the law, without betraying the richness of its organization and the limits that the latter provides to what the law, as a social subsystem, is capable of producing in terms of rationality. This is impossible because, to account for it, one should be able to summarize in one single formula the complexity of the system it constitutes: we should be able to understand it in its entirety in one swoop. For example, what I said about the norm-distinguishing criterion as postulating a rationality requirement cannot be fully understood unless we understand the normative production process. But, conversely, this process can only be understood if we understand that the law assumes a rationality requirement. There is circularity in the structure of the whole, which makes it impossible to isolate any one of its elements to define it by itself, and which to the same extent prevents the whole from being defined without taking its elements organization into account.

NOTES

Baranzini and Allisson, 'Introduction'

1. In the original French: 'il faut savoir ce que l'on fait. Si l'on veut récolter à bref délai, il faut planter des carottes et des salades; et si l'on a l'ambition de planter des chênes, il faut être assez sage pour se dire: [La postérité] me devra cet ombrage.'

1 Lallement, 'Walras between Holism and Individualism'

1. Text translated by Dominique Macabies.
2. Arrow notes that when it comes to assessing economic research, to report on an article or recruit a colleague, economists widely adopt the criterion that, in principle, proposed economic explanations and economic policies necessarily involve individuals and not other social entities. In other words, Arrow recognizes the universality of methodological individualism in standard economic theory: individual agents' economic decisions are therefore the only explanatory variables.

    Arrow gives a simple definition of methodological individualism: all explanations in social sciences must be made exclusively in individual terms. If such a minimal definition is sufficient for Arrow's purpose, debates about methodological individualism have led to more sophisticated formulations (see J. Agassi, 'Institutional Individualism', *British Journal of Sociology*, 26:2 (1975), pp. 144–55; G. Hodgson, 'Meanings of Methodological Individualism', *Journal of Economic Methodology*, 14:2 (2007), pp. 211–26, amongst many others).
3. K. J. Arrow, 'Methodological Individualism and Social Knowledge', *American Economic Review*, 84:2 (1994), pp. 1–9, on p. 1.
4. Walras obviously does not use the modern term holism: he speaks, as the case may be, of 'collectivism' or 'communism' (see L. Walras, 'Méthode de conciliation et de synthèse', in *Études d'économie sociale* (1896), in A. Walras and L. Walras, *Œuvres économiques complètes* (hereafter *OEC*), published by P. Dockès, P.-H. Goutte, C. Hébert, C. Mouchot, J.-P. Potier and J.-M. Servet, 14 vols (Paris: Économica, 1987–2005), vol. 9, pp. 151–73. L. Walras, 'Esquisse d'une doctrine économique et sociale', in *Études d'économie politique appliquée* (1898), *OEC*, vol. 10, pp 405–41.
5. L. Walras, 'Théorie générale de la société', in *Études d'économie sociale, OEC*, vol. 9, p. 90. The 'Théorie générale de la société' is a set of six lectures delivered by Walras between October 1867 and March 1868, initially published in the journal *Le Travail*, and later republished by Walras in his *Études d'économie sociale* (1896), C. Mouchot, J.-P. Potier and J.-M. Servet, 14 vols (Paris: Économica, 1987–2005)).

6. Walras, 'Théorie générale de la société', p. 90.
7. Ibid. We will see below that humanitarian facts and social facts are two perfectly suited synonyms for Walras, insofar as he cannot dissociate man from society.
8. 'However, if, neglecting the study of man as an animal that breathes, digests and reproduces, feels, perceives and resolves, who was born, grows and dies, we strive to study him exclusively to discern in what his virtual human faculties are typically human and their manifestations active, we will see two facts that emerge in him, which are the basis of the physiology and psychology of man's ability to division of labour and moral personality. These two facts ... are like two doors through which one moves from the field of nature to the field of humanity' (Walras, 'Théorie générale de la société', p. 90).
9. Among these features, the opposition of the thumb to the other fingers. If Walras's developments on the specificity of the human versus the animal may now seem rather naive, they in any case express very clearly Walras's position on man's irreducible specificity.
10. Sensitivity puts man in a position to experience the outside world caused by emotions and develop feelings for his fellow men. Walras's view of intelligence, largely borrowed from Kant, allows for an implementation of reason, necessary to know the world.
11. Walras, 'Théorie générale de la société', p. 102.
12. Ibid., p. 105.
13. Social wealth, which is the subject of political economics, is defined by Walras as all rare things, i.e. useful things that are in limited supply; it has been thoroughly studied once there is a theory of exchange and value, a production theory and a theory for the distribution of social wealth.
14. Morals here mean not so much an individual ethics as the science of mores and society, which the nineteenth century readily called moral sciences, as opposed to physics or natural sciences.
15. Later, Walras introduced in his trilogy a new distinction between pure morals and applied morals (see J.-P. Potier, 'Classification des sciences et divisions de l'"économie politique et sociale" dans l'œuvre de Walras: une tentative de reconstruction', *Economies et Sociétés*, série PE, 20–1(1994), pp. 223–77 and R. Baranzini and E. Tatti, 'Léon Walras e il metodo matematico dell'economia pura: al di là della forma', *Economica politica*, 19:1 (2002), pp. 65–89).
16. The presentation can be found in the 'Théorie générale de la société' (1867–8), but also in the *Éléments d'économie politique pure* (1874–7).
17. Walras, 'Théorie générale de la société', p. 130.
18. Ibid.
19. These laws are subjective in that they express humanitarian facts that depend on men's far-sighted reason and free will, implying that these facts are, not necessary and immutable as natural facts, but rather are subject to change and progress. This theme of human progress is very important for Walras: it is what allows him to affirm the future possibility of a science of society. Men are free, they can change society and move towards the best to achieve the social ideal in practice (e.g. Walras, 'Théorie générale de la société', pp. 147–8).
20. Ibid., p. 130.
21. 'A highly educated man professes favourable feeling to freedom of international trade, to banks of issue, to a Liberal and Democratic government, but another who passes for no less educated is a declared supporter of the protectionist system, of the monopoly of banknotes issuance and of aristocratic and authoritarian regime' (Ibid., pp. 130–1).
22. Ibid., p. 131.

23. Ibid.
24. Ibid.
25. In the early nineteenth century, theodicy (the science of God, established by the light of reason, without recourse to Revelation) is one of the four parts of philosophy as taught in secondary schools. A freethinker, Walras is bound to deny the divine origin of society.
26. Ibid., p. 133. Though a freethinker, Walras does not refrain from referring to the New Testament, here to the Acts of the Apostles (17, 28). But the practice was common in the nineteenth century: Frédéric Bastiat, for example, uses the same quote in Chapter 2 (*Deux morales*) of the second series of *Sophismes économiques*, see 'Deux morales', in *Œuvres complètes, tome IV, Sophismes économiques, 2ᵉ série* (Paris: Guillaumin, 1863), pp. 148–56.
27. 'Man can exist only in society and thanks to society. The real man is man in society.' L. Walras, 'Méthode de conciliation et de synthèse', p. 171.
28. Ibid., p. 131.
29. Ibid., pp. 134–5.
30. L. Walras, *Éléments d'économie politique pure*, in *OEC*, vol. 8, p. 62.
31. Walras regretted that these two ideals of the French Revolution had not yet been implemented when he wrote: 'In truth, although three quarters of a century has elapsed since the day when these two words were proclaimed, I am forced to admit that we have never been able to separate them, but have not yet managed to reconcile them either in science, nor in politics, and that all our systems are still tossed from individualism to communism, as are all our governments, from unequal liberalism to authoritarian democracy' (Walras, 'Théorie générale de la société', pp. 135–6).
32. Ibid., p. 131.
33. Ibid., p. 134.
34. Ibid., p. 137.
35. The following will explain these paradoxical formulations. For now, we can just say, with a vocabulary that is not exactly Walrasian, that he prescribes equality of individuals before the State's authority while simultaneously advocating the right to difference for each individual.
36. Walras, 'Théorie générale de la société', p. 138.
37. This means, among other things, equality of chances.
38. By comparison, Gossen's barter does not comply with commutative justice but performs distributive justice.
39. Walras, 'Théorie générale de la société', p. 140.
40. P. Dockès, *La société n'est pas un pique-nique* (Paris: Économica, 1996), p. 96.
41. Walras, 'Méthode de conciliation et de synthèse'.
42. Walras, 'Théorie générale de la société', p. 134. Please remember that, together with the individual, general social conditions and particular personal positions, the State is one of the four concepts necessary to develop the theory of society according to Walras.
43. Walras, 'Théorie générale de la société', p. 136.
44. Ibid., p. 137.
45. Ibid. Walras here evokes natural law as he also does about ownership of the land (which belongs by natural law to the State) and about personal faculties (which belong by natural law to individuals). If Walras often refers to the 'lawyers' good old natural law' (see P. Dockès and J.-P. Potier, *Léon Walras: vie et œuvre économique* (Paris: Économica, 2001), p. 23), it seems that here, this reference does not point to natural law with the lawyers' meaning, but an observation: 'nature has given the earth to us all and our personal capabilities to each of us' (L. Walras, 'Esquisse d'une doctrine économique et sociale', p. 424). Walras

simply wants to emphasize that the state and the individual are factual givens, i.e. natural, and therefore the attributes of these entities, which follow logically from their natural character as givens, are natural facts themselves, too.

46. Walras, 'Méthode de conciliation et de synthèse', p. 171.
47. Walras, 'Théorie générale de la société', p. 137. Walras still maintains the confusion insofar as he continues his comparison with the army, but now it is not society that is compared to the army, but the State. 'The army already existed before the oldest soldiers had joined it, and it will still exist after the youngest of them is released. Similarly, the State has a life of its own', ibid., p. 137.
48. Ibid., p. 144.
49. Simplifying a lot, we say that the quarrel of universals opposed realists, who recognized the real existence of universals (concepts such as collective rights, or whiteness) to nominalists, who argued that these universal terms were just shortcuts of language to describe unique collections of objects, which alone have real existence.
50. K. Popper, *Misère de l'historicisme* (Paris: Plon, 1956), p. 133.
51. Ibid.
52. F. Hayek, *Scientisme et science sociale* (1953; Paris: Plon, 1991), p. 52.
53. Ibid.
54. Ibid., p. 83.
55. Walras, 'Théorie générale de la société', p. 163.
56. It is worth pointing out that they both take the same example, the army, to underpin two opposed theses: Walras to justify his realism and Popper to vindicate his nominalism.
57. While the theories of individualism are explicitly stated and claimed as their own (by social contract theorists, Hayek and Popper, amongst others), holism is much more difficult to define, and proponents of individualism are usually the ones that define a form of holism an intentional supporter of which is difficult to find among authors. Moreover, it should be noted that when he speaks of individualism or communism, Walras does not explicitly distinguish between different levels of analysis of individualism and holism (ontological, methodological and political) as Popper and Hayek will, at least partially. Walras's vocabulary reflects this lack of differentiation; he speaks of communism (sometimes collectivism) to describe an ontological postulate or a holistic policy position as well as methodological choices.
58. Hence, as mentioned earlier, Walras is neither an individualist nor a holist.
59. Walras, 'Méthode de conciliation et de synthèse', p. 145.
60. Ibid., p. 146.
61. Walras, 'Théorie générale de la société', pp. 134ff.
62. Walras, 'Méthode de conciliation et de synthèse', p. 143.
63. Walras, 'Esquisse d'une doctrine économique et sociale', p. 434.
64. Walras, 'Théorie générale de la société', p. 11.
65. Walras, 'Esquisse d'une doctrine économique et sociale', p. 426.
66. Ibid., pp. 426–7.
67. See the very comprehensive article by Alain Béraud, 'Walras et l'économie publique', *Œconomia. History, Methodology, Philosophy*, 1:3 (2011), pp. 351–92.
68. Walras, 'Esquisse d'une doctrine économique et sociale', p. 427.
69. Walras acknowledges and accepts responsibility for the major role he assigns the State to help markets to work, which departs quite drastically from the usual liberal dogma. 'My socialism leans towards the restoration of the State against the invasion of the individual' (Walras, 'Théorie générale de la société', p. 143).

70. Ibid., p. 142.
71. Ibid., pp. 392, 397.
72. Ibid., p. 143.
73. Ibid., pp. 142–3.
74. The growth of the rent, linked to the absolute limitation of the earth, insures the State growing means to perform its missions.
75. Ibid., p. 143.

2 Dos Santos Ferreira, 'The Case against Market Perfection: The Two Bertrands' Objections are One'

1. See P. Bridel, *Le Chêne et l'architecte: Un siècle de comptes rendus bibliographiques des Éléments d'économie politique pure de Léon Walras,* text prepared with the collaboration of R. Baranzini (Geneva: Droz, 1996), pp. 163–9, for a full discussion of Bertrand's contribution.

2. See P. Bridel and E. Huck, 'Yet another Look at Léon Walras's Theory of *Tâtonnement*', *European Journal of the History of Economic Thought*, 9:4 (2002), pp. 513–40.

3. L. Walras, *Éléments d'économie politique pure* (Lausanne: Corbaz, 1874), as in *Auguste et Léon Walras. Œuvres économiques complètes*, vol. 8 (Paris: Economica, 1988), §42, p. 72, my emphasis.

4. A. A. Cournot, *Recherches sur les Principes Mathématiques de la Théorie des Richesses* (Paris: L. Hachette, 1838); translated by N. T. Bacon, *Researches into the Mathematical Principles of the Theory of Wealth* (New York: Macmillan, 1897).

5. 'In his critique of Cournot, Bertrand (1883) suggested that price rather than quantity be taken as the independent variable' (M. Shubik, *A Game-Theoretic Approach to Political Economy*, vol. 2 of *Game Theory in the Social Sciences* (Cambridge, MA: MIT Press, 1984), p. 135). 'A natural objection to the Cournot quantity model is that in practice businesses choose prices rather than quantities as their strategic variables ... Bertrand (1883), in his review of Cournot's book, was the first to criticize Cournot on these grounds, and his name has since been attached to simple pricing games, just as Cournot's is with simple quantity games' (C. Shapiro, 'Theories of Oligopoly Behavior', in R. Schmalensee and R. Willig (eds), *Handbook of Industrial Organization*, vol. 1 (Amsterdam: North-Holland, 1989), pp. 329–414, on p. 343). 'Bertrand (1883) objected to Cournot's analysis on the basis that firms actually do set prices, and thus considered a model where prices are the strategic variables' (J.-P. Bénassy, 'Monopolistic Competition', in W. Hildenbrand and H. Sonnenschein (eds), *Handbook of Mathematical Economics*, vol. 4 (Amsterdam: North-Holland, 1991), pp. 1998–2045, on p. 2001).

6. R. W. Dimand and M. H. I. Dore, 'Cournot, Betrand, and Game Theory: A Further Note', *Atlantic Economic Journal*, 27:3 (1999), pp. 325–33.

7. J. Bertrand, '"Théorie mathématique de la richesse sociale" par Léon Walras; "Recherches sur les principes mathématiques de la théorie des richesses" par Augustin Cournot', *Journal des Savants*, 67 (1883), pp. 499–508, trans. J. W. Friedman, in A. F. Daughety (ed.), *Cournot Oligopoly: Characterization and Applications* (Cambridge: Cambridge University Press, 1988), pp. 73–81.

8. J. Magnan de Bornier, 'The "Cournot–Bertrand Debate": A Historical Perspective', *History of Political Economy*, 24:3 (1992), pp. 623–56.

9. Cournot, *Recherches sur les Principes Mathématiques de la Théorie des Richesses*, in Bacon, *Researches into the Mathematical Principles of the Theory of Wealth*, ch. 7.

10. Ibid., pp. 51–2n, with translator's 'unrestricted commerce' replaced by Cournot's '*free trade*'.

11. Ibid., p. 79.

12. Ibid., p. 80, my emphasis, and with replacement of translator's 'his' by Cournot's 'the'.

13. Ibid., my emphasis.

14. Ibid., p. 80.

15. D. M. Kreps and J. A. Scheinkman, 'Quantity Precommitment and Bertrand Competition Yield Cournot Outcomes', *Bell Journal of Economics*, 14:2 (1983), pp. 326–37.

16. Notice that both maximization problems have, under the market-clearing condition $D_i + D_j = F(p)$, the same first order necessary condition: marginal revenue $p + D/F'(p)$ should be zero (see J. Magnan de Bornier, 'Magnan de Bornier on Cournot-Bertrand: A Rejoinder to Clarence Morrison', *History of Political Economy*, 33:1 (2001), pp. 167–74).

17. Some 'facilitating practices' like the *best price guarantee*, which automatically ensures downward price adjustments, or the *public advance notification of price increases*, which facilitates upward price adjustments, are known to contribute in practice to price manipulability by market participants (see C. d' Aspremont, R. Dos Santos Ferreira and L.-A. Gérard-Varet, 'Pricing Schemes and Cournotian Equilibria', *American Economic Review*, 81:3 (1991), pp. 666–73). But this goes largely beyond Cournot's analysis, which does not extend to the process of price adjustments, except possibly in the form of alternate pricing moves in the case of a duopoly.

18. Bertrand, '"Théorie mathématique de la richesse sociale', in Daughety (ed.) *Cournot Oligopoly*, p. 77, my emphasis.

19. Ibid.

20. Ibid.

21. See Bridel and Huck, 'Yet another Look at Léon Walras's Theory of *Tâtonnement*', for the implications of such extension.

22. The *Principle of a Mathematical Theory of Exchange* was read to the Academy of Moral and Political Sciences in 1873, and was published the following year in the *Compte-rendu des séances et travaux* of this Academy. It was later incorporated, in 1877, as the first of four memoirs composing the *Mathematical Theory of Social Wealth*, to which three more memoirs were added in the 1883 edition.

23. L. Walras, *Théorie mathématique de la richesse sociale* (Lausanne: Corbaz, 1883), as in *Auguste et Léon Walras. Œuvres économiques complètes*, vol. 11 (Paris: Economica, 1993), pp. 25–133, on p. 37.

24. Ibid., p. 40.

25. Ibid., p. 43.

26. Ibid., pp. 43–4, my emphasis.

27. Ibid., p. 33. During a short verbal exchange between Walras and Bertrand, in 1877, the latter expressed the impression given to him by Walras's efforts, that of addressing the hydraulics of a muddy liquid. Walras answered that the impression was right, except that he was abstracting from the mud, that is, 'from all the circumstances disrupting exchange and production' (quoted by Bridel, *Le chêne et l'architecte*, p. 164).

28. Walras, *Théorie mathématique de la richesse sociale*, pp. 37, 66.

29. Ibid.

30. Ibid.

31. L. Walras, 'Un économiste inconnu: Hermann-Henri Gossen', *Journal des Economistes* (1885), as in *Auguste et Léon Walras. Œuvres économiques complètes*, vol. 9 (Paris: Economica, 1990), pp. 311–30, on p. 312n, my emphasis.

32. Bertrand, '"Théorie mathématique de la richesse sociale, in Daughety (ed.) *Cournot Oligopoly*, p. 79.

33. Ibid.

34. Ibid., p. 80.

3 Dockès, 'Walras, Marx and the Philosophy of History'

1. L. Walras, *Cours d'économie sociale, Cours, Œuvres économiques complètes*, vol. 12 (Paris: Economica, 1996), pp. 164–5.

2. K. Marx, *Le Capital, Critique de l'économie politique*, Volume 1 (1867), Postface to the second edition, *Œuvres, Économie*, vol. 1 (Paris: Gallimard, 1963), p. 555.

3. L. Walras, *Études d'économie sociale, Œuvres économiques complètes*, vol 9 (Paris: Economica, 1990); *Studies in Social Economics*, translated by J. van Daal and D. A. Walker (New York: Routledge, 2010), p. 5, lii.

4. The young Walras (in 1863) was still a naïve materialist (P. Dockès, *La Société n'est pas un pique-nique; L. Walras et l'économie sociale* (Paris: Economica, 1996), p. 40). In 1868 (Walras, *Recherche de l'idéal social*, 1990, p. 69, p. 162; 2010, p. 48, p. 122), he wants to *synthetize* materialism and spiritualism, or utilitarianism and moralism, or Interest and Justice. But, Walras is idealist in the sense of Plato and Hegel: ideas exists ontologically (*realism* in the old medieval signification), he is explicitly essentialist (holist), anti-nominalist.

5. See Walras, 'Théorie de la propriété', 1990, p. 206; 2010, p. 158.

6. On Walras's method see R. Arena and L. Ragni, 'Libre concurrence et méthodologie walrasienne: une tentative de mise en relation', *Economies et sociétés – Cahiers de l'ISMEA, series PE*, 28:20–1 (1994), pp. 161–82; R. Baranzini, 'La concurrence et le tâtonnement à la lumière du réalisme walrassien', in R. Baranzini, A. Legris and L. Ragni (eds), *Léon Walras et l'équilibre économique général, Recherches récentes* (Paris: Economica, 2011); P. Bridel, 'Juglar, Walras et Pareto: Measurement without Theory *vs* Theory without Measurement?', *Revue européenne des sciences sociales*, 47:143 (2009), pp. 87–94; P. Dockès, *La Société n'est pas un pique-nique; L. Walras et l'économie sociale* (Paris: Economica, 1996); J. Lallement, 'Walras et les mathématiques, un malentendu persistant', in R. Baranzini, A. Diemer and C. Mouchot (eds), *Études walrassiennes* (Paris: L'Harmattan, 2004), p. 81–104, on p. 81ff); D. A. Walker, *Walrasian Economics* (Cambridge: Cambridge University Press, 2006), ch. 1.

7. J.-P. Potier, 'Léon Walras, un économiste socialiste libéral', in J.-L. Fournel, J. Guillaumou and J.-P. Potier (eds), *Liberté(s), libéralisme(s). Formation et circulation des concepts* (Lyon: ENS-Editions, 2012), pp. 117–35.

8. Walras, 'Théorie de la Propriété', 1990, p. 207ff; 2010, p. 135ff; Walras, 'L'économique appliquée et la défense des salaires', 1992, p. 250ff; 2005.

9. For Walras, the land service is *rent*, its price is *tenant farming*, the artificial capital service is *profit*, its price is *interest*.

10. P. Dockès and J.-P. Potier, 'Léon Walras and the Significance of Free Competition', The Sixth conference of the International Walras Association: The International Diffusion of Walras's Economics: Influence, Interpretations and Controversies, Kyoto University, September 11–13 (2008); J.-P. Potier, 'Léon Walras et les exceptions au principe

de la libre concurrence', *Economies et Sociétés-Cahiers de l'I.S.M.E.A.*, series PE, 40:38 (December 2006), pp. 1813–26.

11. Dockès, *La Société n'est pas un pique-nique*, p. 219ff; J.-P. Potier, 'L'économie politique appliqué walrassienne: principe de la libre concurrence et intervention de l'Etat', *Revue européenne des sciences sociales, Cahiers Vilfredo Pareto*, 37:116 (1999), pp. 51–72.

12. Dockès, *La Société n'est pas un pique-nique*.

13. K. Marx, *La Guerre civile en France*, in *Œuvres complètes* (Paris: Ed. sociales, 1968), pp. 64–7.

14. K. Marx, *Manifeste du parti communiste*, in K. Marx, *Œuvres Économie I* (Paris: Gallimard, 1963), pp. 157–95, on p. 182.

15. K. Marx, 'La nationalisation de la terre', Appendice, in *Œuvres, Économie I* (Paris: Gallimard, 1963), pp. 1476–9. Marx is favourable to the collectivization of land but completely opposed to the Walrasian idea of renting it in small plots afterwards to small farmers or producers' associations, at least under a bourgeois government (it would be different under communism as we saw) (Marx, 'La nationalisation de la terre', p. 1478). See the comments of Maximilien Rubel (p. 1475) noting Marx's criticisms of Henry George's *Progress and Poverty* in 1881 that apply to Walras's programme.

16. Marx, *Manifeste*, pp. 175–6. It is not a case of taking from anybody the 'right to appropriate oneself social produce' (ibid., p. 177), or abolish the personal appropriation of work production (p. 176) – that is not the abolition of 'all kinds of ownership, but the abolition of bourgeois ownership' (p. 175).

17. Ibid., p. 181.

18. Ibid., p. 175.

19. The famous Saint-Simon sentence was taken up in Friedrich Engels's *Anti-Dühring* (1878) and *Socialism: Utopian and Scientific* (1880).

20. Marx, *Manifeste*, p. 192; see K. Marx, *Misère de la philosophie*, in *Œuvres, Économie I* (1847; Paris: Gallimard, 1963), pp. 7–136, on p. 136.

21. Marx, *Le Capital*, Volume 1, p. 613.

22. Ibid., '*The Fetishism of Commodities and the Secret thereof*', p. 604.

23. Marx, 'La nationalisation de la terre'.

24. Ibid., p. 1479.

25. K. Marx, *Critique du programme de Gotha*, in *Œuvres, Économie I* (Paris: Gallimard, 1963), pp. 1411ff, 1418–20. The first edition of this text, in *Neue Zeit*, 9:1, n. 18, pp. 563–75.

26. Marx, *Critique du programme de Gotha*, p. 1419.

27. Ibid., pp. 1411ff, 1418–20.

28. Ibid., p. 1420.

29. In the 1880s, Walras was interested in Marx, although his readings are unknown, and his interest remained vivid in the 1890s. On 22 October 1895, one of Walras's notebooks shows that he has 'read Marx' (Walras, 'Théorie de le propriété', p. 195, n. 14).

30. Walras, 'Le problème fiscal', 1990, p. 424, n. 43.

31. Walras criticizes the Marxian idea of moving from complex labour to simple labour by a coefficient representative of the relative lengths of training; he does not take the time to form what is considered an 'easy' refutation, but notes that Marxism could leave the price of the different forms of labour be determined 'by the mechanism of outbidding [*enchères*] or underbidding [*rabais*]', thereby getting rid of this 'second mistake' whilst retaining the idea of product prices being equal to the cost of wages. Moreover, Walras notes that the price of products should take into account the depreciation (and insurance) of the means of production.

32. Dockès, *La Société n'est pas un pique-nique*, pp. 219–21.
33. Not being able to produce luxury products is condemning society to stagnation and men to mediocrity. This anti-populist provocation would exasperate Charles Péguy (Dockès, *La Société n'est pas un pique-nique*, pp. 257–8).
34. Walras, 'Théorie de la propriété', p. 204.
35. Walras, 'L'économique appliquée et la défense des salaires', 1992, p. 251. Walras notes that if Marxist collectivism accepted that wages for different types of labour were set by 'outbidding' [*enchères*] or 'underbidding' [*rabais*]', men would move automatically, unless 'certain constraints' were used.
36. Walras does not know the German philosophy directly and his surpassing of Vacherot is made possible only by his readings of Etienne Vacherot, *Métaphysique et la science, ou Principes de métaphysique positive* (Paris: Chamerot, 1858). Walras admits it was his bedside reading as soon as it was published and during his entire lifetime ('Esquisse d'une doctrine économique et sociale', p. 414).
37. As Walras summarizes himself (ibid., p. 414), there is in Vacherot a theory of 'two separate worlds': on the one hand, a real physical and moral world, a necessary, infinite, continuous yet imperfect whole that is given to us by external and intimate experience; on the other hand, an ideal world, that of 'universal, necessary, infinite and perfect substance' – that is God – which is given to us by Reason, and this perfect idea excludes all true existence. Walras considers that if the real being is not perfect, 'he is improving' through man's will (ibid., p. 441). 'The world is God being fulfilled by the will of man' (ibid., p. 414). The link between ideal and real is forged by history.
38. Dockès, *La Société n'est pas un pique-nique*, p. 40, 65ff.
39. K. Marx, *Manuscrits de 1844*, in *Œuvres, Economie II* (Paris: Gallimard, 1968), pp. 76–90; K. Marx and F. Engels, *L'Idéologie allemande* (Paris: Ed. sociales, 1968), pp. 31–4, theses 1, 3, 7; Marx, *Critique de l'économie politique*, pp. 272–4. See also 'the opposition of the materialist and idealist conception' (Marx and Engels, *Idéologie allemande*, ch. 1 on Feuerbach, pp. 44–54, 60–2). 'Social relations are intimately linked to productive forces. By acquiring new productive forces, men change their mode of production, and by changing the mode of production, the way of earning a living, they change all of their social relations. The arm mill will give a society with an overlord, the steam mill a society with a capitalist industrialist' (Marx, *Misère de la philosophie*, ch. 2, §1 Method, pp. 78–9).
40. Marx and Engels, *Idéologie allemande*, thesis 3, p. 32.
41. F. Engels, 'Letter to Borgius, 25th January 1894', in *Marx-Engels Werke*, vol. 39 (Berlin: Dietz Verlag, 1973–7), pp. 205ff.
42. Ibid.
43. Marx, *Manifeste*, p. 161.
44. According to the expression constantly used by Walras and that is criticized by Marx and Engels (*Idéologie allemande*, pp. 105–6).
45. Marx, *Capital*, L. I, p. 1239.
46. L. Walras, *L'Economie politique et la justice*, *Œuvres économiques complètes*, vol. 5 (Paris: Economica, 1996), p. 152.
47. L. Walras, *Éléments d'économie politique pure*, *Œuvres économiques complètes*, vol. 8 (Paris: Economica, 1988), p. 40. In the various editions of *Elements* except the first. See also Walras, *Cours d'économie sociale, Cours, Œuvres économiques complètes*, p. 147, where he adds that the truth of pure moral science is 'historic truth' (n. 104, 108, n. 3). In 'Esquisse d'une doctrine économique et sociale' (pp. 405–43), after his reading of F. H. Giddings (in 1896–7), Walras will give different content to pure moral science. '*General*

coenonic' ('la cénonique générale') becomes an abstract and rational science of man and society, comparable to pure economics. He therefore keeps two definitions of pure moral science: *a priori* history and 'general coenonic'.

48. Walrasian philosophy of history is not to the author's mind completely *a priori* reasoning because observation first remains necessary as in any pure science.

49. 'Mankind is a planet which creates its own trajectory in the moral world. This is achieved by way of a double effort and double progress: the effort of human reason, which seeks a social ideal, and the effort of human will which achieves this ideal; the progress of scientific ideas and the progress of political facts' (Walras, *Études d'économie sociale, Œuvres économiques complètes*, p. 146).

50. Dockès, *La Société n'est pas un pique-nique*, pp. 47–54.

51. Walras, *Études d'économie sociale, Œuvres économiques complètes*, pp. 4–5.

52. Ibid., p. 147.

53. L. Walras, 'Théorie générale de la société', in A. Walras and L. Walras, *Études d'économie sociale*, vol. 9, p. 147.

54. 'L'économie appliquée et la défense des salaires', 1992, p. 250 and n. 12.

55. Walras, Théorie de la propriété, 1990, p. 192. Nuances are introduced in the second edition.

56. Walras, L'industrie moderne et l'économie politique, 1987, p. 136, 144–6.

57. Walras, *Cours d'économie sociale, Cours, Œuvres économiques complètes*, S. 3, L. 22, § 114, n. 100.

4 Arena, 'Sraffa without Walras'

1. My sincerest thanks go to P. Bridel, R. Baranzini, A. Cot, P. Dockès, F. Donzelli, R. Dos Santos Ferreira, H. Kurz, A. Legris, N. Naldi, N. Salvadori and all the participants of the fifth International Walras Conference – where a first version of this contribution was presented – for their help and/or comments. I am also grateful, once more, to Jonathan Smith, the curator of the Wren Library, as well as all the team for their competent support, availability and friendly reception.

2. G. C. Harcourt, *Some Cambridge Controversies on the Theory of Capital* (Cambridge: Cambridge University Press, 1972).

3. C. Napoleoni, *L'Equilibrio Economico GeneraleI* (Turin: Bollati Boringhieri, 1965).

4. Ibid., p. 7.

5. V. Walsh and H. Gram, *Classical and Neo-classical Theories of General Equilibrium* (Oxford: Oxford University Press, 1980).

6. Ibid., p. xii.

7. Ibid., p. 3.

8. Ibid., ch. 10.

9. See ibid., ch. 10.

10. F. Hahn, 'Revival of Political Economy: The Wrong Issues and the Wrong Argument', *Economic Record*, 51:3 (1975), pp. 360–4, on p. 362.

11. F. Hahn, 'The Neo-Ricardians', *Cambridge Journal of Economics*, 6:4 (1982), pp. 353–74.

12. Ibid., p. 363.

13. Ibid., p. 365.

14. Ibid., p. 354.

15. P. Sraffa, 'The Laws of Returns under Competitive Conditions', *Economic Journal*, 36:144 (1926), pp. 535–50, on p. 541.

16. Again, Harcourt, *Some Cambridge Controversies on the Theory of Capital*, but also P. Garegnani, 'Heterogeneous Capital, the Production Function and the Theory of Distribution', *Review of Economic Studies*, 37:3 (1970), pp. 407–36.

17. P. Garegnani, *Il capitale nelle teorie della distribuzione* (Milan: Giuffrè, 1959–1960) and Garegnani, 'Heterogeneous Capital, the Production Function and the Theory of Distribution'.

18. B. Schefold, *Mr Sraffa on Joint Production and Other Essays* (London: Unwin Hyman, 1989), p. 267.

19. Ibid., p. 259.

20. Ibid., p. 273.

21. Ibid., p. 296.

22. *Sraffa's Library*, Walras/2213.

23. Ibid., Walras/2217.

24. Ibid., Walras/2216.

25. Ibid., Walras/2215.

26. Ibid., Walras/2214.

27. Ibid., Walras/2186.

28. See J. P. Potier, *Piero Sraffa, Biografia* (Rome: Editori Riuniti, 1965), p. 122, n. 47 concerning the content and meaning of this letter.

29. W. Jaffé, 'Letter to Piero Sraffa dated September, 20th 1956', *Sraffa Archives*, Cambridge: Wren Library, Trinity College [hereafter *SA*], H3/33 (1956), pp. 19–20.

30. Ibid., p. 21.

31. Ibid., pp. 22–3)

32. Sraffa, 'The Laws of Returns under Competitive Conditions', p. 541.

33. Schefold, *Mr Sraffa on Joint Production and Other Essays*, p. 275, n. 11 – italics added.

34. See Sraffa, *SA*, D 2/4, p. 44 and annex 6.

35. Ibid., p. 27.

36. Ibid.

37. Ibid., p. 33.

38. Sraffa, *SA*, D 3/12, 13:2.

39. Sraffa, *SA*, D 2/4, p. 27.

40. Ibid., p. 28.

41. Ibid., p. 44.

42. Ibid., p. 28.

43. Ibid., annex 3.

44. Ibid., p. 28.

45. Sraffa, *SA*, D 3/12 n.

46. Ibid., 3:5.

47. Ibid., 3:15.

48. Ibid., 10:48.

49. Sraffa, *SA*, D 1/11, p. 27.

50. Garegani, *Il capitale nelle teorie della distribuzione* and Garegnani, 'Heterogeneous Capital, the Production Function and the Theory of Distribution'.

5 Backhouse and Medema, 'Walras in the Age of Marshall: An Analysis of English-Language Journals, 1890–1939'

1. P. Bridel, *Le Chêne et l'architecte: Un siècle de comptes rendus bibliographiques des 'Éléments d'économie politique pure' de Leon Walras* (Geneva: Droz, 1996). D. A. Walker, *The Legacy of Leon Walras* (Cheltenham: Edward Elgar, 2001). See in particular pp. xii–xxix for Walker's discussion of Walras's influence between 1890 and 1930.

2. A notable feature of this correspondence was that the British and American economists invariably wrote in English, and Walras replied in French, implying that each had at least a reading knowledge of the other language.

3. American Economic Association, *Publications of the American Economic Association*, 10:3 (1895), pp. 7–35.

4. We take for granted that Walras was well known in continental Europe.

5. These figures have not been normalized with respect to some measure of the total number of articles published, which was presumably increasing. Instead, we have sought to confine our comments to claims that do not depend on this. As well as giving a rough idea of the main trends, the data show where Walras was being discussed. One reason for thinking that percentages would not give significantly more information is that an equally important factor is changes in relationship between journal articles and other types of publication. In this period, journals did not have the high status that they now have – indeed, in the inter-war period, there were times when the *American Economic Review* struggled to fill its pages. To estimate percentages would be to imply that journal publication had an unchanging significance that it did not have. Even more important, JSTOR's incomplete coverage, especially of non-English-language journals, makes it difficult to attach much significance to proportions.

6. Bridel, *Le Chêne et l'architecte*.

7. See R. E. Backhouse, 'The Transformation of U.S. Economics, 1920–1960, Viewed through a Survey of Journal Articles', *History of Political Economy*, 30 (Supplement, 1998), pp. 85–107, and M. S. Morgan, *The World in the Model: How Economists Work and Think* (Cambridge: Cambridge University Press, 2012).

8. For example W. Caldwell, 'Review of *Grundbegriffe und Grundlagen der Volkswirthschaft: Zur Einführung in das Studium der Staatswissenschaften* by Lehr, J.', *Journal of Political Economy*, 2:2 (1894), pp. 303–4, on p. 303.

9. 'Personal Notes', *Annals of the American Academy of Political and Social Science*, 6 (1895), pp. 94–109.

10. 'Personal Notes', *Annals of the American Academy of Political and Social Science*, 4 (1894), pp. 155–68, on p. 165.

11. Ibid., p. 166.

12. A. Oncken, 'Letter from Switzerland', *Economic Journal*, 6:22 (1896), pp. 308–14, on p. 311.

13. F. Y. Edgeworth, 'Review of *Researches into the Mathematical Principles of the Theory of Wealth* by Augustin Cournot; Nathaniel T. Bacon; Irving Fisher; *A Brief Introduction to the Infinitesimal Calculus, Designed Especially to Aid in Reading Mathematical Economics and Statistics* by Irving Fisher', *Economic Journal*, 8:29 (1898), pp. 111–14, on p. 114.

14. I. Fisher, 'Cournot and Mathematical Economics', *Quarterly Journal of Economics*, 12:2 (1898), pp. 119–38, on p. 120.

15. H. L. Moore, 'Paradoxes of Competition', *Quarterly Journal of Economics*, 20:2 (1906), pp. 211–30, on p. 218.

16. E. R. A. Seligman, 'On Some Neglected British Economists', *Economic Journal*, 13:51 (1903), pp. 335–63, on p. 357.

17. H. L. Moore, 'The Personality of Antoine Augustin Cournot', *Quarterly Journal of Economics*, 19:3 (1905), pp. 370–99, on p. 373, emphasis added.

18. Fisher, 'Cournot and Mathematical Economics', p. 123.

19. J. Schumpeter, 'On the Concept of Social Value', *Quarterly Journal of Economics*, 23:2 (1909), pp. 213–32, on p. 213.

20. Fisher, 'Cournot and Mathematical Economics', p. 125.

21. H. L. Moore, 'Review of *Cours d'Économie Politique* by Vilfredo Pareto', *Annals of the American Academy of Political and Social Science*, 9 (1897), pp. 128–31, on p. 130.

22. G. M. Fiamingo, 'The Measure of the Value of Money according to European Economists', *Journal of Political Economy*, 7:1 (1898), pp. 42–77.

23. A. W. Flux, 'Review of *Über Wert, Kapital Und Rente nach der neueren nationalökonomischen Theorien* by Knut Wicksell; *Essay on the Co-ordination of the Laws of Distribution* by P. H. Wicksteed', *Economic Journal*, 4:14 (1894), pp. 305–13, on p. 305.

24. A. W. Flux, '*Review of Cours d'Economie Politique*, Tome Premier. by Vilfredo Pareto', *Economic Journal*, 6:22 (1896), pp. 249–53, on p. 249.

25. F. D. Merritt, 'Review of *Cours d'Economie Politique* by Vilfredo Pareto', *Journal of Political Economy*, 6:4 (1898), pp. 549–52, on p. 549.

26. F. Y. Edgeworth, 'Theory of International Values III', *Economic Journal*, 4:16 (1894), pp. 606–38, on p. 634; F. Y. Edgeworth, 'Theory of International Values II', *Economic Journal*, 4:15 (1894), pp. 424–43, on p. 442.

27. F. Y. Edgeworth, 'The Theory of Distribution', *Quarterly Journal of Economics*, 18:2 (1904), pp. 159–219, on p. 162.

28. Ibid., pp. 174, 175–6, 177.

29. E. R. A. Seligman, 'On the Shifting and Incidence of Taxation', *Publications of the American Economic Association*, 7:2/3 (1892), pp. 7–191, on p. 84.

30. A. C. Pigou, 'Monopoly and Consumers' Surplus', *Economic Journal*, 14:55 (1904), pp. 388–94, on p. 388.

31. A. S. Johnson, 'The Relation of Monopoly Price to the Rate of Interest', *Quarterly Journal of Economics*, 22:3 (1908), pp. 384–98, on p. 385.

32. Ibid., p. 388.

33. J. R. Commons, 'Bullion Notes and an Elastic Currency', *Annals of the American Academy of Political and Social Science*, 4 (1893), pp. 99–101, on pp. 99–100; 'Variorum Notes on Indian Currency', *Economic Journal*, 3:11(1893), pp. 517–22, on pp. 521–2.

34. C. P. Sanger, 'Review of *Geldzins und Güterpreise* by Knut Wicksell', *Economic Journal*, 8:31 (1898), pp. 384–6, on p. 386.

35. C. P. Sanger, 'Review of *Clue to the Economic Labyrinth* by Michael Fürscheim', *Economic Journal*, 13:51 (1903), pp. 403–5, on p. 405.

36. Commons, 'Bullion Notes and an Elastic Currency', pp. 99–100.

37. Significant attention was also paid to technical details of Walras's monetary theory (C. A. Conant, 'The Law of the Value of Money', *Annals of the American Academy of Political and Social Science*, 16 (1900), pp. 13–35; C. A. Conant, 'What Determines the Value of Money', *Quarterly Journal of Economics*, 18:4 (1904), pp. 551–69; I. Fisher, 'The Mechanics of Bimetallism', *Economic Journal*, 4:15 (1894), pp. 527–37; I. Fisher, 'Senses of "Capital"', *Economic Journal*, 7:26 (1897), pp. 199–213).

38. I. Fisher, 'What is Capital?', *Economic Journal*, 6:24 (1896), pp. 509–34, on p. 512.

39. Ibid., p. 528.

40. F. A. Fetter, 'Recent Discussion of the Capital Concept', *Quarterly Journal of Economics*, 15:1 (1900), pp. 1–45, on p. 3.

41. Fisher, 'What is Capital?', p. 528.
42. Ibid., p. 529. This point is also made in Fisher, 'Senses of "Capital"'.
43. Fisher, 'What is Capital?', p. 525.
44. Ibid., p. 535.
45. Ibid., p. 534. Fisher also noted that a businessman would be astonished to find that Walras did not include the businessman's fuel in his capital stock (likewise for others who did not include raw materials, land, or perishable goods in capital). I. Fisher, 'Precedents for Defining Capital', *Quarterly Journal of Economics*, 18:3 (1904), pp. 386–408, on p. 399.
46. These banks, as Gide later noted, were 'a kind of bank intended to propagate and organise cooperative associations of production' (C. Gide and G. J. G., 'Obituary', *Economic Journal*, 6:22 (1896), pp. 318–23, on p. 320).
47. E. Cummings, 'Co-operative Production in France and England', *Quarterly Journal of Economics*, 4:4 (1890), pp. 357–86, on p. 365.
48. A. Oncken, 'Letter from Switzerland', *Economic Journal*, 7:26 (1897), pp. 288–93, on p. 292.
49. C. Gide, 'Productive Co-operation in France', *Quarterly Journal of Economics*, 14:1 (1899), pp. 30–66, on p. 34.
50. C. Gide, 'Has Co-operation Introduced a New Principle into Economics?', *Economic Journal*, 8:32 (1898), pp. 490–511, on p. 498. Different conclusions were reached on Walras's views on socialism. Gide ('Review of *The Physiocrats. Six Lectures on the French Économistes of the 18th Century* by Henry Higgs', *Economic Journal*, 7:26 (1897), pp. 245–8, on p. 247) suggested that the physiocrats 'paved the way for the Socialists, or at least for those who, like Henry George and Walras, look to the appropriation of rent by the State as the solution of the social problem'. In contrast, Sidney Ball ('Review of 1. *Un Socialisme en Harmonie Avec La Doctrine Économique Libérale* (Bibliothèque Sociologique Internationale) by Rignano, E., 2. *Christian Socialism in England* by Woodworth, A. V.', *Economic Journal*, 14:53 (1904), pp. 88–95, on p. 91) noted that Walras had demonstrated the 'impracticability' of collectivism on the grounds of its doing away with both competition and freedom of contract.
51. V. Pareto, 'The New Theories of Economics', *Journal of Political Economy*, 5:4 (1897), pp. 485–502, on p. 491.
52. Oncken, 'Letter from Switzerland' (1897), p. 292.
53. For example A. Oncken, 'Letter from Switzerland 1897–98', *Economic Journal*, 8:30 (1898), pp. 269–73, on p. 271; I. Fisher, 'Review of Pure Economics by Maffeo Pantaleoni', *Annals of the American Academy of Political and Social Science*, 12 (1898), pp. 122–5, on p. 123.
54. F. Wieser, 'The Austrian School and the Theory of Value', *Economic Journal*, 1:1 (1891), pp. 108–21, on p. 108.
55. E. von Böhm-Bawerk, 'The Austrian Economists', trans. H. Leonard, *Annals of the American Academy of Political and Social Science*, 1 (1891), pp. 361–484, on p. 367.
56. F. Y. Edgeworth, 'Review of *Natural Value* by Friedrich von Wieser; William Smart; Christian A. Malloch', *Economic Journal*, 4:14 (1894), pp. 279–85, on pp. 282–3.
57. I. Fisher, 'Davenport's Value and Distribution', *Journal of Political Economy*, 16:10 (1908), pp. 661–79, on p. 663.
58. M. H. R., H. Higgs, A. T. H. and I. F., 'Personal and Miscellaneous Notes', *Economic Bulletin*, 3:2 (1910), pp. 131–44, on p. 143.
59. Ibid., p. 144.
60. V. Pareto, 'Obituary: Walras', *Economic Journal*, 20:77 (1910), pp. 137–40, on p. 139.

61. D. F. Houston et al., 'Money and Prices: Discussion', *American Economic Review*, 1:2 (1911), pp. 46–70, on p. 68.

62. F. Y. Edgeworth, 'Applications of Probabilities to Economics II', *Economic Journal*, 20:79 (1910), pp. 441–65, on p. 461.

63. A. A. Young, 'Jevons' "Theory of Political Economy"', *American Economic Review*, 2:3 (1912), pp. 576–89, on p. 579.

64. V. Pareto, 'Review of *Introduction Mathematique a l'Etude de l'Economie Politique* by L. Leseine; L. Suret', *Economic Journal*, 21:82 (1911), pp. 261–3, on p. 262. See also H. E. Mills, 'Review of *The Economics of Everyday Life* by T. H. Penson; *Elements of Economics* by Henry Reed', *American Economic Review*, 3:4 (1913), pp. 894–6, on p. 896; P. H. Wicksteed, 'Review of *Political Economy* by S. J. Chapman', *Economic Journal*, 23:89 (1913), pp. 72–5, on p. 72 and A. C. Pigou, 'Monopoly and Consumers' Surplus', *Economic Journal*, 14:55 (1904), pp. 388–94 on this point.

65. W. C. Mitchell, 'The Role of Money in Economic Theory', *American Economic Review*, 6:1 (1916), pp. 140–61, on p. 144.

66. A. A. Young, 'Marshall on Consumers' Surplus in International Trade', *Quarterly Journal of Economics*, 39:1 (1924), pp. 144–50, on p. 148.

67. F. Y. Edgeworth, 'Professor Cassel's Treatise', *Economic Journal*, 30:120 (1920), pp. 530–6, on p. 532.

68. A. W. Zotoff, 'Notes on the Mathematical Theory of Production', *Economic Journal*, 33:129 (1923), pp. 115–21.

69. I. Fisher, 'Comment on President Plehn's Address', *American Economic Review*, 14:1 (1924), pp. 64–7 and Fetter, 'Recent Discussion of the Capital Concept'.

70. M. Tappan, 'Review of *The Mathematical Groundwork of Economics* by A. L. Bowley', *Economica*, 15 (1925), pp. 334–38.

71. E. B. Wilson, 'Review of *Principles of Methods of Statistics* by Robert E. Chaddock; *An Introduction to the Methods of Economic Statistics* by William L. Crum; Alson C. Patton; *Statistical Analysis* by Edmund E. Day; *A First Course in Statistical Method* by G. Irving Gavett; *An Introduction to Statistical Methods* by Horace Secrist; *Elementary Statistical Methods* by William G. Sutcliffe', *American Economic Review*, 17:1 (1927), pp. 145–8, on p. 146.

72. J. Schumpeter, 'The Instability of Capitalism', *Economic Journal*, 38:151 (1928), pp. 361–86.

73. H. L. Moore, 'Partial Elasticity of Demand', *Quarterly Journal of Economics*, 40:3 (1926), pp. 393–401.

74. H. L. Moore, 'Pantaleoni's Problem in the Oscillation of Prices', *Quarterly Journal of Economics*, 40:4 (1926), pp. 586–96, on p. 586.

75. H. L. Moore, 'A Theory of Economic Oscillations', *Quarterly Journal of Economics*, 41:1 (1926), pp. 1–29, on p. 3.

76. Ibid.

77. C. F. Roos, 'A Dynamical Theory of Economics', *Journal of Political Economy*, 35:5 (1927), pp. 632–56.

78. H. Schultz, 'Mathematical Economics and the Quantitative Method', *Journal of Political Economy*, 35:5 (1927), pp. 702–6, on pp. 702–3.

79. H. Schultz, 'Review of *Vilfredo Pareto: Sa Vie et Son Oeuvre* by G. H. Bousquet', *Journal of Political Economy*, 36:6 (1928), pp. 740–2, on p. 741, quoting the book under review.

80. H. Schultz, 'Marginal Productivity and the General Pricing Process', *Journal of Political Economy*, 37:5 (1929), pp. 505–51.

81. Tappan, 'Review of *The Mathematical Groundwork of Economics* by A. L. Bowley'.

82. F. A. von Hayek, 'Carl Menger', *Economica*, 1:4 (1934), pp. 393–420, on p. 403.

83. R. G. D. Allen, 'The Foundations of a Mathematical Theory of Exchange', *Economica*, 36 (1932), pp. 197–226.

84. J. R. Hicks, 'Marginal Productivity and the Principle of Variation', *Economica*, 35 (1932), pp. 79–88.

85. Ibid., p. 84.

86. H. Schultz, 'Marginal Productivity and the Lausanne School', *Economica*, 37 (1932), pp. 285–96.

87. Hicks, 'Marginal Productivity and the Principle of Variation', p. 299.

88. Ibid., p. 300.

89. J. Schumpeter, 'The Common Sense of Econometrics', *Econometrica*, 1:1 (1933), pp. 5–12, on p. 9.

90. Ibid., p. 10.

91. R. Roy, 'Cournot et l'école mathématique', *Econometrica*, 1:1 (1933), pp. 13–22.

92. M. Ezekiel, Some Considerations on the Analysis of the Prices of Competing or Substitute Commodities', *Econometrica*, 1:2 (1933), pp. 172–80, on p. 173.

93. G. H. Bousquet, 'Les trois notions de l'équilibre économique', *Econometrica*, 1:2 (1933), pp. 190–6, on p. 190.

94. J. Tinbergen, 'Annual Survey of Significant Developments in General Economic Theory', *Econometrica*, 2:1 (1934), pp. 13–36, on p. 13.

95. P. T. Homan et al., 'Economic Theory-Institutionalism: What It is and What It Hopes to Become', *American Economic Review*, 21:1 (1931), pp. 134–41, on p. 140.

96. G. R. Davies, 'The Significance of Economic Law', *American Economic Review*, 21:3 (1931), pp. 450–62.

97. W. Jaffe, 'Imperfect Competition', *American Economic Review*, 24:1 (1934), pp. 27–30.

98. P. T. Ellsworth, 'Review of *Interregional and International Trade* by Bertil Ohlin', *American Economic Review*, 23:4 (1933), pp. 680–3.

99. B. Ohlin, *Interregional and International Trade* (Cambridge, MA: Harvard University Press, 1933).

100. P. G. Wright, 'Moore's "Synthetic Economics"', *Journal of Political Economy*, 38:3 (1930), pp. 328–44.

101. C. F. Roos, 'A Mathematical Theory of Price and Production Fluctuations and Economic Crises', *Journal of Political Economy*, 38:5 (1930), pp. 501–22.

102. H. Schultz, 'Review of *Mathematische Volkswirtschaftslehre* by O. Weinberger', *Journal of Political Economy*, 40:3 (1932), pp. 422–4.

103. H. Schultz, 'Frisch on the Measurement of Utility', *Journal of Political Economy*, 41:1 (1933), pp. 95–116.

104. J. A. Schumpeter and A. J. Nichol, 'Robinson's Economics of Imperfect Competition', *Journal of Political Economy*, 42:2 (1934), pp. 249–59.

105. A. W. Marget, 'Léon Walras and the "Cash-Balance Approach" to the Problem of the Value of Money', *Journal of Political Economy*, 39:5 (1931), pp. 569–600 and C. Whitney, 'The Equation of Exchange and the Price Stabilization Problem', *American Economic Review*, 22:2 (1932), pp. 231–40.

106. L. Rogin, 'Werner Sombart and the "Natural Science Method" in Economics', *Journal of Political Economy*, 41:2 (1933), pp. 222–36.

107. There was an article on statistical demand curves (E. W. Gilboy, 'Demand Curves in Theory and in Practice', *Quarterly Journal of Economics*, 44:4 (1930), pp. 601–20), a substantial and supportive review of Moore (M. Ezekiel, 'Moore's Synthetic Economics', *Quarterly*

Journal of Economics, 44:4 (1930), pp. 663–79), and in reviewing Mitchell on the business cycle, Schumpeter (J. Schumpeter, 'Mitchell's Business Cycles', *Quarterly Journal of Economics*, 45:1 (1930), pp. 150–72) noted his dismissal of both Marshall and Walras.

108. R. S. Howey, 'Review of *Etudes d'Economie Politique Appliquée (Théorie de la Production de la Richesse Sociale); Etudes d'Economie Sociale (Théorie de la Répartition de la Richesse Sociale)* by Léon Walras', *American Economic Review*, 27:3 (1937), pp. 536–8.

109. 'Address of the Econometric Society to the University of Lausanne', *Econometrica*, 2:4 (1934), p. 337.

110. 'Facsimile of the Address of the Econometric Society to the University of Lausanne', *Econometrica*, 3:1 (1935), p. 128; '[Photograph]: Specimen of Walras' Correspondence', *Econometrica*, 2:4 (1934); L. Walras, A. Cournot, S. Jevons and E. Antonelli, 'Léon Walras et sa correspondance avec Augustin Cournot et Stanley Jevons', *Econometrica*, 3:1 (1935), pp. 119–27.

111. W. Jaffé, 'Unpublished Papers and Letters of Léon Walras', *Journal of Political Economy*, 43:2 (1935), pp. 187–207; A. W. Marget, 'The Monetary Aspects of the Walrasian System', *Journal of Political Economy*, 43:2 (1935), pp. 145–86. The session is summarized in C. F. Roos, 'Meetings of the Econometric Society in Chicago and Pittsburgh, December, 1934', *Econometrica*, 3:3 (1935), pp. 345–52, on p. 348–50.

112. Roos, 'Meetings of the Econometric Society in Chicago and Pittsburgh, December, 1934', p. 348.

113. Marget, 'The Monetary Aspects of the Walrasian System', pp. 145–6.

114. This assessment is consistent with the lack of references to this aspect of Walras's work that we find in the US/UK literature of the 1890s and early 1900s, discussed above.

115. J. M. Keynes, 'Alfred Marshall, 1842–1924', *Economic Journal*, 34:135 (1924), pp. 311–72.

116. Roos, 'Meetings of the Econometric Society in Chicago and Pittsburgh, December, 1934', pp. 349–50.

117. J. R. Hicks, 'Léon Walras', *Econometrica*, 2:4 (1934), pp. 338–48, on p. 338.

118. Ibid., p. 341.

119. Ibid., p. 347.

120. Ibid.

121. G. Stigler, 'Production and Distribution in the Short Run', *Journal of Political Economy*, 47:3 (1939), pp. 305–27; G. Stigler, 'The Economics of Carl Menger', *Journal of Political Economy*, 45:2 (1937), pp. 229–50.

122. See P. H. Douglas, 'Henry Schultz as Colleague', *Econometrica*, 7:2 (1939), pp. 104–6; H. Hotelling, 'The Work of Henry Schultz', *Econometrica*, 7.2 (1939), pp. 97–103; T. O. Yntema, 'Henry Schultz: His Contributions to Economics and Statistics', *Journal of Political Economy*, 47:2 (1939), pp. 153–62, T. E. Gregory on Cannan ('Edwin Cannan: A Personal Impression', *Economica*, 2:8 (1935), pp. 365–79) and L. Amoroso on Pareto ('Vilfredo Pareto', *Econometrica*, 6:1 (1938), pp. 1–21).

123. See I. Fisher, 'Cournot Forty Years ago', *Econometrica*, 6:3 (1938), pp. 198–202; A. J. Nichol, 'Tragedies in the Life of Cournot', *Econometrica*, 6:3 (1938), pp. 193–7; R. Roy, 'L'œuvre économique d'Augustin Cournot', *Econometrica*, 7:2 (1939), pp. 134–44.

124. W. Jaffé, 'Review of *Abrégé des Eléments d'Economie Politique Pure* by Léon Walras; Gaston Leduc', *Economica*, 5:20 (1938), pp. 474–6; A. W. Marget, 'Note on a New Edition of the Works of Léon Walras', *Econometrica*, 5:1 (1937), pp. 103–4.

125. D. Durand, 'Some Thoughts on Marginal Productivity, with Special Reference to Professor Douglas' Analysis', *Journal of Political Economy*, 45:6 (1937), pp. 740–58, on p.

742, W. Leontief, 'The Significance of Marxian Economics for Present-Day Economic Theory', *American Economic Review*, 28:1 (1938), pp. 1–9, on p. 2.

126. K. E. Boulding, 'Time and Investment: A Reply', *Economica*, 3:12 (1936), pp. 440–2, on p. 440.

127. E. B. Wilson, 'Pareto versus Marshall', *Quarterly Journal of Economics*, 53:4 (1939), pp. 645–50, on p. 650.

128. W. Leontief, 'The Fundamental Assumption of Mr. Keynes' Monetary Theory of Unemployment', *Quarterly Journal of Economics*, 51:1 (1936), pp. 192–7, on p. 196.

129. O. Lange, 'The Rate of Interest and the Optimum Propensity to Consume', *Economica*, 5:17 (1938), pp. 12–32.

130. F. V. Waugh, E. L. Burtis and A. F. Wolf, 'The Controlled Distribution of a Crop among Independent Markets', *Quarterly Journal of Economics*, 51:1 (1936), pp. 1–41, on p. 36.

131. J. Marschak, 'Money and the Theory of Assets', *Econometrica*, 6:4 (1938), pp. 311–25, on p. 312.

132. J. Åkerman, 'Annual Survey of Economic Theory: The Setting of the Central Problem', *Econometrica*, 4:2 (1936), pp. 97–122, on p. 100.

133. H. Schultz, 'Interrelations of Demand, Price, and Income', *Journal of Political Economy*, 43:4 (1935), pp. 433–81.

134. D. H. Leavens, 'Report of the Atlantic City and Indianapolis Meetings, December 27–30, 1937', *Econometrica*, 6:2 (1938), pp. 180–92; W. Leontief, 'Interrelation of Prices, Output, Savings, and Investment', *Review of Economics and Statistics*, 19:3 (1937), pp. 109–32.

135. Leavens, 'Report of the Atlantic City and Indianapolis Meetings, December 27–30, 1937', p. 188.

136. G. Tintner, 'Review of *Dynamic Economics: Theoretical and Statistical Studies of Demand, Production and Prices* by Charles Frederick Roos', *Journal of Political Economy*, 44:3 (1936), pp. 404–9, on p. 406.

137. J. Tinbergen, 'Annual Survey: Suggestions on Quantitative Business Cycle Theory', *Econometrica*, 3:3 (1935), pp. 241–308, on p. 308.

138. P. Lorenz, 'Annual Survey of Statistical Technique: Trends and Seasonal Variations', *Econometrica*, 3:4 (1935), pp. 456–71, on p. 456.

139. P. A. Samuelson, 'The Empirical Implications of Utility Analysis', *Econometrica*, 6:4 (1938), pp. 344–56.

6 Walker and van Daal, 'The English Translation of Léon Walras's *Études d'économie sociale*'

1. L. Walras, *Études d'économie sociale (Théorie de la répartition de la richesse sociale)*, 2nd edn (1896; Lausanne: F. Rouge, Paris: R. Pichon and R. Durand-Auzias, 1936).

2. Likewise, he gave up his plan to write a comprehensive treatise on applied economics; see L. Walras, *Études d'économie politique appliquée (Théorie de la production de la richesse sociale)*, 2nd edn (1898; Lausanne: F. Rouge, Paris: R. Pichon and R. Durand-Auzias, 1936).

3. L. Walras, *Élements of Pure Economics or the Theory of Social Wealth*, trans. and annot. W. Jaffé (Homewood, IL: Irwin, London: Allen and Unwin, 1954).

4. A. Walras and L. Walras, *Œuvres économiques complètes*, *Œuvres économiques complètes*, ed. P. Dockès, P.-H. Goutte, C. Hébert, C. Mouchot, J.-P. Potier and J.-M. Servet under

the auspices of the Centre Auguste et Léon Walras, 14 vols (Paris: Économica, 1987–2005), vol. 9, *Economica* (1990).

7 Mornati, 'Pareto: A Possible Forerunner of the Studies on Social Complexity'

1. V. Pareto, 'Delle logiche delle nuove scuole economiche', in V. Pareto, *Ecrits sociologiques mineurs*, ed. G. Busino (1877; Geneva: Droz, 1980), pp. 75–100, on p. 79.
2. V. Pareto, 'Letters from Italy. I', in V. Pareto, *Ecrits épars*, ed. G. Busino (1888; Geneva: Droz, 1974), pp. 15–24, on p. 15.
3. V. Pareto, *Premier Cours d'économie politique appliquée*, ed. G. Busino (Geneva: Droz, 1982), pp. 8–10.
4. Ibid., p. 8.
5. Ibid., pp. 11–12.
6. Ibid., p. 111.
7. Ibid., p. 112.
8. Ibid., p. 114.
9. Ibid., pp. 117–18.
10. Ibid., p. 118.
11. Ibid., p. 117; V. Pareto, 'De l'économique', in V. Pareto, *Marxisme et Economie pure*, ed. G. Busino (1894; Geneva: Droz, 1987), pp. 115–19.
12. V. Pareto, G. H. Bousquet and G. Busino (eds), *Cours d'économie politique* (1896–7; Geneva: Droz, 1982), §§ 592, 598, 601: having reminded us that the result of the phenomenal interdependence is represented by the equilibrium of a system (either mechanic or economic), he insisted that the variables' equilibrium values are simply co-determined by the equation system they belong to, thus making a meaningless exercise of the pretence that one of these values causes the remaining ones without any reaction.
13. Ibid., §580.
14. Ibid., §581.
15. Ibid., §592. Pareto initially defined social science as the study of human characters, different from those studied by political economy, and therefore made up by the sciences of law, religions, ethics, intellectual development, aesthetics and the organization of societies.
16. Ibid., §582.
17. Ibid., §602.
18. Ibid., §584.
19. Ibid., §619.
20. V. Pareto, 'Il compito della sociologia fra le scienze sociali', in V. Pareto, *Ecrits sociologiques mineurs*, ed. G. Busino (1897; Geneva: Droz, 1980), pp. 130–9, on p. 131.
21. Ibid., p. 133.
22. Ibid., p. 137.
23. Ibid., p. 134.
24. V. Pareto, 'Comment se pose le problème de l'économie politique pure', in V. Pareto, *Marxisme et Economie pure*, ed. G. Busino (1898; Geneva: Droz, 1987), pp. 102–9.
25. Ibid., pp. 104–6.
26. V. Pareto, *Lettere a Maffeo Pantaleoni (1897–1906)*, ed. G. De Rosa (Geneva: Droz, 1984), p. 73.

27. V. Pareto, *Traité de Sociologie Générale (1917–1919)*, ed. P. Boven (Geneva: Droz, 1968), §2079.
28. Ibid., §§2079, 2083.
29. Ibid., §2082.
30. Ibid., §2172.
31. Ibid., §2062.
32. Ibid., §1732.
33. Ibid., §2068.
34. Ibid., §2205.
35. Ibid., §2206.
36. Ibid., §2206.
37. Ibid., §2207.
38. Ibid., §2207.
39. Ibid., §2219.
40. Ibid., §2208.
41. Ibid., §2208.
42. Ibid., §2208.
43. Ibid., §2210.
44. Ibid., §2210.
45. Ibid., §2209.
46. Ibid., §2211.
47. Ibid., §2212.
48. Ibid., §2215.
49. Ibid., §2217.
50. Ibid., §2216.
51. Ibid., §2227.
52. Ibid., §2269.
53. Ibid., §2274.
54. Ibid., §2276.
55. Ibid., §2225.
56. Ibid., §2228.
57. Ibid., §2228.
58. Ibid., §2231.
59. Ibid., §2232.
60. Ibid., §2232.
61. V. Pareto, 'L'opera scientifica di Leone Walras', in *Ecrits d'économie politique pure*, ed. G. Busino (1910; Geneva: Droz, 1982), pp. 644–6, on p. 645.
62. V. Pareto, 'Du matérialisme historique', in V. Pareto, *Marxisme et Economie pure*, ed. G. Busino (1898; Geneva: Droz, 1987), pp. 94–9, on p. 94.
63. Ibid., pp. 95–6.
64. Ibid., p. 97.
65. C. H. Powers and R. A. Hanneman, 'Pareto's Theory of Social and Economic Cycles: A Formal Model and Simulation', *Sociological Theory*, 1 (1983), pp. 59–89, on p. 62.
66. Ibid.
67. Ibid., p. 63.
68. Ibid., pp. 82–5.
69. Ibid., p. 65.
70. Ibid., pp. 66–75.

71. Ibid., p. 75.
72. Ibid., p. 77.
73. Ibid., pp. 80–1.
74. Ibid., p. 81.
75. Ibid.

8 Allisson, 'Samsonoff on Rent Theory: Or, Yet Another Member of the Lausanne School?'

1.   B. Samsonoff, 'Esquisse d'une théorie générale de la rente, suivie d'une critique des principales opinions émises sur le même sujet' (PhD dissertation, University of Lausanne, 1912). I would like to thank Olivier Robert and Sabine Utz from the Archival Department of the University of Lausanne for their help in locating papers related to Samsonoff; the librarians of the St Petersburg Russian State Library, for helping me in locating Bilimovic's 1918 obituary of Samsonoff with very incomplete references; Fiorenzo Mornati and Thomas Müller for comments on a first version of this text; and Pascal Bridel, who was my PhD supervisor, and who, a few years ago, gave me a copy of Samsonoff's dissertation. At that time, I had no idea of who Samsonoff was. In this essay, I try to fill this gap.

2.   E. Lowenthal, 'Review of Esquisse d'une Théorie Générale de la Rente by B. Samsonoff', *American Economic Review*, 3:4 (1913), pp. 897–8; F. A. Fetter, 'Review of Esquisse d'une Théorie Général [*sic*] de la Rente by B. Samsonoff', *Political Science Quarterly*, 29:2 (1914), pp. 336–7.

3.   P. B. Struve, *Khozjâjstvo i cena* [Economy and Price] (St Petersburg and Moscow: Šreder, 1913); A. Bilimovic, 'V. V. Samsonov. Nekrolog [Obituary of B. Samsonoff]', *Izvestiâ Rossijskoj Akademii Nauk*, 4 (1918), pp. 176–9.

4.   G.-H. Bousquet, *Pareto (1848–1923): le savant et l'homme* (Lausanne: Payot, 1960), p. 121; G. Busino, 'Materiali per l'edizione dell'epistolario', in V. Pareto, *Œuvres complètes*, ed. G. Busino, 32 vols (Geneva: Droz, 1964–2005), vol. 19.1 (1975), pp. 1–53, on p. 28; F. Mornati, *Pasquale Boninsegni e la Scuola di Losanna* (Torino: UTET, 1999), pp. 265–6, 316, 350.

5.   A. I. Paškov (ed.), *Istoriâ russkoj ekonomičeskoj mysli* [History of Russian Economic Thought] (Moscow: Socekgiz, 1966), vol. 3, part 1, p. 164; quoted by V. Barnett, *E. E. Slutsky as Economist and Mathematician: Crossing the Limits of Knowledge* (Abingdon: Routledge, 2011), p. 14.

6.   J. A. Schumpeter, *History of Economic Analysis* (1954; London: Routledge, 2006), p. 906n.

7.   These biographical details are collected here for the first time. The sources on Samsonoff's Russian period consist only of Bilimovic, 'V. V. Samsonov. Nekrolog [Obituary of B. Samsonoff]', pp. 176–9. On the Lausanne period, there are several sources: the administrative archives of the University of Lausanne (*Catalogues des étudiants, Fiches d'immatriculations*, and *Inscription de cours*, two local newspapers (*Gazette de Lausanne* and *Feuille d'avis de Lausanne*), the letter of Samsonoff to Pierre Boven as published by Busino, 'Materiali per l'edizione dell'epistolario', p. 28 and some letters from Pierre Boven and from Vilfredo Pareto as published in Bousquet, *Pareto (1848–1923)*, p. 121 and by Busino (in Pareto, *Œuvres*, vol. 19.2, pp. 723, 728–32, 775–7).

8.   *Gazette de Lausanne*, 24 January 1907, p. 3.

9.   *Feuille d'avis de Lausanne*, 20 August 1930, p. 13.

10. Ibid.

11. Their daughter, Nadine Aruffo, later known as Nadine Karpouchko-Aruffo (or Nadejda Antonovna Karpouchko-Aruffo) after she married Pierre Karpouchko, was the organizer of the social and intellectual life of the whole Russian community in Lausanne. She held a circle in her flat, rue de Cour, for several decades, until her death in 2010. The legacy of this circle is today continued by the *Association Léman Russe*.

12. *Gazette de Lausanne*, 29 May 1913, p. 5.

13. *Feuille d'avis de Lausanne*, 13 June 1922, p. 14.

14. *Gazette de Lausanne*, 22 April 1970, p. 9, and *Feuille d'avis de Lausanne*, 22 April 1970, p. 40.

15. Letter of Samsonoff to Boven, 10 July 1911, in Busino, 'Materiali per l'edizione dell'epistolario', p. 28.

16. Letter of Pareto to Boven, 14 July 1912, in Pareto, *Œuvres*, vol. 19.2, p. 775.

17. Sensini also published *La teoria della rendita* in 1912, and Pareto managed that Boven and Samsonoff received the proofs in 1911 (Letter of Vilfredo Pareto to Guido Sensini, 7 June 1911, in Pareto, *Œuvres*, vol. 19.2, p. 728).

18. *Feuille d'avis de Lausanne*, 27 June 1912, p. 15.

19. *Gazette de Lausanne,* 14 April 1910, p. 3.

20. *Gazette de Lausanne*, 15 July 1912, p. 3.

21. Unfortunately, the journal ceased to exist during World War I. The manuscript was therefore not published, and has not yet been located.

22. Bilimovic, 'V. V. Samsonov. Nekrolog [Obituary of B. Samsonoff]', p. 177–8.

23. Ibid., p. 176.

24. On these Russian economists, see F. Allisson, 'V*alue and Prices in Russian Economic Thought (1890–1920)'* (PhD dissertation, University of Lausanne, 2012), chs 3, 6.

25. Samsonoff, '*Esquisse d'une théorie générale de la rente*', p. 3.

26. Gossen, Cournot and Dupuit for the Ancients. Jevons, Walras, Pantaleoni, Pareto, Marshall, Böhm-Bawerk, Wieser and Schumpeter for the Moderns.

27. Samsonoff, 'Esquisse d'une théorie générale de la rente', p. 2.

28. Ibid., p. 12.

29. Ibid., p. 9.

30. Samsonoff detected in the literature a third one, the *historical thesis*, according to which the most fertile lands would first be cultivated, explaining the rent through fertility. This is reducible, according to Samsonoff, to the static theory (ibid., pp. 88–95).

31. Ibid., p. 111.

32. Ibid., p. 95.

33. Ibid., p. 180.

34. There are also two pages on Molinari, who had an influence on Pareto (ibid., pp. 219–21).

35. Ibid., p. 21.

36. Ibid., p. 37.

37. Ibid., p. 43.

38. Ibid., p. 68, quoting P. Boven, 'Les applications mathématiques à l'économie politique' (PhD dissertation, University of Lausanne, 1912), p. 153.

9 Steiner, 'Administration and Œconomic Government in Quesnay's Political Economy'

1. F. Quesnay, *Œuvres économiques complètes et autres textes* (1767; Paris: INED, 2005), p. 232.

2. M.-F. Piguet, *Histoire du mot et genèse du concept des Physiocrates aux historiens de la Restauration* (Lyon: Presses universitaires de Lyon, 1996).

3. P. Steiner, *La 'Science nouvelle' de l'économie politique* (Paris: Presses universitaires de France, 1998).

4. P. Napoli, *Naissance de la police moderne. Pouvoir, normes, société* (Paris: La Découverte, 2003).

5. P. Minard, *La fortune du colbertisme. État et industrie dans la France des Lumières* (Paris: Fayard, 1998).

6. L. Charles and P. Steiner, 'Entre Montesquieu et Rousseau: la Physiocratie aux origines de la Révolution française', *Études Jean-Jacques Rousseau*, 11 (1999), pp. 83–159.

7. See Appendix to this chapter, p. 134.

8. See ibid.

9. Quesnay, *Œuvres économiques complètes et autres textes*, p. 154.

10. Ibid., pp. 141, 148ff.

11. Ibid., pp. 211, 223, 231, 272, 301ff.

12. Ibid., p. 296.

13. Ibid., pp. 147, 153, 154, 201, 202, 272, 273ff.

14. Ibid., pp. 274–5.

15. P. Steiner, 'Quesnay et le commerce', *Revue d'économie politique*, 107:5 (1997), pp. 695–713; P. Steiner, 'Wealth and Power: Quesnay's Political Economy of the "Agricultural Kingdom"', *Journal of the History of Economic Thought*, 24:1 (2002), pp. 91–110.

16. Quesnay, *Œuvres économiques complètes et autres textes*, p. 294.

17. Ibid., p. 308.

18. Ibid., p. 205.

19. Ibid., p. 259.

20. Ibid., pp. 297, 306.

21. Ibid., p. 316.

22. Ibid., p. 183.

23. Ibid., p. 232.

24. Ibid., pp. 266, 297.

25. Ibid., p. 244; see also pp. 220, 256.

26. Ibid., p. 232.

27. Ibid., p. 259.

28. Ibid., p. 302.

29. Ibid., p. 297.

30. Ibid., p. 226.

31. Ibid., p. 230.

32. Ibid., p. 231.

33. Ibid., p. 305.

34. These two complex issues are presented in connection with financial reform in eighteenth-century France (A. Decroix, *Question fiscale et réforme financière en France (1749–1789). Logique de la transparence et recherche de la confiance publique* (Aix en Provence, Presses universitaires d'Aix-Marseilles, 2006)) and with the drawing up of a cadastral register (A. Alimento, *Réformes fiscales et crises politiques dans la France de Louis XV. De la taille tarifée au cadastre général* (Brussels: Peter Lang, 2008)).

35. J. Swann, 'Malesherbes et la critique parlementaire du despotisme, de la bureaucratie et de la monarchie administrative', in L. Charles, F. Lefebvre and C. Théré (eds), *Le cercle de Vincent de Gournay. Savoirs économiques et pratiques administratives en France au milieu du XVIIIᵉ siècle* (Paris: INED, 2011), pp. 111–29.

36. Apart from the theoretical relevance of the concept of net product and the use of the *Encyclopédie* entry 'Impôt' in the body of the book, the entry 'Grains' is mentioned at various points in the *Théorie de l'impôt* as a means of calculating the wealth of the kingdom.

37. V.-R. Mirabeau, *Théorie de l'impôt* ([n.p.]: [n.p.], 1761), p. 248.

38. These two taxes were proportional (respectively, 5 per cent and 10 per cent) to the revenues of taxpayers.

39. Mirabeau, *Théorie de l'impôt*, p. 252.
40. G.-F. Le Trosne, *De l'administration provinciale et la réforme de l'impôt*, 2 vols (1779; Bâle and Paris: Duplain, 1788), vol. 1, p. v.
41. L. Charles and P. Steiner, 'Entre Montesquieu et Rousseau: la Physiocratie aux origines de la Révolution française', *Études Jean-Jacques Rousseau*, 11 (1999), pp. 83–159.
42. Le Trosne, *De l'administration provinciale et la réforme de l'impôt*, vol. 1, pp. 67–8.
43. P.-P. Le Mercier de la Rivière, *L'ordre naturel et essentiel des sociétés politiques* (1767; Paris: Fayard, 2001).
44. Steiner, *La 'Science nouvelle' de l'économie politique*, pp. 96–116.
45. Le Trosne, *De l'administration provinciale et la réforme de l'impôt*, vol. 1, p. 128.
46. Ibid., p. 139.
47. Ibid., p. 129.
48. See Mirabeau's *Précis de l'organisation ou Mémoire sur l'administration provinciale* and his *Réponse aux objections contre le mémoire sur les états provinciaux*, published as the fourth part of *L'Ami des hommes*. It is important to bear in mind the fact that Quesnay himself was not opposed to a synthesis between enlightened central administration and provincial administration, as this is plainly stated in the end of the entry 'Impôt': 'If the administration is placed in difficulty by the detail and the difficulty of proportional taxation, it can avoid this detail and difficulty by asking the provinces to assess taxes in their part of the country: they would do a better job than dedicated administrators, and this task is too important to be badly done' (Quesnay, *Œuvres économiques complètes et autres textes*, p. 256). And in the following sentence, Quesnay suggests reading the *Mémoire de l'administration provinciale*.
49. Le Trosne, *De l'administration provinciale et la réforme de l'impôt*, vol. 1, p. 177.
50. Ibid., pp. 146–7.
51. Ibid., pp. 538–40, 567–71.
52. Le Trosne, *De l'administration provinciale et la réforme de l'impôt*, vol. 2, pp. 161–7.
53. Ibid., vol. 1, p. 159.
54. Ibid., p. 592.
55. Ibid., pp. 205, 530.
56. Ibid., vol. 2, p. 217.
57. Charles and Steiner, 'Entre Montesquieu et Rousseau'.
58. P. Steiner, 'Foucault and Weber and the History of the Economic Agent', *European Journal of the History of Economic Thought*, 15:3 (2008), pp. 503–27.
59. M. Foucault, *Sécurité, territoire et population* (1977; Paris: Gallimard – Seuil, 2004).
60. J. Necker, *De l'administration des finances de la France* ([n.p.]: [n.p.], 1785).
61. G. Faccarello and P. Steiner, 'Interest, Sensationism and the Science of the Legislator: French "philosophie économique", 1695–1830', *European Journal of the History of Economic Thought*, 15:1 (2008), pp. 1–23.
62. Quesnay, *Œuvres économiques complètes et autres textes*, p. 572.

10 Sofia and Dal Degan, 'Constant as a Reader of Sismondi'

1. Francesca Sofia is the author of section 1, and Francesca Dal Degan is the author of section 2.
2. All translations from French to English are by the authors unless otherwise indicated. [Translation: a circle that its members have at no time sought to baptize]. S. Balayé, *Le Groupe de Coppet: conscience d'une mission commune*, in S. Balayé and J.-D. Candaux

(eds), *Le Groupe de Coppet*. Actes et documents du deuxième colloque de Coppet, 10–13 juillet 1974 (Geneva and Paris: Slatkine-Champion, 1977), pp. 29–45, on pp. 28–9.

3. [Translation: a crossing point between Southern and Northern Europe, between Latin and German, and also between the monarchic forms of government and the republican regimes (both patrician and popular)]. E. Hofmann and F. Rosset, *Le Groupe de Coppet. Une constellation d'intellectuels européens* (Lausanne, Presses polytechniques et universitaires romandes, 2005), p. 13.

4. K. Kloocke, *L'atelier d'édition aux* Principes de politique *dans le cadre des* Œuvres complètes de Benjamin Constant, *Annales Benjamin Constant*, 33 (2008), pp. 11–24, on p. 12.

5. See E. Paulet-Grandguillot, *Libéralisme et démocratie. De Sismondi à Constant, a partir du* Contrat social *(1801–1806)* (Geneva: Slatkine, 2010).

6. [Translation: I consider tyrannical the usurpation made by the community of all its members' rights. To give some examples, I consider tyrannical the sale of five thousand of Athens' citizens, deprived of their rights and enslaved under Pericles's administration, because they were born of a stranger; atrocious decree which, assuming it was true, does not exceed the power left by Rousseau to society. I consider tyrannical many of Lycurgus's institutions which hinder the privacy of every single citizen. I consider tyrannical most of the laws emanated in modern Europe according to the fatal mercantile system and all the restrictions on trade and industry which originate from it. I consider tyrannical, despite its futility, even Czar Peter's law which forces his subjects to give up their beards.] J. C. L. Sismondi, *Recherches sur les constitutions des peuples libres*, ed. M. Minerbi (Geneva: Droz, 1965), p. 112.

7. [Translation: When this authority extends to objects outside its sphere, it becomes illegitimate. The sale of 5,000 citizens under Pericles because they were born of a stranger was tyrannical. Lycurgus's institutions on the privacy of citizens were tyrannical. Our laws on mercantile system are tyrannical ... Peter the First's law ordering his subjects to cut their beards was tyrannical.] B. Constant, *Principes de politique applicables à tous les gouvernements représentatifs (texte de 1806)*, ed. K. Kloocke *Œuvres complètes, Œuvres*, vol. 9:2 (Berlin and New York: De Gruyter, 2011), pp. 133–4.

8. [Translation: I do not know why I interfere to offer advice to you, to you who, only 30 years old, have already raised a magnificent building to the good principles and gathered more knowledge than it is necessary to compose twelve of our most educated publicists.] Constant, *Correspondance générale*, 4, *1803–1805*, ed. P. Delbouille, D. Wood and A. Tooke, *Œuvres complètes, Œuvres*, vol. 5 (Tübingen: Niemeyer, 2007), p. 96.

9. Sismondi, *Recherches sur les constitutions des peuples libres*, pp. 275–6, n. 2.

10. See B. Constant, *De la possibilité de la constitution républicaine dans une grand pays (1799–1803)*, ed. M. L. Sánchez Meija and K. Kloocke *Œuvres complètes, Œuvres*, vol. 4 (Tübingen: Niemeyer, 2005), p. 418; Constant, *Principes de politique applicables à tous les gouvernements représentatifs (texte de 1806)*, p. 360; and B. Constant, *Textes de 1818: lectures à l'Athénée; Annales de la session de 1817 à 1818; Cours de politique constitutionnelle; La Minerve française; Affaires W. Regnault et C. Lainé; Élections de 1818*, ed. E. Hofmann, *Œuvres complètes, Œuvres*, vol. 11 (Berlin and New York: De Gruyter, 2011), p. 323.

11. [Translation: I know that these principles are opposed to those of our legislators during the Revolution, but they appear to me such a manifest result of the entire Italian history, that I could not hide them.] Sismondi, *Recherches sur les constitutions des peuples libres*, p. 112.

12. [Translation: At the foundation of the French Republic, the aim was, like in the Italian republics of the Middle Ages, to reject the conquerors rather than giving equal rights to citizens, and the consequence was to momentarily offer the nobility a new sign of dis-

tinction, the persecution. Strengthened by this privilege, the noblesse was able to fight with advantage the institutions that oppressed her.]

13. Sismondi, *Recherches sur les constitutions des peuples libres*, p. 285.

14. [Translation: We need a constitutional power able to maintain what was useful in the Ballia without what was dangerous, that is, a power neither legitimate to condemn nor imprison, rob or exile, but with the only capacity of depriving men or assemblies of the power that they can no longer use it without danger.]

15. [Translation: It is necessary, as was the practice in Venice, that the first attack forces them to immediately return into the ranks of citizens, that they are deprived of the power of damaging, instead of thinking of punishing them. Let's deprive them of this power through the mere refusal of the vote, which does not expose anybody to their revenge, and which does not require the deployment of a large civil courage.] J. C. L. Sismondi, *Histoire des Républiques italiennes du Moyen-Age*, vols 1–16 (Paris: Nicolle, Treuttel and Würtz, 1809–1818), vol. 4, pp. 371–2.

16. [Translation: In a republic, the honour of governing is an adequate reward for the job of the government; when the good reputation is the only remuneration of an official, everyone tries to get it; on the contrary, if they receive a salary, their main goal is reached when they are paid, and their employment does not seem fruitless, even if they have not conquered either the people's love, or the posterity's respect.] Sismondi, *Histoire des Républiques italiennes du Moyen-Age*, vol. 5, p. 368.

17. The Republic of Consigal comes from the acronyms of Victor Constant, Benjamin's cousin, Sismondi himself and the Gallatin brothers. It was created by them at the age of twelve in imitation of the Republic of Geneva and the Roman Republic (see J.-D. Candaux, *L'Histoire de la République de Consigal, premier écrit de Sismondi, 1785*, in *Atti del Colloquio internazionale sul Sismondi*, Pescia 8–10 settembre 1970 (Rome: Accademia nazionale dei Lincei, 1973).

18. [Translation: Long live the Republic of Consigal ... this is almost the only State in the world where there is still talent, nobility and energy.] B. Constant, *Correspondance générale, 6, 1806–1807*, ed. P. Delbouille *Œuvres complètes* (Tübingen: Niemeyer, 2008), p. 409.

19. [Translation: the first difference between the social condition of the ancients and that of the moderns.] Constant, *Principes de politique applicables à tous les gouvernements représentatifs (texte de 1806)*, p. 601.

20. [Translation: However, two things are worthy of note in this republican despotism. The first is the consolation that citizens can find in the loss of civil liberties by obtaining or sharing a great power. This compensation only exists in a state where citizens are few, and where, therefore, the chance to achieve supreme power is large enough or close enough to soften the daily sacrifice that every citizen makes of his rights to this power. Thus, in the republics of antiquity, there was no civil liberty; the citizen recognized himself slave of the nation to which he belonged; he settled in full into the decisions of the sovereign, without challenging the legislator the right to control all his actions, to compel his wishes completely; but on the other hand, it was itself, in turn, this sovereign and this legislator. He knew the value of his vote in a nation small enough so that every citizen was an estate, and he felt that it was to himself, as a sovereign, that he sacrificed as a subject his civil liberty.] Sismondi, *Histoire des Républiques italiennes du Moyen-Age*, vol. 4, pp. 369–70.

21. See G. Paoletti, *Benjamin Constant et les Anciens. Politique, religion, histoire* (Paris: Champion, 2006), pp. 90–8 and G. Paoletti, 'Introduction to B. Constant', in B. Constant, *Principes de politiques...* (2011), pp. 19–86, on p. 35.

22. See Sismondi, *Recherches sur les constitutions des peuples libres*, pp. 160–3.

23. [Translation: History, by allowing you a sentence only after a fact, marks a track that preserves from digressions and at the same time is useful for talent, because it forces you to be accurate.] In a letter dated 13 May: Constant, *Correspondance générale, 4, 1803–1805*, p. 106.

24. See E. Hofmann, *Constant et l'histoire de son temps. A propos du dernier chapitre des* Mélanges de littérature et politique, *Annales Benjamin Constant*, 28 (2004), pp. 51–67.

25. [Translation: in which he describes the distinction expressed by the author between the freedom of the ancients and that of the moderns, and between the industrial state and the military one as very ingenious, although he admitted that it was not original: 'Several writers, including M. Sismondi and the author of this essay, fourteen years ago have said the same things in almost the same words'.] B. Constant, *Mélanges de littérature et de politique*, ed. F. Rosset *Œuvres complètes, Œuvres*, vol. 33 (Berlin and New York: De Gruyter, 2012), p. 257.

26. [Translation: The freedom of the ancients, as their philosophy – Sismondi wrote – aimed at virtue; the freedom of the moderns, like their philosophy, aims at nothing but happiness. The best lesson to draw from the comparison between the two systems should be to learn how to combine the one with the other ... Today the legislator has to bear in mind citizens' safety, and the guarantees that the moderns have reduced to an habit; but he ought to remember also that he must look for their greatest moral development ... And it is by multiplying their rights, by inviting them to share the sovereignty, by redoubling their interest in public affairs, that he will also teach them to know their duties, and he will give them at the same time the desire and the ability to fulfill them.] Sismondi, *Histoire des Républiques italiennes du Moyen-Age*, vol. 16, pp. 405–6.

27. [Translation: So, Gentlemen, far from renouncing one or the other of the two kinds of freedom which I told you of, it is necessary, as I have demonstrated, to learn to combine them ... By respecting their individual rights, by providing them independence, by not disturbing their occupations, they must nevertheless consecrate their influence on public affairs, call them to concur, with their determinations and their votes, in the exercise of power, grant them the right to control and supervise through the expression of their opinions, and thereby forming them through the practice at these elevated functions, give them at the same time the desire and the ability to fulfill them.] B. Constant, *De la liberté des anciens comparée à celle des modernes*, in *Cours de politique constitutionnelle*, 4 (Paris and Rouen: Béchet, 1820), pp. 238–374, on pp. 373–4.

28. Revolution broke out at the end of 1792 in Geneva, see E. Chapuisat, *Des le Terreur à l'annexion. Geneva et la République française* (Geneva and Paris: Atar/Champion, [1912]). On reaction in Geneva, see B. Fontana, *Benjamin Constant e il pensiero post-rivoluzionario* (Milan: Baldini & Castoldi, 1996).

29. See F. Sofia, 'Sul pensiero politico-costituzionale del giovane Sismondi', *Rassegna Storica del Risorgimento*, 68 (1981), pp. 131–47.

30. H. O. Pappe, 'Introduction to Sismondi Jean-Charles Léonard', in *Statistique du département du Léman* (*c.* 1802; Geneva: A. Julien, 1971), p. 6.

31. See M. Minerbi, 'Introduction to Sismondi, J. C. L.', in *Recherches sur les constitutions des peuples libres* (Geneva: Droz, 1965) and Sofia, 'Sul pensiero politico-costituzionale del giovane Sismondi'.

32. 'Ce qui fait le prix de [la réflexion des grands libéraux du XIXe siècle] ce ne sont pas tellement les principes *économiques* libéraux, qui, chez les plus grands, ne constituent nullement un thème central, c'est plutôt leur conscience aiguë des difficultés de la *condition politique* de l'homme moderne' (P. Raynaud, 'Préface', in B. Constant, *De la Force du*

gouvernement actuel de la France et de la nécessité de s'y rallier. Des Réactions politiques. Des Effets de la Terreur (Paris: Flamarion, coll. 'Champs', 1988), p. 8).

33. J. C. L. Sismondi, *De la richesse commerciale ou principes d'économie politique, appliqués à la Législation du Commerce*, ed. P. Bridel, F. Dal Degan and N. Eyguesier, *Œuvres Economiques Complètes*, vol. 2 ([1803]; Paris: Economica, 2012), p. 6.

34. Constant, *Principes de politique applicables à tous les gouvernements représentatifs (texte de 1806)*, p. 469.

35. Ibid., pp. 326, 338.

36. J. C. L. Sismondi, *Essais sur les constitutions des peuples libres*, in R. Di Reda (ed.), *Libertà e scienza, del governo in Sismondi* (Rome: Jouvence, 1998), pp. 568–9.

37. Constant, *Principes de politique applicables à tous les gouvernements représentatifs (texte de 1806)*, p. 442.

38. Ibid., p. 324.

39. Ibid., p. 339.

40. Sismondi, 'De la richesse commerciale ou principes d'économie politique, appliqués à la Législation du Commerce', p. 138.

41. Constant, *Principes de politique applicables à tous les gouvernements représentatifs (texte de 1806)*, p. 340.

42. Ibid., p. 367.

43. Ibid., p. 275.

44. In relation to the concept of liberty understood as the outcome of the historical process of civilization after the rupture of feudal bonds which transforms individual differences (*les intérêts divers*) into common values and ideas (*opinion publique*), see Pappe, 'Introduction to Sismondi Jean-Charles Léonard', while for the Scottish historical school which has many affinities with Sismondi's idea of liberty see F. Meinecke, *Le origini dello storicismo* (Florence: Sansoni, 1954), p. 155–96 and D. Cantimori, *Studi di Storia* (Torino: Einaudi, 1959), pp. 557–63.

45. In *Ressources de la Toscane* (1799) Sismondi writes: 'les devoirs civiles sont anéantis, le contrat social n'est plus qu'une fiction cruelle, pour l'individu qui meurt de misère' (Bridel, DalDegan and Eyguesier (eds), *Oeuvres économiques complètes - Ecrits d'économie politique*, p. 26.)

46. Constant, *Principes de politique applicables à tous les gouvernements représentatifs (texte de 1806)*, p. 351.

47. Ibid., p. 353.

48. Ibid., p. 458.

49. Ibid., p. 455.

50. Ibid., p. 469.

51. Ibid.

52. Thus, as Sismondi said in a letter addressed to his mother in 1817, in the wake of Mme de Stael's burial: 'C'en est donc fait de ce jour où j'ai tant vécu, où je me croyais si bien chez moi! C'en est fait de cette société vivifiante, de cette lanterne magique du monde que j'ai vu s'éclairer là pour la première fois et où j'ai tant appris de choses!'.

53. Citing the title of the book edited by K. Szmurlo, *Germaine de Staël: Forging a Politics of Mediation* (Oxford: Voltaire Foundation, 2011).

54. S. Tenenbaum and F. Tilkin (eds), *Le groupe de Coppet et le monde moderne – Conceptions, Images, Débats* (Geneva: Droz, 1998), p. 226.

55. See A. Hirschman, 'Rival Interpretations of Market Society: Civilizing, Destructive, or Feeble?', *Journal of Economic Literature*, 20 (1982), pp. 1463–84, on p. 1463.

11 Potier, 'French Liberal Economists and the "Labour Question" before and during the Revolution of 1848'

1. J.-A. Schumpeter, *History of Economic Analysis* (New York: Oxford University Press, 1954), p. 497.

2. C. Dunoyer, *De la liberté du travail*, 3 vols (Paris: Guillaumin, 1845), book 4, ch. 10, vol. 1, pp. 380–1.

3. According to Dunoyer, we must not have the aim of eradicating misery, because it is useful for the right working of the 'social order': 'It is good that there are in society inferior places where the families that behave badly are supposed to fall, from whence they cannot rise without behaving well. Misery is this frightening hell' (C. Dunoyer, 'Des objections qu'on a soulevées dans ces derniers temps contre le régime de la concurrence', *Journal des économistes*, 1 (1841), pp. 13–43, 129–46, on p. 136).

4. L. Wolowski, 'Communication au Congrès des économistes de Bruxelles', in *Congrès des économistes de tous les pays. Première réunion à Bruxelles (16, 17 et 18 septembre 1847)*, *Journal des économistes*, 18 (October 1847), pp. 254–56, on p. 255; M. Chevalier, *Lettres sur l'organisation du travail, ou Etudes sur les principales causes de la misère et sur les moyens proposés pour y remédier* (Paris: Capelle, 1848), pp. 12–13, 162–163, 300, 423. Concerning L. Wolowski, see M. Lutfalla, 'Louis Wolowski ou le libéralisme positif', in Y. Breton and M. Lutfalla (eds), *L'économie politique en France au XIXe siècle* (Paris: Economica, 1991), pp. 185–201 and concerning M. Chevalier, see Y. Breton, 'Michel Chevalier. Entre le saint-simonisme et le libéralisme', in Y. Breton and M. Lutfalla (eds), *L'économie politique en France au XIXe siècle* (Paris: Economica, 1991), pp. 247–75 and P. Steiner, 'Production, répartition, et passion de l'égalité: l'économie politique de Michel Chevalier', *Revue européenne des sciences sociales*, 36:110 (1998), pp. 97–119.

5. According to Turgot, 'Dieu, en donnant à l'homme des besoins, en lui rendant nécessaire la ressource du travail, a fait du droit de travailler la propriété de tout homme, et cette propriété est la première, la plus sacrée et la plus imprescriptible de toutes' [God, by giving to man needs and making him dependent upon the resources of labour, had made the 'droit de travailler' the property of each man and this property is primary, the most sacred and most imprescriptible of all] (*Œuvres de Turgot, et documents le concernant*, ed. G. Schelle, vol. 5 (Paris: F. Alcan, 1923), p. 242).

6. L. Wolowski, *Cours de législation industrielle, Conservatoire des Arts et Métiers, Première leçon (27 novembre 1844), De l'organisation du travail*, extracted from *Revue de législation et de jurisprudence* (Paris: Au bureau de la Revue de législation et de jurisprudence, 1844), p. 11; J. Garnier, *Le droit au travail, quelques mots d'explication et d'histoire; introduction à la discussion qui a eu lieu au sein de l'Assemblée nationale* (Paris: Guillaumin, 1848b), pp. v–vi; L. Faucher, *Du droit au travail* (Paris: Guillaumin, 1848), p. 29.

7. See N. Sigot, 'Utility and Justice: French Liberal Economists in the Nineteenth Century', *European Journal of the History of Economic Thought*, 17:4 (October 2010), pp. 759–92.

8. See, for example, F. Bastiat, 'Propriété et loi', *Journal des économistes*, 20 (15 May 1848), pp. 177–91 and Chevalier, *Lettres sur l'organisation du travail*, p. 158.

9. See J.-P. Potier, 'L'Assemblée Constituante et la question de la liberté du travail: un texte méconnu, la loi Le Chapelier', in J.-M. Servet (ed.), *Idées économiques sous la Révolution (1789–1794)* (Lyon: Presses universitaires de Lyon, 1989), pp. 235–54.

10. The arbitrage of conflicts was made through the *conseil des prud'hommes*, created by decree in 1806.

11. See J. Garnier, *Eléments de l'économie politique. Exposé des notions fondamentales de cette science* (1846; Paris: Guillaumin, 1848).
12. G. de Molinari, *Les soirées de la Rue Saint Lazare* (Paris: Guillaumin, 1849), pp. 109–10, 117–21.
13. Ibid., pp. 121–4.
14. Nothing would change before the law of 25 May 1864, which legalized the strikes under certain conditions, and the law of 21 March 1884, which legalized the trade unions.
15. F. Bastiat, Discours sur la répression des coalitions industrielles', in *Œuvres complètes de Frédéric Bastiat*, ed. P. Paillotet and R. de Fontenay, vol. 5 (1849; Paris: Guillaumin, 1863), pp. 494–512, on p. 501.
16. See Y. Guin, 'Au cœur du libéralisme: la loi du 22 mars 1841 relative au travail des enfants employés dans les manufactures, usines ou ateliers', in J.-P. Le Crom (ed.), *Deux siècles de droit du travail* (Paris: Editions de l'Atelier, 1998), pp. 29–43.
17. Wolowski, *Cours de législation industrielle*, pp. 15–16.
18. A. Blanqui, 'De la concurrence et du principe d'association', *Séances et travaux de l'Académie des sciences morales et politiques* (ASMP), vol. 9, p. 418, quoted by S.-A. Leterrier, *L'institution des sciences morales (1795–1850)* (Paris: L'Harmattan, 1995), p. 231.
19. Chevalier, *Lettres sur l'organisation du travail*, pp. 249–50.
20. A. Blanqui, *Des classes ouvrières en France, pendant l'année 1848* (Paris: Pagnerre/Paulin/Firmin Didot, 1849), p. 202.
21. See F. Jarrige and B. Reynaud, 'La durée du travail, la norme et ses usages en 1848', *Genèses*, 85 (December 2011), pp. 70–92, on p. 72.
22. L. Faucher, Discours prononcés dans la discussion du projet de loi tendant à abroger le décret du 2 mars 1848, relatif à la fixation des heures de travail [séance du 4 septembre 1848]', in *Mélanges d'économie politique et de finances, vol. 2, Economie politique* (1848; Paris: Guillaumin, 1856), pp. 175–84, on pp. 177–80.
23. Chevalier, *Lettres sur l'organisation du travail*, pp. 115–16.
24. Ibid., pp. 107–11.
25. F. Bastiat, *Harmonies économiques* (Paris: Guillaumin, 1850), p. 382.
26. Ibid., p. 384.
27. M. Chevalier, *Question des travailleurs. L'amélioration du sort des ouvriers. Les salaires. L'organisation du travail*, extracted from *Revue des Deux Mondes*, 15 mars 1848 (Paris: Au bureau de la Revue des Deux Mondes, 1848), pp. 24–7.
28. According to Louis Blanc: 'que chacun produise selon son aptitude et ses forces, que chacun consomme selon ses besoins' (Speech in Luxembourg published in *Le Moniteur*, 3 April 1848).
29. Chevalier, *Lettres sur l'organisation du travail*, pp. 76–84.
30. Faucher, *Du droit au travail*, pp. 29–31 and L. Faucher, 'Droit au travail', in C. Coquelin and G.-U. Guillaumin (eds), *Dictionnaire de l'économie politique* (Paris: Guillaumin, 1852), pp. 605–19, on p. 612.
31. P.-J. Proudhon, *Le droit au travail et le droit de propriété* (Paris: L. Vasbenter, 1848).
32. Garnier, *Le droit au travail*, p. viii.
33. In his book *Pages d'histoire de la révolution de février 1848* (Paris: Au bureau du Nouveau Monde, 1850), p. 31, Louis Blanc said: 'En rédigeant ce décret, je n'ignorais pas jusqu'à quel point il engageait le gouvernement; je savais à merveille qu'il n'était applicable qu'au moyen d'une réforme sociale ayant l'association pour principe et pour effet l'abolition du prolétariat. Mais à mes yeux, c'était là justement la valeur du décret' [While I was writing this decree, I was not unaware of up to which point it committed the government; I

knew perfectly that it was applicable only by means of a social reform having association for principle and abolition of the proletariat for effect. But according to me, it was there precisely the value of the decree].

34. In *The Class Struggles in France* (1850), Karl Marx treats them as 'English workhouses out in the open'!

35. See J. Garnier, 'Quelques mots d'explication et d'histoire au sujet des principales formules socialistes', *Journal des économistes*, 20:83 (July 1848), pp. 375–80 and A. Clément, *Des nouvelles idées de réforme industrielle et en particulier du projet d'organisation du travail de M. Louis Blanc* (Paris: Guillaumin, 1848).

36. See Blanqui, *Des classes ouvrières en France, pendant l'année 1848*; Chevalier, *Question des travailleurs* and Chevalier, *Lettres sur l'organisation du travail*.

37. J. Godechot (ed.), *Les Constitutions de la France depuis 1789* (Paris: Garnier-Flammarion, 1970), pp. 264–5.

38. Faucher, *Du droit au travail*, p. 13.

39. L. Blanc, *Le socialisme. Droit au travail. Réponse à M. Thiers*, 3rd edn (Paris: Au bureau du Nouveau Monde, 1849), p. 54).

40. Faucher, *Du droit au travail*, p. 4.

41. See Leterrier, *L'institution des sciences morales (1795–1850)*, pp. 315–21 and M. S. Staum, 'French Lecturers in Political Economy, 1815–1848: Varieties of Liberalism', *History of Political Economy*, 30.1 (Spring 1999), pp. 95–120, on p. 111. In this collection of twelve 'petits traités de l'Académie des sciences morales et politiques', we find in good place the following books: A. Thiers, *De la propriété*, H. Passy, *Des causes de l'inégalité des richesses* et A. Blanqui, *Des classes ouvrières en France, pendant l'année 1848*.

42. See also the entry 'Droit du travail' in the *Dictionnaire Universel* of Pierre Larousse.

12 Marcuzzo, 'Whatever Happened to the Keynesian Multiplier?'

1. C. Borio, 'The Financial Cycle and Macroeconomics: What Have we Learnt?', BIS Working Papers No 395 (2012), at http://www.bis.org/publ/work395.pdf, p. 1 [accessed 14 May 2014].

2. G. Davies, 'High Fiscal Multipliers Undermine Austerity Programmes', *Financial Times*, 21 October 2012, at http://blogs.ft.com/gavyndavies/2012/10/21/high-fiscal-multipliers-undermine-austerity-programmes, p. 3 [accessed 14 May 2014].

3. R. F. Kahn, *The Making of Keynes's* General Theory (Cambridge: Cambridge University Press, 1984), p. 91.

4. R. F. Kahn, 'The Relation of Home Investment to Unemployment', *Economic Journal*, 411:62 (1931), pp. 173–98.

5. See R. J. Kent, 'A 1929 Application of Multiplier Analysis by Keynes', *History of Political Economy*, 39:3 (2007), pp. 529–43.

6. J. Meade, 'The Relation of Mr Meade's Relation to Kahn's Multiplier', *Economic Journal*, 103:418 (1993), pp. 664–5.

7. Kahn, *The Making of Keynes's* General Theory, p. 99, emphasis added.

8. R. F. Kahn, 'The Financing of Public Works: A Note', *Economic Journal*, 42:167 (1932), pp. 492–5, on p. 494.

9. See J. M. Keynes, 'The Means to Prosperity', in *The Collected Writings*, 30 vols (London: Macmillan, 1971–1989), vol. 9; see M. C. Marcuzzo, 'The Collaboration between J. M. Keynes and R. F. Kahn from the *Treatise* to the *General Theory*', *History of Political Economy*, 34:2 (2002), pp. 421–47.

10. Quoted in N. G. Mankiw, 'The Macroeconomist as Scientist and Engineer', *Journal of Economic Perspectives*, 20:4 (2006), pp. 29–46, on p. 34.

11. V. Ramey, 'Can Government Purchases Stimulate the Economy?', *Journal of Economic Literature*, 49:3 (2011), pp. 673–85, on p. 673.

12. J. M. Keynes, 'The General Theory of Employment, Interest and Money', in *The Collected Writings*, vol. 6, p. 293.

13. Ibid., pp. 293–4.

14. M. C. Marcuzzo, 'Re-embracing Keynes: Admirers, Scholars and Sceptics in the Aftermath of the Crisis', in T. Hirai, M. C. Marcuzzo and P. Mehrling (eds), *Keynesian Reflections: Effective Demand, Money, Finance and Policies in the Crisis* (New Delhi: Oxford University Press, 2013), pp. 3–23.

15. A. Alesina, 'Fiscal Policy after the Great Recession', *Atlantic Economic Journal* 40:4 (2012), pp. 429–35, on p. 431.

16. Keynes, 'The General Theory of Employment, Interest and Money', p. 122.

17. J. Bailly, 'Consumption, Investment and the Investment Multiplier', in C. Gnos and L. Rochon (eds), *The Keynesian Multiplier* (Aldershot: Routledge, 2004), pp. 127–50, on p. 130.

18. M. Chinn, 'Fiscal Multipliers' (2012), mimeo at http://www.ssc.wisc.edu/~mchinn/Fiscal%20Multipliers.pdf [accessed 6 June 2014].

19. Alesina, 'Fiscal Policy after the Great Recession', p. 431.

20. R. E. Hall, 'Comment on "Fiscal Multipliers in Recession and Expansion"', in A. Alesina and F. Giavazzi (eds), *Fiscal Policy after the Financial Crisis* (Chicago, IL: NBER, 2013), pp. 98–102.

21. R. J. Barro, 'Government Spending Is No Free Lunch', *Wall Street Journal*, 22 January 2009.

22. J. Sachs, 'It is Time to Plan for the World after Keynes', *Financial Times*, 8 June 2010.

23. Marcuzzo, 'Re-embracing Keynes'.

24. M. Seccareccia, 'Keynes's Legacy: Fiscal Activism through Public Investment as the Principal Macroeconomic Tool to Achieve Sustained Economic Growth', INET's Bretton Woods Conference (2011), at http://ineteconomics.org/sites/inet.civicactions.net/files/BWpaper_SECCARECCIA_040811.pdf [accessed 14 May 2014].

25. B. de Long and L. Summers, 'Fiscal Policy in a Depressed Economy', *Brookings Papers on Economic Activity* (Spring 2012), pp. 233–74, on p. 233.

26. G. Corsetti, A. Meier and G. Muller, 'What Determines Government Spending Multipliers?', *Economic Policy*, 27:91 (2012), pp. 521–65, on pp. 521, 558.

27. IMF, *Word Economic Outlook* (Washington: IMF, October 2012), p. 43.

28. European Union, 'Report on Public Finances in EMU', *European Economy*, 4 (2012), p. 5.

29. Ibid., p. 123.

30. Ibid., p. 126.

31. Ramey, 'Can Government Purchases Stimulate the Economy?', p. 683.

32. IMF, *Word Economic Outlook*, p. 43.

33. E. T. Swanson and J. C. Williams, 'Measuring The Effect of the Zero Lower Lower Bound On Medium and Longer Term Interest Rates', *Federal Reserve Bank of San Francisco*, Working Paper 2012-02 (2012), p. 2.

34. Chinn, 'Fiscal Multipliers', p. 12.

35. N. Shapiro, 'Keynes, Steindl, and the Critique of Austerity Economics', *Monthly Review*, 64:3 (2012), pp. 103–13, on p. 110.

36. T. Pusch, 'Fiscal Spending Multiplier Calculations based on Input–Output Tables – an Application to EU Member States', *European Journal of Economics and Economic Policies*, 9:1 (2012), pp. 129–44.

37. A. García-Lizana and S. Pérez-Moreno, 'Consumption and Income Distribution: A Proposal for a New Reading of Keynes' Thinking', *European Journal of the History of Economic Thought*, 19:1 (2012), pp. 45–65.

38. Alesina, 'Fiscal Policy after the Great Recession', p. 430.

39. Keynes, 'The General Theory on Employment, Interest and Money', p. 96.

40. J. M. Keynes, 'The General Theory and After: Defence and Development', in *The Collected Writings*, vol. 14, pp. 188–9.

41. P. Mirowski, *Never Let a Serious Crisis Go to Waste: How Neoliberalism Survived the Financial Meltdown* (London: Verso, 2013), p. 240.

13 Porta, 'Sundry Observations and New Findings on the Anglo-Italian Tradition of Economic Thought'

1. I wish to record a special debt (with the usual disclaimer) to Mauro Baranzini and Geoff Harcourt, who – through the years – have provided fundamental inspiration and encouragement to my continuing research on the sources and the legacy of the Anglo-Italian School. Geoff Harcourt, in particular, has given me useful comments on the present essay. The preparation of this essay has required the study of the Sraffa papers at Trinity. I am grateful to The Master and Fellows of Trinity College, Cambridge, for granting access to their Collections and to the late Professor Pierangelo Garegnani for permission to make use of the unpublished materials.

2. It is well-known that J. M. Keynes, in his celebrated biographical essay, has reason to call Malthus 'the first of the Cambridge economists'. We do not go back as far as Malthus and his emphasis on the 'practical application' of the economic principles. Bruni and Zamagni (*Economia civile. Efficienza, equità, felicità pubblica* (Bologna: il Mulino, 2004), ch. 5 § 4, pp. 117 ff.) are doing that.

3. L. L. Pasinetti, *Keynes and the Cambridge Keynesians: A 'Revolution in Economics' to be Accomplished* (Cambridge: Cambridge University Press, 2007).

4. As Colander recalls, Keynes should also be put in the number of those disclaiming being a follower of himself (D. Colander, "Was Keynes a Keynesian or a Lernerian", *Journal of Economic Literature*, 22 (1984), pp. 1572–5).

5. In the same vein, the *Cambridge Journal of Economics* launched the Conference 'New Perspectives on the Work of Piero Sraffa' in 2010 for the fiftieth anniversary of *Production of Commodities*. In introducing the relevant Special Issue (November 2012), the editors emphasize (p. 1267) that the initiative 'was aimed at Sraffa scholars who had taken the opportunity to engage with materials in the Sraffa Archives and who were interested in exploring their potential for revisiting and placing PCMC in the wider context of ongoing debates on economic philosophy, economic theory and economic policy' (*Cambridge Journal of Economics*, 'New Perspectives on the Work of Piero Sraffa', 36:4, special issue (2012), pp. 1267–578).

6. Pasinetti, *Keynes and the Cambridge Keynesians*. I refer the reader here also to Harcourt (G. C. Harcourt, *The Structure of Post-Keynesian Economics: The Core Contributions of the*

Pioneers (Cambridge: Cambridge University Press, 2006)), a book which is complementary to Pasinetti.

7. L. L. Pasinetti, *Structural Change and Economic Growth: A Theoretical Essay on the Dynamics of the Wealth of Nations* (Cambridge: Cambridge University Press, 1981); and L. L. Pasinetti, *Structural Economic Dynamics: A Theory of the Economic Consequences of Human Learning* (Cambridge: Cambridge University Press, 1993), pp. x–xi. Pasinetti describes Kaldor to be 'always bubbling with new ideas' and Sraffa 'the real master of all critics'. Beyond the names mentioned by Pasinetti, I should add Maurice Dobb here, particularly his book of 1973.

8. A. Graziadei, *La teoria del valore* (Milan: A.N.S., 1935), esp. pp. 17–18 – my translation.

9. See P. L. Porta, 'I postkeynesiani di Cambridge e la tradizione italiana di economia politica nel dopoguerra' (Paper presented at the conference *Gli economisti postkeynesiani di Cambridge e l'Italia*, Roma: Accademia Nazionale dei Lincei, 11–12 marzo 2009), in *Atti dei Convegni Lincei*, 261 (Rome: Scienze e Lettere Editore, 2011), pp. 393–408; P. L. Porta, 'Highlights on the Cambridge School: The Italian Connection', in H. M. Krämer, H. D. Kurz and H.-M. Trautwein (eds), *Macroeconomics and the History of Economic Thought: Festschrift in Honour of Harald Hagemann* (London: Routledge, 2012), pp. 145–57.

10. On the development of Sraffa's thought from the early years, see Pasinetti, *Keynes and the Cambridge Keynesians*, esp. ch. 6.3 on continuity and change in Sraffa's economic thought). See also P. L. Porta, 'Piero Sraffa's Early Views on Classical Political Economy', *Cambridge Journal of Economics*, 36:6 (2012), pp. 1357–84.

11. P. L. Porta and R. Scazzieri, 'A Revolution to be Accomplished: Keynes and the Cambridge Keynesians', *Economia politica. Journal of analytical and institutional economics*, 3 (December 2008), pp. 455–80.

12. See also, among other references, M. Baranzini and G. C. Harcourt (eds), *The Dynamics of the Wealth of Nations: Growth, Distribution and Structural Change, Essays in honour of Luigi Pasinetti* (London: Macmillan, 1983).

13. Pasinetti, *Keynes and the Cambridge Keynesians*, p. 219.

14. P. L. Porta, 'The History of Economics: Highlights from the Italian Tradition', in A. Agnati, G. Marangoni, A. Montesano and A. Pellanda (eds), *Dinamica economica e istituzioni. Studi in onore di Davide Cantarelli* (Padova: CEDAM, 2005), pp. 387–99.

15. For example N. Bellanca, *Dinamica economica e istituzioni* (Milan: F. Angeli, 2000); R. Faucci, *Economic Knowledge for Political Action. Political Economy in Italy from the Sixteenth Century to the resent* (London: Routledge, 2014).

16. Pasinetti, *Keynes and the Cambridge Keynesians*.

17. Ibid.; L. L. Pasinetti, *Keynes e i keynesiani di Cambridge: una 'rivoluzione in economia' da portare a compimento* (Rome: Laterza, 2010), pp. xi–xiv.

18. Ibid., pp. xii–xiii.

19. Ibid., p. xv.

20. See Bruni and Zamagni, *Economia civile. Efficienza, equità, felicità pubblica*.

21. See Pasinetti, *Keynes and the Cambridge Keynesians*, p. 275.

22. Ibid.

23. See V. Zamagni, 'What is the Message of "Understanding the Process of Economic Change" for Economic Historians', *Structural Change and Economic Dynamics*, 21:2 (May 2010), pp. 157–63.

24. See also Porta and Scazzieri, 'A Revolution to be Accomplished', esp. pp. 475–7.

25. A. Quadrio Curzio, *Economisti ed economia. Per un'Italia europea: paradigmi tra il XVIII e il XX secolo* (Bologna, il Mulino, 2007).

26. See A. Quadrio Curzio and C. Rotondi, 'Sulle ricerche di economia politica in Cattolica', in G. Garofalo, and A. Graziani (eds), *La formazione degli economisti in Italia* (Bologna: Mulino, 2004), pp. 361–422, on pp. 406–7.

27. See Pasinetti, *Keynes and the Cambridge Keynesians*, p. 325. See also Pasinetti's recent acknowledgement of Francesco Vito's dynamic studies. The trade cycle was prominent in Francesco Vito's own research agenda and in general Vito had transmitted the idea to his pupils that economics was to be conceived with a view to policy, i. e. as a study of the ways to improve the conditions of mankind: *l'economia al servizio dell'uomo* (1954) is one of Vito's better-known titles. Let me just mention here that, in a recent essay of his, Pasinetti has reconsidered those years and he finds that the focus of Vito's own economic reflection lay in 'permanent human learning, in terms of production of new technologies, new products, new consumption models and new spare time use patterns, which has become available' (D. Parisi and C. Rotondi, 'Keynesian Elements in a Long-Term Analysis: Two Views of Two Influencial Pre- and Postwar Italian Economists', in L. L. Pasinetti and B. Schefold (eds), *The Impact of Keynes on Economics in the 20th Century* (Cheltenham and Northampton, MA: Edward Elgar, 1999), pp. 153–9).

See also Pasinetti's endorsement of the recent revival of happiness studies in economics, when he argues that the 'revival of interest in the relation between economic theory and human happiness ... might contribute to a resurgence of the long-forgotten Classical approach to Political Economy: ... an approach which seems to me now to emerge as much more suitable for dealing with the richness and freedom of human action'.

28. M. Blaug, 'The Trade-Off between Rigour and Relevance: Sraffian Economics as a Case in Point', *History of Political Economy*, 41:2 (2009), pp. 219–47, on p. 234.

29. See G. Becattini, 'L'interpretazione sraffiana di Marshall', in R. Bellofiore (ed.), *Tra teoria economica e grande cultura europea: Piero Sraffa* (Milan: F. Angeli, 1986), pp. 29–58; P. D. Groenewegen, 'Marshall's Interpretation of the "Classics"', in T. Raffaelli, G. Becattini and M. Dardi (eds), *The Elgar Companion to Alfred Marshall* (Cheltenham: Edward Elgar, 2006), pp. 116–23.

30. Quadrio Curzio, *Economisti ed economia*.

31. Ibid.

32. The best evidence on this point is contained in Piero Sraffa's 'Lectures on the Advanced Theory of Value' (Manuscript: Trinity College Archives, Cambridge, Classmark D2/4). The Lectures were first delivered in 1928 and are announced to appear in the first volume of Sraffa's works to be published by Cambridge University Press. The pages of interest here are from 51 to 59[8] of the Manuscript (as numbered in Sraffa's hand), where the different concepts of cost (Marshall's on one side and the Classical economists' on the other) are contrasted and discussed.

33. R. Arena and P. L. Porta, 'Structural Dynamics and Contemporary Growth Theory': An Introductory Essay to *Structural Dynamics and Economic Growth*, ed. R. Arena and P. L. Porta (Cambridge: Cambridge University Press, 2012), pp. 1–31.

14 Danthine, 'Financial Stability: The Role of Central Banks'

1. I would like to thank Till Ebner for his very valuable support in drafting this essay.

2.   A term introduced by J. H. Stock and M. W. Watson in 'Has the Business Cycle Changed and Why?', in M. Gertler and K. Rogoff (eds), *NBER Macroeconomics Annual 2002*, 17 (Cambridge, MA and London: MIT Press, 2003), pp. 159–230 to designate the period since the mid-1980ies characterized by reduced business cycle amplitude and lower volatility of the GDP growth rate.

3.   See, for instance, A. Alesina and L. H. Summers, 'Central Bank Independence and Macroeconomic Performance: Some Comparative Evidence', *Journal of Money, Credit, and Banking*, 25:2 (1993), pp. 151–62 and J. Klomp and J. de Haan, 'Inflation and Central Bank Independence: A Meta-Regression Analysis', *Journal of Economic Surveys*, 24:4 (Oxford: Blackwell Publishing, 2010), pp. 593–621.

4.   See IMF, 'The Interaction of Monetary and Macroprudential Policies', *IMF Policy Paper* (Washington, DC: International Monetary Fund, 2012) and IMF, 'The Interaction of Monetary and Macroprudential Policies', *Background Paper* (Washington, DC: International Monetary Fund, 2012), and references therein.

5.   See C. Borio and H. Zhu, 'Capital Regulation, Risk-taking and Monetary Policy: A Missing Link in the Transmission Mechanism?', *BIS Working Paper 268* (Basel: Bank for International Settlements, 2008).

6.   See C. Bean et al., 'Monetary Policy After the Fall', *Paper Presented by C. Bean, Deputy Governor of the Bank of England at the Federal Reserve Bank of Kansas City Annual Conference* (Jackson Hole, WY: 28 August 2010). The simulation exercise assumes that US interest rates are about 200 basis points higher than actually observed.

7.   See S. Ingves, 'Monetary Policy Entails a Balancing Act', Speech Held at the Norrland County Administrative Board (Luleå: 4 December 2012). Household debt – predominantly mortgage debt – amounted to approximately 170 per cent of disposable income in 2012.

8.   See L. E. O. Svensson, 'Monetary Policy and Employment: Monetary Policy is Too Tight', *Speech held at the Swedish Trade Union Confederation* (Stockholm: 16 January 2013).

9.   See J. Tinbergen, 'On the Theory of Economic Policy' (Amsterdam: North-Holland Publishing Co., 1952).

10.   C. Crowe et al., 'Policies for Macrofinancial Stability: Options to Deal with Real Estate Booms', *IMF Staff Discussion Note 11/02* (Washington, DC. International Monetary Fund, 2011) provide a discussion of different policy options to reduce the risks associated with real estate booms.

11.   See C. Borio, 'The Financial Cycle and Macroeconomics: What Have We Learnt?', *BIS Working Paper 395* (Basel: Bank for International Settlements, 2012) and M. Schularick and A. Taylor, 'Credit Booms Gone Bust: Monetary Policy, Leverage Cycles, and Financial Crises, 1870–2008', *American Economic Review*, 102:2 (2012), pp. 1029–61.

12.   See Crowe et al., 'Policies for Macrofinancial Stability' and Committee on the Global Financial System, 'Macroprudential Instruments and Frameworks: A Stocktaking of Issues and Experiences', *CGFS Papers 38* (Basel: Bank for International Settlements, 2010).

13.   See Basel Committee on Banking Supervision, 'An Assessment of the Long-Term Economic Impact of Stronger Capital and Liquidity Requirements' (Basel: Bank for International Settlements, 2010).

15 Laidler, 'The Fisher Relation in the Great Depression and the Great Recession'

1. This essay builds upon a section of an earlier and longer paper: 'Two Crises, Two Ideas and One Question' (EPRI Working Paper 2012–4) and incorporates material from it. Correspondence and discussion with Michael Belongia, Lars Christensen, Tim Congdon, Peter Howitt, Thomas Humphrey, Douglas Irwin, Richard Lipsey, Perry Mehrling, Edward Nelson and Michael Parkin are gratefully acknowledged.

2. Robert Dimand and Rebeca Gomez-Betancourt survey this early history, and the later roles played by Fisher's ideas in the evolution of macroeconomics (Dimand and Gomez-Betancourt, 'Irving Fisher's *Appreciation and Interest* (1896) and the Origins of Modern Macroeconomics', *Journal of Economic Perspectives,* 26:4 (Fall 2012), pp. 185–96).

3. Equation 1 is obviously written in deterministic form. In modern dynamic stochastic general equilibrium analysis, R is treated not as a constant, but as a long run steady state value of the real rate of interest, around which its actual value varies in response to various shocks, to productivity, for example. Whether this steady state value is itself constant depends upon the particular model, of course, but again as a practical matter it often is so presented. Discussion with Michael Parkin on this point has been very helpful.

4. Though it is really Marshall's, including the vocabulary of real and nominal, as Fisher himself acknowledged (see A. Marshall, 'Remedies for Fluctuations in General Prices', *Contemporary Review* (March 1887). It is a somewhat paradoxical feature of the subsequent development of the Cambridge tradition in monetary economics, that though expectations of rising prices played a key role in expositions of its analysis of monetary elements in the cycle well into the early 1930s, with the exception of Hawtrey (*Good and Bad Trade* (London: Constable, 1913)), these did not make explicit use of the real-nominal interest rate distinction. Bridel (*Cambridge Monetary Thought* (London: Macmillan, 1987)) is a classic source on the development of this tradition, parallel to the one explored here, which is not dealt with in any detail below.

5. A. H. Meltzer, *A History of the Federal Reserve* (Chicago, IL: University of Chicago Press, 2003), vol. 1, pp. 412–13.

6. C. D. Romer and D. H. Romer, 'Friedman and Schwartz's' Monetary Explanation of the Great Depression: Old Challenges and New Evidence' (Preliminary draft of paper presented at the ASSA meetings, San Diego, 2013).

7. J. M. Keynes, *A Tract on Monetary Reform* (London: Macmillan, 1923), p. 20.

8. I. Fisher, 'The Theory of Interest', ch. 19, pp. 399–451 [pp. 439–95]). In all references to Fisher, two sets of page numbers are given, those in the original printing, and in square brackets, those in the relevant volume of the Barber, Dimand and Foster's edition of his works. See *The Works of Irving Fisher*, ed. W. J. Barber, R. W. Dimand and K. Foster, 14 vols (London: Pickering & Chatto, 1997).

9. Fisher, 'The Theory of Interest', p. 494 [p. 538]).

10. H. Thornton, *An Enquiry into the Nature and Effects of the Paper Credit of Great Britain*, ed. F. H. von Hayek (1802; London: Allen and Unwin, 1939).

11. R. G. Hawtrey, *Currency and Credit* (London: Longmans Group, 1919).

12. For example K. Wicksell, *Lectures in Political Economy, Vol. 2*, 2nd edn, trans. E. Claassen (1915; London: Routledge and Kegan Paul, 1935).

13. F. G. Steindl, *Monetary Interpretations of the Great Depression* (Ann Arbor, MI: University of Michigan Press, 1995), chs 1, 3.

14. Hawtrey (for example R. G. Hawtrey, *The Art of Central Banking* (London: Longmans Group, 1932)).

15. Lauchlin Currie (for example *The Supply and Control of Money in the United States* (Cambridge, MA: Harvard University Press, 1934)).

16. Fisher, 'The Theory of Interest', pp. 493–4 [pp. 537–8], italics in original.

17. Meltzer, *A History of the Federal Reserve*.

18. Of course the effect in question is anything but asymmetrical if debtors are unable to pay off their real losses, and hence creditors to collect their gains, and this is surely what Fisher had in mind.

19. See I Fisher, 'The Money Illusion', in *The Works of Irving Fisher* ([1928] 1997), vol. 8.

20. I. Fisher, 'Booms and Depressions', in *The Works of Irving Fisher* ([1932] 1997), vol. 10, p. 211 [p. 271].

21. And which lay directly in the Cambridge tradition of discussions of the effect of inflation on investment documented by Bridel in *Cambridge Monetary Thought*.

22. J. M. Keynes, *The General Theory of Employment, Interest and Money* (London: Macmillan, 1936), p. 142.

23. See ibid., p. 140.

24. Ibid., pp. 142–3, italics in original.

25. R. F. Harrod, *Money* (London: Macmillan, 1970), pp. 179–80.

26. It is nevertheless an unexplained puzzle in the Keynesian literature that the *Radcliffe Report* itself (Committee on the Working of the Monetary System (the Radcliffe Committee), *Report* (London: HMSO, 1959)) of all documents, provided an exception to the general tenor of British Keynesian discussions of these matters, by suggesting (p. 211) that sustained inflation in the 2 per cent range might create expectations that would raise the above-mentioned normal value of the long run rate of interest from 3 to 5 per cent. The *Report* made nothing further of this point, however.

27. J. R. Hicks, *A Market Theory of Money* (Oxford: Oxford University Press, 1992), p. 79.

28. H. G. Johnson, 'The Keynesian Revolution and the Monetarist Counter-Revolution', *American Economic Review*, 61:2 (May 1971), pp. 212–25.

29. M. Friedman, 'The Quantity Theory of Money, a Restatement', in *Studies in the Quantity Theory of Money* (Chicago, IL: University of Chicago Press, 1956), pp. 9–10. That Friedman took this warning seriously is confirmed by the fact that the nominal rate of return on bonds and the expected rate of inflation figured as separate variables in that essay's equation (11) which restated the quantity theory as a theory of the demand for money.

30. Keynes, *A Tract on Monetary Reform*.

31. M. Friedman, 'The Role of Monetary Policy', *American Economic Review*, 58:1 (March 1968), pp. 1–19, on p. 6.

32. M. Friedman, 'The Optimum Quantity of Money', in *The Optimum Quantity of Money* (London: Macmillan, 1969), p. 41.

33. P. Cagan, 'The Monetary Dynamics of Hyper-Inflation', in M. Friedman (ed.), *Studies in the Quantity theory of Money* (Chicago, IL: University of Chicago Press, 1956), pp. 25–117.

34. See D. Laidler and J. M. Parkin, 'Inflation – a Survey', *Economic Journal*, 85 (December 1975), p. 741–809, as reprinted in Royal Economic Society and Social Science Research Council, *Surveys of Applied Economics* (London: Macmillan, 1977), vol. 2, p. 216; W. Gibson, 'Price Expectations Effects on Interest Rates', *Journal of Finance*, 25:1 (March 1970), pp. 19–34; and W. P. Yohe and D. S. Karnowsky, 'Interest Rates and Price Level Changes', *Federal Reserve Bank of St. Louis Review*, 51 (December 1969), pp. 18–38.

35. M. Feldstein and G. Chamberlain, 'Multimarket Expectations and the Rate of Interest', *Journal of Money, Credit and Banking* 5:4 (November 1973), pp. 873–902.

36. Friedman, 'The Optimum Quantity of Money'.

37. M. J. Bailey, *National Income and the Price Level* (New York: McGraw Hill, 1962); R. J. Mundell, 'Inflation and Real Interest', *Journal of Political Economy*, 71 (June 1963), pp. 280–3.

38. Friedman, 'The Optimum Quantity of Money'.

39. Laidler and Parkin, 'Inflation – a Survey'.

40. Miguel Sidrauski (1967).

41. Friedman for one immediately recognized this, witness his moving memorial speech delivered at a 1968 American Bankers Association conference, and reprinted in Gordon (ed.) (1974), a volume dedicated to Sidrauski's memory.

42. Laidler and Parkin, 'Inflation – a Survey', p. 178, n.

43. Ibid., p. 200. Though this author recalls that the degree of scepticism expressed here was to some extent the result of Brian Reddaway's editorial reactions to earlier drafts of the relevant section.

44. Ibid., pp. 217–18.

45. Though as Michael Parkin has pointed out to me, these developments paid little if any attention to questions about the term structure of inflation expectations that we had tentatively raised in 1975 (Laidler and Parkin, 'Inflation – a Survey'), and as he has also stressed, this inattention was not obviously an advance.

46. The key papers of what is usually called the 'Rational Expectations Revolution' are conveniently gathered in a single edited volume (R. E. Lucas, Jr and T. J. Sargent (eds), *Rational Expectations and Econometric Practice* (Minneapolis, MS: University of Minnesota Press, 1981)) whose rather austere title does not do full credit to its wide range. But it was not just New Classical economists who took to embedding versions of equation 1 in their models, and uncritically assuming a constant long run equilibrium real rate of interest. The current author must also confess to having done so in a number of places. See for example, D. Laidler, 'Some Macroeconomic Implications of Price Stickiness', *Manchester School*, 56:1 (March 1988), pp. 37–54, reprinted in D. Laidler, *Taking Money Seriously* (Deddington: Philip Allen, 1990), p. 88, eq. 13.

47. See, for example, R. J. Barro, 'Unanticipated Money, Output and the Price Level in the United States', *Journal of Political Economy*, repr. in Lucas and Sargent (eds) *Rational Expectations and Econometric Practice*.

48. See, for example, M. Friedman, 'Lessons from the 1978–82 Monetary Policy Experiment', *American Economic Review*, 84 (Papers and proceedings, May 1984) pp. 395–400.

49. Friedman's forecast was in error largely because he overlooked the effect that rapidly falling inflation, expectations, were having on the demand for money. Ironically, the mechanism at work here had been much stressed in his earlier writings (e.g. *The Optimum Quantity of Money* of 1969), albeit in the context of rising, rather than falling, inflation.

50. M. Sidrauski, 'Rational Choice and Patterns of Growth in a Monetary Economy', *American Economic Review*, 57:2 (May 1967), pp. 534–44.

51. M. Woodford, *Interest and Prices: The Theory of Monetary Policy* (Princeton, NJ: Princeton University Press, 2003).

52. L. Summers, 'How Should Long-Term Monetary Policy be Determined', *Journal of Money, Credit and Banking*, 23:3 (August 1991), pp. 623–31.

53. The relative merits of inflation and price-level targeting are discussed along these lines by Parkin (J. M. Parkin, *What is the Ideal Monetary Policy Regime? Commentary #279*

(Toronto: C. D. Howe Institute, 2009)), while Scott Sumner (2012) makes the current case for nominal GDP targeting (S. Sumner, 'The Case for Nominal GDP Targeting' (Working Paper, Fairfax, VA: Mercatus Centre, George Mason University, 2012).

54. J. B. Taylor, *Getting Off Track* (Stanford, CA: Hoover Institution Press, 2011).

55. Ibid.

56. This is not a debate to be settled here, but permit me the luxury of quoting my own pre-crisis (early 2006) view of this matter: 'Local experts know more about how strong a case can be made for the existence of a housing market bubble, and about how much of it can be attributed to monetary policy as opposed to other features of the US scene ... but even so, perhaps a Fed constrained by, say, a 2 per cent inflation target for the CPI (as opposed to some measure of core inflation) would not have responded to the "dot com" collapse quite so vigorously and for quite so long, while still managing to maintain financial stability in its wake'. D. Laidler, Comment, in Bank of Canada, Inflation Targeting: Problems and Opportunities, Proceedings of a Conference Co-Sponsored by the Bank of Canada and the New York Association of Business Economists (2006), at http://www.bankof-canada.ca/publications-research/research/conferences/ [accessed 12 February 2014].

57. This quotation was attributed to Kocherlakota by Steven Williamson, and caused Nicholas Rowe to 'lose it' – in Paul Krugman's well-chosen phrase (see N. Rowe, 'Why everyone should be forced to take Intro Economics', at http://worthwhile.typepad.com/worthwhile_canadian_initi/2010/08/why-everyone-should-be-forced-to-take-intro-eco-nomics.html [accessed 12 February 2014]). See Williamson, as quoted by Rowe, as quoted by Paul Krugman (P. Krugman, 'Nick Rowe loses it', *New York Times,* 25 August 2010).

58. S. Schmitt-Grohe and M. Uribe, 'Liquidity Traps: An Interest Rate Based Exit Strategy', *NBER Working Paper,* 16514 (2010), at http://www.nber.org/papers/16514 [accessed 12 February 2014], p. 12.

59. P. W. Howitt, 'Interest Rate Control and Non-Convergence to Rational Expectations', *Journal of Political Economy,* 100:4 (August 1992), pp. 776–800.

60. Specifically, Howitt showed that the equilibrium time paths along which today's interest rate settings determine the future time path of inflation are unstable, in the sense that any disturbance to them, including of course an unanticipated change in the interest rate itself, would set up dynamics that take the economy away from, rather than back towards, its equilibrium path.

16 Cartelier, 'Endogenous Money in an Elementary Search Model: Intrinsic Properties versus Bootstrap'

1. Many thanks are due to Régis Breton and Randall Wright for their help and criticism. I am grateful also to Andrès Alvarez, Vincent Bignon, Richard Dutu, Bertrand Gobillard, Ryan Love and Stefania Vanacore for their helpful remarks on a preliminary version. The usual disclaimer applies.

2. See N. Kiyotaki and R. Wright, 'A Search-Theoretic Approach to Monetary Economics', *American Review,* 83 (1993), pp. 63–77.

3. In standard theory the quantity of coined gold is given by the equation of exchange, the price of gold (and therefore the value of money) being determined as for any other commodity through market equilibrium conditions (see, for example, J. Niehans, *The Theory of Money* (Baltimore, MD: The Johns Hopkins University Press, 1978), p. 140).

4. Tooke's interpretation of the gold standard may help the modern reader to grasp this point.

5. F. R. Velde, W. E. Weber and R. Wright, 'A Model of Commodity Money with Applications to Gresham's Law and the Debasement Puzzle', *Review of Economics Dynamics*, 2 (1999), pp. 291–323.

6. B. Peterson, 'Endogenous Liquidity, Currency Flows, and Currency Substitution' (Mimeo, 2001).

7. Y. Li, 'A Search Model of Money and Circulating Private Debt with Applications to Monetary Policy', *International Economic Review*, 12 (2001), pp. 925–46.

8. Kiyotaki and Wright, 'A Search-Theoretic Approach to Monetary Economics'.

9. Such an assumption rules out the possibility of 'melting' money. By symmetry with the gold standard, 'melting' money may be introduced by supposing a specific cost and a probability x of getting a consumption good from doing so. It seems, however, to be a very artificial question in our monetary system. Note that free disposal of money is not a relevant problem here since money is not imposed upon agents. In a sense, free disposal of money is a way of questioning the existence of money equivalent (but not complementary) to that of minting.

10. See Rupert et al. for more details ('Generalized Search-Theoretic Models of Monetary Exchange', *Journal of Monetary Economics*, 48 (2001), pp. 605–22). Only K models will be considered here without loss of generality.

11. For a comparison between symmetric mixed strategy equilibria and asymmetric pure strategy equilibria, see R. Wright, 'A Note on Asymmetric and Mixed Strategy Equilibria in the Search-Theoretic Model of Fiat Money', *Economic Theory*, 14 (1999), pp. 463–71.

12. It is worth noting that barter value is $x(u - c)/r$ and not $x(1 - M)(u - c)/r$ as in the Kiyotaki and Wright model.

13. In model S we have:
$$W(M^{ooo}) = 1/r[-(u - c)(1 - x)M^2 + (u - c)(1 - x)M + x(u - c)] \quad (11)$$
It turns out that $M^* = 1/2$ which does not depend on particular values of the parameters. The reason for that is straightforward. In an economy where nobody is crowded out of production by holding money, the best situation occurs when a money holder meets a non-money holder with the same probability as a non-money holder meets a money holder. In order to have M^* monetary authority must choose $s^* = [(u - c)(1 - x) - 2rc] / (1 + r)$.

17 Morvant-Roux and Servet, '*Digression* on the Relations between Anthropology and Economics on the Topic of "Primitive" Currencies: A Page in the History of Thought'

1. Outdated should here be understood as fundamental (J.-M. Servet, 'Compte-rendu de K. Polanyi, La subsistance de l'Homme. La place de l'économie dans l'histoire et dans la société', *Œconomia – History/Methodology/Philosophy*, 2:4 (December 2012), pp. 538–43).

2. Ibid.

3. P. Einzig, *Primitive Money in its Ethnological, Historical and Economic Aspects* (London: Eyre/Spottiswoode, 1949), p. v.

4. A. H. Quiggin, *A Survey of Primitive Money* (London: Methuen, 1949), p. 1.

5. Beccaria is known today as the first recipient of a dedicated chair in the new discipline that economics was at the time (J.-M. Servet, 'Possibilité et nécessité de pensées interdiscipli-

naires en temps de crise', *Journal of Interdisciplinary History of Ideas*, 1:2 (2012), pp. 3–7, at www.ojs.unito.it/index.php/jihi/article/download/179/198 [accessed 6 June 2014].)

6. J.-M. Servet, 'Les figures du troc du XVIe au XIXe siècle. Cahier AEH no. 12' (Thèse de 3e cycle Université Lyon 2, 1977); J.-M. Servet, 'Le troc primitif, un mythe fondateur d'une approche économiste de la monnaie', *Revue numismatique* (2001), pp. 15–32.; D. Graeber, *Debt: The First Five Thousand Years* (Brooklyn, NY: Melville House, 2011).

7. See G. Simmel, *The Philosophy of Money* (1907; London: Routledge, 1978).

8. J. Rivallain, *Echanges et monnaies en Afrique du XIVe au XIX siècle d'après les récits de voyageurs* (Paris and Lyon: Musée de l'Homme and Musée de l'Imprimerie et de la Banque, 1994).

9. S. Jevons, *Money and the Principles of Exchange* (1876).

10. E. G. Schwimmer, 'Cultural Consequences of a Volcanic Eruption Experienced by the Mount Lamington Orokaiva' (Department of Anthropology, Report 9, University of Oregon, 1969), p. 82, quoted by A. Iteanu, *La ronde des échanges. De la circulation aux valeurs chez Les Orokaiva* (London and Paris: Cambridge University Press/Ed. de la Maison des Sciences de l'Homme, 1983), p. 267.

11. Quiggin, *A Survey of Primitive Money*, p. 186.

12. F. Boas, *The Social Organization and the Secret Societies of the Kwakiutl Indians* (Washington, DC: Smithsonian Institution US Nat. Museum, 1897). See also the links already highlighted by John Locke between money and ownership. Money is what allows one to appropriate a good or service, to give up a property in order to convert it into another property, and to preserve this possibility of acquisition over time.

13. It would be interesting to deepen the analysis by using Justinian law in order to determine who in an exchange is the one who buys and who is the one that sells, reciprocity not being mandatory.

14. Servet, 'Compte-rendu de Karl Polanyi, La subsistance de l'Homme'; J.-P. Warnier, 'Unicité et pluralité paléomonétaire en Afrique centrale', Contribution au Séminaire La monnaie entre unicité et pluralité, ouvrage à paraître sous la direction de Jérôme Blanc etBruno Théret, Paris, CDC, 24 May 2013.

15. The work begins with a preliminary summary of the works of the seminar at the origin of this meeting, the work of which had been little disseminated.

16. See, for example, Graeber's reading.

17. B. Théret (ed.), *La monnaie dévoilée par ses crises* (Paris: Éditions de l'École des Hautes Etudes en Sciences Sociales, 2007), p. 20.

18. This is probably the reason why it was welcomed and debated by anthropologists and historians in *L'Homme* (2002, vol. 162, 2009, no. 190) and *Les Annales* (2000, vol. 6). C. Baroin, 'Testart Alain (dir.), Aux Origines de la monnaie', *Compte-rendus, Journal des Africanistes*, 73:1 (2003), p. 184 rightly remarks that A. Testart (ed.), *Aux Origines de la monnaie* (Paris: Errance, 2001) very surprisingly ignores the thesis of *La monnaie souveraine*. Reading this work would have certainly prevented taking a functional approach to currency and failing to understand the theoretical and historical link between credit and currency. All credit relationships by nature have a monetary dimension.

19. See the further development of this section of the text in the lectures delivered by Jacques Birouste for the preparation of the introduction of the Euro for the DG XXIV of the European Commission, and in France for the Ministry of Economic Affairs and Finance, the Caisse des Dépôts et Consignations, and for finance funds.

20. R. Boyer, 'Bruno Théret (Dir.), La monnaie dévoilée par ses crises, Éditions de l'EHESS, Paris, 2008', *Revue de la régulation [En ligne]*, 2nd semester, 3:4 (Autumn 2008), at http://regulation.revues.org/4813, p. 5 [accessed 6 June 2014]. when reviewing *La Monnaie dévoilée par ses crises*, a work which in some ways serves as a sequel to *La monnaie souveraine*, remarks that Bruno Théret mainly uses the different forms of trust from this initial theoretical tripod to analyse monetary crisis. The concepts of sovereignty, and

particularly of life debt, read as underdeveloped in his conclusion on modern currency, although his work on social protection and particularly retirement plans had led one to believe that he would use the concepts much more extensively.

21. If the contribution of *La monnaie souveraine* to economic anthropology and socio-economics could be reduced to this critique, the work would indeed be ill-fitted for differently understanding the monetary practices Karl Polanyi discusses.

22. J.-M. Servet, 'Monnaie: quand la dette occulte le partage', *Revue Française de Socio Economie*, 2:12 (2013), pp. 125–47.

23. B. Courbis, E. Froment and J.-M. Servet, 'A propos du concept de monnaie', *Cahier d'Economie politique*, 18 (1990), pp. 5–29; B. Courbis, E. Froment and J.-M. Servet, 'Enrichir l'économie politique de la monnaie par l'histoire', *Revue économique*, 42 (1991) pp. 315–38; J.-M. Servet, 'Genèse des formes et pratiques monétaires' (PhD dissertation, Université Lyon 2, 1981); J. Blanc, *Les monnaies parallèles* (Paris: L'Harmattan, 2001).

24. K. Polanyi, *The Livelihood of Man* (New York, San Francisco, CA, and London: Academic Press, 1977); K. Polanyi, *La subsistance de l'homme*, ed. B. Chavance (Paris, Le Seuil, 2011), p. 179; Servet, 'Compte-rendu de Karl Polanyi, La subsistance de l'Homme'; J.-M. Servet, *Les Monnaies du lien* (Lyon: PUL, 2012), pp. 315–17.

25. We can cite from the many works addressing this question, C. Barraud, 'De la résistance des mots. Propriété, possession, autorité dans des sociétés de l'Indo-Pacifique', in A. Iteanu (ed.), *La cohérence des sociétés* (Paris: Maison des Sciences de l'Homme, 2010), pp. 83 146 and the research she quotes (C. Hann (ed.), *Property Relations. Renewing the Anthropological Tradition* (Cambridge: Cambridge University Press, 1998)).

26. See Melanesian theory, the confusion such as the purchase of skin in Armstrong's view, which is a symbolic ceremony for John Liep; see the cited passage in the link of money (Servet, *Les Monnaies du lien*, pp. 314, 350).

27. S. Morvant-Roux, 'Processus d'appropriation des dispositifs de microfinance : un exemple en milieu rural mexicain' (Thèse de doctorat en sciences économiques, Université Lumière Lyon 2, 2006).

28. A. Bergeret, 'La quête d'autonomie des paysans mayas-q'eqchi' de Cahabón (Guatemala), 1944–2011. Trois perspectives sur les conflits de terre et les politiques de développement agricole', 2 vols (PhD dissertation, Université Sorbonne Nouvelle Paris 3, November 2012), p. 754.

29. Morvant-Roux, 'Processus d'appropriation des dispositifs de microfinance'.

30. O. Favereau, 'Développement et économie des conventions', in P. Hugon, G. Pourcet and S. Quiers-Valette (eds), *L'Afrique des incertitudes* (Paris: PUF/IEDES, 1995), p. 186.

31. Bergeret, 'La quête d'autonomie des paysans mayas-q'eqchi' de Cahabón (Guatemala), 1944–2011'.

32. F. Zanotelli, 'La circulación social de la deuda: códigos culturales y usura rural en Jalisco', in M. Villareal (ed.) *Antropología de la deuda, crédito, ahorro, fiado y prestado en las finanzas cotidianas* (Mexico: CIESAS, 2004).

33. J.-B. Greenberg, 'Medio Mileno de Credito entre los Mixes de Oaxaca', *Cuadernos del Sur*, 10 (2004), pp. 31–50.

34. J.-M. Servet, 'Le *Chicago Plan* revisité par les monnaies complémentaires, le microcrédit solidaire et les tontines', in B. Hours and P. Ould-Ahmed (eds), *Dette de qui, dette de quoi? Une économie anthropologique de la dette* (Paris: L'Harmattan, 2013), pp. 45–71.

35. Unlike the so-called 'natural' sciences, where patents conferring property rights can be made, knowledge in the social sciences and humanities is made freely available for use provided that the sources are correctly quoted. Such knowledge can thus be considered as a public good (its use does not diminish but rather increases its value).

36. E. Ostrom, *Understanding Institutional Diversity* (Princeton, NJ, and Oxford: Princeton University Press, 2005), pp. 23–7.

37. Servet, 'Possibilité et nécessité de pensées interdisciplinaires en temps de crise'.

18 Witztum, 'The Economics of Ethics and the Ethics of Economics in Adam Smith'

1. See, for instance, J. Evensky, 'The Two Voices of Adam Smith: Moral Philosopher and Social Critic', *History of Political Economy*, 19:3 (1987), pp. 447–68; J. Evensky, 'The Evolution of Adam Smith's Views of Political Economy', *History of Political Economy*, 21:1 (1989), pp. 123–45; J. Evensky, 'Ethics and the Classical Liberal Tradition in Economic', *History of Political Economy*, 24:1 (1992), pp. 61–77; S. Fleischacker, *A Third Concept of Liberty: Judgment and Freedom in Kant and Adam Smith* (Princeton, NJ: Princeton University Press, 1999); P. Force, *Self-Interest before Adam Smith: A Genealogy of Economic Science* (Cambridge: Cambridge University Press, 2003); C. L. Griswold, *Adam Smith and the Virtues of Enlightenment* (Cambridge: Cambridge University Press, 1999); S. J. Pack, *Capitalism as a Moral System: Adam Smith's Critique of the Free Market Economy* (London: Edward Elgar, 1991); G. Vivenza, *Adam Smith and the Classics: The Classical Heritage in Adam Smith's Thought* (Oxford: Oxford University Press, 2001) and J. Young, 'Natural Price and the Impartial Spectator: A New Perspective on Adam Smith as a Social Economist', *International Journal of Social Economics*, 12:6–7 (1985), pp. 118–21; J. Young, 'The Impartial Spectator and Natural Jurisprudence: An Interpretation of Adam Smith's Theory of the Natural Price', *History of Political Economy*, 18:3 (1986), pp. 365–82) to name a few.
2. J. Young, *Economics as a Moral Science: The Political Economy of Adam Smith* (Cheltenham: Edward Elgar, 1997).
3. See, for instance, a discussion of this in A. Witztum, 'Distributional Consideration in Smith's Concept of Economic Justice', *Economics and Philosophy*, 13 (1997), pp. 242–59.
4. *EPS*-HA, p. 45. As mentioned, *EPS* stands for the *Essays on Philosophical Subjects* and HA stands for the 'History of Astronomy', one of the works contained in it.
5. *EPS*-HA, pp. 33–105.
6. LRBL, p. 58.
7. Ibid.
8. Ibid., p. 139.
9. Ibid.
10. *EPS*-HA, pp. 33–105; 'History of Ancient Physics' [hereafter HAP], *EPS*, pp. 106–17; 'History of Ancient Logic and Metaphysics' [hereafter HALM], *EPS*, pp. 118–29.
11. *EPS*-HA, p. 48.
12. *EPS*-HAP, p. 106.
13. These characteristics are put forward in sections 1 and 2 in the 'History of Astronomy' (*EPS*-HA, pp. 34–7).
14. A discussion of this issue can be found in the general introduction, by Raphael and Skinner, to the *EPS* (p. 2). They also refer to Schumpeter.
15. *EPS*-HALM, pp. 118–20.
16. *EPS*-HA, pp. 38–9.
17. D. Hume, *A Treaties of Human Nature* (Oxford: Oxford University Press, 2007), p. 274.
18. *EPS*, p. 278.
19. In an 'empiricist' sense I should use the word 'Classification' rather than universals. But this is only a semantic difference in what concerns my purpose.
20. Why it is that I believe this to be the principle of the *WN* rather than 'self-interest' will be explained below. In any case, either this propensity or 'self-interest' will serve the purpose of what I have to say here.

21. In the Lectures on Jurisprudence (*LJ*) Smith argues that the real foundation of this propensity is the 'principle of persuasion' in human nature (*LJ*, pp. 493–4).
22. Which is, of course, part of his drive to be socially approved.
23. *TMS*, p. 185.
24. Again, all these points will be properly explored below. It is nevertheless important to present them here as they intend to give the sense of Smith's use of universals.
25. *LJ*, pp. 401–2.
26. Ibid., p. 493.
27. *WN*, pp. 65–6.
28. A different kind of argument in support of the 'labour theory of value' being approved by the 'impartial spectator' can be found in Young, 'The Impartial Spectator and Natural Jurisprudence'. It is also interesting to note that the idea that exchange should reflect labour ratios is not unrelated to Smith's discussion of property rights. In Smith's discussion of property rights in the Hunters's stage he says: 'All agree that it is a breach of property to break in on the chase of a wild beast which another has started, tho' some are of opinion that if another should wound the beast in its flight he is entitles to a share, as he rendered the taking it more easy on the whole' (*LJ*, pp. 459–60). Which means that the 'labour theory of value' is also somewhat hidden behind a right which is strongly related to conventions about social organization. These conventions are bound to be dependent on people's disposition towards others.
29. *TMS*, p. 9.
30. Ibid., p. 218.
31. Ibid., p. 9.
32. Ibid., p. 21.
33. Ibid., p. 44.
34. Ibid., p. 13.
35. Ibid., p. 18/67, my emphasis.
36. *LJ*, p. 401.
37. *TMS*, p. 185.
38. I assume here, quite crudely, that the composition of the two aspects in a person's character must add up to unity. Namely, a benevolent person employs 'sympathy' in 90 per cent of his judgements (or observations) of the others while only 10 per cent of such an activity is affected by utility. In 90 per cent of the cases the benevolent person will judge people by trying to put himself in their position. In 10 per cent of the cases he will judge them by the general impression that the system will have on him.
39. *TMS*, p. 185.
40. Ibid., p. 188.
41. Griswold, *Adam Smith and the Virtues if Enlightenment*, p. 261.
42. Already in J. Viner, 'Adam Smith and Laissez-faire', *Journal of Political Economy*, 35:2 (1927), pp. 198–232.
43. See, for example, J. R. Davis, 'Adam Smith on the Providential Reconciliation of Individual and Social Interests: Is Man Led by an Invisible Hand or Misled by a Sleight of Hand?', *History of Political Economy*, 22:2 (1990), pp. 341–52; Evensky, 'The Two Voices of Adam Smith'; 'The Evolution of Adam Smith's Views of Political Economy'; J. Evensky, 'Ethics and the Classical Liberal Tradition in Economic', *History of Political Economy*, 24:1 (1992), pp. 61–77; Pack, *Capitalism as a Moral System*; A. Witztum, 'A Study into Smith's Conception of the Human Character: Das Adam Smith Problem Revisited', *History of Political Economy*, 30:3 (1998), pp. 489–513; L. Montes, 'Das Adam Smith

Problem: Its Origins, the Stages of the Current Debate, and One Implication for our Understanding of Sympathy', *Journal of the History of Economic Thought*, 25:1 (2003), pp. 62–90 and Force, *Self-Interest before Adam Smith*.

44. N. Rosenberg, 'Adam Smith on the Division of Labour: Two Views of One?', *Economica*, 33 (1965), pp. 127–39; N. Rosenberg, 'Adam Smith and the Stock of Moral Capital', *History of Political Economy*, 22:1 (1990), pp. 1–118; E. G. West, 'Adam Smith's Two Views on the Division of Labour', *Economica*, 31 (1964), pp. 22–32; E. G. West, 'Adam Smith on the Cultural Effects of Specialisation: Splenetics versus Economics', *History of Political Economy*, 28:1 (1996), pp. 83–105.

45. P. H. Werhane, *Adam Smith and his Legacy for Modern Capitalism* (Oxford: Oxford University Press, 1991), p. 31.

46. Ibid., p. 20.

47. Evensky, 'The Two Voices of Adam Smith'.

48. J. Evensky, 'Adam Smith on the Human Foundation of a Successful Liberal Society', *History of Political Economy*, 25:3 (1993), pp. 395–412, on p. 396.

49. Witzum, 'A Study into Smith's Conception of the Human Character'.

50. This view is, of course, held by non-Smith specialists and the list is very long. See, for instance, J. M. Buchanan, 'The Justice of Natural Liberty', in F. R. Glahe (ed.), *Adam Smith and the Wealth of Nations: 1776–1976 Bicentennial Essays* (Boulder, CO: Colorado Associated University Press, 1978) and G. Stigler, *The Economist as a Preacher* (Chicago, IL: University of Chicago, 1982).

51. See, for instance, *TMS*, pp. 269–70.

52. See Werhane, *Adam Smith and his Legacy for Modern Capitalism*, p. 179.

53. In his *Theory of Justice* Rawls proposes to counter the often difficult-to-defend reign of Utilitarianism as the predominant moral theory. Utilitarianism is a teleological theory where the *right* is derived from the *good*. Rawls's attempt is deontological where, in broader terms, that which is *right* is determined independently from that which is *good* (see a discussion in J. Rawls, *A Theory of Justice* (Oxford: Oxford University Press, 1973), ch. 7).

54. Young, 'The Impartial Spectator and Natural Jurisprudence'.

55. See Witztum, 'Distributional Consideration in Smith's Concept of Economic Justice'; A. Witztum and J. Young, 'The Neglected Agent: Justice, Power and Distribution in Adam Smith', *History of Political Economy*, 38:3 (2006), pp. 437–71.

56. Aristotle, *Nicomachean Ethics*, trans. J. A. K. Thomson (Sydney: Allen & Unwin, 1953), pp. 176–7.

57. *TMS*, p. 168.

58. Ibid., p. 92.

59. As a matter of fact Smith's entire moral theory is based on the principle of 'propriety'. However, following his own structuring, I distinguish between propriety and merit although in both cases the measure of moral approval can be said to be propriety.

60. *TMS*, p. 18.

61. This is consistent with Smith's analysis of the three types of passions which rests in all humans; the social, unsocial and selfish (see *TMS*, pp. 34–42). This distinction is obviously based on the attitudes toward the others which is embedded in each type of sentiment.

62. Notice, however, that Smith's analysis is in the discrete form. Namely, there are no *degrees* of benevolence or malevolence.

63. With respect to Smith's analysis of action, the idea of the 'impartial spectator' seems to resemble the Kantian notion of the 'Universal test' (See I. Kant, *Ground Work of*

the Metaphysic of Morals (1785; New-York: Harper and Row, 1964), p. 88). Kant also explicitly uses an idea of the 'impartial spectator' in his *Reflection on Anthropology*. There, however, he describes the 'impartial spectator' as the observer who views things from the point of view of society without giving any account of *how* this spectator formulates society's point of view.

64. *TMS*, p. 92.
65. 'To the intention or affection of the heart, therefore, to the propriety or impropriety, to the beneficence or hurtfulness of the design, all praise or blame ... must ultimately belong' (ibid., p. 93).
66. Ibid., p. 96.
67. This knowledge, in Smith, probably means the action that would have been taken by someone who is not directly involved and, thus, whose judgement is not clouded by emotions.
68. The discussion of resentment and the general problem with unsocial sentiments can be found in *TMS*, pp. 34–8.
69. Here too we may find some resemblance to the Kantian idea of the 'universal test'. For the 'impartial spectator's' approval of sentiments we needed a universal test in the sense that all would have felt the same had they been in place of the subject of approbation. Here, however, we are concerned with action. The 'universal test' means to ask 'what if everyone acted in this way?' which is perhaps even closer to the Kantian idea and use of the Universal test.
70. *TMS*, p. 82.
71. Ibid., p. 86.
72. Ibid., p. 18.
73. Ibid., p. 67.
74. Obviously it is possible to consider situations where individuals behave differently, in other words, where they might feel resentment in spite of a beneficent outcome. All this is basically taken care of by the argument β of S^2. It will be up to the 'impartial spectator' to determine whether or not the particular circumstances of the person who is being acted upon allow a reversed respond from what an innocent observer might expect.
75. *TMS*, p. 69.
76. Ibid., pp. 71–2.
77. Ibid., pp. 85–6, my emphasis.
78. Ibid., p. 79.
79. Ibid., p. 80.
80. See also Witztum and Young (2006, section 5).
81. *TMS*, p. 81.
82. In Witztum and Young, 'The Neglected Agent', we show how politics interfered with the transmission of what would constitute justice in the eyes of an 'impartial spectator' onto law.
83. *TMS*, p. 96.
84. Ibid., p. 79.
85. 'The preservation and healthful state of the body seem to be the object which Nature first recommends to the care of every individual' (*TMS*, p. 212).
86. The logical foundations of such a view have been rigorously contested in Witztum, "A Study into Smith's Conception of the Human Character".

87. In *TMS*, on p. 96 Smith specifies what is required for moral evaluation. Someone feeling either gratitude or resentment is one of the conditions.
88. Viner, 'Adam Smith and Laissez-faire', pp. 198–232.
89. Young, 'Natural Price and the Impartial Spectator'; Young, 'The Impartial Spectator and Natural Jurisprudence'.
90. In our case we needed the wheat to serve as seeds as well as the food for the capitalist and labourer, during the period of production. By food to the people involved in the process of production, I mean the level of physical subsistence.
91. Note that we are examining the beneficence of the action, which is a dynamic concept, rather than the beneficence of the situation. Someone may feel grateful for what he has in comparison to what he might have had. Nevertheless, the action itself has not brought about any change in his conditions. There is no reason to suppose that as a result of a stationary state a person will attribute his position to actions which merely preserve what he has already been enjoying before.
92. I shall assume that when surplus prevails, no capitalist will reduce his labourer's wages below subsistence.
93. 'It is to no purpose that the proud and unfeeling landlord views his extensive fields, and without a thought for the wants of his bretherns in imagination consumes himself the whole harvest that grows upon them ... The capacity of his stomach bears no proportion to the immensity of his desires, and will receive no more than that of the meanest peasant. The rest he is obliged to distribute among those, who prepare in the nicest manner, that little which he himself makes use of ... The produce of the soil maintains at all times nearly that number of inhabitants which it is capable of maintaining. The rich only select from the heap what is most precious and agreeable. They consume little more than the poor ... They are led by an invisible hand to make nearly the same distribution of the necessaries of life, which would have been made, had the earth been divided into equal portions among all its inhabitants' (*TMS*, pp. 184–5).
94. By the action of production I also mean the productive labourer's remuneration. I refer to it as part of production because the subsistence of the productive labourer is part of the reproduction of the whole process. Obviously, the capitalist can share the surplus with his own labourer, and increase his wages above subsistence, but, as it might affect production (in terms of productivity) I shall not discuss it here. This sort of analysis must be carried out in a more complete model of Smith's economic system. For the moment, we may distinguish between the remuneration of the productive labour, as part of production, while, the unproductive labourer receives his remuneration in the process of the exchange of surplus.
95. In the previous case 20 workers produced 200 and now 100 'workers' produce the same quantity.
96. A discussion of whether there is symmetry in the rationality of agents can be found in Witztum, 'Natural Price and the Impartial Spectator'.
97. *WN*, p. 96.
98. Ibid., p. 87.
99. P. Samuelson, 'A Modern Theorist's Vindication of Adam Smith', *American Economic Review*, 67:1 (February 1977), pp. 42–9.

19 Livet, 'Why do Economists and Philosophers Resort to the History of their Discipline?'

1. G. Debreu and H. Scarf, 'A Limit Theorem on the Core of an Economy', *International Economic Review*, 4:3 (September 1963), pp. 235–46.

20 Picavet, 'Interest-Based Prediction and Mutual Expectations: Reflections on the Normative Value of Hobbesian Methodology'

1. This essay has its origins in the author's epistemological involvement in a Paris-based research project, NORMA. Support from regional research and education structure 'Hesam' and the Sorbonne Centre for Contemporary Philosophy (PhiCo) is gratefully acknowledged.

2. For an analysis of Hobbes's doctrine which takes economic knowledge into account, see especially P. Dockès, *Hobbes. Economie, terreur et politique* (Paris: Economica, 2008).

3. See P. Bridel, *Money and General Equilibrium Theory. From Walras to Pareto (1870–1923)* (Cheltenham: Edward Elgar, 1997) and P. Bridel and F. Mornati, 'De l'équilibre général comme "branche de la métaphysique"; ou de l'opinion de Pareto sur le projet walrasien', *Revue économique*, 60:4 (2009), pp. 869–90.

4. Quotations are from R. A. Dahl and C. E. Linblom, *Politics, Economics, and Welfare* (New York: Harper and Row, 1953, 2nd edn, Harper Torchbooks, 1963), p. 223).

5. See especially D. Schulthess, Réflexions sur la motivation économique', in R. Damien and A. Tosel, *L'action collective. Coordination, conseil, planification*, Annales littéraires de l'université de Franche-Comté, AGON series, 12:653 (Besançon: Presses de l'université de Franche-Comté, 1998), pp. 247–57. Dahl and Linblom, by the way, fairly acknowledge that '[o]ne of the difficulties of maintaining a price system is that the "self interest" role is one that individuals do not play in their noneconomic activities and do not find entirely congenial when they must assume it in the market' (ibid.).

6. A. O. Hirschman, *The Passions and the Interests: Political Arguments for Capitalism before its Triumph* (Princeton, NJ: Princeton University Press, 1977).

7. P. Bridel, 'Passions et intérêts revisités: la suppression des "sentiments" est-elle à l'origine de l'économie politique?', *Revue européenne des sciences sociales* (special issue 'Rationalités et émotions: un examen critique', 14th interdisciplinary colloquium of research group 'Raison et Rationalités'), 47:144 (2009), pp. 135–50.

8. In the phrase of P. Bridel, ibid.

9. Ibid.

10. On this, see Y.-C. Zarka, *Philosophie et politique à l'âge classique* (Paris: Presses universitaires de France, 1998), p. 129ff.

11. F. Cunningham, 'Homo democraticus: pour une perspective anti-échangiste', in R. Damien and A. Tosel (eds), *L'action collective. Coordination, conseil, planification,* Annales littéraires de l'université de Franche-Comté, AGON series, 12:653 (Besançon: Presses de l'université de Franche-Comté, 2008), pp. 403–21.

12. Aristotle, *Magna Moralia*, I.xxxiii.27ff.

13. Aristotle, *Nicomachean Ethics*, V.

14. *Nicomachean Ethics*, V.11.1136b.

15. Ibid.

16. Hobbes, *Leviathan*, ch. XIV.

17. Ibid., ch. XV.

18. Cicero, *De officiis*, X.32.

19. They are unlike conventions as understood by D. Lewis in this respect; see D. K. Lewis, *Convention: A Philosophical Study* (Cambridge, MA: Harvard University Press, 1969).

20. Following the path-breaking contributions of Jack Hirschleifer and others; see J. Hirshleifer, 'Theorizing About Conflict', in K. Hartley and T. Sandler (eds), *The Handbook of Defense Economics*, 1 (Amsterdam: Elsevier Science, 1995).

21. As I have extensively argued elsewhere: see E. Picavet, *La Revendication des droits* (Paris: Classiques Garnier, 2011).

22. This has been argued in C. Guibet Lafaye and E. Picavet, 'Do We Gain from Exchange at all? On Some Lessons to be Drawn from Rousseau', in R. Ege and H. Igersheim (eds), *Freedom and Happiness in Economic Thought and Philosophy* (London and New York: Routledge, 2011), ch. 15, pp. 243–55, and in E. Picavet and C. Guibet Lafaye, 'Les limites du droit de contracter', in G. Lewkowicz and M. Xifaras (eds), *Repenser le contrat* (Paris: Dalloz, 2009), pp. 135–55.

23. A. Gibbard, 'A Pareto-Consistent Libertarian Claim', *Journal of Economic Theory*, 7 (1974), pp. 595–605.

24. See C. Seidl, 'Foundations and Implications of Rights', in K. J. Arrow, A. K. Sen and K. Suzumura (eds), *Social Choice Re-Examined*, 2 (New York: St Martin's Press, 1997), pp. 53–77.

21 Besomi, 'Tempests of the Business World: Weather Metaphors for Crises in the Nineteenth Century'

1. I am grateful to an anonymous referee for suggestions on a preliminary version of this chapter. The usual caveats apply.

2. [Anon.], 'A Patch of Blue', *Le Follet: Journal du Grand Monde, Fashion, Polite Literature, Beaux Arts &c. &c.*, 324 (1 September 1873), p. 68.

3. The poor state of the theory of crises in Britain is well illustrated by the entries on the subject in Palgrave's *Dictionary of Political Economy*. For a discussion see P. Bridel, 'Of the "Old" Palgrave Entries on Crises', in D. Besomi, *Crises and Cycles in Economic Dictionaries and Encyclopedias* (London: Routledge, 2011), pp. 332–42. The situation was better in France and especially in Germany.

4. The medical analogy is examined in D. Besomi, 'Disease of the Body Politick: A Metaphor for Crises in the History of Nineteenth-Century Economics', *Journal of the History of Economic Thought*, 33: 1 (March 2011), pp. 67–118, while other metaphors will be the subject of further studies.

5. Tornadoes and cyclones, for instance, are evoked in the United States but only rarely in Britain.

6. These two approaches, to be described in detail in the text, do not exhaust the list of interpretations of crises held during the nineteenth century. Some writers maintained that the nature of business is intrinsically oscillating under the continuous changes affecting demand and the conditions of production, which sometimes give rise to major fluctuations if accidentally co-occurring, or if amplified by institutional frictions. Other writers maintained instead that crises should be understood as part of a cycle. For a general exposition of the approaches to crises see D. Besomi, '"Periodic Crises": Clément

Juglar between Theories of Crises and Theories of Business Cycles', *Research in the History of Economic Thought and Methodology*, 28A (2010), pp. 169–283, on pp. 225–39.

7. The latter term was used to describe crises up to the 1837 panic, typically focusing on the consequences rather than on the event itself: see D. Besomi, 'Naming Crises: A Note on Semantics and Chronology', in D. Besomi (ed.), *Crises and Cycles in Economic Dictionaries and Encyclopedias* (London: Routledge, 2011), pp. 54–132, on pp. 59–60.

8. [Anon.], 'Commercial Matters', *New-York Daily Tribune*, 27 January 1858, p. 8.

9. I. S. Homans, 'Sugar', in I. S. Homans (ed.), *A Cyclopedia of Commerce and Commercial Navigation* (New York: Harper & Brothers, 1859), pp. 1766–78.

10. M. J. Lamb, *Wall Street in History* (New York: Funk & Wagnalls, 1883), p. 75.

11. J. West, 'Redemption work at Euroa', *Australasian*, 1511 (16 March 1895), p. 488.

12. [Anon.], 'The History of Yankee Jim', *Watchman and Southron* (3 October 1882), p. [1].

13. G. L. Craik and C. MacFarlane, *The Pictorial History of England during the Reign of George the Third: Being a History of the People as well as a History of the Kingdom*, vol. 3 (London: Knight, 1843), p. 645.

14. J. G. Gibbons, *The Banks of New York, their Dealers, the Clearing House, and the Panic of 1857. With a Financial Chart* (New York: Appleton, 1858), p. 346. The passage was cited by other writers: D. Green, *Facts and Suggestions Relative to Finance and Currency, Addressed to the President of the Confederate States* (Augusta, GA: J. T. Paterson & Co, 1864), p. 15, H. C. Carey, *The Way to Outdo England without Fighting her. Letters to the Hon. Schuyler Colfax ... on the Paper, the Iron, the Farmer's, the Railroad, and the Currency Questions* (Philadelphia, PA: Henry Carey Baird, 1865), p. 149, and – in a slightly modified and unacknowledged form – Lamb, *Wall Street in History*, p. 75.

15. [Anon.], 'Effects of the Panic', *Nashville Union and American* (2 February 1859), p. [1].

16. [Anon.], 'The Financial Question', *St. Paul Daily Globe* (Christmas Number, 25 December 1887), p. 28.

17. É. de Laveleye, *Le marché monétaire et ses crises depuis cinquante ans* (Paris: Guillaumin, 1865), p. 6, my translation.

18. E. T. Freedley, *Opportunities for Industry and the Safe Investment of Capital; or, A Thousand Chances to Make Money. By a Retired Merchant* (Philadelphia, PA: J. B. Lippincott & Co, 1859), p. 12.

19. See Besomi, 'Disease of the Body Politick'.

20. J. A. Blanqui, 'Crise commerciale', *Encyclopédie des gents du monde*, 7 (Paris: Librairie de Treuttel et Würtz, 1836), pp. 257–9, on p. 257, my translation.

21. G. de Molinari, 'La crise financière et commerciale en Angleterre', *Journal des Économistes*, first series, 17 (June 1847), pp. 274–84, on p. 274, my translation.

22. [Anon.], 'Business of 1873. Careful and Candid Review by a Good Hand – The Outlook Generally Cheerful', *Memphis Daily Appeal* (6 January 1874), p. [2].

23. [Anon.], 'After the Storm: The Financial Flurry Over, the Markets Settling Down to Regular Business ...', *Daily Globe* (3 March 1881), p. [2].

24. [Anon.], 'The Late Panic', *National Republican* (10 October 1873), p. [2].

25. [Anon.], 'The Financial Situation', *Anderson Intelligencer* (2 October 1873), p. [2].

26. A. de Broglie, 'De la question vinicole, et de l'urgence de la résoudre dans la crise actuelle', *Journal des Économistes*, 22:96 (15 March 1849), pp. 363–73, on p. 372, my translation.

27. Besomi, 'Diseases of the Body Politik'.

28. United States, House of Representatives, Committee to Investigate Bank of the United States, *Bank of the United States* ([n.p.]: [n.p.]. 1832), p. 434.

29. [P. Colquhoun], *Reflections on the Causes which have Produced the Present Distress in Commercial Credit: with Suggestions Relative to the Means of Remedying the Evil in Future and of Granting Immediate and Effectual Relief to the Merchants and Manufacturers* (London: J. Sewell, J. Debrett, J. Downes, 1793), p. 10.

30. T. Joplin, *An Examination of the Report of the Joint Stock Bank Committee: ... to which is Added an Account of the Late Pressure in the Money Market, and Embarrassment of the Northern and Central Bank of England*, 3rd edn (London: J. Ridgway and Sons, 1837), p. 67.

31. [Anon.], 'Symptoms of the Coming Crash', *New York Herald* (22 May 1857), p. 4, col. E.

32. [Anon.], 'Financial Storm Gathering in Montreal', *Daily Globe* (9 June 1879), p. [1].

33. Cited in [Anon.], 'Finance and Commerce – The Storm', *Daily Phoenix* (19 February 1867), p. [2].

34. Cited in [Anon.], 'A Panic', *Keowee Courier* (2 June 1866), p. [2].

35. [Anon.], 'Money Market', *Capital and Labour*, 97 (29 December 1875), pp. 794–5.

36. P. S. Du Pont de Nemours, *Sur la Banque de France, les causes de la crise qu'elle a éprouvé ... avec une théorie des banques: Rapport fait à la Chambre de commerce par une commission spéciale, à Paris, en 1806* (Paris: Delance, 1806; Reprinted London: J. Hatchard, 1811), p. 65, my translation.

37. J. Laing, *The Theory of Business* (London: Longmans, Green & Co., 1867), p. 237.

38. [Anon.], 'The Monetary Crisis', *Victoria Herald, a Magazine for the People*, 1 (1865), pp. 141–4, on p. 141.

39. Boston Merchant, 'From a Boston Correspondent', *Niles' Weekly Register*, 16:588 (21 December 1822), pp. 243–5, on p. 244.

40. T., 'The Rate of Exchange', *Niles' Weekly Register*, 23:591 (11 January 1823), pp. 29–30, on p. 29.

41. Boston Merchant, 'Rate of Exchange, &c.' *Niles' Weekly Register*, 23:595 (18 February 1823), pp. 356–8, on p. 358.

42. *The Parliamentary Debates*, 14 (London: Hansard, 2 February to 17 March 1826), 1826, p. 1305.

43. [Anon.], 'Meeting of Merchants at the Mansion House, upon the Subject of the Existing Distress in the City', *Observer* (18 December 1825), p. 2.

44. C. Stebbins et al., 'Assembly No 74, January 22, 1835. Report Submitted by the Bank Commissioners', *Documents of the Assembly of the State of New York, 58th Session* (Albany: Croswell, 1835), p. 8.

45. [Anon.], 'The Moral of the Crisis', *United States Magazine and Democratic Review*, 1 (October 1837), pp. 108–22, on p. 109.

46. [Anon.], 'Weekly Epitome of News', *Friend of India*, issue 679 (6 January 1848), pp. 4–8, on p. 5.

47. M. B. Begbie, *Partnership 'en commandite', or, Partnership with Limited Liabilities (according to the Commercial Practice of the Continent of Europe, and the United States of America) for the Employment of Capital, the Circulation of Wages, and the Revival of our Home and Colonial Trade* (London: E. Wilson, 1848), p. 5.

48. Overstone, however, may have had this in mind when he wrote that 'So long as human nature remains what it is, and hope springs eternal in the human breast, speculations will occasionally occur, and bring with them their attendant train of alternate periods of excitement and depression. Those who expect to find, even in the most perfect management of the circulation, the magic power to secure perpetual ease and undisturbed steadiness in commercial affairs, are like the alchymists in search of their mysterious

secret; and the discovery, if made, would prove equally useless. Storms and tempests are not more certain and inevitable in the material world, than are the periodical convulsions of commercial affairs; and they both answer similarly useful purposes' (S. J. Loyd (Overstone), *Remarks on the Management of the Circulation and on the Condition and Conduct of the Bank of England and of the Country Issuers, during the Year 1839* (London: P. Richardson, 1840), p. 104). He did not, however, specify which purpose was served by storms and crises.

49. [Anon.], 'The United States', *Morning Chronicle*, 28320 (28 September 1857).

50. [Anon.], 'Financial Crime in England', *New York Observer and Chronicle*, 35:47 (19 November 1857), p. 373.

51. [Anon.], 'The Commercial Panic', *Harbinger* (December 1857), p. 197.

52. D. M. Evans, *The History of Commercial Crisis, 1857–58 and the Stock Exchange Panic of 1859* (London: Groombridge, 1859), p. 121.

53. S. Jubb, *The History of the Shoddy-Trade: Its Rise, Progress, and Present Position* (London: Houlston and Wright; Manchester: John Heywood; Batley: J. Fearnsides, 1860), p. 115.

54. K. Marx, *Zur Kritik der politischen Oekonomie* (Berlin: Duncker, 1859); English trans. *A Contribution to the Critique of Political Economy* (Moscow: Progress Publishers), at Marxists.org, 1999 [accessed 13 February 2014], ch. 4, n. C.

55. W. Roscher, *Ansichten der Volkswirthschaft aus dem geschichtlichen Standpunkte* (Leipzig and Heidelberg: C. F. Winter'sche Verlagshandlung, 1861), p. 361, my translation.

56. M. Wirth, *Geschichte der Handelskrisen* (Frankfurt: Sauerländer, 1858), p. 461, my translation.

57. Ibid., 1890, 4th edn of 1858, p. 16.

58. M. I. Tugan-Baranovsky, *Studien zur Theorie und Geschichte der Handelskrisen in England* (Jena: Fisher, 1901), p. 415, my translation. German enlarged translation of the second Russian edition, 1900, of *Promyshlennye krizisy v sovremennoi Anglii, ikh prichiny i blizhaishie vliyaniya na narodnuyu zhizn* (St Petersburg, 1894).

59. M. I. Tugan-Baranovsky, '[Economic crises]' (in Russian), in F. A. Brockhaus and I. A. Efron (publishers), *Enciklopedicheskij slovar'* [Encyclopaedic dictionary] (St Petersburg: Efron, 1890–1907, 1895), p. 744, English trans. in F. Allisson, 'From Crises to Cycles: Tugan-Baranovsky and the Brockhaus–Efron (1895–1915)', in D. Besomi (ed.), *Crises and Cycles in Economic Dictionaries and Encyclopedias* (London: Routledge, 2011), pp. 343–60, on p. 348.

60. [Anon.], 'The Funds', *Observer* (11 January 1858), p. 4.

61. Cited in [Anon.], 'Prospects of Trade', *Manchester Guardian* (11 February 1868), p. 6.

62. [Anon.], 'A Financial Storm Brings Disaster to a Chosen Few, but its Very Violence will Soon Clear the Atmosphere ...', *Pittsburg Dispatch* (12 November 1890), p. [1].

63. [Anon.], 'The Business Outlook: A Sensible View of the Situation', *Burlington Weekly Free Press* (24 August 1883), p. 2.

64. [J. W. Michie], 'The History and Principles of Banking. Chapter Fifteenth: The Panics of 1857 and of 1866', *Bankers' Magazine and Statistical Register*, 7:12 (June 1873), pp. 937–67, on p. 942.

65. [Anon.], 'When Shall We have Good Times again?', *New-York Daily Tribune* (23 February 1858), p. 4.

66. A fourth view held in the nineteenth century interpreted crises as the result of the accidental superimposing of small fluctuations, occasionally summing up their effects rather than cancelling them out. This perspective relied on different metaphors, such as the waves of the sea or the oscillation of a pendulum: not the mathematical one to which theorists

of the cycle referred, but the actual pendulum subject to friction and tending towards a position of rest unless further disturbed. This view was consistently held by a minority of writers throughout the century, and was carried over through the twentieth century. Arguably, real business cycle theories are the modern incarnation of this approach.

67. F. Louçã, 'Intriguing Pendula: Founding Metaphors in the Analysis of Economic Fluctuations', *Cambridge Journal of Economics*, 25:11 (January 2001), pp. 25–55, and F. Louçã, *The Years of High Econometrics: A Short History of the Generation that Reinvented Economics* (London and New York: Routledge, 2007).

68. Expressions such as financial, commercial or economic storm(s) or tempest(s), or other similar expressions implicitly comparing economic and meteorological phenomena, recur frequently in the literature, both popular or of a higher standard. In JSTOR, for instance, the string 'financial storm' is cited 100 times in full text between 1869 and 2010, Econlit lists 15 results (in titles and abstracts) between 1993 and January 2012; at the other end of the spectrum, Newspaperarchive.com lists 4,521 articles containing the expression published between 1825 and 2011, and 2,158 more using it in the plural (1840–2011), almost 90 of which in the third millennium. Inserting expressions such as a 'economic storm' or 'financial tempest' in Google n-grams gives a visual image of the remarkable resilience of such terms in the literature.

22 Akhabbar, 'Samuelson and the Non-Substitution Theorem: Some Methodological Remarks'

1. P. A. Samuelson, 'Economists and the History of Ideas', *American Economic Review*, 52:1 (1962), pp. 1–18, on p. 10.

2. A first version of this essay was presented in July 2006 at the *Meetings of the International Input-Output Association* at Sendaï (Japan).

3. In philosophy of science, operationism is synonymous to operationalism. See P. W. Bridgman, *The Logic of Modern Physics* (New York: MacMillan, 1927) and W. Bridgman, 'Operational Analysis', *Philosophy of Science*, 5:2 (1938), pp. 114–31 and R. Carnap, 'Testability and Meaning', *Philosophy of Science*, 3:4 (1936), pp. 419–71, and R. Carnap, 'Testability and Meaning Continued', *Philosophy of Science*, 4:1 (1937), pp. 1–40.

4. P. Bridel, 'Homo oeconomicus: Rerum cognoscere causas? ou du principe de rationalité comme instrument de connaissance en théorie économique', *Revue européenne des sciences sociales*, 37:113 (1999), pp. 149–67; P. Bridel, 'Le rôle de la mesure dans la construction de l'objet théorique et comment l'objet théorique devient ... mesure', *Revue européenne des sciences sociales*, special issue (2007), pp. 143–52.

5. Bridel, "Le rôle de la mesure dans la construction de l'objet théorique et comment l'objet théorique devient ... mesure'.

6. P. Bridel and C. Salvat, 'Reason and Sentiments: Review of Emma Rothschild's *Economic Sentiments: Adam Smith, Condorcet and the Enlightenment*', *European Journal of the History of Economic Thought*, 11 (2004), pp. 131–45.

7. All the analyses developed here belong to the static and atemporal framework.

8. N. Salvadori, 'Non-Substitutions Theorems', in J. Eatwell, M. Milgate and P. Newman (eds), *The New Palgrave, A Dictionary of Economics* (London: Palgrave MacMillan, 1987).

9. See W. Leontief, 'Interrelations of Prices, Output, Savings and Investment', *Review of Economic Statistics*, 19:3 (1937), pp. 109–32; W. Leontief, 'Output, Employment, Con-

sumption, and Investment', *Quarterly Journal of Economics*, 58:2 (1944), pp. 290–314; W. Leontief, 'Structural Matrices of National Economies', *Econometrica*, 17: Supplement: *Proceedings of the International Statistical Conferences* (1949), pp. 273–82.

10. L. Walras, *Éléments d'économie politique pure, OEC*, vol. 7 (Paris: Economica, 1986).

11. See K. Arrow, 'Alternative Proof of the Substitution Theorem for Leontief Models in the General Case', in T. C. Koopmans (ed.), *Activity Analysis* (Chicago, IL: Cowles Commission for Research in Economics, Monograph 13, 1951), pp. 155–64; G. Dantzig, 'Programming of Interdependent Activities: II Mathematical Model', *Econometrica*, 17:3/4 (1949), pp. 200–11; G. Dantzig and K. W. Marshall, 'Programming of Interdependent Activities: I General Discussion', *Econometrica*, 17:3/4 (1949), pp. 193–9; T. C. Koopmans, 'Introduction', in Koopmans (ed.), *Activity Analysis*, pp. 1–12 and P. A. Samuelson, 'Abstract of a Theorem Concerning Substitutability in Open Leontief Models', in Koopmans (ed.), *Activity Analysis*, pp. 142–6.

12. P. A. Samuelson, 'A Modern Treatment of the Ricardian Economy: I. The Pricing of Goods and of Labor and Land Services', *Quarterly Journal of Economics*, 73:1 (1959), pp. 1–35, on p. 18.

13. A. d' Autume, 'Le rôle intime de la demande dans la production jointe', in R. Arena and J.-L. Ravix (eds), *Sraffa, trente ans après* (Paris: Presses Universitaires de France and CNRS-Université de Nice, 1990), p. 246.

14. See K. Arrow, *General Equilibrium*, Collected Papers of K. J. Arrow, vol. 2 (Oxford: Blackwell, 1983); L. McKenzie, *Classical General Equilibrium Theory* (Cambridge, MA: MIT Press, 2002); R. Weintraub, 'On the Existence of a Competitive Equilibrium: 1930–1954', *Journal of Economic Literature*, 21:1 (1983), pp. 1–39.

15. See M. Blaug, *The Methodology of Economics* (Cambridge: Cambridge University Press, 1980) and J. Cohen, 'Samuelson's Operationalist-Descriptivist Thesis', *Journal of Economic Methodology*, 2:1 (1995), pp. 53–78.

16. See P. A. Samuelson, 'The Empirical Implications of Utility Analysis', *Econometrica*, 6:4 (1938), pp. 344–56; P. A. Samuelson, 'A Note on the Pure Theory of Consumer's Behavior', *Economica*, 5:17 (1938), pp. 61–71; P. A. Samuelson, 'The Numerical Representation of Ordered Classifications and the Concept of Utility', *Review of Economic Studies*, 6:1 (1938), pp. 65–70; P. A. Samuelson, 'How *Foundations* Came to Be', *Journal of Economic Literature*, 36:3 (1998), pp. 1375–86.

17. Samuelson's demonstration was first presented in 1949 at the 'Linear Programming' conference organized at Chicago by the Cowles Commission under the direction of Tjalling C. Koopmans. Samuelson's proof was published in 1951 in the Cowles Commission monograph *Activity Analysis*, edited by Koopmans, which gathered a selection of the linear programming conference papers. Afterwards, Samuelson published a series of papers to develop the theoretical consequences of his theorem (see P. A. Samuelson, 'Wages and Interest: A Modern Dissection of Marxian Economic Models', *American Economic Review*, 47:6 (1957), pp. 884–912; P. A. Samuelson, 'A Modern Treatment of the Ricardian Economy: I. The Pricing of Goods and of Labor and Land Services', *Quarterly Journal of Economics*, 73:1 (1959), pp. 1–35, P. A. Samuelson, 'A Modern Treatment of the Ricardian Economy II: Capital and Interest Aspects of the Pricing Process', *Quarterly Journal of Economics*, 73:2 (1959), pp. 217–31). Samuelson also expanded the NST to an intertemporal framework (P. A. Samuelson, 'A New Theorem on Non-Substitution', in J. Akerman and H. Hegelan (eds), *Money, Growth and Methodology* (Lund: CWK Gleerup, 1961)).

18. Samuelson, 'Abstract of a Theorem Concerning Substitutability in Open Leontief Models'.

19. The non-substitution theorem was first named 'substitution theorem'. For an interesting interpretation of this title change, see L. L. Pasinetti, 'On "Non-Substitution" in Production Models', *Cambridge Journal of Economics*, 1:4 (1977), pp. 389–94.
20. That is to say, to allow multiple primary factors and joints production.
21. Samuelson, 'Abstract of a Theorem Concerning Substitutability in Open Leontief Models', pp. 142–3.
22. Ibid., p. 143.
23. Samuelson defined this in 'The Empirical Implications of Utility Analysis'.
24. H. Schultz, 'Rational Economics', *American Economic Review*, 18:4 (1928), pp. 643–8.
25. Ibid., p. 647.
26. Bridgman, *The Logic of Modern Physics*.
27. Also called operationism or operational analysis; see Bridgman, 'Operational Analysis'.
28. In Bridgman's words: 'We mean by any concept nothing more than a set of operations; the concept is *synonymous* with the corresponding set of operations' (Bridgman, *The Logic of Modern Physics*, p. 5, our emphasis). In economics, Schultz noticed: 'As long as our fundamental concepts are not synonymous with corresponding sets of operations (and, hence, do not admit of the possibility of experimental verification), it is wrong to speak of economics as an experimental science' (Schultz, 'Rational Economics', p. 647).
29. Behaviourism is particularly influenced by operationism.
30. Carnap, a German citizen, emigrated in 1935 from Czechoslovakia to the United States. Though Carnap was a professor of philosophy at the University of Chicago (1936–1952), he spent the years 1939–41 at Harvard as a visiting professor. From 1934 on, Carnap has been close to the Harvard professor Willard Van Orman Quine. The works from Carnap on operationism we refer to are his 'Testability and Meaning', *Philosophy of Science*, 3:4 (1936), pp. 419–71 and 'Testability and Meaning – Continued', *Philosophy of Science*, 4:1 (1937), pp. 1–40.
31. We consider in what follows that Carnap's version of operationism is the general one (and not Bridgman's).
32. Samuelson, 'The Empirical Implications of Utility Analysis'.
33. W. Leontief, 'Structural Matrices of National Economies', *Econometrica*, 17: Supplement: *Proceedings of the International Statistical Conferences* (1949), pp. 273–82.
34. Samuelson, 'The Empirical Implications of Utility Analysis', p. 344, our emphasis.
35. P. A. Samuelson, *Foundations of Economic Analysis* (Cambridge, MA: Harvard University Press, 1947).
36. Samuelson, 'The Empirical Implications of Utility Analysis', p. 344, our emphasis.
37. Ibid., p. 345, our emphasis.
38. Samuelson, 'How *Foundations* Came to Be', p. 1380.
39. Samuelson, 'A Note on the Pure Theory of Consumers' Behavior', p. 61.
40. See M. Blaug, *The Methodology of Economics* (Cambridge: Cambridge University Press, 1980); Cohen, 'Samuelson's Operationalist-Descriptivist Thesis'; P. Mongin, 'Les préférences révélées et la formation de la théorie du consommateur', *Revue Économique*, 51:5 (2000), p. 1125–52; A. Akhabbar, 'La fonction de production et la signification opérationnelle des théories: une alternative à la méthode des tests?', in A. Berthoud, B. Delmas and T. Demals (eds), *Y a-t-il des lois en économie?* (Lille: Presses Universitaires du Septentrion, 2007), pp. 371–89; A. Akhabbar, 'Leontief et l'économie comme science empirique: la signification opérationnelle des lois', *Économies et Sociétés*, série PE, 39 (2007), pp. 1745–88; and W. Hands, 'Introspection, Revealed Preference, and Neo-

classical Economics: A Critical Response to Don Ross on the Robbins–Samuelson Argument Pattern', *Journal of the History of Economic Thought*, 30:4 (2008), pp. 453–78.

41. Blaug, *The Methodology of Economics*.

42. Karl Popper is considered to be the father of falsificationism. This methodology doesn't permit one to find the empirical meaning of a concept but only to say if it is a scientific one and if it is not yet falsified.

43. Cohen, 'Samuelson's Operationalist-Descriptivist Thesis'.

44. Popper, *The Logic of Scientific Discovery* (1959).

45. Cohen, 'Samuelson's Operationalist-Descriptivist Thesis', p. 66.

46. Samuelson, 'A Note on the Pure Theory of Consumer's Behavior', p. 62.

47. About the epistemological status of the optimization process, see P. A. Samuelson, 'Maximum Principle in Analytical Economics', *American Economic Review*, 62:3 (1972), pp. 249–62.

48. Samuelson's methodology is understandable as a methodology concerning the validity of assumptions. Here, he replaced an unoperational assumption (a function of utility based on introspection) by an operational assumption (a utility function based on market data).

49. As noticed above, in contrast to Bridgman's operationism, Samuelson's methodology is not based on a meaning criterion.

50. T. C. Koopmans, 'Measurement without Theory', *Review of Economic Statistics*, 29:3 (1947), pp. 161–72.

23 Coenen-Huther, '*Homo Oeconomicus* and *Homo Sociologicus* as Contrasted Ideal-Types'

1. The expression 'ideal-type' belongs currently to the standard vocabulary of sociology. Its use should not be construed as the preamble of a specific Weberian approach; see on this J. Coenen-Huther, 'Le type idéal comme instrument de la recherche sociologique', *Revue française de sociologie*, 44:3 (2003), pp. 531–47.

2. R. Dahrendorf, 'Homo Sociologicus. On the History, Significance, and Limits of the Category of Social Role', translated from German in *Essays in the Theory of Society* (London: Routledge and Kegan Paul, 1968), p. 19.

3. Ibid.

4. P. Bridel, 'Cumulativité des connaissances et science économique', *Revue européenne des sciences sociales*, 131 (2005), pp. 63–79, on p. 67.

5. E. Durkheim, *La science sociale et l'action*, ed. and intro. J.-C. Filloux (1970; Paris: Puf, 1987). See also my *Comprendre Durkheim* ((Paris: Armand Colin, 2010).

6. P. Berger, *Pyramids of Sacrifice: Political Ethics and Social Change* (Harmondsworth: Penguin, 1977), p. 223.

7. Ibid.

8. For some of my experiences with kibbutz life in the seventies, see my book *Observation participante et théorie sociologique* (Paris: L'Harmattan, 1995).

9. M. Mauss, 'Essai sur le don', *Sociologie et anthropologie* (1925; Paris: Puf, 1950, 1983).

10. Berger, *Pyramids of Sacrifice*, pp. 214–15.

11. R. Boudon, *L'idéologie ou l'origine des idées reçues* (Paris: Fayard, 1986), pp. 11–16.

12. M. Mamdani, *The Myth of Population Control* (New York: Monthly Review Press, 1972).

13. K. Bradsher, 'Betting it all on Education', *International Herald Tribune*, 18 February 2013.

14. On rationality and coherence, see my recent book *Les paradoxes de la sociologie* (Paris: L'Harmattan, 2012). See also J. Coenen-Huther, 'The Postulate of Rationality between Universality and Diversity', in M. Cherkaoui and P. Hamilton (eds), *Raymond Boudon: A Life in Sociology*, Vol. 2 (Oxford: The Bardwell Press, 2009), pp. 111–24 and J. Coenen-Huther, 'Les sociologues et le postulat de rationalité', *Revue européenne des sciences sociales*, 145 (2010), pp. 5–16.

15. B. Keller, 'A Protégé of Mandela, Back in the Power Circle', *International Herald Tribune*, 26–7 January 2013.

24 Gaudin, 'Social Sciences in Front of "Broad Questions"'

1.   G. Bachelard, *La formation de l'esprit scientifique* (Paris: Vrin, 1971).

2.   Association for Interdisciplinary Studies (1979).

3.   K. Popper, *La connaissance objective* (Paris: Flammarion, 1999).

4.   A. Negri and M. Hardt, *Empire* (Paris: Exils, 2000).

5.   See for example the Center for the Study of Interdisciplinarity at Texas University.

6.   J.-P. Gaudin, *L'action publique* (Paris: Presses de Sciences Po/Dalloz, 2004).

7.   See bounded rationality.

8.   P. Schmitter, F. Scharpf and G. Marks, *Governance in the European Union* (London: Sage, 1996).

9.   G. Majone, 'The Rise of the Regulatory State in Europe', *West European Politics*, 14:3 (1994), pp. 77–101.

10. A. Benz and R. Eberlein, 'The Europeanization of Regional Policy Patterns of Multilevel Governance', *Journal of European Public Policy*, 6:2 (1999), pp. 329–48.

11. G. Marks and L. Hooghe, *Multilevel Governance and European Integration* (Oxford: Rowman, 2001); T. Risse and A. Boerzel, *Governance without State* (New York: Colombia University Press, 2004).

12. See Schmitter, Scharpf and Marks, *Governance in the European Union*.

13. J.-P. Worms, 'Le préfet et ses notables', *Sociologie du travail*, 3 (1966), pp. 246–75.

14. P. Grémion, *Le pouvoir périphérique* (Paris: Le Seuil, 1976).

25 Busino, 'Sociology: An Infirm Science?'

1.   R. Boudon, *La crise de la sociologie* (Geneva: Droz, 1971), pp. 9–47.

2.   Montesquieu, *L'Esprit des Lois* (1748).

3.   R. Aron, *Les étapes de la pensée sociologique. Montesquieu – Comte – Marx – Tocqueville – Durkheim – Pareto – Weber* (Paris: Gallimard, 1967), pp. 27–76.

4.   A. Ferguson, *The Origin of the Distinction of Rank* (1771).

5.   H. H. Jogland, *Ursprünge und Grundladen der Soziologie bei Adam Fergusson* (Berlin: Dunker und Humblot, 1959).

6.   See W. C. Lehmann, *John Millar of Glasgow, 1735–1801: His Life and Thought and his Contribution to Sociological Analysis* (London: Cambridge University Press, 1960).

7.   W. Lepenies, 'Sur la guerre des sciences et des Belles-Lettres à partir du 18è siècle', *MSH Informations*, 54 (1988), pp. 6–17; W. Lepenies, 'Contributions à une histoire des rapports entre la sociologie et la philosophie', *Actes de la recherche en sciences sociales*, 47–8 (June 1983), pp. 37–44.

8.   A detailed reconstruction of the formation of this problematic has been made by P. Dockès, *L'espace dans la pensée économique. Du XVIe au XVIIIe siècles* (Paris: Flam-

marion, 1969). On the history of social physics, see P. Sorokin, *Contemporary Sociological Theories* (New York: Harper and Row, 1966).

9. P. F. Lazarsfeld, *Philosophie des sciences sociales* (Paris: Gallimard, 1970), pp. 78–102.

10. G. Busino, 'Marx et la sociologie', in G. Seel (ed.), *Actes du Colloque de Neuchâtel, le 16 et 17 décembre 1983. Marx et les sciences humaines* (Lausanne: l'Age d'Homme, 1987), pp. 138–150.

11. W. Lepenies, *Die Drei Kulturen. Soziologie zwischen Literatur und Wissenschaft* (Munich: Carl Hanser Verlag, 1985).

12. W. Lepenies (ed.), *Geschichte der Soziologie. Studien zur kognitiven, sozialen und historischen Identität einer Disziplin* (Frankfurt: Suhrkamp, 1981).

13. R. Brown, *A Poetic for Sociology: Toward a Logic Discovery for the Human Sciences* (New York: Cambridge University Press, 1977).

14. D. N. Levine, *The Flight from Ambiguity* (Chicago, IL: Chicago University Press, 1985).

15. D. C. Phillips, *Holistic Thought in Social Science* (Stanford, CA: Stanford University Press, 1985).

16. T. Parsons, *Societies. Evolutionnary and Comparative Perspectives* (Englewood Cliffs, NJ: Prentice-Hall, 1966).

17. J. Lopreato, *Human Nature and Biocultural Evolution* (Boston, MA: Allen and Unwin, 1984) as well as the sections of the *Revue européenne des sciences sociales*, 23:69 (1985) and 23:73 (1986).

18. G. Busino, 'Raymond Aron et la sociologie', *L'Année sociologique*, 36 (1986), pp. 291–315.

19. I developed this point in G. Busino, 'Sociology in Crisis', *Diogenes,* 135 (July–September 1986), pp. 79–92.

20. The emptiness of this affirmation has been proved by J. Monnerot, *Les faits sociaux ne sont pas des choses*, 6th edn (Paris: Gallimard, 1946).

21. See on this subject the brilliant pages of S. Moscovici, *La machine à faire des Dieux. Sociologie et psychologie* (Paris: Fayard, 1988).

22. Parsons, *The Social System* (1951).

23. G. Busino, 'La théorie et le fait', *Cahiers internationaux de sociologie*, 71:28 (July–December 1981), pp. 309–19.

24. P. Sorokin, *Fads and Foibles in Modern Sociology and Related Sciences* (Chicago, IL: Regnery, 1956).

25. I have fully analysed this problematic in G. Busino, 'De quelques apports de l'histoire à la sociologie et de la sociologie à l'histoire', *Revue européenne des sciences sociales*, 11:30 (1973), pp. 91–122.

26. A. Inkeles, *What is Sociology?* (Englewood Cliffs: Prentice Hall, 1964), p. 21.

27. G. Busino, 'Le passage des sociétés traditionnelles aux sociétés industrielles. Quelques réflexions pour un débat', *Bulletin de M.A.U.S.S.*, 1:17 (March 1986), pp. 45–69.

28. P. Abrams, 'History, Sociology, Historical Sociology', *Past and Present*, 87 (1980), pp. 3–16 as well as the article by G. Noirel, 'Pour une approche subjective du social', *Annales* (November–December 1989), pp. 1435–59. See also the works of T. Skocpol, *Theory and Method in Historical Sociology* (Cambridge: Cambridge University Press, 1983); T. Skocpol, *States and Social Revolutions* (Cambridge: Cambridge University Press, 1979).

29. G. S. Becker, *The Economic Approach to Human Behaviour* (Chicago, IL: Chicago University Press, 1976), p. 205.

30. Ibid., p. 14.

31. See L. J. D. Wacquant and C. J. Calhoun, 'Intérêt, Rationalité et Culture. A propos d'un récent débat sur la théorie de l'action', *Actes de la recherche en sciences sociales*, 78 (June

1989), pp. 41–60 and especially J. S. Coleman, *Foundation of Social Theory* (Cambridge, MA: Harvard University Press, 1990).

32. R. Boudon, 'L'individualisme méthodologique', in *Encyclopedia Universalis. Symposium Les enjeux* (Paris: Encyclopédie universelle, 1988), pp. 644–7; R. Boudon, 'Individualisme et Holisme: un débat méthodologique fondamental', in H. Mendras and M. Verret (eds), *Les champs de la sociologie française* (Paris: A. Colin, 1988), pp. 31–45.

33. See H. Schwartz and J. Jacobs, *Qualitative Sociology: A Method to the Madness* (New York: Free Press, 1979) as well as J.-B. Grize, *Logique et langage* (Paris: Ophrys, 1990).

34. J. Freund, *Philosophie Philosophique* (Paris: Ed. de la Découverte, 1990), esp. pp. 312–17.

26 Ingrao, 'Imaginative Intelligence: Cognition in the Visual Arts versus Rationality in Economics'

1. H. Gardner, *Frames of Mind: The Theory of Multiple Intelligences* (1993; New York: Basic Books, 2011).

2. 'The rationality assumption consists of two components: first individuals are assumed to form, on average, correct beliefs about events in their environment and about other people's behaviour; second, given their beliefs, individuals choose those actions that best satisfy their preferences' (C. F. Camerer and E. Fehr, 'When Does "Economic Man" Dominate Social Behavior?', *Science*, 311:6 (January 2006), pp. 47–52, on p. 47).

3. G. Gigerenzer and D. G. Goldstein, 'Reasoning the Fast and Frugal Way: Models of Bounded Rationality', *Psychological Review*, 103:4 (1996), pp. 650–69.

4. T. Raffaelli, 'Marshall on Mind and Society: Neurophysiologic Models Applied to Industrial and Business Organisation', *European Journal of the History of Economic Thought*, 8:2 (June 2001), pp. 208–29; T. Raffaelli, *Marshall's Evolutionary Economics*, Studies in the History of Economics, vol. 59 (New York and London: Routledge, 2003).

5. J. A. Schumpeter, *The Theory of Economic Development: An Inquiry into Profits, Capital, Credit, Interest, and the Business Cycle* (1934; New York: Oxford University Press, 1961), ch. 2, pp. 83–4. 'This is so because all knowledge and habit once acquired becomes as firmly rooted in ourselves as a railway embankment in the earth ... Everything we think, feel, or do often enough becomes automatic and our conscious life is unburdened by it' (ibid., p. 84).

6. F. A. Hayek, *The Sensory Order: An Inquiry into the Foundations of Theoretical Psychology* (London: Routledge, 1952); F. A. Hayek, 'Notes on the Evolution of Rules of Conduct', in F. A. Hayek, *Studies in Philosophy, Politics and Economics* (1967; London: Routledge and Kegan Paul, 1978), pp. 66–81.

7. P. M. Todd and G. Gigerenzer, 'Bounding Rationality to the World', *Psychological Review*, 103:24 (2003), pp. 143–65, on p. 148.

8. F. Knight, *Risk, Uncertainty, and Profit* (Boston, MA, and New York: Houghton Mifflin Co, The Riverside Press, 1921); O. Morgenstern, 'Vollkommene Voraussicht und wirtschaftliches Gleichgewicht', *Zeitschrift für Nationalökonomie*, 6:3 (1935), pp. 337–57. English translation: 'Perfect Foresight and Economic Equilibrium', in *Selected Economic Writings of Oskar Morgenstern* (New York: New York University Press, 1976), pp. 169–83; F. A. Hayek, 'Economics and Knowledge', *Economica*, 4 (1937 [1948]), pp. 33–54, in F. A. Hayek, *Individualism and Economic Order*, pp. 33–56 (Chicago, IL: University of Chicago Press, 1948); J. M. Keynes, 'The General Theory of Employment', *Quarterly Journal of Economics*, 51 (February 1937), in *The Collected Writings of John Maynard Keynes*, 30 vols (London: Macmillan 1973), vol. 14, pp. 109–23.

9. M. Augier and K. Kreiner, 'Rationality, Imagination and Intelligence: Some Boundaries in Human Decision-Making', *Industrial and Corporate Change*, 9:4 (2000), pp. 659–81; M. Klaes and E. M. Sent, 'A Conceptual History of the Emergence of Bounded Rationality', *History of Political Economy*, 37 (2005), pp. 27–59; S. Fiori, 'Forms of Bounded Rationality: The Reception and Redefinition of Herbert A. Simon's Perspective', *Review of Political Economy*, 23:4 (2011), pp. 587–612; Y.-F. Kao and K V. Velupillai, 'Origins and Pioneers of Behavioural Economics', *Interdisciplinary Journal of Economics and Business Law*, 1:3 (2012), pp. 47–73; Y.-F. Kao and K V. Velupillai, 'Behavioural Economics: Classical and Modern', *European Journal for the History of Economic Thought*, forthcoming (2014), published online 26 September 2013 at www.tandfonline.com.

10. Kao and Velupillai distinguish 'Classical' and 'Modern' behavioural economics to oppose Simon's vision of problem solving, based on procedural rationality and satisficing, to the literature in behavioural economics that adopts best optimization techniques as the reference model of perfect rationality. They argue that Simon's procedural rationality encompasses optimization as a special case (Kao and Velupillai, 'Origins and Pioneers of Behavioural Economics'; Kao and Velupillai, 'Behavioural Economics').

11. A. M. Turing, 'Computing Machinery and Intelligence', *Mind*, 49 (1950), pp. 433–60.

12. In his critique of substantive rationality in neoclassical economics, Simon wrote that psychology, as opposed to economics, is concerned 'with both the rational and the irrational aspects' of behaviour (H. A. Simon, 'Rationality in Psychology and Economics', *Journal of Business*, 59:4 (1986), pp. 209–24, on p. 209). He mentioned 'nonrational processes (e.g. motivations, emotions and sensory stimuli)' as influences on the focus of attention and the definition of the situation by the problem solver (ibid., p. 210). In his definition of bounded rationality, Simon highlights the normative aspects of bounded rationality, that is, the relatively efficient procedures to reach satisficing goals in the environment the problem solver is facing, given the human limits in time, computational capacity and informational resources.

13. 'If individuals exhibit, however, systematically biased beliefs about external events or other people's behavior or if they systematically deviate from the action that best satisfy their preferences, we speak of bounded rationality' (Camerer and Fehr, 'When Does "Economic Man" Dominate Social Behavior?', p. 47).

14. 'In the past 25 years, this stronghold [the perfect rationality approach] came under attack by proponents of the heuristics and biases program, who concluded that human inference is systematically biased and error prone, suggesting that the laws of inference are quick-and-dirty heuristics and not the laws of probability (D. Kahneman, P. Slovic and A. Tversky (eds), *Judgement under Uncertainty: Heuristsics and Biases* (Cambridge: Cambridge University Press, 1982)). This second perspective appears diametrically opposed to the classical rationality of the Enlightenment, but this appearance is misleading. It has retained the normative kernel of the classical view. For example, a discrepancy between the dictates of classical rationality and actual reasoning is what defines a *reasoning error* in this programme. Both views accept the laws of probability and statistics as normative, but they disagree about whether humans stand up to these norms'(Gigerenzer and Goldstein, 'Reasoning the Fast and Frugal Way', p. 650).

15. Biases are systematic errors in intuitive judgement, which recur predictably in given circumstances.

16. D. Kahneman, 'Maps of Bounded Rationality: Psychology for Behavioral Economics', *American Economic Review*, 93:5 (December 2003), pp. 1449–75, on p. 1469.

17. 'The guiding ideas are (i) that most judgements and most choices are made intuitively; (ii) that the rules that govern intuition are generally similar to the rules of perception. Accordingly, the discussion of the rules of intuitive judgements and choices will rely extensively on visual analogies' (ibid., p. 1450).

18. Ibid., p. 1452.

19. Ibid., pp. 1452ff.

20. Ibid., p. 1454.

21. The analogy is, by contrast, with the assumption of reference-independent final utility in expected utility maximization.

22. Kahneman, 'Maps of Bounded Rationality', pp. 1450, 1453, 1467, 1469.

23. D. Kahneman, *Thinking, Fast and Slow* (New York: Farrar, Straus & Giroux, 2011).

24. This is the good reason why, in the eighteenth century, enlightened scholars recommended the universal instruction of children in primary education, a result which is far from being achieved in the contemporary world and included among the Millennium Development Goals.

25. F. A. Hayek, 'Individualism: True and False', in B. Caldwell (ed.), *Studies on the Abuse and Decline of Reason: Texts and Documents,* vol. 13, *The Collected Works of F. A. Hayek* (1946; London: Routledge, 2010), pp. 46–76. 'The fundamental assumption, here as elsewhere, is the unlimited variety of human gifts and skills and the consequent ignorance of any single individual of most of what is known to all the other members of society taken together. Or, to put this fundamental contention differently, human Reason, with a capital R, does not exist in the singular, as given or available to any particular person, as the rationalist approach seems to assume, but must be conceived as an interpersonal process in which anyone's contribution is tested and corrected by others' (ibid., p. 60). In Hayek's view of free competition, diverse capabilities and differential access to local information are the source of opportunities and innovation in market economies, more than at the origin of market imperfections (F. A. Hayek, 'Economics and Knowledge', *Economica*, 4 (1937), pp. 33–54, in F. A. Hayek, *Individualism and Economic Order*, pp. 33–56 (Chicago, IL: University of Chicago Press, 1948); F. A. Hayek, 'Competition as a Discovery Procedure', in F. A. Hayek, *New Studies in Philosophy, Politics, Economics and the History of Ideas* (1978; London: Routledge, 1990), pp. 179–90).

26. G. Steiner, 'Ten (Possible) Reasons for the Sadness of Thought', *Salmagundi*, 146–7 (Spring–Summer 2005), pp. 3–32.

27. Both George Shackle and James March underlined the role of imagination in building personal identity (Augier and Kreiner, 'Rationality, Imagination and Intelligence'; R. Patalano, *La mente economica. Immagini e comportamenti di mercato* (Bari: Laterza, 2005)). The subject has a long history in philosophy and human sciences.

28. Faithful to the artificial intelligence programme, Simon argued that problem solving that would be regarded as 'creative' if reached by human beings 'can be produced by computer programs that use weak methods to search very selectively in unfamiliar problem domains and that are able, with the help of such methods, to detect interesting laws in data and to invent new interesting concepts' (H. A. Simon, 'Discovery, Invention and Development: Human Creative Thinking', *Proceedings National Academy of Science*, 80 (1983), pp. 4569–71, on p. 4570). The assertion is clearly not substantiated by the history of natural sciences, also for the obvious reason that the attribution of meaning to concepts is a task that only the human mind performs. Simon pretended that 'scientific discovery can be understood as a natural phenomenon and that it follows laws already

made familiar by other research in cognitive psychology' (ibid., p. 4571). An ample philosophical debate deals with this controversial issue.

29. On the history of the creative borrowing involving the images of Achilles, Meleager
and Christ, see M. L. Catoni et al., *Tre figure. Achille, Meleagro e Cristo* (Milan: Feltrinelli, 2013).

30. K. Clark, *The Nude: A Study in Ideal Form* (1956; Princeton, NJ: Princeton University
Press, 1984).

31. K. Clark, *Landscape into Art* (London: John Murray, 1949).

32. R. Patalano devoted a well-argued book to imagination in economics (R. Patalano, *La
mente economica. Immagini e comportamenti di mercato* (Bari: Laterza, 2005)).

33. J. Mokyr, *The Lever of Riches: Technological Creativity and Economic Progress* (New York:
Oxford University Press, 1990).

34. R. L. Gregory and P. Heard, 'Giocare con gli occhi', in *Inganni ad Arte. Meraviglie del
trompe-l'oeil dall'antichità al contemporaneo* (Florence: Mandragora, 2009), pp. 299–
305, on pp. 299–300.

35. In his book *The Mind's Eye* the neurologist Oliver Sacks narrates stories of people who
suffered losses of visual or other sensorial abilities, including his own experience of losing
sight on one side, and explores the complex links between the conscious mind and sensorial perceptions (O. Sacks, *The Mind's Eye* (New York: Knopf, 2010)).

36. Gregory and Heard, 'Giocare con gli occhi', p. 303.

37. 'La prima intenzione del pittore è fare che una superficie piana si dimostri un corpo rile-
vato e spiccato da esso piano' [The first objective of a painter is to make a simple flat
surface appear like a relievo, and some of its parts detached from the ground] (L. da
Vinci, *A Treatise on Painting*, trans. J. F. Rigaud (*c.* 1498, London: J. B. Nichols and Son,
1835), p. 136).

38. 'La cosa bianca si dimostrerà più bianca se sarà in campo più oscuro, e si dimostrerà più
oscura se sarà in campo più bianco ... Delle cose d'ugual chiarezza, quella si dimostrerà di
minor chiarezza, la quale sarà veduta in campo di maggior bianchezza; e quella parrà più
bianca, che campeggerà in campo più oscuro; e l'incarnata parrà pallida in campo rosso, e
la pallida parrà rosseggiante essendo veduta in campo giallo, e similmente i colori saranno
giudicati quello che non sono mediante i campi che li circondano' [Anything white will
appear whiter, by being opposed to a dark ground: and, on the contrary, darker, upon a
light ground ... Of two objects equally light, one will appear less so if seen upon a whiter
ground; and, on the contrary, it will appear a great deal lighter if upon a space of a darker
shade. So flesh colour will appear pale upon a red ground, and a pale colour will appear
redder upon a yellow ground. In short, colours will appear what they are not, according
to the ground which surrounds them] (Ibid., pp. 117, 145).

39. E. H. Gombrich, *Shadows: The Depiction of Cast Shadows in Western Art* (London:
National Gallery Publications Ltd, 1995), p. 43.

40. Kahneman, 'Maps of Bounded Rationality', pp. 1452ff.

41. Ibid., p. 1454.

42. J. Poirier, *Artnica* (1997).

43. A. Pinotti, *Estetica della Pittura* (Bologna: Il Mulino, 2007).

44. R. Wollheim, *Painting as an Art* (Princeton, NJ: Princeton University Press, 1987), p.
45.

45. Ibid., p. 46.

46. Ibid., p. 47. It is a plain experience to whoever approaches too close to the surface of a painting; the fascination of the image is lost, and only strokes or rough stains of colour are visible.
47. R. Wollheim, *On Drawing an Object* (1965; London: University College, 1967), pp. 72–3.
48. E. H. Gombrich, *Art and Illusion: A Study in the Psychology of Pictorial Representation* (Washington, DC: Trustees of the National Gallery of Art, 1959); Wollheim, *On Drawing an Object*. In *Art and Illusion*, Gombrich denied the possibility of twofoldness. He examined the image that may be read either as a duck or as rabbit, arguing that the visual decoding is alternatively the duck or the rabbit (Gombrich, *Art and Illusion*; Wollheim, *On Drawing an Object*, p. 360, n. 6).
49. C. Cappelletto, *Neuroestetica. L'arte del cervello* (Bari: Laterza, 2009). Ample literature deals with the neuronal basis of the empathic reaction to images based on mirror neurons.
50. J. Ruskin, *The Elements of Drawing* (1857; New York: Dover, 1971), pp. 81ff.
51. Gombrich, *Shadows*.
52. A. Giusti (ed.), *Inganni ad Arte. Meraviglie del trompe-l'oeil dall'antichità al contemporaneo* (Florence: Mandragora, 2009).
53. Pinotti, *Estetica della Pittura*, pp. 38–40.
54. S. Alpers, *The Art of Describing: Dutch Art in the Seventeenth Century* (Chicago, IL: University of Chicago Press, 1983). On the use of optical instruments by painters, the controversy continues and opinions are not concordant.
55. Clark, *The Nude*, p. 8.
56. Pinotti, *Estetica della Pittura*, pp. 35–6.
57. T. Pericoli, *Robinson Crusoe di Daniel Defoe* (Milan: Adelphi, 2007), pp. 153ff.
58. T. Pericoli, *L'anima del volto* (Milan: Bompiani, 2005), pp. 63–4.
59. The intended effect of the cappella San Severo was to create wonder ('meraviglia').
60. L. Benevolo, *Introduzione all'architettura* (Bari: Laterza, 1990), pp. 25ff.
61. www.illusionworks.com [accessed 1 March 2014].
62. *Art of Illusion* is an open source software programme that creates effects of 3D visual illusion on screen (www.ArtofIllusion.org [accessed 1 March 2014]). The images are more or less incisive depending on the artist's inner world and innovative style. Many images of illusion art are built just for fun or for experimental purposes.
63. A. Seckel, *Masters of Deception: Escher, Dalí, and other Artists of Optical Illusion* (New York: Sterling Publications, 2004).
64. The compelling perceptive illusion of a *trompe-l'oeil* painting requires 'context dependence', such as the real size of portrayed objects, the nature of the frame, the environment in which it is visible (M. Milman, 'Esiste il "vero" *trompe l'oeil* ?', in A. Giusti (ed.), *Inganni ad Arte. Meraviglie del trompe-l'oeil dall'antichità al contemporaneo* (Florence: Mandragora, 2009), pp. 21–32, on pp. 21–2).
65. Ibid., p. 21.
66. Benevolo, *Introduzione all'architettura*, pp. 18–19, 168ff.

27 Tortajada, 'Realism and Reality: The Arguments of Cinema'

1. Text translated by Franck Le Gac.
2. This is apparent in a recent publication, D. Andrew and H. Joubert-Laurencin (eds), *Opening Bazin: Postwar Film Theory and Its Afterlife* (Oxford and New York: Oxford University Press, 2011). See also D. Andrew, *André Bazin* (1978; Oxford and New York: Oxford University Press, 2013).

3. A. Bazin, *What is Cinema?*, trans. H. Gray, 2 vols (1967; Berkeley, CA: University of California Press, 2005).

4. Laurent Le Forestier's work (2010) attempts to reintegrate Bazin within this discursive network. See L. Le Forestier, 'La Transformation Bazin ou Pour une histoire de la critique sans critique', *1895*, 62 (December 2010), pp. 9–27.

5. Jean Desternes authored several articles in La Revue du cinéma between 1946 and 1948. He occasionally collaborated to *Cahiers du cinéma* in 1954, reporting on the Venice Film Festival (issues 39 and 40). Antoine de Baecque refers to him as one of the 'progressive dandies' in his overview of the journal's editorial make-up, together with Jacques Doniol-Valcroze, Pierre Kast and Lo Duca. A. de Baecque, *Cahiers du cinéma. Histoire d'une revue, vol. 1, 1951–1959* (Paris: Cahiers du cinéma, 1991), p. 295.

6. J. Desternes, 'Débat sur le réalisme', *La revue du cinéma*, 18 October 1948, p. 49.

7. Ibid., pp. 49–50.

8. Ibid., p. 50.

9. Still, it is not rare to find the term 'verisimilitude' in the discursive space on realism, but what matters here is to outline the historical limit of the concept.

10. Desternes, 'Débat sur le réalisme', p. 50. Emphasis mine.

11. Ibid., pp. 50–1. Emphasis mine.

12. I am thinking of Flaubert's work in *Madame Bovary*, for instance, where the issue of who sees, knows or speaks is so central. See S. Kracauer, *Theory of Film: The Redemption of Physical Reality* (1960; Princeton, NJ: Princeton University Press, 1997) with an introduction by Miriam Bratu Hansen.

13. In *Dissemination*, Jacques Derrida writes: 'it is, to speak in a post-Cartesian manner, the copy inside me, the representation of the thing through thought, the ideality – for a subject – of what is'. In this case, Derrida adds, 'the relation of imitation and the value of adequation [between who imitates and what is imitated] remain intact since it is still necessary to imitate, represent, or "illustrate" the idea' (J. Derrida, *Dissemination*, trans. B. Johnson (Chicago, IL: University of Chicago Press, 1981), pp. 194–5).

14. See the quotation referenced in n. 11, above.

15. This was the case of Jacques Doniol-Valcroze, for instance, as he substituted the notion of 'film bearing witness' for this term (see J. Doniol-Valcroze, 'Le film témoin', *La revue du cinéma*, 4 January 1947, pp. 58–65).

16. Barkan wrote regularly in *Europe*, but also in the 'Images de la vie' [Images of life] department of *L'Écran français* and in *Action*. Besides his activity as a film critic, he authored several novels. For more detail, see the entry devoted to him in M. Ciment and J. Zimmer (eds), *La critique de cinéma en France. Histoire, anthologie, dictionnaire* (Paris: Ramsay, 1997), p. 283.

17. R. Barkan, 'Chronique du cinéma. L'exemple du "Point du jour"', *Europe*, 27:43 (July 1949), p. 133.

18. Ibid., p. 136.

19. Ibid., p. 133.

20. Ibid., p. 134.

21. The metaphor of the windowpane could be added: 'While superbly recreating outdoor and indoor settings, André Bac's exceptional talent in photography gives us the impression of a windowpane behind which we see the doings of people in the mining village' (Barkan, 'Chronique du cinéma. L'exemple du "Point du jour"', p. 138) This analysis of reflection does not express the range of representational approaches developed in relation to Marxist theory. The Brechtian 'demonstration' or Althusser's proposition of a

'materialist theatre' conflict with the idea of representation as reflection. See Bertolt Brecht's writings on theatre, in particular B. Brecht, *The Messingkauf Dialogues [1939–1955]*, trans. J. Willet (London: Methuen, 1965); and L. Althusser, 'The Piccolo Teatro: Bertolazzi and Brecht. Notes on a Materialist Theatre', in *For Marx [1965]*, trans. B. Brewster (1969; London: Verso, [1969] 2005), pp. 129–52.

22. 'However, how important it is for the camera to turn into a witness of this moving phenomenon that is the emergence of a nation in the midst of the twentieth century'. The quotation can be found in (R. Barkan, 'Chronique du cinéma. L'arme du réalisme dans le combat pour le progrès', *Europe*, 27:40 (April 1949), p. 136).

23. 'More than any other art, cinema needs to draw its themes from this prodigious material ceaselessly changing that is reality – or risk wilting' (ibid., p. 137).

24. Barkan, 'Chronique du cinéma. L'exemple du "Point du jour"', p. 136.

25. Barkan, 'Chronique du cinéma. L'arme du réalisme dans le combat pour le progrès', p. 137.

26. I am also thinking of the other type of projection, that of the camera obscura, and its analysis by Sarah Kofman in relation to Karl Marx, ideology and the question of reflection. See S. Kofman, *Camera Obscura. Of Ideology*, trans. W. Straw (1973; London: The Athlone Press, 1998).

27. L. Hjelmslev, *Prolegomena to a Theory of Language* (Madison, WI: University of Wisconsin Press, 1961).

28. Barkan, 'Chronique du cinéma. L'exemple du "Point du jour"', p. 138.

29. A. Bazin, 'For a Realist Aesthetic', in *French Cinema of the Occupation and Resistance: The Birth of a Critical Aesthetic*, trans. S. Hochman (New York: Ungar, 1982), p. 37. The text originally appeared in *Information universitaire*, 6 (November 1943).

30. The definition of Italian neorealism sparked debates which opposed, to put it briefly, those who adhered to a 'stylistic' definition and those who approached the films according to the discourse of social, committed critique. On the relation with Aristarco, see D. Wehrli, 'Bazin/Aristarco. Une relation en montage alterné', *1895*, 67 (Sumer 2012), pp. 63–93.

31. A. Bazin, 'On Realism', in *French Cinema of the Occupation and Resistance: The Birth of a Critical Aesthetic*, pp. 70–2. The text originally appeared in *Information universitaire*, 15 (April 1944).

32. 'A. Bazin, 'The Myth of Total Cinema (1944–1958)', in Bazin, *What Is Cinema?*, vol. 1, p. 22. The text originally appeared in *Critique*, 6 (November 1946).

33. A. Bazin, 'Ontology of the Photographic Image (1945–1958)', in Bazin, *What Is Cinema?*, vol. 1, p. 12. The text first appeared in G. Diehl, *Les Problèmes de la peinture* (Bordeaux: Confluences, 1945). I will mention differences between versions, with the exception of changes in grammatical agreement or punctuation.

34. This Bazin calls 'technical realism': 'Let us, however, begin by distinguishing the technical 'realism' of the image from the 'realism' of the plastic or dramatic content. Thus *Les Visiteurs du soir* is no less 'realistic' in the first sense of the word than Le Corbeau, since both these works are cast in the objectivity of photographic matter; but the marvellous and the fantastic of Carné's is in opposition to the 'realistic' observation of Clouzot's' (Bazin, 'On Realism', p. 71).

35. Bazin, 'Ontology of the Photographic Image', p. 13.

36. Ibid., p. 15.

37. Ibid., p. 12. This text also appears as a note in the 1945 version – where it directly bears on the notion of 'ontology' of the image, however (Diehl, *Les Problèmes de la peinture*, p. 408). In 'Ontology of the Photographic Image' Bazin also refers to the Holy Shroud of

Turin, which 'combines the features alike of relic and photograph' (Bazin, 'Ontology of the Photographic Image', p. 14).

38. 'Montage interdit' ('The Virtues and Limitations of Montage') goes over this at length. See Bazin, *What Is Cinema?*, vol. 2. The piece originally appeared in *Cahiers du cinéma*, 65 (December 1956).

39. Bazin, 'Ontology of the Photographic Image', pp. 14–15, emphasis mine. The 1945 version is slightly different here: 'Viewed in this perspective, cinema appears as the culmination of the object – the limited photograph – in time', insisting all the more on the objectification of the image (Diehl, *Les Problèmes de la peinture*, p. 409). In his 1944 article, the figure was that of the fossil: 'Film, on the contrary, remains by its very nature anchored in the moment of its birth. What is conserved in the layer of film gelatin is only fossilized time' (Bazin, 'On Realism', p. 71).

40. Bazin, 'Ontology of the Photographic Image', p. 14. See also H. Bergson, *Matter and Memory* (1896; New York: Zone Books, 1990), ch. 1.

41. Bazin, 'Ontology of the Photographic Image', p. 14, emphasis mine.

42. Ibid., pp. 15–16. There is the participation of cinema in the existence of reality evoked by Francesco Casetti in his *Theories of Cinema 1945–1995* (Austin, TX: University of Texas Press, 1999), p. 32.

43. Bazin, 'Ontology of the Photographic Image', p. 16. This was also confirmed in the expression used in 1945: 'the object – the limited photograph'. See n. 39, above.

44. Bazin, 'Ontology of the Photographic Image', p. 13. The 1945 version read: 'whose natural or earthly origins' (Diehl, *Les Problèmes de la peinture*, p. 408).

45. Bazin, 'Ontology of the Photographic Image', pp. 13–14. Save for some minor difference in punctuation, the 1945 version also used the phrase 'actually re-presented' (Diehl, *Les Problèmes de la peinture*, p. 409). Translator's note: the italicized emphasis on 're-' does not appear in the original French text.

46. This formulation matches Eric Rohmer's Bazinian realism as 'theorized' in his films. On the subject, see my analysis of *The Green Ray* as a representational model for ontological realism in M. Tortajada, *Le spectateur séduit. Le libertinage dans le cinéma d'Eric Rohmer et sa fonction dans une théorie de la représentation filmique* (Paris: Éditions KIME, 1999), pp. 208–31. On the issue of belief, see P. Rosen, 'Belief in Bazin', in Andrew and Joubert-Laurencin (eds), *Opening Bazin*, pp. 107–26.

47. Writing on works by Murnau (*Tabou*) and Max Linder, Bazin wrote: 'both are saved by their submission to realism. Cinema cannot escape its essence. It can achieve the eternal only by unreservedly searching for it in the exactitude of the instant' (Bazin, 'On Realism', p. 72). This is a form of Christian redemption transposed to the economy of representation.

48. More specifically Gombrich, *Art and Illusion*; R. Jakobson, 'On Realism in Art', in *Language in Literature* (Cambridge, MA: Harvard University Press, 1987), pp. 19–27; N. Goodman, *Languages of Art: An Approach to a Theory of Symbols* (1968; Indianapolis, IN: Hackett, 1976).

28 De Vroey, 'A Reflection on the Social Utility of Modern Macroeconomics'

1. R. Skidelsky, *John Maynard Keynes: The Economist as Saviour 1920–1937* (London: McMillan, 1992), p. 344.

2. A. Leijonhufvud, *On Keynesian Economics and the Economics of Keynes* (Oxford: Oxford University Press, 1968), p. 31.

3. It is intentionally that I have spoken of congeniality. A theory is a conceptual apparatus or, to use a metaphor, a language, that is, a set of syntax rules. In so far as one respects these, one can say whatever one wants. Because of the premises upon which it is built, Keynesian macroeconomics may well bend towards mitigated liberalism, but this association is not automatic. The language can be forced away from it: models using the Keynesian apparatus can be constructed that end up vindicating laissez faire. The best example of this is Milton Friedman's work.

4. Walras's annotation on p. 17 of his copy of Cournot's *Principes de la théorie de la richesse*, held at the Centre Walras-Pareto at the University of Lausanne, where he wrote 'la théorie pure n'attend aucune confirmation de la réalitie' [pure theory requires no confirmation from reality]. Quoted in R. Baranzini and P. Bridel, 'L'Ecole de Lausanne, l'utilité marginale moyenne et l'idée de marché', in G. Bensimon (ed.), *Histoire des représentations du marché* (Paris: Houdiard, 2005), pp. 347–65, on p. 360, n. 3.

5. R. E. Lucas, Jr, 'Expectations and the Neutrality of Money', *Journal of Economic Theory*, 4:2 (April 1972), pp. 103–24.

6. R. E. Lucas, Jr, *Models of Business Cycle* (Oxford: Basil Blackwell, 1987), p. 107.

7. J. M. Keynes, *The General Theory of Employment, Interest, and Money* (London: Macmillan, 1936), p. 33.

8. R. E. Lucas, Jr, 'Understanding Business Cycles', in *Studies in Business Cycle Theory* (1977; Cambridge, MA: The MIT Press, 1981), pp. 215–39, on p. 219.

9. F. Kydland and E. Prescott, 'Time to Build and Aggregate Fluctuations', *Econometrica*, 50:6 (November 1982), pp. 1345–70.

10. R. Lipsey, 'IS-LM, Keynesianism, and the New Classicism', in R. Backhouse and A. Salanti (eds), *Macroeconomics and the Real World,* vol. 2 *Keynesian Economics, Unemployment and Policy* (Oxford: Oxford University Press, 2000), pp. 57–92, on p. 76.

11. D. Cass, 'Interview with David Cass by S. Spear and R. Wright', *Macroeconomic Dynamics*, 2:3 (1988), pp. 533–58, on p. 546.

12. F. Hahn, 'Why I am not a Monetarist', in F. Hahn, *Equilibrium and Macroeconomics* (1982; Oxford: Basil Blackwell, 1984), pp. 307–26, on p. 308.

13. R. E. Lucas, Jr, various, Box 23, Barro folder, Lucas Archives. Duke's University Special Archives Division.

14. R. E. Lucas, 'Review of Milton Friedman and Anna J. Schwartz's "A Monetary History of the United States, 1867–1960"', *Journal of Monetary Economics*, 34 (1994), pp. 5–16, on p. 13.

15. M. Obstfeld and K. Rogoff, *Foundations of International Macroeconomics* (Cambridge, MA: The MIT Press, 1996), p. 627.

29 Fontana, 'Failing to Control: Accountability in Historical Perspective'

1. See Plato, *Republic*, ed. P. Shorey, Loeb Classical Library, 2 vols (London: Heinemann, 1987), vol. 1, pp. 108ff.; Aristotle, *The Politics*, ed. S. Everson (Cambridge: Cambridge University Press, 1988), book V, pp. 109ff.; see also M. C. Nussbaum, *The Fragility of Goodness: Luck and Ethics in Greek Tragedy and Philosophy* (Cambridge: Cambridge University Press, 1986); J. Annas, *The Morality of Happiness* (Oxford: Oxford University Press, 1993). For an overview of Christian writers, see A. MacIntyre, *After Virtue* (London: Duckworth, 1981) and C. Taylor, *Sources of the Self: the Making of Modern Identity* (Cambridge: Cambridge University Press, 1989).

2. T. Hobbes, *Leviathan*, ed. R. Tuck (1651; Cambridge: Cambridge University Press, 1991).

3. Ibid., part 2, chs 17, 18, pp. 117ff.

4. Long before the publication of *Leviathan* the Florentine diplomat Nicolò Machiavelli, in his provocative work *Il Principe* (1513), had detailed with unforgettable vividness the infinite duplicity and the criminal strategies to which the sovereign was bound to resort in the exercise of power (N. Machiavelli, *The Prince*, ed. Q. Skinner and R. Price (Cambridge: Cambridge University Press, 1988)).

5. To simplify the argument I am placing in the same category regimes which were not strictly speaking 'democratic' in the modern sense of the term, since, though elective, they allowed only a restricted electoral suffrage, and contemporary democracies founded upon universal suffrage. See B. Fontana (ed.), *The Invention of the Modern Republic* (Cambridge: Cambridge University Press, 1994) and J. Dunn (ed.), *Democracy, The Unfinished Journey* (Oxford: Oxford University Press, 1992).

6. J. Locke, *Two Treatises of Government*, ed. P. Laslett (Cambridge: Cambridge University Press, 1988), *Second Treatise*, ch. 19, §425, p. 415.

7. Cicero, *De Legibus*, trans. C. W. Keyes (1928; Cambridge, MA, and London: Loeb Classical Library, 1988), III.5, pp. 461–3.

8. See B. Manin, *Principes du gouvernement représentatif* (Paris: Calmann-Lévy, 1995).

9. In this respect Switzerland is an exception reminiscent of the practices of ancient republics: the service of deputies is considered as a 'part-time' activity (and compensated accordingly); it is compatible with other forms of public or professional employment.

10. B. Constant, *Political Writings*, ed. B. Fontana (Cambridge: Cambridge University Press, 1988), ch. 3, 'On the Right to Dissolve Representative Assemblies', p. 195. On Constant's views on responsibility see also B. Fontana, *Benjamin Constant and the Post-Revolutionary Mind* (New Haven, CT, and London: Yale University Press, 1991), pp. 81–97.

11. A. Pizzorno, *Le radici della politica assoluta* (Milan: Feltrinelli, 1993), ch. 8.

12. For an overview of the issue of responsibility in relation to democracies see J. Dunn, *Interpreting Political Responsibility* (Cambridge: Polity Press, 1990).

13. A. L. Moote, *The Revolt of the Judges* (Princeton, NJ: Princeton University Press, 1971); O. Ranum, *The Fronde, A French Revolution, 1648–1652* (New York: Norton & Co., 1993). On the functioning of *parlements* see R. Mousnier, *Les Institutions de la France sous la monarchie absolue*, 2 vols (Paris: PUF, 1980).

14. Montesquieu, *De l'Esprit des Lois*, in *Œuvres Complètes*, ed. R. Caillois, 2 vols (Paris, Bibliothèque de la Pléiade, 1951).

15. Ibid.

16. This notion that delay would be a good thing may seem surprising to us, given the modern obsession to speed up and simplify bureaucracy; the inefficiency of bureaucracy was in fact a problem also in Montesquieu's own time; but it was counterbalanced by the ominous power of the sovereign to act instantly against his subjects by, for example, secret orders of arrest or the sudden enforcement of new taxation.

17. See M. Troper, *La séparation des pouvoirs et l'histoire constitutionnelle française* (Paris: Librairie Générale de Droit et Jurisprudence, 1980).

18. On the different dimensions of the separation of powers see S. Baume and B. Fontana (eds), *Les usages de la séparation des pouvoirs* (Paris: Michel Houdiard Editeur, 2008).

19. B. Manin, 'Checks, Balances and Boundaries', in B. Fontana (ed.), *The Invention of the Modern Republic* (Cambridge: Cambridge University Press, 1994), pp. 27–62.

20. D. Hume, 'The Independency of Parliament' (1741).

21. In D. Hume, *Essays, Moral, Political and Literary*, ed. E. F. Miller (Indianapolis, IN: Liberty Press, 1985), p. 43.

22. J. Madison, *Federalist Papers* (1788).

23. A. Hamilton, J. Madison and J. Jay, *The Federalist Papers*, ed. I. Kramnick (Harmondsworth: Penguin Books, 1987), X, p. 125.

24. On the recent developments in Italian parties see I. Diamanti, *Un salto nel voto, Ritratto politico dell'Italia di oggi* (Bari: Laterza, 2013).

25. M. H. Hansen, *The Athenian Democracy in the Age of Demosthenes* (Oxford: Blackwell, 1991), ch. 8.

26. C. Nicolet, *Le métier de citoyen dans la Rome républicaine* (Paris: Gallimard, 1976), ch. 8.

27. According to Aristotle the citizen of a democracy was defined by his double role as a juror (*dikastes*) and a member of the Assembly (*ekklesiastes*). It is helpful to keep in mind that in ancient Greece or Rome private litigation, and even criminal cases, seldom came to the attention of tribunals and were generally settled out of court; with the exception of a small number of serious crimes, courts were mostly concerned with public issues; modern tribunals, on the other hand, work predominantly to judge private litigation.

28. On these new approaches see: P. Rosanvallon, *La contre-démocratie, La politique à l'âge de la défiance* (Paris: Seuil, 2006); Y. Sintomer, *Le pouvoir au peuple, Jurys citoyens, triage au sort et démocratie participative* (Paris: La Decouverte, 2007); H. Landemore, *Democratic Reason: Politics, Collective Intelligence and the Rule of the Many* (Princeton, NJ: Princeton University Press, 2012).

29. See B. Fontana, 'A New Kind of Federalism, Benjamin Constant and Modern Europe', in M. Albertone and A. De Francesco (eds), *Rethinking the Atlantic World* (Basingstoke: Palgrave Macmillan, 2009), pp. 163–79.

30. G. de Staël, 'De l'influence des passions sur le bonheur des individus et des nations', in *Œuvres complètes, series 1, vol. 1* (Paris: Honoré Champion, 2008), pp. 131–302, on p. 163.

31. Y. Papadopoulos, *Complexité sociale et politiques publiques* (Paris: Montchrestien, 1995), pp. 35ff.

32. B. Constant, *Political Writings*, ed. B. Fontana (Cambridge: Cambridge University Press, 1988), ch. 1, 'Of the Sovereignty of the People', pp. 179–80.

30 Baume, 'Does Transparency Engender the Confidence of the Governed? A Contribution to Political Thought'

1. In this essay, I consider transparency and publicity as quasi-equivalent. However, when I refer to a specific author or corpus, I use the word as used by its source, and when I refer to the general phenomenon I use the word transparency. For more details, see n. 5, below.

2. See S. Baume, 'Exposer les affaires publiques au regard des citoyens: les raisons justificatives du principe de transparence', in M. Pasquier (ed.), *La transparence en Suisse et dans le monde. Contributions à l'action publique* (Lausanne: PPUR, 2013), pp. 3–18.

3. R. Hardin, *Trust and Trustworthiness* (New York: Russell Sage Foundation, 2002), p. 1.

4. In this quotation by Bentham, the notion of transparency doesn't receive a different meaning than the word publicity: 'Opakeness. Want of transparency, disturbance given [to] the transparency of the whole business hence facilities afforded throughout for the secret and successful operation of sinister interest' (J. Bentham, *First Principles Preparatory to Constitutional Code* (Oxford: Clarendon Press, 1989), p. 102) and 'In the darkness of secrecy, sinister interest and evil in every shape, have full swing ... Where there is no publicity there is no justice' (J. Bentham, 'Constitutional Code', in J. Bowring (ed.), *The Works of Jeremy Bentham*, 11 vols (New York: Russell & Russell, 1962), vol. 9, p. 493).

5. See S. Baume, 'La transparence dans la conduite des affaires publiques. Origines et sens d'une exigence', *Raison publique*, 44 (2011), pp. 1–26, notably 'Transparence versus publicité'.

6. '[C]'est toute la pensée "révolutionnaire" qui est animée de la croyance en une transparence de la société à elle-même' (M. Richir, 'Révolution et transparence sociale', in J. Fichte, *Considérations sur la Révolution française* (1793; Paris: Payot, 1973), p. 10, my translation).

7. M. Foucault, 'The Eye of Power', in C. Gordon (ed.), *Power/Knowledge: Selected Interviews and Other Writings 1972–1977* (New York: Pantheon Books, 1980), pp. 146–65, on p. 153.

8. J. Starobinski, *Transparency and Obstruction* (Chicago, IL, and London: University of Chicago Press, 1988), p. 3.

9. '[S]ociété de représentation où chacun devait tenir sa place [... elle] était la scène par excellence de ce jeu de rôles' (S. Wahnich, *L'impossible citoyen. L'étranger dans le discours de la Révolution française* (Paris: Albin Michel, 1997), p. 32).

10. 'In the "law" the quintessence of general, abstract, and permanent norms, inheres a rationality in which what is right converges with what is just; the exercise of power is to be demoted to a mere executor of such norms ... Historically, the polemical claim of this kind of rationality was developed, in conjunction with the critical public debate among private people, against the reliance of princely authority on secrets of State. Just as secrecy was supposed to serve the maintenance of sovereignty based on *voluntas*, so publicity was supposed to serve the promotion of legislation based on *ratio*' (J. Habermas, *The Structural Transformation of the Public Sphere: An Inquiry into a Category of Bourgeois Society* (1963; Cambridge: MIT Press, 1991), p. 53).

11. See the section 'Trust and transparency today' in this chapter, p. 430.

12. C. Schmitt, *The Crisis of Parliamentary Democracy* (1923; Cambridge, MA: MIT Press, 1988), pp. 37–50.

13. J. Bentham, 'Of Publicity', in J. Bentham, *Political Tactics*, ed. M. James and C. Blamires (Oxford: Clarendon Press, 1999), p. 30.

14. 'Publicity is farther useful as a security for the reputation of the judge (if blameless) against the imputation of having misconceived, or, as if on pretence of misconception, falsified, the evidence. Withhold this safeguard, the reputation of the judge remains a perpetual prey to calumny, without the possibility of defence: apply this safeguard, adding it as an accompaniment and corroborative to the security afforded (as above) by registration – all such calumny being rendered hopeless, it will in scarce any instance be attempted – it will not in any instance be attempted with success' (J. Bentham, 'Rationale of Judicial Evidence, Specially Applied to English Practice', in *The Works of Jeremy Bentham*, ed. J. Bowring, 11 vols (New York: Russell & Russell, 1962), vol. 6, p. 355).

15. 'But in an open and free policy, what confidence and security – I do not say for the people, but for the governors themselves! Let it be impossible that anything should be done which is unknown to the nation – prove to it that you neither intend to deceive nor to surprise – you take away all the weapons of discontent. The public will repay with usury the confidence you repose in it. Calumny will lose its force; it collects its venom in the caverns of obscurity, but it is destroyed by the light of day' (Bentham, 'Of Publicity', p. 30).

16. Ibid., pp. 38–9.

17. Ibid., p. 31.

18. B. Constant, 'Principles of Politics Applicable to All Representative Governments', in B. Fontana (ed.), *Political Writings* (Cambridge: Cambridge University Press, 1988), pp. 232–3.

19. Constant, 'Principles of Politics Applicable to All Representative Governments', p. 233. Similarly, 'In England too there are, in the House of Commons, ranters and troublemakers. Yet what happens? They talk, no one listens to them, and they fall silent. The same interest which makes an assembly attached to its own dignity teaches it to restrain its members without seeking to stifle their voices. Let it get its own education. It must do so. To interrupt it is simply to retard its progress' (Constant, 'Principles of Politics Applicable to All Representative Governments', pp. 233–4).

20. Bentham, 'Of Publicity', p. 31.

21. Ibid.

22. Ibid., p. 39.

23. Bentham, 'Rationale of Judicial Evidence, Specially Applied to English Practice', vol. 6, p. 360.

24. 'It is objected against the régime of publicity, that it is a system of *distrust*? This is true; and every good political institution is founded upon this base. Whom ought we to distrust, if not those to whom is committed great authority, with great temptations to abuse it?' (Bentham, 'Of Publicity', p. 37).

25. M. Cleary and S. Stokes, 'Trust and Democracy in Comparative Perspective', in K. Cook et al., *Whom Can We Trust* (New York: Russell Sage Foundation, 2009), pp. 308–38, on p. 308.

26. R. Hardin, 'Do We Want Trust in Government?' in M. Warren (ed.), *Democracy and Trust* (Cambridge: Cambridge University Press, 1999), pp. 22–41, on pp. 22–3.

27. N. Luhmann, 'Trust: A Mechanism for the Reduction of Social Complexity', in *Trust and Power: Two Works by Niklas Luhmann* (Chichester: John Wily and Sons, 1979), pp. 4–103, on p. 46.

28. Ibid., p. 54.

29. D. Naurin, 'Transparency, Publicity, Accountability – The Missing Links', *Swiss Political Science Review*, 12 (3, 2006), pp. 91–2.

30. R. Zajonc, 'On the Primacy of Affect', *American Psychologist*, 39:2 (1984), pp. 117–23.

31. S. Grimmelikhuijsen, 'Linking Transparency, Knowledge and Citizen Trust in Government: An Experiment', *International Review of Administrative Sciences*, 78 (2012), pp. 50–73, on p. 57.

32. Ibid., p. 67.

33. S. Baume and Y. Papadopoulos, 'Transparency as a Requirement of Good Governance: A Historical Perspective', Paper presented at the CAST Workshop '*National Security, Risk Management, and the Transformation of Bureaucratic Ethics*', 23–4 May 2013.

34. O. O'Neill, *A Question of Trust: The BBC Reith Lectures 2002* (Cambridge: Cambridge University Press, 2003), p. 75.

35. Baume and Papadopoulos, 'Transparency as a Requirement of Good Governance: A Historical Perspective'.

36. Y. Papadopoulos, *Democracy in Crisis: Politics, Governance and Policy* (Basingstoke: Palgrave, 2013), § 2.

37. R. Dalton, *Democratic Challenges, Democratic Choices: The Erosion of Political Support in Advanced Industrial Democracies* (Oxford: Oxford University Press, 2004), p. 71.

38. S. Coleman and J. Blumler, *The Internet and Democratic Citizenship: Theory, Practice and Policy* (Cambridge: Cambridge University Press, 2009).

39. Foucault, 'The Eye of Power', p. 161.

40. O'Neill, *A Question of Trust: The BBC Reith Lectures 2002*, p. 66.

41. 'If we want to increase trust we need to avoid deception rather than secrecy. Although some ways of increasing transparency may indirectly reduce deception, many do not. Unless there has been prior deception, transparency does nothing to reduce deception; and even if there has been deception, openness is not a sure-fire remedy. Increasing transparency can produce a flood of unsorted information and misinformation that provided little but confusion unless it can be sorted and assessed. It may add to uncertainty rather than to trust' (O'Neill, *A Question of Trust: The BBC Reith Lectures 2002*, pp. 72–3).

42. P. Rosanvallon, *La légitimité démocratique: impartialité, réflexivité, proximité* (Paris: Seuil, 2008), pp. 11–12.

43. Bentham, 'Of Publicity', p. 37. See n. 24.

31 Dongois and Swaton, 'The Enterprise Face to the Environmental Challenge: Straddling the Fence Between Social Responsibility and Penal Responsibility'

1. Text translated by Dominique Macabies.

2. As an emblematic example, the destruction of forests caused by the growing use of palm oil is a matter that has been denounced by Greenpeace since 2008. While that NGO obtained a seat at the negotiation table with the cosmetic industry group Unilever and Kraft Foods group, such was not the case with Nestlé. Indeed, despite pressures, Nestlé continued its operations that caused the massive destruction of forests. Greenpeace opted for a radical response: on 17 March 2010, it posted a video on *YouTube* showing Nestlé's operations. Relayed by social networks, the video has been a great success, to the point that Nestlé called for its immediate removal. Yet the commercial implications were already looming and threats of boycott were made. While the group turned a deaf ear for two years, faced by such media pressure, it took only one month for Nestlé to air its commitment to use sustainable palm oil by 2015. A partnership with 'The Forest Trust' was signed in the bargain to fight deforestation in the Amazon.

3. The phrase 'corporate societal responsibility' is also common, a term used in Belgium and recently adopted by the Ministry of Ecology, Energy and Sustainable Development in France. For an overview of the concept of CSR, see the eponymous article on this website: www.humanrights.ch [accessed 11 July 2013].

4. European Commission, *Promouvoir un cadre européen pour la responsabilité sociale des entreprises. Livre vert* [Promoting a European framework for corporate social responsibility. Green Book] (July 2001).

5. The report of the measures taken by countries to fight poverty and protect the environment – including a report that can be consulted on this website: http://www.un.org/french/events/wssd/coverage/summaries/envdev33.htm [accessed 11 July 2013] – expressed the Swiss position: 'The observer for Switzerland expressed his country's satisfaction for the consensus that led to reaffirm our commitment to achieving sustainable development. It also shows our commitment to economic development, social development and environmental protection, at a time when the world is distracted by security concerns. The precautionary principle, to Switzerland's satisfaction, has not been questioned.'

6. Principle 27 in the appendix to the Declaration available on this site: http://www.francophonie.org/IMG/pdf/Johannesburg.pdf [accessed 11 July 2013]. Besides, Principle 29 states: 'We agree on the view that private sector companies must operate within a transparent and stable regulatory framework'.

7. In this contribution we have to face this lack of definition.
8. In the same way as Greenpeace, mentioned above, but also like 'Friends of Nature', the 'International Union for the Conservation of Nature', 'Climate Action Network', 'SB Alliance' and 'World Wildlife Fund'.
9. This will be defined further (see p. 437).
10. We here use 'liability' as a legal term. But it is also an alternative word for 'responsibility'.
11. For more details about OCDE recommendations, see M. Prieur, *Droit de l'environnement* (Paris: Dalloz, 2011), p. 176.
12. Ibid., p. 176, n. 165 and quoted reference.
13. For example, N. Gardères and T. Porcher, 'Les limites du pollueur payeur', *L'Humanité* (13 January 2011).
14. D. Mullenex, 'Pollueur payeur: La CJUE persiste et signe ...', *LeFigaro*, 14 March 2010.
15. To be more explicit, we might use here the term 'neoclassical paradigm'.
16. S. Swaton, *Une entreprise peut-elle être sociale dans une économie de marché?*, n. 72 (Charmey: De l'Hèbe, La Question, 2011).
17. A. B. Carroll, 'A Three-Dimensional Conceptual Model of Corporate Performance', *Academy of Management Review*, 4:4 (1979), pp. 497–505.
18. Even if some pioneer companies such as Patagonia or Nature et Découvertes are really focused on the ecological issue. E. Laville, *L'entreprise verte* (Paris: Pearson Education France, 2009).
19. S. Mercier, *L'éthique dans les entreprises* (Paris: Repères, La Découverte, 2004).
20. Thus, the United Nations Global Compact in 2000, the ILO Tripartite Declaration of Principles concerning Multinational Enterprises and the 1997 and 2000 Social Policy, or then again the OECD Guidelines for Multinational Enterprises. More recently, a White Paper was published in 2009 on its website by the European Commission, entitled: 'Adapting to Climate Change: Towards a European Framework for Action'. In 2007, the European Commission also published a Green Book, entitled: *Adapting to Climate Change in Europe: Opportunities for Action by the European Union*.
21. For a historical overview and details of the various standards (ISO, GRI, ESRB), see the sites www.humanrights.ch and www.actares.ch [accessed 11 July 2013]. Regarding CSR, it is ISO 26 000, published recently, that stipulates the integration of social responsibility standards, governance and ethics. But it is not yet certifiable.
22. These principles include issues related to child labour, prohibition of forced labour, consumer protection or the protection of the environment by promoting, on this point, sustainable development, for example.
23. This concept, which consists in combining economic efficiency and considerations of environmental concerns aims at educating companies first, but is also relevant in a wider context: states' economic and industrial policies, the European Union in particular. Indeed, the promotion of the eco-efficiency concept stems from an action by the World Business Council for Sustainable Develpment and European Partners for the Environment in partnership with the European Commission. For more information, see http://www.wbcsd.org/home.aspx [accessed 11 July 2013].
24. For example, the AFAQ 1000 model that certifies the ISO 26 000 standard relatively to CSR.
25. This can be translated as 'Suez, the non-sustainable sustainable development!'. Original quote in *Libération*, 11 January 2003.
26. See A. Macaluso, 'Commentaire de l'article 102 CP', in R. Roth and L. Moreillon (eds), *Commentaire romand, Code pénal I*, 1–110 CP (Helbing Lichtenhahn: 2009).

27. This provision applies to legal persons of private law (art. 102 al.4 let. A), legal persons under public law (excluding territorial institutes) (letter b), corporations (letter c), sole proprietorships (letter d). For more details see, amongst others, Macaluso, 'Commentaire de l'article 102 CP' and the references cited therein.

28. Ibid.

29. The existence of a link between the agent and the company is one of the conditions of companies' criminal liability: it is therefore necessary for the offense to have been committed by a person maintaining a link with the enterprise that it is hierarchical or organizational, for it to be recognized that the offense was committed 'within' the company, in accordance with the provisions of paragraph 1 of Article 102 CP. The person can be a member of the said company's *de facto* body or body of law, a top executive but a mere employee as well. On this point, see M. Forster, *Die strafrechtliche Verantwortlichkeit des Unternehmens nach Art. 102 StGB* (Bern: Stämpfli, 2006), pp. 154ff. See also A. Macaluso, 'Principes et commentaire des articles 100^{quater} et 100^{quinquies} CP', *La responsabilité pénale des entreprises* (Geneva, Basel and Zurich: Schulthess, 2004), pp. 719ff.

30. Organization failure is assessed in terms of what should have been done in terms of delineation of duties, of procedures for delegation, of the business's management, and so forth. On this point, see Macaluso, 'Commentaire de l'article 102 CP'.

31. Article 105 CP expressly mentions this exclusion.

32. There are indeed many criminal offenses relating to the environment (see art. 60s EPL, for example). Consequently, it is worth asking to what extent they are covered by Article 102 al. 1 CP. Under that provision, offenses (felonies or misdemeanours) must have been committed that are within the purview of both of the *Code Pénal* and of accessory law. In accordance with what is set out in sections 333 al. 1 and 335 s. CP 2, Article 102 al. 1 CP allows it to seek the company's criminal liabibility to all the accessory offenses in the legislation or, within certain limits, cantonal law (On this point, see Macaluso, 'Commentaire de l'article 102 CP', ad art. 102, N64). In these circumstances, therefore, it is sufficient to ensure that the criminal offenses under the EPA have been committed in connection with the sale of goods or the provision of services for profit sought by the company in question. We will no longer analyse this point in more detail since the aim of this contribution is to see if companies'criminal liability as provided in section 102CP could apply to breaches of CSR environmental principles, which means that these principles are previously criminalized. We will therefore focus on this last point.

33. A connection with the for-profit sale of goods or provision of services is then required. On this point, see A. Niggli and D. R. Gfeller, 'Commentaire de l'article 102 CP', in *BSK Strafrecht I* (Basel: Helbing Lichtenhahn Verlag, 2013), ad 102 comments PC, N76ss; it is also necessary that the activity in which the offense was committed should be consistent with the lawful objectives of the company, which limits the type of offenses. On this point, see Macaluso, 'Commentaire de l'article 102 CP', ad art. 102, N34s.

34. These words have been coined by Professor Macaluso (see Macaluso, 'Commentaire de l'article 102 CP', ad art. 102, N55, and references cited therein).

35. The precautionary principle is a legal document but was also analysed by the supporters of political ecology based on philosopher Hanz Jonas's work on the ethics of responsibility. In case of risk to the environment, the responsibility principle should be accompanied by a requirement for companies to refrain from any toxic activity. But the

precautionary principle is less demanding: a minimum level of knowledge is sufficient to allow a company to act.

36. So-called social and solidarity companies in Switzerland provide for that environmental dimension in their objectives. In these companies, it is difficult to account for entrepreneurs' and employees' motivations on the basis of profit maximization. Besides, the environment is part of a company's mission rather than of its strategy, which the European Commission did not fail to point out elsewhere in its Green Book.

37. Also called evolutionist theses, alluding to the theory of evolution as illustrated by Darwin or Spencer.

38. C. Borzaga and E. Tortia, 'Les organisations d'économie sociale dans la théorie de la firme', in A. Noya and E. Clarence, *Pour une économie sociale, Créer de la richesse par l'intégration sociale* (Lonrai: Economica, 2009), on p. 21.

39. Ibid.

40. See N. Postel et al., *La Responsabilité Sociale de l'Entreprise, Nouvelle régulation du capitalisme?* (Grenoble: Presses Universitaires du Septendrion, 2011).

41. See S. Swaton, *Une entreprise peut-elle être sociale dans une économie de marché?* (Charmey: De l'Hèbe, La Question, 2011), no. 72.

42. See F. Quairel, 'L'influence des parties prenantes sur les dispositifs de notation sociale', in M. Bonnafous-Boucher and Y. Pesqueux (eds), *Décider avec les parties prenantes* (Paris: La Découverte, 2006), pp. 141–53, on p. 142.

43. M. Capron and F. Quairel-Lanoizelée, *La responsabilité sociale des entreprises* (Paris: Repères, La Découverte, 2011).

44. M. Fleurbaey, *Capitalisme ou démocratie?* (Paris: Grasset, 2006).

45. See the website: http://eradicatingecocide.com/ [accessed 11 July 2013]: 'Ecocide is the extensive damage to, destruction of or loss of ecosystem(s) of a given territory, whether by human agency or by other causes, to such an extent that peaceful enjoyment by the inhabitants of that territory has been or will be severely diminished'.

46. A company's misconduct should be established (intent or negligence) rather than institute strict company's liability. In addition, the criminal penalty articulates with the civil penalty (reparation) to which the company may be liable for the damage it has caused.

32 Moor, 'Law as a System of Normative Production. Law and Semiotics'

1. Text translated by Dominique Macabies.

2. For more developments, see P. Moor, *Pour une théorie micropolitique du droit* (Paris: Presses Universitaires de France, 2005); P. Moor, *Dynamique du système juridique – Une théorie générale du droit* (Geneva, Brussels and Paris: Schulthess, Bruylant and L. G. D. J., 2010).

INDEX

For Product Safety Concerns and Information please contact our EU
representative GPSR@taylorandfrancis.com Taylor & Francis Verlag GmbH,
Kaufingerstraße 24, 80331 München, Germany

Printed and bound by CPI Group (UK) Ltd, Croydon, CR0 4YY
04/05/2025
01860539-0001